Organizational Advancements through Enterprise Information Systems:
Emerging Applications and Developments

Angappa Gunasekaran
University of Massachusetts—Dartmouth, USA

Timothy Shea
University of Massachusetts—Dartmouth, USA

BUSINESS SCIENCE REFERENCE

Hershey · New York

Director of Editorial Content:	Kristin Klinger
Senior Managing Editor:	Jamie Snavely
Assistant Managing Editor:	Michael Brehm
Publishing Assistant:	Sean Woznicki
Typesetter:	Michael Brehm, Michael Killian
Cover Design:	Lisa Tosheff
Printed at:	Yurchak Printing Inc.

Published in the United States of America by
Business Science Reference (an imprint of IGI Global)
701 E. Chocolate Avenue
Hershey PA 17033
Tel: 717-533-8845
Fax: 717-533-8661
E-mail: cust@igi-global.com
Web site: http://www.igi-global.com/reference

Library of Congress Cataloging-in-Publication Data

Organizational advancements through enterprise information systems : emerging applications and development / Angappa Gunasekaran and Timothy Shea, editors.
    p. cm.
  Includes bibliographical references and index.
  Summary: "This book provides a comprehensive assessment of the latest developments in the EIS revolution. including Enterprise Resource Planning (ERP) adoption, the integration of enterprise systems, personalized ERP, and the Semantic Web, and ideas and solutions for the future of the global enterprise"--Provided by publisher.
  ISBN 978-1-60566-968-7 (hardcover : alk. paper) -- ISBN 978-1-60566-969-4 (ebook : alk. paper) 1. Information technology--Management. 2. Management information systems. 3. Business planning. 4. Information resources management. I. Gunasekaran, A. II. Shea, Timothy, 1954- III. Title.

  HD30.2.O73773 2010
  658.4'038011--dc22

2009042278

British Cataloguing in Publication Data
A Cataloguing in Publication record for this book is available from the British Library.

All work contributed to this book is new, previously-unpublished material. The views expressed in this book are those of the authors, but not necessarily of the publisher.

Advances in Enterprise Information Systems (AEIS) Series

ISBN: 1935-3111

Editor-in-Chief: Angappa Gunasekaran, University of Massachusetts—Dartmouth, USA

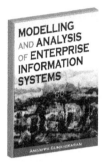

Modelling and Analysis of Enterprise Information Systems

Angappa Gunasekaran, University of Massachusetts—Dartmouth, USA

IGI Publishing * copyright 2007 * 392pp * H/C (ISBN: 978-1-59904-477-4)

Insight into issues, challenges, and solutions related to the successful applications and management aspects of enterprise information systems may provide to be a hardship to researchers and practitioners. Modelling Analysis of Enterprise Information Systems presents comprehensive coverage and understanding of the organizational and technological issues of enterprise information systems.

Modelling Analysis of Enterprise Information Systems covers current trends and issues in various enterprise information systems such as enterprise resource planning, electronic commerce, and their implications on supply chain management and organizational competitiveness.

Techniques and Tools for the Design and Implementation of Enterprise Information Systems

Angappa Gunasekaran, University of Massachusetts—Dartmouth, USA

IGI Publishing * copyright 2008 * 303pp * H/C (ISBN: 978-1-59904-826-0)

Inter-organizational information systems play a major role in improving communication and integration between partnering firms to achieve an integrated global supply chain. Current research in enterprise resource planning and electronic commerce is crucial to maintaining efficient supply chain management and organizational competitiveness.

Techniques and Tools for the Design & Implementation of Enterprise Information Systems enables libraries to provide an invaluable resource to academicians and practitioners in fields such as operations management, Web engineering, information technology, and management information systems, providing insight into the effective design and implementation of enterprise information systems to improve communication and integration between partnering firms to achieve an integrated global supply chain.

Global Implications of Modern Enterprise Information Systems: Technologies and Applications

Angappa Gunasekaran, University of Massachusetts—Dartmouth, USA

Information Science Reference * copyright 2008 * H/C (ISBN: 978-1-60566-146-9)

Many companies have encountered pitfalls in their attempts to successfully implement enterprise resource planning (ERP) that have proven nearly insurmountable, due to lack of techniques and tools for the design and implementation of enterprise information systems (EIS) that are properly aligned with business models and strategic objectives.

Global Implications of Modern Enterprise Information Systems: Technologies and Applications presents useful strategies, techniques, and tools for the successful design, development, and implementation of enterprise information systems (EIS). By assimilating the truly international perspective, this collection constructs on this ascending area of research in an array of related fields will greatly benefit from these cutting-edge findings on modern enterprise information systems.

The Advances in Enterprise Information Systems (AEIS) Book Series aims to expand available literature in support of global markets and the globalized economy surrounding Enterprise Information Systems. The Series provides comprehensive coverage and understanding of the organizational, people and technological issues of EIS. Design, development, justification and implementation of EIS including ERP and EC will be discussed. Global markets and competition have forced companies to operate in a physically distributed environment to take the advantage of benefits of strategic alliances between partnering firms. Earlier, information systems such as Material Requirements Planning (MRP), Computer-Aided Design (CAD) and Computer-Aided Manufacturing (CAM) have widely been used for functional integration within an organization. With global operations in place, there is a need for suitable Enterprise Information Systems (EIS) such as Enterprise Resource Planning (ERP) and E-Commerce (EC) for the integration of extended enterprises along the supply chain with the objective of achieving flexibility and responsiveness. Companies all over the world spend billions of dollars in the design and implementation of EIS in particular ERP systems such as Oracle, Peoplesoft, SAP, JD Edwards and BAAN with the objective of achieving an integrated global supply chain. Inter-organizational information systems play a major role in improving communication and integration between partnering firms to achieve an integrated global supply chain. The Advances in Enterprise Information Systems (AEIS) Book Series endeavors to further this field and address the growing demand for research and applications that will provide insights into issues, challenges, and solutions related to the successful applications and management aspects of EIS.

Hershey · New York

Order online at www.igi-global.com or call 717-533-8845 x 10 –
Mon-Fri 8:30 am - 5:00 pm (est) or fax 24 hours a day 717-533-8661

Editorial Advisory Board

Table of Contents

Preface xviii

Chapter 1
Critical Success Factors in Enterprise Resource Planning Implementations........................ 1
Joseph R. Muscatello, Kent State University, USA
Injazz J. Chen, Cleveland State University, USA

Chapter 2
The Paradox of Complex ERP Systems used in Simplified Organisations such
as Small and Medium Enterprises.. 18
Catherine Equey, Haute Ecole de Gestion de Genève, Switzerland
Emmanuel Fragnière, Haute Ecole de Gestion de Genève, Switzerland

Chapter 3
Requirements Management for ERP Projects... 29
S. Parthasarathy, Thiagarajar College of Engineering, Madurai, India
Muthu Ramachandran, Leeds Metropolitan University, UK

Chapter 4
Requirements Elicitation for Personalized ERP Systems: A Case Study 46
Lex van Velsen, University of Twente, The Netherlands
Corrie Huijs, M&I/Partners, The Netherlands
Thea van der Geest, University of Twente, The Netherlands

Chapter 5
Specifying General Activity Clusters for ERP Projects Aimed at Effort Prediction 57
Guy Janssens, Open Universiteit Nederland, The Netherlands
Rob Kusters, Eindhoven University of Technology, The Netherlands
Fred Heemstra, KWD Result Management, The Netherlands

Chapter 6

Time, Attitude, and User Participation: How Prior Events Determine User Attitudes
in ERP Implementation 80

Lene Pries-Heje, IT University of Copenhagen, Denmark

Chapter 7

ERP Selection: Effect of Product and Organizational Constructs 99

Uzoka Faith-Michael Emeka, Mount Royal University, Canada
Abiola Richard Oladele, Federal University of Technology, Nigeria

Chapter 8

A SOA-Based Approach to Integrate Enterprise Systems 120

Anne Lämmer, University of Potsdam, Germany
Sandy Eggert, University of Potsdam, Germany
Norbert Gronau, University of Potsdam, Germany

Chapter 9

The Underlying Test—Human, Organisational and Technical Considerations adjoined
with Critical Success Factors when Implementing ERP: A Case Study of a UK SME 134

Jonathan D. Owens, University of Lincoln, UK
Julie Dawson, University of Lincoln, UK

Chapter 10

The Role of Enterprise Perceptions in Acceptance of Information Systems 156

Blanca Hernández, University of Zaragoza, Spain
Julio Jiménez, University of Zaragoza, Spain
M. José Martín, University of Zaragoza, Spain

Chapter 11

Modeling and Implementation of Formal Power Structures in Enterprise Information Systems 174

Alexei Sharpanskykh, Vrije Universiteit Amsterdam, The Netherlands

Chapter 12

Enhancing Traditional ATP Functionality in Open Source ERP Systems:
A Case Study from the Food & Beverages Industry 188

Ioannis T. Christou, Athens Information Technology, Greece
Stavros Ponis, National Technical University of Athens, Greece

Chapter 13

Developing an Enterprise Wide Knowledge Warehouse: Challenge of Optimal Designs
in the Media Industry 203

Amit Mitra, Cranfield University, UK
Laura Campoy, University of the West of England, UK

Chapter 14

Exploring the Influence Sources of ERP Adoption and the Y2K Effect in Taiwan 224
  Hsiu-Hua Chang, National Central University and Tajen University, Taiwan
  Chun-Po Yin, Haiching Vocational High School of Technology and Commerce and Cheng Shiu
    University, Taiwan
  Huey-Wen Chou, National Central University, Taiwan

Chapter 15

IS Success Factors and IS Organizational Impact: Does Ownership Type Matter in Kuwait? 239
  Abdulrida Alshawaf, Kuwait University, Kuwait
  Omar E. M. Khalil, Kuwait University, Kuwait

Chapter 16

An ASP-Based Product Customization Service Systems for SMEs: A Case Study
in Construction Machinery 261
  Yan Su, Nanjing University of Aeronautics and Astronautics, China
  Wenhe Liao, Nanjing University of Aeronautics and Astronautics, China
  Yu Guo, Nanjing University of Aeronautics and Astronautics, China
  Shiwen Gao, Nanjing University of Aeronautics and Astronautics, China
  Huibin Shi, Nanjing University of Aeronautics and Astronautics, China

Chapter 17

Monitoring Enterprise Applications and the Future of Self-Healing Applications............................278
  Shuchih Ernest Chang, National Chung Hsing University, Taiwan
  Boris Minkin, National Chung Hsing University, Taiwan

Chapter 18

Managing the Implementation of Business Intelligence Systems: A Critical
Success Factors Framework.. 291
  William Yeoh, University of South Australia, Australia
  Andy Koronios, University of South Australia, Australia
  Jing Gao, University of South Australia, Australia

Chapter 19

Rule-Based Approach for a Better B2B Discovery 308
  Youcef Aklouf, University of Science and Technology –USTHB, Algeria
  El Kindi Rezig, University of Science and Technology –USTHB, Algeria

Chapter 20

Generic Object Oriented Enterprise Modeling Approach Utilizing a Strategic
Abstraction Mechanism 322
  Islam Choudhury, Kingston University, Kingston-upon-Thames, UK
  Sergio de Cesare, Brunel University, UK
  Emily Di Florido, Brunel University, UK

Chapter 21
Semantic Web Services for Simulation Component Reuse and Interoperability:
An Ontology Approach 336
    Simon J. E. Taylor, Brunel University, UK
    David Bell, Brunel University, UK
    Navonil Mustafee, Brunel University, UK
    Sergio de Cesare, Brunel University, UK
    Mark Lycett, Brunel University, UK
    Paul A. Fishwick, University of Florida, USA

Compilation of References 353

About the Contributors 387

Index 397

Detailed Table of Contents

Preface xviii

Chapter 1
Critical Success Factors in Enterprise Resource Planning Implementations.. 1
Joseph R. Muscatello, Kent State University, USA
Injazz J. Chen, Cleveland State University, USA

This chapter seeks to further the study of the critical success factors of ERP implementations by using statistical analysis to further delineate the patterns of adoption of the various concepts. Through the use of a cross-sectional mail survey, the authors offer empirical evidence of critical success factors that will enable practitioners to improve their chances of ERP project success. Additionally, this study furthers the academic theory of ERP implementations that can benefit future studies.

Chapter 2
The Paradox of Complex ERP Systems used in Simplified Organisations such
as Small and Medium Enterprises.. 18
Catherine Equey, Haute Ecole de Gestion de Genève, Switzerland
Emmanuel Fragnière, Haute Ecole de Gestion de Genève, Switzerland

This chapter further develops and generalises findings from the authors' July 2008 chapter in the International Journal of Enterprise Information Systems (IJEIS) by adding organisational issues such as business process reengineering (BPR). The authors argue that enterprise resource planning (ERP) systems are complex management tools that impose standard business processes from larger manufacturing firms. The authors test whether these systems can be adapted effectively to more simplified organisations such as small and medium enterprises (SMEs). The authors found that SMEs tend to have a high perceived level of satisfaction when using these complex tools, independent of size or sector. However, they cannot clearly establish that SMEs having applied BPR while implementing an ERP system are more satisfied than those that did not.

Chapter 3

Requirements Management for ERP Projects...29

S. Parthasarathy, Thiagarajar College of Engineering, Madurai, India
Muthu Ramachandran, Leeds Metropolitan University, UK

ERP software standardizes an enterprise's business processes and data. The software converts trans-actional data into useful information and collates the data so that they can be analyzed. Requirements engineering is an important component of ERP projects. In this chapter, the authors propose: (1) An ERP maturity model (EMM) for assessing the ERP maturity within the organization and (2) A Requirements Engineering Method (REM) for ERP system requirements to capture the requirements from the different types of users of an ERP system, verifying and validating them. The EMM consists of three levels and each level has a focus and a key process area. Key indicators of ERP functionality identified by a major ERP vendor have been used to apply the EMM to an enterprise. This identifies the level of the EMM to which an enterprise belongs. Then the REM is used to enable the enterprise to assess its ERP system requirements and refine it using a knowledge database to reach a higher level in the EMM than the present one. The authors deem that this model can benefit users across all the ERP projects.

Chapter 4

Requirements Elicitation for Personalized ERP Systems: A Case Study 46

Lex van Velsen, University of Twente, The Netherlands
Corrie Huijs, M&I/Partners, The Netherlands
Thea van der Geest, University of Twente, The Netherlands

For small and medium-sized companies the fit between their business processes and their Enterprise Resource Planning (ERP) system is a critical success factor. The functions and features for essential tasks must be geared to the demands and skills of the individual users. This chapter reports on the usefulness of several methods for eliciting user input which served as a basis for requirements for a personalized ERP system. It describes the yield of heuristic evaluations, both by experts and by developers, and a focus group with six users representing the main user types. The focus group consisted of an identification of the most important functions, task demonstrations, and a mini design workshop. As a demonstration of the results of the various user-focused methods, some noteworthy findings on the personalization of ERP systems are presented.

Chapter 5

Specifying General Activity Clusters for ERP Projects Aimed at Effort Prediction 57

Guy Janssens, Open Universiteit Nederland, The Netherlands
Rob Kusters, Eindhoven University of Technology, The Netherlands
Fred Heemstra, KWD Result Management, The Netherlands

ERP implementation projects affect large parts of an implementing organization and lead to changes in the way an organization performs its tasks. The costs needed for the effort to implement these systems are hard to estimate. Research indicates that the size of an ERP project can be a useful measurement for predicting the effort required to complete an ERP implementation project. However, such a metric does not yet exist. Therefore research should be carried out to find a set of variables which can define the size of an ERP project. The authors hypothesize that ERP projects consist of a collection of clusters of activities with their own focus on implementation costs and project size. This was confirmed in a survey among domain experts. This chapter describes a first step in retrieving these clusters. It shows 21 logical clusters of ERP implementation project activities based on 405 ERP implementation project activities retrieved from literature. Logical clusters of ERP project activities can be used in further research to find variables for defining the size of an ERP project.

Chapter 6

Time, Attitude, and User Participation: How Prior Events Determine User Attitudes in ERP Implementation 80
Lene Pries-Heje, IT University of Copenhagen, Denmark

Assimilation of a standard ERP system to an organization is difficult. User involvement seems to be the crux of the matter. However, even the best intentions for user involvement may come to nothing. A case study of a five-year ERP implementation process reveals that a main reason may be that the perception of usefulness of the system in any given phase of the implementation is heavily dependent on preceding events—the process. A process model analysis identifies eight episodes and nine encounters in the case showing that the user's attitude towards the ERP system changes between acceptance, equivocation, resistance and rejection depending on three things: (1) the dynamic between user and consultants, (2) the dynamic between different user groups, and (3) the understanding of technical, organizational and socio-technical options. When relating the empirical findings to existing theory on user participation, it is argued that the changes could be explained as a slide from influential user participation toward pseudo participation and back to influential participation, and that user participation in the context of ERP implementations raises new issues regarding user participation. Thus further research regarding new approaches and/or new techniques and tools for user participation in the context of ERP implementations is needed.

Chapter 7

ERP Selection: Effect of Product and Organizational Constructs 99
Uzoka Faith-Michael Emeka, Mount Royal University, Canada
Abiola Richard Oladele, Federal University of Technology, Nigeria

Previous studies have shown that Enterprise Resource Planning (ERP) systems have significantly impacted positively on the productivity of the organization. However, there exists a cost-failure paradox. ERP systems are very expensive and constitute a huge budgetary component, yet the failure rate of ERPs is very high. The selection process of ERPs is a critical success factor. This study focuses on the product and organizational constructs that affect the selection of ERP systems. The authors utilized an extension of technology acceptance model (TAM) by elements of the information systems (IS) success model. The study evaluated the impact of system quality, information quality, service quality, and support quality as key determinants of cognitive response, which influences ERP system purchase/use. Industry, firm size, buying center, and product experience were introduced as organizational constructs. The results of the study indicate that system quality, information quality and software support are significant product qualities that affect an organization's decision to adopt an ERP product. Among the organizational constructs, only firm size was found to be statistically significant. The results also indicate that multi department committees and the IT department are the major buying centers responsible for vendor selection. In terms of information source, vendor reference and adverts are major information sources, while government standards and popularity/experience of vendors are important considerations in vendor selection.

Chapter 8
A SOA-Based Approach to Integrate Enterprise Systems 120
Anne Lämmer, University of Potsdam, Germany
Sandy Eggert, University of Potsdam, Germany
Norbert Gronau, University of Potsdam, Germany

This chapter presents a procedure for the integration of enterprise systems. Therefore enterprise systems are being transferred into a service oriented architecture. The procedure model starts with decomposition into Web services. This is followed by mapping redundant functions and assigning of the original source code to the Web services, which are orchestrated in the final step. Finally, an example is given how to integrate an Enterprise Resource Planning System with an Enterprise Content Management System using the proposed procedure model.

Chapter 9
The Underlying Test—Human, Organisational and Technical Considerations adjoined
with Critical Success Factors when Implementing ERP: A Case Study of a UK SME 134
Jonathan D. Owens, University of Lincoln, UK
Julie Dawson, University of Lincoln, UK

Enterprise Resource Planning (ERP) systems are pervasive information systems that have been fundamental in organisations for the past two decades. ERP systems may well count as the most important development in technology in the 1990s. There are many ERP success stories; equally there are as many failure stories. However, organisations encounter obstacles when implementing ERP systems. This chapter intends to explore some of the problems that occur throughout the implementation of an ERP system.

Chapter 10
The Role of Enterprise Perceptions in Acceptance of Information Systems 156
Blanca Hernández, University of Zaragoza, Spain
Julio Jiménez, University of Zaragoza, Spain
M. José Martín, University of Zaragoza, Spain

This study analyzes current and future enterprise use of various Information Systems (IS), such as management software, employing a technology acceptance model (TAM) optimized by the inclusion of technological compatibility with previous IS and Web procurement. It also examines whether relationships in the model change according to the sector to which an enterprise belongs (i.e., if there exists a moderating effect of industry). The study applies two types of analyses: structural and multisample. The results show that Technological compatibility, Web procurement, Perceived usefulness and Perceived ease of use influence upon future use of business IS. Enterprises need to be aware that interrelationships exist among the various IS. Investment in a specific system may facilitate the acceptance and subsequent performance of other applications. Furthermore, the "industry effect" modifies two important TAM relationships, and consequently it affects enterprise behaviour regarding IS

Chapter 11

Modeling and Implementation of Formal Power Structures in Enterprise Information Systems....... 174
Alexei Sharpanskykh, Vrije Universiteit Amsterdam, The Netherlands

The concepts of power and authority are inherent in human organizations of any type. In some organizations power relations on individuals are defined explicitly and formalized in organizational documentation. In other organizations power relations are implicit, less strict and may change depending on contextual conditions. As power relations have important consequences for organizational viability and productivity, they should be considered explicitly in enterprise information systems (EISs). Although organization theory provides a rich and very diverse theoretical basis on organizational power, still most of the definitions for power-related concepts are too abstract, often vague and ambiguous to be directly implemented in EISs. To create a bridge between informal organization theories and automated EISs, this chapter proposes a formal logic-based specification language for representing power- (in particular authority) relations and their dynamics. The use of the language is illustrated by considering authority structures of organizations of different types. Moreover, the chapter demonstrates how the formalized authority relations can be integrated into an EIS.

Chapter 12

Enhancing Traditional ATP Functionality in Open Source ERP Systems:
A Case Study from the Food & Beverages Industry... 188
Ioannis T. Christou, Athens Information Technology, Greece
Stavros Ponis, National Technical University of Athens, Greece

Available-to-promise (ATP) procedures in today's enterprise information systems usually involve a simple search for available or planned inventory of a particular product in a particular depot at a particular time. In this chapter, ATP is viewed as a dynamic and more complex problem of deciding whether to accept a customer order request given the available inventory and planned production plus the remaining production capacity and business rules for covering demand from certain customer classes, for given products and time window. Whenever this is not possible, the production schedule is modified, by utilizing "reserved" capacity and resources, to cover extra demand. A prototype tool has been designed and implemented based on this approach, that can be easily integrated into existing ERP systems enhancing their functionality and increasing the level of customer service. The elaborated prototype is pilot tested in a case company in the food industry and is loosely integrated within the Open Source Compiere 2, ERP system extended to handle manufacturing. The prototype produces almost real time results on modern commodity-off-the-shelf computers, thus enhancing sales personnel performance and efficiency and increasing the level of customer service and satisfaction.

Chapter 13

Developing an Enterprise Wide Knowledge Warehouse: Challenge of Optimal Designs
in the Media Industry 203

Amit Mitra, Cranfield University, UK

Laura Campoy, University of the West of England, UK

It has been common practice among organisations to develop standard operating procedures to gain advantages like standardisation, ensure continuity, and deal with contingency needs. Over time, processual perspectives of activity within organisations have enabled appreciation of such practices through what is commonly referred to as organisational knowledge. Whilst the process of knowledge development can be unique to the context, practical dimensions of development may be considerably different from those suggested by established theory. The present chapter firstly reviews different frameworks that have come to be recognised as being effective in categorising organisational knowledge. Secondly, in the light of experiences of both authors in developing an interactive knowledge warehouse, the present chapter discusses usefulness of these frameworks. Prevalence of non-disclosure conditions would mean that the mentioned organisation would need to remain anonymous. For the purposes of the present chapter, the chosen organisation would be referred to as Kadrosi.

Chapter 14

Exploring the Influence Sources of ERP Adoption and the Y2K Effect in Taiwan 224

Hsiu-Hua Chang, National Central University and Tajen University, Taiwan

*Chun-Po Yin, Haiching Vocational High School of Technology and Commerce and Cheng Shiu
University, Taiwan*

Huey-Wen Chou, National Central University, Taiwan

Based on diffusion-of-innovation models, in this study, the authors investigate the influence sources of ERP adoption in Taiwan and explore if the Y2K can be viewed as a critical point. The results demonstrate that the main influence source of ERP adoption is the mixed influence source for all adopters. Before the Y2K, the internal model shows the higher power of explanation. And after the Y2K, the main influence becomes external influence source. With different diffusion patterns before and after the Y2K, the results confirm that the Y2K is a critical point. Besides contributing to the application of diffusion-of-innovation in Taiwan's ERP adoption, the results of this study can provide suggestions for ERP suppliers' marketing strategy.

Chapter 15

IS Success Factors and IS Organizational Impact: Does Ownership Type Matter in Kuwait? 239

Abdulrida Alshawaf, Kuwait University, Kuwait

Omar E. M. Khalil, Kuwait University, Kuwait

This research investigated the possible ownership type effect on the information systems (IS) success factors and IS impact on organizational performance in Kuwaiti organizations. Four IS success factors—IS strategy and resources, end user support, IS sophistication and IS organizational level & user involvement—and three IS organizational impact factors—improving work efficiency, improving decision making, and improving work effectiveness—were identified. Ownership type was found to affect the profiles of the IS success factors and IS organizational impact. Public organizations tend to commit less IS resources; their managers get less involved in IS strategy formulation, and their users get less involved in systems development. Yet, they tend to rate their IS organizational impact higher. This "IS expectation-performance gap" is further explained in the chapter, along with research implications, limitations, and future research.

Chapter 16

An ASP-Based Product Customization Service Systems for SMEs: A Case Study
in Construction Machinery 261

Yan Su, Nanjing University of Aeronautics and Astronautics, China
Wenhe Liao, Nanjing University of Aeronautics and Astronautics, China
Yu Guo, Nanjing University of Aeronautics and Astronautics, China
Shiwen Gao, Nanjing University of Aeronautics and Astronautics, China
Huibin Shi, Nanjing University of Aeronautics and Astronautics, China

A product customization system with integrated application services is helpful for small to medium-sized enterprises (SMEs). The mode of application service provider (ASP) particularly targets SMEs by providing integrated applications. The current product customization system seldom considers integrating with ASPs and orienting product lifecycle. In this chapter, an ASP-based product customization service system operating in lifecycle-oriented customization mode is proposed. Resource share, product data transform, and product configuration are three important aspects for effectively supporting lifecycle-oriented product customization service. A resource collection method for distributed resource share is put forward. An XML-based data mapping model for isomeric/isomorphic product data transform is presented. A new algorithm for rapid product configuration is designed, and an interactive virtual environment for collaborative configuration is suggested. Using this system, SMEs can develop their Internet-based sales and customization systems smoothly, in a short time, and at low cost. A construction machinery oriented product customization service platform is introduced as a case study.

Chapter 17

Monitoring Enterprise Applications and the Future of Self-Healing Applications 278

Shuchih Ernest Chang, National Chung Hsing University, Taiwan
Boris Minkin, National Chung Hsing University, Taiwan

With the drastic growth of the Internet and the advance of hardware and software technologies, the enterprise information systems supporting business operations and functions have become more and more complex. The need of monitoring the behavior of such systems is becoming apparent, since it allows detecting problems early and resolving them before they become fatal and affect business seriously. In addition to covering the concept and related technologies of various monitoring approaches and their corresponding advantage and disadvantages, this chapter illustrates how self-healing application monitoring can facilitate the performance and availability management of Java based enterprise applications. The creating of enterprise strength monitoring solutions, together with the criteria of monitoring technology adoption and vendor selection, is also presented in this chapter.

Chapter 18

Managing the Implementation of Business Intelligence Systems: A Critical
Success Factors Framework..291

William Yeoh, University of South Australia, Australia
Andy Koronios, University of South Australia, Australia
Jing Gao, University of South Australia, Australia

The implementation of a BI system is a complex undertaking requiring considerable resources. Yet there is a limited authoritative set of CSFs for management reference. This chapter represents a first step of filling in the research gap. The authors utilized the Delphi method to conduct three rounds of studies with 15 BI system experts in the domain of engineering asset management organizations. The study develops a CSFs framework that consists of seven factors and associated contextual elements crucial for BI systems implementation. The CSFs are committed management support and sponsorship, business user-oriented change management, clear business vision and well-established case, business-driven methodology and project management, business-centric championship and balanced project team composition, strategic and extensible technical framework, and sustainable data quality and governance framework. This CSFs framework allows BI stakeholders to holistically understand the critical factors that influence implementation success of BI systems.

Chapter 19

Rule-Based Approach for a Better B2B Discovery 308

Youcef Aklouf, University of Science and Technology –USTHB, Algeria
El Kindi Rezig, University of Science and Technology –USTHB, Algeria

This chapter presents an approach that targets the discovery of organizations' Web services according to what they provide to other organizations that might become potential partners using a functionality-based model. The proposed model attempts to express without ambiguity the functionalities of the organization's Web services operations by using an ontology. Moreover, the proposed approach exploits expert systems that aim at adding new business functionalities to Web services according to their rule-base defined by the organization knowledge engineer or the system administrator. The authors have also added a semantic layer between the ontology and the expert systems to make them more ontology-aware. A JAVA implementation has been done to validate the authors' proposal.

Chapter 20

Generic Object Oriented Enterprise Modeling Approach Utilizing a Strategic
Abstraction Mechanism 322

Islam Choudhury, Kingston University, Kingston-upon-Thames, UK
Sergio de Cesare, Brunel University, UK
Emily Di Florido, Brunel University, UK

A Generic Object-Oriented Enterprise Modeling Process (GOOEMP) is a set of partially ordered steps intended to reach the objective of building a fully integrated, dynamic, object-oriented model of the enterprise. An abstraction mechanism is proposed to enable this process. The process is generic because it applies to most types of enterprises. Enterprise models are the products developed from the process and these can be used by various stakeholders in an organization to: a) give them an understanding of the enterprise; b) design integrated information systems; c) respond to business changes by evolving their enterprise models and information systems in a coordinated and coherent manner; and d) enable the enterprise models built within a particular industry to be reused and applied to many other industries.

Chapter 21
Semantic Web Services for Simulation Component Reuse and Interoperability:
An Ontology Approach 336
    Simon J. E. Taylor, Brunel University, UK
    David Bell, Brunel University, UK
    Navonil Mustafee, Brunel University, UK
    Sergio de Cesare, Brunel University, UK
    Mark Lycett, Brunel University, UK
    Paul A. Fishwick, University of Florida, USA

Commercial-off-the-shelf (COTS) Simulation Packages (CSPs) are widely used in industry primarily due to economic factors associated with developing proprietary software platforms. Regardless of their widespread use, CSPs have yet to operate across organizational boundaries. The limited reuse and interoperability of CSPs are affected by the same semantic issues that restrict the inter-organizational use of software components and web services. The current representations of Web components are predominantly syntactic in nature lacking the fundamental semantic underpinning required to support discovery on the emerging Semantic Web. The authors present new research that partially alleviates the problem of limited semantic reuse and interoperability of simulation components in CSPs. Semantic models, in the form of ontologies, utilized by the authors' Web service discovery and deployment architecture provide one approach to support simulation model reuse.

Compilation of References 353

About the Contributors 387

Index 397

Preface

Enterprise Information Systems (EIS) allow for the sharing and coordination of information across an organization. Given the global nature of today's business, it has become necessary to develop strategic alliances and promote inter-organizational communication. This collection, entitled *Organizational Advancements through Enterprise Information Systems: Emerging Applications and Developments*, provides a comprehensive assessment of the latest developments in the EIS revolution. Individual chapters, which focus on Enterprise Resource Planning (ERP) adoption, the integration of enterprise systems, personalized ERP, and the Semantic Web, offer ideas and solutions for the future of the global enterprise.

Chapter 1, "*Critical Success Factors in Enterprise Resource Planning Implementations*," by Joseph R. Muscatello and Injazz J. Chen seeks to further the study of the critical success factors of ERP implementations by using statistical analysis to further delineate the patterns of adoption of the various concepts. Through the use of a cross-sectional mail survey, the authors offer empirical evidence of critical success factors that will enable practitioners to improve their chances of ERP project success. Additionally, this study furthers the academic theory of ERP implementations that can benefit future studies.

Chapter 2, "*The Paradox of Complex ERP Systems used in Simplified Organisations such as Small and Medium Enterprises*," by Catherine Equey and Emmanuel Fragnière further develops and generalises findings from the authors' July 2008 paper in the International Journal of Enterprise Information Systems (IJEIS) by adding organisational issues such as business process reengineering (BPR). The authors argue that enterprise resource planning (ERP) systems are complex management tools that impose standard business processes from larger manufacturing firms. The authors test whether these systems can be adapted effectively to more simplified organisations such as small and medium enterprises (SMEs). The authors found that SMEs tend to have a high perceived level of satisfaction when using these complex tools, independent of size or sector. However, they cannot clearly establish that SMEs having applied BPR while implementing an ERP system are more satisfied than those that did not.

Chapter 3, "*Requirements Management for ERP Projects*," by S. Parthasarathy and Muthu Ramachandran proposes: (1) An ERP maturity model (EMM) for assessing the ERP maturity within the organization and (2) A Requirements Engineering Method (REM) for ERP system requirements to capture the requirements from the different types of users of an ERP system, verifying and validating them. The EMM consists of three levels and each level has a focus and a key process area. Key indicators of ERP functionality identified by a major ERP vendor have been used to apply the EMM to an enterprise. This identifies the level of the EMM to which an enterprise belongs. Then the REM is used to enable the enterprise to assess its ERP system requirements and refine it using a knowledge database to reach a higher level in the EMM than the present one. The authors deem that this model can benefit users across all the ERP projects.

Chapter 4, "*Requirements Elicitation for Personalized ERP Systems: A Case Study*," by Lex van Velsen, Corrie Huijs, and Thea van der Geest reports on the usefulness of several methods for eliciting user input which served as a basis for requirements for a personalized ERP system. It describes the yield of heuristic evaluations, both by experts and by developers, and a focus group with six users representing the main user types. The focus group consisted of an identification of the most important functions, task demonstrations, and a mini design workshop. As a demonstration of the results of the various user-focused methods, some noteworthy findings on the personalization of ERP systems are presented.

Chapter 5, *"Specifying General Activity Clusters for ERP Projects Aimed at Effort Prediction,"* by Guy Janssens, Rob Kusters, and Fred Heemstra hypothesizes that ERP projects consist of a collection of clusters of activities with their own focus on implementation costs and project size. This was confirmed in a survey among domain experts. This chapter describes a first step in retrieving these clusters. It shows 21 logical clusters of ERP implementation project activities based on 405 ERP implementation project activities retrieved from literature. Logical clusters of ERP project activities can be used in further research to find variables for defining the size of an ERP project.

Chapter 6, *"Time, Attitude, and User Participation: How Prior Events Determine User Attitudes in ERP Implementation,"* by Lene Pries-Heje discusses the difficulty in assimilating an ERP system to an organization. User involvement seems to be the crux of the matter. However, even the best intentions for user involvement may come to nothing. A case study of a five-year ERP implementation process reveals that a main reason may be that the perception of usefulness of the system in any given phase of the implementation is heavily dependent on preceding events—the process. A process model analysis identifies eight episodes and nine encounters in the case showing that the user's attitude towards the ERP system changes between acceptance, equivocation, resistance and rejection depending on three things: (1) the dynamic between user and consultants, (2) the dynamic between different user groups, and (3) the understanding of technical, organizational and socio-technical options. When relating the empirical findings to existing theory on user participation, it is argued that the changes could be explained as a slide from influential user participation toward pseudo participation and back to influential participation, and that user participation in the context of ERP implementations raises new issues regarding user participation. Thus further research regarding new approaches and/or new techniques and tools for user participation in the context of ERP implementations is needed.

Chapter 7, *"ERP Selection: Effect of Product and Organizational Constructs,"* by Uzoka Faith-Michael Emeka and Abiola Richard Oladele focuses on the product and organizational constructs that affect the selection of ERP systems. The authors utilized an extension of technology acceptance model (TAM) by elements of the information systems (IS) success model. The study evaluated the impact of system quality, information quality, service quality, and support quality as key determinants of cognitive response, which influences ERP system purchase/use. Industry, firm size, buying center, and product experience were introduced as organizational constructs. The results of the study indicate that system quality, information quality and software support are significant product qualities that affect an organization's decision to adopt an ERP product. Among the organizational constructs, only firm size was found to be statistically significant. The results also indicate that multi department committees and the IT department are the major buying centers responsible for vendor selection.

Chapter 8, *"A SOA-Based Approach to Integrate Enterprise Systems,"* by Anne Lämmer, Sandy Eggert, and Norbert Gronau presents a procedure for the integration of enterprise systems. Therefore enterprise systems are being transferred into a service oriented architecture. The procedure model starts with decomposition into Web services. This is followed by mapping redundant functions and assigning of the original source code to the Web services, which are orchestrated in the final step. Finally, an example is given how to integrate an Enterprise Resource Planning System with an Enterprise Content Management System using the proposed procedure model.

Chapter 9, "*The Underlying Test—Human, Organisational and Technical Considerations adjoined with Critical Success Factors when Implementing ERP: A Case Study of a UK SME,*" by Jonathan D Owens and Julie Dawson intends to explore some of the problems that occur throughout the implementation of an ERP system. Enterprise Resource Planning (ERP) systems are pervasive information systems that have been fundamental in organisations for the past two decades. ERP systems may well count as the most important development in technology in the 1990s. There are many ERP success stories; equally there are as many failure stories. However, organisations encounter obstacles when implementing ERP systems.

Chapter 10, "*The Role of Enterprise Perceptions in Acceptance of Information Systems,*" by Blanca Hernández, Julio Jiménez, and M. José Martín analyzes current and future enterprise use of various Information Systems (IS), such as management software, employing a technology acceptance model (TAM) optimized by the inclusion of technological compatibility with previous IS and Web procurement. It also examines whether relationships in the model change according to the sector to which an enterprise belongs (i.e., if there exists a moderating effect of industry). The study applies two types of analyses: structural and multisample. The results show that Technological compatibility, Web procurement, Perceived usefulness and Perceived ease of use influence upon future use of business IS. Enterprises need to be aware that interrelationships exist among the various IS. Investment in a specific system may facilitate the acceptance and subsequent performance of other applications. Furthermore, the "industry effect" modifies two important TAM relationships, and consequently it affects enterprise behaviour regarding IS.

Chapter 11, "*Modeling and Implementation of Formal Power Structures in Enterprise Information Systems,*" by Alexei Sharpanskykh proposes a formal logic-based specification language for representing power- (in particular authority) relations and their dynamics to create a bridge between informal organization theories and automated EISs. The use of the language is illustrated by considering authority structures of organizations of different types. Moreover, the chapter demonstrates how the formalized authority relations can be integrated into an EIS.

Chapter 12, "*Enhancing Traditional ATP Functionality in Open Source ERP Systems: A Case Study from the Food & Beverages Industry,*" by Ioannis T. Christou and Stavros Ponis views Available-to-promise (ATP) procedures as a dynamic and more complex problem of deciding whether to accept a customer order request given the available inventory and planned production plus the remaining production capacity and business rules for covering demand from certain customer classes, for given products and time window. Whenever this is not possible, the production schedule is modified, by utilizing "reserved" capacity and resources, to cover extra demand. A prototype tool has been designed and implemented based on this approach, that can be easily integrated into existing ERP systems enhancing their functionality and increasing the level of customer service. The elaborated prototype is pilot tested in a case company in the food industry and is loosely integrated within the Open Source Compiere 2, ERP system extended to handle manufacturing. The prototype produces almost real time results on modern commodity-off-the-shelf computers, thus enhancing sales personnel performance and efficiency and increasing the level of customer service and satisfaction.

Chapter 13, "*Developing an Enterprise Wide Knowledge Warehouse: Challenge of Optimal Designs in the Media Industry*" by Amit Mitra and Laura Campoy first reviews reviews different frameworks that have come to be recognised as being effective in categorising organisational knowledge. Secondly, in the light of experiences of both authors in developing an interactive knowledge warehouse, the present chapter discusses usefulness of these frameworks. Prevalence of non-disclosure conditions would mean that the mentioned organisation would need to remain anonymous. For the purposes of the present chapter, the chosen organisation would be referred to as Kadrosi.

Chapter 14, "*Exploring the Influence Sources of ERP Adoption and the Y2K Effect in Taiwan*," by Hsiu-Hua Chang, Chun-Po Yin, and Huey-Wen Chou investigates the influence sources of ERP adoption in Taiwan and explore if the Y2K can be viewed as a critical point. The results demonstrate that the main influence source of ERP adoption is the mixed influence source for all adopters. Before the Y2K, the internal model shows the higher power of explanation. And after the Y2K, the main influence becomes external influence source. With different diffusion patterns before and after the Y2K, the results confirm that the Y2K is a critical point. Besides contributing to the application of diffusion-of-innovation in Taiwan's ERP adoption, the results of this study can provide suggestions for ERP suppliers' marketing strategy.

Chapter 15, "*IS Success Factors and IS Organizational Impact: Does Ownership Type Matter in Kuwait?*" by Abdulrida Alshawaf and Omar E. M. Khalil, investigates the possible ownership type effect on the information systems (IS) success factors and IS impact on organizational performance in Kuwaiti organizations. Four IS success factors—IS strategy and resources, end user support, IS sophistication and IS organizational level & user involvement—and three IS organizational impact factors—improving work efficiency, improving decision making, and improving work effectiveness—were identified. Ownership type was found to affect the profiles of the IS success factors and IS organizational impact. Public organizations tend to commit less IS resources; their managers get less involved in IS strategy formulation, and their users get less involved in systems development. Yet, they tend to rate their IS organizational impact higher. This "IS expectation-performance gap" is further explained in the article, along with research implications, limitations, and future research.

Chapter 16, "*An ASP-Based Product Customization Service Systems for SMEs: A Case Study in Construction Machinery*," by Yan Su, Wenhe Liao, Yu Guo, Shiwen Gao, and Huibin Shi proposes an ASP-based product customization service system operating in lifecycle-oriented customization mode. Resource share, product data transform, and product configuration are three important aspects for effectively supporting lifecycle-oriented product customization service. A resource collection method for distributed resource share is put forward. An XML-based data mapping model for isomeric/isomorphic product data transform is presented. A new algorithm for rapid product configuration is designed, and an interactive virtual environment for collaborative configuration is suggested. Using this system, SMEs can develop their Internet-based sales and customization systems smoothly, in a short time, and at low cost. A construction machinery oriented product customization service platform is introduced as a case study.

Chapter 17, "*Monitoring Enterprise Applications and the Future of Self-Healing Applications*," by Shuchih Ernest Chang and Boris Minkin illustrates how self-healing application monitoring can facilitate the performance and availability management of Java based enterprise applications. The creating of enterprise strength monitoring solutions, together with the criteria of monitoring technology adoption and vendor selection, is also presented in this chapter.

Chapter 18, "*Managing the Implementation of Business Intelligence Systems: A Critical Success Factors Framework*," by William Yeoh, Andy Koroios, and Jing Gao represents a first step of filling in the research gap. The authors utilized the Delphi method to conduct three rounds of studies with 15 BI system experts in the domain of engineering asset management organizations. The study develops a CSFs framework that consists of seven factors and associated contextual elements crucial for BI systems implementation. The CSFs are committed management support and sponsorship, business user-oriented change management, clear business vision and well-established case, business-driven methodology and project management, business-centric championship and balanced project team composition, strategic and extensible technical framework, and sustainable data quality and governance framework. This CSFs framework allows BI stakeholders to holistically understand the critical factors that influence implementation success of BI systems.

Chapter 19, *"Rule-Based approach for a Better B2B Discovery,"* by Youcef Aklouf and El Kindi Rezig, presents an approach that targets the discovery of organizations' Web services according to what they provide to other organizations that might become potential partners using a functionality-based model. The proposed model attempts to express without ambiguity the functionalities of the organization's Web services operations by using an ontology. Moreover, the proposed approach exploits expert systems that aim at adding new business functionalities to Web services according to their rule-base defined by the organization knowledge engineer or the system administrator. The authors have also added a semantic layer between the ontology and the expert systems to make them more ontology-aware. A JAVA implementation has been done to validate the authors' proposal.

Chapter 20, *"Generic Object Oriented Enterprise Modeling Approach Utilizing a Strategic Abstraction Mechanism,"* by Islam Choudhury, Sergio de Cesare, and Emily Di Florido reports on the Generic Object-Oriented Enterprise Modeling Process (GOOEMP), a set of partially ordered steps intended to reach the objective of building a fully integrated, dynamic, object-oriented model of the enterprise. An abstraction mechanism is proposed to enable this process. The process is generic because it applies to most types of enterprises. Enterprise models are the products developed from the process and these can be used by various stakeholders in an organization to: a) give them an understanding of the enterprise; b) design integrated information systems; c) respond to business changes by evolving their enterprise models and information systems in a coordinated and coherent manner; and d) enable the enterprise models built within a particular industry to be reused and applied to many other industries.

Chapter 21, *"Semantic Web Services for Simulation Component Reuse and Interoperability: An Ontology Approach,"* by Simon J. E. Taylor, David Bell, Navonil Mustafee, Sergio de Cesare, Mark Lycett, and Paul A. Fishwick presents new research that partially alleviates the problem of limited semantic reuse and interoperability of simulation components in Commercial-off-the-shelf (COTS) Simulation Packages (CSPs). Semantic models, in the form of ontologies, utilized by the authors' Web service discovery and deployment architecture provide one approach to support simulation model reuse.

Organizational Advancements through Enterprise Information Systems: Emerging Applications and Developments aims to provide contemporary coverage of enterprise information systems with a focus on how these systems help to achieve a global supply chain. Through investigations of different types of planning and implementation, the collection aims to inform researchers of best practices in the application and management of enterprise information systems.

Chapter 1
Critical Success Factors in Enterprise Resource Planning Implementations

Joseph R. Muscatello
Kent State University, USA

Injazz J. Chen
Cleveland State University, USA

ABSTRACT

Search for Enterprise Resource Planning (ERP) systems and one will find a plethora of information on both successful and unsuccessful systems implementations. The benefits of successful ERP implementations have been verified by numerous studies. However, the critical success factors, those that truly help lead an organization to success, are still being researched. This chapter seeks to further the study of the critical success factors of ERP implementations by using statistical analysis to further delineate the patterns of adoption of the various concepts. Through the use of a cross-sectional mail survey, the authors offer empirical evidence of critical success factors that will enable practitioners to improve their chances of ERP project success. Additionally, this study furthers the academic theory of ERP implementations that can benefit future studies.

INTRODUCTION

Enterprise resource planning (ERP) systems are implemented to eliminate disparate **systems** and to provide one common data source for all business (Muscatello et al., 2003; Chen, 2001; Hicks and Stecke, 1995). They also are used to replace legacy **systems** that are aging piecemeal solutions created by IS departments or older off-the-shelf packages that have become difficult to maintain and no longer

meet the needs of the organization (Bradley, 2008). This trend does not appear to be slowing down. The **ERP** market is forecasted to hit $US 1 trillion by 2010 (Hunter and Lippert, 2007) and a survey by the Society for Information Management showed that **ERP** spending is among the top application and developments of its members (Luftman et al., 2006). Given the level of spending on **ERP systems**, it is imperative that studies on **ERP implementation** successes and failures continue so as to provide a proven path to success in the future.

DOI: 10.4018/978-1-60566-968-7.ch001

The promises of gains from **ERP** are unbounded. **ERP systems** offer tremendous opportunities to more consistently provide information to organizations in a standardized, centralized and cost efficient manner (Muscatello and Parente, 2006; Olson, et al., 2005). **ERP systems** improve efficiency within the four walls of an enterprise by integrating and streamlining internal **processes** (Nicolaou and Bhattacharya, 2006; Somers and Nelson, 2004; Davenport and Brooks, 2004; Koch 2001; Anderson, 2000; Brakely, 1999; Davenport, 1998, 2000). **ERP** has also been found to be effective in reducing inventory costs, improving efficiency and increasing profitability (Muscatello, 2006; Brakely, 1999; Appleton, 1997). In addition, **ERP** has been credited with reducing manufacturing lead times (Davenport and Brooks, 2004; Goodpasture, 1995). Other potential benefits of **ERP** include drastic declines in inventory, breakthrough reductions in working capital, abundant information about customer wants and needs, and the ability to view and manage the extended enterprise of suppliers, alliances, and customers as an integrated whole (Muscatello, 2006; Muscatello, et al., 2003). Clearly, the integrated information **technology** of **ERP software** has the potential to provide manufacturing firms with extensive new competitive capabilities, especially since the real-time information can improve the speed and precision of enterprise response. Given the widespread popularity of **ERP software**, and the spectacular successes achieved by a few firms, an open question remains: Why has the effective deployment of **ERP systems** proven to be elusive for the majority of firms? (Stratman and Roth, 2002).

Despite the promise of **ERP systems**, these **software** solutions have proven to be expensive and difficult to implement, as they often impose new logic and **processes** and completely change a company's strategy and culture (Bradley, 2008; Muscatello, 2006; Pozzebon, 2000). **Implementation** of an **ERP** does not come without significant technical and managerial challenges, huge financial investments, and a great deal of organizational change. Operational problems at Dell, Hershey Foods, Whirlpool, FoxMeyer Drugs and more recently Hewlett Packard, Mobile Europe and W.L. Gore & Associates have been blamed on poor **implementations** of **ERP** solutions (Bradley, 2008). **ERP** also has the reputation of being notoriously over-sold and under-delivered (Millman, 2004). Cliffe (1999) even reported that 65% of executives believed that **ERP** could be harmful to their organizations and Failure rates can approach 50% (Muscatello and Parente, 2006).

Many **researchers** have attempted to identify the set of **factors** that are critical for ensuring success with **ERP implementations**. A lot of these efforts have been case study driven and have had important but not necessarily comprehensive conclusions for critical success **factors** of **ERP implementations**. Employing a large scale survey, this paper seeks to ascertain how businesses receive these concepts and, more specifically, which concepts are practiced widely and which are not. With this goal in mind, we first identify and develop pertinent constructs of **ERP implementations** based on a critical review of business and managerial literature in section 2. We then explain the **research** design including data collection in section 3. Section 4 presents the results along with implications of the study findings. In the concluding section, we highlight the limitations of the study along with guidelines for future **research**.

THEORETICAL ERP IMPLEMENTATION CONSTRUCTS

Key **factors** have been developed of **ERP implementations** based on a critical review of both scholarly and managerial literature. These constructs include strategic initiatives, executive commitment, human resources, **project** management, information **technology**, business **process**, **training**, **project** support and communications, and **software** selection and support. The constructs developed by the authors are very similar to the ones developed by Stratman and Roth (2002), further validating the **research** effort undertaken here.

Strategic Initiatives

Business success is not guaranteed by the successful integration of the internal functions of the business. End-to-end **processes** that transfer information from module to module will not in themselves improve cost effectiveness and efficiency. The ability to use the information to drive the business is the key to successful integration. Performance measurements must be developed to measure the impact of the **ERP** system on the business. It has been suggested that an **ERP** system that is not strategically tied into the supply chain will lack the ability to provide the type of business intelligence that is needed to grow the business (Muscatello, 2006; Davenport and Brooks, 2004; Melnyk and Stewart, 2002; Koch, 1999; Carr, 1999; Hickes and Stecke, 1995;)Therefore, it is essential that firms must have strategic goals in place before undertaking an **ERP implementation** (Motwani et al., 2002).

Executive Commitment

Top management is consistently identified as the most important success **factor** in **ERP** system **implementations** (Bradley 2008; Bowen et al., 2007; Gupta, 2000; Rao, 2000; Bancroft et al., 1998; Davenport 1998; Sumner, 1999; Bingi et al., 1999; Welti, 1999;). It can be inferred from the literature that executives and managers believe that **ERP systems** help their company achieve greater business benefits. However, they are mystified as to how to design, implement and manage an **ERP project**. When it comes to **ERP projects**, Fortune 500 companies are beginning to sound like children in the back seat of a car on a long drive—"Are we there yet? Are we done yet? No!

We're not there and we are not done. And we may never be done." (Koch, 1999).

Any executive planning the **implementation** of an **ERP** system needs to make some savvy decisions, from identifying what business needs the **ERP** system must meet to preparing for post-**implementation** maintenance and user support (Musson, 1998). Many executives are having a hard time understanding that **ERP implementation** is not simply a package installation. It is a long journey of fine-tuning, upgrading, and continual learning, not a sprint. Therefore it may lead to a sense of frustration and anger at the system and in some cases total abandonment. Unlike any other **software project**, an **ERP** system doesn't merely change employees' computer screens the way previous generations of **software** did; it changes the way they do their jobs and how the company does business. Top management, therefore, must fully understand the degree of the changes and supports needed for the new **project** and be comfortable with the fact that the decisions their planners make will have a profound impact on the entire supply chain (Chen, 2001).

Human Resources

The most recurring theme in management literature concerning the failure of **ERP systems** is the inability of firms to take into account the new organizational, interdepartmental, and personnel aspects of work organizations. Unintended consequences include the emotional fallout when employees are suddenly given much greater responsibilities. Managers sometimes neglect to assess not only the skill development needed by employees but also the organizational changes required of them (Muscatello 2006; Appleton, 1997). This can be very difficult for employees as the **project** seems to be 'never ending.' It is also felt that the low Information **Technology** (IT) staff levels are inadequate for the rigorous and extensive IT **training** and development requirements of an **ERP project** because the expertise is usually low

(Hill, 1997). In many cases of **ERP implementations**, consultants are required to help meet the **project**s' needs (Muscatello, et al., 2003).

Project Management

Project managers must be veterans, with positive experiences, to lead an **ERP project** (Bradley 2008; Brown and Vessey, 2003). A **project** team must be flexible and deal with the problems as they arise in the **implementation process**. Anyone who revisits the charter documents of a large-scale **ERP project** will see that the ultimate product is almost always shaped by unanticipated and late breaking circumstances. It is a fact of business life that important things come up later rather than earlier in complex new **project**s (Cliffe, 1999). However, these interruptions should not encourage "scope creep," when **processes** or functions are added after the **project** has begun. As mentioned, unanticipated circumstances are the norm; however, wholesale changes such as adding an additional **process**, module or department after the **project** has been scoped and started may lead to a "never ending" **project**. To prevent scope problems, firms need to make sure a **project** charter or mission statement exists. It is paramount to nail down the **project** requirements and have them documented and signed by the senior management and users. Furthermore, it is essential for firms to clearly define change control procedures and hold everyone to them. Tight change control procedures may end up causing tension between the **project** team and those who do not get the changes they want. Ultimately, though, the **project** will not be successful if the **project** team is trying to hit a constantly moving target (Trepper, 1999).

A survey by the Meta Group found that it takes an average of 31 months before an **ERP** system will show benefits (Muscatello, 2006). There is no magic in implementing **ERP systems**, but, when they are carefully conceived and executed, **ERP systems** can radically changed the way companies do business. In many companies, it would now be unthinkable to manage financials, customer relationships and supply chains without **ERP** (Oliver, 1999).

Information Technology

Information **technology** has moved from a support function to an integrated core of business. Knowledge management, data analysis and quick response methodologies are now the future of business. IT/business alignments are required for business success (Bowen et al., 2007; Stevens Institute of **Technology**, 2007; Whalen 2007; Luftman et al., 2006;) Deloitte Consulting (2000) reports that the second largest **ERP implementation** challenge related people issues is internal staff adequacy. If a firm's existing **technology** will run the new **ERP** system, then the **technology training** may be an upgrade of the skill set. If a wholesale change is required, such as moving from an IBM mainframe to a Sun Microsystem, then an in-depth **hardware** and **software training** program must be implemented. In fact, some firms have selected their **ERP systems** based on their current **technology** and business **process**, and **research** has showed this approach to be a mistake since it is very limiting (Anderson, 2000). Because some firms may not be willing to change current **technology**, they may consequently report a lower significance on **technology training** for **ERP implementation**. Firms who account for business **processes** first and **technology** fit second reflect IT **training** positively (Davenport 2000).

Managers cannot minimize the importance of **technology training** regardless if it is an upgrade of current **software** and **hardware** or a complete **technology** change. An upgrade of current **software** usually includes new file structures, report writers, functional modules and other changes. An upgrade of current **hardware** usually involves a re-installation of the operating system or at least installing the operating system changes, new functionality and new modules. If a complete **technology** change (**hardware** and/or **software**) is required, then a much larger commitment must be undertaken to insure that the proper employees can manage the **technology** after going live. In either case, managers must be proactive in securing the **technology training** to insure that their technical employees can run the **ERP** system effectively. The consequences of not having enough technical **training** can be catastrophic and lead to outright failure of the **ERP** system (Evangelista, 1998; Hill, 1997).

Business Process

As suggested by Hammer and Champy (1993), reengineering of business **process** activities focuses the firm on identifying and improving the efficiency of critical operations, on restructuring important non-value-adding operations and on eliminating inefficient **processes**. Reengineering should be undertaken to insure that the strategic objectives mentioned earlier are feasible. The reengineering effort should create a uniform response from all aspects of the business. When goals are common, improvement becomes a shared task (Hill, 2000). Using reengineering techniques to develop a homogeneous vision depicting the company's **processes** after the **ERP implementation**, a firm is more likely to minimize uncertainty and achieve success. **Researchers** have found a strong correlation between the attention paid to business **process** improvement and the likelihood of **ERP** success (Muscatello and Parente 2006; Muscatello, 2006; Olson et al., 2005; Millman, 2004; Muscatello et al., 2003; Carton and Adams 2003; Motwani et al., 2002;).

Training

Radical **process** changes brought about by **ERP implementation** have made providing sufficient and timely **training** to **project** persons and users a critical requirement in **ERP implementation**

(Bradely, 2008; Davenport, 2000). Assessing the needs for **training** usually uncovers several **training** and skills deficiencies. Rectification of **training** deficiencies can be accomplished in three ways: reassignment, outsourcing or replacement of staff, hiring of new personnel with substantial knowledge in **ERP systems**, or **training** of managers and key employees. In most cases, a firm implementing **ERP** engages in two types of **training**: fundamental **ERP systems** education and technical **training** in the usage of the **ERP software** (Yusuf, 2004; Sarkis and Sundarraj, 2003; Muscatello, 2002; Evangelista, 1998). In international cases, language and cultural barriers can be a technical hindrance that requires additional **training** (Al-Mashari, 2000).

Project Support and Communications

Ongoing communication to all employees affected by the new **ERP** system is a must. Olsen et al., (2005) found that it is necessary to inform organizational employees of how the system can help them do their jobs better. They also found that all retained employees are going to find their jobs changed. **ERP** applications lock the operating principles and **processes** of the adopting organization into **software systems**. If organizations fail to reconcile the technological imperatives of the enterprise **systems** with their business needs, the logic of the system may conflict with the logic of business **processes** (Davenport, 1998). Needless to say, managers have found **ERP implementation projects** the most difficult **systems** development **projects** (Kumar et al., 2003). People are naturally resistant to change and it is very difficult to implement a system within an organization without some cooperation. Effective communication and ongoing support has also been noted by several **researchers** (e.g., Muscatello et al., 2003; Sarkis and Sundarraj 2003; Motwani et al., 2002;).

Software Selection and Support

One of the major challenges an adopting organization faces is that **software** does not fit all their requirements (Davenport, 1998). **ERP systems** are **software** packages, generically designed, keeping the industry-wide needs and best practices in mind (Kumar et al., 2003). A systematic "needs assessment" therefore must be commissioned to determine the specific **ERP** modules, subsystems and **hardware** that are required to achieve the desired level of **systems** integration. Where there is a lack of internal knowledge of **ERP systems** and their operating requirements (either at the corporate or division level), management should solicit the help of knowledgeable outside consultants for the assessment (Chen, 2001, Davenport, 2000, Booker, 1999). Firms that analyze their **software** "fit" and individual module needs can enhance the likelihood of a successful **ERP implementation** (Yusuf, et al., 2004).

RESEARCH DESIGN

Data Collection

Based on a thorough review of the literature, the theoretical constructs identified by this study are well grounded in existing theory (Muscatello et al., 2003). The theoretical constructs are made up of 4 or more items using a 7 point Likert scale with a score of 1 labeled "not important" and a score of 7 labeled "very important."

A cross sectional mail survey was conducted in the United States, during 2006, drawing from members of the American Production and Inventory Control Society (APICS), The National Association of Accountants (NAA), the American Productivity and Quality Center (APQC) and the Institute for Supply Management (ISM) because of their potential involvement in an **ERP implementation**. The survey was very clear that

only those with **ERP implementation** experience should respond.

A modified version of Dillman's total design method was followed in order to increase the response rate (Dillman, 1978). All mailings were first class mail including a cover letter, survey and postage paid return envelope. Three weeks after the initial mailing, reminder cards were sent to all potential respondents. Of the 973 surveys mailed, 28 came back due to address discrepancies. From the new sample size of 945, 203 were received resulting in a response rate of 21.5%. A total of 6 were discarded for incompleteness/damage for an effective response rate of 197/945 or 20.8%. Considering that this is a lengthy survey, this response rate is acceptable and correlates well with recent empirical studies in operations management (OM) and supply chain management (SCM) (e.g., Paulraj and Chen, 2005, 23.2%; Krause et al, 2001, 19.6%).

Respondent and Firm Profiles

The profile of the final sample of 197 included top executives (17%), middle managers (73%) and others (10%). Almost half of the firms had been in business for over 30 years (48%) and most were engaged in end product manufacturing (49%), followed by subassembly (30%), components (19%) and others (2%). Firm size was

Table 1. Respondent profile

Title	Count	Percent
Manufacturing/Business Executives CEO,CFO,COO,CIO President, Vice-President, Director	34	17%
Manufacturing/Business Middle Manager Purchasing Manager Operations/production Manager	143	73%
Other Buyers, Planners Supervisors	20	10%

Table 2. Company profile

Years in Operation	Count	Percent
Less than 5	55	28%
6-15	39	20%
16-30	8	04%
30 or more	95	48%
Types of Products Produced	**Count**	**Percent**
Components	37	19%
Sub Assemblies	59	30%
End Products	97	49%
Other	4	02%
Annual Sales Volume	**Count**	**Percent**
Less than $10m	16	08%
$10m-$100m	12	06%
$100m-$500m	37	19%
$500m-$1b	59	30%
$1b-$20b	61	31%
Greater than $20b	12	06%
Number of Employees	**Count**	**Percent**
Less Than 100	14	07%
101-250	14	07%
251-500	10	05%
501- Up	159	81%
Number of ERP Implementations	**Count**	**Percent**
1	154	78%
2	35	18%
3 or more	8	04%
Multiple ERP Systems in the Same Facility	**Count**	**Percent**
No	171	87%
Yes	26	13%

fairly evenly distributed between large and small firms with respondents with sales of over $20B (6%), $1B~$20B (31%), $500M~$1B (30%), $100M~$500M (19%), $10M~$100M (6%) and under $10M (8%). Most firms employed 500 or more employees (81%). The vast majority of the respondents were working on their first **ERP** system (78%) with some (22%) on their second or third system. Furthermore, most had not worked

on multiple **ERP systems** (87%), but some had multiple **systems** in the same facility (13%). The distribution of the sample regarding respondent and firm profiles are presented in Table 1 and Table 2, respectively.

RESULTS AND DISCUSSIONS

Exploratory **factor** analysis (EFA) was performed to empirically test the nine strategic **ERP** constructs included in this study using the principle component method. Items with a **factor** loading of 0.3 or greater were retained for further analysis (Flynn et al., 1994; Hair et al, 1998). Reliability analyses were performed to test whether random measurement errors varied from one question to another (Judd et al., 1991). Reliability was measured using Cronbach's alpha internal consistency method where reliability coefficients of 0.60 or higher are considered acceptable (Cronbach, 1951). All of the reliability coefficients are greater than 0.658 after the removal of questions 2 and 3 from the "Human Resource" construct and question 9 from the "**Software** Selection and Support" construct. Reliability Statistics and **factor** loadings are shown in Appendix A.

All questions were analyzed using a seven point Likert scale with a score of 1 labeled 'not important," a score of 4 labeled "neither important nor unimportant," and a scale of 7 labeled "very important." This study uses simple mean-based ranking of the indicators within each theoretical construct. Further analysis was conducted to provide additional insight into the results. The following sub-sections present the current state of practice for each of the theoretical constructs.

Strategic Initiatives

Table 3 presents the results for strategic initiatives. The mean response for the seven indicators ranged from 5.33 to 5.79. This result is a pleasant surprise in that many **researchers** have written about **ERP**

implementations being relegated to the information **technology** departments; to the contrary, this **research** shows that firms are now attaching a strategic component to their **ERP implementations** and that the decision to implement an **ERP** system is now being made at a cross functional executive level which includes inputs from all functional business areas. Further, the respondents concur that the **ERP implementation** should be tied to achieving strategic goals. The fact that two-thirds (67%) of the respondents came from firms with sales in excess of $500 million may further explain the increased desire for a strategic component. Larger firms have the resources to fully integrate **ERP systems** as opposed to just automating **processes** (Muscatello, 2002). These larger firms may have access to information and **research** that smaller firms do not and thus have common strategic goals and when goals are common, improvement becomes a shared task (Hill, 2000). The low standard deviation further shows the uniformity of this opinion.

Executive Commitment

Executive commitment has been documented to be of great importance in achieving any major business improvement **project**. The response to this survey re-confirms the need for executive commitment for **ERP implementations** identified by on past **research**. Seventy three percent (73%) of the respondents classified themselves

as middle-managers and 17% classified themselves as Director or above. However, a test of the means between the respondents produced no discernable difference, verifying that all levels of management consider executive commitment important. Table 4 presents the results for executive commitment and support. The mean response for the seven indicators ranged from 4.68 to 5.53. The highest responses came from the question on long-term executive commitment showing the high regard they have for executives who realize the complexity and time commitment necessary for a successful **implementation**. The lowest indicator showed that while executives deemed the **ERP implementation** very important, they still expected the operational concerns to be addressed in the interim.

Human Resources

Indicator number 2, 'low IT skills are an obstacle to successful **ERP implementations**' and Indicator 3, 'Executives with little knowledge of **ERP** should be minimally involved' were eliminated from the **research** to improve the Cronbach's alpha to 0.677 from 0.606. The mean responses of the remaining six indicators ranged from 4.57 to 5.76 and are presented in table 5. From the human resource side, there appears to be strong commitment to gaining the knowledge required to successfully implement **ERP systems** via **training** and education of current employees or hiring

Table 3. Strategic initiatives

Indicator	Mean	Std Dev
We constantly review our IT capabilities against strategic goals	5.79	1.148
Strategic IT planning is a continuous process	5.60	1.260
Written guidelines exist to structure strategic IT planning in our organization	5.33	1.369
Strategic IT planning includes inputs from all business functional areas	5.49	1.244
ERP is integrated into the strategic plans of all business functional areas	5.53	1.210
ERP was chosen to support the organization's strategic plans	5.59	1.124
Managers evaluate the potential of ERP when building strategic plans	5.40	1.181

of outside consulting help. Significant **research** has noted that **ERP** education and **training** is required for successful **implementation**. This **research** offers a new insight: respondents saw little difference between gaining the knowledge via education and **training** or through consulting help. The lowest responses came from the idea of replacing ineffective employees or managers who are not able to adapt to the new system. This could present a problem in some smaller firms where key managers have multiple tasks. Possible explanations for the low response rate for employee replacement includes the reluctance of many firms to terminate people for incompetence if they are well liked and committed. It is noted that Hammer and Champy (1993) also openly reject the idea of eliminating jobs through reengineering. Thus, many managers and consultants may still hold true to this idea.

Project Management

Respondents were asked about **ERP project** management issues including the responsibilities of **project** team members and the capabilities of the **project** leader. Table 6 presents the results for **Project** Management. The mean response for the seven indicators ranged from 5.51 to 5.64. This shows a strong commitment for **project** management skills in **project** definition, scope, tracking and status. It reveals that **project** management skills were grossly underestimated in **ERP implementation** in the past and are now becoming a critical skill set for ever changing business needs. The fact that 81% of the responding firms had more than 500 employees could also explain this response. Larger firms have more internal expertise to draw from and thus are more likely to be equipped with **project** management champions.

Table 4. Executive commitment

Indicator	Mean	Std Dev
The need for long term ERP support resources is recognized by management	5.53	1.100
Executive management is enthusiastic about the possibilities of ERP	5.29	1.144
Executives have invested the time needed to understand ERP's benefits	5.23	1.222
Executives mandate that ERP requirements have priority over functional concerns	4.68	1.387
Top management has clearly defined the ERP entity's business goals	5.31	1.378
All levels of management support the overall goals of the ERP entity	5.24	1.313
Executives continuously champion the ERP project	5.07	1.35

Table 5. Human resources

Indicator	Mean	Std Dev
The ability of the IT workforce to learn is critical to an ERP implementation	5.64	1.076
Low IT skills are an obstacle to successful ERP implementations	5.35	1.179
Executives with little knowledge of ERP should be minimally involved	4.86	1.711
Ineffective employees are moved or replaced if they are not able to adapt	4.57	1.396
Ineffective managers are moved or replaced if they are not able to adapt	4.83	1.445
The ERP team members need to understand the project has priority	5.74	1.040
Consultants are used where in-house knowledge is inadequate or not available	5.76	1.135
Compensation and incentives should be given to high achieving team members	5.57	1.170

Information Technology

Software and **hardware** expertise has been documented to be of great importance to a successful **ERP implementation** and this survey shows the same high level of importance with a range of the means from 5.41 to 5.69 with very low standard deviations. The results are presented in Table 7. Somewhat unique to this **research** is the attempt to find out the importance of the skill sets of the current information **technology** (IT) staff, which are deemed very important, and the use of consultants if the skill sets are not internal. The results show that firms are willing to supplement their IT staff with consultants when necessary. This acceptance of outside help shows an understanding of internal limitations of a firm and a sense of urgency and willingness to acquire it externally.

Business Process

ERP implementation has been referred to as an "organization wide revolution" due to the large number of changes it brings to an organization (Hammer and Stanton, 1999; Bingi et al., 1999). The strong connections that **researchers** have proposed between business **process** redesigns and successful **ERP implementation** have been confirmed by our results. The means ranged from 5.45 to 5.74 with low standard deviations are presented in Table 8. Interestingly, the high means for all seven indicators suggest that the connection **researchers** have preached is being accepted by the practitioners. Ross (1999) suggested that firms believed that **ERP software** would solve their problems by imposing discipline and **process** integration on their organization. This **research** confirms that practitioners now

Table 6. Project management

Indicator	Mean	Std Dev
The tasks to be performed during the ERP project are clearly defined	5.61	1.149
The responsibilities of project team members are clearly defined	5.64	1.167
There is a formal management process to track external contractor activities	5.59	1.173
Measurements are used to determine the status of project tasks	5.51	1.105
The ERP project leader is able to track project tasks to completion	5.58	1.102
The ERP project leader is experienced in project management	5.60	1.128
The ERP project leader is able to minimize project scope creep	5.57	1.031

Table 7. Information technology

Indicator	Mean	Std Dev
There is a high degree of technical expertise in the IT organization	5.49	1.137
Internal It members understand custom ERP software programs	5.52	1.062
The IT staff are able to efficiently implement ERP system upgrades	5.65	1.036
The IT staff are able to analyze the technical impact of proposed system changes	5.53	1.268
The IT organization provides a service to the business	5.47	1.296
Consultants are hired to supplement internal IT staff when necessary	5.63	1.165
The IT staff is continuously updating their technical skills through training	5.74	1.092

disagree with that assessment and realize that **software** is not a substitute for good business **processes**. The "business **process**" indicators indicate that **process** knowledge and redesign, cross functional management and driving out inefficiencies that improve customer benefits are all strongly accepted as necessary for a successful **implementation**. Hammer and Champy's (1993) work on reengineering and the wide-spread use of their practices as a change enabling tool helps confirm the positive use of reengineering in **ERP implementations**.

Training

The importance of **training** was echoed by most of our respondents. As expected, based on current **research**, **training** was a highly regarded component of **ERP implementations**. The means of the eight indicators ranged from 5.45 to 5.70 with low standard deviations and are presented in table 9. Again we asked the question if external expertise in the form of consulting should be used to supplement internal knowledge and the answer was strongly yes. Firms supported the need for formal, customized **training** on both **ERP** knowledge and specific job duties. They also strongly supported on-going education programs which has not always been the case for some firms who are risk adverse. The high percentage of respondents in larger firms (81% had 500 or more employees, and 86% had sales over $100 million) may explain the high level of interest in outside consulting help, since larger firms usually have greater access to resources. Smaller firms, without the access to **ERP** resources, need to establish whether or not they can obtain the resources or postpone the **implementation** since it is documented that

Table 8. Business process

Indicator	Mean	Std Dev
Employees understand how their actions impact the operations of other functions	5.45	1.171
There is a high level of business process knowledge within the ERP entity	5.52	1.123
Managers are skilled at analyzing business processes for customer benefits	5.65	1.036
Business process redesign is performed before ERP implementation	5.53	1.268
The operational processes of the ERP entity are formally documented	5.47	1.296
Business process redesign teams are cross functional	5.63	1.165
Redesigned business processes are used to drive out inefficiency	5.74	1.092

Table 9. Training

Indicator	Mean	Std Dev
Specific user training needs were identified early in the implementation	5.70	1.020
A formal training program has been developed to meet the ERP users requirements	5.53	1.276
Training materials have been customized for each specific job	5.45	1.158
Training materials target the entire business task, not just the ERP screens/reports	5.49	1.284
Employees are tracked to insure they have received the appropriate ERP training	5.51	1.194
All users have been trained in basic ERP system skills	5.69	1.130
Consultants are used to supplement training when internal expertise does not exist	5.55	1.239
ERP training and education is ongoing and available to refresh users skills	5.60	1.194

overcoming an **ERP** failure is difficult and often fatal (Muscatello et al, 2003)

Project Support and Communications

Lack of strong support for a massive **project** like **ERP** creates enormous challenges for the **project** team such as buy-in from users. A recent study revealed that 25% of organizations adopting **ERP systems** faced significant resistance from staff and that 10% of the organizations also encountered resistance from managers (Kumar et al., 2003). Table 10 presents the results for **project** support and communication. The means range from 5.57 to 5.86. This **research** supports extant **research** on employee relations and change management

in that the respondents felt it very important to actively communicate how employees fit into the new **ERP**-oriented environment and to actively work to alleviate employee concerns. Respondents also agree that cultural changes need to be managed to ensure shared values and common aims conducive to both employee and firm success. A user support group with employee comments and reactions should be used to help employees manage through the cultural changes.

Software Selection and Support

Even with today's state of the art **technology**, organizations find that not all their requirements are met by the **ERP systems** they adopt. The remaining nine indicators are strong with means from 5.64

Table 10. Project support & communications

Indicator	Mean	Std Dev
Employees understand how they fit into the new ERP entity	5.71	1.112
Management actively works to alleviate employee concerns about ERP	5.65	1.153
The roles of all employees under the ERP system have been clearly communicated	5.57	1.161
An ERP support group is available to answer concerns about ERP job changes	5.57	1.093
Effective communication is critical to ERP implementations	5.63	1.110
User input should include requirements, comments, reactions and approvals	5.86	1.025
Enterprise wide culture and structure change should be managed	5.77	1.033
A culture with shared values and common aims is conducive to success	5.66	1.111

Table 11. Software selection & support

Indicator	Mean	Std Dev
An analysis should be performed to select the appropriate business modules	5.86	1.079
The modules selected should be able to share information freely	5.80	1.137
The ERP system should eliminate the need for redundant entry of data	5.79	1.033
If ERP experience does not reside in house then consultants should be used	5.79	1.135
The overall ERP architecture should be established before deployment	5.66	1.134
The firm should work well with vendors and consultants to resolve software issues	5.64	1.101
Vigorous and sophisticated software testing eases implementation	5.85	1.085
There should be a plan for migrating and cleaning up data	5.64	1.062
ERP software development, testing and troubleshooting is essential	5.83	1.310

to 5.86 and the results are presented in Table 11. These indicators confirm current **research** that shows a strong relationship between successful **ERP implementations** and **software** fit. Interestingly, the **research** again confirms that firms are willing to use outside consultants if **software** selection experience is not available internally. Again, this set of indicators show a new willingness amongst **ERP** implementers to realize their firm's limitations in this difficult endeavor. Also of note is a strong resolve to work with vendors to ensure proper module and **process** fit, as well as vigorous **software** testing, troubleshooting and a plan for migrating and data clean up after the initial installation.

CONCLUSION

Enterprise resource planning (**ERP**) **systems** continue to grow in popularity with organizations based on the need to remove disparate **systems**, interconnect suppliers and customers and leverage speed and knowledge for profitability. Academics and practitioners continue to study successful and unsuccessful **ERP** efforts in hopes of providing a proven path for success. This study aimed to understand the critical success **factors** of **ERP implementations** using a large scale survey. A cross sectional mail survey of business executives with **ERP implementation** experience was used to capture the degree of adoption of various ERP concepts. Statistical analysis was conducted on this empirical data to examine the adaptation. Although this analysis was based on simple statistical methods, it provides a clearer picture of the beliefs of current **ERP implementation**. These constructs can also help guide future **research** for academics and practitioners in the **ERP** environment.

The results show that the **implementation** of **ERP systems** has grown from the belief that it was a simple information system **implementation** of new **software** into a realization that it is a strategic and tactical revolution which requires

a total commitment from all involved. This is in stark contrast to studies as recent as five years ago, which concluded that firms believed that the **ERP software** would automatically drive the strategic and tactical changes. Firms now realize that business **process** changes and **project** management are strongly linked to the success of the **ERP implementation**. Moreover, these two factors are as important as **software** and **hardware** knowledge. Another new finding is that firms now strongly believe that the use of outside consultants to supplement internal staff is an acceptable and desirable practice. This is likely a result of the documented cases of **ERP implementation** failure where firms failed to take stock of their internal competencies and shortcomings and the increased knowledge and experience of **ERP** consultants. Taken together, these results suggest that firms are realizing that **ERP implementations** are a long journey and that results may not be readily apparent until well into the future.

This **research** adds value to both the practitioner and academic communities by providing insight into the current practice of **ERP implementations.** While this study does not offer solutions to specific industries, it has paved a solid foundation on which to build future **research** in this area. Future **research** may focus on longitudinal studies and the collective impact of these critical success **factors**.

REFERENCES

Al- Mashari. M. (2000). Constructs of Process Change Management in ERP Context: A Focus on SAP R/3. In *Proceedings of AMICS*.

Anderson, G. (2000). From Supply Chain to Collaborative Commerce Networks: The Next Step in Supply Chain Management. []. Montgomery Research Inc.]. *Achieving Supply Chain Excellence Through Technology*, 2, 101–105.

Appleton, E. L. (1997). How to Survive ERP. *Datamation, 43*(3), 50–53.

Bancroft, N., Seip, H., & Sprengel, A. (1998). *Implementing SAP R/3: How to introduce a large system into a large organization.* Manning Publishing Company, USA.

Bingi, P., Sharma, M., & Godla, J. (1999). Critical Issues Affecting an ERP Implementation. *Information & Management*, 7–14.

Booker, E. (1999). Web to ERP - - ERP Stage II: Outsiders Invited In. *Internet Week*, October 25, pp. 86.

Bradley, J. (2008). Management Based Critical Success Factors in the Implementation of Enterprise Resource Planning Systems. *International Journal of Accounting Information Systems, 9*, 175–200. doi:10.1016/j.accinf.2008.04.001

Brakely, H. H. (1999). What makes ERP Effective? *Manufacturing Systems, 17*(3), 120.

Brown, C. V. (2003). Managing the Next Wave of Enterprise Systems. *MIS Quarterly, 2*(1), 65–77.

Carr, S. (1999). The Intelligence Game. *Upside, 11*(10), 75–78.

Carton, F., & Adam, F. (2003). Analysing the Impact of ERP Systems Roll-Outs in Multi-National Companies. *Electronic Journal of Information Systems Evaluation, 6*(2), 21–32.

Chen, I. J. (2001). Planning for ERP Systems: Analysis and Future Trend. *Business Process Management Journal, 7*(5), 374–386. doi:10.1108/14637150110406768

Cliffe, S. (1999). ERP Implementation. *Harvard Business Review*, (January-February): 16–17.

Davenport, T. H. (1998). Putting the enterprise into the enterprise system. *Harvard Business Review*, (July-August): 121–131.

Davenport, T. H. (2000). *Mission Critical: Realizing the Promise of Enterprise Systems*. Harvard Business School Publishing.

Davenport, T. H., & Brooks, J. (2004). Enterprise Systems and the Supply Chain. *Journal of Enterprise Information Management, 17*(1), 8–19. doi:10.1108/09576050410510917

Deloitte Consulting (2000). ERP's Second Wave.

Evangelista, P. (1998). ERP Systems Strategies. *American Production and Inventory Control Society- Cleveland Chapter*, Speech Proceedings, June.

Ferman, J. E. (1999). Strategies for Successful ERP Connections. *Manufacturing Engineering, 123*(4), 48–60.

Flynn, B. B., Schroeder, R. G., & Sakakibara, S. (1994). A framework for quality management research and an associated measurement instrument. *Journal of Operations Management, 11*(4), 339–575. doi:10.1016/S0272-6963(97)90004-8

Goodpasture, V. (1995). Easton Steps up to the Plate. *Manufacturing Systems, 13*(9), 58–64.

Gupta, A. (2000). Enterprise Resource Planning: The Emerging Organizational Value System. *Industrial Management & Data Systems, 100*(3), 114–118. doi:10.1108/02635570010286131

Hair, J. E., Anderson, R. E., Tatham, R. L., & Black, W. C. (1998). *Multivariate Data Analysis* (5th ed.). Englewood Cliff, NJ: Prentice Hall.

Hammer, M., & Champy, J. (1993). *Reengineering the Corporation*. New York: Harper Business.

Hicks, D. A., & Stecke, K. E. (1995). The ERP Maze: Enterprise Resource Planning and Other Production and Inventory Control Software. *IIE Solutions, 27*(8), 12–16.

Hill, S. (1997). The Wait is Over. *Manufacturing Systems, 15*(6), 11–X.

Hill, T. (2000). *Manufacturing Strategy*. Boston: McGraw-Hill.

Holland, C., & Light, B. (1999). A critical success factors model for ERP implementation. *IEEE Software, 16*(3), 30–36. doi:10.1109/52.765784

Hunter, M. G., & Lippert, S. K. (2007). Critical Success Factors of ERP implementation. *Information Resources Management Proceedings*. Hershey, PA: IGI Publishing.

Judd, C. M., Smith, E. R., & Kidder, L. H. (1991). *Research Methods in Social Relations* (6th ed.). Fort Worth, TX: Harcourt Brace Jovanovich.

Koch, C. (1999). The Most Important Team in History. *CIO, 13*(2), 40–52.

Krause, D. R., Pagell, M., & Curkovic, S. (2001). Toward a Measure of Competitive Priorities for Purchasing. *Journal of Operations Management, 19*, 497–512. doi:10.1016/S0272-6963(01)00047-X

Kumar, V., Maheshwari, B., & Kumar, U. (2003). An investigation of critical management issues in ERP implementation: empirical evidence from Canadian organizations. *Technovation, 23*, 793–807. doi:10.1016/S0166-4972(02)00015-9

Luftman, J., Kempaiah, R., & Nash, E. (2005). Key Issues for IT Executives . *MIS Quarterly, 5*(2), 81–99.

Melnyk, S.A., & Stewart, D.M. (2002). Managing Metrics. *APICS- The Performance Advantage, 12*(2), 23-26.

Millman, G.J. (2004). What did you get from ERP and what can you get? *Financial Executive*, May, 38-42.

Motwani, J., Mirchandani, D., Madan, M., & Gunasekaran, A. (2002). Successful Implementation of ERP Projects: Evidence From Two Case Studies. *International Journal of Production Economics, 75*(1-2), 83–96. doi:10.1016/S0925-5273(01)00183-9

Muscatello, J. R. (1999). ERP and its Effects on the Supply Chain. APICS Manufacturing Symposium, Erie, PA.

Muscatello, J. R. (2002). The Potential Use of Knowledge Management for Training: A Review and Direction of Future Research. *Business Process Management Journal, 9*(3), 382–394. doi:10.1108/14637150310477948

Muscatello, J. R. (2006). The Usefulness of Reengineering for Enterprise Resource Planning (ERP) Systems Implementations: A Comparison of Practitioners and Consultants Beliefs. *Applied Computing and Informatics, 2*, 54–66.

Muscatello, J. R., & Parente, D. H. (2006). Enterprise Resource Planning (ERP): A Post Implementation Cross Case Analysis. *Information Resources Management Journal, 7*(3), 61–80.

Muscatello, J. R., Small, M. H., & Chen, I. J. (2003). Implementing Enterprise Resource Planning (ERP) Systems in Small and Midsize Manufacturing Firms. *International Journal of Operations & Production Management, 23*(8), 850–871. doi:10.1108/01443570310486329

Nicolaou, A. I., & Bhattacharya, S. (2006). Organizational Performance Effects of ERP Systems Usage: The Impact of Post-Implementation Changes. *International Journal of Accounting Information Systems, 7*, 18–35. doi:10.1016/j.accinf.2005.12.002

Oliver, R. (1999). ERP is Dead! Long Live ERP. *Management Review, 88*(10), 12–13.

Olson, D. L., Chae, B., & Sheu, C. (2005). Issues in Multinational ERP Implementations. *International Journal of Services and Operations Management, 1*(1), 7–21. doi:10.1504/IJSOM.2005.006314

Paulraj, A., & Chen, I. J. (2005). Strategic Supply Management: Theory and Practice. *International Journal of Integrated Supply Management, 1*(4), 457–477. doi:10.1504/IJISM.2005.006306

Pozzebon, M. (2000). *Combining a Structuration Approach with a Behavioral Based Model to Investigate ERP Usage*. Presentation at the Association of Information Systems.

Rao, S. (2000). Enterprise Resource Planning: Business Needs and Technology. *Industrial Management & Data Systems, 100*, 81–88. doi:10.1108/02635570010286078

Ross, J. W. (1999). Clueless executives still keep ERP from delivering value. *Computer World*, September 20, p.30.

Sarkis, J., & Sundarraj, R. P. (2003). Managing Large-Scale global Enterprise Resource Planning Systems: A Case Study at Texas Instruments. *International Journal of Information Management, 23*(5), 431–442. doi:10.1016/S0268-4012(03)00070-7

Somers, T. M., & Nelson, K. G. (2004). A Taxonomy of Players and Activities Across the ERP Project Life Cycle. *Information & Management, 41*, 257–278. doi:10.1016/S0378-7206(03)00023-5

Stratman, J.K., & Roth, A.V. (2002). Enterprise Resource Planning (ERP) Competence Constructs: Two-Stage Multi-item Scale Development and Validation. *Decision Sciences*, Fall.

Sumner, M. (1999). Critical Success Factors in Enterprise Wide Information Management Systems Projects. In *Proceedings of SIGCPR*, New Orleans, LA, USA

Trepper, C. (1999). ERP Project Management is Key to a Successful Implementation. Retrieved from http://www.erphub.com.

Welti, N. (1999). *Successful SAP R/3 Implementation: Practical Management of ERP Projects*. Addison Wesley Publications.

Whalen, P. J. (2007). Strategic and Technology Planning on a Roadmapping Foundation. *RES Technology Management*, May-June, pp. 40-51.

Yusuf, Y., Gunasekaran, A., & Althorpe, M. S. (2004). Enterprise Information Systems Project Implementations: A Case Study of ERP in Rolls-Royce. *International Journal of Production Economics, 87*(3), 251–266.doi:10.1016/j.ijpe.2003.10.004

APPENDIX A

Reliability Measurements

Table 12.

Item	Cronbach's Alpha
Strategic Initiative	.797
Executive Commitment	.788
Human Resources	.658
Project Management	.784
Information Technology	.818
Business Process	.810
Training	.807
Project Support and Communication	.761
Software Selection and Support	.830

Chapter 2

The Paradox of Complex ERP Systems used in Simplified Organisations such as Small and Medium Enterprises

Catherine Equey
Haute Ecole de Gestion de Genève, Switzerland

Emmanuel Fragnière
Haute Ecole de Gestion de Genève, Switzerland

ABSTRACT

This chapter further develops and generalises findings from the authors' July 2008 paper in the International Journal of Enterprise Information Systems (IJEIS) by adding organisational issues such as business process reengineering (BPR). The authors argue that enterprise resource planning (ERP) systems are complex management tools that impose standard business processes from larger manufacturing firms. The authors test whether these systems can be adapted effectively to more simplified organisations such as small and medium enterprises (SMEs). The authors found that SMEs tend to have a high perceived level of satisfaction when using these complex tools, independent of size or sector. However, they cannot clearly establish that SMEs having applied BPR while implementing an ERP system are more satisfied than those that did not.

INTRODUCTION

Since the late 1990s, vendors of integrated management tools called ERPs (enterprise resource planning) have found their primary market, mainly large companies, is saturated. To find new customers, they have begun to market these products to small and medium enterprises (SMEs) (generally with about

100 to 500 employees) (Deep, Guttridge, Dani & Burns, 2007; Muscatello, Small & Chen, 2003).

However, it seems few SMEs have actually implemented an ERP (a fact this survey confirms). But is this due to the rigid framework of ERP systems, which were initially created for larger manufacturing firms (Basoglu, Daim & Kerimoglu, 2007; Botta-Genoulaz & Millet, 2006)? We aim to determine whether ERP systems can be fitted ef-

DOI: 10.4018/978-1-60566-968-7.ch002

fectively to more simplified organisations such as SMEs, and how the organisational constraints of ERP systems affect SME user satisfaction.

Research has found that ERP systems implementation and IT issues can differ vastly depending on industry sector, business type or country (i.e., culture), and company size (Velcu, 2007; Snider, Silveira & Balakrishnan, 2009; Raymond, Uwizeymungu & Bergeron, 2005). Thus, we cannot really apply the extant academic research on ERP system implementation directly to SMEs without further research (Snider et al., 2009).

We aim to enhance the research on ERP implementation in SMEs, as well as to obtain more generalizable results. To that end, we conducted a questionnaire-based survey about the level of implementation and use of ERP systems in Swiss SMEs. Our main findings were published in the *International Journal of Enterprise Information Systems* (*IJEIS*) in July 2008, in a paper called "Elements of Perception Regarding the Implementation of ERP Systems in Swiss SMEs." We extend here the work done for that paper by adding new descriptive statistics about business process reengineering (BPR) used by SMEs during ERP systems implementation.

To our knowledge, this is the first study of its kind to have been conducted in Switzerland. The work further adds to the literature by the qualitative aspects addressed in the questionnaire, such as the value-added provided by ERP systems in terms of satisfaction, as well as the managerial and organizational difficulties encountered when implementing and using these systems.

For example, we found that the main difficulties cited during the implementation phase were related to "complexity." In terms of difficulty of use, companies listed primarily "resistance to change" followed by "lack of training." We found that ERP satisfaction did not differ significantly among small and medium-sized companies, or among industry types.

On the other hand, however, we found that many companies were required by their parent company to adopt ERPs. Furthermore, the decision to implement an ERP system in an SME is clearly linked to firm size or sector.

We provide our findings in the form of summarized descriptive statistics and hypothesis testing. For the latter, we focus on ERP user satisfaction regarding implementation in SMEs. The chapter is organized as follows. The first section presents a literature review of the organizational implications of ERP systems in companies, and specifically in SMEs. In the second section, we briefly present the questionnaire and the sampling strategy. The third section presents the main descriptive statistics obtained from our survey, as well as results related to the topic of organizational complexity. We formulate and test hypotheses in the fourth section. We also confirm the need for specific research involving SMEs. Finally, in the fifth section, we conclude by discussing the limitations of this study, and providing directions for future research.

LITERATURE REVIEW

The first part of this literature review focuses on academic findings regarding business process reengineering and organizational change due to ERP systems implementation and use. The second part summarises the main subjects developed specifically for SMEs in order to examine BPR and SME satisfaction with ERP implementation. We find that the paradox of using complex ERP systems in simplified organisations has not been addressed sufficiently thus far in the literature. There is a critical need to bridge this research gap.

ERP and Organizational and Structural Changes

The main advantage of an ERP system is clearly the improved organization wide spread of information, which should enhance management decision-making (Davenport, 1998; Scapens &

Jazayeri, 2003; Kumar, Maheshwari & Kumar, 2002; Equey, 2006; Botta-Genoulaz & Millet, 2006; El Sayed, 2006). However, as Willcocks and Skykes (2000) note, ERP system implementation changes the way "business is done," and "is dependent also on major human, cultural and organizational changes."

We noted earlier that respondents cited "resistance to change" and "lack of training" as the two primary risks of ERP implementation. Kumar et al. (2002), who conducted a study of perceived risks of an ERP implementation in ten Canadian government organizations, found the third-highest risk is "high degree of organizational change" (named by 40% of respondents). Their findings suggest ERP implementation "faces more behavioural and management related challenges than pure technical glitches."

According to Davenport (1998), the number of failed ERP implementations is quite large (in both number and U.S. dollars). He notes that failures are usually due to the difficulty in matching the "technological imperatives of the enterprise system with the business needs of the enterprise itself." He further argues that ERP *imposes its own logic on a company's strategy, organization and culture.*" Overall, however, ERP, which imposes somewhat "generic" processes on companies, is meant to integrate a company's "best practices."

The question arises of whether a company's business processes *must* be adapted to the ERP's way of doing business, or whether it would be better to customize the ERP to the specific business. Davenport (1998) found that the answers to these questions are not simple.

On the one hand, an ERP's business process is supposed to represent the best way to perform tasks. It is generally believed to improve an enterprise's performance. On the other hand, "there is a very real risk that an enterprise system could dissolve their [the company's] sources of advantage" (Davenport, 1998).

In fact, loss of competitive differentiation is one of the major risks raised by Davenport (1998), at least "for companies that compete on distinctive products or superior customer service." For companies that compete mainly on price, standard ERP may be more suitable. Above all, ERP system implementation is not only a question of "technical criteria," but strategic and organizational purposes.

ERP systems are generally built around business process standards (Scapens & Jazayeri, 2003; Rikhardsson & Kraemmergaard, 2006). Thus it is widely believed that business process re-engineering (BPR) is used in ERP implementation projects. However, as Granlund and Malmi (2002) note, only two out of ten firms indicated that "their ERP project was clearly connected with a BPR initiative." Even if BPR is not undertaken before the implementation, it could be performed afterward, and would also be likely to result in changes (Koch, 1996). Thus, Granlund and Malmi (2002) outlined that organisational independence and responsibility change in the context of ERP implementation.

The main impacts of BPR on a company are: 1) integration (of business processes), 2) standardization, and 3) use of procedures. BPR is a chance to enhance a company's processes, but it can also be problematic for individuals in the organization (Rikhardsson & Kraemmergaard, 2006).

Finally, Basoglu et al. (2007) claim that DeLone and McLean's (1992) success model is particularly applicable to an ERP system. This model links "user satisfaction" with "organisational impact," and ultimately with ERP implementation success. In reviewing the literature, we found that organisational impact is clearly a major issue in ERP system implementation.

ERP and SMEs

Because we have no scientific results regarding the loss of competitive differentiation due to the use of standard business processes (see Davenport, 1998), we posit that this may be more of a risk for SMEs than for large companies. SMEs often feature a more informal organizational structure. This could be viewed as a competitive advantage over larger companies, however, whose more rigid organizational structures could be destroyed by the standard business processes imposed by ERP systems.

Despite the rich and varied literature on ERP and SMEs, we find little information on the use of business process reengineering applied in SMEs. For larger companies, the major research topics are: 1) critical success factors (Muscatello et al., 2003; Sun, Yazdani & Overend, 2005; Loh & Koh, 2004; Snider et al., 2009); 2) ERP system implementation (Muscatello et al., 2003); 3) project management (Loh & Koh, 2004; Muscatello et al., 2003); and 4) training (Muscatello et al., 2003).

Other Subjects have been Studied with a Comparison to Large Companies

Buonanno, Faverio, Pigni, Ravarini, Sciuto and Tagliavini (2005) studied the factors affecting ERP adoption, and compares SMEs with large companies. They demonstrate a strong correlation between company size and ERP adoption.

Bernroider and Koch (2001) analyze differences in ERP system selection processes between SMEs and larger organizations. The main differences relate to "a different approach to staffing the group performing the selection process"(for example, larger organizations tend to engage more employees in decision making processes than SMEs). SMEs also tended to choose ERPs with less complex models and less expensive methods.

The literature is also rather scarce concerning SME satisfaction with ERP system use. A recent study by Esteves (2009) focused on the benefits of ERPs for SMEs. However, the concept of

perceived benefits is not necessarily the same as a guarantee of satisfaction (especially because any disadvantages of ERP systems must also be considered).

Esteves (2009) uses Shang and Seddon's (2000) ERP benefits list in order to gauge the benefits lifecycle (i.e., with a time perspective on benefits realisation). He finds that the main benefits of ERP tended to occur during the second stage (e.g., 6-18 months after the "go-live," or the completion of the installation). We can categorize the dimensions of the benefits as 1) operational, 2) managerial, 3) involving information technology infrastructure, and 4) organizational.

However, Esteves (2009) also found that the strategic dimension of the ERP's benefits was only realized at the third stage (e.g., 12-24 months after the "go-live"). And his study did not deal with benefits cited by SMEs themselves.

As far as we know, only three sets of authors have addressed BPR and ERP implementation in an SME context. Muscatello et al. (2003) argued that SMEs needed "re-engineering prior to selection of the ERP." Their research was based on multiple case studies on U.S. manufacturing SMEs.

Quiescenti, Bruccoleri, La Commare, Noto La Diega and Perrone (2006) worked with an ERP systems vendor to develop "a structured approach to the design and configuration of ERP systems for small enterprises." Their aim was to adapt ERP processes to SMEs.

Finally, Newman and Zhao (2008) conducted a case study on two Chinese SMEs. One had successfully implemented an ERP system; the other had not been successful. Newman and Zhao (2008) noted some important factors to success: 1) involvement of top management, 2) the clear need for a new system, and 3) the decision regarding BPR (the firm that successfully implemented an ERP system had performed BPR during the implementation). However, all of these findings need to be confirmed on a larger scale.

In summary, because the literature about BPR during ERP implementation in SMEs is so scarce, we omit generalizable results. Research on SME satisfaction with ERP system use is also insufficient, and is generally not based on inductive approaches.

METHODOLOGY

We used a questionnaire to address our research questions. In the first phase, we conducted in-depth interviews with Swiss-French companies. These multiple case studies (Equey & Rey, 2004) led to the development of a small number of research questions, as well as associated research hypotheses. This material was then used to design the questionnaire.

The first version of the questionnaire was built with the help of senior consultants from Abacus (the leading ERP vendor for SMEs in the German-speaking part of Switzerland), Microsoft, Oracle, and SAP. The final version was comprised of seven major parts: contacts, activities and financial information about the enterprise, specifics of the ERP implemented, description of the project, organisation of the project, benefits of and outcomes related to the ERP system, and the difficulties and problems encountered.

From November 2005 to April 2006, we asked more than 4,000 Swiss SMEs (spread equally throughout the Swiss territory) to take part in the study. The questionnaire was administered by mail, and an online version was also available. The questionnaire was provided in four languages: French, German, Italian, and English. The French version is included in the appendix of the French technical report (Equey, 2006).

We obtained Swiss SME addresses from the Swiss Federal Office of Statistics (OFS), and we made selections based on two criteria: size (number of employees), and linguistic area.

The stratification of the sample was as follows: 75% of the companies came from the German-speaking section of Switzerland, 20% came from the French-speaking section, and 5% came from the Italian-speaking section. Moreover, 84% of the companies employed 1 to 49 employees, and 16% employed 50 to 249 employees.

To maximize our participation rate, we conducted follow-up telephone interviews. Ultimately, we obtained a 17.2% response rate, or a total of 687 Swiss SMEs. Of those 687, 18.2% (or 125) reported using an ERP, 81.5% (560) did not use an ERP, and there was no response from 0.3% (2). This indicates a low level of penetration in Swiss SMEs (less than 20%). We analysed the data using the STATA and SPSS statistical packages.

DESCRIPTIVE STATISTICS

The main part of the questionnaire was dedicated to companies that use an ERP. However, we also asked companies that had not implemented an ERP about their motivations. The main reasons cited by Swiss SMEs were "high costs" (21%), "non-necessity," (11%) and "lack of knowledge" (5%). More than 40%, however, did not respond to this question, indicating a certain lack of concern about ERP systems.

The next section highlights results relating to organisational issues that were not published in our previous *IJEIS* article.

As indicated in the literature review, Buonanno et al.'s (2005) findings are based on a survey that compares a sample of large companies with a sample of SMEs. They reject the hypothesis that SMEs are less likely to implement ERPs because of a lack of business complexity. Indeed, they show the main reason is a perception of high cost.

As we discuss later in this article, it is important to note that the reasons given by SMEs for not implementing ERPs are *not* similar to the difficulties met by ERP users in comparable companies. SMEs that implement an ERP are frequently dissatisfied with the complexity of the tools.

On the other hand, our study shows that cost is rarely the reason for dissatisfaction among ERP users. Based on the 40% non-response rate noted above, we posit that the perception of high cost comes from a lack of knowledge of ERP systems. However, this point needs to be investigated further to validate this hypothesis.

We skip here most of the detailed results relating to ERP software specifics (for more information, readers are referred to Equey, 2006). We consider here only the main figures. The following descriptive statistics are drawn from the sample of 125 ERP user respondents who provided the most answers to the questionnaire.

The decision to implement an ERP was not related to the cultural or linguistic characteristics of the companies. This was confirmed via the language and canton (i.e., Swiss states) of residence, and by the variables capturing cultural differences.

We found that the size of an SME, in terms of number of employees, is important to explaining the adoption of an ERP system. These descriptive statistics indicate that larger SMEs are more likely to adopt an ERP system.

Most respondents indicated they are in a growth phase. Only 7% acknowledged a reduction in sales revenue. Of these, 75% had installed their ERP system more than five years earlier, a period during which their financial situations may have been different.

Given the predominance in Switzerland of the tertiary sector (services, tourism), industry (the secondary sector) is overrepresented in our sample. This may be because ERP systems are built on the material requirement planning (MRP) structure, and are therefore naturally more involved in manufacturing.

Note that 36% of our sample are Swiss subsidiaries, while 19% are foreign subsidiaries. On the whole, 44% defined themselves as part of a larger group. From this, we assume that the parent company likely imposed the ERP system on the subsidiary. We expect that otherwise the use of ERPs by SMEs would be even weaker.

A significant percentage (50.4%) of companies listed "Other" when asked which vendor installed their ERP systems (rather than better-known vendors such as SAP or Oracle). It is noteworthy that no particular program dominates the "Other" category. To ensure business sustainability, we expected companies to be more likely to rely on higher-profile software providers.

Another surprising point is that several companies cited programs that are not actually ERPs (e.g., AS400, Clipper). This confirms the lack of clarity about what ERP systems are.

And regarding the choice of ERP system itself, we found that Swiss-French and Swiss-German companies differed significantly. Swiss-French companies used primarily Oracle; Swiss-German companies were more likely to use Abacus or Microsoft. Thus we note the Swiss market for ERP systems is segmented into two distinct markets (the results for the Swiss-Italian region were insignificant).

The duration of an ERP installation lasted less than one year for 80% of the respondents, and less than six months for 53%. Nevertheless, for 4.6%, the installation required more than eighteen months, and may have thus been inordinately problematic.

In addition, the number of consultants (as opposed to internal human resources) does not appear to be related to the duration of the ERP installation. However, it is important to ensure a minimum of one consultant for each employee involved in the implementation project. 71% of the respondents cited a need for external assistance.

The level of involvement of upper management also had only a moderate impact on the duration of the installation (although we noted that a higher level of involvement contributed to dramatically reducing the probability that the installation would last more than eighteen months.

Regarding organizational issues, we found that more than half the sample undertook a BPR during their ERP system implementation. We also found that larger SMEs (in terms of number of employees) tended to revise their processes more. In fact, for SMEs, an ERP implementation implied an average of 54% (total and partial) business process revisions. Furthermore, approximately 62% of respondents planned to formalize business processes during ERP implementation, with the main areas being finance (30%-35%), customer service (25%), and manufacturing (20%).

In terms of difficulties encountered during the implementation phase, 45% of respondents cited the "complexity" of the system. This was followed by "work overload" (38%), and "difficulty adapting the ERP system to your process (customization)" (32%). In terms of difficulties using the ERP system, 32% of respondents cited "resistance to change," followed by "lack of training" (29%), and, again, the "complexity" of the system (25%). Technical difficulties tended to rank at the bottom. We thus conclude that managerial issues are the predominant difficulties associated with ERP systems implementation.

HYPOTHESIS TESTING

The main research question developed in our earlier *IJEIS* paper was: "Is the satisfaction regarding the benefits provided by ERP systems evenly spread among Swiss SMEs?" We focus here on only one of the qualitative aspects developed in our survey. We believe the originality of this study lies in the measurement of qualitative variables, such as user satisfaction with ERP systems and difficulties encountered (e.g., resistance to change).

We first test the following hypothesis scheme:

H0: Satisfaction with ERP systems is not dependent on the size or sector of the SME.

Ha: Satisfaction with ERP systems is dependent on the size and sector of the SME.

The satisfaction variable corresponds to the average for all ERP modules (finance, SCM,

HR, inventory, production, etc.) used by each respondent. This variable is expressed on a Likert scale, where 1 is the lowest value, and 5 is the highest. The size variable is broken down into four categories: 10 to 49 employees, 50 to 99 employees, 100 to 199, and 200 to 249. The sector variable is defined as either the secondary or the tertiary sector.

To analyze the hypotheses, we compare mean values (of satisfaction) for every sample of size and sector (see Table 1). We note that perceived satisfaction is generally quite high. We then conduct an analysis of variance (ANOVA) for the size case, by which we compare the means of more than two independent samples. For the sector case, we perform a t-test on two independent samples. We find a 5% significance level for type 1 errors.

We obtained a p-value of 0.355 for the size case, which indicates that the null hypothesis cannot be rejected at a 5% significance level. We thus conclude that satisfaction is not affected by size. We further obtained a (two-tailed) p-value of 0.09 for the sector case, which also indicates the null hypothesis cannot be rejected. This is less clear than for the size case, but we conclude that ERP satisfaction is generally high for SMEs, regardless of size or sector.

We can conduct other statistical tests that deal with variables defined on a nominal scale (e.g., "yes" or "no"), which is often the case with qualitative variables. Table 2 gives descriptive statistics about different attributes of the perceived value-added from ERP systems.

For example, we can explore the relationship between the "time savings" variable and the size and sector variables (see Bryman and Cramer, 2001). We can use a chi-square test (which is useful with nominal variables) to determine whether there is a relationship between time saved and an SME's size or sector.

Here, a detailed analysis would likely show there is no relationship between time saved and size or sector variables. We find that satisfaction is on average quite high and homogeneous

Table 1. Satisfaction means and standard deviations for size and sector

Size	N	Mean	Standard Deviation
10 to 49	64	3.76	0.83
50 to 99	25	3.66	0.48
100 to 199	22	4.02	0.57
200 to 249	9	3.86	0.70
Total	120	3.80	0.72
Sector	N	Mean	Standard Deviation
Secondary	63	3.69	0.78
Tertiary	57	3.91	0.63
Total	120	3.80	0.72

Table 2. Value-added from ERP systems

Value-added	Yes	No	No response
Improved information	96%	3%	1%
Cost savings	48%	38%	14%
Time savings	74%	20%	6%
Improved work quality	95%	5%	0%

among the Swiss SME population (we also tested other aspects besides size and sector, such as language). The same results hold for the benefits from using an ERP system (except perhaps for cost savings, because only 48% answered yes to that question).

We can thus infer that it would be beneficial for vendors and consultants to specifically address the needs and expectations of Swiss SMEs. On the other hand, because of its homogeneity, there is no need to segment the SME market.

Discussion

The influence of company size or sector on IT and ERP issues is worth further discussion. Authors such as Raymond et al. (2005) clearly found differences between large and small companies. They argued that the extant literature on ERP needs to be adapted to SMEs. This recommendation was mostly confirmed by our research.

We found that the decision to implement an ERP system in an SME is clearly linked to the size or sector of the firm. The correlation between size and ERP adoption had already been noted by Buonanno et al. (2005). We also note that BPR was more likely to be used by larger SMEs. These two findings confirm size differences in ERP implementation projects.

On the other hand, our results for the perceived satisfaction of ERP use are clearly the same for SMEs. Therefore, size does not appear to be important for these issues. We recommend further research to determine whether differences exist on other important issues between large companies and SMEs.

From our sample, we also found that companies that implemented an ERP system along with a BPR approach seem to have higher levels of user satisfaction. However, because of the limited size of our sample, our test results are not significant. A new survey should be conducted to further test and confirm this finding.

CONCLUSION

We present here the initial results of a national survey we conducted on the implementation and use of ERP systems in Swiss SMEs. We selected SMEs because they make up the largest part of the Swiss economy. Our main contribution is that we have examined the perceptions of SMEs about the qualitative aspects of implementing and using ERP systems.

ERP systems lead to important organizational changes in companies. Existing literature on BPR and satisfaction in SMEs is scarce, and based primarily on case studies. We believe that qualitative variables studied via a questionnaire-based approach provide a valuable addition to the current knowledge.

We show that the satisfaction of ERP users within Swiss SMEs is generally high, and quite homogeneous in terms of industry type and size. We also show that BPR tends to be implemented more often by larger SMEs. However, the correlation between satisfaction and BPR use among SMEs was not significant. Therefore, we believe this point should be a subject of subsequent research.

Empirical research that attempts to measure business perceptions always has limitations. Perception biases are inevitable, and findings need to be interpreted with caution. Our study also emphasizes managerial and practical implications. In particular, we recommend that developers and consultants emphasize the accessibility of these systems to SMEs.

We also observe that general ERP systems knowledge among SMEs is rather weak. This point should also be investigated further. But the few SMEs that use an ERP system seem to be satisfied, and they cite important benefits such as improved information and work quality. Consequently, we believe ERP systems for SMEs could become a growing and sustainable market if managed properly.

ACKNOWLEDGMENT

The authors thank Loïc Marchand for his valuable contributions.

REFERENCES

Basoglu, N., Daim, T., & Kerimoglu, O. (2007). Organizational adoption of enterprise resource planning systems: A conceptual framework. *The Journal of High Technology Management Research, 18*, 73–97. doi:10.1016/j.hitech.2007.03.005

Bernroider, E., & Koch, S. (2001). ERP selection process in midsize and large organizations. *Business Process Management, 7*(3), 251–257. doi:10.1108/14637150110392746

Botta–Genoulaz, V., & Millet, P. (2006). An investigation into the use of ERP systems in the service sector. *International Journal of Production Economics, 99*, 202–221. doi:10.1016/j.ijpe.2004.12.015

Bryman, A., & Ducan, C. (2001). *Quantitative data analysis with SPSS Release 10 for Windows*. London: Routlege Publishing.

Buonanno, G., Faverio, P., Pigni, F., Ravarini, A., Sciuto, D., & Tagliavini, M. (2005). Factors affecting ERP system adoption. A comparative analysis between SMES and large companies. *Journal of Enterprise Information Management, 18*, 384–426. doi:10.1108/17410390510609572

Davenport, T. (1998). *Putting the Enterprise into the enterprise system*. Harvard Business Review.

Deep, A., Guttridge, P., Dani, S., & Burns, N. (2007). Investigating factors affecting ERP selection in made-to-order SME sector. *Journal of Manufacturing Technology Management, 19*(4), 430–446. doi:10.1108/17410380810869905

DeLone, W., & McLean, E. (1992). Information systems success: The quest for the dependent variable. *Information Systems Research, 3*(1), 60–95. doi:10.1287/isre.3.1.60

El Sayed, H. (2006). ERPs and accountant's expertise: the construction of relevance. *Journal of Enterprise Information Management, 19*(1), 83–96. doi:10.1108/17410390610636896

Equey, C. (2006). *Etude du comportement des PME/PMI suisses en matière d'adoption de système de gestion integré* (HES-SO/HEG-GE/C Working paper series N° 06/12/1-CH). HEG: Dept. of Economie d'Entreprise.

Equey, C., & Rey, A. (2004*). La mise en place d'une solution de gestion moderne (ERP/PGI), quels enjeux pour une PME/PMI? 1ère partie: étude de cas détaillés*, (HES-SO/HEG-GE/C Working paper series N° 06/1/4-CH). HEG: Dept. of Economie d'Entreprise.

Esteves, J. (2009). A benefits realisation roadmap framework for ERP usage in small and medium-sized enterprises. *Journal of Enterprise Information Management, 22*(1), 25–35. doi:10.1108/17410390910922804

Granlund, M., & Malmi, T. (2002). Moderate impact of ERPs on management accounting: a lag or permanent outcome? *Management Accounting Research, 13*, 299–321. doi:10.1006/mare.2002.0189

Koch, C. (1996, June 15). Flipping the switch. *CIO, 9*(17), 43–66.

Kumar, V., Maheshwari, B., & Kumar, U. (2002). ERP systems implementation: Best practices in Canadian government organizations. *Government Information Quarterly, 19*, 147–172. doi:10.1016/S0740-624X(02)00092-8

Loh, T. C., & Koh, S. C. L. (2004). Critical elements for a successful ERP implementation in SMEs. *International Journal of Production Research, 42*(17), 3433–3455. doi:10.1080/00207540410001671679

Muscatello, J. R., Small, M. H., & Chen, I. J. (2003). Implementing enterprise resource planning (ERP) systems in small and midsize manufacturing firms. *International Journal of Operations & Production Management, 23*, 850–871. doi:10.1108/01443570310486329

Newman, M., & Zhao, Y. (2008). The process of enterprise resource planning implementation and business process re-engineering: Tales from two Chinese small and medium-sized enterprises. *Information Systems Journal, 18*, 405–425. doi:10.1111/j.1365-2575.2008.00305.x

Quiescenti, M., Bruccoleri, M., La Commare, U., Noto La Diega, S., & Perrone, G. (2006). Business process-oriented design of Enterprise Resource Planning (ERP) systems for small and medium enterprises. *International Journal of Production Research, 44*(18-19), 3797–3811. doi:10.1080/00207540600688499

Raymond, L., Uwizeymungu, S., & Bergeron, F. (2005). *ERP adoption for e-government: An analysis of motivations*. e-Government Workshop '05 (eGOV05), Brunel University.

Rikhardsson, P., & Kraemmergaard, P. (2006). Identifying the impacts of enterprise system implementation and use: Examples from Denmark. *International Journal of Accounting Information Systems, 7*, 36–49. doi:10.1016/j.accinf.2005.12.001

Scapens, R., & Jazayeri, M. (2003). ERP systems and management accounting change: opportunities or impacts? *European Accounting Review, 12*(1), 201–233. doi:10.1080/0963818031000087907

Shang, S., & Seddon, P. (2000, August 10-13). *A comprehensive framework for classifying the benefits of ERP systems*. Paper presented at the 6th America's Conference on Information Systems, Long Beach, California.

Snider, B., Silveira, G., & Balakrishnan, J. (2009). ERP implementation at SMEs: Analysis of five Canadian cases. *International Journal of Operations & Production Management, 29*, 4–29. doi:10.1108/01443570910925343

Sun, A., Yazdani, A., & Overend, J. (2005). Achievement assessment for enterprise resource plan-ning (ERP) system implementations based on critical success factors. *International Journal of Production Economics, 98*(2), 189–203. doi:10.1016/j.ijpe.2004.05.013

Velcu, O. (2007). Exploring the effects of ERP systems on organizational performance. *Industrial Management & Data Systems, 107*, 1316–1334. doi:10.1108/02635570710833983

Willcocks, L., & Skykes, R. (2000). Enterprise resource planning: The role of the CIO and its function in ERP. *Communications of the ACM, 43*(4), 32–38. doi:10.1145/332051.332065

Chapter 3
Requirements Management for ERP Projects

S. Parthasarathy
Thiagarajar College of Engineering, Madurai, India

Muthu Ramachandran
Leeds Metropolitan University, UK

ABSTRACT

ERP software standardizes an enterprise's business processes and data. The software converts transactional data into useful information and collates the data so that they can be analyzed. Requirements engineering is an important component of ERP projects. In this paper, we propose: (1) An ERP maturity model (EMM) for assessing the ERP maturity within the organization and (2) A Requirements Engineering Method (REM) for ERP system requirements to capture the requirements from the different types of users of an ERP system, verifying and validating them. The EMM consists of three levels and each level has a focus and a key process area. Key indicators of ERP functionality identified by a major ERP vendor have been used to apply the EMM to an enterprise. This identifies the level of the EMM to which an enterprise belongs. Then the REM is used to enable the enterprise to assess its ERP system requirements and refine it using a knowledge database to reach a higher level in the EMM than the present one. The authors deem that this model can benefit users across all the ERP projects.

INTRODUCTION

ERP is a packaged software solution that addresses the enterprise needs taking the process view of an organization to meet the organizational goals tightly integrating all functions of an enterprise. It is a set of application software that integrates manufacturing, finance, sales, distribution, HR and other business functions with a single comprehensive database that collects data from and feeds data into modular applications supporting all the company's business activities, across these functions, across business units, across the world.

Enterprise systems are complex and expensive and create dramatic organizational change. Learning from high performance projects is crucial for software process improvement. Last, but not least, by determining the crucial factors of a successful

DOI: 10.4018/978-1-60566-968-7.ch003

ERP system, we create incentives that likely will yield higher performance. Weinberg (Weinberg, 1971) demonstrated many years ago that the proverb "You get what you measure" also is highly valid in the software engineering field. ERP projects are a subclass of software projects (Erik Stensrud et al., 2003). According to a report by Advanced Manufacturing Research (AMR) (www.amrresearch.com), we find that the entire enterprise applications market which includes Knowledge Management (KM), Customer Relationship Management (CRM) and Supply Chain Management (SCM) software will top $70 billion by 2007. Many researchers and practitioners have suggested that it is easier and less costly to mold business processes to ERP systems rather than vice versa (Davenport, 1998; Holland & Light, 1999). A high failure rate in implementing ERP systems has been widely cited in the literature (Davenport, 1998), but research on critical success factors in ERP implementation is rare and fragmented.

To date, little has been done to theorize the important factors for initial and ongoing ERP implementation success (Brown et al., 1999). Enterprise Resource Planning (ERP) systems (Fiona Fui-Hoom et al., 2001) have emerged as the core of successful information management and the enterprise backbone of organizations. ERP implementation is a lengthy and complex process and there have been many cases of unsuccessful implementations which have had major impacts on business performance (Parr & Shanks, 2000). Also ERP applications require the capability to link all internal transactions (Hiquet, 1998). Though the ERP implementation and its critical issues, success factors and implementation problems have been identified (Markus et al., 2000), but no empirical studies and no explicit proposition are evaluated so far.

One study of mid-size to large companies conducted by AMR research found that 67% of these companies are implementing some form of ERP, while another 21% are evaluating potential ERP systems solutions. As a growing number of companies adopt ERP systems, the performance of ERP systems is identified as one of the top five IT priorities among global CIOs according to independent surveys conducted by the Morgan Stanley (Togur et al., 2003) and Deloitte & Touche/IDG Research Services Group (Deloitte Touche, 2002).

In this paper, we propose: (1) An ERP maturity model (EMM) for assessing the ERP maturity within the organization and (2) A Requirements Engineering (RE) method for ERP system requirements (ERPRE) to capture the requirements from the different types of users of an ERP system, verifying and validating them. The EMM consists of three levels and each level has a focus and key process area. Key indicators of ERP functionality identified by a major ERP vendor have been used to apply the EMM to an enterprise. This identifies the level of the EMM to which an enterprise belongs. Then the ERPRE is used to enable the enterprise to assess its ERP system requirements and refine them using a knowledge database to reach a higher level in the EMM than the present one. The EMM and ERPRE proposed in this paper have been validated and the upshot of the study is that the proposed method to handle requirements engineering and an exclusive ERP maturity model for ERP projects is set to enhancement the performance of the ERP projects.

LITERATURE REVIEW

Requirements engineering comprises those processes by which a client's requirements are analyzed and then transformed into precise specifications. The final specifications include functions, interfaces, performance and constraints. Often the requirements analysis activity utilizes data flow diagrams (DFD) and data dictionary (DD), while the final requirements are specified using the natural language and formal notation. One standard for organizing the requirements specification is the IEEE/ANSI 830-84 standards.

Often, the requirements specification document is found to be a voluminous report. Studies conducted by the Standish Group (www.standish-group.com) found a striking 74 percent project failure rate, while 28 percent of projects were cancelled completely. The study suggests that the top factors of failure are related to requirements problems, including lack of user input, lack of a clear statement of requirements, and incomplete and changing requirements.

Software requirements analysis and specification is also an activity that is error prone (Jalote 2002). It is also seen that 56% of the bugs detected at testing can be traced to errors made at the requirements stage (Tavolato et al 1984). According to the Naval Research Lab (Basili et al 1981), 77% of all requirements errors are non-clerical. Of these 49% are usually incorrect facts, 31% omissions, 13% inconsistencies, 5% ambiguity and 2% misplacements. It is clear that the current tools, methods and practices for software requirements leave a lot to be desired.

The requirements analysis activity can be considered as possessing two sub-phases – analysis and specifications (Jalote 2002). In requirements analysis, the requirements of the client are understood, analyzed and given a form susceptible to logical reasoning (Cohen 1989). In the requirements specification, the analyzed requirements are precisely specified in the software requirements specification (SRS) document. The first sub-phase can be viewed as converting the requirements in the minds of the customers into a DFD or DD, and the second sub-phase can be considered as converting the DFD or DD based analysis into SRS.

Unlike traditional software projects, where the software is developed for one customer, in the case of ERP projects, a packaged software is developed for different types of users such as Customer Relationship Management (CRM) users, ERP users and Supply Chain Management (SCM) users. Hence more efforts are required to manage the requirements from these customers' and if an exclusive requirement engineering method is de-signed for the ERP projects, then it is certain that the ERP implementation team will greatly benefit from this mechanism. There is no such method in practice to aid ERP projects. Some of today's CASE (Computer Aided Software Engineering) tools support specific activities in a single life cycle phase like analysis, requirements tracing, prototyping, data modeling, design, testing, code generation, and reengineering or restructuring (Oman 1990).

Some requirements tools have real time extensions with finite state machines, decision tables and decision trees, program design language (PDL), state charts, requirements engineering validation system (REVS), requirements language processor (RLP), specification and description language (SDL) and petrinets. There are some languages like the Latex with commands to specify the SRS. The existing methods and tools are just sufficient for the traditional software projects and the large scale information system projects like the ERP projects are yet to get a requirements engineering method where the requirement engineering problems encountered by the ERP implementation team are slightly challenging and different from the regular one (Davis 1990). Small-to-medium enterprises (SMEs) demand effective, efficient requirements engineering practice because they must adhere to delivery dates and provide the same quality as large organizations, but with a smaller budget and staff. Moreover, these companies are highly affected by each customer's specific needs, and they must react accordingly (Dorr et al 2008).

Requirements compliant software is becoming a necessity. Fewer and fewer organizations will run their critical transactions on software that has no visible relationship to their requirements. Businesses wish to see their software being consistent with their policies. Moreover, partnership agreements are pressuring less mature organizations to improve their systems. Businesses that rely on web services, for example, are vulnerable to the problems of their web service providers.

Table 1. Literature review on requirements management for ERP projects

S.No.	Related Work	Observation
1	Dorr et al (2008)	Requirements engineering can help assure success for projects and their products.
2	Manish Agrawal et al (2007)	There is need to reexamine the various factors affecting the software project development outcomes.
3	Oslen et al (2007)	Major problem for an ERP system is that it has an inherent business model that may not conform to the needs of the company.
4	Pitts et al (2007)	Information Systems projects' success is dependent upon the effectiveness of requirements elicitation.
5	Maya Daneva et al (2006)	How to align ERP application components and business requirements for coordination and cooperation is hardly known.
6	Neil Maiden (2006)	Ensuring that the software complies with the requirements is very important for the success of software projects.
7	Daniela Damian et al 2006	Requirements engineering is an important component of effective software engineering, yet more research is needed to demonstrate the benefits to development organizations.
8	Maya Daneva (2004)	Among the keys to success are applying a Requirements Engineering Model in the client's context and installing processes to support key RE activities.
9	Procaccino et al (2002)	Attention to upfront requirements activities has been said to produce benefits for software development projects.
10	Brooks (1987)	Requirements Engineering – the elicitation, definition, and management of requirements – is often cited as one of the most important, but difficult, phases of software development.

While electronic commerce has increased the speed of on-line transactions, the technology for monitoring requirements compliance – especially for transactions – has lagged behind. To address the requirements engineering problem for the enterprise information systems such as an ERP system, its requirement analysis method has to be different from the traditional software projects. Requirements engineering has traditionally assumed that the system to be designed is under the control of a single stakeholder who (at least in principle) determines a consistent set of requirements. Modern information systems, however, do not fit this mold, and so requirements engineering must adapt it to handle them.

In any organization, past experience plays a key role in improvement and management. How effectively past experience can be leveraged depends on how well this experience is captured and organized to enable learning and reuse. Systematically recording data from projects, deriving lessons from them, and then making the lessons available to other projects can enhance this reuse. This can be done through the creation of a knowledge database for ERP projects. A knowledge database is the repository of the crucial information of an ERP project such as the business processes fulfilled by the ERP software, the data and system integration architecture of the ERP system, ERP customization approaches and the application of Business Process Reengineering (BPR) in standardizing business processes. This is maintained in every IT company involved in ERP implementation but under different banners and is found isolated. Hence the creation of a knowledge database for a completed ERP project is simple and useful for future ERP projects to do the requirements management effortlessly. An ERP project, being a large scale software project, can improve its performance by effectively utilizing the knowledge database.

REQUIREMENTS ENGINEERING

To define a requirements engineering method for the requirements management of ERP projects, the requirements engineering concept of the software engineering is used in this research study. Requirements engineering and domain analysis deal with gathering and analysis of requirements which eventually lead to a decision on "what to build". Each deserves serious studies in its own right. We turn our attention to a study of specification as a means of dealing with the inherent difficulties stated above. In systems engineering and software engineering, requirements analysis (Pressman 2006) encompasses those tasks that go into determining the needs or conditions to meet for a new or altered product, taking account of the possibly conflicting requirements of the various stakeholders, such as beneficiaries or users. Requirements analysis is critical to the success of a development project.

Systematic requirements analysis is also known as requirements engineering. It is sometimes referred to loosely by names such as requirements gathering, requirements capture, or requirements specification. Requirements must be measurable, testable, related to identified business needs or opportunities, and defined to a level of detail sufficient for system design. Conceptually, requirements analysis includes three types of activity:

- **Eliciting requirements:** the task of communicating with customers and users to determine what their requirements are.
- **Analyzing requirements:** determining whether the stated requirements are unclear, incomplete, ambiguous, or contradictory, and then resolving these issues.
- **Recording requirements:** Requirements may be documented in various forms, such as natural-language documents, use cases or process specifications.

New systems change the environment and relationships between people, so it is important to identify all the stakeholders, take into account all their needs and ensure they understand the implications of the new systems. Analysts can employ several techniques to elicit the requirements from the customer. Historically, this has included such things as holding interviews, or holding focus groups and creating requirements lists. More modern techniques include prototyping, and use cases. Where necessary, the analyst will employ a combination of these methods to establish the exact requirements of the stakeholders, so that a system that meets the business needs is produced.

Stakeholder interviews are a common method used in requirement analysis. Some selection is usually necessary, cost being one factor in deciding whom to interview. These interviews may reveal requirements not previously envisaged as being within the scope of the project, and requirements may be contradictory. However, each stakeholder will have an idea of his expectation or will have visualized his requirements. Requirements often have cross-functional implications that are unknown to individual stakeholders and often missed or incompletely defined during stakeholder interviews. These cross-functional implications can be elicited by conducting discussions in a controlled environment, facilitated by a Business Analyst, wherein stakeholders participate in discussions to elicit requirements, analyze their details and uncover cross-functional implications. A dedicated scribe to document the discussion is often useful, freeing the Business Analyst to focus on the requirements definition process and guide the discussion.

An use case is a technique for documenting the potential requirements of a new system or a software change. Each use case provides one or more scenarios that convey how the system should interact with the end user or another system to achieve a specific business goal. Use cases typically avoid technical jargon, preferring instead the language of the end user or domain expert. Use cases are often co-authored by requirements engineers and stakeholders.

A software requirements specification (SRS) is a complete description of the behavior of the system to be developed. It includes a set of use cases that describe all of the interactions that the users will have with the software. Use cases are also known as functional requirements. In addition to the use cases, the SRS also contains nonfunctional (or supplementary) requirements. Non-functional requirements are requirements which impose constraints on the design or implementation (such as performance requirements, quality standards, or design constraints).

An ERP system has four types of users namely ERP users, Supply Chain Management (SCM) users, Customer Relationship Management (CRM) users and Knowledge Management (KM) users. The requirements management activity primarily involves requirements verification and requirements validation. For the traditional software projects, these activities would be carried out during the requirements analysis phase. Large scale information system projects like the ERP projects where we have different types of users require a different approach. The requirements engineering phase of the software development lifecycle is the base for the requirements management of a software project. Hence, in this research study, the requirements engineering concept is used to define a new requirements engineering method for the ERP projects.

REQUIREMENTS MANAGEMENT IN ERP PROJECTS

One of the main goals of software engineering is the production of software that successfully works in the environment where it is intended to be used. The development process of a large, complex software system necessitates the gathering and the management of a vast amount of data on the application domain, processes, people, and product descriptions. In order to cope with the numerous objects that arise and the enormous amount of information generated while managing them, abstraction and decomposition have been found to be useful tools. The best software practices

are useless if they are focused on implementing the wrong functions. The essential role of the requirements phase is to ensure that the users' need is properly understood before designing and implementing a system to meet them.

The job of developing software requirements involves gathering relevant information on the users' needs and distilling the critical items. This job is difficult because generally it is hard to distinguish between what is needed and what is wanted. This is further complicated by the fact that the users' functional needs are essentially unlimited. The only limitation on requirements content is thus the cost and the time needed for the system implementation. Requirements will thus continually expand until the project's economic limits are reached.

Software that fails to deliver its promised functionality can have devastating consequences (Amrit Tiwana et al 2006). The opening of the Denver International Airport was delayed over a year because of software that did not do what it was intended to do; software problems wrecked a $500 million European satellite; functionality problems with the infamous London's stock exchange TAURUS system cost taxpayers £1.6 billion; and elsewhere it destroyed a NASA Mars Mission. While the operational consequences of dysfunctional software are not always so dramatic, the financial consequences are, in the aggregate, quite dramatic: Nearly 40% of the $2.5 trillion spent in the United States on IT in the past few years is estimated to be gambled on such underperforming projects (Amrit Tiwana et al 2006). While some projects are judged to be outright failures, more often, they fall into a gray area somewhere between complete success and abject failure.

ERP systems are the latest in information systems that have been developed to help coordinate the information flow that parallels the physical flow of goods from raw materials to finished goods. Requirements engineering is an important component of ERP projects. To manage the requirements engineering process in the ERP projects, the following are developed in this research study. They are:

1. An ERP Maturity Model (EMM) for assessing the ERP maturity within the organization and

2. A Requirements Engineering Method (REM) for ERP Projects to capture the requirements from the different types of users of an ERP system, verifying and validating them.

The EMM consists of three levels and each level has a focus and a key process area. The key indicators of ERP functionality identified by a major ERP vendor have been used to apply the EMM to an enterprise. This identifies the level of the EMM to which an enterprise belongs. Then the newly defined REM is used to enable the enterprise to assess its ERP system requirements and refine it using a knowledge database to reach a higher level in the EMM than the present one. It is observed that this model can benefit users across all the ERP projects.

REQUIREMENTS ENGINEERING METHOD FOR ERP PROJECTS

ERP vendors pick up these so-called best practices not because they have precisely quantifiable values, but rather because successful ERP project organizations commonly use them in Requirements Engineering (RE) (Maya Daneva, 2003). A RE model recommends a set of defined processes, suggests process stakeholders, specifies steps involved in getting something accomplished, indicates RE task dependencies, and offers some standard tool support for ERP Requirements Engineering process. Essentially, such an off-the-shelf process is composition and reconciliation: the logic behind it is to start with a general set of business process and data requirements and then explore standard ERP functionality to see how closely it

matches the company's process and data needs. The client's staff involved in ERP Requirements Engineering process acts as consumers who integrate the ERP components they buy into a solution that meets the needs of the organization.

In the SAP Requirement Engineering (SAPRE), (SAP AG, 1999) the requirements engineering process has been extensively elaborated. According to the SAPRE, the requirements engineering process for ERP projects can be modeled as a spiral (Figure 1) (Maya Daneva, 2003; SAP AG, 1999) with four iterations showing the increasing collection of information by three types of activities: (i) requirements elicitation activities which are concerned with finding, communication and validation of facts and rules about the business, (ii) enterprise modeling activities which are concerned with the business processes and data analysis and representation, and (iii) requirements negotiation activities which are concerned with the validation of process and data architectures, the resolution of process and data issues, and the prioritization of the requirements.

In this SAP RE process shown in Figure 1, the very first iteration results in a clear picture of the company's organizational structure based on the pre-defined organization units in the SAP System. The second iteration is to define aims and scope for business process standardization based on the SAP R/3 application components. The third iteration leads to company-specific business process and data architectures based on the SAP reference process and data models (Curran et al., 2000). Finally, the fourth iteration results in the specification of data conversion, reporting and interfaces requirements. The major actors in these activities are business process owners who are actively supported by the SAP consultants and the internal process and data architects. The final deliverable they produce is the business blueprint for the project. The software development process has to go through many phases. The important phases are software requirements analysis and design, preliminary design, detailed design, cod-

Figure 1. SAP RE process

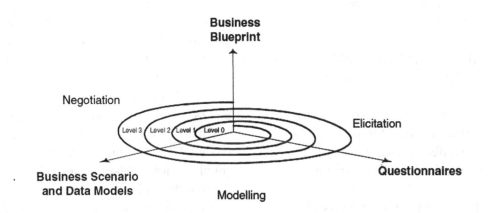

ing, unit testing, integration testing, system testing, delivery and deployment, maintenance and enhancement (Pressman 2006; Demarco 1978; Jalote 1999). The requirements analysis phase is now recognized as one of the hardest activities, errors in which can cause major cost and schedule overrun (Boehm et al 1988). The final output of this phase is the software requirements specification document.

The software requirements specification document plays an important role in all the activities related to software development. The document (i) establishes the basis for agreement between the customers and the supplier on what the software product is to do, (ii) provides a basis for estimating costs and schedule (iii) provides a baseline for validation and verification and, (iv) serves as a basis for maintenance and enhancement. Software continues to play a prominent and critical role in large business applications, technical endeavors in space missions, and control systems for airlines, railways, and telecommunications. Software for managing these applications is complex to construct. The source of complexity of a software product lies in the set of stringent requirements, system integrity constraints, and the vast amount of knowledge necessary to adequately describe the expected interaction of the software

with its environment. When all the requirements are not properly understood, recorded, and communicated within the development team, there is a gap between the documented requirements and the requirements actually needed for correct discrepancy, which is the root cause of software errors. Precise documentation of requirements with sufficient detail to cover unexpected worst-case scenarios is a good defense against errors (Alagar et al 1998). More than two decades ago, Brooks (Brooks 1975) recognized the difficulties in developing large complex software and likened the development of large system software to a great beast thrashing in a tar pit. It was relatively easy to get hold of any particular component of the software, but pulling the whole out of the tar was nearly impossible. Twelve years later, Brooks (Brooks 1987) wrote that not only has there been little change, but there is not even a "silver bullet" in sight: a method, a software tool, development in technology, or management technique that would dramatically improve productivity. This situation was attributed to the essential difficulties that are inherent in the nature of software: invisibility, complexity, conformity, changeability. Acknowledging that there may be no "silver bullet" in this area, one of the promising attacks on these essential difficulties is to rigorously deal with the problem of gathering and specifying the requirements of a software product. Software life cycle models decompose the entire development process into a series of phases and associate a specific task with each phase. Although the boundaries and the ordering of these phases differ in different models, the specification activity in each phase produces a more precise definition of system attributes. Since object description, properties of the object, and operations must be dealt with as a whole for every object in the system during its entire evolution, we may regard specification as a multistage activity rather than a one-time activity.

ERP projects integrate three major areas of Information Technology (IT) projects–knowledge management (KM), customer relationship management (CRM), and supply chain management systems (SCM). This is shown in Figure 2 as ERP systems integration. Knowledge Management (KM) comprises a range of practices used by organizations to identify, create, represent, and distribute knowledge for reuse, awareness and learning. Therefore the issues of identifying the requirements for an ERP project become much more complicated than traditional software projects. The growing number of horror stories found in the literature about failed ERP projects clearly indicates that the existing requirements capturing methods are inadequate. As shown in Figure 2, the Requirements Engineering Method (REM) for ERP Projects has more of a multi-user perspective than the usual software projects which integrates the requirements from the ERP end users, the supply chain systems users, the CRM users, and the KM users. Every IT company normally possesses a process database. This is a repository of process performance data from successful projects, which can be used for project planning, estimation, analysis of productivity and quality and other purpose (Grady et al 1999; Humphrey 2005). Similarly the knowledge database forms the quantitative knowledge of successfully completed ERP projects. The data captured in the process database can be classified into the fol-

lowing categories: Project characteristics, Project schedule, Project effort, Size and Defects (Jalote 1999; Jalote 2002). Similar to a process database, in our research study, the creation of a knowledge database is recommended for the ERP projects, as it is very much essential to effectively carry out the requirements analysis process during the ERP implementation. We define the knowledge database for an ERP project as the repository of the crucial informations of an ERP project such as the business goals fulfilled by the ERP software, the data and system integration architecture used in the ERP system, ERP customization approaches adopted in the ERP implementation and the application of Business Process Reengineering (BPR) to standardize the business processes of an enterprise. These data will be available with every ERP vendor and all that is required is to collect it and create a knowledge database to hold it for future. The Capability Maturity Model (CMM) requires that the organization have a database which is used for planning, monitoring and effective software process management though the CMM does not specify what this database contains. The EMM will be useful to highlight the various expected performance indicators for ERP projects thereby making the ERP systems implementation, integration, and testing much faster and more reliable.

In Figure 3, we have developed an exclusive requirements engineering method for ERP projects. ERP projects involve four different types of users namely ERP system users, SCM system users, CRM users and KM system users. Mostly the information system projects like the ERP projects consider the requirements of the ERP system users only. In this requirements engineering method for ERP projects, provision is made for multi-perspective user validation and refined improvements are obtained from the different users of the ERP system. This will help the ERP implementation team to develop a complete ERP solution for the enterprise. In this requirements engineering method, the business goals of differ-

Figure 2. ERP systems integration

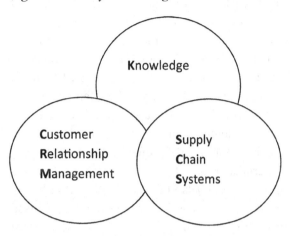

ent types of users of an ERP system are captured. Business Process Reengineering (BPR) is defined as the fundamental rethinking and radical redesign of business processes of an enterprise. The BPR requirements to meet the business goals of four different users of the ERP system namely ERP user, CRM user, KM user and SCM user are analyzed in the proposed requirements engineering method. The ERP software, being an integrated software package, its data and system integration requirements to fulfill the business goals of its

users are verified. Then, the process of elicitation is done by the consultants to make decisions on how to manage the customization during the ERP implementation. Once all these activities are carried out successfully, the next phase of work is to validate these captured data from the different users of ERP through a knowledge database. This database will assist the ERP team members in fine tuning the business goals of the ERP system users and other pre-requisites of the ERP software to meet these goals. The outcome of this process is the improved ERP systems requirements. The significance of the proposed requirements engineering method for the ERP projects is: (i) The requirements captured from different types of users of the ERP system are analyzed in two different perspectives namely, technological and business. (ii) These requirements are validated using a knowledge database and fine tuned. The maturity of these requirements before and after the application of the knowledge database can be assessed using the EMM. The business goals, BPR, data & system integration requirements and customization of the different users of an ERP system are indicated in Figure 3 in a single layered box

Figure 3. Requirements engineering method (REM) for ERP projects

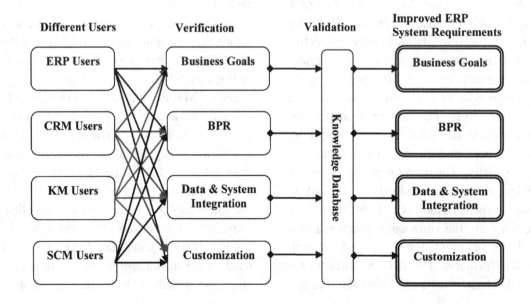

before it is scanned using a knowledge database. These are shown in a double layered box when they are fine tuned after validating them using a knowledge database.

In Figure 4, similar to the CMM model used in the traditional software projects, we have proposed an ERP Maturity Model (EMM). This model is meant to help the ERP implementation team to assess the maturity of an ERP system in an enterprise and accordingly apply the REM in Figure 3 to improve the maturity level of the ERP system. Each level of the EMM has got an individual focus on the ERP system and a key process area has been identified for each level to improve the processes focused at each level

as shown in Table 2. The ERP Maturity Model consists of three levels which consist of Legacy, Designed, and Improved systems. Level 1 is a **Legacy System** which deals with manual and ad-hoc processes involved in the ERP projects; Level 2 **Designed** involves understanding the existing system, assessing it, identifying the scope for improvement, introduction of new technology, and integration of systems. Level 3 **Improved** deals with the implementation of the proposed requirements engineering method. From Figure 4, we find that the ERP Maturity Model is found suitable for small-to-medium enterprises (SMEs).

Figure 4. ERP maturity model (EMM)

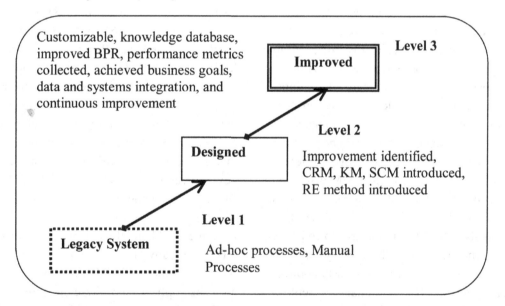

Table 2. EMM's key process areas

Level	Focus	Key Process Areas
3	Continuous process Improvement	Knowledge database applied to BPR, Business Goals, Data & System Integration
2	Process Standardization, requirements engineering method introduced	Improvement identified in KM, SCM and CRM's processes
1	Ad-hoc Processes, Manual Processes	Existing Business Processes

APPLICATION

A case study was conducted at the ABC Company to apply the proposed requirements engineering method and the ERP maturity model. The survey was conducted with the employees in the technical as well as managerial positions who were employed during the ERP implementation and the members of the ERP vendor deputed to the ABC for ERP implementation. The ABC, a Company dealing with giant food and pharmaceuticals, carried out their operations through their branches opened all over the world. The company had more than 250,000 employees at 500 facilities in ninety countries. The team decided to use the following ERP modules: purchasing, finance, sales and distribution modules. All of these modules would be installed in every division of the company. The company later contracted with an ERP vendor to purchase and deploy the new version of their software. The company decided to create up to five computer centers around the world to run the new ERP package containing financial, accounts payable, accounts receivable, planning, production management, supply chain management and business intelligence software. The problem started when the employees could not reap the real benefits of the ERP system. The EMM discussed here were applied to the ABC Company to assess the impact of the ERP implementation in the ABC. Then to enable the ABC Company to improve their performance through the ERP system, the requirements engineering method was applied. The results show a positive climate for deployment of the EMM and the REM in an enterprise during ERP implementation. Key indicators of ERP functionality (Table 3) identified by a major ERP vendor Intuitive Manufacturing Systems (http://www.intuitivemfg.com) have been used to apply the EMM to an enterprise. This identifies the level of EMM to which an enterprise belongs. Then the REM is used to enable the enterprise to assess its ERP system requirements and refine it to reach a higher level in the EMM than the present one. In the Table 3, eighteen key factors are present and a score (Shown in Table 4) is given to the response from an enterprise for each of these key factors. After rounds of analysis, the ERP vendor Intuitive Manufacturing System has fixed the score an enterprise has to secure for each of the key indicators of ERP functionality. Then the REM in Figure 3 is applied to the enterprise with reference to the EMM's key process areas shown in Table 3. This is done to collect the improved requirements for the ERP system and design an improved ERP system to enhance its performance. The minimum score for each response obviously indicates the success of the ERP implementation leading to the conclusion that the benefits of the ERP implementation can be fully reaped by the enterprise. From the analysis done by the ERP vendor "Intuitive Manufacturing Systems" among a set of companies using the ERP software, it is found find that only 6% of the companies lie in level 3 of the EMM, 19% in level 2 and 75% in level 1 of the EMM. The total score obtained by an enterprise is used to determine to which level of the EMM model, the enterprise belongs. The percentage shown in Table 3 for each of the key indicators shows the percentage of companies that have chosen that response for the respective key indicators. To validate the ERP Maturity Model (EMM) and the Requirements Engineering Method (REM) for ERP projects discussed here, the EMM and the REM were applied to the ABC Company and a comparison was made on the performance of the ABC Company before and after the application of these methods.

The ABC Company's ERP team members as well as the end users were given the score sheet given in Table 3 and the score obtained by the ABC Company was 53. This shows that the Company is in Level 2 of our EMM model. This indicates that the ERP software does not completely reflect the business processes of the enterprise and the different types of users of the ERP system are not satisfied with the ERP implementation. Then the REM (Refer to Figure 3) was applied to the ABC

Table 3. Key indicators of ERP functionality

Key Indicators of ERP Functionality		Scoring: 1 = Strongly Disagree and 5 = Strongly Agree				
K1	Inventory accuracy for finished goods, work-in-progress or raw material is not satisfactory.	1 10%	2 10%	3 20%	4 24%	5 37%
K2	Too much of manual reconciliation required between our accounting and inventory systems.	1 9%	2 11%	3 22%	4 25%	5 33%
K3	On-time delivery performance is not satisfactory.	1 12%	2 14%	3 25%	4 24%	5 26%
K4	It is not easy to track job status on the shop floor.	1 7%	2 12%	3 23%	4 23%	5 34%
K5	We do more than two physical inventories per year.	1 26%	2 14%	3 19%	4 12%	5 28%
K6	We are constantly rescheduling work orders.	1 9%	2 13%	3 26%	4 27%	5 25%
K7	Our purchasing activity is not integrated with accounts payable.	1 18%	2 13%	3 19%	4 20%	5 31%
K8	We do not have access to real-time status of key performance indicators.	1 7%	2 7%	3 16%	4 20%	5 50%
K9	Material planning process does not automatically include actual and projected sales orders.	1 10%	2 10%	3 16%	4 22%	5 41%
K10	We constantly have part shortages.	1 11%	2 16%	3 30%	4 20%	5 23%
K11	There is no link between our customer sales orders and our accounting system.	1 20%	2 12%	3 22%	4 16%	5 29%
K12	We have a very limited view of vendor performance.	1 9%	2 12%	3 21%	4 29%	5 30%
K13	Our shipping process does not automatically update our general ledger.	1 14%	2 11%	3 17%	4 18%	5 40%
K14	It is not easy to adjust schedules to incorporate new customer orders.	1 9%	2 15%	3 27%	4 24%	5 25%
K15	We aren't able to accurately manage work center capacity.	1 10%	2 11%	3 22%	4 29%	5 28%
K16	We can't easily review product cost.	1 8%	2 13%	3 18%	4 24%	5 37%
K17	We have too much cash tied up in inventory.	1 11%	2 15%	3 25%	4 21%	5 27%
K18	We don't have good visibility of material and capacity requirements.	1 8%	2 9%	3 24%	4 27%	5 33%

Table 4. Score summary for EMM

Score Summary	
Score Obtained	Level in the ERP Maturity Model (EMM)
18 – 36	03
37 – 54	02
55 – 90	01

Company to collect the improved requirements from the different users of the ERP system and to refine the ERP system. After a certain period, the same score sheet shown in Table 3 was given to the ERP team members and end users of the ABC Company. The score obtained by the ABC Company was 27. This shows that the company has improved from Level 2 to Level 3 in the EMM model. This result is compelling and poses a positive climate for the usage of the EMM and the REM for ERP projects to improve the performance of the ERP software for an enterprise. Figure 5 shows the score obtained by the ABC Company based on their response to the key indicators mentioned in Table 3. In Figure 5, series 1 and series 2 show the score obtained by the ABC Company before and after the application of the requirements engineering method and the EMM respectively. It is observed that the total score secured by the ABC Company are 53 and 27 according to series 1 and series 2 respectively. It is evident that the application of the proposed requirements engineering method for the ERP projects will produce refined and improved ERP software to suit the needs of the different types of users of the ERP system. From Figure 5, it is evident that there is a substantial improvement in the ERP's performance of the ABC Company

after applying the EMM and the REM. The ABC Company has moved from Level 2 of the EMM to Level 3. It is found that the ERP team will be able to address the following using our requirements engineering method and the ERP maturity model. They are: (i) Defining what ERP is to achieve. (ii) Checking whether all the business processes are well defined and understood. (iii) To identify the gaps and bottlenecks in the ERP Project. (iv) Identifying the performance metrics for the ERP project. (v) The need to do BPR and (vi) Feasibility to execute data and system integration. The application of the EMM and the REM is very straightforward, but should be applied in the early stage of ERP implementation to get the full benefits out of it. The EMM when applied to the ABC's ERP system gave their ERP team clarity of comprehension of the ERP system and the ability to reason the reengineered business processes logically and clearly. It acts as a catalyst to draw a road map for capturing the requirements from the different types of users of the ERP system and improving them to produce customer specific ERP software. Most of the enterprises involved in the ERP implementation nowadays lie in Level 1 or Level 2 of our EMM but only those that could reach Level 3 will be able to reap the full benefits of an ERP integrated system. Defining

Figure 5. Applications of the EMM and the REM

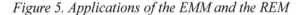

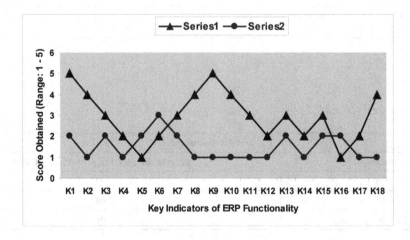

business requirements and then determining how to configure them into the software are an iterative process. During the initial implementation of an ERP system, many organizations choose to customize the standard ERP software modules to meet implementation dates and to match their unique business requirements. Failure to handle customization, poor software process management and the absence of historical information on successfully implemented ERP projects make it difficult for the development team to match the business process and the packaged software, resulting in failure.

CONCLUSION

The exploratory case study highlights the significance of the ERP Maturity Model (EMM) for assessing the ERP maturity within the organization and the Requirements Engineering Method (REM) for ERP system requirements. These methods are found to yield fruitful results to the ERP team since it possesses the following features: (i) The REM relies on user-defined requirements and also contains a couple of requirements engineering-based performance measures validated by the various stakeholders. (ii) The EMM provides the base to study the existing business processes, identify and define new processes with the feasibility to redesign and improve them continuously to meet the performance metrics and the challenges for data and system integration to come in the later part of the ERP implementation.

Only a few articles document the actual cause for ERP failure (Willcocks et al 2000). It is observed that technical factors contribute to the high success rate of ERP projects (Bingi et al 1999). The present research demonstrates the importance of the different types of user's requirements for the success of the ERP system. From a research perspective, we have shown that requirements

engineering forms an important component of the ERP implementation. In the present work, we have proposed a REM and an EMM to make ERP implementation successful through effective requirements gathering and subsequently verifying and validating them using a knowledge database.

All the IT companies involved in ERP implementation are required to maintain a knowledge database. The usage of this database effectively by the IT Companies decides their success rate. From a practical standpoint, prior research has shown that providing focus and structure to requirements gathering results in more accurate and complete outcomes (Agarwal et al 1990; Marakas et al 1998). In this research study, we have demonstrated that the requirements engineering method coupled with the EMM will enable the ERP implementation team to meet the requirements of the different types of users of the ERP system.

There are several important practical implications to be gained from this research. First, applying the EMM to the ERP of an enterprise to assess its maturity. Second, the application of the requirements engineering method to elevate the ERP system in the EMM from the present level to a higher level. The findings from the case study are very gripping. The ERP vendors and the organizations in the process of launching ERP should remember to integrate the technical factors with other managerial factors to deliver a quality ERP system on time as well as within budget.

REFERENCES

Agarwal, R., & Tanniru, M. R. (1990). Knowledge acquisition using structured interviewing: an empirical investigation. *Journal of Management Information Systems*, 7, 123–140.

Agrawal, M., & Chari, K. (2007, March). Software Effort, Quality and Cycle Time: A Study of CMM Level 5 Projects. *IEEE Transactions on Software Engineering, 33*(3), 145–156. doi:10.1109/TSE.2007.29

Alagar, V. S., & Periyasamy, K. (1998). Specification of Software Systems. New York: Springer-Verlag.

Basili, V. R., & Weiss, D. M. (1981). Evaluation of a software requirements document by analysis of change data. In *Proceedings of 5th International Conference on Software Engineering* (pp. 314-323).

Bingi, P., Sharma, M. K., & Godla, J. K. (1999). Critical success factors affecting an ERP implementation. *Information Systems Management.*

Boehm, B. W., & Papaccio, P. N. (1988). Understanding and controlling software costs. *IEEE Transactions on Computers*, 1462–1467.

Brooks, F. P. (1975). *The Mythical Man-month: Essays on Software Engineering*. Reading, MA: Addison-Wesley Publishing Company

Brooks, F. P. (1987). No Silver Bullet: Essence and Accidents of Software Engineering. *IEEE Computer, 20*(4), 10–19.

Brooks, F. P. (1987). No Silver Bullet: Essence and Accidents of Software Engineering. *IEEE Computer, 20*(4), 10–19.

Brown, C., & Vessey, I. (1999). ERP implementation approaches: toward a contingency framework. In *Proceedings of the International Conference on Information Systems* (pp. 411-416).

Cohen, B. (1989). Justification of formal methods for systems specifications. *Software Engineering Journal, 4*(1), 26–35. doi:10.1109/32.21723

Curran, T., & Lad, A. (2000). *SAP R/3 Business Blueprint* (2nd ed.). Prentice Hall.

Damian, D., & Chisan, J. (2006). An Empirical Study of the Complex Relationships between Requirements Engineering Processes and Other Processes that Lead to Payoffs in Productivity, Quality, and Risk Management. *IEEE Transactions on Software Engineering, 32*(7), 433–453. doi:10.1109/TSE.2006.61

Daneva, M. (2003). Lessons Learnt from Five Years of Experience in ERP Requirements Engineering. In *Proceedings of the 11th IEEE International Requirements Engineering Conference.*

Daneva, M. (2004). ERP Requirements Engineering Practice: Lessons Learned. *IEEE Software*, 26–33. doi:10.1109/MS.2004.1270758

Daneva, M., & Wieringa, R. J. (2006). A Requirements engineering framework for cross-organizational ERP systems. *Requirements Engineering, 11*, 194–204. doi:10.1007/s00766-006-0034-9

Davenport, T. H. (1998, July-August). Putting the enterprise into the enterprise system. *Harvard Business Review*, 121–131.

Davis, A. M. (1990). *Software Requirements–Analysis and Specification*. Prentice Hall.

Deloitte Touche (2002). *Achieving, Measuring and Communicating IT value, and IDG Research Services Group report.*

DeMarco, T. (1978). *Structured analysis and system specification*. New York: Yourdon press.

Grady, R., & Caswell, D. (1999). *Software Metrics: Establishing a Company-wide program*. Prentice Hall.

Hiquet, B., & Kelly, A. F. (1998). SAP R/3 implementation guide: A manager's guide to understanding SAP. India: Macmillan Technical.

Holland, C. P., & Light, B. (1999, May/June). A Critical success factor model for ERP implementation. *IEEE Software*, 30–36. doi:10.1109/52.765784

Humphrey, W. (2005). *Managing the software process*. Addison-Wesley.

Jalote, P. (1999). *CMM in Practice, Processes for executing project at Infosys*. Addison-Wesley

Jalote, P. (2002). *Software Project Management in Practice*. Addison-Wesley.

Maiden, N. (2006). Improve you Requirements: Quantify them. *IEEE Software*, 68–69. doi:10.1109/MS.2006.165

Marakas, G., & Elam, J. (1998). Semantic structuring in analyst acquisition and representation of facts in requirements analysis. *Information Systems Research*, *9*, 37–63. doi:10.1287/isre.9.1.37

Markus, L., Axline, S., Petrie, D., & Tanis, C. (2000). Learning from Adopters' Experience with ERP Problems Encountered and Success Achieved. *Journal of Information Technology*, 245–265. doi:10.1080/02683960010008944

Nah, F. F.-H., & Lau, J. L.-S. (2001). Critical factors for successful implementation of enterprise systems. *Business Process Management Journal*, *7*(3), 285–296. doi:10.1108/14637150110392782

Oman, P. W. (1990). CASE Analysis and Design Tools. *IEEE Software*, *7*, 37–44. doi:10.1109/52.55226

Oslen, K. A., & Saetre, P. (2007). IT for niche companies: Is an ERP system the solution? *Information Systems Journal*, *17*, 37–58. doi:10.1111/j.1365-2575.2006.00229.x

Parr, A., & Shanks, G. (2000). A Model of ERP Project Implementation. *Journal of Information Technology*, 289–303. doi:10.1080/02683960010009051

Pitts., M. G., & Browne, G.J. (2007). *Improving requirements elicitation: An empirical investigation of procedural prompts*, 17, 89-110.

Pressman, R. S. (2006). Software Engineering, A Practitioner's Approach, India: Tata McGraw-Hill.

Procaccino, J., Verner, J., Overmyer, S., & Darter, M. (2002). Case Study: Factors for early prediction of software development success. *Information and Software Technology*, *44*, 53–62. doi:10.1016/S0950-5849(01)00217-8

SAP AG. (1999). ASAP Methodology for Rapid R/3 Implementation: User Manual, Walldorf.

Stensrud, E., & Myrtveit, I. (2003, May). Identifying High Performance ERP Projects. *IEEE Transactions on Software Engineering*, *29*(5). doi:10.1109/TSE.2003.1199070

Tavolato, P., & Vincena, K. (1984). A prototyping methodology and its tool (pp. 334-346). Springer-Verlag.

Tiwana, A., & Keil, M. (2006). Functionality risk in Information Systems Development: An Empirical Investigation. *IEEE Transactions on Engineering Management*, *53*(3), 412–425. doi:10.1109/TEM.2006.878099

Togur, D. M., & Bloomberg, E. (2003). *CIO Survey Series: Release 4.5*, Morgan Stanley Research Report, 2003.

Weinberg, G. (1971). *The Psychology of Computer Programming*. New York: van Nostrand Reinhold Co.

Willcocks, L. P. (2000). The role of the CIO and IT function in ERP. *Communication of ACM*.

Chapter 4
Requirements Elicitation for Personalized ERP Systems:
A Case Study

Lex van Velsen
University of Twente, The Netherlands

Corrie Huijs
M&I/Partners, The Netherlands

Thea van der Geest
University of Twente, The Netherlands

ABSTRACT

For small and medium-sized companies the fit between their business processes and their Enterprise Resource Planning (ERP) system is a critical success factor. The functions and features for essential tasks must be geared to the demands and skills of the individual users. This paper reports on the usefulness of several methods for eliciting user input which served as a basis for requirements for a personalized ERP system. It describes the yield of heuristic evaluations, both by experts and by developers, and a focus group with six users representing the main user types. The focus group consisted of an identification of the most important functions, task demonstrations, and a mini design workshop. As a demonstration of the results of the various user-focused methods, some noteworthy findings on the personalization of ERP systems are presented.

INTRODUCTION

Enterprise Resource Planning (ERP) systems often place huge demands on their users. The wide variety of functions and features offered throughout the system often lead to systems that are far from intuitive and may hinder efficient use. Moreover, many users need only a part of the functions to fulfill their work tasks effectively. Therefore, from the perspective of a specific user, providing all the options makes the system more complicated than necessary. The **usability** problems which are the result of the complexity of an ERP system may be reduced by personalizing it (Benyon, 1993). Another

DOI: 10.4018/978-1-60566-968-7.ch004

benefit of personalization of business software is that it enables handicapped employees to function like every other employee, as it can tailor system output to cater for an employee's special needs (Hardt & Schrepp, 2008).

Personalization deals with presenting each user with tailored system output (for an elaborate discussion of personalization, see Brusilovsky (2001) or Jameson (2007)). Such output can be based upon user behavior in which case it is implicitly collected. This kind of tailoring is called adaptivity. Or the tailored output can be based upon the user wishes, needs or context which the user explicitly provided to the system. This kind of tailoring is called adaptability. A system is personalized when it includes adaptive and / or adaptable features. A personalized ERP system can, for example, provide quick links to the automatically generated reports which a user normally creates at the end of each week, and only show these links on Thursdays and Fridays. As a basis for personalization, knowledge about the users, their domain and their contexts is required. This paper reports our attempts to create this basis in a sound empirical manner, by applying a set of design-supporting, user-centered methods.

The system that is the focus of this case study is an **ERP** system that is developed for Small and Medium-sized Enterprises (SMEs) in the metal industry; we will refer to it as M-ERP. As the development of such a system is highly dependent on the context in which it is to be used, a **case study** is a valuable source of information for practitioners, as well as researchers in the field of ERP system design (Yin, 2003). Our activities show that users expect that the M-ERP system would benefit from tailored output and it demonstrates how to approach personalization in a re-design process. In order to create a basis for the personalization effort, we concentrated on the requirements engineering stage in the re-design of the M-ERP system.

TAILORING ERP SYSTEMS

ERP systems are mostly Commercial-off-the-Shelf (COTS) systems. The investment that is needed for fine-tuning such COTS systems is often the reason that implementation budgets are exceeded (Scheer & Habermann, 2000). Fine-tuning of COTS systems can be done by configuration or customization. Configuration deals with adjusting system parameters and user rights. Customization, in this domain, focuses on changing the package code (Light, 2005).

Vendors and buyers of ERP systems are hesitant to customize because of high development and maintenance costs and the high risks of software failure. Furthermore, every time that a new version of a customized ERP is installed, it needs to be customized again. As a result, most organizations purchase COTS systems and only configure those (Brehm et al., 2001). Configuration is focused on business processes and not on the individuals executing the business processes or their specific tasks. The fit between business processes and the ERP system has been identified as the most important success factor for SMEs (Everdingen et al., 2000), but a lack of focus on the individual may result in a disparity between the configured system's functions and the user's perceptions of goals and tasks. Because of the many tasks the relatively few employees of SMEs have to perform, a fit between business processes and ERP system in this domain means focusing on a single user's tasks and context. Personalization may be an approach that is particularly helpful in this case, since it may increase this fit between ERP system, tasks and context of a particular user, hence increasing user efficiency.

METHOD

In order to optimize the fit between user tasks, context and the ERP system, the requirement phase of the development process needs a strong focus on the user and his or her context. Without **user involvement** the system functionality will not fit with user tasks and goals (Wright & Wright, 2002). Furthermore, user involvement results in more accurate **requirements** (Kujala, 2003).

In the case of the ERP system described in this paper, we applied a number of user-focused methods (derived from Maguire (2001)) to evaluate the current version of M-ERP and to elicit requirements. In this chapter, we will first discuss the ERP system that is dealt with in this study. Second, we discuss the methods used in the requirements elicitation process and their application to this specific case.

M-ERP

M-ERP is an ERP system for SMEs in the metal industry. Besides normal ERP functionality, M-ERP has features that are specifically designed for the metal industry, such as a calculator for material prices. Most of the enterprises that use M-ERP are small enterprises, which mean that only one or a few employees within each enterprise are actual users of the system. Figure 1 shows a part of the M-ERP screen (text is in Dutch). The developers of M-ERP decided that a complete re-design of their system was needed. The first version of the system had grown over the years, and with many new opportunities in technology, the moment had come to reconceptualize and work towards a new version of M-ERP. This decision offered them the occasion to create a version that was more adapted to the needs of the users and offered possibilities for personalization. Since they realized that their expertise was in the domain of the metal industry business processes, they asked an 'innovation coach' to act as project manager for the re-design process and sought support in academia for realizing the user-centered approach to the design.

Figure 1. Part of an M-ERP screen

We, the academia, proposed the following activities to create the basis for a user-centered, personalized re-design:

- Heuristic evaluation of the interface by experts, as well as by developers; and
- A focus group which includes the identification of the most important functions, task demonstrations by users, a mini design workshop and the setting of priorities.

Before conducting these activities we asked the developers to analyze their customer database and distinguish the different types of M-ERP users. They came up with six types:

1. **Account manager:** the user who manages customer contacts, (e.g., makes offers, informs customers about delivery, etc.) with M-ERP;
2. **General manager:** the user who does his administration with M-ERP;
3. **Financial bookkeeper:** the user who keeps his books with M-ERP;
4. **Jack-of-all-trades:** the user who has to use all parts of M-ERP (e.g., the owner of a very small enterprise);
5. **Office manager:** the user who manages procurement, sales and personnel data with M-ERP; and

6. **Product planner:** the user who plans and controls the production work in the metal workshop with M-ERP.

This typology was used as input for the design of the heuristic evaluation and the focus group, but can also serve as input when one wants to determine group characteristics on which tailored output can be based.

Heuristic Evaluation

A **heuristic evaluation** is a systematic evaluation of an interface guided by a set of (preferably validated) guidelines (Nielsen, 1994). The evaluation results in an assessment of whether an interface complies with rules of good design. Heuristics evaluations are either conducted with prototypes, as part of the iterative design process, or with complete versions of a system to generate input for interface re-design. An advantage of the method is that the evaluation can be done by just a handful of experts. The trade-off is that the method may not elicit all the problems that real users would have uncovered (De Jong & Van der Geest, 2000).

Setup of the Heuristic Evaluation

1. *Heuristic evaluation by experts.* We, as academics, performed a heuristic evaluation of the most important screens of M-ERP, using the interface usability principles of Nielsen as guidelines (Nielsen, 1994). We found that most of the **usability** problems in the system could be detected and discussed with a selection of four typical screens from M-ERP, which would also be used for the heuristic evaluation with developers. We wrote down our evaluation, but did not report it to the developers yet. Inconsistency of navigation between pages and within pages, mismatch between real-world activities and system functions, and lack of intuitiveness

were recognized as main sources of potential usability problems.

2. *Heuristic evaluation by developers, role-playing for typical users.* Our aim with the heuristic evaluation of M-ERP by its developers was threefold. First, we wanted them to generate input for the redesign of the system concerning the user interface. Second, we wanted to ensure that the various perspectives of different types of users were taken into account. We wanted to let the developers actually experience differences in user expectations and use of the system. We saw an awareness concerning differences among users within designers as a prerequisite for successful development of a personalized system. Our third aim was making the developers aware of a set of basic usability principles, like minimalist design and a need for visibility of the system status.

The four developers were asked to take the role of either, Jack-of-all-trades, product planner, account manager or office manager. The external project manager was given the role of temporary employee since she had no experience with the system. Consequently, she would notice different issues than the developers since the latter are used to seeing the interface and as a result, may consider some parts of the design as good and logical because they have always seen and made them this way. When we showed the participants each screen, we asked them to comment on it as their assigned counterparts would. They had to indicate what functionality they would use on each screen and whether the supplied functionality and information was useful or not.

3. *Icon quiz.* In order to create awareness for the importance of intuitiveness, we set up a game with the icons used in the current version of the system. A large part of the

icons used in the system were listed and their caption was removed. This list of icons was given to all the participants and they were asked to write down the meaning for all the icons.

Results of the Heuristic Evaluation

The heuristic evaluation resulted in the acknowledgement of inconsistency of navigation and a lack of intuitiveness as main aspects to give attention to in the redesign of M-ERP. A lack of intuitiveness was the result of an identified difficulty for users to orientate themselves within and between pages in M-ERP. Realization of the lack of intuitiveness was strengthened by the icon game, which many designers found hard to complete satisfactory. It was an eye-opener for the developers that without the descriptions some of the icons were identical and that the meaning of an icon was not always clear at first glance, even though the icons were used in the system they developed themselves. Finally, as a result of the role play, the designers realized that different users demand different functionality in order to fulfill their tasks most efficiently.

Focus Group

A **focus group** is a group discussion with six to nine people and is led by a moderator. A great advantage of this method is that participants feel the need to explain their answers to the group and provide a thorough rationale for their thinking (Morgan, 1996). For the design of personalized systems, such discussions can be held as a part of the **requirements** engineering process or to evaluate low-fidelity prototypes (Van Velsen et al., 2008). During requirements engineering, focus groups can serve as a means to receive input for functional, data, user and environment analysis (Gena & Weibelzahl, 2007). In combination with a paper prototype, a focus group can generate feedback on design ideas in a very early stage of

the design process (Karat et al., 2003). During this stage in the design process, it is important to have a prototype or earlier version of a system to show to participants since they find it hard to imagine functionality that does not exist yet (Weibelzahl et al., 2006).

A focus group is often combined with other methods (Morgan, 1996). We will discuss two of these methods which we combined with our focus group: task demonstrations and a mini design workshop. Task demonstration is a way to observe tasks as they are performed by actual users. Users often have difficulty explaining what they do with a system. Demonstrating what they do is easier for them (Lauesen, 2002). Demonstrations by users can serve as input for task analysis. Task analysis concerns the breaking down of processes in small steps and identifying the user rationale behind each step. During requirements engineering for personalized systems, task demonstrations can produce helpful input for functional, data and task knowledge analysis (Gena & Weibelzahl, 2007). A design workshop brings together users and developers (Lauesen, 2002). Cooperatively they design (part of) an interface. Many design workshops are focused on a system that is to be used in one organization and workshop participants are employees of this organization. This approach has not been applied to the design of personalized systems yet. We think this method may generate useful information concerning the actual need for personalization, the visual lay-out of a system and can provide input for functional, data, user and environment analysis.

Setup of the Focus Group

The quality of the results of the focus group depends on the variety of answers a group of participants provide. One needs a heterogeneous group of participants in order to collect multiple views on a given topic. Therefore, each different type of user the developers identified was present in the focus group. One of the users (the Financial bookkeeper) had used the system for only a very short while. The place of venue was a conference room in a hotel. Time reserved for the focus group was four hours.

The focus group consisted of five parts:

1. *Identification of the most important M-ERP functions.* We asked each participant to list the top 3 of activities they performed most with M-ERP. We also handed them the print-outs of the most used M-ERP screens. They had to choose which screens corresponded with each activity in their top 3 best. Next, they had to place plusses and minuses on these print-outs on aspects of these screens they valued positively or negatively. Then, every print-out was discussed and we asked the participants whether they used each screen and to what avail. They were also given the opportunity to tell where they placed plusses and minuses on each screen and why. By means of this activity, we wanted to identify the functions that were widely used and to assess the weak and strong points of the interface that offers these functions.

2. *Task demonstrations.* From the collected M-ERP activity top 3s we choose two activities that were listed often and used a wide variety of system functions. For each scenario, one participant was asked to use the M-ERP system (which was projected on a big screen) to perform the activity while thinking-aloud. The other participants were asked to write down what (dis)advantages they saw in M-ERP for this activity, and how M-ERP could be improved upon to support the demonstrated activity better. After a demonstration, the notes each participant made were discussed. By means of this activity, we wanted to identify the amount of support M-ERP gives for the performance of primary tasks and the weak and strong points of the current M-ERP interface in these contexts.

3. *Mini-design workshop*: '*My M-ERP*'. We started this part of the session with a demonstration of 'iGoogle', which is an application that can be personalized. The participants were explained that 'iGoogle' is a web page filled with applets containing self-chosen information which are constantly being updated by their provider. Then we asked each participant to create their own 'My M-ERP' page on a white A3 paper sheet, by using post-its and markers. They could come up with chunks of information, or direct links to information they wanted on their M-ERP starting screen. By means of this activity, we wanted to identify the diversity of applets with information users want to have on their personalized starting page.

4. *Proactive notifications.* For some time, the M-ERP developers toyed with the idea of providing proactive notifications to their users. While working with M-ERP, a user should receive reports containing meta-information that help to conduct their professional task. The user should be able to chose which reports he or she wants to receive and to customize them as well. Examples include a critical liquidity position or an upcoming delivery date. The participants were given a short presentation of this idea. Next, they were asked what they thought about it. By means of this activity we wanted to gather their opinions about this idea. Furthermore, we wanted to assess the domain the participants thought of when presented with the possibility of personalized proactive notifications.

5. *Setting priorities.* During the focus group, the participants provided us with many wishes and demands. In order to get a feeling for priority, we asked the participants to give the developers just one piece of advice which should really be taken into account in M-ERP redesign.

Results of the Focus Group

For each activity we will discuss here what kind of information it provided to us.

1. *Identification of the most important M-ERP functions.* This activity was undertaken to elicit a list of the functions that were widely used, as well as the strong and weak points of the M-ERP interface. Besides these kinds of information, the discussion resulted in other kinds of feedback that could be used for functional and environment analysis. Many comments were directed at the shortcomings of current functionality or the lack of desired functions. An example of such a comment was made by the General manager about the planning of hours:

"[This function] works well, it's just that it doesn't give me the information I need -- who comes in late, who is ill, etc. Those are things I'd like to know at the end of the day."

Comments that could function as input for environment analysis focused on the harmony between the system and the real life of the metal industry enterprise. The Jack-of-all-trades, for example, commented on the usefulness of the planning module:

"It doesn't give me an overview. When a customers walks into my office I can't just tell him whether I can plan something in at short notice."

2. *Task demonstrations.* The task demonstrations were supposed to provide information on the support M-ERP provides to users for some, frequently executed, tasks. Again, strong and weak points of the current interface were to be assessed. Besides these gains, the task demonstrations also proved

to be useful input for task analysis. The participants were able to 'walk through' the other participants and the moderator through their tasks with stunning accuracy, providing a thorough rationale for their actions. The subsequent discussion among participants resulted in many comments which were useful for environment analysis, since they focused on how the demonstrated tasks were performed in their enterprises and how M-ERP supports them. For example, a demonstration by a participant showing how a product was treated in her enterprise, from product offer to production order, resulted in the following discussion:

General manager: "We don't use the product offer part. And I don't see it happening either, way too complicated. In my case it starts with the sales offer."

Product planner: "In our company, this is divided over several people."

Financial bookkeeper: "In our company, someone else does the calculation and I do the rest."

Such comments can be used to determine characteristics of a group of users. Personalization can use these characteristics for the tailoring of output. During this discussion, the Jack-of-all-trades even spoke out the wish for M-ERP to be adaptive:

"There should be intelligence behind this screen [...] It should automatically close the screen after I acknowledge it. After a while it should know what I want, right?"

Figure 2. 'My M-ERP' page created by the general manager

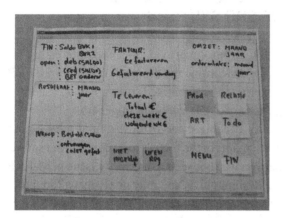

Figure 3. 'My M-ERP' page created by the product planner

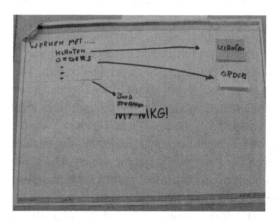

3. *Mini-design workshop: 'My M-ERP'.* We conducted a mini-design workshop to identify the diversity of applets containing information users want on their personalized M-ERP starting page. Figure 2 and Figure 3 show examples of screens that were created.

The applets with information each participant desired, were for a large part related to their professional function. They wanted quick access to the information necessary for main tasks. The Financial bookkeeper, for example, told he would like to see his liquidity, delivery terms and planning. He also wanted this page be interoperable, desiring links with Outlook and his bank accounts. These comments can serve as input for data analysis. They inform us of what kind of output the user desires and based on this information, one can derive the required system input and what kind of data needs to be stored internally. Besides the applets with information directly related to work, many participants would like to see their coworkers' birthdays on their starting page, as well as links to newspapers.

In general, the participants were enthusiastic about the idea of a personalized starting page. The General manager stated that:

"A 'My M-ERP' starting page is very tempting. I would like to have some important data on my screen."

4. *Proactive notifications.* Here, we wanted to receive feedback on the idea of proactive notifications and to establish the domain it should support. Participants did not have a clear opinion about the idea. Many examples of notifications they came up with, regarded the information the participants wanted on their 'My M-ERP' starting page. However, they indicated they did like the idea.

5. *Setting priorities.* We asked the participants for one advice for the system developers, in order to identify priority issues. These issues ranged from the switching between keyboard and mouse as input device, to the inclusion of specific features, to the updating of system documentation. Interestingly, nobody mentioned any of the personalized features we presented to the participants during the session ('My M-ERP' starting page, proactive notifications).

EXPERIENCES WITH THE APPLIED METHODOLOGY

As we stated before, the **heuristic evaluation** by the developers fulfilled an important condition for successful development of personalization. They made the developers aware of the fact that a user population consists of different kinds of users, in different kinds of enterprises who all interact with the system in their own way. Besides a tool to evaluate an earlier version of a system, this method is also a means to contribute to a state of mind, necessary to develop a personalized system.

The **focus group** provided useful input for functional, data, user and environment analysis. However, we think that the usefulness of this focus group was, in large part, the result of the combination of the group discussion with other methods (in our case task demonstrations and a mini design workshop). Each combination elicited different kinds of comments which were useful for different kinds of analyses. Using the focus group as a single method may limit its usefulness in this phase of the system development.

The discussion of the proactive notifications was not as lively as the discussion about the 'My M-ERP' starting page. The participants mostly repeated the ideas they came up with for their 'My M-ERP' page and had difficulty formulating an opinion about the proactive notifications without involving the 'My M-ERP' starting page. The discussion suffered from the fact that we consecutively questioned two personalized features. Moreover, these features were very much alike. They both supply the user with (meta)information. A 'My M-ERP' page is adaptable and supplies tailored output on a stable place in the system (the starting page). Proactive notifications are adaptive as well as adaptable and provide information on diverse places in the system (where the user happens to be). Based on our experience in this project, we advise evaluators not to question several similar personalized features in one (group) interview.

SOME NOTEWORTHY FINDINGS ON PERSONALIZATION OF ERP SYSTEMS

The focus group provided us with interesting insights concerning the design of personalized ERP systems, or personalized software to be used in a professional environment in general.

As became clear from the final advices the participants of the focus group gave us, **personalization** was not seen as a priority issue in M-ERP (re)design. This result may imply that an adaptive or adaptable feature is only a wish of ERP users when the system itself works properly and satisfies the basic user needs. However, we did not address personalization as a function to satisfy these basic user needs which may have influenced results. In order to generate a better understanding of the priority personalization should be given in the (re)design process of an ERP system, more research should be conducted.

It was striking to see that many participants saw personalized features as a means to compensate weak personal capabilities. Examples include not having an overview of everything that happens within the organization, or forgetting birthdays.

The application of personalization in a professional environment poses stakeholders with an important issue that is not as emphatically present in the domain of educational or entertainment systems (the domains in which personalization is very popular). A personalized system tailors output for each person. This does not only change the system behavior, but the user behavior as well. The user will act in a way that complies best with the system. In the education or entertainment domain, loss of the user of a personalized system will probably not affect an organization much. In a professional environment it will. A new employee will be placed in a working environment which is geared upon his or her predecessor's working habits. The personalized system will provide output based on the predecessor's working patterns and these working patterns, on their turn, have influenced the way an organization works, especially in SMEs. Two things can be done to gear system, user and organization upon each other now. First, the new user can start with a clean user profile. Then, the system and the organization will have to learn about the user's working habits and adapt to it to create a well-functioning working routine. Second, the new user can use the user profile of the former user and learn to work with it. In this case only the user will have to learn to create a well-functioning working routine, but the personalization will not be personal anymore. Furthermore, the new user may not function optimally because system output is not geared upon his or her characteristics. A second, related issue, concerns the relation between organizational structures and intelligent systems. Many organizational structures rely on the assumption that systems are stable tools to conduct tasks with. With the introduction of personalized systems, these organizational structures may have to change, since they must be able to cope with changing working routines, using tools tailored to individuals.

At the moment of writing, only a very small number of issues that may hinder effective and efficient use of personalized systems in professional environments have been identified. These issues mostly concern the interface of and interaction with the system. Skov and Høegh (2006), for example, found that a lack of control over the personalization of output can lead to a disruption in work processes. The organizational structures or individual roles that change due to the introduction of personalization are not a topic of discussion yet. Therefore, how to cope with the aforementioned consequences of using personalized systems in professional environments remains a challenge for the future.

CONCLUSION

Our sessions with the system developers and users have shown that **personalization** may be a promising feature for ERP systems that may contribute to enhanced efficiency and quality of work in a professional environment. However, good **usability** appeared to be more important than the inclusion of personalized features. Employees may benefit from the personalization of an ERP system in the form of a personalized starting page containing meta-information. This meta-information can compensate personal weaknesses and thus, improve the quality of work.

In this study, the methods we applied for eliciting comments that can serve as input for **requirements**, have proven their worth. Nonetheless, other methods may be fruitful as well or may elicit other kinds of input that can be very beneficial in the design process. In order to generate a full understanding of the different methods' worth, more research in an immature field is needed.

ACKNOWLEDGMENT

We would like to thank the Metaal Kennis Groep (MKG) in Hengelo, the Netherlands, for providing us with the opportunity to conduct this study.

REFERENCES

Benyon, D. (1993). Adaptive systems: A solution to usability problems. *User Modeling and User-Adapted Interaction*, 3(1), 65–87. doi:10.1007/BF01099425

Brehm, L., Heizl, A., & Markus, L. (2001). Tailoring ERP systems: a spectrum of choices and their implications. In *Proceedings of the 34th Hawaii International Conference on System Sciences*, Hawaii, USA (pp. 8017-8025).

Brusilovsky, P. (2001). Adaptive hypermedia. *User Modeling and User-Adapted Interaction*, 11(1/2), 87–110. doi:10.1023/A:1011143116306

De Jong, M., & Van der Geest, T. (2000). Characterizing web heuristics. *Technical Communication, 47*(3), 311–326.

Gena, C., & Weibelzahl, S. (2007). Usability engineering for the adaptive web. In P. Brusilovsky, A. Kobsa & W. Nejdl (Eds.), *The adaptive web* (pp. 720-762). Berlin: Springer.

Hardt, A., & Schrepp, M. (2008). Making business software usable for handicapped employees. In K. Miesenberger, J. Klaus, W. Zagler & A. Karshmer (Eds.), *Computers helping people with special needs* (pp. 502-509). Berlin: Springer.

Jameson, A. (2007). Adaptive interfaces and agents. In J.A. Jacko & A. Sears (Eds.), *Human-computer interaction handbook* (pp. 433-458). Mahwah, NJ: Erlbaum.

Karat, M., Brodie, C., Karat, J., Vergo, J., & Alpert, S. R. (2003). Personalizing the user experience on ibm.com. *IBM Systems Journal, 42*(4), 686–701.

Kujala, S. (2003). User involvement: a review of the benefits and challenges. *Behaviour & Information Technology, 22*(1), 1–16. doi:10.1080/01449290301782

Lauesen, S. (2002). *Software requirements. Styles and techniques.* London: Addison-Wesley.

Light, B. (2005). Going beyond 'misfit' as a reason for ERP package customization. *Computers in Industry, 56,* 606–619. doi:10.1016/j.compind.2005.02.008

Maguire, M. (2001). Methods to support human-centred design. *International Journal of Human-Computer Studies, 55*(4), 587–634. doi:10.1006/ijhc.2001.0503

Morgan, D. L. (1996). Focus groups. *Annual Review of Sociology, 22,* 129–153. doi:10.1146/annurev.soc.22.1.129

Nielsen, J. (1994). Heuristic evaluation. In J. Nielsen & R.L. Mack (Eds.), *Usability inspection methods* (pp. 25-62). New York: John Wiley & Sons.

Scheer, A., & Habermann, F. (2000). Making ERP a success. *Communications of the ACM, 43*(4), 57–61. doi:10.1145/332051.332073

Skov, M. B., & Høegh, R. Th. (2006). Supporting information access in a hospital ward by a context-aware mobile electronic patient record. *Personal and Ubiquitous Computing, 10*(4), 205–214. doi:10.1007/s00779-005-0049-0

Van Everdingen, Y., Van Hillegersberg, J., & Waarts, E. (2000). Enterprise resource planning experiences and evolution – ERP adoption by European midsize companies. *Communications of the ACM, 43*(4), 27–31. doi:10.1145/332051.332064

Van Velsen, L., Van der Geest, T., Klaassen, R., & Steehouder, M. (2008). User-centered evaluation of adaptive and adaptable systems: a literature review. *The Knowledge Engineering Review, 23*(3), 261–281. doi:10.1017/S0269888908001379

Weibelzahl, S., Jedlitschka, A., & Ayari, B. (2006). Eliciting requirements for an adaptive decision support system through structured interviews. In *Proceedings of the 5th Workshop on User-Centred Design and Evaluation of Adaptive Systems,* Dublin, Ireland (pp. 470-478).

Wright, S., & Wright, A. (2002). Information system assurance for enterprise resource planning systems: unique risk considerations. *Journal of Information Systems, 16,* 99–113. doi:10.2308/jis.2002.16.s-1.99

Yin, R. K. (2003). *Case study research. Design and methods* (3rd ed.). Thousand Oaks, CA: Sage publications.

Chapter 5
Specifying General Activity Clusters for ERP Projects Aimed at Effort Prediction

Guy Janssens
Open Universiteit Nederland, The Netherlands

Rob Kusters
Eindhoven University of Technology, The Netherlands

Fred Heemstra
KWD Result Management, The Netherlands

ABSTRACT

ERP implementation projects affect large parts of an implementing organization and lead to changes in the way an organization performs its tasks. The costs needed for the effort to implement these systems are hard to estimate. Research indicates that the size of an ERP project can be a useful measurement for predicting the effort required to complete an ERP implementation project. However, such a metric does not yet exist. Therefore research should be carried out to find a set of variables which can define the size of an ERP project. The authors hypothesize that ERP projects consist of a collection of clusters of activities with their own focus on implementation costs and project size. This was confirmed in a survey among domain experts. This chapter describes a first step in retrieving these clusters. It shows 21 logical clusters of ERP implementation project activities based on 405 ERP implementation project activities retrieved from literature. Logical clusters of ERP project activities can be used in further research to find variables for defining the size of an ERP project.

INTRODUCTION

Globalization has put pressure on organizations to perform as efficiently and effectively as possible in order to compete in the market. Structuring their internal processes and making them most efficient by integrated information systems is very important for that reason. In the 1990s organizations started implementing ERP systems in order to replace their legacy systems and improve their business processes. This change is still being implemented. ERP is a key ingredient for gaining competitive

DOI: 10.4018/978-1-60566-968-7.ch005

advantage, streamlining operations, and having "lean" manufacturing (Mabert, Soni, & Venkataramanan, 2003). A study of Hendricks indicates that research shows some evidence of improvements in profitability after implementing ERP systems (Hendricks, Singhal, & Stratman, 2006). Forecasters predict a growth in the ERP market.

Several researchers also indicate that much research is still being carried out in this area (Botta-Genoulaz, Millet, & Grabot, 2005; Møller, Kræmmergaard, & Rikhardsson, 2004). Although the research area is rather clearly defined, many topics still have to be researched and the usefulness of results for actual projects has to be designed.

ERP projects are large and risky projects for organizations, because they affect great parts of the implementing organization and lead to changes in the way the organization performs its tasks. The costs needed for the effort to implement these systems are usually very high and also very hard to estimate. Many cases are documented where the actual required time and costs exceeded the budget, that is to say the estimated costs, many times. There are even cases where ERP implementation projects led to bankruptcy (Holland & Light, 1999; Scott, 1999). Francalanci states that software costs only represent a fraction of the overall cost of ERP projects within the total costs of the implementation project, that is to say, less than 10% over a 5-year period (Francalanci, 2001). In addition Willis states that consultants alone, can cost as much as or more than five times the cost of the software (Willis, Willis-Brown, & McMillan, 2001). This is confirmed by von Arb, who indicates that consultancy costs can be 2 to 4 times as much as software license costs (Arb, 1997). This indicates that the effort required for implementing an ERP system largely consists of effort-related costs. Von Arb also argues that license and hardware costs are fairly constant and predictable and that only a focus on reducing these effort-related costs is realistic. The conclusion is legitimate that the total effort is the most important and difficult factor to estimate in an

ERP implementation project. Therefore the main research of the authors only focuses on the estimation of the total effort required for implementing an ERP system.

In every project there is a great uncertainty at the start, while at the end there is only a minor uncertainty (Meredith & Mantel, 2003). In the planning phase the most important decisions are made that will affect the future of the organization as a whole. As described earlier, a failure to implement an ERP system can seriously affect the health of an organization and even lead to bankruptcy. This means that it would be of great help if a method would exist that could predict the effort required for implementing the ERP system within reasonable boundaries. The method should not be too complex and should be quick. Its outcomes should support the rough estimation of the project and serve as a starting point for the detailed planning in the set-up phase of the project phase and for the first allocation of the resources. Moreover, if conditions greatly change during a project, the method could be used to estimate the consequences for the remaining effort required for implementing the ERP system.

The aim of this chapter is to answer which activities exist in ERP projects according to literature and how these can be clustered as a basis for defining the size of an ERP project.

In this chapter the approach and main goal of our research will first be described, followed by a literature review on ERP project activities. After that it will present the clustering approach and results followed by conclusions and discussion.

RESEARCH APPROACH

When examining more or less successful methods for predicting software development effort, it is to be expected, that with regard to implementing ERP systems, it will also be possible to find measurements for predicting implementation efforts.

However, Stensrud (Stensrud, 2001) already indicated that although many effort prediction systems exist, none unfortunately have been specifically devised for ERP projects. Kusters and Heemstra (R. Kusters & Heemstra, 2007; R. J. Kusters, Heemstra, & Jonker, 2009) collected candidate cost driver variables from literature and asked experts in two major companies what they thought about the relevance of these variables. One of their conclusions was that the size of an ERP implementation is a major cost driver in ERP implementation projects. In software development the size of the software can be expressed in a single variable such as number of program lines or function points (Stensrud, 2001). By using this variable in a formula with several parameters, useful predictions of the development effort can be made. Can similar variables be found for predicting the implementation effort in an ERP project? According to Stensrud several variables together should be used to express this size. Francalanci (Francalanci, 2001) used three variables for her size definition: organizational size, configuration size and technical size. Von Arb (Arb, 1997) used two variables for size definition in his dissertation: number of users and number of ERP (sub) modules. As far as the authors can conclude from studying available publications on this topic, no further research has been carried out in defining the size of an ERP implementation project. All the mentioned researchers concluded that size cannot be expressed as a single variable as in software development, but should be expressed as a multidimensional variable. ERP implementation projects are complex projects where successful organizational, technical and people strategies are critical factors for success (Aladwani, 2001; Ngai, Law, & Wat, 2008). Because an ERP implementation project is confronted with many different aspects, the authors postulate the hypothesis that an ERP implementation project consists of a collection of clusters of activities with their own focus on implementation costs and project size. Clusters of activities include: the preparation

of the appropriate technical infrastructure, the business process redesign or the installation of the software. Of course these clusters of activities will be related to each other, but the authors expect that they will influence the total cost of the implementation project fairly independently. If size variables can be found for these clusters and these variables could be used as an estimator for the prediction of the effort required for these clusters, these variables could be the dimensions of the multidimensional variable which defines the size of an ERP implementation project.

For the development of regular information systems several methodologies exist, which support the project manager in deciding what needs to be done in the project. In these methodologies, all relevant activities are described and defined in terms of goals, results and necessary resources. In software development projects, activities that are relevant in that specific situation are selected from this methodology and planned. It goes without saying that not all activities are relevant in every project. There is no reason to expect that an ERP implementation project will be different in that matter. Therefore this research is based on the assumption that a range of activities exists which represents the most relevant activities in an ERP project.

The authors research approach in finding the most relevant activities in ERP implementation projects is to retrieve them from published research. Although several authors showed the phases in an ERP project and activities in these phases (Robey, Ross, & Boudreau, 2002), a complete list of all relevant activities in an ERP implementation project was not found, unfortunately. Several authors pointed out activities which where relevant according to their point of view in their paper, but none of them intended to collect all possible relevant activities. Therefore papers were collected which listed activities within an ERP implementation project. By examining papers with different views the authors of this chapter expect to have found the most relevant activities.

In this chapter the authors try to lay a foundation for defining the size of an ERP project. Because it is expected that the costs for the effort to implement an ERP system will constitute the greatest part of the total costs of an ERP implementation project, the first logical step is to define which activities that require human effort are important in an ERP project. Activities are always performed for a reason, i.e. to reach a certain goal and can be grouped into logical clusters which contribute to the same intermediary product or products. For instance, an intermediary product such as 'trained users' can be achieved by a cluster of activities such as: 'prepare training material', 'train the trainers', 'set up training infrastructure', 'train users' etcetera.

OBJECTIVE OF THIS RESEARCH

The objective of this research is to define logical clusters of ERP project activities.

This chapter will show the method and results in retrieving important ERP activities and the results of this first formal attempt to cluster these activities into clusters which contribute to similar intermediate products. This chapter aims at answering the next research questions:

1. Is the hypothesis of the authors, that ERP projects consist of a collection of clusters of activities with their own focus on implementation costs and project size, supported by domain experts?
2. Which activities in general exist in ERP projects according to literature?
3. What is a useful method to cluster these activities?
4. What is the result of a first clustering of these activities?

IS THE HYPOTHESIS OF THE AUTHORS, THAT ERP PROJECTS CONSIST OF A COLLECTION OF CLUSTERS OF ACTIVITIES WITH THEIR OWN FOCUS ON IMPLEMENTATION COSTS AND PROJECT SIZE, SUPPORTED BY DOMAIN EXPERTS?

The main research question of the authors focuses on the estimation of the effort-related costs needed for the implementation project of an ERP system. However, is it a relevant research question? That is to say, are the results of this research relevant in the empirical world? In order to detect the relevancy, the authors executed a small survey in the period September until November 2007. In this survey they also checked the reasonableness of their assumptions on a model for estimation of effort-related costs.

Goals of the Survey

With this survey the authors aimed at retrieving a clear answer from professionals with sufficient knowledge and experience in ERP implementation projects for the following questions:

1. Is it difficult to estimate the total costs of an ERP implementation project?
2. Is it important to estimate the total costs of an ERP implementation project?
3. Could a model support the estimation of the total costs of an ERP implementation project?
4. If there existed a model with clusters of activities and it would be possible to estimate the effort-related costs per cluster, would this be a basis for estimating the effort-related costs for an entire ERP implementation project?
5. If this model would be useful, out of how many clusters would it exist and how many of these clusters would cause the largest part of the effort-related costs?

Survey Content

The survey consisted of 2 groups of Dutch questions and general instructions.

The first group of questions aimed at retrieving information about the authors' main research questions i.e. whether it is useful doing research at methods for being able to predict the effort-related costs in an ERP implementation project. The purpose of the second group of questions was to verify the assumption that the total cost of the human labor could be predicted by adding the estimated costs from every activity cluster. Also in this group the respondents were asked to estimate out of how many clusters of activities an ERP project consists and how many of these clusters would cause the largest part of the total cost.

Finally the respondents were asked whether they would be willing to participate in other similar surveys.

Target Group of Participants and Survey Tool

For this survey the authors aimed at a group of professionals with substantial experience, knowledge of and insight in ERP implementation projects.

Because SAP is a commonly used ERP software and is used by big and complex organizations, individuals with experience and knowledge of SAP implementation projects were suitable participants for this survey. Therefore this survey was submitted at a small Dutch conference on the subject of the costs of the maintenance of SAP implementations. The participants could be expected to fit the requirements.

The respondents all attended the conference. The authors chose to use an online survey as their research tool. Mainly because they expected that more participants would respond to an online survey than to a paper based survey submitted during or at the end of the conference. LimeSurvey was selected as the online survey tool. LimeSurvey

(http://www.limesurvey.org/) is an open source survey tool under GNU General Public License.

Survey Results

Initially 42 e-mails were sent to the participants of the conference. From these 42 participants 2 replied that according to their view they had insufficient knowledge for completing the survey and would therefore not participate. From the remaining 40 participants 20 finished the survey in the period September 13, 2007 until November 7, 2007.

Survey Conclusion and Discussion

The respondents provided unambiguous answers to the research questions:

1. It is rather difficult to estimate the total effort-related costs of an ERP implementation project. (65%)
2. It is important to estimate the total effort-related costs of an ERP implementation project. (85%)
3. A model could support the estimation of the total effort-related costs of an ERP implementation project. (90%)
4. A model with clusters of activities that can be used to estimate the effort-related costs per cluster, can be a basis for estimating the total effort-related costs for an ERP implementation project. (65%)
5. There are around 10 clusters of activities in an ERP project.
6. From these clusters less then half account for the largest part of the effort-related costs.

This indicates that the main research question of the authors is useful and also that the research direction, by defining activity clusters, is plausible.

The authors are fully aware that the number of respondents is low. Of course a larger group could make the outcomes more reliable. On the other hand, the quality of the respondents is also an important factor. Since the conference was by invitation only, it provided a good quality filter for the participants. On this basis we believe we can have confidence in the results of this survey.

A discussion of this survey in more detail is available as a working paper (Janssens, Kusters, & Heemstra, 2008).

WHICH ACTIVITIES IN GENERAL EXIST IN ERP PROJECTS ACCORDING TO LITERATURE?

Literature Review on ERP Project Activities

A literature search was performed aiming at finding papers in which activities within an ERP implementation project were listed. From these papers a collection of names and expressions of activities was retrieved. The papers were retrieved from a collection of about 200 papers which were composed of papers selected from 'A Comprehensive ERP bibliography - 2000-2004' from Møller et al. (Møller et al., 2004) and a separate literature search for papers about implementation projects of ERP systems. Within this collection of about 200 papers a paper was selected if it showed at least one list of activities performed in ERP selection, implementation or maintenance. In most cases papers were found that enumerated the important activities in a regular project phase of an ERP implementation project. A total of 24 papers were found with lists of ERP activities. These papers can be divided into three categories:

A.　Papers which relate risk factors and Critical Success Factors (CSF's) or other influencing factors to activities and/or project phases.
B.　Papers about cases which describe the phases and activities of the actual projects.

C.　Papers which describe standard project phases and activities from consultancy firms or ERP software suppliers.

It can be expected that these three types of papers will show the important project activities.

Appendix A shows the list of the retrieved papers and the classification into the three categories.

The next section will discuss the retrieved papers grouped by the three categories.

Although the authors aimed at activities that are part of the implementation project, activities were also recorded in this literature study that belong to the pre-implementation phase and maintenance phase of an ERP system.

Papers with Research-Based Phases and Activities

These research studies relate risk factors, critical success factors or other influencing factors to activities and/or project phases. These authors based their framework of the standard activities and project phases on other scientific research and in some cases performed interviews with experts to enhance their framework.

A first example of this type of research is by Parr and Shanks (Parr & Shanks, 2000). The purpose of their research was to create a project phase model (PPM) of ERP project implementation. They based their model on other process models of ERP implementation from other researchers and tried to synthesize these models into one model which also recognizes the importance of the planning and post-implementation stages. They used the model in 2 case studies to examine the relationship between the CSF's from their earlier research and the phases to the PPM.

Rajogopal (Rajagopal, 2002) used a stage model to analyze six manufacturing firms that had one of the widely used ERP systems to retrieve factors of influence in the various stages of ERP implementation. He based his stage model on a six-stage model from Kwon and Zmud (Kwon & Zmud, 1987) and other authors.

Al-Mashari et al. (Al-Mashari, Al-Mudimigh, & Zairi, 2003) presented a novel taxonomy of the critical success factors in the ERP implementation process. They based their taxonomy on a comprehensive analysis of ERP literature combining research studies and organizational experiences. In their taxonomy they showed three major ERP phases. In these phases they also described project activities based on an analysis of ERP literature.

Ehie and Madsen (Ehie & Madsen, 2005) studied 38 critical issues in ERP implementation to measure the critical factors of ERP implementation. They developed a questionnaire based on five stages of ERP implementation. Stages are based on reviews of literature and extensive personal interviews with ERP consultants.

In their investigation on critical management issues in ERP implementation Kumar et al. (Kumar, Maheshwari, & Kumar, 2003) divided the project activities into 2 phases 'dollars to assets' and 'assets to impacts'. They described the typical activities within these phases. They based their phase and activities on innovation process stage models from other authors. They used these activities in open-ended questions in a questionnaire for ERP project managers of 20 Canadian organizations. The aim of the questionnaire was to find critical management issues.

Hallikainen et al. (Hallikainen, Kimpimäki, & Kivijärvi, 2006) developed and tested a model to support the decision which modules are implemented and in which order. They based their model on the phase model of Bancroft.

In their paper in which they seek to provide a conceptual model that explains the complexity of an ERP system to project managers in a non-technical manner, Marnewick and Labuschagne (Marnewick & Labuschagne, 2005) also present an ERP implementation methodology, which consists of 5 steps.

Somers and Nelson (Toni M. Somers & Nelson, 2004) examined the ERP project from different viewpoints: Players, ERP Project Life Cycle Stages and Activities. Their main purpose was to analyze the importance of key players and activities across the ERP life cycle by designing a questionnaire, which was returned by 116 companies. They adopted the six-stage model from Rajagopal (Rajagopal, 2002). For every phase they derived the key activities from other research studies.

The same six-stage model was used by Somers and Nelson (T.M. Somers & Nelson, 2001). They questioned 86 organizations in order to retrieve the impact of Critical Success Factors (CSF's) across the stages of ERP implementations. The top CSF's that were listed for every ERP implementation stage largely consist of project activities.

Umble et al. (Umble, Haft, & Umble, 2003) identified CSF's, software selection steps and implementation procedures critical to a successful implementation. Based on available resources and own experiences, including a case study, they showed the most important activities for ERP system selection and implementation steps.

The activities for selecting an ERP system were presented by Wei and Wang (Wei & Wang, 2004). They constructed a comprehensive framework for selecting an ERP system and applied it to a case in Taiwan. This was followed by a research paper in which they presented a comprehensive framework for selecting a suitable ERP system, which was based on the analytic hierarchy process (AHP) method from Saaty (Wei, Chien, & Wang, 2005).

Wagner and Antonucci (Wagner & Antonucci, 2004) studied whether there are different ERP implementation approaches and models for a large-scale integrated ERP system in the public sector as compared to the private sector. For their research they used a generalized structured implementation.

Markus and Tanis (Markus & Tanis, 2003) described various subjects of ERP systems for educational purposes. They based their phases on other models from other authors. For every phase they described typical activities, common errors or problems, typical performance metrics and possible outcomes.

Latvanen and Ruusunen (Latvanen & Ruusunen, 2001) used a socio-technical model of risk management of ERP projects.

Mabert et al. (Mabert, Soni, & Venkataramanan, 2005) compared and evaluated the use of regression analysis, logistic (logit) models, discriminate analysis and data envelopment analysis (DEA), for empirical data from ad surveys of ERP implementations in the US manufacturing sector. For this they applied key planning, decision and implementation management variables for the implementation phases. They did not specify important activities within these phases.

Sumner (Sumner, 2000) identified risk factors unique to ERP projects by interviewing ERP project managers in 7 companies. For this research she used 5 ERP project phases.

Francalanci (Francalanci, 2001) tested whether technical size and organizational complexity of SAP/R3 projects could be used to predict the implementation effort. She used ERP implementation phases that were consistent with the reference manuals of most commercial packages.

Weston (Weston, 2001) discussed project management issues related to 4 ERP implementation stages.

Esteves and Pastor (Esteves & Pastor, 2001) analyzed the relevance of critical success factors along SAP implementation phases. They used the 5 implementation phases from the ASAP implementation methodology.

Papers with Case-Based Phases and Activities

These research studies present case studies of ERP implementation projects. The purpose of these studies is to show in detail what happened in an actual case or to use a case to test a construct.

Berchet and Habchi (Berchet & Habchi, 2005) studied an ERP implementation project at Alcatel. The project was carried out according to a five-stage model. They also described important activities for every phase.

In describing the ERP implementation at Rolls-Royce, Yusuf et al. (Yusuf, Gunasekaran, & Abthorpe, 2004) carried out an in-depth study of the issues behind the process of implementation. The implementation plan at Rolls-Royces consisted of 4 main phases. In their description of these phases the main activities were also described.

Sarker and Lee (Sarker & Lee, 2003) tested three critical success factors in a case. They concluded that only the CSF 'strong and committed leadership' could be empirically established as a necessary condition. The case company implemented ERP according to three phases.

Tchokogué et al. (Tchokogué, Bareil, & Duguay, 2005) performed a case study and showed the lessons learned in that organization at a strategic, tactical and operational level. The project studied had 5 phases.

Papers with Project Phases from Consultancy Firms and ERP Suppliers

One paper specifically described ERP implementation methodologies used by consultancy firms or ERP suppliers.

Bruges (Bruges, 2002) showed the phases and main activities from three methodologies: AcceleratedSAP (ASAP), The Total Solution (Ernest & Young) and The Fast Track Workplan (Deloitte & Touche).

Retrieve Activities

The list of activities was retrieved from these three types of papers. Because the intention is to cluster these activities into logical units, no attention was paid to the phases mentioned in the papers. As shown above there is a variety of the numbers and names for project phases. Therefore only the activity names were retrieved.

With regard to every ERP activity that was discovered, the following was recorded: the paper title, the name of the ERP phase as mentioned in the paper (if present), and the name of the ERP activity itself.

In total 402 activities were recorded. Of course the same activity was mentioned more than once. Double names, synonyms or homonyms were not filtered out for reasons as discussed below in the metaplan session. These activities should be categorized unbiased. A filtering of the activities before the session would result in activities that would be selected and named by the personal preference of the researchers.

WHAT IS A USEFUL METHOD TO CLUSTER THESE ACTIVITIES?

A grouping technique was needed in order to be able to categorize the retrieved activities into coherent clusters of activities. As mentioned before, the selection and testing of the clustering technique was also a research goal.

The only categorization found in literature was grouping of activities by formal project phases. Unfortunately, there is no generally accepted phasing for ERP implementation projects. Besides, although activities may be started in a particular project phase, activities can still go on during other phases of the project. Project phases are based on a time-based view of the project. In the concept behind this research the time-based view is not relevant, only what has to be done in the project.

Categorization of project activities by applying objective attributes of these activities, for instance the duration of an activity, was also not possible. Except for its name and in most cases the project phase name, no more properties of an activity were available. However, people with sufficient knowledge of ERP projects should understand

an activity. Therefore the clustering can only be done by human judgment.

The number of established activities (402) also implies the need for a formal technique. For this type of clustering a card sorting technique seems appropriate. Card sorting has proven its usefulness in many concept mapping studies (Trochim, 1989). If card sorting is done by one human individual, bias and limited knowledge will influence the result. Judgment by several individuals and group interaction will improve the quality of the results. Unfortunately members of freely interactive groups are often dissatisfied with group interaction (Howard, 1994). According to Howard, a Nominal Group Technique (NGT) improves the output and satisfaction of the group members (Howard, 1994). Therefore, the metaplan technique for the clustering was chosen in this phase of the research. The metaplan technique uses card sorting and can be viewed as a Nominal Group Technique (NGT). The metaplan technique was developed by Wolfgang and Eberhard Schnelle. It is a simple visual technique which can be used by groups to structure thinking processes within the context of group work. A moderator leads the group discussion. Ideas are generated by group members and noted on cards. Finally, these cards are organized into categories and may show new results of which the single persons were not aware. The moderator leads the organizing into categories.

Metaplan is a technique in which cards are sorted by a group of people in a formal way. There is a formal interaction within the group with regard to the categorization. Moreover, sorting of a large number of cards can be done in a relatively short period of time. Last but not least, a metaplan session is easy to setup and requires only a few resources. By using this method, the authors could quickly see whether card sorting by a group would be a useful tool for the clustering. In the next step of the main research the most appropriate method and tool for the clustering should be selected.

This metaplan session was performed as a first step in categorizing i.e. clustering ERP activities in clusters which are logical groups of activities in an ERP implementation project which contribute to the production of the same intermediary products. Of course the activities found in the papers are not comprehensive. However, it is reasonable to expect that the activities mentioned in these papers are important activities in an ERP implementation project and will influence the total project effort. Furthermore, it is not the purpose of this research to find all possible activities. This research tried to find only important activities because they will influence the total project effort most likely. The goal of this first session was to find out whether activities can easily be clustered and if a technique such as the metaplan technique can be used in future to improve the clustering by more experts.

The first step in a regular metaplan session is a brainstorming part from which ideas are generated and noted on cards. In this case there was no brainstorming session for retrieving possible ERP activities. This was replaced by retrieving activities from relevant scientific papers in which phases and activities within these phases were described. The list retrieved from these activities is probably more complete and relevant than by brainstorming. Of course there are many synonyms and homonyms, but this also will be the case in an actual brainstorming session. Only the categorizing part of the metaplan technique was used. Of these activities the following data were printed: name, project phase (if present) and title of the paper. Some examples of these stickers are shown in appendix B. Not only the name was printed on these stickers, because if the name itself would be confusing, it would be possible in the metaplan session to retrieve the paper from which the activity originated to obtain some clarification. The stickers were stuck to 402 Post-it notes which where used in the metaplan session.

The metaplan session was performed by the authors of this paper in a 3-hour meeting. The session was prepared by the first author who selected the useful papers and recorded the activity names, project phases and paper names in an Excel spreadsheet. From these data the stickers were printed and stuck to post-it notes.

The participants of this session were instructed to categorize these post-it notes into logical clusters by sticking them on a wall. The participants had to categorize these notes by bearing strongly in mind that clusters should not relate to project phases, but that activities within a cluster should strongly contribute to the same intermediate product or products of an ERP implementation. After assigning all relevant activities to a cluster, the clusters were studied by the group in detail, which resulted in some rearranging of activities and also in some subgroups within the main clusters.

In this session the first author of this chapter served as a facilitator/moderator by taking a Post-it note, reading aloud the name of the activity. After that, the group decided under which cluster of activities the activity belonged. If a cluster did not exist yet, the name of the cluster was mutually decided upon and written on a blank Post-it note. This was stuck to the wall and the activities belonging to this cluster were stuck below. If an activity resulted in a new cluster, some already categorized activities were, if necessary, moved to this cluster. Some activities were regarded as not being part of the scope of an ERP project or very confusing to the group. They were stuck on a wall separately in an 'out of scope' section. Near the end of the session all relevant activities were assigned to a cluster. After that the clusters were studied by the group in detail, which led to some rearranging of the activities and also to some subgroups within the main clusters. After the session the clusters and activities in these clusters were recorded in a spreadsheet. In addition, obvious double activities and synonyms were removed in a two hour separate session by the first two of the authors. In this session also the cluster names and logical sequence were enhanced.

From the outcomes of the session it can be concluded that the metaplan technique is a suitable technique for clustering ERP activities. The activities taken from literature were categorized according to their name. In the papers there was often no more information available about the exact content of the activity. Therefore in some cases the metaplan group had to further discuss the activity.

Preparing the session was a labor-intensive process. The session itself took about 3 hours, mainly caused by the large number of activities (402). The categorizing itself was not a difficult task. Sometimes there hardly was any discussion about the naming of the clusters and the assignment of the activities to the clusters. The method could also be useful in subsequent research where other experts should perform the same exercise. Although for practical reasons it would be advisable to perform this session by applying a method and software to do the clustering independent from time and place. Experts are hard to persuade to participate in these sessions. If experts could perform the clustering whenever they want and wherever they want, the willingness to participate will be higher. As shown by Howard as well, support of this process by a Group Decision Support System (GDSS), which can support clustering in different locations and/or at different times, leads to the same quality of results (Howard, 1994). Therefore the authors will try to set up a GDSS for this purpose in the next step.

WHAT IS THE RESULT OF A FIRST CLUSTERING OF THESE ACTIVITIES?

Figure 1 shows the found clusters and subclusters.

Appendix C shows all results, i.e. the clusters and subclusters with all activities and the references from which the activity was derived for every activity.

Figure 1 also shows that 208 unique activities were assigned to the clusters and/or subclusters. In the second session the homonyms and synonyms were removed, which resulted in 208 unique activities.

In the second session the clusters were also categorized in three groups: 'project', 'system', 'organization', as shown in Figure 1. The group 'project' shows the clusters which contain activities required for the proper operation of the project, for instance the project management. The group 'system' shows clusters of activities required for the configuration an implementation of the ERP system itself. Finally the group 'organization' shows clusters of activities required for the organizational changer for the implementation. These points of view can be used in future research for crosschecking whether all relevant activities and clusters are taken into account.

CONCLUSION AND DISCUSSION

The small survey among ERP experts confirmed the hypothesis of the authors, that ERP projects consist of a collection of clusters of activities with their own focus on implementation costs and project size. It also gave a first indication of the number of clusters. Research into defining clusters of activities of ERP projects is therefore relevant and if the estimated number of clusters by these experts is reasonable, this number can lead to a practical prediction method. The clustering of the authors took place before the survey, therefore the authors where not biased by the outcome of the survey. It is remarkable that the number of activity clusters fairly corresponds with the estimated number of clusters by the correspondents of the survey. A number of approximately 10 clusters seems reasonable.

Figure 1. Found clusters and subclusters

Clusters	Subclusters	Group view			Number of unique activities
		Project	System	Organization	
Selection	Vendor selection		✓		4
	Product selection		✓		16
Project configuration		✓			19
Project management	Management	✓			4
	Communication to organization	✓			4
Organizational and system design	Current state analysis			✓	5
	Organizational requirements			✓	7
	Requirements ERP system		✓	✓	8
	High level Design		✓	✓	6
Configuration and installation	System configuration		✓		17
	Data conversion		✓		4
	System integration		✓		9
	ERP system testing		✓		14
Customizing			✓		7
Infrastructure			✓		14
Reorganization				✓	11
System implementation				✓	21
Training	Training Implementation Staff	✓			2
	Training users			✓	9
	Training maintenance staff			✓	2
Set up maintenance			✓		25
TOTAL					208

The most important results of the research described in this chapter are clusters of activities. It forms a basis for further research on this subject. The clustering has been done by the three authors. Although this is a small group and they share collective opinions, the clustering has been done in a sound manner and the results are a good indication of what the final result of clustering could be. It will be used as a starting point for further clustering.

The results will be validated in future research by increasing the clustering group of people. Validation will also take place by checking these activities against activities retrieved from real-life projects and checking whether activities from real-life projects can be categorized according to the established clusters of activities. It should of course also be checked whether the activities that can be found in real-life project documentation occur in the list of activities from the literature search.

As described before, the metaplan technique was found in principle to be a suitable technique for clustering these activities. Unfortunately, the preparation is very time consuming and it will also be difficult to arrange this type of session with several experts in this field of knowledge. The use of a GDSS (Group Decision Support System) can facilitate this. It will also have to be researched which GDSS will be the most appropriate and what type of NGT (Nominal Group Technique) should be used. Online open card sorting combined with Delphi technique characteristics could be an option (Paul, 2008).

The results of this chapter will be used to perform a first exploration into the practical use of the clusters for defining variables which could be used to define the size of an ERP implementation project. As discussed in the research approach, the size of an ERP implementation project should be expressed in a multidimensional variable. At this point in time the authors assume that the clusters can serve as the dimensions according to which an ERP implementation project can be viewed. Validated clusters are homogeneous groups of activities which can facilitate estimation of the important parts of an ERP implementation project.

The first impression of the authors is that the subclusters and not the clusters should be the starting point for the definition of variables, because the level of detail of the clusters seems to be too low to be able to easily find variables. However, this has to be verified in further research.

REFERENCES

Al-Mashari, M., Al-Mudimigh, A., & Zairi, M. (2003). Enterprise resource planning: A taxonomy of critical factors. *European Journal of Operational Research, 146*(2), 352–364. doi:10.1016/S0377-2217(02)00554-4

Aladwani, A. M. (2001). Change management strategies for successful ERP implementation. *Business Process Management Journal, 7*(3), 266–275. doi:10.1108/14637150110392764

Arb, R. v. (1997). *Vorgehensweisen und Erfahrungen bei der Einführung von Enterprise-Management-Systemen dargestellt am Beispiel von SAP R/3*. Institute für Wirtschaftsinformatik der Universität Bern.

Berchet, C., & Habchi, G. (2005). The implementation and deployment of an ERP system: An industrial case study. *56*(6), 588-605.

Botta-Genoulaz, V., Millet, P. A., & Grabot, B. (2005). A survey on the recent research literature on ERP systems. *Computers in Industry, 56*(6), 510–522. doi:10.1016/j.compind.2005.02.004

Bruges, P. (2002). ERP Implementation Methodologies. *MSIS, 488.*

Ehie, I. C., & Madsen, M. (2005). Identifying critical issues in enterprise resource planning (ERP) implementation. *56*(6), 545-557.

Esteves, J., & Pastor, J. A. (2001). Analysis of critical success factors relevance along SAP implementation phases. *Seventh Americas Conference on Information Systems*.

Francalanci, C. (2001). Predicting the implementation effort of ERP projects: empirical evidence on SAP/R3. *Journal of Information Technology, 16*(1), 33–48. doi:10.1080/02683960010035943

Hallikainen, P., Kimpimäki, H., & Kivijärvi, H. (2006). Supporting the Module Sequencing Decision in the ERP Implementation Process. In *Proceedings of the 39th Hawaii International Conference on System Sciences - 2006*, 1-10.

Hendricks, K. B., Singhal, V. R., & Stratman, J. K. (2006). (in press). The impact of enterprise systems on corporate performance: A study of ERP, SCM, and CRM system implementations. [*Corrected Proof.*]. *Journal of Operations Management*.

Holland, C. R., & Light, B. (1999). A critical success factors model for ERP implementation. *Software, IEEE, 16*(3), 30–36. doi:10.1109/52.765784

Howard, M. S. (1994). *Quality of Group Decision Support Systems: a comparison between GDSS and traditional group approaches for decision tasks*. Eindhoven University of Technology, Eindhoven.

Janssens, G., Kusters, R., & Heemstra, F. (2008). A small survey into the importance of and into a concept for estimating effort-related costs of ERP implementation projects. *Working papers Management Sciences, 14.*

Kumar, V., Maheshwari, B., & Kumar, U. (2003). An investigation of critical management issues in ERP implementation: empirical evidence from Canadian organizations. *Technovation, 23*(10), 793–807. doi:10.1016/S0166-4972(02)00015-9

Kusters, R. J., Heemstra, F. J., & Jonker, A. (2009). ERP Implementation Costs: A Preliminary Investigation. In *Enterprise* []. Berlin: Springer.]. *Information Systems, 12*, 95–107.

Kwon, T. H., & Zmud, R. W. (1987). Unifying the fragmented models of information systems implementation. In *Critical issues in information systems research* (pp. 227-251). John Wiley & Sons, Inc.

Latvanen, H., & Ruusunen, R. (2001). Management of Risks in an ERP Implementation Project. In T. S. o. Economics (Ed.), (pp. 20).

Mabert, V. A., Soni, A., & Venkataramanan, M. A. (2003). Enterprise resource planning: Managing the implementation process. *European Journal of Operational Research, 146*(2), 302–314. doi:10.1016/S0377-2217(02)00551-9

Mabert, V. A., Soni, A., & Venkataramanan, M. A. (2005). Model based interpretation of survey data: A case study of enterprise resource planning implementations. *In Press, Corrected Proof.*

Markus, M. L., & Tanis, C. (2003). The Enterprise System Experience - From Adoption to Success. *Pinnaflex Educational Resources* 173-207.

Marnewick, C., & Labuschagne, L. (2005). A conceptual model for enterprise resource planning (ERP). *Information Management & Computer Security, 13*(2), 144–155. doi:10.1108/09685220510589325

Meredith, J. R., & Mantel, S. J. J. (2003). *Project management: a managerial approach* (5ᵗʰ ed.). John Wiley & Sons Inc.

Møller, C., Kræmmergaard, P., & Rikhardsson, P. (2004). A Comprehensive ERP bibliography - 2000-2004. *Department of Marketing, Informatics and Statistics, Aarhus School of Business, IFI Working paper series*(12), 54.

Ngai, E. W. T., Law, C. C. H., & Wat, F. K. T. (2008). Examining the critical success factors in the adoption of enterprise resource planning. *Computers in Industry, 59*(6), 548–564. doi:10.1016/j.compind.2007.12.001

Parr, A., & Shanks, G. (2000). A model of ERP project implementation. *Journal of Information Technology, 15*(4), 289–303. doi:10.1080/02683960010009051

Paul, C. L. (2008). A modified delphi approach to a new card sorting methodology. *Journal of Usability Studies, 4*(1), 24.

Rajagopal, P. (2002). An innovation-diffusion view of implementation of enterprise resource planning (ERP) systems and development of a research model. *Information & Management, 40*(2), 87–114. doi:10.1016/S0378-7206(01)00135-5

Robey, D., Ross, J. W., & Boudreau, M.-C. (2002). Learning to Implement Enterprise Systems: An Exploratory Study of the Dialectics of Change. *Journal of Management Information Systems, 19*(1), 17–47.

Sarker, S., & Lee, A. S. (2003). Using a case study to test the role of three key social enablers in ERP implementation. *Information & Management, 40*(8), 813–829. doi:10.1016/S0378-7206(02)00103-9

Scott, J. E. (1999). The FoxMeyer Drugs' Bankruptcy: Was it a Failure of ERP? *Americas Conference on Information Systems, August 13-15, Milwaukee*, 223-225.

Somers, T. M., & Nelson, K. G. (2001). The Impact of Critical Success Factors across the Stages of Enterprise Resource Planning Implementations. In *Proceedings of the Annual Hawaii International Conference on System Sciences.*

Somers, T. M., & Nelson, K. G. (2004). A taxonomy of players and activities across the ERP project life cycle. *Information & Management, 41*(3), 257–278. doi:10.1016/S0378-7206(03)00023-5

Stensrud, E. (2001). Alternative approaches to effort prediction of ERP projects. *Information and Software Technology, 43*(7), 413–423. doi:10.1016/S0950-5849(01)00147-1

Sumner, M. (2000). Risk factors in enterprise-wide/ERP projects. *Journal of Information Technology, 15*(4). doi:10.1080/02683960010009079

Tchokogué, A., Bareil, C., & Duguay, C. R. (2005). (in press). Key lessons from the implementation of an ERP at Pratt & Whitney Canada. [*Corrected Proof.*]. *International Journal of Production Economics.*

Trochim, W. (1989). Concept Mapping: Soft Science or Hard Art? In W. Trochim (Ed.), *A Special Issue of Evaluation and Program Planning, 12,* 1-16.

Umble, E. J., Haft, R. R., & Umble, M. M. (2003). Enterprise resource planning: Implementation procedures and critical success factors. *European Journal of Operational Research, 146*(2), 241–257. doi:10.1016/S0377-2217(02)00547-7

Wagner, W., & Antonucci, Y. L. (2004). An analysis of the imagine PA public sector ERP project. *System Sciences, 2004. Proceedings of the 37th Annual Hawaii International Conference on,* 8.

Wei, C.-C., Chien, C.-F., & Wang, M.-J. J. M.-J. J. (2005). (in press). An AHP-based approach to ERP system selection. [*Corrected Proof.*]. *International Journal of Production Economics.*

Wei, C.-C., & Wang, M.-J. J. (2004). A comprehensive framework for selecting an ERP system. *International Journal of Project Management, 22*(2), 161–169. doi:10.1016/S0263-7863(02)00064-9

Weston, F. C. W. J. (2001). ERP implementation and project management. *Production and Inventory Management Journal, 42*(3/4), 75.

Willis, T. H., Willis-Brown, A. H., & McMillan, A. (2001). Cost containment strategies for ERP system implementations. *Production and Inventory Management Journal, 42*(2), 36.

Yusuf, Y., Gunasekaran, A., & Abthorpe, M. S. (2004). Enterprise information systems project implementation: A case study of ERP in Rolls-Royce. *International Journal of Production Economics, 87*(3), 251–266. doi:10.1016/j.ijpe.2003.10.004

APPENDICES

Appendix A: Used Papers with Lists of Activities within an ERP Implementation Projects

Number	Paper	Category
1.	Al-Mashari, M., Al-Mudimigh, A., & Zairi, M. (2003). Enterprise resource planning: A taxonomy of critical factors. European Journal of Operational Research, 146(2), 352-364.	A
2.	Berchet, C., & Habchi, G. (2005). The implementation and deployment of an ERP system: An industrial case study. 56(6), 588-605.	B
3.	Bruges, P. (2002). ERP Implementation Methodologies. MSIS, 488.	C
4.	Ehie, I. C., & Madsen, M. (2005). Identifying critical issues in enterprise resource planning (ERP) implementation. 56(6), 545-557.	A
5.	Esteves, J., & Pastor, J. A. (2001). Analysis of critical success factors relevance along SAP implementation phases. Seventh Americas Conference on Information Systems.	A
6.	Francalanci, C. (2001). Predicting the implementation effort of ERP projects: empirical evidence on SAP/R3. Journal of Information Technology, Volume 16(1), 33 - 48.	A
7.	Hallikainen, P., Kimpimäki, H., & Kivijärvi, H. (2006). Supporting the Module Sequencing Decision in the ERP Implementation Process. Proceedings of the 39th Hawaii International Conference on System Sciences - 2006, 1-10.	A
8.	Kumar, V., Maheshwari, B., & Kumar, U. (2003). An investigation of critical management issues in ERP implementation: empirical evidence from Canadian organizations. Technovation, 23(10), 793-807.	A
9.	Latvanen, H., & Ruusunen, R. (2001). Management of Risks in an ERP Implementation Project. In T. S. o. Economics (Ed.), (pp. 20).	A
10.	Mabert, V. A., Soni, A., & Venkataramanan, M. A. (2005). Model based interpretation of survey data: A case study of enterprise resource planning implementations. In Press, Corrected Proof.	A
11.	Markus, M. L., & Tanis, C. (2003). The Enterprise System Experience - From Adoption to Success. Pinnaflex Educational Resources 173-207.	A
12.	Marnewick, C., & Labuschagne, L. (2005). A conceptual model for enterprise resource planning (ERP). Information Management & Computer Security, 13(2), 144-155.	A
13.	Parr, A., & Shanks, G. (2000). A model of ERP project implementation. Journal of Information Technology, 15(4), 289-303.	A
14.	Rajagopal, P. (2002). An innovation--diffusion view of implementation of enterprise resource planning (ERP) systems and development of a research model. Information & Management, 40(2), 87-114.	A
15.	Sarker, S., & Lee, A. S. (2003). Using a case study to test the role of three key social enablers in ERP implementation. Information & Management, 40(8), 813-829.	B
16.	Somers, T. M., & Nelson, K. G. (2004). A taxonomy of players and activities across the ERP project life cycle. Information & Management, 41(3), 257-278.	A
17.	Sumner, M. (2000). Risk factors in enterprise-wide/ERP projects. Journal of Information Technology, 15(4).	A
18.	Tchokogué, A., Bareil, C., & Duguay, C. R. (2005). Key lessons from the implementation of an ERP at Pratt & Whitney Canada. International Journal of Production Economics, In Press, Corrected Proof.	B
19.	Umble, E. J., Haft, R. R., & Umble, M. M. (2003). Enterprise resource planning: Implementation procedures and critical success factors. European Journal of Operational Research, 146(2), 241-257.	A
20.	Wagner, W., & Antonucci, Y. L. (2004). An analysis of the imagine PA public sector ERP project. System Sciences, 2004. Proceedings of the 37th Annual Hawaii International Conference on, 8.	A
21.	Wei, C.-C., Chien, C.-F., & Wang, M.-J. J. M.-J. J. (2005). An AHP-based approach to ERP system selection. International Journal of Production Economics, In Press, Corrected Proof.	A
22.	Wei, C.-C., & Wang, M.-J. J. (2004). A comprehensive framework for selecting an ERP system. International Journal of Project Management, 22(2), 161-169.	A
23.	Weston, F. C. W. J. (2001). ERP implementation and project management. Production and Inventory Management Journal, 42(3/4), 75.	A
24.	Yusuf, Y., Gunasekaran, A., & Abthorpe, M. S. (2004). Enterprise information systems project implementation: A case study of ERP in Rolls-Royce. International Journal of Production Economics, 87(3), 251-266.	B

Appendix B: Examples of Stickers

analyze business processes 2. Analysis phase A conceptual model for enterprise resource planning (ERP)
user training 2. Deployment and integration of the ERP system The implementation and deployment of an ERP system: An industrial case study
training of project team members and acquisition of supportive skills 2. The project (Configure&Rollout) The Enterprise System Experience—From Adoption to Success
build networks 2.5 Project Installation A model of ERP project implementation

Appendix C: Clusters and Subclusters with Activities and References

Cluster	Subcluster	Activity Number	Activity	Reference number from appendix A
Selection				
	Vendor selection			
		1	Select consulting company	3
		2	Selecting implementation partner	9
		3	Establish contracts	2, 3, 19
		4	Interview vendors and collect detailed information	22
	Product selection			
		5	Select ERP vendor	14, 23
		6	Identify the ERP system characteristics	21
		7	Choose appropriate technology	14
		8	Define expression of requirements and specifications	2
		9	Create the request for proposal (RFP)	19
		10	Construct the structure of objectives	21
		11	Create a software candidate list	19
		12	Analyse functionality, price, training and maintenance service	3, 19, 21, 22, 23
		13	Analyze current Business Processes and selecting ERP-system	4
		14	Select ERP package	1, 3, 14, 16, 19, 22
		15	Define contractual agreement	3
		16	Produce request for proposal (to vendors software)	23
		17	Make evaluation scheme for comparing and ranking vendor responses	23
		18	Check references ERP vendors	23
		19	Selection of ERP product, project manager and implementation partners	8
		20	Collect all possible information about ERP vendors and systems. Filter out unqualified vendors	22

Cluster	Subcluster	Activity Number	Activity	Reference number from appendix A
Project configuration				
		21	Develop project plan	1, 3, 4, 5, 7, 8, 9, 11, 13, 17, 18, 23, 24
		22	Compose team	3, 4, 5, 7, 8, 9, 11, 12, 13, 16, 21, 24
		23	Select the project leader	9
		24	Form steering committee	7, 9, 13, 24
		25	Format budget	2, 9, 24
		26	Develop project deliverables	23
		27	Define project objectives	3
		28	Define areas of responsibility	23
		29	Develop project charter	23
		30	Plan for project reviews	23
		31	Planning Variables	10
		32	Scoping & Planning	20
		33	Address change control procedures	23
		34	Address planning and implementation tools	23
		35	Development of the project's guiding principles	7
		36	Decision to proceed, approval of project plan	11
		37	Reporting mechanisms	13
		38	Develop metrics (for revenues implementation ERP system)	23
		39	Address tools to measure performance results	21, 23
Project management				
	Management			
		40	Ongoing project management	6, 11, 16
		41	Interdepartmental cooperation	16
		42	Proceed planning	23
		43	Change management	16
	Communication to organization			
		44	Interdepartmental communication	16
		45	Communication to organization	11
		46	Constant communication with users	13
		47	Create communication plan	1
Organizational and system design				
	Current state analysis			
		48	Current state analysis (may be deferred or not done)	11
		49	Analyse current business processes	7, 13
		50	Map business processes on to ERP functions	7
		51	Evaluate processes in place	18
		52	Analyse organizational processes and compare them with the procedures embedded in the ERP package	6

Cluster	Subcluster	Activity Number	Activity	Reference number from appendix A
	Organizational requirements			
		53	Business process reengineering	1, 4, 5, 16, 18, 22
		54	Identify process redesign	12
		55	Current and/or future business process modelling and reengineering, if any	11
		56	High level design review (analyse the enterprise model, and develop ' Vanilla' prototype)	24
		57	Develop metrics (for revenues implementation ERP system)	23
		58	Address tools to measure performance results	21, 23
		59	Develop initial audit procedures	3
	Requirements ERP system			
		60	Definition of system requirements	3, 9, 12, 13
		61	Identify operational needs	12
		62	Review functional and technical requirements to determine the system build needs	12
		63	Requirements analysis	17
		64	Create a feature/function list	19
		65	Identifying modules needed	9
		66	Determine the software components of the ERP system	12
		67	Finalize requirement definition stage (scope, schedule, resource requirements quality concerns, risk concerns, organizational issues	23
	High level design			
		68	Define business processes (blueprint)	3, 5
		69	High-level design	2, 7, 9, 12, 13, 20
		70	Evaluate alternatives to comprehensive engineering project	3
		71	Craf "best-fit" approach	3
		72	Business processes into ERP system	9
		73	Preliminary design review (developing a design and implementation strategy, defining the scope of the project, and developing the business process model)	24
Configuration and installation				
	System configuration			
		74	Systems desig	7, 13, 17
		75	Customize and parameterization of ERP software	3, 5, 6, 11, 18
		76	Install ERP	7, 13, 14
		77	High-level design	13
		78	Configure baseline system	3
		79	Mastering ERP system (functionality, configuration)	4
		80	Development of a comprehensive configuration	7
		81	Identify functionality delivery options	12
		82	Configurator implementation	15
		83	Starting preparation	2

Cluster	Subcluster	Activity Number	Activity	Reference number from appendix A
		84	Reduce the number of specific programs	2
		85	Develop comprehensive configuration	13
		86	Write and test reports	13
		87	Install the software and perform the computer room pilot	19
		88	Establish security and necessary permissions	19
		89	Define the system hierarchy	9
		90	Install prototype system	24
	Data conversion			
		91	Convert data	5
		92	Data analysis and conversion	16
		93	Data cleanup and conversion	11
		94	Transfer data from legacy systems	24
	System integration			
		95	Identify data and system interfaces	9, 13
		96	Build and test interfaces	7, 9, 13
		97	Integrate with other systems	1, 3, 11
		98	Analyze legacy systems	1
		99	Determine the software components of the ERP system interact with each other	12
		100	Integrate functional units	14
		101	Technology integration and implementation	17
		102	Ensure that all data bridges are sufficiently robust and the data are sufficiently accurate	19
		103	Replace legacy systems	24
	ERP system Testing			
		104	Test ERP system	1, 3, 5, 7, 9, 13, 18
		105	Test reports	7, 9
		106	Population of the test instance with real data	7, 13
		107	Test with real data	9
		108	Acceptance test	23
		109	Create test scenario	1
		110	Build & Test	20
		111	Evaluate the process model and the information system build against each other	12
		112	Testing, bug fixing, and rework	11
		113	Critical design review (integration testing)	24
		114	Implementation realisation (user acceptance testing)	24
		115	Technical/operation review (user acceptance testing)	24
		116	Post implementation review (system deployment, systems conversion, user training before the ' Go Live')	24
		117	Test all modules against requirements as well as quality parameters	6

Cluster	Subcluster	Activity Number	Activity	Reference number from appendix A
Customizing				
		118	Interactive prototyping	7, 9, 13
		119	Specify functional and data requirements	6
		120	Customization	11, 16
		121	Custom programming and documentation	23
		122	Technical development (modifications, interfaces, data conversion)	4
		123	Detailed design, realisation, and prototype validation	2
		124	Develop and verify software code for modules that need reprogramming	6
Infrastructure				
		125	Establish contracts	2
		126	Hardware acquisition	23
		127	Determine operating system	23
		128	Decide on wireless requirements	23
		129	Plan infrastructure	1
		130	Infrastructure up gradation	8
		131	IT integration at global levels realized	14
		132	Architecture choices	16
		133	Selection of software, hardware platform, networking, database, implementation partner, project manager (may be partially or totally deferred to project phase)	11
		134	Build networks	13
		135	Install desktops	13
		136	Install and test any new hardware	19
		137	Inventory existing hardware and software	9
		138	Investigate incompatibility	14
Reorganization				
		139	Change culture+structure organization	1
		140	Software configuration and "fit with the organization" (Current and/or future business process modelling and reengineering, if any, Execution of change management plan, if any, Software configuration, Software customization if any, System integration, Integration of software bolt-ons and/or legacy systems, if any, Data cleanup and conversion, Documentatio	8
		141	Identify change ownership	12
		142	Make final changes to business processes, policies and procedures and system builds tot prepare for a go-live	12
		143	Observe user resistance	14
		144	Realize organizational integration	14
		145	Organizational structure and culture change	15
		146	Organizational changes and/or incentives related to enterprise system and/or organizational performance improvement, if any (may be deferred)	11
		147	Execution of change management plan, if any	11
		148	Process and procedure changes	11
		149	User communications and gaining acceptance	9

Cluster	Subcluster	Activity Number	Activity	Reference number from appendix A
System implementation				
		150	Implement	2, 20, 22, 24
		151	Go live	4, 23
		152	Testing, bug fixing, and rework	11
		153	Conference room pilot (prototyping and adjustment toward final system)	4
		154	Rollout and start-up	8
		155	Make systems available for usage	14
		156	Use systems in individual units	14
		157	Increase use of systems	14
		158	Users accept the systems	14
		159	use of systems become a routine activity	14
		160	Correct flaws	14
		161	Implementation of core modules of the selected ERP package	15
		162	Users understand, assimilate and then appropriate their new tool	2
		163	Rollout and start-up	11
		164	Systems implementation/maintenance	17
		165	Run a pre-implementation pilot	19
		166	Review the pre-implementation process to date	19
		167	Bring the entire organization on-line, either in a total cutover or in a phased approach	19
		168	Celebrate	19
		169	Cutover from the old systems	18
		170	Usage of the system is not an 'out of the ordinary' situation	14
Training				
	Training implementation staff			
		171	Train the project team	3, 7, 9, 13
		172	Training of project team members and acquisition of supportive skill	8, 11
	Training users			
		173	Prepare end-user training	5
		174	Begin training activities	14
		175	Train users	1, 2, 3, 5, 8, 11, 16, 23
		176	Educate and train critical mass (on processes, data discipline and modules)	4
		177	Train users more	14
		178	Education on new business processes	16
		179	Managing user training and support	13
		180	Attend system training	19
		181	Train on the conference room pilot	19
	Training maintenance staff			
		182	Problem resolution (adding hardware capacity, process and procedure changes, user acceptance, retraining, additional training)	8
		183	Create support for tangible operational processes and information system	12

Cluster	Subcluster	Activity Number	Activity	Reference number from appendix A
Set up maintenance				
		184	Optimize tool	2, 4, 11, 19
		185	Correct malfunctions	3, 11, 13, 23
		186	Fine tune system	3
		187	Enhance original implementation	23
		188	Create additional metrics	23
		189	Go & Live Support	5
		190	Adjust system	3
		191	Use product	3
		192	Maintain product	3
		193	Meet special optimisation requests	3
		194	Tuning and testing (finalize processing options, profiles, menus, and testing robustness)	4
		195	Testing, bug fixing, and rework	8
		196	Challenges (bug fixing, rework, system performance tuning	8
		197	Problem resolution (adding hardware capacity, process and procedure changes, user acceptance, retraining, additional training)	8
		198	Create support for tangible operational processes and information system	12
		199	Modify systems to fit user needs carried out	14
		200	Enhance compatibility	14
		201	Operational starting with production	2
		202	Detect key processes of improvement	2
		203	Start potential modifications	2
		204	Optimise the ERP deployment process itself	2
		205	Adding hardware capacity	11
		206	Retraining, additional training	11
		207	Adding peopet accommdate learning and shakedown needs	11
		208	Extension and transformation	13

Chapter 6
Time, Attitude, and User Participation:
How Prior Events Determine User Attitudes in ERP Implementation

Lene Pries-Heje
IT University of Copenhagen, Denmark

ABSTRACT

Assimilation of a standard ERP system to an organization is difficult. User involvement seems to be the crux of the matter. However, even the best intentions for user involvement may come to nothing. A case study of a five-year ERP implementation process reveals that a main reason may be that the perception of usefulness of the system in any given phase of the implementation is heavily dependent on preceding events—the process. A process model analysis identifies eight episodes and nine encounters in the case showing that the user's attitude towards the ERP system changes between acceptance, equivocation, resistance and rejection depending on three things: (1) the dynamic between user and consultants, (2) the dynamic between different user groups, and (3) the understanding of technical, organizational and socio-technical options. When relating the empirical findings to existing theory on user participation, it is argued that the changes could be explained as a slide from influential user participation toward pseudo participation and back to influential participation, and that user participation in the context of ERP implementations raises new issues regarding user participation. Thus further research regarding new approaches and/or new techniques and tools for user participation in the context of ERP implementations is needed.

INTRODUCTION

When the organization Alfa decided to implement an ERP system, it also decided that there should be user participation in all phases of the implementation. Alfa's top management and the ERP project manager considered user participation essential for the quality of the solution as well as necessary for assimilation of the system in the organization. Thus during the project users participated in requirements specification, evaluation of candidate systems, scoping of the project, configuration of the system, testing of the system, and user training in the new system. The ERP system was implemented on time and within budget, but despite the user participation, the quality and the assimilation of the system in the organization was problematic, seen from the user point of view. When interviewing project participants and end-users, it became clear that the attitude toward the system changed during the project and so did user involvement in the project. When the ERP project was initiated, both the system as well as the implementation approach had wide support in Alfa's organization, but at the time of go-live, this had changed dramatically, and in the years following go-live, Alfa struggled to achieve quality in use and in getting the intended user groups to use the system. It took two years after going live before the users' attitude toward the system had changed in a somewhat more positive direction.

This article takes an outset in the empirical situation explained above. The aim of the research is to better understand the issues related to user participation during Alfa's ERP implementation in order to identify better alternative approaches. Thus the research questions for this article are:

1. How and why are the users' attitudes toward the system changing over time in Alfa's ERP lifecycle?

2. Why did user participation *not* provide the intended user involvement and the intended quality of the system?

The remainder of this article is organized as follows. The next section provides a theoretical reference for understanding user participation and user involvement in software projects in general and ERP implementations in particular. In the two sections thereafter, we describe the research method followed by the section where we discuss the case and the case analysis. In the last two sections, we discuss the findings related to the theoretical understanding and then conclude our article.

THEORETICAL FOUNDATIONS FOR USER PARTICIPATION IN SOFTWARE DEVELOPMENT AND ERP IMPLEMENTATIONS

Having users participate and being involved in ERP implementations is considered essential for success (Kawalek & Wood-Harper, 2002; Robey, Ross, & Boudreau, 2002; Nah, Zuckweiler, & lau, 2003) and is expected to provide a better fit of user requirements, achieving better system quality, use, and acceptance (Esteves-Sousa & Pastor-Collado, 2000). It has been argued that implementing ERP package software products is different from traditional IT-system development and therefore needs a different implementation approach, namely adapting the organizational processes to those implied by the ERP Package (Lucas, Walton & Ginzberg, 1988; Markus & Tanis, 2000; Parr & Shanks, 2003). The design team should be balanced or cross-functional, and comprise a mix of external consultants and internal staff; the internal staff should develop the necessary skills for design and implementations (Holland, Light, & Gibson, 1999; Summer, 1999; Shanks et al., 2000). Both business and technical knowledge are important (Summer, 1999; Shanks et al., 2000). Sharing information among the various parties involved is vital and requires partnership trust (Stefanou, 1999), and the team should be empowered to make quick decisions (Shanks et al., 2000). Research on how to organize and support user participation in the context of ERP implementations is, however, very limited.

Within the field of participatory design (PD), issues related to the nature and reasons for user participation can be thought of in terms of three distinguished arenas (Gärtner & Wagner, 1996): (1) The *individual project arena* where specific systems are designed and new organizational forms are created; (2) the *company arena* where "breakdowns" or violations of agreements are diagnosed and hitherto stable patterns of organizational functioning are questioned and redesigned; and (3) the *national arena* where the general legal and political framework is negotiated which defines the relations between the various parties. In the context of ERP implementations, all three levels could be relevant, however, in this article, only level (1) and (2) will be addressed. In the individual arena (the work situation level), technology is used as an instrument and communication media supporting local work, the current organization of work is often taken for granted, and user participation is aimed at improving the work situation. In the company arena, the use of technology depends on how different activities are coordinated and integrated in the local organization. Conflicting interests between stakeholders is not only being played out during development, but may also articulate themselves in the discussion of the overall organizational goals, which in many cases guide the selection of the technology and the local design (Bjerkness & Bratteteig, 1995). When implementing ERP systems, the scope of the system is often the organization as a whole, thus the ERP system can be seen as a common system serving many heterogeneous user groups at the same time. When considering design politics and user participation, the totality of the system could be addressed using a management perspec-

tive or it could be emphasized that there are several differing perspectives depending on various stakeholders' organizational positions and roles (Bjerkness & Bratteteig, 1995). Using the later perspective, the realization of the system would be a compromise between interests and needs of many different user groups, and the goal would be to balance these interests. This perspective is similar to the socio-technical approach which takes as a premise that employers and employees have a common interest in developing useful computer systems (Bjørn-Andersen & Hedberg, 1977; Markus, 1983; Mumford, 2003). The socio-technical approach also addresses the organization as a whole, and within socio-technical research techniques for stakeholder participation in the organizational arena it has been discussed and developed. Although PD and socio-technical design might disagree on the existence and nature of a labor-capital conflict, in practice it is difficult to see the difference between the two approaches (Bjerkness & Bratteteig, 1995).

Three main issues have dominated the field of PD (Kensing & Blomberg, 1998): (A) the politics of design, (B) the nature of participation, and (C) methods, tools and techniques for carrying out design projects. Most of the work within PD has been directed at the individual arena. In this article, the politics of design (A) is not playing a significant role, the two other areas (B and C), however, is considered very relevant for discussion of the issues of user participation, user involvement and user attitude toward the system in the context of ERP implementations. Within the PD discourse, participation of the intended users in technology design is thought to increase the likelihood that the system will be useful and well integrated into the work practices of the organization (Kensing & Blomberg, 1998). In order to develop a meaningful and productive relation between the user and the technology designer, the latter needs knowledge about the actual use context and the user needs knowledge of possible technological options. In technology development projects, the arguments for why and how users participate vary. At one end of the spectrum, workers participate solely to provide (professional) designers with an understanding of the local work situation. The design work is initiated by management or design professionals, and is carried out by designers. Users have no or very limited influence on the design and they are only participating when their input is considered valuable to the designer. At the other end of the spectrum, users participate not only because their knowledge is considered valuable, but also because their interests in the design outcome are acknowledged. Thus users participate in negotiating and deciding on how projects are negotiated and supported, and they participate in all phases of a project. In a review of ten PD projects, Clement and Van den Besselar (1993) outline five basic requirements for user participation (the first three reiterated from Kensing & Blomberg, [1998]): (1) access to relevant information, (2) the possibility for taking an independent position on the problems, (3) participation in decision making, (4) the availability of appropriate participatory development methods, and (5) room for alternative technical and/or organizational arrangements. Over the years, different tools and techniques for participatory design have been developed within PD research.

Also using different lenses, user participation and user involvement is an important factor in systems' success, for example, studying the decision processes around system development and implementation (Robey & Farrow, 1982; Ives & Olson, 1984) or when studying organizational change (Zmud & Cox, 1979; Baroudi, Olson, & Ives, 1986). User participation and user involvement has been defined as two distinct terms by Barki and Hartwick (1989) in relation to IT systems development. *User participation* refers to the behaviors and activities that users perform in the systems implementation process, and *User involvement* refers to a psychological state of the individual, and is defined as the importance and personal relevance of a system to a user. Barki

and Hartwick (1989) found that the influence of user participation on system use is mediated by user involvement and attitudes concerning use. Following this, Vidgen et al. (1993) argue that there is a socially constructed element to IS-use quality that is culturally influenced and dynamic. Thus in the context of IT development, user involvement and user participation is understood to be important, playing a key role in success or failure, although there still are some contradictions in the findings. Successful user participation is, however, not easy. Newman and Noble (1990) found that conflict may arise from differences in perspective, or when users have insufficient influence or power to control the development and implementation process. Along the same line of thinking, Robey and Farrow (1982) pointed out that participation without influence is unlikely to lead to success. Cavaye (1995) found that when tasks were unstructured and only described at the strategic level, then the urgency for user involvement increased, where as Ives and Olson (1984) found that if a system is well-structured and well-defined, then it is not necessary to involve users for the purposes of system quality but perhaps for system acceptance. Finally, Noyes et al. (1996) highlighted the difficulties of deciding how to involve users, and when they should be involved.

RESEARCH METHOD

To answer the questions "How and why are the users' attitudes toward the system changing over time in Alfa's ERP lifecycle?" "Why did user participation not provide the intended user involvement and the intended quality of the system?", I decided to carry out a case study within the interpretive tradition of information technology studies (Klein & Myers, 1999). I adopted an inductive approach, and did not specify theory a priori to guide my data collection. As the data were analyzed, relevant theories were investigated. I entered the research with a bias: being aware of the practical difficulties taking advantage of pre-defined ERP software and a wish to understand how ERP systems can be implemented in a way that provides useful and easy to use software for multiple groups of end users. As the analysis progressed, I consulted different streams of literature that could provide insight into my empirical observations, for example, literature which consider ERP implementations, user participation, user involvement, quality of use, and design politics.

The study was carried out in the Danish headquarter of an international engineering company called Alfa (pseudonym). In January 2001, Alfa initiated the process of selecting and implementing a standard ERP system, and in October 2003, they went live. In the following years, Alfa struggled to stabilize the system and improve the use and usability of the system. In October 2007, an upgraded version of the ERP package software was implemented.

Data Collection

Data collection was carried out through interviews with the ERP project manager, users serving as team leaders during the implementation (some of them now in the internal ERP competence centre), managers and end-users from all functional areas within the scope of the project, a consultant participating in the project on the vendor side, and the vendor's solution architect. All 18 interviews were semi-structured and lasted 1½ to 2 hours. The interviews were taped, transcribed and verified by the interviewee. See Table 1 for details.

It has not been possible to follow the project from its beginning, although it had been preferable. Thus to cover the part of the implementation taking place before February 2005, the interviews have been conducted with a retrospective focus. One of the issues using this approach is that the interviewees' interpretations of the history are influenced by events taking place after the situation at which is being focused. Written project documentation has therefore been used to verify the interviews where possible, and contradictions and conflicting statements have been put forward for the interviewees to comment on. Alfa has provided elaborate documentation including detailed requirements specification, documented workshop evaluations of the candidate systems, business cases, gap analysis, and issue-log and change requests.

Table 1. ERP system interviews

Role in the ERP implementation	Number of interviews	Interview periods
ERP Project Manager	3 interviews	February 2005 January 2006 May 2007
4 people from the internal ERP competence centre	1-2 interviews each	August-November 2005 June-August 2006
Vendors solution architect and a consultant	1-2 interviews each	November 2005 February 2006 July 2006
7 people from the end user organization	1 interview each	February 2006-June 2006
In Total	18 interviews each lasting 1.5 to 2 hours	

Figure 1. Alfa's process model adapted from Newman & Robey (1992)

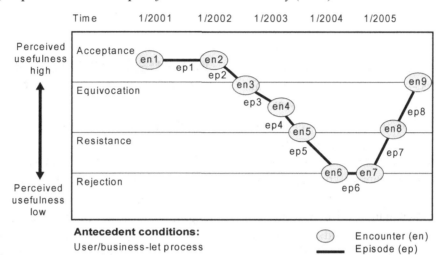

Data Analysis

The data analysis has been an iterative process going back and forth between coding and collecting data allowing gaps to be identified and addressed, and different interviewees' interpretations to be commented and reflected on by others. Thus a hermeneutic interpretive approach (Klein & Myers, 1999) has been used.

My research in Alfa was originally initiated by a desire to understand the misfits Alfa experienced after going live, and investigate their relation to factual properties of the IT artifact. However, after the first six or seven interviews, it became clear that different actors in the organization had very different understandings of whether something qualified as a misfit or not, and when asking into the origin of the misfits, the implementation process, rather then the initial factual properties of the IT artifact, seemed to be an issue. Thus the focus of the research changed from the artifact to the implementation process. Slowly, a paradox emerged; Alfa had been very conscious about having users participate throughout the implementation process, the organizational policy of design seemed to fit an approach having users participate not just to provide knowledge to professional designers, but also to influence the

design. However, the interviews left an impression of users becoming more and more frustrated as the process moved forward, and the initial analysis revealed that actions and events in the case were strongly influenced by prior events. Thus I was looking for a way to analyze the data allowing me to focus on points in time where the users' attitude toward the system and the implementation process had changed and try to understand why these changes had happened. Therefore, another round of analysis was conducted using a process model inspired by Newman and Robey (1992). This process model focuses on sequences of events over time in order to explain how and why particular outcomes are reached. The constructs in the process model are *antecedent conditions*, *episodes* (a series of events that stand apart from each others), *encounters* (mark the beginning and end of an episode), and *outcome* over the course of time (see Figure 1). The historic context of the ERP implementation is expressed through the antecedent conditions. During each episode, the antecedent conditions of the episode may be challenged (in this case the design policy of having users influence the design) and the users may choose to respond by changing their involvement and attitude toward the new system. So in this article I use the process model to analyze how and why user involvement and attitude toward the ERP implementation changes over time.

I adopted Newman and Robey's four categories of episodes which are: (1) episodes led by the IT-expert—focus on the technology; (2) episodes led by the users—focus on the organizational practice; (3) episodes of joint development, and (4) *wait-and-see* episode where both parties are uncommitted. As possible, responses to each episode four categories of user attitude are used: (1) acceptance of the system, (2) equivocation, (3) resistance, and (4) rejection. Category 1, 2 and 4 are included in Newman and Robey's original process model, however, I found that a fourth category was necessary; rejecting a system or parts of a system may not be an option for the users, but resisting or enacting the system in order to minimize the use or the consequences is a milder but still powerful way to express non-acceptance. So I added "(3) resistance" to my analysis.

Using the process model as a tool, I went through the interview transcripts again looking for points in time where interviewees expressed a change in attitude toward the system or the process. A change in the users' attitude toward the system could be expressed literally, for example, *"At the time of go-live I would give the system an F (failed) and now it is properly a D."* Or it may be expressed more indirectly such as: *"It was very difficult to report back to my colleges, when all I had was bad news!"* The encounters could not be defined based on a unified view of all participants; therefore I choose the encounters so that they reflect the more general opinion; as a result eight episodes and nine encounters were found. Having identified the encounters, I looked in the interviews again to investigate whether the dynamic between the users and the consultants could explain the changes in attitude? Two other themes kept coming up interlinked to the dynamic between users and consultants: the dynamic between different stakeholders (user groups) and, knowledge about the system. The result of the

analysis using the process model and the three themes is presented later in the article.

IMPLEMENTATION OF AN ERP SYSTEM AT ALFA ENGINEERING

Introduction to the Case

The case organization Alfa is an engineering company with more than 80 years of experience—a leading supplier of systems, consultancy and engineering services to the pharmaceutical and biotechnological industry. The organization has 1,200 employees in Europe, China and the USA. Employees typically have a degree from a technical university. Alfa is not manufacturing or selling materials for the projects, they are overseeing the projects—being responsible for the project management of the projects. Most of the work in Alfa is conducted in large projects lasting several years and costing billions of U.S. dollars. Thus project managers are quite powerful and influential.

The ERP project started in January 2001 at Alfa's headquarter in Denmark. A project manager with extensive ERP project management experience was hired to manage the project. From the very beginning it was clear that this was a common project for management and employees in Alfa. It was never questioned if users should participate throughout the project and in all aspects of the project. A project organization was set up and user representatives from all functional areas included in the project scope were appointed.

Alfa's core business is project administration and project management on behalf of their customers. Alfa was aware that ERP systems in general are not targeted at their line of business. Therefore, a thorough evaluation and selection process was conducted to ensure that the standard system met their needs. In fact, Alfa spent almost a year specifying requirements, evaluating candidate systems and finally selecting a system.

Further, Alfa spent 9-10 months to configure and customize the system before going live in October 2003.

A Process Model for Alfa's ERP Experience

In this section, Alfa's ERP process model is described and a graphical representation is depicted in Figure 1.

Antecedent Conditions: Up until the decision to buy and implement the ERP system, Alfa had no experience with integrated systems, and very limited experience with standard systems. Historically, software had been developed specifically for functional areas and the users were allowed significant influence on the design of the software.

Encounter 1- project initiated: In order to improve the quality of services offered to the customers, improve resource management, and provide better financial control. Alfa had come to the conclusion that an integrated ERP package providing real-time sharing of data was necessary. Managers as well as users were aware that it would require the organization to adapt to the ERP system, but at the same time they wanted to continue the appreciated tradition of user participation. Therefore, an approach involving the users throughout the project was decided on:

- **Users' attitude toward the system:** Users, the ERP project manager and top management at Alfa acknowledged the need for a new system and the intended approach, thus the project started out with wide acceptance.
- **Dynamic between users and consultants/ system:** In general, relations are good; users have over the years cooperated directly with developers.

- **Dynamic between the users:** No open conflicts
- **Knowledge about the technical options and design possibilities:** Very limited

Episode 1-Alfa business processes and requirements specification: First, all business processes that should be part of the new system were described including finance, purchase, project administration and resource management. A large number of users throughout the organization were involved in the process, and a number of simple business process models on different levels were produced using Power Point as a tool. For each of the four areas, knock-out criteria were defined. After the business processes were defined, they served as a common reference for discussing the requirements focusing on input (data) triggering a process, steps within a process and output from a process. More detailed requirements for each area were defined in a dialogue between the project manager and the participating users. It was a long and difficult process especially because it involved a large number of users who had little or no experience defining requirements. The requirements should at the same time reflect existing processes and be open towards processes within a standard system. The users did not know what to expect from a standard system, and to inspire them, a couple of standard systems were demonstrated by different vendors.

Alfa defined more than 800 detailed requirements which were simple and prioritized on a scale from 1-4. Finally, all the requirements were included in a spreadsheet and mailed to the candidate vendors.

Encounter 2–Finalized requirements specification: The requirement specification is finished; users from the four functional areas were in charge of the requirement process and the users influence on the process has not been challenged:

- **Users' attitude toward the system:** Acceptance (no changes from the antecedent conditions). There personal involvement is high and the expectations to the new system high.
- **Dynamic between users and consultants/ system:** Users and organizational practice are in focus.
- **Dynamic between the users:** Good; they worked separately in different groups.
- **Knowledge about the technical options and design possibilities:** Limited knowledge about ERP package software in general

Episode 2-Evaluating candidate ERP systems: The vendors performed a written reply and for each requirement they defined to what degree the system could meet the requirement; they used four categories: "Fully as standard," "Customization included in future upgrades," "Customization not included in future upgrades," "Not at all".

Parallel with the requirements definition, a set of criteria for evaluating the vendor were defined and knowledge about the industry and the vendors desire to understand Alfa's situation were among the more important criteria.

The three pre-qualified vendors were invited to demonstrate there system in an all-day workshop using scenarios defined by Alfa. Ten to 15 users participated in the workshops evaluating the system and vendor performance using an evaluation framework. Finally, one to two reference customers for each vendor were visited. An evaluation report comparing the three candidate systems and the tenders from the vendors were composed. The results from the evaluation process were summarized and presented as quantitative and qualitative scores in a number of different areas.

Encounter 3-Evaluation: Alfa's board of directors decided to follow the recommendation given by the project group and Oracle was chosen as Alfa's new ERP system.

- **Users' attitude toward the system:** The attitudes toward the systems are somewhat mixed. Some users developed an equivocate attitude, but acceptance is still the domination attitude.
- **Dynamic between users and consultants/ system:** The users were in charge of the evaluation and the analysts were in charge of the demo. Some users, especially form project management, realize that the systems may not fulfill there needs. They have started to realize that the approach for this implementation minimizes customization and requires the organization to adapt to the ERP package, which will challenge there historical influence on the systems design, and therefore their anticipated usefulness of the system changes slightly.
- **Dynamic between the users:** The dynamic is still good, however, some of the participants started to realize that they had to compromise to allow others to have their needs fulfilled.
- **Knowledge about the technical options and design possibilities:** The users gained some knowledge about the ERP package software during the demos, but most of the participants admit that the evaluation of the ERP packages was based on a god filing rather than on an understanding of the capabilities of the candidate ERP packages.

Episode 3-Re-scoping: Due to financial difficulties in the organization as a whole, the ERP project was asked to cut the project cost by 5 million DKK before even starting. To re-scope the project, Alfa's ERP project manager and user representatives from the four functional areas together with consultants from Oracle implemented a 'Conference Room Pilot,' a quick examination of the original requirements and scope. For each requirement, the implementation consultants would show the solution in Oracle, and the possibility of cutting something was discussed. This process very quickly made it visible that it would be necessary to add as well as cut requirements and scope. In the original requirements specification process, the users had relied on assumptions about what a standard system would provide. Therefore, the requirements now appeared to be incomplete. At the end of the two weeks, the 5 million cuts were found and a contract was signed defining scope, price, and so forth.

Encounter 4–Contract signed: A fixed price contract is signed with the vendor based on the original requirements specification with adjustments decided on during episode 3.

- **Users' attitude toward the system:** Equivocation and some resistance, most users have started to feel that the historic participation tradition has changed. The users got to make the re-scoping decisions, but the final result has to be approved by the steering committee.
- **Dynamic between users and consultants/ system:** The project manager is driving the process very strictly to cut project cost and the users have to rely on the consultants' knowledge and judgment about the ERP system. Most users have now realized that the requirements specifications will not necessarily help them achieve significant influence on the system's capability, and a feeling that the system will not provide what they asked for is emerging. The process is now challenging the users' traditional position of having significant influence.
- **Dynamic between the users:** Conflicting interests have started to surface.
- **Knowledge about the technical options and design possibilities:** There is limited knowledge about individual modules within

the ERP package. There is no ability to see cross-module issues.

Episode 4-Configuration: In the following nine months, three conference room pilots were conducted. In each pilot, the system "to-be" was (re-)scoped at a more detailed level and the configuration decisions were documented. The work was conducted in small workshops where user representatives and consultants worked together; the users provided knowledge about the existing work practice (requirements) and the consultants their knowledge about the standard system. The processes embedded in the ERP package were guiding the work and the process tool accompanying the ERP system was used. The requirements specification was used as a checklist.

Encounter 5–The first version of the new ERP system is finished:

- **Users' attitude toward the system:** Resistance and some rejection. Most of the user representatives are disappointed with the results and know it will be difficult to "sell" it to the users in their department. The functionality within resource management is considered so poor that the users have started rejecting the system as a whole.
- **Dynamic between users and consultants/ system:** The consultants were in charge of the implementation process; the capability of the ERP package is constraining the design and the requirements specification is used to evaluate the progress of the work. The users lack experience in the configuration process and knowledge about the capabilities of ERP package; they are totally dependent on the consultants. Users have realized that the new system will not meet the expectations of their peers and some of them feel precarious and stressed reporting back to their peers. Conflicting interests among the users is also influencing the process; most of

the user representatives feel that the financial department is too dominant.

- **Dynamic between the users:** Open conflicts between user groups have surfaced. Other user groups perceived as dominating the process and the decisions, especially the finance people.

- **Knowledge about the technical options and design possibilities:** The users are primarily providing knowledge for the consultants; their understanding of the technological possibilities is limited and their ability to see the larger picture of the design decisions are very limited especially if it involves cross-functional processes. Customizations are programmed in India or China, and the possibility of understanding how their implementation will affect the existing functionality is difficult. Some cross-module testing is performed with consultants and user representatives in one room, but it is very close to going live and only for some parts of the system.

Episode 5-Training and testing: The project is under extreme time pressure. Within Alfa's concern, one is not allowed to implement a new financial system in the last quarter of a financial year; therefore the system has to go live at the beginning of October. Thus the training of the users takes place alongside the final testing and data conversion.

Encounter 6-October 8, 2003 Alfa's Oracle solution went live:

- **Users' attitude toward the system:** A lot of resistance toward the system is building up in the organization during episode 6. The users succeed at this late stage in having the resource management module taken out of the implementation because the functionality in their opinion is too poor, and project

managers refused to participate in training and using the system.

- **Dynamic between users and consultants/ system:** The consultants were in charge of the configuration of the system and the modifications to the system. However, the user representatives have taken over responsibility regarding training and testing and the overall responsibility for the socio-technical design.

- **Dynamic between the users:** The conflicts that broke out during episode 4 have not been resolved.

- **Knowledge about the technical options and design possibilities:** Difficulties caused by customizations corrupting data is influencing the quality of the training, and some users (especially Alfa's project managers) get a very poor impression of the new system. The attendance to the next rounds of training is poor which then results in sparse diffusion of knowledge about the ERP system throughout the organization.

Episode 6-Go live and stabilizing the system: Because of the time pressure, many reports (to be generated by the system) were still outstanding and a lot of promising functionality was left to be implemented in a later phase. During the next months, the users struggled with the system. Some parts of the system they learned to manage but other parts they refused to use or used incorrectly, thereby causing data quality problems as well as system malfunction in other areas. After a very turbulent period, the system was stabilized and the most important reports were developed.

Encounter 7-An internal ERP-competence centre was formed: An ERP competence center is formed. It is headed by the ERP project manager and has some of the user representatives who worked in the ERP project, a former ERP consultant and some technical IT experts as members. At the same time, it is decided to improve the usefulness of the system, and a follow-up project is initiated:

- **Users' attitude toward the system:** Resistance/rejection. Many users are not using the system or only use it functionality when they are forced to use. However, those who actually use the system became more convinced that parts of the system had to be redesigned to support their daily work. The users use their political power to have changes made and as the system is redesigned, their attitude is slowly getting more positive.
- **Dynamic between users and consultants/system:** No significant pattern in some areas, however, the use has more focus. The members of the new competence center have now taken on the consultants' role.
- **Dynamic between the users:** Many conflicts from episode 4 are still unresolved.
- **Knowledge about the technical options and design possibilities:** As the users are using the system, they get more knowledge about the technological possibilities.

Episode 7-The follow-up project: Some of the consultants participating in the configuration had moved on to a new project and some were still helping out correcting errors. Members of the new internal ERP competence center were assigned the roles of technology experts. The fit of the system was in some areas more problematic then in others. Meetings were set up where people from the competence center met all user groups within Alfa. The analysts met the users with an open mind and all issues reported were noted without considering the relevance or the reason, which resulted in a list of more than 500 issues. Afterwards, the reasons for the issues were discussed and the appropriate action decided. Some issues were handled with end-user education and some with reconfiguration or customizations of the system; some were researched thoroughly, but

could not be solved due to the design of standard system.

Encounter 8-follow-up project was completed:

- **Users' attitude toward the system:** More functionality is accepted. In general, the perceived usefulness of the system increased and some of the rejected functionality were re-designed or just re-introduced and now accepted.
- **Dynamic between users and consultants/system:** The users in general gained more self-confidence and they started to fight to get more influence on the socio-technical design of the new system. Alfa project managers are still fighting what they perceive to be a very poor system design refusing to use some functionalities and have project assistances and secretaries use the system on their behalf.
- **Dynamic between the users:** Friendships across user groups are providing some understanding for other groups' work situation and some of the open conflicts find a resolution, although the memory of what happened during episode 4 is still causing many angry outbreaks.
- **Knowledge about the technical options and design possibilities:** Friendships and work-related corporation across the functional areas and across user groups, provide better understanding of cross-functional processes in the system, although the users still complain that it is extremely difficult to grasp the complexity of the system.

Episode 8-Continuous improvement: Users throughout Alfa and members of the competence center are working to increase the quality of use. To do so, they are customizing the software to change the original capabilities of the ERP package, reconfiguring the system and enacting the

Table 2. Summarizing changes in encounters over time

Encounter	User-consultants/ system dynamic	Dynamic between user groups/stakeholders	Knowledge about the technical possibilities/design suggestions
Encounter 1 *project initiated*	Users dominating–organizational practice in focus	No conflicts related to the ERP project	No knowledge about the future ERP system
Encounter 2 *Finalized requirements specification*	Users dominating– organizational practice in focus	No conflicts related to the ERP project	Very limited knowledge about ERP systems in general
Encounter 3 *Evaluation of ERP packages conducted*	Consultants/system dominating-organizational needs used for scooping	Minor conflicts of interest surfaced	User representatives: Superficial knowledge related to functional modules End users: No knowledge
Encounter 4 *Contract signed*	Consultants/system in dominating-requirements specification in focus	Open conflicts between user groups	User representatives: Some understanding related to modules End users: No or very limited knowledge (end users were invited to demos/ test but did in general not participate)
Encounter 5 *The first version of the new ERP system is finished*	Consultants/system in dominating	Open conflicts between user groups	End users: No or limited knowledge
Encounter 6 *Go live*	No significant pattern-organizational use more in focus	Open conflicts between user groups	End users: Some practical knowledge related to own use
Encounter 7 *An internal ERP-competence centre was formed*	No significant pattern-organizational use in focus	Resolution of minor conflicts	End users: More practical knowledge related to own use, and limited understanding for others use
Encounter 8 *follow-up project completed*	Users more influence-organizational use in focus	Resolution of more conflicts although the history is still influencing the relationships	More interaction across user groups.

software. The relationship between the users and the competence center is in some areas problematic, but in other areas the relation is very good and fruitful based on a more joint development approach.

Outcome: While focusing on what is often understood as the core ERP project (episode 3-5), the project is considered a success from a project management point of view. Cost and time estimates were met, and the promised functionality (it is a vague definition) was delivered; after a chaotic go live, the system is used in the organization and more functionality is implemented as an ongoing process. Users participated in the selection process, the scoping of the system, the

configuration and implementation, and last but not least the users' issues that remained after the go-live phase were collected and seriously addressed. Participation was encouraged and organized for. However, the quality of the solution is being questioned throughout the organization, many users are still complaining, that they lack knowledge to use the system correctly. More powerful users resist using functionality with what they consider poor functionality or user interface. Users participating in ongoing implementation of new functionality are complaining about not being able to understand the capabilities of the software and the consequences of different design possibilities. User representatives participated in different activities in the project, but the relation to the remainder of the users in the organization were problematic throughout the project, and during episodes 3-6, the user representatives could not or would not get too deeply involved. Episode 3 and 4 left the organization with a lot of internal conflicts and frustration, influencing the users' behavior in the following episodes, and causing a lot of re-design and customizations years after the ERP system went live. (see Table 1)

The users' attitude toward the system is changing over time as depicted in Figure 1. Analysis revealed that three entangled issues contributed to the change of attitude: (1) The dynamic between the users/organizational practice and the consultants/the system, (2) the dynamic between different user groups, and (3) knowledge about the technical and socio-technical options.

As the project was initiated, Alfa was aware that it could be challenging to "fit" the ERP system into their organization, because the organization's way of doing business was believed to differ from the mainstream of the organization's adoption of ERP systems. Thus it was considered important to:

- have a thorough requirements specification as a basis for the contract
- allow necessary customizations to the system
- choose an implementation partner recognizing the uniqueness of the organizations way of operation
- have users and consultants work as one team—as partners.

Although there was some awareness that the ERP package software would constrain the design possibilities, there was initially genuine confidence that it would be possible to influence the design in a satisfactory way. Having no prior experience in implementing ERP systems and no or very limited knowledge about technical and socio-technical options related to the specific ERP package, the users (or user representatives)

did not challenge the contradiction implementing a pre-developed system and having it fit the organizational practice. No interest conflicts surfaced due to the fact that work was conducted in four user groups isolated from the others. Thus up until episode 3, user participation was instantiated in user involvement, and a satisfactory expected usefulness and ease of use of the new system

As the user representatives obtained more knowledge about the ERP package in episode 3 and discussed technical options with the consultants, they realized that their expectations about usefulness and ease of use had been based on assumptions about ERP package software. At the same time, they started to realize that having the system guide the design process (despite the consultants' willingness to understand and recognize the organizational practice) would make it very difficult to maintain a focus on the organizational practices. And although users were still participating, the personal involvement became more difficult. Especially, Alfa's more experienced project managers dissociate themselves from the project.

The configuration and customization process in episode 4 caused many difficulties involving user representatives and users (not just participating). They relied on the vendor's tool box and the consultants' experience with ERP. In short, this meant that users provided knowledge about the organization to the consultants and that consultants then configured the system and showed it to the user representatives who then evaluated the usefulness. However, prior to episode 4 and during episode 4, some necessary customizations which are profound to the ERP package's way of operating had been defined. This means that the consultants as well as the user representatives had difficulties visualizing how parts of the technical and socio-technical solution would work. Although the customizations were supposed to improve the usefulness of the system, they were at the same time challenging the "tested-ness" and "proven-ness" of the work design (especially coordination mechanisms) built into the system. In this situation, the consultants could no longer trust the system to "consider" everything for them when it came to work design. Further, the users could not embrace the complexity of the system and evaluate the usefulness of the customized system. Thus both consultants and user representatives lacked sufficient knowledge to design and evaluate possible solutions in a good way. At the end of episode 4, an integration test of the four different modules was performed and interest conflicts became visible. The users' difficulties in understanding the technical solution as well as evaluating the socio-technical implications made them more reluctant to become involved in the process and to promote the solution to the remainder of the organization. Although end users were invited to information meetings and demos of the system and to participate in testing the system, very few end users actually became engaged. Thus actual knowledge about the new system was not diffused in the organization. Conflicts between stakeholders were not resolved, and the general perception of the quality of use was that it was very poor.

Given the lack of personal involvement for most users and user representatives in episode 4, their influence on and knowledge about the technical design was limited. Thus their possibility of "testing" it against the organization's way of working (or new ways of working) was very limited. So despite Alfa's intention of involving the users, it did not materialize.

After the go live, the users gained knowledge about the technical design, and they started to try out different socio-technical possibilities. After a period of time, the users had more knowledge about the ERP package and the external consultants had left the organization; then the technical design as well as the socio-technical design was negotiated in the context of the organization. However, for a long time the lack of trust between one user group and other user groups and IT professionals was complicating the process.

CONCLUSION AND DISCUSSION

The aim of this article is to answer the research questions:

- How and why are the users' attitudes toward the system changing over time in Alfa's ERP lifecycle?
- Why did user participation *not* provide the intended user involvement and the intended quality of the system?

The most interesting theoretical *contribution* of the case analysis was that the users' attitudes toward the system change between acceptance, equivocation, resistance and rejection over time depending on three things: (1) Dynamic between users/organizational practice and consultants/the system, (2) Dynamic between different user groups, and (3) Understanding of technical and socio-technical options. Having users participate was more difficult than expected, and although users are asked to participate, and are given time to do so, in practice the majority do not get involved before go live. The analysis of the case confirm prior findings in the literature, namely that user participation without influence will not result in involvement, and without involvement there will be no or limited effect on the quality of the product and no or limited knowledge diffusion.

The second interesting theoretical *contribution* is the answer to the second research question. In short, the answer is that the users' change in behavior and attitude in episode 3 and 4 can be explained by a reaction to what I call *pseudo participation. Pseudo participation* is defined as a situation where users are asked to participate but not given the possibility to influence the design. Pseudo participation may not always be intentional. Unexpected events or using inappropriate techniques and tools could cause user participation to become pseudo participants.

Although, Alfa at the outset had a sincere wish to involve the users and let them influence at least part of the design. Pseudo participation became a reality during episode 4. In Alfa's case, the following process characteristics lead to pseudo participation:

- Requiring a large part of the ERP package implemented without customizations (having the system dominate the design)
- Using inappropriate techniques and tools to support the users' gain of knowledge about technical and socio-technical options (resulting in lack of knowledge in order to develop and evaluate design suggestions)
- Not resolving interest conflicts between user groups (meaning that some user groups felt dominated by others)
- Time constraints (no implementation the last quarter of a financial year)
- Resource constraints (cutting the original budget)

Pseudo participation coupled with low perceived usefulness and a strong power position in the organization caused especially the influential project managers to avoid participating in the configuration and customization project. Also, the participation in information meetings, demonstrations of the system and training were avoided. Thus the ERP project became detached from the remainder of the organization. At the time of go live, the users were able to resist or reject the system based on arguments of poor design. At the initiation of the follow-up project (episode 7), the factors leading to pseudo participation had changed. Customizing the system to the work situation was now the objective in order to make, for example, the project managers use the system. Secretaries, project assistants, controllers, finance people, purchase assistants and other users now had practical experience with the

system. Thus the organizational knowledge about technical options had improved. Interest conflicts were still not resolved, but some resolution had begun. The time and resource constraints had been loosened.

Furthermore, the case analysis points to an interesting dilemma when having two conflicting design perspectives in use at the same time. Alfa's organization (management, the ERP project manager, and users) valued some of the organization's unique business processes (central to what it meant to be doing business in Alfa) and agreed on having them implemented in the system, while more secondary processes were expected to be adapted to the system. Thus for some part of the implementation, the organizational practice was expected to guide the work design and in other parts the system was supposed to guide. Customizing the software is technically challenging in itself and on top of that it seems to pose a challenge on how to organize user participation, as well as which tools and techniques to use to support two different design strategies at the same time. The vendor's general recommendation is not to customize the software and have the ERP package guide the design of work processes. If no customization is decided on it may— from a management perspective—be sufficient to have users participate primarily for assimilation purposes. However, some organizations like Alfa will need to have customizations made for strategic purposes or because they simply do not fit all parts of the template used to design the ERP package software. In that case, user participation may also be mandatory for design.

As stated in a previous section, not much research on user participation has been conducted in the organizational arena and even less in the context of ERP implementations. The case study is pointing to a need for further research regarding new approaches to support the user organization's generation of knowledge about the technical options and the socio-technical options during configuration and customization, and to investigate how different tools and techniques can allow conflicts of interests to be analyzed and reconciled when the design space is constrained by packaged standard software such as an ERP system.

Prior research on user participation primarily addresses two design strategies—one allowing the organizational practice to influence and inform the design and another having design professionals being responsible for the design. As I see it, ERP package software, however, could provide a different design strategy letting the system inform the design. User participation related to such an approach would need further research.

One practical *contribution* of the case study is the awareness that customizing the software is not just technically challenging, but it is also requires conscious work design. Thus the organization will have to decide whether users or design professionals should be given the task and to what extent the organizational practice should guide the design. Furthermore, profound customizations will make vendors' "template" approach for implementation projects somewhat problematic. Thus the organization will have to explicitly address the issue of handling two different design politics at the same time, and at the same time they have to think about how they can avoid pseudo participation.

REFERENCES

Barki, H., & Hartwick, J. (1989). Rethinking the concept of user involvement. *MIS Quarterly, 13*(1), 55-63.

Baroudi, J., Olson, M., & Ives, B. (1986). An empirical study of the impact of user involvement on system usage and information satisfaction. *Communications of the ACM, 29*(3), 232-238.

Bjerkness, G., & Bratteteig, T. (1995). User participation and democracy: A discussion of Scandinavian research on system development. *Scandinavian Journal of Information Systems, 7*(1), 73-98.

Bjørn-Andersen, N., & Hedberg, B. (1977). Designing information systems in an organizational perspective. *Studies in the Management Sciences Perscriptive Models of Organizations, 5.*

Boudreau, M., & Robey, D. (2005). Enacting integrated information technology: Human agency perspective. *Organization Science, 16*(1), 3-18.

Cavaye, A. (1995). User participation in system development revisited. *Information Management, 29,* 311-323.

Clement, A., & Van den Besselar, P. (1993). A retrospective look at PD projects. *Participatory Design: Special Issue of the Communications of the ACM, 36,* 29-39.

Davenport, T. (1998). Putting the enterprise into the enterprise system. *Harvard Business Review.*

DeLone, W., & McLean, E. (1992). Information systems success: The quest for the dependent variable. *Information Systems Research, 3*(1), 60-95.

Esteves-Sousa, J., & Pastor-Collado, J. (2000). Towards the unification off critical success factors for ERP implementations. *Proceedings of the 10th Annual Business Information Technology conference.* Manchester, UK.

Gärtner, J., & Wagner, I. (1996). Mapping actors and agendas: Political frameworks of systems design and participation. *Human-Computer Interaction, 11*(3).

Holland, C., Light, B., & Gibson, N. (1999). A critical success model for enterprise resource planning implementation. *Proceedings of the 7th European Conference on Information Systems.* Copenhagen, Denmark: Copenhagen Business School.

Ives, B., & Olson, M. (1984). User involvement and MIS success: A review of research. *Management Science, 30*(5), 586-603.

Kawalek, P., & Wood-Harper, T. (2002). Finding of thorns: User participation in enterprise system implementation. *Advances in Information Systems, 33*(1), 13-22.

Kensing, F., & Blomberg, J. (1998). Participatory design: Issues and concerns. *Computer Supported Cooperative Work, 7,* 167-185.

Kien, S., & Soh, C. (Eds.). (2003). An exploratory analysis of the sources and nature of misfits in ERP implementations (1st ed.). In: G. Shanks, P. Seddon, & L. Willcocks (Eds.), *Second-wave enterprise resource planning systems, implementing for effectiveness* (pp. 373-387). Cambridge, UK: Cambridge University Press.

Klein, H., & Myers, M. (1999). A set of principles for conducting and evaluating interpretive field studies in information systems. *MIS Quarterly, Special Issue on Intensive Research, 23*(1), 67-93.

Lucas, H., Walton, E., & Ginzberg, M. (1988). Implementing package software. *MIS Quarterly, 12*(4), 537-549.

Markus, L. (1983). Power, politics and MIS implementation. *Communication of the ACM, 26*(6), 430-444.

Markus, M., & Tanis, C. (2000). The enterprise system experience—from adoption to success. In: R. Zmud & M. Price (Eds.), *Framing the domains of IT management: Projecting the future through the past.* Cincinnati, OH: Pinnaflex Educational Resources.

Mumford, E. (2003). *Redesigning human systems* (p. 303). Hershey, PA: Information Science Publishing.

Nah, F., Zuckweiler, K., & lau, J. (2003). ERP implementation: Chief information officers' perceptions of critical success factors. *International Journal of Human-Computer Interaction, 16*(1), 5-22.

Newman, M., & Noble, F. (1990). User involvement as an interaction process: A case study. *Information Systems Research, 1*(1), 89-113.

Newman, M., & Robey, D. (1992). A social process model of user-analyst relationships. *MIS Quarterly, 16*(2), 249-266.

Noyes, J., Starr, A., & Frankish, C. (1996). User involvement in the early stages of the development of an aircraft warning system. *Behaviour & Information Technology, 15*(2), 67-75.

Parr, A., & Shanks, G. (2003). Critical success factors revisited: A model for ERP project implementation. In: G. Shanks, P. Seddon, & L. Willcocks (Eds.), *Second-wave enterprise resource planning systems.* Cambridge, UK: Cambridge University Press.

Pries-Heje, L. (2006). ERP misfits: What is it and how do they come about?. *Proceedings of the 17th Australasian Conference on Information Systems.* Adelaid, Australia.

Robey, D. & Farrow, D. (1982). User involvement in information system development: A conflict model and empirical test. *Management Science, 28*(1), 73-85.

Robey, D., Ross, J., & Boudreau, M. (2002). Learning to implement enterprise systems: An exploratory study of the dialectics of change. *Journal of Management Information Systems, 19*(1), 17-46.

Shang, S., & Seddon, P. (2002). Assessing and managing the benefits of enterprise systems: The business manager's perspective. *Information Systems Journal, 12,* 271-299.

Shanks, G., et al. (2000). Differences in critical success factors in ERP systems implementations in Australia and China: A cultural analysis. *Proceedings from the 8th European Conference on Information Systems*. Venna, Austria.

Stefanou, C. (1999). Supply chain management (SCM) and organizational key factors for successful implementation of enterprise resource planning (ERP) systems. *Proceedings of Americas Conference on Information Systems*. Milwaukee, WI.

Summer, M. (1999). Critical success factors in enterprise-wide information management systems projects. *Proceedings of the Americas Conference on Information Systems*. Milwaukee, WI.

Vidgen, R., Wood-Haper, T., & Wood, R. (1993). A soft systems approach to information systems quality. *Scandinavian Journal of Information Systems, 5,* 97-112.

Zmud, R., & Cox, J. (1979). The implementation process: A change approach. *MIS Quarterly, 3*(2), 35-43.

Chapter 7
ERP Selection:
Effect of Product and Organizational Constructs

Uzoka Faith-Michael Emeka
Mount Royal University, Canada

Abiola Richard Oladele
Federal University of Technology, Nigeria

ABSTRACT

Previous studies have shown that Enterprise Resource Planning (ERP) systems have significantly impacted positively on the productivity of the organization. However, there exists a cost-failure paradox. ERP systems are very expensive and constitute a huge budgetary component, yet the failure rate of ERPs is very high. The selection process of ERPs is a critical success factor. This study focuses on the product and organizational constructs that affect the selection of ERP systems. The authors utilized an extension of technology acceptance model (TAM) by elements of the information systems (IS) success model. The study evaluated the impact of system quality, information quality, service quality, and support quality as key determinants of cognitive response, which influences ERP system purchase/use. Industry, firm size, buying center, and product experience were introduced as organizational constructs. The results of the study indicate that system quality, information quality and software support are significant product qualities that affect an organization's decision to adopt an ERP product. Among the organizational constructs, only firm size was found to be statistically significant. The results also indicate that multi department committees and the IT department are the major buying centers responsible for vendor selection. In terms of information source, vendor reference and adverts are major information sources, while government standards and popularity/experience of vendors are important considerations in vendor selection.

INTRODUCTION

Competition, globalization, and digitization have compelled organizations to resort to information

systems as a major driver of other business processes (O'Brien and Marakas 2007). Enterprise Resource Planning (ERP) systems have become major tools in organizational efficiency and strategic advantage through the synergistic integration of fragments of data in hundreds of previously disparate systems

DOI: 10.4018/978-1-60566-968-7.ch007

that degraded organizational efficiency and business performance (Laudon and Laudon 2007). Global expenditure on information and communications technology (ICT) infrastructure grows tremendously, with growth in software investment averaging from 30% to 40% per year (Eckhouse 1999). ERP acquisition is a high expenditure activity that consumes a substantial portion of an organization's capital budget (Verville *et al.* 2005) and shakes the structural and cultural foundations of the organization. It is therefore not surprising that organizations take some time to think and plan the adoption of ERP.

Most organizations have had a successful ERP implementation, but a sizable number of organizations have failed to derive benefits from ERP (O'Brien and Marakas 2007). The costs and risks of failure in implementing a new ERP are huge. The paradox that in spite the high failure rates of ERP systems they are still being soled and are becoming more expensive, proves that ERPs are very vital to organizations and their selection, a key managerial decision (Kerimoglu *et al.* 2008). A number of researchers have focused on implementation and post implementation issues, while the acquisition process is for the most part being ignored (Verville and Halingten 2003). Most of the failures in ERP implementation result from poor selection process that ignores contextual organizational factors. Since an ERP system imposes its own logic on a company's strategy, organization and culture, it is imperative that ERP selection be made with care in order to avoid failure, which could result from technology-business needs/process mismatch (Umble *et al.* 2003). For researchers, the challenge would then be to ascertain the correlation between the acquisition process and the implementation process, the results of which could be beneficial to practitioners (Estevez and Pastor 2001).

It is important that developers of ERP systems align their development strategies to the needs, business processes and purchasing behavior of their clients. This is an uphill goal especially for off-the-shelf ERPs. However, a basic understanding of the factors influencing the organization's choice of ERP systems is extremely vital. In most cases, these factors vary across organizations. Issues such as size of the organization, available capital budget, business processes, international outlook, and data enrichment needs are of importance (Bernroider and Koch 2001, Verville *et al.* 2005, Adelman *et al.* 2005).

This study aims at examining critical ERP selection factors and processes in a developing country (Botswana) that has a high level of information technology (IT) utilization (Toure 2007) using a triangulation of the technology acceptance model (TAM), Information systems (IS) success model, and elements of organizational buying behavior. It would provide insight to ERP developers on issues to be addressed when tailoring ERP systems to the needs of organizations and attempt to contribute towards filling the literature gap that exists in ERP research in developing countries. Most of the studies on ERP selection have been carried out in the developed world (E.g. Verville and Halingten 2002, Kostopoulos *et* al. 2004, Amoako-Guyampah and Salam 2004, Buonanno *et* al. 2005). Section 2.0 examines some existing literature in ERP selection, while in Section 3.0, a research framework is presented. The materials and methods employed in the study are presented in Section 4.0, while the results are presented in Sections 5.0. In Section 6.0 the results are discussed and some conclusions are drawn.

REVIEW OF RELATED LITERATURE

The acquisition of ERP is a complex, involving, and intensive activity, which could take months and a number of personnel in planning and deciding on critical concomitants that should go into the decision matrix. In [Verville and Halingten 2003], a six step process of ERP selection is presented (Figure 1). The MERPAP consists of planning, which is a continuous exercise throughout the

Figure 1. The model of ERP acquisition process (MERPAP) Key: Dotted lines indicate information flow while solid lines indicate sub process interrelationships

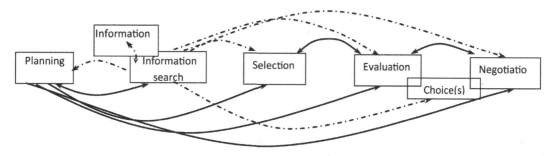

selection process; information search, which provides information used in subsequent steps; selection, which includes shortlisting of vendors and technologies; evaluation, which includes vendor, functional and technical evaluation of potential candidates in order to make a *choice*, which eventually culminates into business and legal *negotiations*. In (Umble *et al*.2003) a fourteen step process is defined, which tends to extend the six step process of Verville and Halingten (2003). It includes the following: vision creation, function list creation, software candidate list creation, candidate list creation, candidate list narrowing (to 4 or 6), request for proposals, proposals review, selection of two or three finalists, finalists package demonstration, winner selection, investment justification, contract negotiation, pre-implementation pilot run, and justification validation. Relevant Business Systems (n.d) outlines the following evaluation steps: review of potential software products, elimination of packages that fail to meet specified needs, creation of a manageable list of vendors, scheduled detailed product demonstration, check on vendors' references, and a visit to 'like' customer site of the final shortlisted vendors. This is a modified subset of the selection process outlined in (Umble *et al.* 2003).

The vendor search, evaluation and selection are very crucial in the ERP selection exercise. There has to be a fit between a vendor's product/ support services and an organization's business strategy, focus, and acquisition/maintenance budget. According to Somers and Nelson (2001), an organization should look for a technology partner that is forward thinking, innovative and can provide a migration path for the business as it grows. Chung and Snyder (1999) outline the most important question an organization needs to ask, "Does the vendor have the functionality to meet the business needs?" An ERP system should not only address the needs an organization has today but also have the ability to accommodate anticipated needs in the future. According to Eckhouse (1999), Economic conditions and vendor consolidations are reshaping the core enterprise resource planning application. The technology transformation to service-oriented architectures will be the most-significant factor redefining ERP marketing. Consolidation among market vendors will continue, therefore, users selecting ERP products should ensure long-term support or at the very least, ensure access to source code in contract negotiations.

The search support and choice behavior of a buyer is analyzed in (Sproule and Archer 2000). The choice behavior is affected by the frequency of purchase, risk involvement, and structuredness of information. Frequent buyers have structured situational information requirements, while new purchase (such as ERP software) utilizes unstructured, concept forming information, needing constructive choice process. In high risky and high consequence trade-offs, buyers choose one of two mechanisms: 1). Problem-focused coping

Table 1. The purchasing situation and choice behavior

	NEW PURCHASE	**FREQUENT PURCHASE**
HIGH RISK	Unstructured process (staged constructive). Risk reduction through problem-focused and emotion focused strategies.	Structured process. Risk reduction through investment reduction and use of familiar suppliers/brands
LOW RISK	Unstructured process (staged constructive). Minimal information processing	Structured process. Very minimal information processing

strategy involving more extensive information processing; and 2). Emotion-focused coping strategy that avoids trade-offs (Bettman *et al.* 1998). Table 1 shows the purchasing situation and choice behavior (Sproule and Archer 2000). The choice of ERP software frequently falls within the high risk, new purchase quadrant that utilizes mostly the problem-focused coping strategy. The success of any ERP implementation depends on factors related to the acquisition process and factors related to people within the process (Verville *et al.* 2003). The evaluation stage of the selection process is very critical because it maps the software intrinsic and extrinsic characteristics to the organization's information, processes, and strategic goals in order to achieve optimum business success (Somers and Nelson 2001).

Lotto (2006) suggests that whether an organization wants to upgrade an existing ERP system or is in the market for the first ERP system, there are a number of factors to consider when selecting an ERP system. The first step is for the organization to do a thorough purchase planning before making a major capital investment. Other factors include organizational needs and goals, risks, benefits, limited resources, relationships between current systems and available alternatives. Kumar and Hillegersberg (2000) say that budget and resources are also key factors to consider. Some of the leading edge technology solutions may initially cost less, but usually end up costing more due to complexity and ongoing maintenance costs. The question of cost always plays a crucial role in any capital expenditure, but the determining factor in the price tag of any ERP system is total cost of ownership. To get an accurate perspective of the

total cost of ownership, an organization should look at how the cost combination of software, implementation, services and maintenance will affect the business over the next five to ten years (Atkinson, 1999).

A number of studies have attempted to identify factors that are considered by organizations in the evaluation and selection of ERP software. Hecht (1997) summarized the factors into six categories, namely; functionality, cost, technical architecture, service and support, vision and ability to execute, while Verville and Hallingten (2002) determined three distinct types of criteria for evaluation: vendor, functionality and technical. Vendor evaluation criteria included size, financial stability, and reputation of vendor etc., functional criteria dealt with the features of the software, and included functionalities specific to front-end interfaces, user friendliness and so on. Technical criteria dealt with the specifics of the systems architecture, integration, performance, and security etc. While vendor criteria may relate to specific characteristics of the vendor and the support provided, functional and technical characteristics of the ERP software would focus on the fit between the ERP product and the organization's corporate characteristics and dynamics. We therefore group the ERP selection criteria into *product constructs* and *vendor constructs*.

Product Constructs

Functionality

Most researchers found functionality to be one of the most important criteria for selecting given ERP software (Hecht 1997, Kumar *et al. 2003;* Baki and Caker 2005). The first issue for the functionality is its comprehensiveness. The solution should have enough or even more modules related to organisations' core activities such as human resources, material management, project management, production planning, supply chain management, etc. (Brewer, 2000). Functional evaluation should be done by a cross-functional team. According to Illa et al. (2000) functionality has three main aspects: which functional areas does the product cover; how flexible the product is with respect to adaptability and openness; and some ERP specific features.

System Reliability

According to the Kumar et al. (2003), system reliability is the second important selection criterion. Incorporating the best business practices of every area as well as the latest trends in IT is important for the new system. Leading ERP vendors have strong alliances with the market leaders in their respective businesses from different areas (Shikarpur, 1997). Organisations should ask some question about reliability such as how long has the vendor been in the core ERP solution business; has its current users been satisfied with the package? (Brewer, 2000)

Technical Criteria

The choice of hardware and software has a major bearing on the acceptance of a system (Poon and Wagner, 2001). The solution should address the current trends in IT. Users need to check the currency of IT trends in the ERP product and examine if the vendor is committed to incorporating the latest trends in IT in the product (Shikarpur, 1997). Technical architecture uncovers the fit between IS and the end user's needs by looking at the environment in which the application is available (database, server, and client environments), the user-interface capabilities, the software archi-

tecture of the application, the development and management tools associated with the application, and the data and process models available within the application (Hecht, 1997). According to Rao (2000) organisations should ensure that the suppliers undertake to upgrade the products to make best use of technologies that are likely to become available in the future. It is important that organisations should use an external consulting group to assist for evaluating the solutions' technical aspects (Verville and Hallingten, 2002).

Compatibility with Other Systems

No single application can do everything an organisation needs. The selected solution has to be integrated along with all the home-grown systems and other specialised software products that organisations may have to use to meet their unique needs. From this view, compatibility/integration is a critical factor for the system success (Bingi *et al.* 1999). Compatibility with the other systems has also been stressed in the literature to be crucial for realising the potential benefits of ERP (Kumar *et al.* 2003).

Ease of Customisation

Most firms need to customise a part of the ERP system in order to suite their businesses needs. Although minor customization is the most common, many firms find customisation to be significant (Mabert et al., 2000). Because of the need to adapt the generic solution to the organisation's specific needs, ERP vendors are required to provide tools and utilities that will allow the firm's in-house IT personnel or independent consulting firms to customise the software (Avshalom, 2000).

Better Fit with Organisational Structure

Selected software should be implemented simply with current organisational structure and human resources. Software requiring more and qualified personnel in the implementation stage may not be preferred. In the selection process, providing compatibility with parent/allied organisations can affect the decision process for some organisations. This compatibility can also affect whole ERP project success. The real benefit of an ERP system is in integration (Shikarpur, 1997). A full integration should be present between the modules. If the integration cannot be achieved, implementation time can extend, implementation cost can increase and finally the effectiveness of the system can decrease.

Cost

Organisations should have pricing strategies and include maintenance and upgrades in the overall price (Brewer, 2000, Adelman *et al.* 2005). Affordability is an important criterion in selecting process; the solution should have attractive prices (Rao, 2000). Setting realistic expectations for the overall cost of the system is essential to gain top management approval in buying process (Hecht, 1997).

Implementation Time

ERP implementation is highly costly and complex company-wide project. According to Mabert et al. (2000), implementation time is closely correlated to the selected implementation strategy. The implementation time can also be changed with implementation scope. Implementation time could be increased with more customisation. Offering industry-specific applications could cut down on the implementation time (Bingi et al., 1999).

Vendor Constructs

Service and Support

Because installation and ongoing costs can reach seven to ten times the initial software cost, the service and support associated with the application becomes vital to the success of the partnership between end user and application vendor (Hecht, 1997). Most organisations face technical or other problems during installation, implementation, or post implementation period. Integration with existing systems, customisation, and security are the most serious problems for the organisations (Themistocleous et al., 2001). To deal with these problems organisations need support from suppliers both in terms of IT expertise and domain knowledge (Rao, 2000). The need for training is recognized in (Kerimoglu *et al.* 2008). Unless training, information sharing, effective communication and help desk activities are available, people cannot have a better understanding of how their jobs are related to other functional areas within the organization, and thus, are not able to effectively utilize the system in contributing to the attainment of corporate objectives.

Vision

In the vendor evaluation process, criteria such as vendor strength and/or reputation, financial stability, vendor's vision is considered (Verville and Hallingten, 2002). Organisations should consider the vendor's vision. Specifically what modification is the vendor planning to make to its products and services over the next three to five years (Hecht, 1997)

Market Position of the Vendor

Learning from past experiences, some organisations lay high stress on vendor reputation and service infrastructure when selecting their ERP systems (Kumar et al., 2003). The world's leading ERP vendors have implemented the best global practices in their ERP products. For this reason the organisations can look at the ERP product as a process advisor (Shikarpur, 1997).

Domain Knowledge of Suppliers

It is important that the software developer or supplier knows the industry and is willing to implement the software for the industry. If the industry is a manufacturing enterprise, company should procure the software from the vendors that have experience in manufacturing industries (Rao, 2000).

References of the Vendor

Sales references, reputation, and internationality of the vendor, and especially completed successful project in the same industry could be considered as important criteria for the selection process (Neves *et* al. 2004, Hurbean 2006).

Irrespective of the steps taken in the evaluation/selection process, it is important to note that organizational peculiarities are key in determining the evaluation criteria and the levels of importance of each criterion. Bernroider and Koch (2001) conducted a study on the differences in characteristics of the ERP system selection between small or medium and large organizations. The study revealed that key differences exist in the kinds of software chosen, weights assigned to different selection criteria, the size and structure of the team responsible for the decision, the methods employed and effort expended. It is noted in (Baki and Caker 2005) that firms in developing countries differ from firms in developed countries in terms of criteria used in evaluation of ERP. This could be obvious considering the differences in size, budget, international outlook, trading mechanisms, and parent/allied organization linkages between organizations in developed and developing countries.

THEORETICAL FOUNDATION

One of the earliest theories of organizational buying decision is the *general model of organizational buying behavior* by Webster and Wind (1972), which suggests that buying takes place in a context that is influenced by budget, cost and profit considerations, and usually involves many people in the decision process with complex interactions among people and among individual and organizational goals. The *general model* identifies four classes of variables determining organizational buying behavior, namely: individual, social, organization, and environment. While the *general model* provides a good insight into the buying process, it seems heavily process centered, and considerably ignores product dimensions that influence the buying decision. The purchasing function is dramatically shifting from the transaction-oriented to relational-oriented philosophy, and it is also shifting from domestic to global sourcing; which in turn, changes the role, process, and strategies of procurement (Sheth 1996). Choffray and Lilien (1980) recognize the inter-organizational differences in selection, while Shainesh (2004) recognizes the market and technological uncertainty vis-à-vis product characteristics especially in software buying process. Previous research in organizational buying focused on the buying centre (e.g. Dawes *et al.* 1998), the decision making process (e.g. Ward and Webster 1991), and factors that influence both the group structure and process (e.g. Ghingold and Wilson 1998).

The influence of product attributes in organizational buying decisions is further recognized in (Kauffman 1996). Lehmann and O'Shaughnessy (1982) had identified standardization, make-up, application, and dollar commitment as being important, while Shaw *et al.* (1989) opine that intangible attributes such as service are more important than product features in the selection process for technically complex products. Complexity, novelty, and importance are key influences in the purchase decision (McQuiston 1989), while Jackson *et al.* (1984) found out that the relative influence of the buying center is constant in different buying classes but changes across product types and decision types. Stephenson and Sage

(2007) identify three basic core elements of an ERP as people, process, and systems. Delone and Mclean (2002) propose a reformulated Information System (IS) success model, which recognizes information quality, system quality, and service quality as key influences to perceived net benefits, which in turn affects the organizations decision to buy. The reformulated IS success model has been utilized by Dobson *et al.* (2007) in making a case for critical realism for enterprise systems evaluation. Perceived benefits (usefulness) and ease of use have been identified in the *technology acceptance model* (TAM) by Davis (1989) as key influences in the adoption and acceptance of a new technology. The TAM has been applied in software/ERP selection and implementation in (Schaik *et al.* 2004, Behrens *et al.* 2005, Ramayah and Lo 2007), while extensions of the TAM are utilized in (Al-Ghanti and King 1999, Mirchandani and Motwani 2001, Amoako-Gyampah and Salam 2003).

This study hybridizes the reformulated IS success model and the TAM (Figure 2) in gaining insight into factors that influence an organization's choice decision in the ERP buying process in a developing country context. It also introduces the *support quality* as a key component in the successful adoption of ERP software. The information quality, system quality, service quality, and support quality are product constructs, which constitute external stimuli that trigger the cognitive response (perceived usefulness and ease of use), which fires a behavioral intention, and consequently, a behavioral response (actual system purchase and use). Due to the product-process centered nature of ERP purchase decision, coupled with its high risk, 'new purchase' nature, we also draw constructs from the field of organizational buying behavior to define some organizational constructs, which may influence the cognitive response that influences the purchase intention of ERP software. The organizational constructs are: *industry type* and *product* experience, which affect the cognitive response; *firm size*, which af-

fects the perceived usefulness of the ERP software to the organization; and *buying centre* influence, which affects the behavioral intention. While the TAM is an individual level theory, it is applied to organizational buying because it is believed that individuals in the organization constitute the buying center that make the actual purchase decision (Dawes *et al.* 1998).

Based on the research model, the following hypotheses were formulated:

H^1: Information quality impacts positively on the cognitive response, which affects an organization's choice of a given ERP software

H^2: System quality is a determining factor in the choice of ERP software

H^3: A vendor's service quality positively impacts on the choice of a vendor and consequently, the ERP software.

H^4: Support quality offered by a vendor is an attracting feature, which positively affects the cognitive response leading to the choice of a vendor/ ERP software.

H^5: The nature of the industry to which a firm belongs ($H^{5.1}$) and the experience in software [ERP] usage ($H^{5.2}$) affects the perceived usefulness and ease of use, and consequently the adoption of an ERP.

H^6: The size of a firm affects its perceived usefulness and consequent adoption of ERP software.

H^7: The buying center influences the choice of a given ERP software.

MATERIALS AND METHODS

Instrument

The instrument for data collection in this study was a structured questionnaire distributed to organizations in both public and private sectors in the three key industrial cities of Botswana,

Figure 2. Research Model

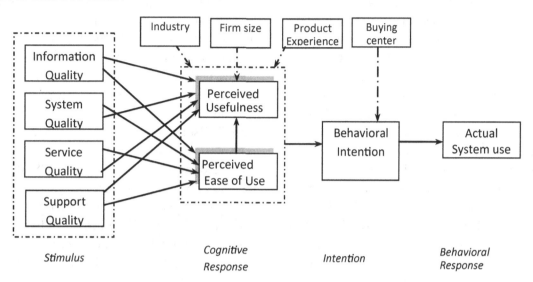

namely: Gaborone, Francistown and Maun. Various industries were included in the population of the study. They include ICT, mining, government, manufacturing, banking and medical among others. The sampling frame is organized according to job positions in the organization, which form the sampling strata. The respondents, all of whom were directly involved in the filing of the questionnaires included managers, technicians and end-users all from different departments such as IT, Finance / Accounting, Sales & Marketing, Human Resource, and who are involved at one level or the other in the organization's software acquisition decision process. One hundred and seventy questionnaires were distributed to staff of forty two organizations which were randomly sampled. One hundred and three questionnaires (60.59% response rate) were properly filled by respondents from thirty eight organizations and used for the purpose of analysis.

Measures

The questionnaire had both close-ended questions and open-ended questions. It was sub-divided into three sections .The first part contained the demographic features such as the respondent's age, gender, position, profession, experience, industry of organization, size of organization and number of employees in the organization. The second section measured twenty variables relating to the criteria used when selecting ERP systems, which were identified through literature search. The selection constructs were measured using multiple items, which were measured on a five point likert type of scale (ranging from 1=irrelevant, 2=not important, 3=fairly important, 4=important, 5=very important).The third section measured eleven other vendor selection and ERP team constructs, also measured on a five point likert scale.

Analysis Procedure

The first part of analysis involves the use of descriptive statistics showing the frequencies and percentages of the demographic variables. The second part of the analysis examined factors considered in the evaluation of ERP software, while the third part examined some vendor selection issues. Exploratory factor analysis was used to reduce the variables into few explainable factors that are considered during the selection process. This was carried out using statistical package for social sciences (SPSS) Version 14.0. Maximum likelihood was utilized as the extraction method while Promax with Kaiser Normalization was used as the rotation method. Variables that did not load on any factor or exhibited cross loading were excluded from the factor analysis. The reliability of the resulting data was measured using the Chronbach's alpha, which is based on the average correlation of items within an instrument and is regarded as an indication of internal consistency. In utilizing factor analysis, it is important to determine the adequacy of the data and the suitability of factor analysis. The Bartlett test of sphericity confirms the adequacy of the sample. The Kaiser Normalization (KMO) measure of sampling indicates the suitability of the application of factor analysis for exploratory purposes. Multiple regressions was further used to test the hypothesis relating to the effects of the factors obtained, while descriptive statistics was utilized in analyzing vendor selection issues.

RESULTS

Respondents Characteristics

Table 2 and Table 3 present descriptive statistics on the data survey. Table 2 highlights the respondents' characteristics. It indicates that the sample is made up mostly of people between ages 25 and 34, accounting for 44.66%, while the age group of 25 and below accounted for 23.30% of respondents. Both males and females actively participated in the survey with only a small margin in favor of the male counterparts. 40.3% of the respondents were management staff, while 59.7% were non-management staff. Database administrators account for the highest respondents profession (17.48%), while systems analysts had the least (5.83%). Most of the respondents had less than 5 years experience in software utilization (58.2%).

32.8% of the respondents were from the ICT industry, followed by government (28.4%), banking (17.9%) and Audit firms (13.4%). Very large organizations like water utilities accounted for the largest percentage (34.3%) of respondents, while medium and small sized had the least (19.4%).

Table 3 shows that 91 respondents (88.35%) used ERP software at some level of usage intensity. The most popularly used ERP was SAP (21.98% of 91), followed by GreatPlains (21.98%), while PeopleSoftHRMS was the least used (5.49%). Majority of the users (29.67%) utilized ERP software to integrate the processes of four departments; namely: Information Technology (IT), Accounting and Finance (AF), Human Resources (HR), and Customer Service (CS); while none of the respondents reported sole utilization of ERP in the HR process.

Factor Analysis

The exploratory factor analysis (Table 4) shows that eighteen out of twenty product related variables loaded on four distinct factors, accounting for a total of 72.887% of the variance in the data. The remaining 27.113% of variance could be attributable to organizational and external variables, which are extraneous to the ERP selection process. The following factors were identified in relation to the research model and considered interpretable: system quality, service quality, information quality and support quality. Table 4 shows the factors and the variables that loaded on them, including the eigenvalues, percentage of variance explained by the factors, and the reliability coefficients (Chronbach's alpha). The results show that *system quality* accounts for the highest variability in the data (46.598%), while *support quality* accounts for the least variability (6.328%). Two variables (language and available platform) were dropped in the analysis because they exhibited cross loading.

Table 2. Respondents characteristics

	Number	Percent
Respondent's Age		
Under 25	24	23.30
25-34	46	44.66
35-44	10	9.71
45-54	17	16.50
55-65	3	2.91
Over 60	3	2.91
Gender		
Male	53	51.46
Female	50	48.54
Position		
Management staff	42	40.3
Non-management staff	61	59.7
Profession		
Technician (Hardware support)	12	11.65
Technician (Software support)	8	7.77
Network administrator	9	8.74
Database administrator	18	17.48
Accountant	8	7.77
Network Engineer	10	9.71
IT Manager	14	13.59
System Analyst	6	5.83
IT consultant	12	11.65
Other	6	5.83
Experience in software Utilization		
0-5 years	60	58.2
6-10 years	32	31.3
11-15 years	6	6.0
Over 15 years	5	4.5
Industry		
Government	29	28.4
Banking	18	17.9
ICT	34	32.8
Audit	14	13.4
Other	8	7.5
Size of Organization		
Small	20	19.4
Medium	26	25.4
Large	22	20.9
Very large	35	34.3

Table 3. ERP Usage

Type of ERP system	Number	Percent
SAP	25	27.47
ACCPAC	15	16.48
SYSPRO	8	8.79
Great Plains	20	21.98
Navision	9	9.89
PeopleSoftHRMS	5	5.49
Others	9	9.89
Total	91	100
Departments' using ERP systems		
Information Technology (IT)	11	12.09
Accounting and Finance (AF)	10	10.99
Customer Service (CS)	6	6.59
IT/HR/AF/CS	27	29.67
IT/AF	10	10.99
Sales and Marketing	8	8.79
IT/CS	7	7.69
HR/AF/CS	7	7.69
Other	5	5.49
Total	91	100
ERP usage		
Not at all	12	11.65
Sparingly	29	28.16
Intensively	19	18.45
Very intensively	18	17.48
Extremely intensively	25	24.27
Total	103	100

Hypotheses Testing

For the purpose of testing the hypothesis, a regression analysis was carried out with product and organizational constructs as independent variables and ERP use as the dependant variable. Table 5, Table 6 and Table 7 show the model summary, ANOVA and the regression statistics respectively.

Table 4. Criteria for choosing ERP systems

Factors	Factor Loads	Eigen value	% of variance explained	Cumulative (%)	Cronbach (α)
Factor 1					
System Quality		1.886	46.598	46.598	0.724
Innovations capability	1.044				
Implementation time	.839				
Adaptability	.802				
Ease of use	.653				
Consistency	.641				
Efficiency	.478				
Factor 2					
Service Quality		1.888	10.342	56.939	0.758
License cost	.880				
Position of vendor	.735				
Attractiveness	.889				
Security	.411				
Factor 3					
Information Quality		1.890	9.620	66.559	0.510
Software capability	.804				
Purpose	.723				
Customization	.563				
Report creation	.588				
Factor 4					
Support Quality		2.67	6.328	72.887	0.664
License warranty	.967				
Manual	.700				
Training support	.559				
Maintenance cost	.502				

Notes: Extraction method: maximum likelihood. Rotation method: Promax with Kaiser Normalization; KMO measure of sampling adequacy =.770; Bartlett test of sphericity (appr.chisquare=2014.720; df=190; sig=.000)

The ANOVA (Table 6) shows an F value of 9.802 (p<0.5) indicating that on the overall the extracted factors significantly affect the dependent variable. In regression analysis, the collinearity statistics determine the levels of correlations among the factors, since one purpose of the study is to estimate the contributions of individual predictors to the model. The result shows a good tolerance level (>0.2) and variance inflation factor (VIF) (< 5) for all predictors.

The t-values (Table 7) indicate that system quality, information quality and software support have statistically significant influence on the selection of a given ERP software ($t \geq |2|$). Service quality affects the decision to select a given ERP software, but not to a statistically significant extent. Of all the organizational variables, only *size of firm* tends to affect the cognitive response and eventually influencing the decision to select a given ERP software. Thus H[1], H[2], H[4] and H[6] are

Table 5. Model summary

Model	R	R Square	Adjusted R Square	Std. Error of the Estimate
1	.359(a)	.129	.121	1.60060
2	.443(b)	.196	.181	1.54508
3	.485(c)	.235	.213	1.51478
4	.527(d)	.278	.249	1.47903

a Predictors: (Constant), System Quality
b Predictors: (Constant), System Quality, Information quality
c Predictors: (Constant), System Quality, Information quality, Software support
d Predictors: (Constant), System Quality, Information quality, Support quality, Size of firm

Table 6. ANOVA

Model		Sum of Squares	Df	Mean Square	F	Sig.
1	Regression	39.896	1	39.896	15.573	.000(a)
	Residual	269.002	105	2.562		
	Total	308.897	106			
2	Regression	60.619	2	30.310	12.696	.000(b)
	Residual	248.278	104	2.387		
	Total	308.897	106			
3	Regression	72.559	3	24.186	10.541	.000(c)
	Residual	236.338	103	2.295		
	Total	308.897	106			
4	Regression	85.770	4	21.443	9.802	.000(d)
	Residual	223.127	102	2.188		
	Total	308.897	106			

a Predictors: (Constant), System Quality
b Predictors: (Constant), System Quality, Information quality
c Predictors: (Constant), System Quality, Information quality, Support quality
d Predictors: (Constant), System Quality, Information quality, Support quality, Size of firm
e Dependent Variable: ErpUsage

supported, while H^3, H^5, and H^7 are not supported. The standardized beta coefficients show that system quality of the software exerts the highest significant influence ($\beta = 0.497$, $p = 0.000$) followed by the Information quality ($\beta = 0.425$, $p = 0.000$), software support ($\beta = 0.286$, $p = 0.006$) and size of firm ($\beta = 0.217$, $p = 0.016$).

Vendor Selection

Table 8 shows the descriptive statistics of the variables considered in vendor selection on a five point scale. Three key constructs examined are the buying center responsible for vendor selection, the information sources that are utilized in vendor selection and variables that influence the buying centre in vendor selection.

The results indicate that multi department committees (mean = 3.597, SD = 1.060) and the

Table 7. Regression statistics

Model		Unstandardized Coefficients		Standardized Coefficients	t	Sig.	Collinearity Statistics	
		B	Std. Error	β			Tolerance	VIF
1	(Constant)	2.972	.334		8.895	.000		
	System Quality	.727	.184	.359	3.946	.000	1.000	1.000
2	(Constant)	2.879	.324		8.886	.000		
	System Quality	.784	.179	.388	4.385	.000	.988	1.012
	Information quality	.466	.158	.261	2.946	.004	.988	1.012
3	(Constant)	2.701	.327		8.257	.000		
	System quality	.895	.182	.443	4.920	.000	.918	1.090
	Information quality	.673	.180	.376	3.745	.000	.737	1.357
	Support quality	.396	.173	.232	2.281	.025	.721	1.387
4	(Constant)	1.838	.475		3.870	.000		
	System quality	1.006	.183	.497	5.489	.000	.862	1.160
	Information quality	.760	.179	.425	4.246	.000	.708	1.412
	Support quality	.488	.173	.286	2.814	.006	.687	1.456
	Size of firm	.203	.082	.217	2.458	.016	.912	1.097

Table 8. Vendor selection

	Mean	Std. Deviation
Buying center responsible		
Managers and shareholders committee	2.9851	1.28502
Multi department staff committee	3.5970	1.05973
Information technology unit only	3.4925	1.21072
Information source		
Survey	3.3881	1.23036
Vendor reference	4.1791	.95228
Decision making committee	3.8358	1.02391
Adverts	4.0149	1.05159
Key considerations		
Expertise	3.4478	1.17142
Government standards	4.1194	.89650
Managerial interest	3.3433	1.36573
Popularity and Experience	3.7164	1.24080

IT department (mean = 3.493, SD = 1.211) are the major buying centers responsible for vendor selection. In terms of information source, vendor reference (mean = 4.179, SD = 0.953) and adverts (mean = 4.015, SD = 1.052) are major information sources, while government standards (mean = 4.119, SD = 0.897) and popularity/experience of vendors (mean = 3.716, SD = 1.241) are important considerations.

DISCUSSION, CONCLUSION AND LIMITATIONS

In this study, we extended the TAM (Davis *et al* 1989) by hybridizing it with the reformulated IS success model (Delone and McLean 2002) with an inclusion of the *support quality* construct. Four organizational constructs; firm size, industry type, buying center, and experience in software /ERP utilization were introduced from organizational buying behavior as variables which could affect the cognitive response and behavioral intention. The extension of the TAM had been previously applied in ERP adoption and implementation to include 'shared beliefs' (Amoako-Gyampah and Salam 2004, Ramayah and Lo 2007). Our study reveals that the system quality, information quality, and support quality significantly influence an organization's decision to purchase and utilize ERP software, while service quality does not impose any significant influence. The results are in line with the outcomes obtained by Hussein *et al.* (2007) and Dobson *et al.* (2007) in confirming system quality and information quality as key constructs that affect 'perceived usefulness' and motivation to adopt a given technology.

The system quality constructs utilized in the study include: innovations capability, implementation time, adaptability, ease of use, consistency, and efficiency. Organizations are interested in utilizing ERP to innovatively gain competitive advantage. Therefore, the ability of ERP to provide such advantage gives it an adoption edge (Molla and Bhalla 2006). Equally, complexity issues such as implementation time, adaptability, ease of use, and consistency are critical (Elbertsen *et al.* 2006) especially in an environment where business continuity is crucial during software transition. The quality of information processed and produced by the ERP is another determining factor in the selection process. Organizations adopt technology in order to increase organizational productivity (Ojedokun 2006), which could be enhanced by the software capability, ease of customization,

report generation ability, and purpose in terms of meeting organizational business processing needs. The importance of information quality in technology adoption has been recognized in (Hussein *et al.* 2007), while compatibility, system capability and purpose have been identified in (Verville and Helignten 2003, Kumar *et al.* 2003, Adelman *et al.* 2005). This study also identified *support quality* as an important factor in the selection process. Usually, organizations that are first time users of ERP are worried about the availability of technical expertise within the organization. A major assurance from the software vendor is the provision of after-sales support for the software. The positive influence of support variables on ERP software selection (especially in SMEs) is in consonance with the results obtained in (Shikapur 1997, Hecht 1997, Bernroider and Koch 2001, Adelman *et al.* 2005). Training is identified as a crucial support function by a vendor that could positively affect perceived ease of use, and consequent acceptance of an ERP software (Al-Gahtani and King 1999, Mirchandani and Motwani 2001, Amoako-Gyampah and Salam 2004). User training support is crucial in assisting the user understand the relationship between his job role and those of other people in the organization who utilize the ERP system (Kerimoglu *et al.* 2008). It is worth noting that ERP vendors that have elaborate support offices in the South African region have better patronage than those that have skeletal services. SAP, Microsoft, and Sage have well established presence in the South African region. This is reflected in the adoption of their products.

Firm size has been identified as being significant in the adoption and selection of ERP software. This is supported by the results obtained by (Bernroider and Koch 2001, Buonanno *et al.* 2005, Laukkanen *et al.* 2005, Elbertsen *et al.* 2006). Differences in managerial and technology leadership play a big role in this regard. According to Laukkanen *et al.* (2005), small companies experience more knowledge constraints than their larger counterparts in ERP adoption. Smaller firms see ERP from the perspective of complexity and cost, while larger firms view ERP from the perspective of 'need' to integrate information across the enterprise in real time in order to optimize decision making (McLaren 2006). Kostopoulos *et al.* (2004) identified lack of financial and human resources, highly centralized structure, and limited technical knowledge of personnel as negative influences on small and medium sized enterprises' (SMEs) ERP adoption process. Buonanno *et al.* (2005) argue that the decision process regarding adoption of ERP systems within smaller firms is affected by exogenous reasons rather than business-related factors. Our survey shows that larger firms utilize more popular, more complex, and more expensive ERPs such as SAP, while smaller firms choose less popular and cheaper software such as Navision and SYSPRO. Other organizational constructs (industry type, experience in software utilization, and buying center influence) do not significantly affect the choice of given ERP software.

The ERP selection committee needs to be appropriately constituted to ensure the inclusion of diverse stake-holders within the organization (Bernroider and Koch 2001). Participation of the people affected by the system, who also know the business processes leads to better decisions and a higher rate of acceptance later on (Guha et al. 1997, Willcocks and Sykes, 2000). From the study, it is clear that both the management and non-management staff participate in usage and selection process therefore having a good contribution from both sides. In most cases, either a multi-department staff committee or the IT department is responsible for vendor/ERP selection. While the use of IT department is encouraged, it is important that other user departments be adequately involved in the decision process, irrespective of their shallow technical knowledge in information systems. Vendor reference and advertisements have been found to be major sources of information in vendor selection. It is important to note that the Government of Botswana requires certain standards from certain organizations that deal directly with the government. One of such standards is the effective utilization of information technology in the storage, processing and transmission of data. Waarts and Everdingen (2005) found out that variables describing national culture and policies significantly explain variations in adoption decisions in addition to traditional micro and meso (industry related) variables. It is believed that government's vendor referencing may play a significant role in the choice of a given ERP by government agencies. Most of the organizations do not conduct intensive survey about the software due to time and resource demands of such surveys. However, a survey may be necessary in order to acquire software that appropriately supports organizational business processes.

The results of this study could provide organizations with valuable knowledge that could prompt them to make significant changes in the manner in which they currently proceed with the selection of any enterprise packaged software, which in turn could result in substantial savings in terms of economics (actual costs, time, and improved administrative procedures). It can serve as the basis for the development or amendment of a formal process policy for complex software selection process. It also provides ERP software developers and vendors with a good knowledge of organizational perspectives to ERP selection as a means of aligning their products and services to the needs of user organizations. Furthermore, this study may also provide some theoretically interesting issues upon which to base future research such as the possibility of a link between the selection process and the suitable software. This will help organizations determine the "cause and effect" relationship that the selection process has on the type of software. Some researchers have established the possibility of utilizing some mathematical models in the ERP selection process. Cebeci (2009) proposed the use of fuzzy-AHP system in the ERP selection process, while Karsak and Ozogul (2009) developed a selection model based on quality function deployment, fuzzy linear regression and zero-one goal programming. Though mathematical models might be lacking in the recognition of organizational peculiarities, they provide structured means of evaluating ERPs. An evaluation process that takes care of structured and unstructured elements in the decision process would be desirable.

Another possibility for this research might be to examine whether the concept of failures in ERP implementation is caused by users simply not utilizing the software correctly or it is from choosing the wrong software for their organization with the focus being on the correlation between final choice of ERP and success of its implementation. Organizations will also be able to identify the key people who need to be involved in the selection process. Kerimoglu *et al.* (2008) identified *technology* followed by *users* and *organization* in terms of capacity value in ERP adoption process.

Finally, this study has some limitations. While our model provides a basis of investigating the possibilities of unifying the TAM with IS success model, it has not been empirically defined to the extent of being generalized. Though we have not found any outcome that significantly deviates from results obtained in developed countries (E.g. Verville and Halingten 2002, Kostopoulos *et al.* 2004, Amoako-Guyampah and Salam 2004, Buonanno *et al.* 2005), we recognize that the data utilized for the study were collected from only one country, Botswana. Though Botswana is considered a nation with high level of IT utilization, it is still not adequate as a basis of drawing conclusions. There is need for cross country data with varying shapes of organizational structure and capabilities. The purpose of our study is to add to the literature on ERP adoption by looking at some dimensions not previously studied extensively, such as effects of information quality, support quality and vendor selection process on adoption and success of ERP implementation, especially in developing countries. Another purpose was to see how organizational buying marries with adoption and

IS success models. Though our model does not possess a very good fit, it is expected that a multi country data could increase the predictive ability of the model. Finally, the TAM is an individual level theory, while organizational buying is a firm level decision. This study extended the TAM as a basis of analysis at individual level based on the strong argument of organizational buying theory that the buying center consists of individuals whose individual opinions and attributes influence the overall buying decision.

REFERENCES

Adelman, S., Moss, L., & Rehm, C. (2005). What are some of the concerns we should be aware of in integrated planning? *DMReview.com*. Retrieved December 20, 2006 from http://www.dmreview.com/article_sub.cfm?articleId=1027080

Al-Gahtani, S., & King, M. (1999). Attitudes, satisfaction and usage: Factors contributing to each in the acceptance of information technology. *Behaviour & Information Technology*, *18*(4), 277–297. doi:10.1080/014492999119020

Amoako-Gyampah, K., & Salam, A. F. (2004). An extension of technology acceptance model in an ERP implementation environment. *Information & Management*, *41*, 731–745. doi:10.1016/j.im.2003.08.010

Atkinson, H. (1999). ERP software requires good planning. *Journal of Commerce*, *9*, 14.

Avshalom, A. (2000); A new approach to ERP customisation. Retrieved April 15, 2009 from www.erpfans.com/erpfans/eshbel.htm

Baki, B., & Caker, K. (2005). Determining the ERP package selecting criteria: The case of Turkish manufacturing companies. *Business Process Management Journal*, *11*(1), 75–86. doi:10.1108/14637150510578746

Behrens, S., Jamieson, K., Jones, D., & Cranston, M. (2005). Predicting system success using the technology acceptance model: A case study. *16ᵗʰ Australian Conference on information Systems*, Nov 9- Dec 2, Sydney

Bernroider, E., & Koch, S. (2001). ERP selection process in midsize and large organizations. *Business Process Management Journal, 7*(3), 251–257. doi:10.1108/14637150110392746

Bettman, R. J., Luce, M. F., & Payne, J. W. (1998). Constructive consumer choice process. *The Journal of Consumer Research, 25*, 187–217. doi:10.1086/209535

Bingi, P., Sharma, M. K., & Godla, J. (1999). Critical issues affecting an ERP implementation. *Information Systems Management, 16*(3), 7–15. doi:10.1201/1078/43197.16.3.19990601/31310.2

Brewer, G. (2000). On the road to successful ERP. *Instrumentation & Control Systems, 73*(5), 49–58.

Buonanno, G., Faverio, P., Pingi, F., Ravarini, A., Sciuto, D., & Tagliavini, M. (2005). Factors affecting ERP system adoption. *Journal of Enterprise Information Management, 18*(4), 384–426. doi:10.1108/17410390510609572

Cebeci, U. (2009). Fuzzy AHP-based Decision Support System for Selecting ERP Systems in Textile Industry by using balanced Scorecard. *Expert Systems with Applications, 36*, 8900–8909. doi:10.1016/j.eswa.2008.11.046

Choffray, J. M., & Lilien, G. L. (1980). Industrial market segmentation by the structure of the purchasing process. *Industrial Marketing Management, 9*, 331–342. doi:10.1016/0019-8501(80)90049-8

Chung, S. H., & Snyder, C. A. (1999). ERP Initiation: A Historical Perspective. In . *Proceedings of Americas Conference on Information Systems, 11*(3), 33–45.

Dawes, P. L., Lee, Y. D., & Dowling, G. R. (1998). Information control and influence in emergent buying centers. *Journal of Marketing, 62*, 55–68. doi:10.2307/1251743

Delone, W. H., & McLean, E. R. (2002). Information Systems success revisited. In *Proceedings of the 35ᵗʰ Hawaii international Conference on Systems Success* (pp. 238-249).

Dobson, P., Myles, J., & Jackson, P. (2007). Making case for critical realism: Examining the implementation of automated performance management systems. *Information Resources Management Journal, 20*(2), 138–152.

Eckhouse, J. (1999, January 25). ERP vendors plot a comeback. *Information Week, 718*, 126–128.

Elbertsen, L., Benders, J., & Nijssen, E. (2006). ERP use: exclusive or complemented? *Industrial Management & Data Systems, 106*(6), 811–824. doi:10.1108/02635570610671498

Esteves, J., & Pastor, J. (2001). Enterprise resource planning systems research: an annotated bibliography. *Communication of AIS, 7*(8), 51–52.

Ghingold, M., & Wilson, D. T. (1998). Buying center research and business marketing practice: meeting the challenge of dynamic marketing. *Journal of Business and Industrial Marketing, 13*(2), 96–108. doi:10.1108/08858629810213315

Guha, S., Grover, V., Kettinger, W. J., & Teng, J. T. C. (1997). Business process change and organizational performance: exploring an antecedent model. *Journal of Management Information Systems, 14*(1), 119–154.

Hecht, B. (1997). Choose the right ERP software. *Datamation, 43*(3), 56–58.

Hurbean, L. (2006). Factors Influencing ERP Projects Success in the Vendor Selection Process. Retrieved June 22, 2009 from http://papers.ssrn.com/sol3/papers.cfm?abstract_id=946746

Hussein, R., Karim, N. S. A., Mohamed, N., & Ahlan, A. R. (2007). The influence of organizational factors on information systems success in e-government agencies in Malaysia. *The Electronic Journal on Information Systems in Developing Countries*, *29*(1), 1–17.

Illa, X. B., Franch, X., & Pastor, J. A. (2000). Formalising ERP selection criteria. In *Proceedings of the 10th International Workshop on Software Specification and Design* (pp.115). IEEE Computer Society, Washington, DC, 5-7 November.

Jackson, D. W., Keith, J. F., & Burdick, R. R. (1984). Purchasing agents' perceptions of industrial buying center influence: a situational approach. *Journal of Marketing*, *48*, 75–83. doi:10.2307/1251512

Karsak, E. E., & Ozogul, C. O. (2009). An integrated decision making approach for ERP system selection. *Expert Systems with Applications*, *36*, 660–667. doi:10.1016/j.eswa.2007.09.016

Kauffman, R. G. (1996). Influences on organizational buying choice process: future research directions. *Journal of Business and Industrial Marketing*, *11*(3/4), 94–107. doi:10.1108/08858629610125496

Kerimoglu, O., Basoglu, N., & Daim, T. (2008). Organizational adoption of information technologies: Case of enterprise resource planning systems. *The Journal of High Technology Management Research*, *19*, 21–35. doi:10.1016/j. hitech.2008.06.002

Kostopoulos, K. C., Brachos, D. A., & Prastacos, G. P. (2004). Determining factors of ERP adoption: an indicative study in the Greek market. In *Proceedings of the IEEE Engineering Management Conference*, Oct 18-21 (pp. 287-291).

Kumar, K., & Hillegersberg, J. (2000). ERP experiences and evolution. *Communications of the ACM*, *43*(4), 23–26. doi:10.1145/332051.332063

Kumar, V., Maheshwari, B., & Kumar, U. (2003). An investigation of crucial management issues in ERP implementation: an empirical evidence from Canadian organizations. *Technovation*, *23*, 793–807. doi:10.1016/S0166-4972(02)00015-9

Laudon, K. C., & Laudon, J. P. (2007). *Essentials of Management Information Systems: Managing The Digital Firm* (6th Ed). NJ: Prentice Hall.

Laukkanen, S., Sarpola, S., & Hallikainen, P. (2005). ERP system adoption – Does the size matter? In *Proceedings of the 38ᵗʰ IEEE Annual Hawaii Conference on System Sciences*, Jan 03-06, 2005. Track 8 (pp. 1-9).

Lehmann, D. R., & O'Shaughnessy, J. (1982). Decision criteria used in buying different categories of products of products. *Journal of Purchasing and Materials Management*, *18*, 9–14.

Lotto, P. (2006). Befriending your ERP system. *Electrical Wholesaling*. Retrieved March 20, 2007 from http://www.infor.com/7343/14397/1 2565/23954/23965

Mabert, V. A., Soni, A., & Venkataramanan, M. A. (2001). Enterprise resource planning: common myths versus evolving reality. *Business Horizons*, *44*(3), 69–76. doi:10.1016/S0007-6813(01)80037-9

McLaren, T. (2006). Why has the adoption of ERPs by SMEs lagged that of larger firms? Retrieved August 5, 2007 from http://www.ryerson. ca/~tmclaren/erpsme.html

McQuiston, D. H. (1989). Novelty, complexity, and importance as critical determinants of industrial buyer behavior. *Journal of Marketing*, *53*, 66–79. doi:10.2307/1251414

Mirchandani, D., & Motwani, J. (2001). End-user perceptions of ERP systems: A case study of an international automotive supplier. *International Journal of Automotive Technology and Management*, *1*(4), 416–420. doi:10.1504/ IJATM.2001.000049

Molla, A., & Bhalla, A. (2006). ERP and competitive advantage in developing countries: The case of an Asian company. *The Electronic Journal on Information Systems in Developing Countries*, *24*(1), 1–19.

Neves, D., Fenn, D., & Sulcas, P. (2004). Selction of Enterprise Resource Planning (ERP) Systems . *South African Journal of Business Management*, *35*(1), 45–52.

O'Brien, J. A., & Marakas, G. M. (2007). *Enterprise Information Systems* (13th ed). Boston: McGraw-Hill International.

Ojedokim, A. A. (2006). *The Impact of Computerization on Productivity in Botswana: A case study of two state corporations*. PhD thesis, Department of Library and Information Studies, University of Botswana.

Poon, P., & Wagner, C. (2001). Critical Success Factors Revisited: Success and Failure Cases of Information Systems for Senior Executives . *Decision Support Systems*, *30*(3), 393–418. doi:10.1016/S0167-9236(00)00069-5

Ramayah, T., & Lo, M.-C. (2007). Impact of shared beliefs on "perceived usefulness" and "ease of use" in the implementation of an enterprise resource planning system. *Management Research News*, *30*(6), 420–431. doi:10.1108/01409170710751917

Rao, S. S. (2000). Enterprise resource planning: business needs and technologies. *Internet and Data Systems*, *100*(2), 81–88. doi:10.1108/02635570010286078

Relevant Business Systems (n.d); The ERP selection process survival guide (2nd ed.). Retrieved February 20, 2007 from http://www.relevant.com/pdf/articles/ERPguide.pdf

Schaik, P. V., Flynn, D., Wersch, A. V., Douglas, A., & Cann, P. (2004). The acceptance of a computerized decision support system in primary care: a preliminary investigation. *Behaviour & Information Technology*, *23*(5), 321–326. doi:10.1080/0144929041000669941

Shainesh, G. (2004). Understanding buyer behavior in software services – strategies for Indian firms. *International Journal of Technology Management*, *28*(1), 118–127. doi:10.1504/IJTM.2004.005056

Shainesh, G. (2004). Understanding Buyer Behavior in Software Services – Strategies for Indian Firms. *International Journal of Technology Management*, *28*(1), 118–127. doi:10.1504/IJTM.2004.005056

Shaw, J., Giglierano, J., & Kallis, J. (1989). Marketing complex technical products: The importance of intangible attributes. *Industrial Marketing Management*, *37*, 50–56.

Sheth, J. N. (1996). Organizational buying behavior: past performance and future expectations. *Journal of Business and Industrial Marketing*, *11*(3/4), 7–24. doi:10.1108/08858629610125441

Shikarpur, D. (1997). The dilemma of buying ERP. *Dataquest India*. Retrieved January 15, 2007 from www.dqindia.com/oct159/3ij1141101.html

Somers, T. M., & Nelson, K. (2001). The impact of critical success factors across the stages of enterprise resource planning implementation. In *Proceedings of the 34th Hawaii international Conference of System Sciences*, Mavis Hawaii, January 3-6, 2001(CD-ROM)

Sproule, S., & Archer, N. (2000). A buyer behavior framework for the development and design of software agents in e-commerce. *Electronic Marketing Applications and Policy*, *10*(5), 396–405.

Stephenson, S. V., & Sage, A. P. (2007). Information and knowledge specifications in systems engineering and management for innovation and productivity through enterprise resource planning. *Information Resources Management Journal*, *20*(2), 44–73.

Themistocleous, M., Irani, Z., & O'Keefe, R. (2001). ERP and application integration: exploratory survey. *Business Process Management Journal*, *7*(3), 195–204. doi:10.1108/14637150110392656

Toure, H. I. (2007). Competitiveness and Information and Communication Technologies (ICTs) in Africa. *World Economic Forum*. Retrieved July 21, 2007 from http://www.weforum.org/pdf/gcr/africa/1.5.pdf

Umble, E. J., Haft, R. R., & Umble, M. M. (2003). Enterprise resource planning: implementation procedures and critical success factors. *European Journal of Operational Research*, *146*, 241–257. doi:10.1016/S0377-2217(02)00547-7

Verville, J., Bernades, C., & Halingten, A. (2005). So you're buying an ERP? Ten critical factors for successful acquisitions. *Journal of Enterprise Information Management*, *18*(60), 665–677. doi:10.1108/17410390510628373

Verville, J., & Halingten, A. (2003). A six-stage model of the buying process of ERP software. *Industrial Marketing Management*, *32*, 585–594. doi:10.1016/S0019-8501(03)00007-5

Ward, S., & Webster, F. E. (1991). Organizational buying behavior. In T.S. Robertson, & H.H. Kassarjian (Eds), *Handbook of Consumer Behavior* (pp. 419-458). Englewood Cliffs, NJ: Prentice Hall.

Webster, F. E., & Wind, Y. (1972). A general model for understanding organizational buying behavior. *Journal of Marketing*, *36*(2), 12–19. doi:10.2307/1250972

Willcocks, L. P., & Sykes, R. (2000). The role of the CIO and IT function in ERP. *Communications of the ACM*, *43*(4), 32–38. doi:10.1145/332051.332065

Chapter 8
A SOA–Based Approach to Integrate Enterprise Systems

Anne Lämmer
University of Potsdam, Germany

Sandy Eggert
University of Potsdam, Germany

Norbert Gronau
University of Potsdam, Germany

ABSTRACT

This chapter presents a procedure for the integration of enterprise systems. Therefore enterprise systems are being transferred into a service oriented architecture. The procedure model starts with decomposition into Web services. This is followed by mapping redundant functions and assigning of the original source code to the Web services, which are orchestrated in the final step. Finally, an example is given how to integrate an Enterprise Resource Planning System with an Enterprise Content Management System using the proposed procedure model.

INTRODUCTION

Enterprise resource planning systems (ERP systems) are enterprise information systems designed to support business processes. They partially or completely include functions such as order processing, purchasing, production scheduling, dispatching, financial accounting and controlling (Monk et. al., 2005). ERP systems are the backbone of information management in many industrial and commercial enterprises and focus on the management of master and transaction data (Sumner 2005). Besides ERP

systems, Enterprise Content Management Systems (ECM systems) have also developed into companywide application systems over the last few years. ECM solutions focus on indexing all information within an enterprise (Rockley, 2003). They cover the processes of enterprise-wide content collection, creation, editing, managing, dispensing and use, in order to improve enterprise and cooperation processes (CMS Watch, 2009). In order to manage information independently, ECM combines technologies such as document management, digital archiving, content management, workflow management, etc. The use of ECM systems is constantly on the rise (Lämmer et. al 2008). This leads to an increasing motivation

DOI: 10.4018/978-1-60566-968-7.ch008

for enterprises to integrate the ECM systems within the existing ERP systems, especially when considering growing international competition. The need for integration is also eminently based on economical aspects, such as the expense factor in system run time (Aier & Schönherr, 2006). For a cross-system improvement of business processes, enterprise systems have to be integrated.

RELATED WORK

Service Oriented Architecture as an Integration Approach

A number of integration approaches and concepts already exist. They can be differentiated by integration level (for example data, functions or process integration) and integration architecture (for example point-to-point, hub & spoke, SOA) (Aier & Schönherr, 2006). This paper presents an approach to integrating enterprise systems by way of building up service oriented architectures. This integration approach is of special interest and will be described in more detail.

The concept of service orientation is currently being intensively discussed. It can be differentiated from component orientation by its composition and index service (repository). Additionally, SOA is suitable for a process oriented, distributed integration (Aier & Schönherr, 2006). However, the addressed goals of component orientation and SOA are similar: different enterprise systems are connected through one interface, and a cross-system data transfer and the re-usage of objects or components is enabled. Thereby a service represents a well defined function which is generated in reaction to an electronic request (Burbeck, 2000). The SOA approach offers a relatively easy way to connect, add and exchange single services, which highly simplifies the integration of similar systems (e.g. enterprise take-over). Moreover, SOA offers a high degree of interoperability and modularity, which increases the adaptability of

enterprise systems (Andresen et. al., 2008), (Lämmer et.al. 2008).

The SOA approach is based on the concept of service. The sender wants to use a service and in doing so he wants to achieve a specific result. Thereby the sender is not interested in how the request is processed or which further requests are necessary. This is the idea of SOA, where services are defined in a specific language and referenced in a service index. Service request and data exchange occur via use of pre-defined protocols (Erl, 2008), (Papazoglou, 2007).

This service orientation can be used on different levels of architecture. The grid architecture is a common example of infrastructure level (Bermann et. al., 2003), (Bry et. al., 2004). On the application level an implementation usually takes place in terms of web services.

The use of web services offers the possibility of re-using raw source code, which is merely transferred to another environment (Sneed, 2000). The benefit of this transfer is the re-usage of perfected (old) algorithms. The main disadvantage is the necessity of revising the raw source code in order to find possible dependencies (Sneed, 2000). This is also true for enterprise systems. It isn't efficient to re-use the entire old system, but rather only significant parts of it. To accomplish this it is necessary to deconstruct the old enterprise system and to locate the source code parts which can effectively be re-used. Our approach uses self-diagnosis for finding these source code locations. This analysis will be considered in the third integration step.

Self-Diagnosis

As just described, our approach uses self-diagnosis for location of useful source code. For this, the method of self-diagnosis will be presented and the differences to other approaches will be shown.

Some approaches for transformation of legacy-systems into a SOA exist already. However, these approaches see the whole system as one service.

The system gets a service description for using this service in a SOA. Our approach differs in that it deconstructs the system for a tailored need. For this, the method of self-diagnosis is used.

Self-diagnosis can be defined as a system's capacity to assign a specific diagnosis to a detected symptom. The detection of symptoms and assignment are performed by the system itself without any outside influence (Latif-Shabgahi et. al., 1999). The mechanism of self-diagnosis has been detected surveying natural systems; it can partly be applied to artificial systems as well.

Self-diagnosis can be seen as an integral part of all self-organising systems. Self-organisation is a generic term for self-x-capabilities also called self-ware. Self-organisation should lead information systems to become self-healing, self-protecting, self-optimizing and self-configuring (Hinchey et. al., 2006), (Garnek, 2007). For reaching these aims, the system has to possess abilities of self-detection or self-diagnosis. Sensors to detect contextual and the environmental changes as well as a monitor for continuous analysis should be a central part of a self-organizing information system and create the basis for the following:

- For self-configuration the possibilities and needs of configuration must be recognized.

- For self-healing the symptoms of an infection must be identified.
- For a self-optimization it is necessary to search for new calculations, algorithms and solution space or process chains.
- The self-protection needs detectors for identification of attacks.

Figure 1 shows a systematization of self-ware.

Beyond this, self-diagnosis can be seen as an integral part of all self-organising systems. Because of the necessity to achieve all aims of self-organising systems, self-diagnosis has to be subordinated to self-management.

Today some approaches for self-diagnosis in computer systems already exist i.e. fault detection in networking communication, or in storage and processor (Sun, 2004). Self-diagnosis also works in infrastructure and load sharing for performance (Mos, Murphy, 2001). In this article a proposal for the implementation of self-diagnosis of enterprise application systems and particularly in the application layer of information systems is presented without using case based reasoning or multi agent systems.

The first step of self-diagnosis is the detection of symptoms. Usually the detection of one existing symptom is not sufficient to make an indisputable diagnosis. In this case, more information and data

Figure 1. Systematization of selfware

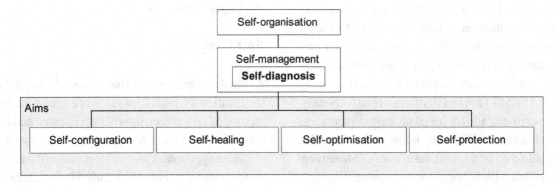

have to be gathered. This can be described as symptom collection. In a second step the symptoms are assigned to a specific diagnosis. Depending on the diagnosis, corresponding measures can be taken (Horling et. al., 2001).

Symptoms are a very abstract part of self-diagnosis. These symptoms can be a high network load in distributed systems, missing signals, or buffer overload of the hardware layer. For enterprise systems the symptoms can be e.g. the frequency of usage of user interface elements by the user, dependencies of code parts or components. Other types of symptoms are possible. In general, the answer to questions concerning the measure of interesting items provides hints for possible symptoms.

Differentiation of Collection

Self-diagnosis can be categorized by symptom acquisition method. Active and passive self-diagnosis must also be distinguished. In this context, the program or source code is the crucial factor for a division between active and passive self-diagnosis. A fundamental basis for either alternative is an observer or monitor.

Using passive self-diagnosis, the monitor detects and collects symptoms and information. It can either be activated automatically or manually (Satzger et. al., 2007). If you know which items need to be observed and the point where this information can be gathered, you only have to monitor this point. This is what passive self-diagnosis does. For example: if you want to know how often a button is pressed, you have to find where the button-event is implemented in the code and observe this button-event.

In active self-diagnosis, the program's function or modules are the active elements. They send defined information to the monitor and act independently if necessary. The monitor is used as receiver and interprets the gathered information and symptoms. The main advantage of active self-diagnosis is the possibility of detecting new symptoms, even if no clear diagnosis can be made before the problems become acute and are forwarded to other systems. In contrast, using passive self-diagnosis, the monitor can only inquire about specific data. In this case, a response or further examination is only possible if the problem is already known. For example: if you don't know the location of all the buttons and or the code component for the button-event, you will have to recognise all events with their initial point and filter them with the monitor. The monitor doesn't have to know how many buttons exist or where their code is located, but the buttons have to "know" to register with the monitor. These are the requirements of active self-diagnosis.

Figure 2. Kinds of acquisition of symptoms for self-diagnosis; a) passive; b) active

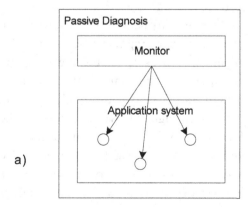

The assembly of diagnosis points depends on application context and software system. The required time and effort cannot be specified; it depends on the design and implementation of the software system.

Self-diagnosis can also be employed for the examination of source-code usage and interdependences. Depending on the desired information, different points of diagnosis have to be integrated into the source-code.

Different points of diagnosis have to be determined in order to allow for the allocation of code parts to various fields and functions. Therefore context, programming language, and software system architecture must be considered.

Differentiation of Layers

Self-diagnosis can be employed for the examination of source code usage and interdependences. According to the desired information different markers have to be integrated into the source-code.

Depending on the desired outcome, source code usage and interdependences could be objects of an analysis.

Three layers can be distinguished: (1) source code layer, (2) component layer and (3) application layer.

For self-diagnosis of the source code layer the markers have to be integrated into the functions or methods. This offers a very specific analysis of the system's bottom, but this is connected with heavy efforts and a deep knowledge about the programming of the system.

Self-diagnosis of the component layer integrates the markers into functional combined code fragments of the components of the information system. The amount of markers is getting smaller accordingly. This implementation is important for the usage of dependencies (detection of causality) about the different components of the system.

The third layer is the application layer. Thereby one marker is used for one application. Usage for this implementation is mainly the surveying of enterprise application landscapes.

Differentiation of Patterns

For self-diagnosis, data are transmitted to a monitor either from the code or the application. Depending on the purpose, patterns can be identified which refer to the frequency (frequency pattern) or markers reporting the dependencies of code fragments (causality pattern).

The frequency pattern provides information about the usage of parts of an application and allows drawing conclusions on user as well as the temporal details. The monitor does not view the content of the message. It counts the frequency of a message and saves the corresponding metadata, e.g. invoking user or instant of the request for information. The application context of the frequency pattern is particularly interesting. In order to supervise the use of code, frequency patterns could be used. By using frequency pattern it is easily possible to analyze the exact usage of certain functions on the code layer. This analysis could be used for maintenance. The maintenance overhead increases at the increasing complexity of operational standard software at any function which was taken over in the standard. In run time it is usually unknown which functions are really used. By detecting the use of frequencies in the runtime a slim down of the software system can be carried out to make sure that the maintenance overhead is done only for the functions which also are needed.

The causality pattern shows the dependencies of certain code fragments between each other. Again, the focus is on the metadata, like for example users and time. Unlike the frequency pattern, the causality pattern collects information of the code fragment invoked before and the code fragment to be invoked. For this the monitor must be able to determine and to save the predecessor and the successor of every message. By analyzing this, dependencies about the code fragments are possible. The causality pattern is particularly important for the examination of a system for the connection to the business process or to the encapsulation of code fragments. An application scenario for the causality pattern at the component layer is found in the area of the system integration. Here the dependencies of the individual components between each other are important for the isolation or reprocess of components and to wrap these into a web service (Sneed, 2000).

The context pattern examines not only the metadata but recognizes messages belonging together. This is a semantic evaluation of the messages. In this case, the cost for developing the monitor is much higher than within the other two detection models. This is due to the fact that messages might have a different wording and be written in different languages.

Our approach uses this method to locate code parts that can be collected into components. As we will demonstrate later in this article, we need to locate functions and enterprise systems business objects.

This method can be used for the detection of code parts which are possible services. Diagnosis points must thereby be integrated into the system source code, and software dependencies analysed.

As discussed earlier the main challenges in integration of legacy enterprise systems like ERP and ECM are, first, the deconstruction and second, the allocation of code. To address these challenges, we have developed a procedure model which will be described next.

PROCEDURE MODEL

In the following, a procedure model that integrates general application systems within a company is presented. The procedure model begins with the deconstruction of systems into web services. This is followed by a mapping of redundant functions and the assignment of original source code to web services, which is orchestrated in the last step.

The process includes taking the old ERP system; deconstructing it into different abstraction levels such as functional entities or business objects, searching for redundant entities, allocating the code fragments dependent on these functional entities, and encapsulating them. This results in many independent functional entities, which can be described as a service. They have different abstraction levels and have to compose and orchestrate with, e.g. BPEL-WS. This composition and orchestration is the way of integration.

Deconstruction of Systems

First, the systems which are to be integrated are deconstructed into services. The challenge of this step depends on the number of particular services, which could span the range from one single service per system, up to a definition of every single method or function within a system as a service. In the case of a very broad definition, the advantages, such as easy maintenance and reuse etc., will be lost. In case of a very narrow definition, disadvantages concerning performance and orchestration develop; the configuration and interdependencies of the services become too complex.

This paper proposes a hierarchical approach which describes services of different granular qualities on three hierarchical levels. *Areas of function* of a system are described as the first of these levels (figure 3, part 1). For example, an area of functions could include purchase or sales in case of ERP systems and, in the case of ECM systems, archiving or content management. An area of function can be determined on the abstract level by posing questions about the general "assigned task" of the system. The differences between the three hierarchical levels can be discovered by answering the following questions:

Figure 3. Procedure model for the integration of application systems

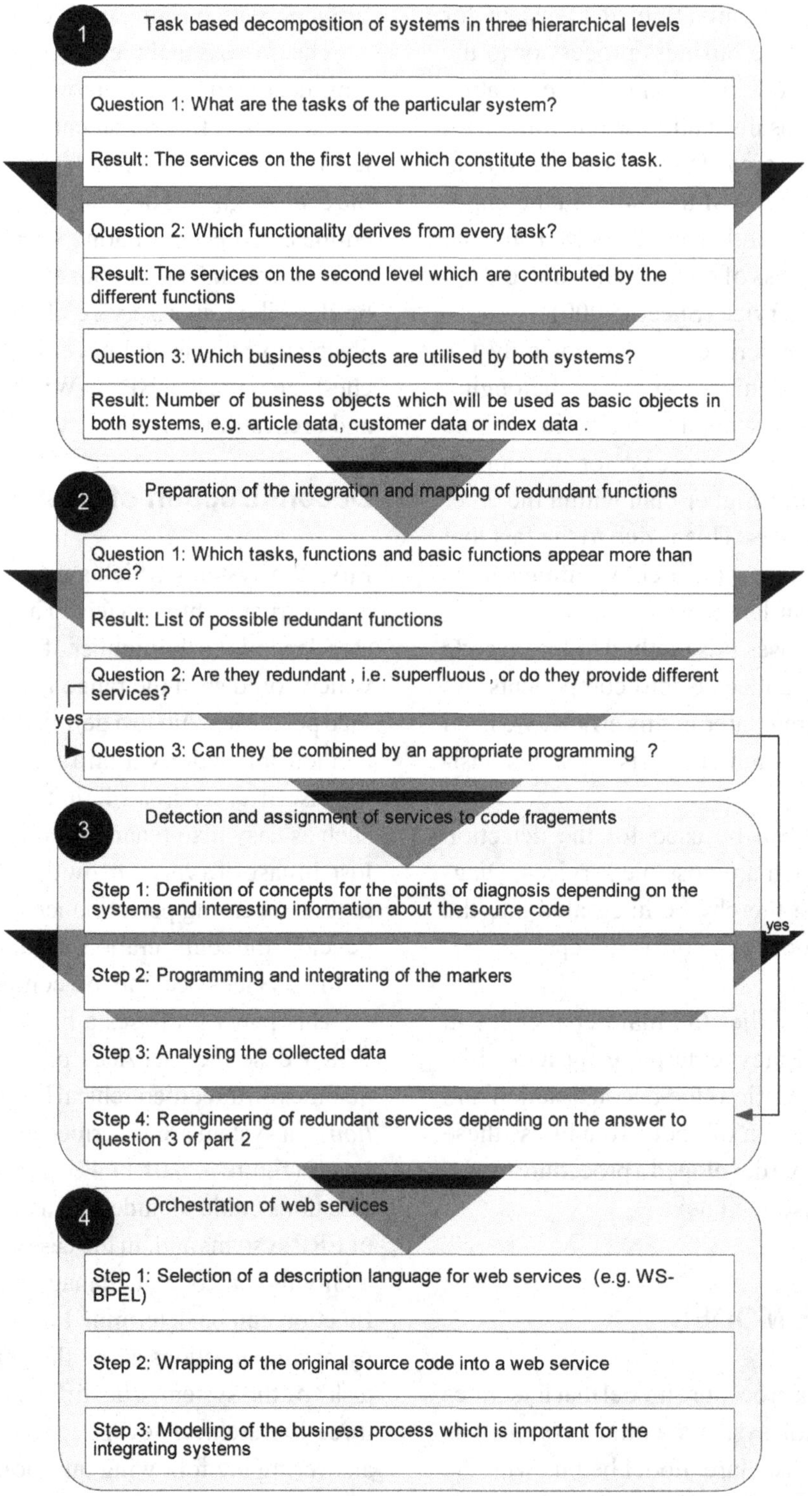

1   Task based decomposition of systems in three hierarchical levels

Question 1: What are the tasks of the particular system?

Result: The services on the first level which constitute the basic task.

Question 2: Which functionality derives from every task?

Result: The services on the second level which are contributed by the different functions

Question 3: Which business objects are utilised by both systems?

Result: Number of business objects which will be used as basic objects in both systems, e.g. article data, customer data or index data .

2   Preparation of the integration and mapping of redundant functions

Question 1: Which tasks, functions and basic functions appear more than once?

Result: List of possible redundant functions

Question 2: Are they redundant , i.e. superfluous , or do they provide different services?

yes

Question 3: Can they be combined by an appropriate programming ?

3   Detection and assignment of services to code fragments

Step 1: Definition of concepts for the points of diagnosis depending on the systems and interesting information about the source code

yes

Step 2: Programming and integrating of the markers

Step 3: Analysing the collected data

Step 4: Reengineering of redundant services depending on the answer to question 3 of part 2

4   Orchestration of web services

Step 1: Selection of a description language for web services (e.g. WS-BPEL)

Step 2: Wrapping of the original source code into a web service

Step 3: Modelling of the business process which is important for the integrating systems

1. **Question:** What are the tasks of the particular system? The answers resulting from this step correspond to services on the first level, which constitute the general task. For example Sales, purchase, inventory management or workflow management, archiving and content management. These tasks are abstract and describe main functionalities. They consist of many other functions which are the objects of the next level.
2. **Question:** Which functionality derives from every single task? The answers to this question correspond to the services on the second level that are contributed by the various functions. These functions are more detailed than the general tasks. They describe what the tasks consist of and what they do, for example: calculate the delivery time, identify a major customer, or constitute check-in and E-Mail functionalities. For these functions the application needs data, which can found in the third level.
3. **Question:** Which business objects are utilised by both systems? This answer constitutes the number of business objects that will be used as basic objects in both systems, e.g. article data, customer data or index data.

In this procedure model, all possible levels of service deconstruction are addressed; yet the realisation on all hierarchical levels constitutes an individual task.

The result of this step is a 3-stage model displaying the services of an application. The data-level, i.e. the integration of databases, is not further examined at this point since it is not an integral part of our model, the aim of which is to wrap functions as web services without altering them or the original source code. The data level is not touched by this process.

Preparation and Mapping

The main advantage of web service architecture is the high degree of possible reuse. By division into three hierarchical levels, a detection of similar functions is made possible, especially on the level of functionality and business objects. In some cases an adjustment of the functions is necessary in order to serve different contexts of use. Therefore, the next step consists of integration on different levels and the mapping of identical functions (figure 3, part 2). This step poses the following questions:

1. **Question:** Which tasks, functions and business objects appear more than once? For example: most applications contain search functions, some applications have functions for check in and check out, ERP systems calculate the time for many things with the same algorithm under different names.
2. **Question:** Are these multiple functions and objects redundant, i.e. superfluous, or do they provide different services? Some functions may have the same name, but perform different tasks.
3. **Question:** Can these multiple functions and objects be combined by way of appropriate programming? For the functions ascertained in question 2 to be similar functions with different names, the possibility of integrating them into one has to be analysed.

The advantage of this mapping is the detection of identical functions, which may by only named differently while completing the same task. In doing so, the benefit of reuse can be exploited to a high degree. Additionally, this part of the survey allows for a minimisation of programming, due to encapsulation of multiple functions. Only those functions which share a high number of similarities, but nevertheless complete different tasks, have to be programmed differently; they can be merged by reprogramming.

It is important to note that this part the deconstruction consists of an abstract level and in the functional view. In the following step, this will change: from a functional view to a code view.

Detection and Assignment of Services to Code Fragments

The next step brings the biggest challenge, namely the transformation of existing applications into service oriented architecture. Until now, services have been identified by their tasks, but the correlation to existing source code still needs to be done. This is going to be accomplished in the next step (figure 3, part 3).

Self-diagnosis is used at this point to integrate earlier defined points of diagnosis into the source code. These points of diagnosis actively collect usage data and facilitate conclusions concerning the fields and functions via their structure. The structure of the points of diagnosis depends on the context of their application and on the software system. It is not possible to describe the complexity of the process, which also depends on the structure and programming of the software systems.

As we discussed earlier in section 2.2, the points of diagnosis depend on what needs to be observed. Here we want to know which code fragments share correspondences and execute the identified functions in the functional view. From this follows the necessity of a monitor. For example, the points can be every method call in the source code of an ERP system. If the user calls a function, the points of diagnosis have to inform the monitor that they were called. The monitor has to recognise and to analyse which method calls belong together.

Now the code fragments are analysed and assigned to the functions identified in part 1, and the wrapping of code fragments into web services can be started. This step necessitates the usage of the existing source code and the description

of relevant parts with a web service description language, making possible the reuse of source code in service oriented architecture.

If redundant services have been detected in part two which need to be reengineered, then the reengineering happens now.

Orchestration of Web Services

The results of stage three are the described web services. These have to be connected with each other depending on the business process. This orchestration takes place in several steps (figure 3, part 4).

First, the context must be defined; second, the service description language has to be selected; and third, the web services need to be combined.

A four-stage procedure model for a service oriented integration of application systems has just been described. This process holds the advantages of a step-by-step transformation. The amount of time needed for this realisation is considerably higher than in a "big bang" transformation, however, a "big bang" transformation holds a higher risk and therefore requires high-quality preparation measures. For this reason, a "big bang" transformation is dismissed, in favour of a step-by-step transformation.

There is yet another important advantage in the integration or deconstruction of application systems into services, when carried out in several steps. First, a basic structure is built (construction of a repository, etc.). Next, a granular decomposition into web services occurs on the first level, thereby realising a basic transformation of a service oriented concept. Following this, web services of the second and third hierarchical level can be integrated step-by-step. This reduction into services provides high quality integration.

The procedure model we just presented is very abstract. Therefore, a practical example for two enterprise systems, ERP and ECM, will be given in part 4.

EXAMPLE OF APPLICATION

It is necessary to develop a general usage approach and to test it on ERP and ECM systems, since no concrete scenario of these technologies in regard to praxis as of yet exists (Gronau, 2003). The aim of this example of use is to describe the integration of both company-wide systems, ERP and ECM, using our presented approach.

In what follows, we present a case study of a situation of integration of two systems: an ERP and an ECM system. A German manufacturer of engines and devices administrate a complex IT landscape. This IT landscape includes, among others, two big enterprise systems. One of them is the ERP system "Microsoft Dynamics NAV" and the other is the ECM system "OS.5|ECM" of Optimal Systems. The ERP System includes modules such as purchase, sales and article management. The ECM system consists of modules such as document management, archiving and workflow management. In the current situation

a bi-directional interface between both systems exists. One example for a business process in which both systems are used is the processing of incoming mails and documents. In order to scan and save the incoming invoices of suppliers, the module of the ECM System "document management" is used. The access to the invoice is made possible through the ERP system.

In the future, a SOA-based integration of both enterprise systems can be reasonably expected under the aspect of business process improvement. Referring to the example mentioned above, the "portal management" component could be used to access, search, and check-in all incoming documents. What now follows is a description, in four parts, of the integration based on the procedure model we presented in part 3.

Figure 4. Segmentation of services

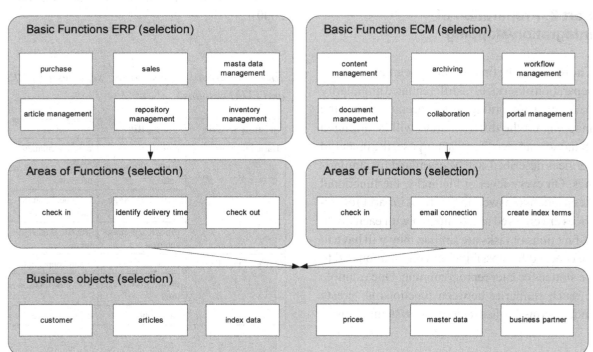

Part 1: Segmentation of ERP and ECM Systems into Services

According to the procedure model (figure 3), the individual systems will be separated into independent software objects, which in each case complete specified functions or constitute business objects. The segmentation is structured in three bottom-up steps (figure 4).

Identification is based on the answers to questions concerning main tasks of specific systems. The basic functions of an ERP system are purchase, sales, master data management, article management und repository management. Document management, content management, records management, workflow management and portal management are basic functions of ECM systems. Subsequently, the areas of functions are disaggregated into separate tasks. Business objects are classified such as the business object "article" or "customer". Thus, segmentation in areas of functions, tasks of functions and business objects is achieved and a basis for the re-usage of services is created.

Part 2: Preparation of Integration/Mapping

The results of the first step of the segmentation are separation of services of differentiated granularity per system. According to the procedure model, the mapping on the different areas will be arranged in the second step. For that purpose, the potential services described will be examined for similarities. On every level of hierarchy, the functional descriptions (answers to questions in part 1) of services are checked and compared with each other. If functions or tasks are similar, they will have to be checked for possibility of combination and to be slotted for later reprogramming. One example of such similarity between functions is "create index terms". Most enterprise systems include the function "create index terms" for documents such as invoices or new articles. The estimation of analogy of different functions, particularly in enterprise systems where implementation is different, lies in the expertise of the developer. Another example is the service "check in/check out". This service is a basic function of both ERP and ECM systems and is now to be examined for possible redundancy. After determining that the services "check in" or "check out" are equal, the service will be registered as a basic function only once. Services which are not equal but related will be checked in another step and either unified with suitable programming or, if possible, spilt into different services. The results of this step are the classification of services from ERP and ECM systems into similar areas and the separation of redundant services. The following table shows examples of separated services.

By this separation of both enterprise systems, a higher degree of re-usage and improved complexity-handling of these systems is achieved. For the application of services, a service-oriented architecture (SOA) which defines the different roles of participants is now required (Burbeck, 2000).

Table 1. Examples of separate services of ERP and ECM systems

Separate services	ERP	ECM
Basic Functions	Purchase	content management
	Sales	archiving
	article management	document management
	repository management	workflow management
Areas of Functions	check in	email connection
	identify delivery time	save document
	check out	create index terms

Part 3: Detection and Assignment of Services to Code Fragments

As already described in the general introduction, the identification of functions to be segmented in the source code constitutes one of the biggest challenges in a transfer to service-oriented architecture. As part of this approach, the method of self diagnosis is suggested. Appropriate points of diagnosis will be linked to the source code in order to draw conclusions from used functions to associated class, method or function in the original source code. Through the use of aspect oriented programming, aspects can be programmed and linked to the classes and methods of the application system. Necessary data, such as the name of the accessed method, can be collected by accessing the respective classes and methods (Vanderperren et. al., 2005).

Based on a defined service, "order transaction", all names of methods which are necessary for the execution of "order transaction", must be identified. To wrap the service "order transaction", i.e. to combine it with a web service description language, the original methods need be searched for and encapsulated. Additionally, the reprogramming of redundant functions is part of the phase of identification and isolation of services. This, as well, is only possible if the original methods are identified.

Part 4: Orchestration of Web Services

The last integration phase is used to compile web services. The previous steps had to be completed in preparation for the procedure model. The web services now are completely described and have an URI to be accessed. Now, only the composition and the chronology of requests of the specific web services are missing. For the orchestration the web service business process execution language (WS-BPEL) is recommended. The WS-BPEL was developed by the OASIS-Group and is currently in the process of standardisation (Cover, 2005). If the web services present a function with a business process, the WS-BPEL is particularly suitable for orchestration of web services (Lübke et. al., 2006). Essentially, BPEL is a language to compose (Leymann & Roller 2000) new web services from existing web services with help of workflow technologies (Leymann, 2003). In BPEL, a process is defined which is started by a workflow system in order to start a business process.

Web services are addressed via a graphical representation with a modelling imagery of WS-BPEL. The business process is modelled independently from the original enterprise systems. Since in the first integration step, the systems were separated by their tasks and functions, now all of the functions are available for the business process as well.

CONCLUSION

Critical Consideration

The procedure model for the integration of application systems as it has been presented in this paper is an approach that has been successfully deployed in one case. Currently the assignment ability and the universality are being tested. The self-diagnosis, i.e. the assignment of source code to services via aspect oriented programming, constitutes a bigger challenge.

A verification of costs and benefit cannot be given sufficiently; however, several examples show convincing results and suggest a general transferability. The complexity in such a realisation cannot be specified. Particularly for bigger and complex systems, the cost to benefit ratio has to be verified. Despite this, it must be recognised that the assignment of code fragments to functions is not an easy task. If one observes every method call, a high number of calls must be analysed. Visualisation can be helpful for analysing, since method calls belonging together will build a cluster in the emerging network. The observation of method calls is possibly not the most optimal way for very complex systems. If the functional view of services in part 1 is not part of the business object layer, but only of the general task layer, one can reduce the numbers of diagnosis points. The possibilities depend on the programming language and their constructs.

Resume

The approach presented above describes a procedure model for service oriented integration of different application systems. The integration proceeds using web services which thereby improve the integration ability, interoperability, flexibility, and sustainability. The reusable web services facilitate the extraction of several functions and combination of these into a new service. This allows for reuse of several software components.

Altogether, Web services improve the adaptability of software systems to the business processes and increase efficiency (Gronau, 2003). To give an example of the realisation of the procedure model, an integration of an ERP- and ECM-system was chosen. The reasons for this choice consist in targeted improvement of business aspects and increasing complexity of both application systems. Dealing with this complexity makes integration necessary. Through mapping, redundant functions can be detected and as a consequence, a reduction of the complexity is made possible. Regarding the adaptability and flexibility of affected application systems, web services are a suitable approach for integration. In particular, it is the reuse of services and an adaptable infrastructure which facilitate the integration.

In addition to all of this, we expect to discover additional advantages concerning maintenance and administration of affected application systems.

REFERENCES

Aier, S., & Schönherr, M. (2006). Evaluating integration architectures – A scenario-based evaluation of integration technologies. In D. Draheim, & G. Weber (Eds.), *Trends in enterprise application architecture, revised selected papers* (LNCS 3888, pp. 2-14).

Andresen, K., Levina, O., & Gronau, N. (2008). *Design of the evolutionary process model for adaptable software development processes*. Paper presented at the European and Mediterranean Conference on Information Systems 2008 (EM-CIS2008)

Berman, F., Fox, G., & Hey, T. (2003). *Grid computing. Making the Global infrastrucure a Reality*. Wiley.

Bry, F., Nagel, W., & Schroeder, M. (2004). Grid computing. *Informatik Spektrum, 27*(6), 542–545.

Burbeck, S. (2000). The Tao of e-business services. *IBM Corporation*. Retrieved October 7, 2006, from http://www.ibm.com/software/developer/library/ws-tao/index.html

CMS Watch. (2009). The ECM Suites Report 2009, Version 3.1. *CMS Works, CMS Watch Olney.*

Cover, R. (2004). *Web standards for business process modeling, collaboration, and choreography*. Retrieved October 7, 2001, from http://xml.coverpages.org/bpm.html.

Erl, T. (2008). *Web service contract design and versioning for SOA*. Prentice Hall International.

Ganek, A. (2007). Overview of autonomic computing: Origins, evolution, direction. In M. Parashar, & S. Harir (Eds.), *Autonomic computing* (pp. 3-18). New York: Taylor & Francis Group.

Gronau, N. (2003). Web services as a part of an adaptive information system framework for concurrent engineering. In R. Jardim-Goncalves, J. Cha, & A. Steiger-Garcao (Eds.), *Concurrent engineering: Enhanced interoperable systems*.

Hinchey, M. G., & Sterritt, R. (2006). Self-managing software. *Computer, 40*(2), 107–111. doi:10.1109/MC.2006.69

Horling, B., Benyo, B., & Lesser, V. (2001). *Using self-diagnosis to adapt organizational structures* (Tech. Rep. TR-99-64). University of Massachusetts.

Kuropka, D., Bog, A., & Weske, M. (2006) Semantic enterprise services platform: Motivation, potential, functionality and application scenarios. In *Proceedings of the tenth IEEE international EDOC Enterprise Computing Conference, Hong Kong* (pp. 253-261).

Lämmer, A., Eggert, S., & Gronau, N. (2008). A procedure model for a SOA-Based integration of enterprise systems. *International Journal of Enterprise Information Systems, 4*(2), 1–12.

Latif-Shabgahi, G., Bass, J. M., & Bennett, S. (1999). Integrating selected fault masking and self-diagnosis mechanisms. In *Proceedings of the Seventh Euromicro Workshop on Parallel and Distributed Processing* (pp. 97-104). IEEE Computer Society.

Leymann, F., & Roller, D. (2000). *Production workflow - Concepts and techniques*. Prentice Hall International.

Leymann, F., & Roller, D. (2006). Modeling business processes with BPEL4WS. *Information Systems and E-Business Management, 4*(3), 265–284. doi:10.1007/s10257-005-0025-2

Lübke, D., Lüecke, T., Schneider, K., & Gómez, J. M. (2006). Using event-driven process chains fo model-driven development of business applications. In F. Lehner, H. Nösekabel, & P. Kleinschmidt (2006), *Multikonferenz Wirtschaftsinformatik 2006* (pp. 265-279). GITO-Verlag.

Monk, E., & Wagner, B. (2005), Concepts in enterprise resource planning (2nd ed.). Boston: Thomson Course Technology.

Mos, A., & Murphy, J. (2001). *Performance monitoring Of Java component-oriented distributed applications*. Paper presented at the IEEE 9th International Conference on Software, Telecommunications and Computer Networks - SoftCOM 2001.

Papazoglou, M. P. (2007). *Web services: Principles and technology*. Prentice Hall.

Rockley, A. (2003). *Managing enterprise content*. Pearson Education.

Satzger, B., Pietzowski, A., Trumler, W., & Ungerer, T. (2007). Variations and evaluations of an adaptive accrual failure detector to enale self-healing properties in distributed systems. In P. Lukowicz, L. Thiele, & G. Tröster (Eds.), *Architecture of computing systems - ARCS 2007* (LNCS 4415, pp. 171-184).

Sneed, H. M. (2000). Encapsulation of legacy software: A technique for reusing legacy software components. *Annals of Software Engineering, 9*, 293–313. doi:10.1023/A:1018989111417

Sumner, M. (2005). Enterprise resource planning. NJ: Pearson Education.

Sun (2004). Predictive self-healing in the Solaris 10 operation system. A technical introduction. Retrieved from http://www.sun.com/bigadmin/content/selfheal/selfheal_overview.pdf

Vanderperren, W., Suvée, D., Verheecke, B., Cibrán, M. A., & Jonckers, V. (2005). Adaptive programming in JAsCo. In *Proceedings of the 4th international conference on Aspect-oriented software development*. ACM Press.

Chapter 9

The Underlying Test—Human, Organisational and Technical Considerations adjoined with Critical Success Factors when Implementing ERP:
A Case Study of a UK SME

Jonathan D. Owens
University of Lincoln, UK

Julie Dawson
University of Lincoln, UK

ABSTRACT

Enterprise Resource Planning (ERP) systems are pervasive information systems that have been fundamental in organisations for the past two decades. ERP systems may well count as the most important development in technology in the 1990s. There are many ERP success stories; equally there are as many failure stories. However, organisations encounter obstacles when implementing ERP systems. This chapter intends to explore some of the problems that occur throughout the implementation of an ERP system. Through the exploration of the literature a framework is constructed considering human, organisational and technical considerations adjoined with critical success factors when implementing ERP. Drawing on empirical evidences from a UK SME, this study then discusses and analyses each problem identified in the framework and its affect on the implementation of their ERP system. The findings of this chapter suggests the fundamental challenge of ERP implementation is not technology but organisational and human problems, which, if not fully understood and addressed, can lead to ERP failure. Finally, this chapter considers the critical success factors that resulted in the failure of the ERP at the case company in the chartering phase of the implementation. It is hoped this chapter will assist in understanding that human, organisational and technical considerations adjoined with critical success factors will encourage practitioners to address these problems and increase their chance of success during ERP implementation.

DOI: 10.4018/978-1-60566-968-7.ch009

INTRODUCTION

In the past two decades, companies around the world have implemented Enterprise Resource Planning (ERP) Systems (Nah *et al* 2006). An ERP system is a commercial software package (Davenport 1998, Markus *et al* 2000) that promotes seamless integration of all the information flowing through a company (Davenport 1998). Laudon and Laudon (2006) explain that an ERP system collects data from various key business processes in manufacturing and production, finance and accounting, sales and marketing, and human resources. The system then stores the data in a single comprehensive data repository where it can be used by other parts of the business. Managers have precise and timely information for co-ordinating the daily operations of the business and a firm wide view of business processes and information flow.

ERP systems have near magical effects when they work as promised (Legare 2002; Laudon and Laudon, 2006), but unfortunately, a significant number of ERP implementation projects do not succeed (Sarker 2002). The fact that many ERP implementations fail or escalate out of control (Davenport 1998), has led academics to concentrate on what makes a successful ERP. Scholars have focused their research on critical success factors (CSF) (Parr *et al* 2000, Somers *et al* 2001, Nah *et al* 2001, Umble *et al* 2002), which focus on the factors that determine whether an ERP implementation will be successful (Umble *et al* 2002). Markus *et al* (2001) explains that most companies experience outcomes that fall some what short of what a "best in class" organisation might achieve. This directs their attention to the problems companies experience when they adopt, deploy, and use ERP systems. Markus' study in 2001 is unusual as it places considerable focus on the problems experienced in ERP implementations as opposed to simply defining CSFs. They explore the aspects of organisations ERP journeys. This study will focus on the problems experienced in

ERP implementations. The authors believe that focusing deeply on ERP problems will produce different findings opposed to focusing on CSFs.

Research suggests that most companies experience problems with their ERP systems, particularly during the implementation phase (Parr 2000). Both technical problems and human and organisational problems can be attributed to ERP failure. "*ERP implementations are affected by both technical and social and organisational aspects*" (Elbanna, 2003, p1). This is because the implementation of an ERP system is a socio-technical challenge (Kansel 2006). Laudon and Laudon (2006) emphasise that information systems are sociotechnical systems. They are composed of machines, devices and 'hard' physical technology, yet they require substantial social, organisational, and intellectual investments to make them work properly.

This paper firstly intends to differentiate between the human and organisational problems and the technical problems in an attempt to explore the presence of the opposing problems in an ERP implementation in a UK SME (Company X). According to Sarker (2002), there is a consensus among researchers that human factors, more than technical are critical to the success of ERP projects, this paper intends to explore this assumption. A combination of the work of Markus *et al* (2001) and Kim *et al* (2005) will be used to construct a framework of Human and Organisational and Technical problems in ERP Implementations during the project phase. Drawing on empirical evidences from company X, this study discusses and analyses each problem identified in the framework and its effect on the implementation of their ERP system.

What is an ERP System?

An Enterprise Resource Planning (ERP) system is a commercial software package (Davenport 1998, Markus and Tanis 2000, Kim *et al* 2005) that promotes seamless integration of all the information flowing through a company (Davenport 1998).

Laudon and Laudon (2006) explain that an ERP system collects data from various key business processes in manufacturing and production, finance and accounting, sales and marketing, and human resources (Fig 1). The system then stores the data in a single comprehensive data repository where they can be used by other parts of the business. Managers have precise and timely information for co-ordinating the daily operations of the business and a firm wide view of business processes and information flow.

Davenport (1998, p2-3) explains how an ERP system can work:

"A Paris-based sales representative for a U.S. computer manufacturer prepares a quote for a customer using an ERP system. The salesperson enters some basic information about the customer's requirements into his laptop computer, and the ERP system automatically produces a formal contract, in French, specifying the products configuration, price and delivery date. When the customer accepts the quote the sales rep hits a key; the system after verifying the customer's credit limit, records the order. The system schedules shipment; identifies the best routing; and then working backward from the delivery date, reserves the inventory; orders needed parts from suppliers;

and schedules assembly in the company's factory in Taiwan."

Why an ERP System?

During the 1990's, ERP systems became the de facto standard for the replacement of legacy systems[1] (Holland and Light 1999). Somers and Nelson (2001) claim there are numerous reasons for the increasing demand of ERP systems, for example, competitive pressures to become a low cost producer, expectations of revenue growth, ability to compete globally and the desire to re-engineer the business. Markus and Tanis (2000) explain that ERP systems are rich in terms of functionality and potential benefits. They continue to explain that companies are implementing ERP systems for many different reasons, some companies have largely technical reasons for investing in ERP systems, other companies have mainly business reasons (Table 1).

ERP Phases

A phase can be described as a point in time (Markus et al 2000). Kim (2005) states that the identification of ERP problems or impediments as they

Figure 1. Enterprise resource planning system (Laudon and Laudon, 2006)

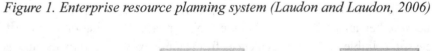

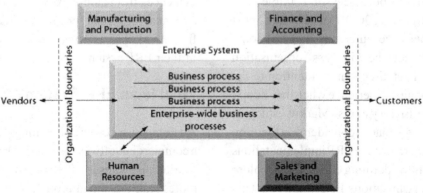

Table 1. Reasons for adopting enterprise systems (Markus and Tanis. 2000)

Technical Reasons	Business Reasons
• Solve Y2K and similar problems • Integrate applications cross- functionally • Replace hard-to-maintain interfaces • Consolidate multiple different systems of the same type (e.g., general ledger packages) • Reduce software maintenance burden through outsourcing • Eliminate redundant data entry and concomitant errors and difficulty analyzing data • Improve IT architecture • Ease technology capacity constraints • Decrease computer operating costs	• Accommodate business growth • Acquire multi language and multicurrency IT support • Provide integrated IT support • Standardize different numbering, naming, and coding schemes • Improve informal and/or inefficient business processes • Clean up data and records through standardization • Standardize procedures across different locations • Reduce business operating and administrative expenses • Present a single face to the customer • Reduce inventory carrying costs and stock outs • Acquire worldwide "available to promise" capability • Eliminate delays and errors in fulfilling customers' orders for merged businesses • Streamline financial consolidations • Improve companywide decision support

call them for each phase provides greater detailed guidelines. Although there have been many definitions of phases across the ERP lifecycle (Esteves *et al* 1999, Parr *et al* 2000), this study will focus on the work of and Markus *et al's* (2000) ideal phases of ERP implementations. In particular the project phase of Markus *et al* (2000) shall be focused on. This is because, as will later become clear, the case study of company X focuses on this period. According to Markus *et al* (2000) the project phase comprises activities intended to get the system up and running in one or more organisational units. Key activities include soft-

ware configuration, system integration, testing, data conversion, training and rollout.

ERP Problems

The ERP implementation problems identified by Markus *et al* (2001) and Kim *et al* (2005) will be detailed in this section. The rationale for using the work of these two authors is that both define the ERP phases using Markus *et al's* (2000) ideal phases and concentrate on the project phase in particular.

Table 2. Challenging problems with ERP adoption in the project phase (Markus et al, 2001)

Challenging Problems	Project Phase
Software Modifications	• Difficulties in operating effectively with systems functionality • Difficulty in getting modifications to work well and arrive in time • Not understanding the ERP system before modifications were made, resulting in unnecessary modifications
System Integration	• Difficulty integrating ERP system with a package of hardware, operating systems, database management systems and telecommunications systems suited to their organisations size, structure and geographic dispersion • Difficulty finding experts to advise on operating requirements
Product and Implementation Consultants	• Few IT products and service firms were willing to take end to end responsibility for project managing all parties (ERP vendor, vendors of supporting hardware, software and telecommunications capabilities and implementations consultants etc) • ERP adopters reluctant to cede authority for project management to an outside party • Conflict between parties • Lack of continuity in personnel assigned to adopter projects • Conflicts between adopting company and IT product or service vendors
Turnover and Project Personnel	• Losing Key IT specialists and user representative

Table 3. Impediments with ERP adoption in the project phase (Kim et al, 2005)

Critical Impediments	Project Phase
Human Resources and Capabilities Management	• Difficulties in building team • Lack of in house resources of project management skills • Difficult to gain outside expertise • Lack of adequate incentives • Imbalanced team composition
Cross Functional Co-ordination	• Lack of co-ordination mechanism to resolve cross-functional differences • Lack of communication across cross-functional units • Lack of communication across internal project teams • Unwillingness to accept changes from other functional units
ERP Software Configuration	• ERP systems that are too difficult to customise • Complexity of ERP systems only a few people understand it beyond a single model which makes design difficult
Systems Development	• Lack of Adequate resources to renew systems • Frequent changes in requirements
Change Management	• Lack of organisational change management expertise • To much effort to redesign business processes, resulting in a heavy burden in reconfiguring the software • Too much effort to align business process to the ERP process resulting in loss of competitive edge
Organisational Leadership	• Perspective of ERP as just a technical system • Inadequate management of stakeholder politics • Lack of adequate monitoring and feedback

Markus *et al* Study

Markus *et al* (2001) conducted a study which reflects the experiences of approximately forty organisations that they have been involved in studying. Markus *et al* (2001) presents findings about adopters' problems with ERP. In the project phase of the ERP lifecycle, they reported that: software modifications, system integration, product and implementation consultants, and turnover of project personnel were the most challenging of problems to overcome. Table 2 details each of these challenging problems in the project phase.

Kim *et al* Study

A later study conducted by Kim *et al* (2005), categorise ERP problems or impediments as they call them, into six different areas. These are: human resources and capabilities management, cross-functional co-ordination, ERP software and configuration, systems development and project management, change management and

organisational leadership. Within these areas they compiled impediments identified from previous ERP implementation studies. Kim *et al* (2005) grouped together the impediments into phases. Kim *et al's* (2005) impediments within the project phase are demonstrated in table 3.

HUMAN AND ORGANISATIONAL PROBLEMS AND TECHNICAL PROBLEMS IN ERP ADOPTIONS

The authors have combined the ERP adoption problems defined by of Markus *et al* (2001) and Kim *et al* (2005) so a united framework of ERP problems in the project phase of the ERP lifecycle can be developed. This framework is then divided into human and organisational problems or technical problems. This is displayed in table 4. This paper defines technical problems as involving the machines, devices and 'hard' physical technology. Human and Organisational problems are categorised as attitudes, management and organisational

Table 4. Human and Organisational Problems and Technical Problems in ERP adoption (Dawson and Owens, 2007)

Human and Organisational Problems	Technical Problems
• Product and Implementation Consultants	• Software Modifications / Software Configuration
• Turnover and Project Personnel	• System Integration
• Human Resources and Capabilities Management	• Systems Development
• Cross Functional Co-ordination	
• Change Management	
• Organisational Leadership	

politics and behaviour. It can be observed that six problems have been identified as human and organisational and three have been identified as technical. This combination of work will be used to analyse company X.

RESEARCH METHODOLOGY AND SETTING

This research belongs to the qualitative school of research in information systems. The case study approach was selected as the methodology for this study. The case study methodology was undertaken because it is effective in studying phenomena in their early stages. The researchers were able to study the phenomena in their natural setting.

An ethnographic approach was adopted. Ethnographies in their most characteristic form involves the ethnographer participating, overtly or covertly, in peoples lives for an extended period of time, watching what happens, listening to what is said, asking questions, in fact, collecting all the data that is available to throw light on the issues that are the focus of the research (Hammersley *et al* 1995). Myers (1999) states that ethnographic research is well suited to providing information system researchers with rich insights into the human, social and organisational aspects of information systems.

The authors were employed by the company X to project manage the adoption of an ERP system.

This gave the authors the opportunity to immerse themselves in the area of study. The ethnography data was collected between November 2005 and April 2006, a six month period. Data was collected via participant observation and social contact with the participants as well as referring to documentation such as project proposals, vendor contracts and company research. Note taking was carried out constantly throughout the ethnographical period. Not only observations were noted, but the impressions and feelings which emerged were also recorded.

Company X

Company X specialise in manufacturing storage furniture for the healthcare industry. They offer a service to the industry in which they design, supply and install not only storage furniture but third party products to equip a hospital room with all the furniture it needs.

The notion of adopting an ERP system in Company X transpired after a systems review exercise in mid 2004. It became apparent that there was an immense need to improve their information systems. Company X's annual growth rate was recorded at approximately twenty percent It was deemed that this level of growth was not sustainable with the current IT infrastructure. The company were acquiring larger projects that increased in complexity and expanded over longer periods of time. Excel spreadsheets were used to an elaborate degree to project manage a project; however the spreadsheets were very large and prone to crashing. The unreliability of Excel spreadsheets increased the need for an advanced IT system. Company X's inventory and purchasing processes were seen as weak areas, processes were manual and relied on the knowledge of employees to know which suppliers to use and what items were currently in stock. A purchasing employee was quoted describing current systems by commenting upon the authors arrival at the company 'System, what system?'

Current systems were restricting the capacity of the recently improved production facilities, improvements needed to be made in the companies order processing and scheduling systems to meet the capacity now available. The quality of management information that could be extracted from current systems was at best limited and often inaccurate and out of date. This aspect needed to be improved considerably to allow management to make informed and timely strategic decisions. The accountancy system utilised in Company X was renowned for its excellence, it was a leading accountancy package. However it was not used to its full potential; this was mainly due to inappropriate implementation and no updates added for approximately five years. Company X spent hours correlating one system with another. For example the delivery note values from the project management system needed to correlate with the invoice values in the accountancy system, the time delay of notifying the accounts department that the delivery had been made to when the accounts department need to raise an invoice might have put both actions in different months. So when monthly sales figures are required, both systems say different things. At the time of the decision to implement an ERP system, the departments within Company X were extremely fragmented. Current systems reflected this as generally each department had their preferred system. The number of different systems for different departments caused excess data entry, a customer enquiry was recorded in three separate computer systems and one paper system by an administrator. It was also observed that a new database was introduced just before the authors arrival at the company. However, the data entry of this database was sporadic for numerous reasons; complexity, lack of training and non buy-in. This list is not exhaustive; Company X saw countless benefits of a unified system, some large some small.

In October 2004 IT exhibitions were attended and ERP vendors were asked to demonstrate their products at the company. After seeing a demonstration of Microsoft Dynamics GP the Company X were suitably impressed. The company were able to compile a case for the ERP system and convince those reluctant parties that an ERP system was the paramount option. In July 2005 a final version of the contract was compiled by the ERP vendor. The contract was later signed between both parties to implement Microsoft Dynamics GP. Company X decided to enlist an external consultant to put together an implementation plan for the ERP system, a plan was compiled before the authors recruitment. In November 2005, the authors were recruited to project manage the implementation of Microsoft Dynamics GP.

The authors were confronted with an ERP system which had been selected and consequently had been contracted to be implemented. An implementation plan had been devised by a consultant and everything was set for the implementation to proceed.

HUMAN, ORGANISATIONAL AND TECHNICAL CONSIDERATIONS FOR COMPANY X DURING ERP IMPLEMENTATION

In this section the human, organisational and technical issues incurred by company X are analysed using the framework compiled in table 4.

Human and Organisational Considerations

Product and Implementation Consultants

Markus *et al* (2001) state that problems might occur because few IT products and service firms were willing to take end to end responsibility for project managing all parties. This problem did not affect company X. The authors were employed to project manage the ERP implementation; they took end to end responsibility for project managing all of the product and service parties involved. Markus *et al* (2001), also states that conflict may occur between parties: the implementation consultant, the ERP vendors and the vendors of existing software. They also state that conflict may occur between the adopting organisation and parties. Company X also did not experience any disputes.

Turnover and Project Personnel

This problem was identified as such by Markus *et al* (2001). Markus *et al* (2001) recognised that internally, adopters are unable to maintain continuity of personnel. Losing Key IT specialists and user representatives was identified as a problem. This was not a problem experienced by company X. The personnel that were involved in the ERP implementation at the beginning of the project were involved in the project at the end.

Human Resources and Capabilities Management

Kim *et al* (2005) firstly state that the problem they define as human resources and capabilities management involves difficulties in building a team. Company X constructed a steering committee of user representatives, directors and project management personnel. The team was encouraged to join together in the first instance by the directors sponsoring the project. At the time of

the recruitment of the authors it appeared that all of members of the steering committee were happy to be part of the team. The building of the team was not a problem for company X. Kim *et al* (2005) suggests the balance of the team may also be a problem. The team at the Company X was well balanced of user representatives, project management personnel and technical personnel. The balance of the team wasn't an issue. Kim *et al* (2005) also points out that lack of in house resources of project management skills can be a problem. According to Loh *et al* (2004), good project management is vital and that the scope of the ERP implementation project should be established and controlled. The authors were well experienced in managing projects, theoretically and practically. This problem was not an issue. Kim *et al* (2005) states that lack of adequate incentives may cause a problem. This was not particularly the case. Company X is an SME, the fact that improvements were going to be made which would improve the business seemed to be incentive enough. The frustration of existing systems motivated the steering committee to contribute to the implementation.

Cross Functional Co-Ordination

Kim (2005) stated that cross functional co-ordination was a problem in the project phase of ERP implementations. An ERP system is cross functional. In the case of the Company X the system was proposed to encompass a large proportion of the business, covering many functions and departments. User representatives from each department were members of the steering committee. The co-ordination mechanism in place to resolve cross functional differences was the steering committee meetings. Communication was encouraged in these meetings. After deciding upon an incremental implementation opposed to a big bang approach, there was a lot of debate as to which departments would see the implementation of the ERP system first. This disagreement was resolved in the steering committee meeting. As company X is an SME, the cross functional co-ordination problems were limited.

Change Management

The authors were fully aware of change management theories and the steps they had to take to make the ERP implementation run smoothly. The project phase, as identified in section two involves: software configuration, system integration, testing, data conversion, training and rollout. Company X only really managed to get as far as the software configuration stage before the project was abandoned. So although the project phase as a whole involves a lot of change, the stage company X managed to get to, did not involve a lot of change. Therefore, there was no real change for the users, so no problems occurred with the management of change.

Organisational Leadership

Kim *et al* (2005) states that perceiving the ERP as just a technical system is a problem for organisational leaders. This point was profound in company X. The user representatives and directors (the leaders) clearly referred to the ERP system as 'the system'. This led the authors to believe that the ERP system was seen by many as just computer software. The managing director saw the ERP implementation simply as an IT improvement, the ERP system wasn't viewed as a social system which would affect the structure, culture and politics of the organisation. The managing director did not really understand the enormity of an ERP system and its effects on the organisation.

Kim *et al* (2005) suggests that the lack of inadequate management of stakeholder politics is an organisational leadership problem for ERP implementations. The politics of information systems can be seen to have evolved from the long tradition of literature on the relationship between information and power (Bull 2003). The

whole ERP implementation at company X had a political dimension. The user representative who was the main leader for getting the ERP approved was a powerful influence. This representative was not necessarily the most informed party on IS, but taking control of vendor selection gave the user representative authority and control. The opposing user representative that was in favour of implementing a best of breed product in company X was also a powerful influence. Although the ERP system was approved and was going ahead, the opposing user representative did not involve themselves in the planning stages (the chartering phase as Markus 2000 would call it). They did not involve themselves in vendor selection and they failed to state their requirements for the ERP system. This is called counter-resistance according to Bull (2003). Consequently the wrong modules were selected and possibly the wrong ERP system had been selected. The process began with trying to correct this. During this process it was established that the ERP system lacked functionality of a product configurator. The ERP vendors proposed a varying degree of options to overcome this problem, from building a bespoke configuration system, using an existing system or linking with another third party product. In making this decision, those opposing the ERP system evidently found an opportunity to discuss abandoning the project. They also began turning up late or make proceedings difficult in steering committee meetings. The management of stakeholder politics should have been focused throughout the project stage and prior to this stage. Because it wasn't, the problem of inadequate management of politics could be associated with the abandonment and consequently the failure of the ERP adoption.

Lack of adequate monitoring and feedback was a problem identified by Kim (2005) under the heading of organisational leadership. The project was monitored and feedback was given by the directors attending the steering committees and offering there opinions and advice. There was not a problem or lack of adequate monitoring and feedback.

Technical Problems

Software Modifications / Software Configurations

The software modifications that were needed to implement Microsoft Dynamics GP were extensive at company X. Holland (1999) states that an organisation should try to purchase the package that fits best into its business processes. They continue to explain that organisations should be willing to change the business to fit the software with minimal modification and work with the existing functionality of the system. Working with the existing functionality in with the Microsoft Dynamics GP would have been impossible. The core capability of company X is that there are few limitations to the dimensions and specification of storage cabinets. Microsoft Dynamics was not specialised enough to manage this functionality, it did not have a product configurator. Company X realised the lack of capabilities of the ERP system very early on in the project, it was a very big problem for the company to overcome.

Markus *et al* (2001) also state that a problem with ERP implementations is the difficulty in getting modifications to work well. The project did not proceed at company X up to the stage where modifications were commissioned. Modifications were discussed in detail, many options and degrees of modification were deliberated, but the ERP adoption was abandoned before any modifications were made.

System Integration

According to Markus *et al* (2001), problems can occur when integrating an ERP system with a package of hardware, operating systems, database management systems and telecommunications systems which are suited to an organisations size, structure and geographic dispersion. These problems were not approached with company X as the implementation of the ERP system did not reach the stage when these aspects were applicable. Company X did not experience difficulty finding experts to advise on operating requirements, which is also a problem defined by Markus *et al* (2001). This again was because they did not reach that stage of implementation.

Systems Development

Kim *et al* (2005) outline the problems that are affected in the project phase. These are lack of adequate resources to renew and maintain systems and frequent changes in requirements. Company X did not progress along the project phase enough to experience problems with lack of adequate resources to renew and maintain systems. However, they did experience considerable problems with frequent changes in requirements. Shortly preceeding the recruitment of the authors it was discovered that the modules of the ERP system that had been contracted to be implemented did not fit the business needs. The business needs initially were decided by a particular function, this function neglected the needs of other functions in company X. Therefore there was a major change in requirements even before the implementation started to take place. The changes had severe impact on the cost of the ERP system, it increased. This change was certainly not welcomed by the Managing Director and the Financial Director.

Chartering Phase of an ERP Implementation

"An organisations experience with an Enterprise Resource Planning System can be described as moving through several phases, characterised by key players, typical activities, characteristic problems, appropriate performance metrics and a range of possible outcomes."(Markus and Tanis, 2000, p189.)

Critical Success Factors

Appendix 1 displays a table which outlines the CSFs defined by thirteen different authors between 1999 and 2006. There are many differences between the CSFs that the authors define this can be observed in Appendix 1. The differences may have occurred because of the varying aims of the research and the research methods. For example those conducting research on an SME enterprise might compile a different set of CSFs to those conducting research on large organisations. It is often the case that authors use different terminology to refer to the same CSF, and even encompass one CSF into what another author defines as two CSFs. The number of CSFs that authors define can vary. Hong and Kim (2002) concentrated on just one CSF for their work, whilst Somers and Nelson (2001) provided a comprehensive list of twenty-two CSFs (although you will notice in Appendix A the twenty-two CSFs have been consolidated to thirteen).

The CSFs that have been uncovered during this content analysis are enlightening. However, these are CSFs which span the whole ERP implementation cycle and this is not the focus of this research. This research intends to uncover the CSFs that are present at the chartering phase of an ERP implementation to analyse the case of Company X.

Critical Success Factors in the Chartering Phase of an ERP Implementation

Only a limited amount of authors have produced research which presents CSFs in the context of their importance in each phase of the implementation process. Namely: Parr and Shanks (2000), Nah *et al* (2001) and Loh and Koh (2004). As a result of their research, Parr and Shanks (2000) state that there are four CSFs which are important in the chartering phase (or as they call it, the planning phase), Nah *et al* (2001) believe that there are seven CSFs, and Loh and Koh (2004) conclude that there are six CSFs in the chartering phase.

This paper has combined the work of Parr and Shanks (2000), Nah *et al* (2001) and Loh and Koh (2004) to obtain a unified framework of CSFs in the chartering phase of an ERP implementation (Table 5) which will be analysed against the case of Company X. By combining the work of these three authors, a framework of the CSFs at the chartering phase of an ERP implementation can be achieved.

Table 5. Unified framework of CSF's at the chartering phase of an ERP implementation (Dawson and Owens, 2008)

CSFs at the *Chartering* Phase	Loh and Koh (2004)	Nah *et al* (2001)	Parr and Shanks (2000)
Project Champion	✓	✓	✓
Project Management	✓	✓	
Business Plan and Vision	✓	✓	
Top Management Support	✓	✓	✓
ERP team and composition	✓	✓	
Effective Communication	✓	✓	
Appropriate Business and Legacy systems		✓	
Commitment to the Change			✓
A Vanilla ERP Approach			✓

Project Champion

Parr and Shanks (2000), state that a project champion is an advocate for the system who is unswerving in promoting the benefits of the new system. The project champion should be a high-level executive sponsor who has the power to set goals and legitimise change (Nah *et al* 2000). It is a CSF that there is a project champion with these attributes involved in the ERP implementation. Subsequently, the project management team (the authors) were mainly responsible for the role as the project champion. As new employees employed to project manage implementation, most questions and queries were directed towards them. The product Company X had chosen to implement was a well known ERP system, Microsoft Dynamics GP. The product had been implemented in many companies worldwide. The project managers were able to promote the product knowing the functionality and the quality of the ERP system. However, as the project progressed and the project managers' confidence in the system dropped due to the mismatch of the system and the companies requirements, the project managers no longer felt the same way about the system and this fact was picked up on by other members of staff.

The project champion should be a high-level executive sponsor who has the power to set goals and legitimise change (Nah et al 2000). However, the project champion was not a high level executive but still had the ability to set goals and legitimise change to a certain extent.

Project Management

According to Loh and Koh (2004), good project management is vital and that the scope of the ERP implementation project should be established and controlled. This includes the system implemented, the involvement of business units and the amount of project re-engineering needed. They continue to explain that the project should be defined in terms of milestones and critical paths. Deadlines should be met to help stay within the schedule and budget and to maintain credibility (Loh and Koh 2004).

Project management at Company X could have been better. At the beginning of the project there was much uncertainty of the tasks that needed to be involved to complete the project. Communication errors had led the ERP vendors to believe they were implementing a smaller system than was required, for example, they had not been informed that any manufacturing modules were required. They were also not enlightened as to the timescales that the company wished to work to, so consequently their initial implementation dates and plans were effectively useless. The company created their own project plan including milestones. Again this suffered from being produced with communication errors as the ERP vendors input were not used. The plan was created not knowing any detail of the ERP system and how long the implementation of the software would actually take. Once the differing project plans were recognised, the problem was addressed. New plans were not drawn up however because the problem of the ERP system not fitting the company was highlighted, and this problem needed to be addressed before any further plans could be made.

Business Plan and Vision

A clear business plan and vision to steer the direction of the project is needed throughout the ERP lifecycle (Buckhout et al 1999). There should be a clear business model, a justification of investment, a project mission and identified goals and benefits (Nah et al 2000).

Upon investigation it was evident Company X did not have a clear business plan and vision for the ERP system. Although some goals and benefits were identified, nothing was documented properly and defined in a united format. In November 2005, at the beginning of the project manager's recruitment, there was no clear idea what the ERP systems intention was. The modules of the ERP system that were purchased contradicted the majority of senior managers' ideas of what the system would do and what was actually required by the system. It was established that a project mission was non existent. The justification of investment was also a subject not approached.

Top Management Support

Parr et al (2000) describe top management support as top management advocacy, provision of adequate resources and commitment to the project. Top management need to publicly and explicitly identify the project as a top priority (Nah 2001). Senior management must be fully committed with its own involvement and have a willingness to allocate valuable resources to the implementation effort (Holland 1999).

The senior management at Company X were committed to the project. Three of the four Directors were members of the Steering Committee, which meant they gave their input on the project on a regular basis. All of the steering committee members were encouraged to be committed to the project by the Directors. The budget for the ERP system had been approved and committed in the form of a contract between Company X and the ERP vendor. Overall time and money was allocated. The project however, may have benefited from top management publicly and explicitly identifying the project as their top priority. As the project progressed, the existing Managing Director left the company. A new Managing Director joined the company. The resources that had previously been allocated for the project were now in question. especially as the project scope looked as if it was going to increase which of course meant the cost of the project would also increase. The concerns from the new Managing Director made the commitment of the other Directors involved in the projects waver. This was evident through lack of attendance in meetings.

ERP Team and Composition

The ERP team should consist of the best people in the organisation (Buckhout et al 1999). Building a cross functional team is also critical (Nah et al 2001). The team should have a mix of consultants and internal staff so that the internal staff can develop the necessary technical skills for design and implementation. Both business and technical knowledge are essential for success (Sumner 1999 cited in Nah et al 2001). Managers should be assigned full time to the implementation and partnerships should be managed with meetings scheduled regularly (Loh et al 2004).

The ERP team, or the Steering Committee as it was known, was cross functional. It consisted of the senior manager of each department and all of the directors that were available. An ERP consultant was also involved at the chartering phase of the project. The ERP consultant's knowledge regarding the chosen ERP system was limited, although he still contributed well to the team. It would have been preferable to assign more than one person to the project full time, however because Company X is an SME this was simply not feasible. All the team were committed and meetings were scheduled regularly. Overall Company X achieved well in terms of ERP team and composition.

Effective Communication

Effective communication is critical to the success of ERP implementations (Loh 2004). Communication includes the formal promotion of project teams and the advertisement of project progress to the rest of the organisation (Holland et al 1999). Expectations at every level need to be communicated (Nah et al 2001). Nah et al (2001) state that communication should penetrate all levels in the company, from upper managers to bottom operators, everyone should know what to expect in the business process change. They continue to explain that communication increases the willingness of people to change and take part.

Company X communicated well within the steering committee group. However, communication to staff outside of the steering committee was limited. Users could find out about the ERP project by asking questions of the steering committee, however no other formal way of communication was identified. In hind sight the project should have had newsletters or made use of notice boards and intranets.

APPROPRIATE BUSINESS AND LEGACY SYSTEMS

Nah et al (2001) believe that appropriate business and legacy systems are important in the initial phase of the project as a stable and successful business setting is essential. They continue to explain that business and IT systems involving existing business processes, organisational structure, culture, and information technology affect success. The existing business and legacy systems determine the IT and organisational change required for success (Holland et al 1999).

Company X had its business faults prior to the ERP system implementation. Some business processes were duplicated or ineffective, especially processes that stretched over departments. Employees were allowed to carry out tasks in their own ways, which led to an array of formats and systems. Business processes did not seem to be the businesses priority. Rightly or wrongly the opinion seemed to be that as long as the job got done, it was ok. The organisational culture was not completely open to a new computer system either. Previous failed implementations of an ERP system had left the organisation guarded. Company X possibly was not the right company to adopt an ERP system, especially at that time.

Commitment to the Change

Parr et al (2000) define the commitment to the change as perseverance. They state that a company should have determination in the face of inevitable problems with implementation.

Company X was committed to the project. All the steering committee gave the project their full attention in terms of attending all the required meetings, doing all of the work required and being positive about the project. When problems occurred with the fit of the ERP system, the steering committee focused on all of the options that were available at the time and came up with the most appropriate solution. The company can be seen as being committed to change from this perspective.

A Vanilla ERP Approach

According to Parr *et al* (2000), a company should have a vanilla ERP approach in order to be successful. Parr *et al* (2000) explains essentially a vanilla approach involves a minimum customisation and an uncomplicated implementation strategy. Organisations should be willing to change the business to fit the software with minimal customisation (Holland et al 1999). Holland (1999) state that an organisation should try to purchase the package that fits best into its business processes.

Company X had a vanilla ERP approach. They realised the time and cost implications of customising an ERP system extensively. They were extremely anti –customisation, this was made clear in all of the initial meetings.

Reviewing the business processes began shortly after the employment of the project manager. It immediately became apparent that the ERP system selected was a bad fit for Company X. Company X manufacture make to order furniture, they needed the flexibility to make almost anything requested. This means that Company X needed an ERP system with a good product configurator. The ERP system selected did not have a product configurator. The vendors did not suggest using an external configurator or integrating the system with the existing bill of material system. It was later discovered that this may have been because the ERP vendor had never implemented the system with a similar manufacturer and the system was mainly marketed towards service organisations not manufacturing. Although Company X had a vanilla ERP approach. This approach was distorted because of the current situation. Company X could not implement the chosen ERP system in a vanilla format because it was a bad fit for the company.

DISCUSSION

This paper is based on only a single exploratory case, so any conceptual insights will need to be verified through subsequent research. With this caution is mind, there do appear to be some interesting theoretical insights that can be derived from the case.

Human, Organisational and Technical Considerations when implementing ERP

The most challenging human and organisational problems encountered by company X were labelled under the heading of Organisational Leadership.

The challenging problems that were defined under the heading of Organisational Leadership were: having the perspective of ERP as just a technical system and inadequate management of stakeholder politics. The most challenging technical problems encountered by company X were labelled under the headings of software modifications / software configurations and systems development. The challenging problem that was defined under the heading of software modifications / software configurations was: difficulties in operating effectively with systems functionality. The challenging problem that was defined under the heading of systems development was: frequent changes in requirements. The challenging problems of the company X are illustrated in table 7.

It should be mentioned a total of six human and organisational problems were identified in table 4 (the framework of organisational problems and technical problems in ERP adoptions) and only three technical problems were identified. This was because the framework was derived from the work of two authors (Markus *et al* 2001, Kim *et al* 2005), and that was what they stated. This point already states that scholars believe that human and behavioural problems are more profound in ERP implementations. However, because two of the

Table 6. Summary of the extent Company X achieved each CSF

CSFs at the Chartering Phase	Company X achieved	Company X partly achieved	Company X did not achieve
Project Champion		✓	
Project Management		✓	
Business Plan and Vision			✓
Top Management Support		✓	
ERP Team and Composition	✓		
Effective Communication		✓	
Appropriate Business and Legacy systems			✓
Commitment to the Change	✓		
A Vanilla ERP Approach		✓	

Table 7. The challenging problems of Company X

Human and Organisation Problems		Technical Problems	
Organisational Leadership	• Perspective of ERP as just a technical system • Inadequate management of stakeholder politics	**Software modifications / software configurations**	• Difficulties in operating effectively with systems functionality
		Systems development	• Frequent changes in requirements

human and organisational problems were found to be relevant to company X, and two technical problems were also found to be relevant, this upon first observation would suggest that the human and organisational problems and the technical problems carry equal importance in the ERP adoption by company X.

However, the findings suggest that the problems experienced due to organisational politics in the planning phase of company X led to the software modification / configuration problems in the project phase. Certain user representatives did not involve themselves in the planning phase because they were resisting the power of the user representatives in favour of the ERP system, therefore an ERP system was selected which did not fit the business in all departments. Markus *et al* (2001) suggests that in practice, it is the case that problems experienced in a prior phase which are not perceived as problems and not rectified will impact on the subsequent phase. This has been the case in company X. Consequently, if the problem of organisational politics had been resolved in the planning stage, a best fit ERP system could have been selected which would have meant that there would have been limited problems with software modifications. The problem of software modifications in the first instance may be perceived as being the cause of the project being abandoned; however, the underlining root cause of the modifications was organisational politics. Because of this point it can be argued that the human and organisational problems caused the technical problems and therefore were more profound in the case of company X.

This study also found that the ERP system in company X was viewed as just a technical system. Viewing the ERP system as a technical system was defined by Kim *et al* (2005) as a problem, this study supports this assumption. The fact that the ERP system was viewed as simply a technical system may have led the adopting organisation to treat the project as unimportant. The organisational politics may not have been managed because the ERP adoption wasn't seen as important enough to provoke conflict. User representatives were left to their own devices in the planning stage, if one user representative did not involve themselves, it wasn't seen as important to encourage their involvement.

The frequent changes in requirements can be seen to originate from the organisational politics too. If the differences between the user representatives were managed, the business requirements would have been accurate. As it was, the requirements were wrong, which led to frequent changes in requirements later on in the project. The changes in requirements led to the cost of the ERP system escalating. This resulted in the Managing Director and the Finance Director seriously questioning the project. There was a budget, and the ERP exceeded this budget. Money was one of the deciding factors that led to the ERP project being abandoned.

Critical Success Factors when implementing ERP

Company X's ERP system failed to be implemented, it failed in the chartering phase. There has been a lot of dispute as to what constitutes ERP failure and success in literature. However it is almost irrefutable that the ERP system at Company X did not succeed.

So why did it fail? Company X successfully achieved the CSFs, ERP team and composition and commitment to the change. They had a cross functional steering committee who were committed to the project, attended scheduled meetings regularly and faced the problems with the ERP system with determination. However, Company X's ERP implementation failed to be implemented; so it appears that achieving two CSFs, team and commitment to the change were not enough to make a successful ERP implementation in the chartering phase.

Company X only partly achieved the CSFs, project champion, project management, top management support, effective communication and a vanilla ERP approach. There was a project champion, however as the project progressed, the project champion's promotion for the project diminished. Project Management of the ERP implementation was not admirable; the project plans differed between the ERP vendor and Company X so the timescales were not defined. The project was clearly supported by three Directors, however top management support was hindered by the existing Managing Director leaving the company. His replacement was a new Managing Director who did not support the project. Communication within the steering committee was good, however, communication outside of the steering committee outside of the project was limited. There was no formal way of communicating the project to users. Although the company had a vanilla ERP approach, the selected ERP system was not a good fit to the company's processes so the vanilla approach was distorted. Company X only partly achieved five CSFs. A partly achieved CSF could have been a reason for the ERP failure. For example, the Project Champion's diminishing support for the project could have led to the rejection of the ERP system by the users which then progressed to the

rejection of the system by the steering committee and a discontinuation of the whole project. Effectively, to only partly achieve can be said to fail in some way, and that partial failure could have led or contributed to the whole system failure.

Company X did not achieve the CSFs, business plan and vision and appropriate business and legacy systems. Although some goals and benefits were identified, nothing was documented properly and defined in a unified format. The company did not have the appropriate business and legacy systems. The culture at Company X was guarded against a new IT system. Failing to achieve these CSFs could have been the reasons for the failure of the ERP in the chartering phase.

This research has distinguished that there is not one reason for the failure of Company X's ERP system. This research has defined seven reasons (five partly achieved CSFs and two not achieved CSFs out of nine), that may have caused failure. Gargeya and Brady (2005) found that factors leading to success and failure are complex and do not occur alone. They explain that they are actually intertwined with one another, and at many times, are hard to separate or isolate. This research supports this finding.

LIMITATIONS

This paper is limited because it fails to identify the importance of each CSF in the chartering phase of ERP implementation, for example whether the non achievement of one CSF is more critical to failure than others. This paper suggests that the failure and partial failure of seven out of nine CSFs can cause ERP failure, however it does not recognise how many non achieved CSF are actually needed to cause failure. This paper also fails to recognise if a particular combination of factors led to the ERP failure, for example if the non achievement of two CSFs together signifies failure.

Only one case study is reported in this research. Care was taken to improve the validity of the case by using multiple sources of data. However this research would be strengthened further if additional cases are addressed. So many companies fail to progress their ERP implementations past the chartering phase. Using the CSFs that are identified in this study with those companies would allow for comparison and validation of the conclusions reached.

CONCLUSION

This paper has identified the problems that are experienced in ERP adoptions using the work of Markus *et al* (2001) and Kim *et al* (2005). A framework was devised from this work clearly stating which problems were human and organisational problems and which were technical problems. Using this framework the case of company X's ERP adoption was analysed. The findings of this paper identify that in the case of company X, the most profound problem was human and organisational. The human and organisational problem was inadequate management of organisational politics, which was not addressed because of another human and organisation problem (perspective of ERP as just a technical system) which instigated the technical problems (difficulties in operating effectively with systems functionality and frequent changes to requirements) which increased the costs of the system and led the ERP adoption to be abandoned.

Also, the considerations of CSFs allowed the exploration of a wide variety of explanations for the ERP failure in the chartering phase of implementation at Company X. Prior to this research, it was deemed by the authors that Company X's ERP demise was simply due to lack of support of the project by the Managing Director. However, looking at the case in terms of CSFs, it was discovered that although lack of top management was a critical factor, it was not the only factor that led to the ERP failure. Company X only partly achieved and did not achieve in total seven CSFs. So in total, this paper has identified seven reasons for the failure of the ERP implementation at Company X.

This research is extremely useful for Company X to understand when they undertake IT projects in the future. Recognising potential failure factors and achieving what the CSFs are and what they need to be achieved will encourage successful IT implementations.

Practitioners can learn from this case. The case study findings emphasise that practitioners need to pay particular attention to human, organisational, technical considerations and CSF'ss when implementing ERP. It also highlights that it is not just one specific area that needs addressing, but a rather a collection. Adapting organisations must make a conscious effort to management organisational politics. If they are not managed appropriately, practitioners ERP adoptions could end up as yet another failed implementation to add to the pile.

REFERENCES

Buckhout, S., Frey, E., & Nemec, J. (1999). Making ERP Succeed: Turning Fear into Promise. *IEEE Engineering Management Review*, Second Quarter, 116-123.

Bull, C. (2003). Politics in Packaged Software Implementations. In *Proceedings of the 11th European Conference on Information Systems, June.*

Cooper, R. B., & Zmund, R. W. (1990). Information Technology Implementation Research: A Technological Diffusion Approach. *Management Science, 36*(2), 123–139. doi:10.1287/mnsc.36.2.123

Davenport, T. H. (1998). Putting the Enterprise into the Enterprise System'. *Harvard Business Review*, (July-August): 121–131.

Dawson, J., & Owens, J. D. (2007). *The Fundamental Challenge: Human and Organisational Factors in an ERP Implementation*. First European Conference on Information Management and Evaluation, University of Montpellier, France, 20-21 September.

Dawson, J., & Owens, J. D. (2008). ERP Non-implementation: A Case Study of a UK Furniture Manufacturer. *International Journal of Enterprise Information Systems*, *4*(3).

DeLone, W. H., & McLean, E. R. (1992). Information Systems Success: The Quest for the Dependent Variable. *Information Systems Research*, *3*(1), 60–95. doi:10.1287/isre.3.1.60

Ehia, I. C., & Madsen, M. (2005). Identifying Critical Issues in Enterprise Resource Planning (ERP) Implementation. *Computers in Industry*, *56*(6).

Elbanna, A. R. (2003). Achieving Social Integration to Implement ERP Systems. In *Proceedings of the 11th European Conference on Information Systems, June*.

Esteves, J., & Pastor, J. (1999). An ERP Life-cycle-based Research Agenda. In *Proceedings of the 1st International Workshop on Enterprise Management and Resource Planning Systems, November*.

Esteves, J., & Pastor, J. (2000). Towards a Unification of Critical Success Factors for ERP Implementations. In *Proceedings of the 10th Business Information Technology Conference, Manchester, UK*.

Esteves, J., & Pastor, J. (2001). Enterprise Resource Planning Systems Research: An Annotated Biography. *Communications of the Association for Information Systems*, *7*(8), 2–52.

Esteves, J., & Pastor, J. (2004). Organisational and Technological Critical Success Factors Behaviour Along the ERP Implementation Phases. In *Proceedings of the 6th International Conference on Enterprise Information Systems, April*.

Fang, L., & Patrecia, S. (2005). *Critical Success Factors in ERP Implementation*. Jonkoping International Business School, Jonkoping University.

Gable, G., & Stewart, G. (1999). *SAP R\3 Implementation Isses for Small to Medium Enterprises*. American Conference on Information Systems, Milwaukee, USA.

Gargeya, V. B., & Brady, C. (2005). Success and Failure factors of adopting SAP in ERP System Implementation. *Business Process Management Journal*, *11*(5), 501–516. doi:10.1108/14637150510619858

Hammersley, M. (1991). *What's Wrong With Ethnography?: Methodological Explorations*. London: Routledge.

Hammersley, M., & Atkinson, P. (1995). *Ethnography: Principles in Practice* (2nd ed.). London: Routledge.

Ho, C. F., Wu, W. H., & Tai, Y. M. (2004). Strategies for the Adaptation of ERP systems. *Industrial Management & Data Systems*, *104*(3), 234–251. doi:10.1108/02635570410525780

Holland, C. P., & Light, B. (1999). A Critical Success Factors Model for ERP Implementation. *IEEE Software*, (May-June): 30–36. doi:10.1109/52.765784

Hong, K. K., & Kim, Y. G. (2002). The Critical Success Factors for ERP Implementation: An Organisational Fit Perspective. *Information & Management*, *40*, 25–40. doi:10.1016/S0378-7206(01)00134-3

Kansel, V. (2006). Enterprise Resource Planning Implementation: A Case Study. *The Journal of American Academy of Business, Cambridge, 9*(1), 165–170.

Kim, Y., Lee, Z., & Gosain, S. (2005). Impediments to Successful ERP Implementation Process. *Business Process Management Journal, 11*(2), 158–170. doi:10.1108/14637150510591156

Laudon, K. C., & Laudon, J. P. (2006). *Management Information Systems*. NJ: Pearson Education.

Law, C.C.H., & Ngai. (2007). ERP systems adoption: An exploratory study of the organizational factors and impacts of ERP success. *Information & Management, 44*(4). doi:10.1016/j.im.2007.03.004

Legare, T. L. (2002). The Role of Organisational Factors in Realising ERP Benefits. *Information Systems Management, 19*(4), 21–42. doi:10.1201/1078/43202.19.4.20020901/38832.4

Loh, T. C., & Koh, S. C. L. (2004). Critical Elements for a Successful Enterprise Resource Planning Implementation in Small and Medium Sized Enterprises. *International Journal of Production Research, 4*, 3433–3455. doi:10.1080/00207540410001671679

Markus, M. L., Axline, S., Petrie, D., & Tanis, C. (2001). Learning From Adopters' Experiences With ERP: Problems Encountered and Success Achieved. *Journal of Information Technology, 15*, 245–265. doi:10.1080/02683960010008944

Markus, M. L., & Tanis, C. (2000). The Enterprise System Enterprise – From Adoption to Success. In R. W. Zmund (Ed.), *Framing the Domains of IT Research* (pp. 173-207). Pinnaflex Educational Resources.

Myers, M. D. (1999). Investigating Information Systems with Ethnographic Research. *Communications of the Association for Information Systems, 2*, 23.

Nah, F. F., & Delgado, S. (2006). Critical Success Factors for Enterprise Resource Planning Implementation and Upgrade. *Journal of Computer Information Systems*, 99–113.

Nah, F. F., & Lau, J. L. S., & Kuang. (2001). Critical Factors for Successful Implementation of Enterprise Systems. *Business Process Management Journal, 7*(3), 285–296. doi:10.1108/14637150110392782

Nah, F. F., & Lau, J. L. S. (2001). Critical Factors for Successful Implementation of Enterprise Systems. *Business Process Management Journal, 7*(3), 285–296. doi:10.1108/14637150110392782

Nah, F. F., & Lau, J. L. S. (2003). ERP Implementation: Chief Information Officers' Perceptions of Critical Success Factors. *International Journal of Human-Computer Interaction, 16*(1), 5–22. doi:10.1207/S15327590IJHC1601_2

Parr, A., & Shanks, G. (2000). A Model ERP project Implementation. *Journal of Information Technology, 15*, 289–303. doi:10.1080/02683960010009051

Ross, J. W. (1999). Surprising Facts about implementing ERP. *IT Professional, 1*(4), 65–68. doi:10.1109/6294.781626

Sarker, S., & Lee, A. (2002). Using a Case Study to Test the Role of Three Key Social Enablers in ERP Implementation. *Information & Management, 40*(8), 813–829. doi:10.1016/S0378-7206(02)00103-9

Soh, C., & Kien, S. S., & Tay-Yap. (2000). Cultural Fits and Misfits: Is ERP a Universal Solution. *Communications of the ACM, 41*(4), 47–51. doi:10.1145/332051.332070

Somers, T. M., & Nelson, K. (2001). The Impact of Critical Success Factors across the Stages of Enterprise Resource Planning Implementations. In *Proceedings of the 34th Hawaii International Conference on System Sciences, January.*

Taube, L. R., & Gargeya, V. B. (2005). An Analysis of ERP System Implementation. *The Business Review Cambridge, 4*(1), 1–6.

Umble, E. J., Haft, R. R., & Umble, M. M. (2003). Enterprise Resource Planning: Implementation Procedures and Critical Success Factors. *European Journal of Operational Research, 146,* 241–257. doi:10.1016/S0377-2217(02)00547-7

Umble, E. J., & Umble, M. M. (2002). Avoiding ERP Implementation Failure. *Industrial Management, January / February,* 25-33.

Wu, J. H., & Wang, Y. M. (2006). Measuring ERP Success: the Ultimate Users View. *International Journal of Operations & Production Management, 26*(8), 882–903. doi:10.1108/01443570610678657

APPENDIX 1

	Holland and Light (1999)	Kim, Lee and Gosain (2005)	Umble, Haft and Umble (2002)	Nah and Lau (2003)	Esteeves and Pastor (2000)	Parr and Shanks (2000)	Gargeya and Brady (2005)	Hong and Kim (2002)	Somers and Nelson (2001)	Nah and Lau and Kuang (2001)	Loh and Koh (2004)	Nah and Delgdo (2006)
Business plan or vision	✓			✓	✓	✓				✓	✓	✓
Communication and co-operation	✓			✓	✓				✓	✓	✓	✓
Top management support	✓		✓	✓	✓	✓			✓	✓	✓	✓
System analysis, selection and technical implementation					✓				✓			✓
Commitment to the change and change management		✓	✓	✓	✓	✓			✓	✓	✓	✓
ERP team composition and skills (steering committee and consultants)	✓	✓	✓	✓	✓	✓	✓		✓	✓	✓	✓
Project management		✓	✓	✓	✓		✓		✓	✓	✓	✓
Strong leadership and empowered decision makers		✓			✓	✓						
Implementation viewed as an ongoing process												
Old systems eliminated												
Achievable implementation schedule and appropriate measurements (goals and objectives)	✓		✓			✓	✓		✓			
Education and training			✓		✓		✓		✓			
Project champion				✓	✓	✓			✓	✓	✓	
Comprehensive BPR					✓				✓			
Minimum customisation, vanilla ERP, smaller scope		✓	✓	✓	✓	✓	✓	✓	✓	✓	✓	
Software development, testing and troubleshooting	✓			✓	✓		✓			✓	✓	
Monitoring and evaluation of performance	✓			✓						✓	✓	
Appropriate business and IT legacy systems	✓			✓						✓		
Adequate ERP Strategy	✓				✓							
User Involvement and participation					✓							
Vendor Partnership and support	✓				✓				✓			
Management of Expectations and acceptance	✓								✓			

Chapter 10
The Role of Enterprise Perceptions in Acceptance of Information Systems

Blanca Hernández
University of Zaragoza, Spain

Julio Jiménez
University of Zaragoza, Spain

M. José Martín
University of Zaragoza, Spain

ABSTRACT

This study analyzes current and future enterprise use of various Information Systems (IS), such as management software, employing a technology acceptance model (TAM) optimized by the inclusion of Technological compatibility with previous IS and Web procurement. It also examines whether relationships in the model change according to the sector to which an enterprise belongs (i.e., if there exists a moderating effect of industry). The study applies two types of analyses: structural and multisample. The results show that Technological compatibility, Web procurement, Perceived usefulness and Perceived ease of use influence upon Future use of business IS. Enterprises need to be aware that interrelationships exist among the various IS. Investment in a specific system may facilitate the acceptance and subsequent performance of other applications. Furthermore, the "industry effect" modifies two important TAM relationships, and consequently it affects enterprise behaviour regarding IS.

INTRODUCTION

The competitive environment requires a continuous process of innovation within enterprises, in both their production and management systems. Information Systems (IS) have become a fundamental tool for the adequate development of corporate activity, significantly affecting production systems and the computerization of their basic functions (Doherty & King, 1998). The IS applied by enterprise are many and varied; some of these have already been sufficiently assimilated (e.g. the telephone and fax), while other more recent innovations have met with varying degrees of acceptance.

DOI: 10.4018/978-1-60566-968-7.ch010

One of the most interesting IS developed in the enterprise environment has been management software, which in addition to facilitating the performance of basic management functions, permits firms to share information with those agents with whom it interacts in the course of its activity, thereby converting the flow of information into bidirectional owing to the use of the Internet. However, despite their numerous advantages and their presentation as attractive business tools, such software has not been generally accepted by enterprises, and the implementation of this software has been subject to serious failures (Wu & Wang, 2006; Park, Suh, & Yang, 2007). Additionally, in some cases, their effects on some performance measures were opposite to expectations (Stoel & Muhanna, 2009).

Understanding the reasons why enterprises adopt new IS has been the subject of considerable interest to researchers and practitioners, as they attempt to correctly define which factors condition such an important decision for enterprises (Bass, 1969; Kositanurit, Ngwenyama & Osei-Bryson, 2006). Most such research is based upon theories related to behaviour and empirically tested models in order to explain the set of actions of users on the basis of their beliefs and/or attitudes: Theory of Reasoned Action, (TRA), Technology Acceptance Model (TAM), Theory of Planned Behaviour (TPB) or Innovation Diffusion Theory (IDT). The most widely used has been TAM (Davis, 1989), which reflects the acceptance of different IS, establishing a connection between users' perceptions and their final decisions.

The present study analyzes the principal factors inherent to enterprises which drive to the current and future acceptance of advanced IS for business management. The results will test the existing relationships between different IS in the business environment (Internet, email, EDI, web procurement and management software) and the effect derived from the firm sector ("industry effect") upon technological behaviour. With this objective in mind, a Technology Acceptance Model (TAM)

has been formulated and extended through new variables such as Technological compatibility and Web procurement.

The following section reviews existing research into IS acceptance, which provides the basis for the research proposals performed in this study. The study then presents the concrete objectives and hypotheses, outlines the methodology and describes the results. Subsequently, we outline the methodology and describe the results. In the final part of the study the conclusions and implications for business are presented.

THEORETICAL BACKGROUND

Technology Acceptance Model

Technology Acceptance Model (TAM) is an extension of the Theory of Reasoned Action (TRA) (Ajzen & Fishbein, 1980), which explains individuals' behaviour on the basis of their beliefs and intentions. TAM concentrates on the analysis of IS and reflects the acceptance of different applications. TAM introduces two key constructs: Perceived Usefulness (PU) and Perceived Ease Of Use (PEOU) (Davis, 1989; Davis, Bagozzi, & Warhaw, 1989). Perceived usefulness is the degree to which users believe the use of a specific IS will improve performance (Davis, 1989; Klopping & McKinney, 2004); ease of use is the perception that using a specific IS will not require additional effort (Davis, 1989; Robinson, Marshall, & Stamps, 2005; Fuller, Hardin, & Scott, 2007). Generally speaking, perceived ease of use has a direct effect on usefulness (Yi, Jackson, Park, & Probst, 2006; Shim & Viswanathan, 2007) and both have an effect on final decisions (Bradley & Lee, 2007; Kamhawi, 2007).

Other new variables influence the effect of usefulness and ease of use upon the variable to be explained and increase the explanatory power of the model. These variables include extrinsic influences, e.g. peer group pressure or business environment, and internal factors e.g. compatibility or technological culture (Achjari & Quaddus, 2003; Bruner & Kumar, 2005).

Technological Compatibility and Web Procurement

The concept of compatibility is common in studies on IS adoption by individual users, as many researchers believe it explains acceptance (Tornatzky & Klein, 1982; Agarwal & Karahanna, 1998; Tung, 2007). Most such research concentrates on subjective individual behaviour and thereby narrows the concept to such a degree that applying it in the business context is difficult (Fitzpatrick, 1998; Miyazaki & Fernández, 2001). Fuller *et al.* (2007) claim that compatibility in the business context refers to the appropriateness of the IS for the task for which it is contemplated. The present study adapts the concept of compatibility, as initially defined by Rogers (1983; 1995), to past and present experiences of enterprises with certain inter-related systems. The systems believed to generate compatibility are closely linked to business activities, and their previous application produces familiarity and influences the adoption of subsequent IS. We have termed this concept Technological compatibility (TC).

Employing the theory of organizational learning, March (1991) believes that experience leads to a wider knowledge base and increases technological capacity, while Barkema and Vermeulen (1998) argue that compatibility increases if a enterprise has a broad range of experience. As experience exists at many levels in organizations, knowledge transfer transcends the individual level to groups, departments, and divisions (Xu & Ma, 2009). Knowledge transfer becomes the process through which one unit is affected by the experience of another person, another situation, or another IS (Argote, 2000).

Factors similar to Technological compatibility were applied to the analysis of other management tools, such as e-CRM (Tung, 2007) and EDI (Ar-

unchalam, 1997; Jiménez & Polo, 1998). Premkumar and Roberts (1999) analyze the intensity of use of various technologies: EDI, online data access, e-mail and Internet. They argue that perceptions explain their application, and observe that the degree of compatibility and previous experience differ between adopters and non-adopters. They consider that both variables therefore significantly differentiate behaviour.

Rogers (1983; 1995) introduces the concept of "technology clustering", subsequently applied by various authors (Leung, 2001; Eastin, 2002), and defines it as the elements of technology that are perceived as interrelated and determine the degree to which other technologies are used. To adequately reflect Technological compatibility, the concept must therefore include not only basic IS, such as Internet and e-mail, but also more complex applications, such as EDI (Premkumar & Roberts, 1999; Emmanouilides & Hammond, 2000; Barwise, Elberse, & Hammond, 2002). Following Liaw and Huang (2003) and Liaw, Chang, Hung, and Huang, (2006), the present study argues that a single construct is insufficient to include such aspects. They represent very different levels of internal technological development, and must be differentiated to be used as indicators, although the joint effect of all applications implemented determines overall Technological compatibility within companies.

The experience acquired in recent years by those enterprises which have used other IS included in the Technological compatibility factor has allowed them to further their knowledge, thereby obtaining a familiarity with IS which may affect the implementation and subsequent development of Web procurement (Lee, Kozar, & Larsen, 2003). We consider that Web procurement should be seen as the technological development of EDI towards more flexible exchanges of information, which allow faster transactions to be made and for business to be directed towards online distribution. Moreover, a review of existing literature on technology adoption reveals that most studies tested the previous model used for EDI as it is similar to e-commerce in that it provides electronic links to customers (Seyal & Rahman, 2003). EDI has many disadvantages, causing some enterprises to look for other similar Internet-based tools, as a viable alternative to previous systems for inter-organizational communication (Angeles & Nath, 2000; Soliman & Janz, 2004).

The Industry Effect

Research on IS diffusion has generally focused on the average impact across industries. However, only a few studies about IS-related have suggested that the nature and significance of their impact may depend on the industry or sector analyzed (Im, Dow & Grover, 2001; Stoel & Muhanna, 2009). The industry in which the enterprise operates can play an important role in enterprise behaviour (Chiasson & Davidson, 2005), so this must be taken into account in the study of enterprise acceptance of IS. The so-called "industry effect" should be included as an explanatory factor of the acquisition of new IS (Goodacre & Tonks, 1995; Dyer, Cho & Chu, 1998; Shore, 2001).

Various studies consider the specific economic activity of an enterprise as being a key element in the determination of the intensity of B2B e-commerce (Goodacre & Tonks, 1995; Shore, 2001). First of all, the industry in which businesses compete influences the efficiency required from their online management; in more technologically developed sectors enterprises must make greater and better use of their IS (Dyer *et al.,* 1998). Secondly, this specific business environment helps to determine the technological benefits which can be obtained from IS.

Other research has analyzed the advance of computerization in enterprises belonging to different industries, concluding that textile enterprises exhibit relatively low technological development, while others, such as electricity companies, typically introduce state-of-the-art IS into their production functions (Shore, 2001). Motiwalla,

Khan and Xu (2005) study the divergence in IS performance for enterprises in three different sectors, in an attempt to highlight the variables which affect them within the e-business context. It can be observed that retail industry experiences a significantly higher percentage of sales growth than those whose activity is the distribution of food, beverages and tobacco or consumer products. Finally, the impact of e-business was stronger on the consumer products industry in terms of net income and sales growth. The logical conclusion is that a particular activity influences the development of similar technological behaviour patterns, which in turn modifies the IS acceptance level. Moreover, other studies, such as the one carried out by Freeman and Soete (1997), emphasize that certain industries (e.g. chemical or computer) differentiate their products through ever-increasing technological innovation, constantly attempting to achieve the greatest possible development within their enterprises.

On a similar note, Premkumar and Roberts (1999) believe that competitive sectorial pressure is a determining factor in the adoption of a greater number of innovations, arguing that to belong to a business sector, which is more technologically competitive, stimulates the implantation of more sophisticated tools, which in addition gives rise to a significant investment of resources in IS (Gatignon & Robertson, 1985; D'aspremont & Jacquemin, 1988). As a result, those activities which are more information-intensive are more likely to implement new systems, due principally to the fact that their employment generates greater strategic advantages (Min & Galle, 2003).

Despite what has been stated above, the relationship which exists between the sector and technological development is not unanimously accepted in the literature on the subject. Other studies conclude that there are no significant differences between the service and manufacturing sectors in the implantation of technologies, and therefore a significant industry effect cannot be said to exist overall (Min & Galle, 2003).

Both sides of the research display the need to test the influence of industry on technological behaviour. We consider that this effect can modify the relationships established between perceptions, acting as a moderating variable.

OBJECTIVES AND HYPOTHESES

The present study analyzes the future company use of advanced IS for business management, testing the TAM framework in the business environment. The study incorporates the typical TAM variables -ease of use, usefulness, and intensity of use- and it also introduces other new and relevant variables such as Technological compatibility and Web procurement. Finally, the moderating effect of industry was tested.

The study has two sub-objectives:

Proposal 1: To extend the TAM proposed by Davis *et al.* (1989) for the business context. We have included some new relationships which potentially affect Technological compatibility and Web procurement, based on the theoretical foundations described in the previous section.

Various studies have analyzed the influence of compatibility upon perceived ease of use and perceived usefulness (Agarwal & Karahanna, 1998; Lu & Yeh, 1998; Venkatesh & Davis, 2000; Tung, 2007). Previous experience with IS and organizational structures adapted to the new systems modify user perceptions (Agarwal & Karahanna, 1998; Chau & Hu, 2002) and influence the adoption of Web procurement (Angeles & Nath, 2000; Lee *et al.,* 2003):

H1: Technological compatibility (TC) has a positive influence on the perceived ease of use (PEOU) of management software.
H2: Technological compatibility (TC) has a positive influence on the perceived usefulness (PU) of management software.

H3: Technological compatibility (TC) has a positive influence on the Web procurement (WP) of the enterprise.

Moreover, the hypotheses connected to the TAM relationships initially proposed by Davis (1989) and Davis *et al.* (1989):

H4: Perceived ease of use (PEOU) within the enterprise has a positive influence on perceived usefulness (PU) of management software.
H5: Perceived usefulness (PU) within the enterprise has a positive influence on intensity of use of management software.
H6: Perceived ease of use (PEOU) within the enterprise has a positive influence on intensity of use of management software.

With regard to the behaviour explained, studies exist on the current use of an IS, future employment, or users' intention to employ it (Henderson & Divett, 2003; Shang, Chen, & Shen, 2005; Wu, Chen, & Lin, 2007). Greater use of an IS produces greater experience and knowledge and an increased influence upon its future use in subsequent periods. Therefore, there exists a cyclical effect in the transmission of knowledge over time which suggests a positive relationship between the intensity of use of various systems (Web procurement and management software, in the present study) and the future intentions to continue applying other advanced IS. We have formulated the following hypotheses:

H7: Intensity of use of management software by the enterprise has a positive influence on future use for advanced technologies.
H8: Web procurement of the enterprise has a positive influence on future use for advanced technologies.

Figure 1 illustrates all of these relationships:

Figure 1. Research model

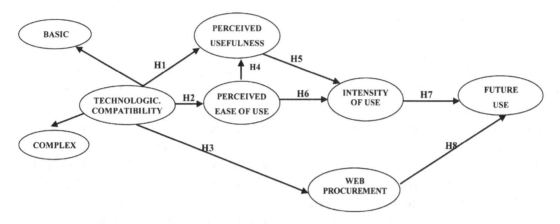

Proposal 2: To analyze whether or not the proposed model displays significant differences depending on the sector to which the enterprise belongs.

The influence of all described variables upon the acceptance level may be modified by the enterprise sector, which would imply that there exists a set of enterprises more predisposed than others to the implantation of sophisticated IS. Such influence has been labelled "industry effect" and would act as a variable which moderates enterprise technological development, influencing the use of management software and enterprise future use of this or other advanced IS.

In consequence, we have distinguished two groups of enterprises according to their activity and we suggest that the relationships described above could be affected by the moderating effect of the industry.

METHODOLOGY

The technique employed to gather information was traditional mail and e-mail, both for a sample of enterprises in the Spanish technological sector (449 enterprises) and for 1,256 enterprises in other economic sectors. This sample was extracted at random from the SABI database, thereby guaranteeing representativeness of sectors and sizes.

After the refining process, a sample of 257 enterprises was obtained, 109 of which belonged to the technological sector and 148 to other sectors (the industrial, service and agriculture sectors, including forestry and fishing). We checked that there was no non-response bias. Differences among early respondents and late respondents were checked through the t-test, analyzing not only demographic characteristics (such as number of employees or number of PCs in the company) but also the independent and dependent variables (Straub, 1989). No significant differences were found, suggesting a non-response bias.

The information refers to each enterprise as a unit, not to each of its employees; managers who are responsible for IS therefore responded on behalf of the enterprise (Riemenschneider, Harrison, & Mykytyn, 2003; Altobello, Grandon, & Mykytyn, 2008) since managerial perceptions play an important role in innovation adoption (To & Ngai, 2007). This is why the questionnaires were sent to the heads of IS departments, those who take decisions regarding systems. It must be remembered that, in the business environment, the decision to adopt a system does not depend on each employee but is taken by a decision-making agent and, subsequently, is implemented at enterprise-wide level (Hartwick & Barki 1994; Holland & Light 1999). As a result, the analysis of enterprise behaviour through the agent who makes IS-related decisions eliminates the effect produced by the coercive nature of acceptance (from the point of view of the employee as end-user).

The study analyzes the principal business functions for which computerization is possible: commercial management, financial accounting, budgetary management and after-sales service. The indicators included in the questionnaire to measure perceived ease of use and perceived usefulness were those most commonly utilized in previous TAM studies (Legris, Ingham, & Collerette, 2003) and also refer to the various types of management software. The future use variable represents the intentions to apply IS in coming years and is an adaptation of those proposed by Riemenschneider *et al.* (2003) and Ajzen and Fishbein (1980).

To measure Technological compatibility, on the one hand the study analyzes aspects of the technological experience with basic and popular IS, such as Internet and e-mail (Emmanouilides & Hammond, 2000; Barwise *et al.,* 2002) and, on the other hand, more complex tools like EDI. To ascertain prior familiarity with these IS, the questionnaire included 9 items regarding their application and further questions about perceptions derived from previous experience (see Appendix); various studies have shown that the degree to which a specific system is diffused depends upon how it is subjectively viewed (Igbaria, Zinatelli, Cragg, & Cavaye, 1997; Lee *et al.,* 2003).

The study measured the variables analyzed using 7-point Likert scales, in which 1 indicates "completely disagree" and 7 "completely agree". The Web procurement measures the percentage of purchases made via the Internet. As this is a directly observable variable, this factor comprises one sole indicator.

EMPIRICAL ANALYSIS

Initial Analysis

Factorial exploratory analyses were performed using the statistical software SPSS/PC (Version 14.0 for Windows) (McDonald, 1981; Hair, Anderson, Tatham, & Black, 1999). This software examines the unidimensionality of the scales. The analyses demonstrate that two differentiated significant factors can be extracted for Technological compatibility: i) a set of indicators linked to the use of the Internet and e-mail, or "compatibility with basic systems"; ii) a set of elements related to the use of EDI, a more sophisticated IS, or "compatibility with complex systems". These factors combine to produce an explained variance of 70.23%, and all their loadings exceed the established minimum of 0.5 (Hair *et al.,* 1999). The remaining factors extracted obtain clearly satisfactory results.

The Cronbach alpha analyses eliminate the indicators related to company after-sales service (USE_4, PU_4, PEOU_4), since the alpha statistics do not exceed the recommended value of 0.7. The constructs which comprise compatibility remain invariant. Following this initial refinement, the scales produce alpha values of 0.928 (BS), 0.884 (CX), 0.743 (USE), 0.765 (PU) and 0.743 (PEOU).

Elimination of these indicators requires the repetition of the exploratory factor analyses. The non-eliminated items are grouped together in the same constructs as in the initial analyses, to retest their stability. The loadings of all factors exceed 0.5 and explained variances surpass 50%.

Confirmatory Analysis of Reliability and Validity

To assess measurement reliability and validity, a confirmatory factor analysis (CFA) containing all the multi-item constructs in our framework was estimated with EQS 6.1 (Bentler, 1995) using the maximum likelihood method. Indicators which do not meet one or more of the three criteria proposed by Jöreskog and Sörbom (1993) have been refined, namely weak convergence, strong convergence and explanatory coefficient. The criterion of weak convergence analyzes the significance of the factor regression coefficients between the indicators and their latent variable, eliminating those which are not significant (t-student >2.58; p=0.01). The criterion of strong convergence requires the elimination of non-substantial indicators, i.e., those whose standardized coefficient is below 0.5 (Hildebrandt, 1987). The explanatory coefficient of the indicator must be greater than 0.3. The e-mail ease of use indicator (BS_6) was excluded. The repetition of the analysis for the remaining indicators rejects the item regarding Internet ease of use (BS_3) due to an insufficient R^2. A further repetition achieves favourable results with regard to all three criteria described. The final measurement model provides a good fit to the data on the basis of a number of fit statistics: GFI= 0.895; RMSR= 0.058; RMSEA= 0.076; CFI= 0.941; CFI robust= 0.948; NFI= 0.914; NNFI= 0.915; X^2 /d.f.= 2.94.

Following the initial testing for the Cronbach alpha, the study tests the reliability of the scales using the composite reliability coefficient (CRC) and average variance extracted (AVE) (Jöreskog, 1971). The results achieved exceed in all cases the

Table 1. Confirmatory analysis

	ITEM	CRC	AVE	R^2	Lambda**	Factors	Interval	Factors	Interval
Basic Systems (BS)	BS_1			0.735	0.857	FU - BS	(0.272- 0.462)	PU - BS	(-0.037- 0.259)
	BS_2			0.707	0.841	FU - CX	(0.150- 0.426)	PU - CX	(0.068- 0.340)
	BS_4	0.908	0.711	0.715	0.845	FU - PEOU	(0.188- 0.476)	PU- PEOU	(0.591- 0.787)
	BS_5			0.688	0.829	FU - PU	(0.187- 0.447)		
Complex Systems (CX)	CX_1			0.833	0.913	FU - USE	(0.180- 0.472)		
	CX_2	0.892	0.735	0.607	0.779	FU - WP	(0.276- 0.508)		
	CX_3			0.765	0.875	WP - BS	(0.159- 0.323)		
Perceived Ease of Use (PEOU)	PEOU_1			0.448	0.669	WP - CX	(0.109- 0.421)		
	PEOU_2	0.749	0.502	0.661	0.823	WP - PEOU	(-0.098- 0.198)		
	PEOU_3			0.369	0.617	WP - PU	(-0.061- 0.191)		
Perceived Usefulness (PU)	PU_1			0.465	0.682	WP - USE	(-0.065- 0.231)		
	PU_2	0.753	0.507	0.672	0.820	USE - BS	(-0.023- 0.277)		
	PU_3			0.384	0.619	USE - CX	(0.106- 0.374)		
Intensity of Use (USE)	USE_1			0.485	0.696	USE - PEOU	(0.791- 0.915)		
	USE_2	0.728	0.474	0.566	0.752	USE - PU	(0.732- 0.888)		
	USE_3			0.369	0.608	CX - BS	(0.129- 0.305)		
Future Use (FU)	FU	-		0.85	0.923	PEOU- BS	(0.013- 0.301)		
Web Procurement	WP	-		0.85	0.923	PEOU- CX	(0.136- 0.380)		

** Significant at level 0.01

recommended limits of 0.6 and 0.5, respectively (Bagozzi & Yi, 1988) (Table 1).

To verify convergent validity, confirmatory analysis must obtain significant standardized loads which exceed 0.5 (Steenkamp & Van Trijp, 1991) (Table 1). If bidimensionality exists (Technological compatibility), the correlations between the two dimensions which measure a single theoretical concept must also be significant at level 0.01. The study thus confirms convergent validity (Table 1). In the case of the discriminatory validity, the study employs two distinct criteria. First of all, none of the intervals of the correlations between different constructs must contain the value 1. Secondly, the average variance extracted from the underlying constructs must be larger than the variance shared with other constructs.

Dimensionality

To contrast the multidimensional structure in the case of Technological compatibility, a rival model strategy (Anderson & Gerbing, 1998) compares two alternative models: the first brings together all the items in a single factor, while the second creates a bidimensional structure ("basic" and "complex"). The results show better goodness-of-fit in the second order model, confirming the bidimensionality of the concept.

The underlying dimensions, nevertheless, reflect a common concept called Technological compatibility. Both factors consequently converge in a single construct, not directly observable, which displays the joint effect of basic and complex tools upon subsequent technological development. Compatibility with "basic systems" obtains a value of 0.303 and "complex systems" 0.737.

Structural Model Analysis

Following verification of the measurement model, the study tests the structural relationships proposed in the working hypotheses, confirming that the model shows appropriate adjustment for the three types of indicators: Absolute (GFI= 0.886; RMSR= 0.068; RMSEA= 0.075; IFI= 0.937), Incremental (NFI= 0.907; NNFI= 0.917; CFI= 0.936; CFI robust= 0.941) and Parsimony ($X^2/$ d.f.= 2.88). The results obtained are shown in Figure 2.

PEOU influences the intensity of use ($\beta5=0.563$) and PU of management software ($\beta4=0.667$); PU explains intensity of use ($\beta6=0.425$). PEOU exerts both a direct and indirect influence upon USE and the findings therefore support H4, H5 and H6.

Technological compatibility significantly influences PEOU ($\beta1=0.373$), and thus the findings support H1. It does not however significantly affect perceived usefulness and the findings do not therefore support H2. The knowledge acquired via the prior use of systems, such as Internet, e-mail and EDI, has a positive influence (0.45) on the proportion of online purchases. Greater Technological compatibility means greater use of the Internet

Figure 2. Results of the structural model and hypotheses test

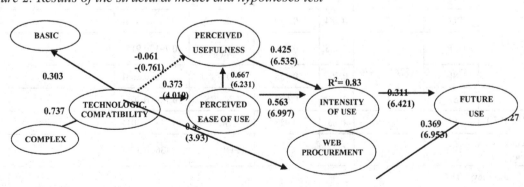

in purchasing and thus the findings support H3. Technological compatibility is a variable that acts as a predecessor for the use of different systems, influencing both the extent of Web procurement and the use of management software via the usefulness and ease of use variables.

The experience gained from current use of such systems directly affects the future use for other IS ($\beta 7=0.311$). Those firms which use Web procurement more intensively make greater future use of IS ($\beta 8=0.369$) and the findings thus support H7 and H8.

In addition to the direct effects reflected through the relationships proposed in the model, future use (final variable) is indirectly influenced by Technological compatibility and by PEOU and PU, via intensity of use, and also by Technological compatibility, via Web procurement. The overall influence of Technological compatibility upon intensity of use is 0.290 and upon future use is 0.256. PEOU influences intensity of use (0.847) and future use (0.264). Finally, the global effect of PU is 0.425 upon intensity of use and 0.132 upon future use. The model displays a considerable explanatory power for the intensity of use ($R^2= 0.83$).

ANALYSIS OF THE INDUSTRY EFFECT

The study next tests the importance of the moderating effect of industry on the process of IS acceptance and analyzes the possible existence of significant differences between the two sub-samples identified (technological and traditional enterprises). As explained earlier, the economic activity undertaken by the company may give rise to specific perceptions of innovations, and these are not necessarily observable in enterprises operating in other industries. In order to test whether or not such an effect exists in the case of IS diffusion, this study employs multisample analysis, based on structural equation models. This analysis

checked the existence of significant inter-sectorial differences in the relationships proposed.

Prior to the analysis of each of the relationships, the adjustment indices for the overall multisample model showed optimum values: CFI 0.898; IFI 0.900; GFI 0.817; RMSEA 0.076; $X^2/$ d.f.= 2.48.

The results obtained verify that the moderating effect of industry can be observed in only two relationships. Both such relationships are analyzed in the leading TAM studies: (1) the influence of ease of use upon intensity of use and (2) the influence of intensity of use upon future use. These relationships vary according to economic sector, which modifies the overall effect of the variables upon future use (Table 2).

DISCUSSION, CONCLUSIONS AND MANAGERIAL IMPLICATIONS

This study analyzes company behaviour regarding the current and future use of new information management systems. It employs a TAM, optimized by the inclusion of new variables (Technological compatibility, Web procurement) which act as predecessors and may help to explain enterprise behaviour. The study tests if the relationships proposed in the model change according to enterprise industry, or whether a "moderating industry effect" exists. The two sub-samples employed distinguish between technological enterprises and the rest of industries. The results obtained can be materialized in important conclusions and have important implications for management.

The significance of Technological compatibility suggests that enterprises should be aware that interrelationships exist among the various IS. Investment in a specific system may facilitate the acceptance and subsequent performance of other IS. As Cho (2006) states, although the adoption of new IS may involve factors different from other IS related to commercial management, they are very similar in nature. Thus, the experience ac-

Table 2. Results of multisample analysis

RELATIONS (diff. between both groups)	X^2	Prob.	RESULTS
TC → PEOU	0.174	0.676	No differences
TC → PU	0.0001	0.976	No differences
TC → WP	2.361	0.124	No differences
PEOU → PU	0.001	0.979	No differences
PEOU → USE	8.588	0.003	Differences**
PU → USE	1.684	0.194	No differences
USE → FU	12.822	0.000	Differences**
WP → FU	1.891	0.169	No differences

** Significant at level of 0.01

cumulated produces a series of synergies derived from the application of mutually complementary systems, allowing enterprises to improve their results in the employment of other IS during business activity. The knowledge the enterprise acquires previously by using other IS should be considered when explaining its future technological behaviour (Bennett, Härtel, & McColl-Kennedy, 2005), since it will increase its motivation and mitigate its resistance to using new applications (Dewar & Dutton, 1986; Kearns & Sabhewarl, 2007). In this way, the learning process undergone will diminish the perception of risk associated with the implementation of a new system, creating overall compatibility which will significantly affect the degree of future development. Some authors, such as Kaefer and Bendoly (2004), have already recommended that such synergies must be exploited by firms wishing to invest in IS, encouraging the acquisition of knowledge which will prove profitable in future activities. This technical aptitude will allow enterprises to correctly evaluate subsequent related projects, assessing the true value of an investment in IS and avoiding financial losses.

However, the technological environment is constantly developing, and the interrelationship which exists between systems varies according to their level of complexity or innovation. The life cycle of a system is ever shorter, meaning it is essential to understand which part of the investment will continue in use and which will become obsolete. As this takes place, it is crucial for the enterprise to accumulate non-measurable benefits derived from knowledge, as these may be reused for the implementation of new applications and, in addition they maintain the current value of the system. In order to not lose the competitive advantage acquired, enterprises must continually invest in this field, concentrating especially on the most important aspects and increasing the efficiency of their management.

Those systems which are considered to be useful in the execution of a particular business function, and are furthermore simple to apply, are more likely to be adopted. Enterprises which promote such systems must be aware that for potential users to acquire an IS it is essential to eliminate the barriers produced by difficulty of use, whether by making their operation simpler or by providing some type of help service (online assistance, etc.). IS must be perceived as useful or capable of facilitating enterprise activity, and thus all possible tools must be employed in order to transmit this message to enterprises.

With regard to the acceptance of IS depending on the industry, the effect of PU is the same for all enterprises. Likewise, the fact of working in a less competitive environment, technologically speaking, does not lead enterprises to ignore the potential advantages a new system may provide. These new systems present an opportunity to improve business and produce greater added value for all enterprises regardless of their activity. Nevertheless, the relevance of ease of use is greater for technological firms, increasing their level of use.

Finally, a future research line would be to analyze over a continuous period the variation in the importance of the constructs which comprise Technological compatibility (basic and complex systems), and the relationships between usefulness, ease of use and the use of software and Web procurement. Such a study would thus measure the use of IS in future years and carry out a more in depth analysis of the adaptation of enterprises to changes in their operating environment. Moreover, we would like to extend the research by including new management software as it comes onto the market. The possibilities offered by new IS to store and manage information improve existing relationships with customers, suppliers and collaborators, as well as offer important business opportunities (Noori & Salimi, 2005; Zablah, Johnston, & Bellenger, 2005).

ACKNOWLEDGMENT

The authors wish to express their gratitude for the financial support received from the Spanish Government CICYT SEC2008-04704, (the Aragón Regional Government (Generés S-09; PI 138/08), and Cátedra Telefónica de la Universidad de Zaragoza (267-184).

REFERENCES

Achjari, D., & Quaddus, M. A. (2003). Roles of formal/informal networks and perceived compatibility in the diffusion of world wide web: The case of Indonesian banks. In *Proceedings of the 36th Hawaii International Conference on System Science*.

Agarwal, R., & Karahanna, E. (1998). The antecedents and consequents of user perceptions in information technology adoption. *Decision Support Systems*, *22*(1), 15–29. doi:10.1016/S0167-9236(97)00006-7

Ajzen, I., & Fishbein, M. (1980). *Understanding attitudes and predicting social behavior*. Prentice Hall.

Altobello, S., Grandon, E., & Mykytyn, P. (2008). Predicting electronic commerce adoption in Chilean SMEs. *Journal of Business Research*, *61*(6), 697–705. doi:10.1016/j.jbusres.2007.06.047

Anderson, J. C., & Gerbing, D. W. (1998). Structural equation modeling in practice: A review and recommend two-step approach. *Psychological Bulletin*, *103*(3), 411–423. doi:10.1037/0033-2909.103.3.411

Angeles, R., & Nath, R. (2000). An empirical study of EDI trading partner selection criteria in customer-supplier relationship. *Information & Management*, *37*, 241–255. doi:10.1016/S0378-7206(99)00054-3

Argote, L. & Ingram, P. (2000). Knowledge transfer: A basis for competitive advantage in firms. *Organizacional behavior and human decision processes, 82*(1), 150-169.

Arunchalam, V. (1997). Electronic data interchange: issues in adoption and management. *Information Resources Management Journal, 10*(2), 22–31.

Bagozzi, R. P., & Yi, Y. (1988). On the evaluation of structural equation models. *Academy of Marketing Science*, *16*(1), 74–94. doi:10.1007/BF02723327

Barkema, H., & Vermeulen, F. (1998). International expansion through start-up or acquisition: A learning perspective. *Academy of Management Journal, 41*(1), 7–26. doi:10.2307/256894

Barwise, P., Elberse, A. & Hammond K. (2002). Marketing and the Internet: A research review. No. 01-801.

Bass, F. M. (1969). A new product growth model for consumer durables. *Management Science, 15*(January), 215–227. doi:10.1287/mnsc.15.5.215

Bennett, R., Härtel, C., & McColl-Kennedy, J. R. (2005). Experience as a moderator of involvement and satisfaction on brand loyalty in a business-to-business setting 02-314R. *Industrial Marketing Management, 34,* 97–107. doi:10.1016/j.indmarman.2004.08.003

Bentler, P. M. (1995). *EQS structural equations program manual.* Inc. CA: Multivariate Software.

Bradley, J., & Lee, C. C. (2007). ERP training and user satisfaction: A case study. *International Journal of Enterprise Information Systems, 3*(4), 33–50.

Bruner, G. C. II, & Kumar, A. (2005). Explaining consumer acceptance of handheld Internet devices. *Journal of Business Research, 58,* 553–558. doi:10.1016/j.jbusres.2003.08.002

Chau, P. Y. K., & Hu, P. J. (2002). Examining a model of information technology acceptance by individual professionals: an exploratory study. *Journal of Management Information Systems, 18*(4), 191–229.

Chiasson, M., & Davidson, E. (2005). Taking industry seriously in IS research. *MIS Quarterly, 29*(4), 591–606.

Cho, V. (2006). Factors in the adoption of third-party B2B portals in the textile industry. *Journal of Computer Information Systems, 46*(3), 18–31.

D'aspremont, C. & Jacquemin, A. (1988). Co-operative and Non-Cooperative R&D Industry with Spillovers. *The American Economic Review, 78*(December), 1133–1137.

Davis, F. D. (1989). Perceived usefulness, perceived ease of use and user acceptance of information technology. *MIS Quarterly, 13*(3), 319–339. doi:10.2307/249008

Davis, F. D., Bagozzi, R., & Warhaw, P. (1989). User acceptance of computer technology: A comparison of two theoretical models. *Management Science, 35*(8), 982–1002. doi:10.1287/mnsc.35.8.982

Dewar, R. D., & Dutton, J. E. (1986). The adoption of radical and incremental innovation: An empirical analysis. *Management Science, 32,* 1422–1433. doi:10.1287/mnsc.32.11.1422

Doherty, N. F., & King, M. (1998). The importance of organizational issues in systems development. *Information Technology & People, 11,* 104–123. doi:10.1108/09593849810218300

Dyer, J. D., Cho, D. S., & Chu, W. (1998). Strategic supplier segmentation: The next 'best practice' in supply chain management. *California Management Review, 40*(2).

Eastin, M. S. (2002). Diffusion of e-commerce: an analysis of the adoption of four e-commerce activities. *Telematics and Informatics, 19,* 251–267. doi:10.1016/S0736-5853(01)00005-3

Emmanouilides, C., & Hammond, K. (2000). Internet usage: predictors of active users and frequency of use. *Journal of Interactive Marketing, 14*(2), 17–32. doi:10.1002/(SICI)1520-6653(200021)14:2<17::AID-DIR2>3.0.CO;2-E

Fitzpatrick, D. (1998). *Regional Development and the Information Society.* TIMMERS.

Freeman, C., & Soete, L. (1997). *The Economics of Industrial Innovation* (3rd ed.). Cambridge, MA: The MIT Press.

Fuller, M. A., Hardin, A. M., & Scott, C. L. (2007). Diffusion of virtual innovation. *The Data Base for Advances in Information Systems*, *38*(4), 40–45.

Gatignon, H., & Robertson, T. S. (1985). A propositional inventory for new diffusion research. *The Journal of Consumer Research*, *11*(4), 859–867. doi:10.1086/209021

Goodacre, A., & Tonks, I. (1995). Finance and technological change. In Stoneman (Ed.), *Handbook of the Economics of Innovation and Technological Change* (pp. 298-341). Oxford: Blackwell

Hair, J. F., Anderson, R. E., Tatham, R. L., & Black, W. C. (1999). *Multivariate Data Analysis*. NJ: Prentice Hall.

Hartwick, J., & Barki, H. (1994). Explaining the role of user participation in information systems use. *Management Science*, *40*(4), 440–465. doi:10.1287/mnsc.40.4.440

Henderson, R., & Divett, M. J. (2003). Perceived usefulness, ease of use and electronic supermarket use. *International Journal of Human-Computer Studies*, *59*(3), 383–395. doi:10.1016/S1071-5819(03)00079-X

Hildebrandt, L. (1987). Consumer retail satisfaction in rural areas: A re-analysis of survey data. *Journal of Economic Psychology*, *8*, 19–42. doi:10.1016/0167-4870(87)90004-3

Holland, C., & Light, B. (1999). A critical success factors model for ERP implementation. *IEEE Software*, *16*(3), 30–36. doi:10.1109/52.765784

Igbaria, M., Zinatelli, N., Cragg, P., & Cavaye, A. L. M. (1997). Personal computing acceptance factors in small firms: a structural equation model. *MIS Quarterly*, *21*(3), 279–302. doi:10.2307/249498

Im, K. S., Dow, K. E., & Grover, V. (2001). A reexamination of IT investment and the market value of the firm: an event study methodology. *Information Systems Research*, *12*(1), 103–117. doi:10.1287/isre.12.1.103.9718

Jiménez, J., & Polo, Y. (1998). International diffusion of a new tool: The case of electronic data interchange in the retailing sector. *Research Policy*, *26*(7-8), 811–827. doi:10.1016/S0048-7333(97)00045-0

Jöreskog, K. (1971). Statistical analysis of sets of congeneric tests. *Psychometrika*, *36*, 109–133. doi:10.1007/BF02291393

Jöreskog, K., & Sörbom, D. (1993). *LISREL 8 Structural Equation Modeling with the Simples Command Language*. Scientific software International, Chicago-Illinois.

Kaefer, F., & Bendoly, E. (2004). Measuring the impact of organizational constraint on the success of business e-commerce efforts: A transactional focus. *Information & Management*, *41*, 529–541. doi:10.1016/S0378-7206(03)00088-0

Kamhawi, E. M. (2007). Critical factors for implementation success of ERP systems. *International Journal of Enterprise Information Systems*, *3*(2), 34–49.

Kearns, G. S., & Sabhewarl, R. (2007). Antecedents and consequences of information systems planning integration. *IEEE Transactions on Engineering Management*, *54*(4), 628–643. doi:10.1109/TEM.2007.906848

Klopping, I., & McKinney, E. (2004). Extending the technology acceptance model the task-technology fit model to consumer e-commerce. *Information Technology . Learning Performance Journal*, *22*(1), 35–48.

Kositanurit, B., Ngwenyama, O., & Osei-Bryson, K.-M. (2006). An exploration of factors that impact individual performance in an ERP environment: an analysis using multiple analytical techniques. *European Journal of Information Systems, 15*, 556–568. doi:10.1057/palgrave.ejis.3000654

Lee, Y., Kozar, K. A., & Larsen, K. R. T. (2003). The technology acceptance model: past, present, and future. *Communications of the Association for Information Systems, 12*, 752–780.

Legris, P. J., Ingham, J., & Collerette, P. (2003). Why do people use information technology? A critical review of the technology acceptance model. *Information & Management, 40*(3), 191–204. doi:10.1016/S0378-7206(01)00143-4

Leung, L. (2001). College student motives for chatting on ICQ. *New Media & Society, 3*(4), 483–500. doi:10.1177/14614440122226209

Liaw, S. S., Chang, W. C., Hung, W. H., & Huang, H. M. (2006). Attitudes toward search engines as a learning assisted tool: approach of Liaw and Huang's research model. *Computers in Human Behavior, 22*(3), 501–517. doi:10.1016/j.chb.2004.10.007

Liaw, S. S., & Huang, H. M. (2003). An investigation of user attitudes toward search engines as an information retrieval tool. *Computers in Human Behavior, 19*(6), 751–765. doi:10.1016/S0747-5632(03)00009-8

Lu, H. P., & Yeh, D. C. (1998). Enterprise's perceptions on business process re-engineering: A path analytic model. *OMEGA . International Journal of Management Science, 26*(1), 17–27.

March, J. (1991). Exploration and exploitation in organizational learning. *Organization Science, 2*(special issue), 71–87. doi:10.1287/orsc.2.1.71

McDonald, R. (1981). The dimensionality of test and items. *The British Journal of Mathematical and Statistical Psychology, 34*, 110–117.

Min, H., & Galle, W. (2003). E-purchasing: profiles of adopters and non-adopters. *Industrial Marketing Management, 32*(3), 227–233. doi:10.1016/S0019-8501(02)00266-3

Miyazaki, A. D., & Fernández, A. (2001). Consumer perceptions of privacy and security risks for online shopping. *The Journal of Consumer Affairs, 35*(1), 27–44.

Motiwalla, L., Khan, M. R., & Xu, S. (2005). An intra- and inter-industry analysis of e-business effectiveness. *Information & Management, 42*(5), 651–667. doi:10.1016/j.im.2003.12.001

Noori, B., & Salimi, M. H. (2005). A decision-support system for business-to-business marketing . *Journal of Business and Industrial Marketing, 20*(4-5), 226–236. doi:10.1108/08858620510603909

Park, J.-H., Suh, H.-J., & Yang, H.-D. (2007). Perceived absorptive capacity of individual users in performance of Enterprise Resource Planning (ERP) usage: The case for Korean firms. *Information & Management, 44*, 300–312. doi:10.1016/j.im.2007.02.001

Premkumar, G. & Roberts. (1999). Adoption of new information technologies in rural small businesses. *Omega, 27*(4), 467–484. doi:10.1016/S0305-0483(98)00071-1

Riemenschneider, C., Harrison, D. A., & Mykytyn, P. P. J. (2003). Understanding ICT adoption decisions in small business: integrating current theories. *Information & Management, 40*(4), 269–285. doi:10.1016/S0378-7206(02)00010-1

Robinson, J. R. L., Marshall, G. W., & Stamps, M. B. (2005). Sales force use of technology: antecedents to technology acceptance. *Journal of Business Research, 58*, 1623–1631. doi:10.1016/j.jbusres.2004.07.010

Rogers, E. M. (1983). *Diffusion of Innovations*. New York: The Free Press.

Rogers, E. M. (1995). *Diffusion of Innovations* (4th ed.). New York: The Free Press.

Seyal, A. H., & Rahman, M. N. A. (2003). A preliminary investigation of e-commerce adoption in small and medium enterprises in Brunei. *Journal of Global Information Technology Management, 6*(2), 6–26.

Shang, R. A., Chen, Y. C., & Shen, L. (2005). Extrinsic versus intrinsic motivations for consumers to shop online. *Information & Management, 42*(3), 401–413. doi:10.1016/j.im.2004.01.009

Shim, S. J., & Viswanathan, V. (2007). User assessment of personal digital assistants used in pharmaceutical detailing: System features, usefulness and ease of use. *Journal of Computer Information Systems, 48*(1), 14–21.

Shore, B. (2001). Information sharing in global supply chain systems. *Journal of Global Information Technology Management, 4*(3).

Soliman, K., & Janz, B. (2004). A exploratory study to identify the critical factors affecting the decision to establish Internet based interorganizational information systems. *Information & Management, 41*(6), 697–707. doi:10.1016/j.im.2003.06.001

Steenkamp, J. P., & Van Trijp, H. C. M. (1991). The use of Lisrel in validating marketing constructs. *International Journal of Research in Marketing, 8*(November), 283–299. doi:10.1016/0167-8116(91)90027-5

Stoel, M. D., & Muhanna, W. A. (2009). IT capabilities and firm performance: a contingency analysis of the role of industry and IT capability type. *Information & Management, 46*, 181–189. doi:10.1016/j.im.2008.10.002

Straub, D. W. (1989). Validating instruments in MIS research. *MIS Quarterly, 13*(2), 147–169. doi:10.2307/248922

To, M., & Ngai, E. W. T. (2007). The role of managerial attitudes in the adoption of technological innovations: an application to B2C e-commerce. *International Journal of Enterprise Information Systems, 3*(2), 23–33.

Tornatzky, L. G., & Klein, K. J. (1982). Innovation characteristics and innovation adoption-implementation: a meta-analysis of findings. *IEEE Transactions on Engineering Management, 29*(1), 28–45.

Tung, F. C. (2007). Using e-CRM Information System in the High-Tech Industry: Predicting Salesperson Intentions. *Journal of American Academy of Business, 11*(2), 131–137.

Venkatesh, V., & Davis, F. D. (2000). A theoretical extension of the technology acceptance model: four longitudinal field studies. *Management Science, 46*(2), 186–204. doi:10.1287/mnsc.46.2.186.11926

Wu, J.-H., & Wang, Y.-M. (2006). Measuring ERP success: the ultimate users' view. *International Journal of Operations & Production Management, 26*(8), 882–903. doi:10.1108/01443570610678657

Wu, J. W., Chen, Y. C., & Lin, L. M. (2007). Empirical evaluation of the revised end user computing acceptance model. *Computers in Human Behavior, 23*(1), 162–174. doi:10.1016/j.chb.2004.04.003

Xu, Q., & Ma, Q. (2008). Determinants of ERP implementation knowledge transfer. *Information & Management, 45*, 528–539. doi:10.1016/j.im.2008.08.004

Yi, M. Y., Jackson, J. D., Park, J. S., & Probst, J. (2006). Understanding information technology acceptance by individual professionals: toward an integrative view. *Information & Management, 43*(3), 350–363. doi:10.1016/j.im.2005.08.006

Zablah, A. R., Johnston, W. J., & Bellenger, D. N. (2005). Transforming partner relationships through technological innovation. *Journal of Business and Industrial Marketing, 20*(7), 355–364. doi:10.1108/08858620510628597

APPENDIX

Table 3. Measurement scale

TECHNOLOGICAL COMPATIBILITY	ITEM	EMP. ANALYSIS*
Basic Systems		
The use of Internet in the performance of the activity is intense	BS_1	Accepted
I consider that Internet is useful for the performance of the activity	BS_2	*Rejected*
Internet is easy to use in the performance of the activity	BS_3	*Rejected*
The use of e-mail in the performance of the activity is intense	BS_4	Accepted
I consider that e-mail is useful for the performance of the activity	BS_5	Accepted
E-mail is easy to use in the performance of the activity	BS_6	*Rejected*
Complex Systems		
The use of EDI in the performance of the activity is intense	CX_1	Accepted
I consider that EDI is useful for the performance of the activity	CX_2	Accepted
EDI is easy to use in the performance of the activity	CX_3	Accepted
INTENSITY OF USE	ITEM	EMP. ANALYSIS*
Customer relationship management software are intensively applied in the performance of the activity	USE_1	Accepted
Accounting software are intensively applied in the performance of the activity	USE_2	Accepted
Budgeting software are intensively applied in the performance of the activity	USE_3	Accepted
After-sales service software are intensively applied in the performance of the activity	USE_4	*Rejected*
PERCEIVED EASE OF USE	ITEM	EMP. ANALYSIS*
In general, customer relationship management software are easy to use in the performance of the activity	PEOU_1	Accepted
In general, accounting software are easy to use in the performance of the activity	PEOU_2	Accepted
In general, budgeting software are easy to use in the performance of the activity	PEOU_3	Accepted
In general, after-sales service software are easy to use in the performance of the activity	PEOU_4	*Rejected*
PERCEIVED USEFULNESS	ITEM	EMP. ANALYSIS*
Customer relationship management software are useful for the performance of the activity	PU_1	Accepted
Accounting software are useful for the performance of the activity	PU_2	Accepted
Budgeting software are useful for the performance of the activity	PU_3	Accepted
After-sales software are useful for the performance of the activity	PU_4	*Rejected*
FUTURE USE	ITEM	EMP. ANALYSIS*
I intend to apply advanced technologies in the course of my activity in the coming months	FU	Accepted

Chapter 11
Modeling and Implementation of Formal Power Structures in Enterprise Information Systems

Alexei Sharpanskykh
Vrije Universiteit Amsterdam, The Netherlands

ABSTRACT

The concepts of power and authority are inherent in human organizations of any type. In some orga-nizations power relations on individuals are defined explicitly and formalized in organizational docu-mentation. In other organizations power relations are implicit, less strict and may change depending on contextual conditions. As power relations have important consequences for organizational viability and productivity, they should be considered explicitly in enterprise information systems (EISs). Although organization theory provides a rich and very diverse theoretical basis on organizational power, still most of the definitions for power-related concepts are too abstract, often vague and ambiguous to be directly implemented in EISs. To create a bridge between informal organization theories and automated EISs, this chapter proposes a formal logic-based specification language for representing power- (in particular authority) relations and their dynamics. The use of the language is illustrated by considering authority structures of organizations of different types. Moreover, the chapter demonstrates how the formalized authority relations can be integrated into an EIS.

INTRODUCTION

The concept of *power* is inherent in human orga-nizations of any type. Power relations that exist in an organization have a significant impact on its viability and productivity. Although the notion of power is often discussed in the literature in social

DOI: 10.4018/978-1-60566-968-7.ch011

studies (Bacharach and Aiken, 1977; Blau and Scott, 1962; Clegg, 1989; Friedrich, 1958; Gulick and Urwick, 1937; Hickson et al., 1971; Parsons, 1947; Peabody, 1964), it is only rarely defined precisely. In particular, power-related terms (e.g., control, authority, influence) are often used interchange-ably in this literature. Furthermore, the treatment of power in different streams of sociology differs significantly. One of the first definitions for power in the modern sociology was given by Max Weber (1958): *Power is the probability that a person can carry out his or her own will despite resistance.* Weber and his followers (Dahl, Polsby) considered power as an inherently coercive force that implied involuntary submission and ignored the relational aspect of power. Other sociologists (Bierstedt, Blau) considered power as a force or the ability to apply sanctions (Blau and Scott, 1962). Such view was also criticized as restrictive, as it did not pay attention to indirect sources and implications of power (e.g., informal influence in decision making) and subordinate's acceptance of power. Parsons (1947) considered power as *a specific mechanism to bring about changes in the action of organizational actors in the process of social interaction.*

Most contemporary organization theories explore both formal (normative, prescribed) and informal (subjective, human-oriented) aspects of power (Clegg, 1989; Peabody, 1964; Scott, 2001). Formal power relations are documented in many modern organizations and, therefore, can be explicitly represented in models on which enterprise information systems (EISs) are based. The representation of formal power in EISs has a number of advantages. First, it allows a clear definition of rights and responsibilities for organizational roles (actors) and a power structure. Second, based on the role specifications, corresponding permissions for information, resources and actions can be specified for each role. Third, explicitly defined rules on power enable the identification of violations of organizational policies and regulations. Fourth, data about power-related actions (e.g., empowerment, authorization) can be stored in an EIS for the subsequent analysis.

For modeling of power relations the rich theoretical basis from social science can be used. Notably many modern EISs implement no or very simplified representations of power relations and mechanisms. In particular, the architecture ARIS (Scheer and Nuettgens, 2000; Davis, 2008) used for development of EISs identifies responsibility and managerial authority relations on organizational roles, however, does not provide general mechanisms for representing such relations and does not address change of these relations over time. Different aspects of authority relations can be specified in ARIS, however no dedicated ontology that would support enterprise architects is proposed. The enterprise architecture CIMOSA (1993) distinguishes responsibilities and authorities on enterprise objects, agents, and processes/activities. However, no precise meaning (semantics) is attached to these concepts, which may be interpreted differently in different applications. Also, different aspects of authorities are not distinguished in CIMOSA (e.g., authority for execution, authority for supervision, authority for monitoring). The Zachman framework (Zachman, 2003) allows defining responsibility relations for roles on functions and access privileges for resources. A number of expressive formalisms were proposed to ensure consistency of this framework (Ostadzadeh et al., 2007). However, from the conceptual point of view, diverse aspects of authority are modeled at a rather abstract level, leaving the specification of precise types of relations to the designer. Furthermore, also the temporal dimension of the formal power is not considered.

Often EISs realize extensive access schemata that determine allowed actions for roles and modes of access of roles to information (Bernus, Nemes and Schmidt, 2003). Normally such schemata are based on power relations established in organizations. Thus, to ensure consistency, unambiguousness and completeness of EISs' access schemata, organizational power relations should be precisely identified and specified using some (formal) language. To this end, theoretical findings on organization power from social science are useful to consider. However, there is an obstacle to the direct implementation of this knowledge in EISs – the absence of operational definitions of power-related concepts in social theories.

The first step to make the concept of power operational is to provide a clear and unambiguous meaning for it (or for its specific aspects). In this chapter this is done by identifying the most essential characteristics and mechanisms of power described in different approaches and by integrating them into two broad categories: formal power (or authority) and informal power (or influence), which are described in the following section. Further this chapter focuses on the formal representation of authority, for which a formal language is described. Moreover, the chapter illustrates how the introduced formal language can be used to model authority systems of different types of organizations. Furthermore, the chapter discusses the integration of formal authority relations into an automated EIS. Finally, the chapter concludes with a discussion.

POWER, AUTHORITY AND INFLUENCE

As in many contemporary social theories (Clegg, 1989; Peabody, 1964), we assume that power can be practiced in an organization either through (formal) *authority* or through (informal) *influence relations*. Authority represents formal, legitimate organizational power by means of which a regulated normative relationship between a superior and a subordinate is established. Usually authority is attached to positions in organizations. For example, authority of some managerial positions provides power to hire or to fire; to promote or to demote; to grant incentive rewards or to impose sanctions. In many approaches it is assumed that authority implies involuntary obedience from subordinates. Indeed, as authority has a normative basis that comprises formal, explicitly documented rules, it is expected that subordinates, hired by the organization, should be aware of and respect these rules, which implies the voluntary acceptance of authority.

All manifestations of power that cannot be explained from the position of authority fall into the category of influence. In contrast to author-

ity, influence does not have a formal basis. It is often persuasive and implies voluntary submission. Some of the bases of influence are technical knowledge, skills, competences and other characteristics of particular individuals. Influence is often exercised through mechanisms of leadership; however, possession of certain knowledge or access to some resources, as well as different types of manipulation may also create influence. Influence may be realized in efforts to affect organizational decisions indirectly.

Although authority and influence often stem from different sources, they are often interrelated in organizations. For example, the probability of the successful satisfaction of organizational goals increases, when a strong leader (meaning a leader that has a great value of influence) occupies a superior position of authority. Furthermore, sometimes patterns of influence that frequently occur in an organization may become institutionalized (i.e., may become authority relations).

Modeling methods for authority and influence are essentially different. While authority relations are often prescriptive and explicitly defined, influence relations are not strictly specified and may vary to a great extent. Therefore, whereas authority relations can be generally represented in EISs, the specification of influence relations is dependant on particular (cognitive) models of agents that represent organizational actors. Relations between authority and influence can be studied by performing simulation with different types of agents situated in different organizational environments. The focus of this chapter is on modeling of formal authority relations. Influence relations and relations between authority and influence will be considered elsewhere.

AUTHORITY: A FORMAL APPROACH

First, a formal language for specifying authority-related concepts and relations is introduced. Then, it will be discussed how the introduced language

Figure 1. Graphical representation of the concepts and relations of the language used for specifying formal authority relations

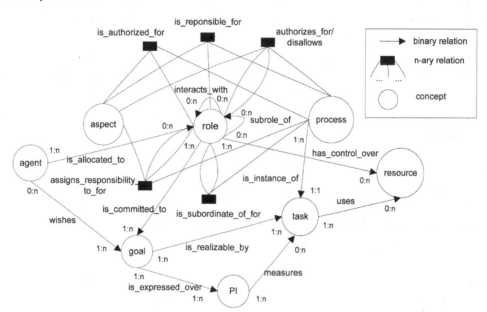

can be used for representing authority structures of organizations of different types.

A Formal Language

Simon (1957) describes three contributions of authority for an organization: (1) the enforcement of responsibility, (2) the specialization of decision-making, and (3) the coordination of activity. Based on this and other theoretical findings that describe power, duties and responsibilities of organizational positions (Mintzberg, 1979), a number of relations for the specification of formal authority can be identified. These relations are defined on positions (or roles), without considering particular agents (individuals). The relations are formalized using the order sorted-predicate language (Manzano, 1996) and are presented graphically in Fig.1.

We represent all activities of an organization (including decision making and personnel-related activities) by processes. Each organizational role is associated with one or more process. Roles may have different rights and responsibilities with respect to different aspects of the process

execution. Furthermore, often several roles may potentially execute or manage certain processes. This is represented by the relation

is_authorized_for: r:ROLE x aspect:ASPECT x a:PROCESS, where aspect has one of the values {execution, monitoring, consulting, tech_des (making technological decisions), manage_des (making managerial decisions), user_defined_aspect}.

All types of decisions with respect to a particular process can be divided into two broad groups: *technological* and *managerial* decisions (inspired by (Bacharach and Aiken, 1977)). Technological decisions concern technical questions related to the process content and are usually made by technical professionals. Managerial decisions concern general organizational issues related to the process (e.g., the allocation of employees, process scheduling, the establishment of performance standards, provision of resources, presenting incentives and sanctions). Managers of different levels (i.e., from the lowest level line managers to strategic apex (top) managers) may be authorized for making different types of managerial decisions varying from in scope, significance and detail. A particular decision type is specified as an aspect in the is_authorized_for relation. The same holds for technological decisions. Whereas consulting has a form of recommendation and implies voluntary acceptance of advices, decisions imposed on a role(s) that execute(s) the process are considered as imperatives with corresponding implications.

Authorization for execution implies that a role is allowed to execute the process according to existing standards and guidelines. Whenever a problem, a question or a deviation from the standard procedures occurs, the role must report about it to the role(s) authorized for making technological/managerial (depending on the problem type) decisions and must execute the decision(s) that will follow.

Monitoring implies passive observation of (certain aspects of) process execution, without intervention.

Notice that other aspects of process execution described in the managerial literature (e.g., control, supervision) can be represented as a combination of already introduced aspects. In particular, control can be seen as the conjunction of monitoring and making technological and/or managerial decisions aspects; supervision can be defined as the combination of consulting and control. Furthermore, the designer is given the possibility to define his/her own aspects and to provide an interpretation to them.

Although several roles in an organization may be authorized for a certain aspect related to some process, only one (or some) of them will be eventually (or are) responsible for this aspect. For example, the responsibility of a certain role with respect to the process execution means that the role is actually the one who will be performing the process and who holds accountability of the process execution. Furthermore, responsibility for the process execution implies allowance to use resources required for the process performance. The responsibility relation is specified as:

is_responsible_for: r:ROLE x aspect:ASPECT x a:PROCESS: process a is under responsibility of role r with respect to aspect (defined as for authorized_for)

Some roles are authorized to make managerial decisions for authorizing/disallowing other roles for certain aspects with respect to process execution. The authorization/ disallowance actions are specified by the following relations:

authorizes_for: r1:ROLE x r2:ROLE x aspect: ASPECT x a:PROCESS: role r1 gives the authority for aspect of process a to role r2.

disallows: r1:ROLE x r2:ROLE x aspect: ASPECT x a:PROCESS: role r1 denies the authority for aspect of process a for role r2.

However, to make a role actually responsible for a certain aspect of the process, another role besides the authority to make managerial decisions should also be the superior of the role with respect to the process. Superior-subordinate relations with respect to organizational processes are specified by: is_subordinate_of_for: r1: ROLE x r2: ROLE x a:PROCESS. Then, responsibility is assigned/ retracted using the following relations:

assigns_responsibility_to_for: r1: ROLE x r2:ROLE x aspect: ASPECT x a:PROCESS: role r1 assigns the responsibility for aspect of process a to role r2.

retracts_responsibility_from_for: r1: ROLE x r2:ROLE x aspect: ASPECT x a:PROCESS: role r1 retracts responsibility from role r2 for aspect of process a.

Using these relations superiors may delegate/ retract (their) responsibilities for certain aspects of processes execution to/from their subordinates, and may restrict themselves only to control and making decisions in exceptional situations.

In (Hickson et al., 1971) control over resources is identified as an important source of power. Therefore, it is useful to identify explicitly which roles control resources by means of the relation has_control_over: r1: ROLE x res:RESOURCE. In the proposed modeling framework the notion of resource includes both tangible (e.g., materials, tools, products) and abstract (information, data) entities.

Our treatment of authority is different from both formal approaches that consider authority as an attribute or a property inherent in an organization (Gulick and Urwick, 1937; Weber, 1958) and from the human-relation view that recognizes authority as an informal, non-rational and subjective relation (e.g., Follett, Mayo, cf. (Clegg, 1989)). As many representatives of converging approaches (e.g., C.I. Barnard, Simon (1957)) we distinguish between the formal authority prescribed by organizational policies and actual authority established between a superior and his/her subordinate in the course of social interactions. In the latter case a special accent lies on the acceptance of authority by a subordinate. In (Clegg, 1989) different cases of the authority acceptance are discussed: orders anticipated and carried out (anticipation); acceptance of orders without critical review; conscious questioning but compliance (acceptance of authority); discusses but works for changes; ignores, evades, modifies orders (modification and evasion); rejection of authority (appeals to co-workers or higher rank for support). Depending on the organizational type, varying administrative sanction may be applied in case an employee does not accept an authoritative communication, when he/she: (a) correctly understands/interprets this communication; (b) realizes that this communication complies with formal organizational documents and/or is in line with organizational goals; (c) is mentally and physically able to perform the required actions. In many modern organizations

rewards and sanctions form a part of authority relation, thus, explicitly defined:

grants_reward_to_for: r1: ROLE x r: REWARD x r2: ROLE x reason: STRING: role r1 grants reward r to role r2 for reason

imposes_saction_on_for: r1: ROLE x s: SANCTION x r2: ROLE x reason: STRING: role r1 imposes sanction s to role r2 for reason

Sometimes authority relations may be defined with respect to particular time points or intervals (e.g., responsibility for some aspect of a process may be provided for some time interval). To express temporal aspects of authority relations the Temporal Trace Language (TTL) (Jonker and Treur, 2003) is used.

TTL allows specifying a temporal development of an organization by a trace. A trace is defined as a temporally ordered sequence of states. Each state corresponds to a particular time point and is characterized by a set of state properties that hold in this state. State properties are formalized in a standard predicate logic way (Manzano, 1996) using state ontologies. A state ontology defines a set of sorts or types (e.g., ROLE, RESOURCE), sorted constants, functions and predicates.

States are related to state properties via the formally defined satisfaction relation |=: state(γ, t) |= p, which denotes that state property p holds in trace γ at time t. For example, state(γ1, t1) |= is_responsible_for(employee_A, execution, p1) denotes that in trace γ1 at time point t1 the employee_A is responsible for the execution of process p1.

Dynamic properties are specified in TTL by relations between state properties. For example, the following property expresses the rule of a company's policy that an employee is made responsible for making technological decisions with respect to process p1 after s/he have been executing this process for two years (730 days):

$\forall \gamma$: *TRACE* $\forall t1$:*TIME* $\forall empl$: *EMPLOYEE* *state($\gamma, t1$) |= is_responsible_for(empl, execution, p1) & $\exists t2$: TIME state($\gamma, t2$) |= assigns_responsibility_to_for(management, empl, execution, p1) & t1-t2 = 730*

$\Rightarrow$ *state($\gamma, t1$) |= assigns_responsibility_to_ for(management, empl, tech_des, p1)*

Other specific conditions (e.g., temporal, situational) under which authority relations may be created/maintained/dissolved are defined by executable rules expressed by logical formulae. The specification of these rules will be discussed further in this chapter.

Modeling Authority Relations in Different Types of Organizations

Authority is enforced through the organizational structure and norms (or rules) that govern the organizational behavior. In general, no single authority system can be equally effective for all types of organizations in all times. An organizational authority system is contingent upon many organizational factors, among which organizational goals; the level of cohesiveness between different parts of an organization, the levels of complexity and of specialization of jobs, the level of formalization of organizational behavior, management style (a reward system, decision making and coordination mechanisms), the size of an organization and its units. Furthermore, the environment type (its uncertainty and dynamism; the amount of competitors), as well as the frequency and the type of interactions between an organization and the environment exert a significant influence upon an organizational authority structure.

In the following it will be discussed how authority is realized in some types of (mostly industrial) organizations and how it can be modeled using relations introduced in the previous section.

Authority in small firms of the early industrial era was completely exercised by their owners through mechanisms of direct personal control. Firm owners were managers and technical professionals at the same time, and, therefore, had authority and responsibility for all aspects related to processes, except for their execution, responsibility for which was assigned to hired workers. This can be expressed using the introduced formal language as follows:

$\forall p$: *PROCESS* $\forall t$: *TIME* $\forall \gamma$: *TRACE* $\exists empl$: *HIRED_EMPLOYEE state(γ, t) |= [is_responsible_for(firm_owner, control, p) & is_responsible_for(firm_owner, supervision, p) & is_responsible_for(empl, execution, p)]*

The owners controlled all resources ($\forall r$: RESOURCE $\forall t$: TIME $\forall \gamma$: TRACE state(γ, t) |= has_control_over(firm_owner, r)). Currently similar types of organizations can be found in family business and small firms.

With the growth of industry, which caused joining of small firms into larger enterprises, owners were forced to hire subcontractors, who took over some of their managerial functions. This can be modeled using the introduced language as assigning responsibility to subcontractors by the owner for some managerial and technological decisions, as well as monitoring and consulting of workers with respect to some processes execution. For example, the responsibility assignment to role subcontractor_A for making managerial and technological decisions related to the process p1 is expressed as

$\forall \gamma$: TRACE $\exists t$: TIME state(γ, t) |= [assigns_responsibility_to_for(firm_owner, subcontractor_A, tech_des, p1) $\wedge$ assigns_responsibility_to_for(firm_owner, subcontractor_A, manage_des, p1)]

The owner reserved often the right to control for himself, which included granting rewards and imposing sanctions to/on subcontractors and workers, realized through superior-subordinate relations. For example, the following rule describes the superior-subordinate relations between the firm owner and subcontractor_A, responsible for making technological decisions related to process p1 and employee_A responsible for execution of process p1.

$\forall \gamma$: *TRACE* $\forall t$: *TIME state(γ, t) |= is_subordinate_of_for(subcontractor_A, firm_owner, p1) & is_subordinate_of_for(employee_B, firm_owner, p1)*

Organizational resources were usually controlled by the owner.

Large industrial enterprises of XX century are characterized by further increase in number of managerial positions structured hierarchically by superior-subordinate relations. Such organizations are often defined as mechanistic (Scott, 2001) and have the following typical characteristics: strong functional specialization, a high level of processes formalization, a hierarchical structure reinforced by a flow of information to the top of the hierarchy and by a flow of decisions/orders from the top. Responsibilities were clearly defined for every position in a hierarchy. In most organizations of this type responsibility for execution was separated from responsibilities to make decisions. Managerial positions differed in power to make decisions depending on the level in the hierarchy. Often, technological decisions were made by managers of lower levels (or even by dedicated positions to which also execution responsibilities were assigned), whereas managerial decisions were made by managers at the apex. For example, the following formal expression identifies one of the upper managers responsible for making strategic decisions related to process p, one of the middle level managers responsible for making tactical decisions related to p and one of the first level managers responsible to making technological decisions related to p:

$\exists manager1$: *UPPER_MANAGER* $\exists manager2$: *MIDDLE_LEVEL_MANAGER* $\exists manager3$: *FIRST_LEVEL_MANAGER* $\forall \gamma$: *TRACE* $\forall t$: *TIME state(γ, t) |= [is_responsible_for(manager1, making_strategic_decisions, p) $\wedge$ is_responsible_for(manager2, making_tactical_decisions, p) $\wedge$ is_responsible_for(manager3, tech_des, p)]*

In many of such organizations managers at the apex shared responsibility for making (some) decisions with lower-level managers. Therefore, decisions that were usually proposed by lower level managers had to be approved by the apex managers. In connection to the previous example the following superior-subordinate relations can be identified: is_subordinate_of_for(manager2, manager1, p) & is_subordinate_of_for(manager3, manager2, p).

Initially such enterprises operated in relatively stable (however, sometimes complex) environmental conditions that reinforced their structure. However, later in the second half of XX century to survive and to achieve goals in the changed environmental conditions (e.g., a decreased amount of external resources; increased competition; diversification of markets) enterprises and firms were forced to change their organizational structure and behavior. In response to the increased diversity of markets, within some enterprises specialized, market-oriented departments were formed. Such departments had much of autonomy within organizations. It was achieved by assigning to them the responsibility for most aspects related to processes, which created products/services demanded by the market. Although department heads still were subordinates of (apex) manager(s) of the organization, in most cases the latter one(s) were restricted only to general performance control over departments. Often departments controlled organizational resources necessary for the production and had the structure of hierarchical mechanistic type.

Although a hierarchical structure proved to be useful for coordination of activities of organizations situated in stable environments, it could cause significant inefficiencies and delays in organizations situated in dynamic, unpredictable environmental conditions. Furthermore, the formalization and excessive control over some (e.g., creative and innovative) organizational activities often can have negative effects on productivity. Nowadays, large enterprises often create project teams or task forces that are given complex, usually innovative and creative tasks without detailed descriptions/prescriptions. As in the case with departments, teams are often assigned the responsibility to make technological and (some) managerial decisions and are given necessary resources to perform their tasks. For example, the following formal expression represents the responsibility assignment to the team_A for making technological and strategic managerial decisions related to the process of development of a design for a new product.

$\forall \gamma$: *TRACE* $\exists t$: *TIME state*(γ, t) $|= [$ *assigns_responsibility_to_for(management, team_A, tech_des, develop_design_new_product_A)* $\land$ *assigns_responsibility_to_for(management, team_A, strategic_managerial_des, develop_design_new_product_A)* $]$

Usually teams have highly cohesive plain structures with participants selected from different organizational departments based on knowledge, skills and experience required for the processes assigned to these teams. Although many teams implement informal communication and participative decision making principles (Lansley, Sadler and Webb, 1975), also formal authority relations can be found in teams. In particular, in some project teams superior-subordinate relations exist between the team manager and team members. In this case, whereas responsibility for making technological decisions is given to team members, the responsibility for most managerial

decisions is assigned to the team manager. Then, the members of such teams, being also members of some functional departments or groups, have at least two superiors. In other teams the team manager plays the integrator role and does not have formal authority over team members. In this case the responsibility for decisions made by a team lies on all members of the team. Sometimes to strengthen the position of a team manager, s/he is given control over some resources (e.g., budgets) that can be used, for example, to provide material incentives to the team members.

The principles on which teams are built come close to the characteristics of the organic organizational form (Scott, 2001). Some of such organizations do not have any formal authority structure, other allow much flexibility in defining authority relations between roles. In the former case formal authority is replaced by socially created informal rules. In the latter case, authority may be temporally provided to the role that has the most relevant knowledge and experience for current organizational tasks. In many organic organizations formal control and monitoring are replaced by informal mutual control and audit. For the investigation of dynamics of organic organization, informal aspects such as influence, leaderships, mental models of employees are highly relevant, which will be discussed elsewhere. Often interactions between organic organizations (e.g., of network type) are regulated by contracts. Usually contracts specify legal relationships between parties that explicitly define their rights and responsibilities with respect to some processes (e.g., production, supply services). Several organizations may be involved in the process execution (e.g., supply chains for product delivery); therefore, it is needed to identify particular aspects of responsibility in contracts for such processes. The introduced language may be used for specifying such responsibilities and their legal consequences through reward/sanctions mechanisms.

AUTHORITY: A FORMAL APPROACH INTEGRATION OF AUTHORITY RELATIONS INTO AN EIS

In our previous work a general framework for formal organizational modeling and analysis is introduced (Popova and Sharpanskykh, 2007c). It comprises several perspectives (or views) on organizations, similar to the ones defined in the Generalized Enterprise Reference Architecture and Methodology (GERAM) (Bernus, Nemes and Schmidt, 2003), which forms a basis for comparison of the existing architectures and serves as a template for the development of new architectures (see Figure 2).

In particular, *the performance-oriented view* (Popova and Sharpanskykh, 2007b) describes organizational goal structures, performance indicators structures, and relations between them. *The process-oriented view* (Popova and Sharpanskykh, 2007a) describes task and resource structures, and dynamic flows of control. In *the organization-oriented view* (Popova and Sharpanskykh, 2007c) organizational roles and relations between them are defined. In *the agent-oriented view* different types of agents with their capabilities are identified and principles for allocating agents to roles are formulated. Concepts and relations within every view are formally described using dedicated formal predicate-based languages. The views are related to each other by means of sets of common concepts. The developed framework constitutes a formal basis for an automated EIS.

To incorporate the authority relations introduced in this chapter into this framework, both syntactic and semantic integration should be performed. The syntactic integration is straightforward as the authority relations are expressed

Figure 2. Relations between the views of the general framework for formal organizational modeling and analysis (Popova and Sharpanskykh, 2007c)

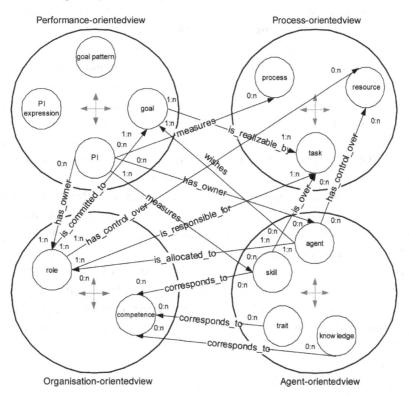

using the same formal basis (sorted predicate logic) as the framework. Furthermore, the authority relations are specified on the concepts defined in the framework (e.g., tasks, processes, resources, performance indicators). For the semantic integration rules (or axioms) that attach meaning, define integrity and other types of organization constraints on the authority relations should be specified. A language for these rules is required to be (1) based on the sorted predicate logic; (2) expressive enough to represent all aspects of the authority relations; (3) executable, to make constraints (axioms) operational. Furthermore, as authority relations are closely related to dynamic flows of control that describe a temporal ordering of processes, a temporal allocation of resources etc., a language should be temporally expressive. A language that satisfies all these requirements is the Temporal Trace Language (TTL). In (Sharpanskykh and Treur, 2006) it is shown that any TTL formula can be automatically translated into executable format that can be implemented in most commonly used programming languages.

In the following the semantic integration rules and several examples of constraints defined for particular organizations are considered.

The first axiom on the authority relations expresses that roles that are responsible for a certain aspect related to some process should be necessarily authorized for this:

Ax1: $\forall r\,ROLE\,\forall a{:}PROCESS\,\forall aspect{:}ASPECT$ $\forall\gamma{:}TRACE\,\forall t{:}TIME\,state(\gamma, t)\mid= [\,responsible\_for(r, aspect, a) \Rightarrow authorized\_for(r, aspect, a)\,]$

Another axiom expresses the transitivity of the is_subordinate_of_for relation: r1: ROLE x r2: ROLE x a:PROCESS:

Ax2: $\forall r1,\ r2,\ r3{:}\ ROLE\ \forall a{:}PROCESS\ \forall\gamma,\ t$ $state(\gamma, t)\mid= [\,is\_subordinate\_of\_for(r2, r1, a)\ \wedge\ is\_subordinate\_of\_for(r3, r2, a)]\Rightarrow is\_subordinate\_of\_for(r3, r1, a)]$

One more axiom (**Ax3**) that relates the interaction (communication) structure of an organization with its authority structure based on superior-subordinate relations expresses that there should be specified a communication path between each superior role and his/her subordinate(s). Such a path may include intermediate roles from the authority hierarchy and may consist of both interaction and interlevel links.

The following axiom expresses that only roles that have the responsibility to make managerial decision with respect to some process are allowed to authorize other roles for some aspect of this process:

Ax4: $\forall r1,r2{:}ROLE\,\forall a{:}PROCESS\,\forall asp{:}ASPECT$ $\forall\gamma,\ t\ state(\gamma, t)\mid=$

$[\ authorizes\_for(r1,\ r2,\ asp,\ a)\ \Rightarrow is\_responsible\_for(r1,\ manage\_des,\ a)\ ]$

In general, rules that describe processes of authorization, assigning/retracting of responsibilities may have many specific conditions. However, to assign responsibility for some aspect of a process a role should necessarily have at least the responsibility to make managerial decisions and be the superior (with respect to this process) of a role, to which the responsibility is assigned. All other conditions may be optionally specified by the designer. Responsibility may be assigned on a temporal basis. To specify that a responsibility relation holds in all states that correspond to time points in the time interval limit, a responsibility persistency rule should be defined:

C1: $\forall asp{:}ASPECT\,\forall r1,r2{:}ROLE\,\forall a{:}PROCESS$ $\forall\gamma,\ \forall t1,\ t2{:}TIME\ state(\gamma, t1)\mid= is\_responsible\_for(r1, asp, a)\ \&\ state(\gamma, t2)\mid= assigns\_responsibility\_to\_for(r1, r2, asp, a)\ \&\ (t1{-}t2) < limit$

$\Rightarrow$ *state(γ, t1+1) |= is_responsible_for(r1, asp, a)*

Using concepts and relations from other organizational views, more complex constraints related to formal authority can be described. For example, "the total amount of working hours for role r1 should be less than a certain limit":

C2: *sum([a:PROCESS], case($\exists$t1 state(γ, t1) |= is_responsible_for(r1, execution, a), a.max_duration, 0)) < limit*

This property can be automatically verified every time when roles are assigned additional responsibilities for some processes. This is particularly useful in matrix organizations (Scott, 2001), in which roles often combine functions related to different organizational formations (departments, teams), and, as a result, their actual workload may not be directly visible.

Another constraint expresses that when the execution of a process begins, for each of the basic aspects for this process (execution, tech_des, and manage_des) a responsible role should be assigned:

C3: *$\forall$a:PROCESS $\forall$$\gamma$, t state($\gamma$, t) |= process_started(a)*

$\Rightarrow$ *$\exists$r1,r2,r3: ROLE state(γ, t) |= [is_responsible_for(r1, manage_des, a) $\wedge$ is_responsible_for(r2, tech_des, a) $\wedge$ is_responsible_for(r3, execution, a)]*

Another example is related to rewards/sanctions imposed on a role depending on the process execution results. As shown in (Popova and Sharpanskykh, 2007b), performance indicators (PIs) may be associated with organizational processes that represent performance measures of some aspects of the tasks execution. Depending on the PIs values, a company may have regula-

tions to provide/impose some rewards/sanctions for roles (agents) responsible for the corresponding processes. Although such rules are rarely completely automated, still an EIS may signal to managers about situations, in which some rewards/sanctions can be applied. For example, the system may detect and propose a reward granting action to the manager, when a role has been keeping the values of some PI(s) related to its process above a certain threshold for some time period [period_start, period_end]. In TTL:

C4: *$\forall$$\gamma$, t1 t1 $\geq$ perod_start & t1 $\leq$ perod_end & state(γ, t1) |= [is_responsible_for(r2, execution, a1) $\wedge$ measures(PI1, a1) $\wedge$ is_subordinate_of_ for(r2, r1, a1) $\wedge$ PI1.value > limit]*

$\Rightarrow$ *state(γ, period_end+1) |= grants_reward_ to_for(r1, bonus_5_procent, r2, excellent_performance_of_a1)*

The axioms Ax1-Ax4 can be checked on a specification of organizational formal authority relations. To this end, simple verification algorthims have been implemented. Whereas the constraints C1-C4 and similar to them need to be checked on actual executions of organizational scenarios (e.g., traces obtained from an EIS). An automated method that enables such types of analysis is described in (Popova and Sharpanskykh, 2007a).

Furthermore, the identified rules can be used to determine for each user of an EIS relevant to him/her information and a set of allowed actions that are in line with his/her (current) responsibilities defined in the system. Moreover, (possible) outcomes of each action of the user can be evaluated on a set of (interdependent) authority-related and other organizational constraints, and based on this evaluation the action is either allowed or prohibited.

DISCUSSION

This chapter makes the first step towards defining the formal operational semantics for power-related concepts (such as authority, influence, control), which are usually vaguely described in organization theory. In particular, this chapter addresses formal authority, different aspects of which are made operational by defining a dedicated predicate logic-based language. It is illustrated how the introduced relations can be used for representing authority structures of organizations of different types.

Modern enterprises can be described along different dimensions/views: e.g., human-oriented, process-oriented and technology-oriented. However, most of the existing EISs focus particularly on the process-oriented view. An extension of the models on which EISs are built with concepts and relations defined within the human-oriented view allows conceptualizing more static and dynamic aspects of organizational reality, thus, resulting in more feasible enterprise models. Among the relations between human actors authority deserves a special attention, as it is formally regulated and may exert a (significant) influence on the execution of enterprise processes. This chapter illustrates how the concepts and relations of authority can be formally related to other organizational views, thus resulting into an expressive and versatile enterprise model. The introduced authority relations may be also incorporated into other existing enterprise architectures that comply with the requirements of the GERAM (e.g., CIMOSA), based on which modern EISs are built. However, to enable semantic integration of the authority concepts, an EIS is required to have formal foundations, which are missing in many existing enterprise architectures and systems.

In the future it will be investigated how the proposed authority modeling framework can be applied for the development of automated support for a separation task (i.e., maintaining a safe distance between aircrafts in flight) in the area of air traffic control. Originally this task was managed by land controllers, who provided separation instructions for pilots. With the increase of air traffic, the workload of controllers rose also. To facilitate the controllers's work, it was proposed to (partially) delegate the separation task to pilots. This proposal found supporters and opponents both among controllers and pilots. The resistance to a large extent was (is) caused by ambiguity and vagueness of issues related to power mechanisms. Such questions as "whom to blame when an incident/accident occurs?", "which part of the task may be delegated?", "under which environmental conditions the task can be delegated?" still remain open. By applying the framework proposed in this chapter one can precisely define responsibilities of both controllers and pilots and conditions under which the responsibility can be assigned/retracted. Notice that these conditions may include relations from different views on organizations (e.g., "current workload is less than x", "has ability a"), which allows a great expressive power in defining constraints.

REFERENCES

Bacharach, S. B., & Aiken, M. (1977). Communication in administrative bureaucracies. *Academy of Management Journal, 18*, 365–377. doi:10.2307/255411

Bernus, P., Nemes, L., & Schmidt, G. (Eds.). (1998). *Handbook on Architectures of Information Systems* Heidelberg: Springer.

Blau, P. M., & Scott, W. R. (1962). *Formal Organizations*. Chandler Publishing.

CIMOSA – Open System Architecture for CIM. *ESPRIT Consortium AMICE* (1993). Berlin: Springer-Verlag.

Clegg, S. R. (1989). *Frameworks of Power*. London: Sage.

Davis, R. (2008) *ARIS Design Platform. Advanced Process Modelling and Administration.* Springer-Verlag.

Friedrich, C. J. (Ed.). (1958). *Authority.* Cambridge: Harvard University Press.

Gulick, L. H., & Urwick, L. F. (Eds.). (1937). *Papers on the Science of Administration.* Institute of Public Administration, New York.

Hickson, D. J., Hinings, C. R., Lee, C. A., Schneck, R., & Pennings, J. M. (1971). A strategic contingency theory of intraorganizational power. *Administrative Science Quarterly, 16,* 216–229. doi:10.2307/2391831

Jonker, C. M., & Treur, J. (2003). A temporal-interactivist perspective on the dynamics of mental states. *Cognitive Systems Research Journal., 4,* 137–155. doi:10.1016/S1389-0417(02)00103-1

Lansley, P., Sadler, P. J., & Webb, T. D. (1975). *Organization Structure, Management Style and Company Performance,* Omega, London.

Manzano, M. (1996). *Extensions of First Order Logic.* Cambridge University Press.

Mintzberg, H. (1979). *The Structuring of Organizations.* Englewood Cliffs, NJ: Prentice Hall.

Ostadzadeh, S. S., Shams Aliee, F., & Ostadzadeh, S. A. (2007) A Method for Consistent Modeling of Zachman Framework Cells. In K. Elleithy (ed.), *Advances and Innovations in Systems, Computing Sciences and Software Engineering* (pp. 375-380). Springer-Verlag.

Parsons, T. (1947). The institutionalization of Authority. In M. Weber (Ed.), *The Theory of Social and Economic organization.* New York: Oxford University Press.

Peabody, R. L. (1964). *Organizational authority: superior-subordinate relationships in three public service organizations.* New York: Atherton Press.

Popova, V., & Sharpanskykh, A. (2007a). Process-Oriented Organization Modeling and Analysis. In: J.C. Augusto, J. Barjis, U. Ultes-Nitsche (Eds.), *Proceedings of the 5th International Workshop on Modelling, Simulation, Verification and Validation of Enterprise Information Systems (MSVVEIS 2007)* (pp. 114-126). INSTICC Press.

Popova, V., & Sharpanskykh, A. (2007b). Modelling Organizational Performance Indicators. In F. Barros, et al. (Eds.), *Proceedings of the International Modeling and Simulation Multiconference IMSM'07* (pp. 165-170). SCS Press.

Popova, V., & Sharpanskykh, A. (2007c). A Formal Framework for Modeling and Analysis of Organizations. In J. Ralyte, S. Brinkkemper, & B. Henderson-Sellers (Eds.), *Proceedings of the Situational Method Engineering Conference, ME'07* (pp. 343-359). Springer Verlag.

Scheer, A.-W., & Nuettgens, M. (2000). *ARIS Architecture and Reference Models for Business Process Management.* In W.M.P. van der Aalst, et al. (Eds.), LNCS 1806, pp. 366-389.

Scott, W. R. (2001). *Institutions and organizations.* Thousand Oaks, CA: SAGE Publications.

Sharpanskykh, A., & Treur, J. (2006) Verifying Interlevel Relations within Multi-Agent Systems. In *Proceedings of the 17th European Conf. on AI, ECAI'06* (pp. 290-294). IOS Press.

Simon, H. A. (1957). *Administrative Behavior* (2nd ed.). New York: Macmillan Co.

Weber, M. (1958). *From Max Weber: Essays in Sociology.* In H.H. Gerth & C. Wright Mills (Eds.). New York: Oxford University Press.

Zachman, J.A. (2003). *The Zachman Framework: A Primer for Enterprise Engineering and Manufacturing.*

Chapter 12
Enhancing Traditional ATP Functionality in Open Source ERP Systems:
A Case Study from the Food & Beverages Industry

Ioannis T. Christou
Athens Information Technology, Greece

Stavros Ponis
National Technical University of Athens, Greece

ABSTRACT

Available-to-promise (ATP) procedures in today's enterprise information systems usually involve a simple search for available or planned inventory of a particular product in a particular depot at a particular time. In this article, ATP is viewed as a dynamic and more complex problem of deciding whether to accept a customer order request given the available inventory and planned production plus the remaining production capacity and business rules for covering demand from certain customer classes, for given products and time window. Whenever this is not possible, the production schedule is modified, by utilizing "reserved" capacity and resources, to cover extra demand. A prototype tool has been designed and implemented based on this approach, that can be easily integrated into existing ERP systems enhancing their functionality and increasing the level of customer service. The elaborated prototype is pilot tested in a case company in the food industry and is loosely integrated within the Open Source Compiere 2, ERP system extended to handle manufacturing. The prototype produces almost real time results on modern commodity-off-the-shelf computers, thus enhancing sales personnel performance and efficiency and increasing the level of customer service and satisfaction.

INTRODUCTION

One of the major challenges enterprises faced during the past decade was the uncontrolled proliferation of ad-hoc, stand-alone computer system applications that supported various functions within different business units. Despite the initial advantages each application offered, managers eventually realized the many dangers this proliferation entailed. In particular, more often than not, the separate—island—applications were producing results of very dubious quality, not only because of possible flaws inside the application itself, but because the application was processing input data that were not coming from original sources. Data produced from one business function were transformed in many uncontrollable ways before being input to an application which required them. In other words, many systems were built around different functions, business units, and even business processes that could not "talk" to each other and thus could not automatically and reliably exchange information. This fragmentation of data among many different isolated systems often translated into reduced business performance or organizational inefficiency, or both, not to mention increased costs of maintenance for each separate application (Laudon & Laudon, 2006).

Enterprise resource planning systems (ERP) (Harreld, 2001) were invented as the response to this growing phenomenon, to provide a single information system for organization-wide coordination and integration of key business functions and processes. They became popular in the mid 90's by vanquishing the old standalone computer systems in manufacturing, finance, human resources, and warehousing and replacing them with a single unified system divided into discrete software blocks (modules) that roughly approximated the old standalone systems. The maturity stage of ERP was reached in the late 90's. By that time ERP systems were extended to include back office functions such as order management,

financial management, warehousing, production, and quality control and front office functions such as sales force and marketing automation (Shehab, Sharp, Supramaniam, & Spedding, 2004).

Currently, ERP systems following the technological wave produced by the advent of new information technologies and mostly the Internet, have been expanded to include the new globalized view of their operations (De Burca, Fynes, & Marshall, 2005). Extended ERP refers to the inclusion of additional modules such as CRM (customer relationship management), SCM (supply chain management), advanced planning and scheduling, integrated e-commerce (including B2B e-marketplaces and B2C portals and Web-stores), sales force automation, content management (including intranets and corporate portals), and decision support (including knowledge management and business intelligence systems) to the core foundation modules of internally focused established ERP systems (McKie, 2001).

In this article, it is argued that despite the acceptance and applicability ERP systems have gained in the last 15 years, the problem of the uncommitted portion of a company's inventory or planned production (available-to-promise) is still confronted, by both commercial off-the-shelf and open source ERP products, in a rather short-sighted manner. The remainder of this article is organized as follows: In the next section, a short but detailed literature review of the ATP problem is elaborated, presenting traditional approaches and explaining their shortcomings in comparison to the dynamic and more complex perspective. Next, a critical review of the ATP functionality in existing commercial and open source ERP packages is presented. In the following section, the proposed ATP model and its solution are presented followed by an evaluation of its performance regarding the necessary processing power and the required solution time. Finally, this myopic view of the ATP problem and the relative performance gap of existing ERP solutions are addressed by designing and implementing a prototype tool that utilises the aforementioned approach and can be loosely integrated into existing ERP systems, thus enhancing their functionality and increasing the level of customer service. In the last section, the results of the prototype implementation in a case company from the food industry are presented followed by a critical discussion on performance measurements, rising issues, and lessons learned from the implementation of the approach.

Description of the ATP Problem

Rapid response to customer needs, high level of customer service, and flexibility to handle uncertainties and fluctuations in both demand and supply are becoming strategic differentiators in the modern marketplace. Organizations that want to achieve these benchmarks require sophisticated approaches to conduct order promising and fulfillment, especially in today's high mix—low volume production environment (Zhao, Ball, & Kotake, 2005). Available-to-promise (ATP) is an approach that allows for customer prioritization and capacity management in order to align the right inventory with the right customer for the right promise date (Cecere, Hofman, Martin, & Preslan, 2005).

The concepts of ATP originate from a set of business practices that were eventually captured in the Association of Operations Management dictionary (APICS, 1987) as the method whereby a firm examines its available finished goods inventory, in order to agree on the quantity and promise a due date against a customer order request. A more recent definition by Gartner (2005), states that ATP is the uncommitted portion of a company's inventory or planned production, a figure that is frequently calculated from the master production schedule (MPS) and is maintained as a tool for order promising.

For decades now, the concepts of ATP were focusing on satisfying the needs of the above definitions by simply searching among the company's depots in an attempt to determine availability of finished goods at certain points of time in the future. As supplier reliability became a prime concern in supply chain and customer relationship management, best practices emerged for the optimal set of policies upon which the company should rely when making promises.

The need for an ATP approach that could assist organizations in the emerging critical task of order promising was an imperative. According to Pibernik (2005), a new improved ATP function should provide a broader scope of functions, such as order quantity and due date quoting on the basis of available supply chain resources and alternative measures in case of an anticipated shortage of finished goods or manufacturing resources. Towards this direction, Ball, Chen, and Zhao (2004) are the first to make the deep observation that the purpose of ATP is to operate on the boundary of push and pull-based controls, and much of the work presented in this article is inspired from the insights provided therein. According to their approach, ATP problems are classified as being either 'push' or 'pull' based.

Push mechanisms include the necessary planning and scheduling processes that a company has to execute in order to fulfil its operational requirements as effectively as possible. The core characteristic of the (traditional) push mechanisms is the forecasting process, by which the marketing and planning functions of the organization predict as accurately as possible, future market needs that the organization should cover. Often, the horizon of the aggregate planning mechanisms becomes greater than 1 or 2 years, which in today's world can be thought as part of strategic decision making. At the other extreme, make-to-order (MTO) business practices are pull-based in the sense that actual orders initiate production. The essence of such business controls is the principle of reacting to demand instead of anticipating it. As work is carried out only on confirmed orders, it is the market that pulls the products from the factory, instead of the factory pushing products to consumers.

Unfortunately, neither of the practices is without risks. MTO and related just-in-time (JIT) practices aim at the reduction of inventory to the minimal possible levels, a practice that can only be successfully applied to environments of relatively steady demand and steady supply. Any sudden demand or supply fluctuations leave the organization unable in the short to medium term to cope with demand. On the other hand, push-based controls run serious risks, especially in the face of turbulent markets. In such situations, push-based inventory controls have no advantage over pull-based ones, other than the higher probability of having somewhat increased inventory levels of raw materials to finished products because of the planning horizons that are covered. In such cases, inventory acts as the buffer that prevents the serious disruption of the supply chain.

In this article, it is argued that a competitive and proactive organization should make every possible effort to combine the advantages of both pull and push based controls into an optimal interplay on the verges of both sides of the customer order decoupling point (CODP). The CODP separates the part of the supply chain geared towards directly satisfying customer orders from the part of the supply chain based on planning (Mason-Jones, Naylor, & Towill, 2000). Recently, it has been shown that a combination of three deterministic optimization models that operate on both sides of the CODP can maximize customer service levels while maintaining more accurate and flexible production plans. The CODP now no longer acts as a barrier between push and pull based ATP approaches but rather as an interconnection point between the static and the dynamic part of the same ATP function (Christou, 2006). This approach can also be seen as a coordination mechanism for the alignment of long-term goals with short-term sales operations decision making. For this approach allows daily order requests from various customers to be checked against long-term planning and scheduling on-the-fly, taking into account the allocated inventory for the particular

customer for the requesting period, the amount of planned production capacity allocated to the customer's class for all periods up to the requesting period, and so on.

Leading research one step further, in this article, a prototype tool integrated in an open source ERP system for implementing the approach in an industrial setting is presented. Before that, in the next section, the gap in the existing ERP functionality is identified followed by a brief description of the selected open source ERP system and the reasons that led the research team to this specific choice. Open source (OS) ERP applications vendors are gradually gaining traction, according to experts. The numbers tell a better story. Framingham, mass.-based IDC estimates that overall market for non-proprietary ERP applications will hit about $36 billion by 2008 (Brunelli, 2005). This hype around open-source ERP systems is justified by their well published benefits over proprietary solutions, such as a) the increased adaptability due to the unrestricted access to the ERP source code, b) the weak reliance on a single supplier and its proprietary source code, and c) the reduced costs gained from lower cost of implementation and hardware platform acquisition. For these reasons, an open source (OS) ERP software was selected for implementing the proposed prototype.

ATP Functionalities in Existing ERP Systems

Traditionally, ATP is a term used in sales and logistics to refer to the level of inventory that is (or will be) available for use on a given date. This narrow definition reduced ATP to a simple easily calculable quantity. Traditional "ATP checking" therefore employed in most current ERP systems, involves considering availability at one or more plants within a sales organization. In the remainder of this section, existing ATP functionalities provided by leading companies of the proprietary ERP systems' market (SAP, Oracle and Microsoft), is presented, followed by a discussion on ATP functionalities provided by OS ERP systems and in particular, Compiere.

SAP's global ATP (GATP) functionality simply extends the concept of ATP to an enterprise-wide basis, by providing the ability to check ATP globally. The GATP module checks product requirements against two things: availability and allocation. Whereas availability considers the total amount of inventory available, allocation considers the amount of product that can be and will be made available to individual customers. Availability is a check against inventory, and allocation is a check against a predetermined amount that has been reserved ("allocated") for a customer (based on forecast, historical off-take, or other business-specific basis). Thus, SAP's perspective on ATP refers to product that is both available and capable of being allocated. If GATP determines that there is insufficient product quantity for either of these reasons, then the order is paused (stays unsaved and thus unconfirmed).

PeopleSoft offers ATP functionality as part of its real-time order promising solution. This module consists of three functions that help planners determine optimal ways for promising (and thus committing to) an order: a) The ATP function determines whether an order can be fulfilled from existing inventory or planned production and purchase receipts, b) The capable-to-promise (CTP) function determines whether the order can be fulfilled by using unallocated capacity and materials when no inventory or planned receipts are available, and c) The profitable-to-promise (PTP) function indicates the costs and margins associated with different order fulfilment scenarios, providing alternatives that are sorted based on user defined business objectives.

Microsoft offers Navision Manufacturing as an add-on to its ERP solution. ATP functionalities are mostly implemented as the (advanced) book-keeping definition of the APICS dictionary with the ability to search in many plant and/or warehouse locations for item availability (APICS,

1987). In particular, the supply planning feature of Navision includes order promising that supports both available-to-promise (ATP) and capable-to-promise (CTP) while multi-location planning facilitates efficient information and material flow through the supply chain.

In the open source ERP arena, ATP functionality is in the best case diminished to a simple quantity calculation. That is also the case for market leading Compiere2, an open-source ERP & CRM system with more than 1 million downloads, an average of 60,000 unique visitors each month and a sum of between 20,000 and 30,000 forum postings, and 70 partners and about 50 code-contributing developers (Ferguson, 2006). Compiere (www.compiere.org) has been published in an open source software repository (Source-Forge.net) since 2001, and is currently installed and running in more than 240 companies. It has a Java Swing rich application interface. The back-end runs under a JBoss server. It also has a limited Web version. Its modules are ideal for organizations in the retail and distribution industries, but as its core distribution lacks MRP/MRPII logic implementations it is not immediately useful in the manufacturing sector. Nevertheless, an extension of Compiere 2.5.2, namely Compiere CMPCS from E-Evolution Inc., does implement the basic manufacturing functionalities an ERP should have. This extension module, which is also open source, provides material planning requirements modules, BOM creation, phantom BOMs, and so forth. Supply chain management functionality is built-in the core Compiere2 system, and is enhanced in the CMPCS solution. ATP in Compiere2 simply looks up the inventory and scheduled receipts to check material availability. For this reason, ATP in Compiere2 can be found under material management and provides no advanced planning capabilities.

Based on the study of existing ERP functionality in proprietary ERP systems, it is safe to argue that this is limited and cannot address the increased needs of companies which utilize an advanced ATP approach in an effort to improve sales and enhance their customer service level. In addition, this situation is more primitive in case of open source systems, where even in the market leading Compiere's case, ATP functionality represents merely a calculative quantity. This ERP performance gap is trying to be addressed by designing and implementing a prototype tool that utilises an advanced ATP approach, based on previous works of the authors. The proposed tool, built in Java, is integrated into an existing ERP system, namely Compiere2. In the next section, the ATP approach, based on which the prototype will be implemented, is presented.

The Proposed Approach to the ATP Problem

From a business point of view, ATP should be the set of processes that allow the company to decide in the best possible way, whether to accept or decline a customer order request, and to (optionally) best negotiate the request fulfilment's due date. These processes should be fast enough so as to allow sales personnel to respond to such requests in time-frames that are deemed acceptable by the customer. In addition, the ATP function should be properly aligned with the company's business model, practices or other hard issues such as production capacity or product life-time constraints.

Inputs that a business takes into account when considering whether or not to accept a customer order are the, a) customer order request data, b) customer significance, which most of the times is based on an ABC analysis classification of their key characteristics such as profitability or sheer size of their account (Christopher, 2004), c) long-term aggregate planning horizon and the decomposition of each aggregate period into fine-grain periods, d) existing current product demand forecasts for the planning horizon, e) production and distribution schedules, f) inventory levels for each warehouse and depot of the company and the

associated geographic considerations and rules, g) existing promised orders and order details, h) factory capacity & personnel work-schedules, i) raw materials and semi-finished goods inventories, together with BOM (bill-of-material) information for each product, j) procurement schedules (raw material availability plans), k) MPS data including scheduled down-times according to maintenance policy, l) product profitability details, and m) the company business rules relating to service levels for each product. A business rule could also indicate that when a request cannot be fulfilled by the due date requested, the system should respond with another proposed later date.

Similarly, a number of parameters that influence the application of ATP in a production business setting are the, a) relative importance of service levels versus product profitability in the form of weighted factors or other means, b) importance of short-term cash-flows versus long-term relationships with customers, c) reserve production capacity or inventory levels, d) safety stock levels, e) product life-times (when dealing with perishable products such as foods and beverages having short expiration dates), and g) the cost (or profit) function to optimize or the exact description of the business priorities for answering an ATP case instance.

Clearly, solving the ATP problem requires deciding whether to accept or deny a customer order request. Besides that, in the event of a positive answer, the solution to the problem has to provide details about which inventory is to be used and what changes to production and distribution scheduling have to be made so that both previously committed orders and the new request can be satisfied. It is worth noting that the Japanese seat production system (Tamura, Fujita, & Kuga, 1997) essentially also aimed at the coordination and integration of the sales and production scheduling functions by deciding whether to accept or decline customer order requests depending on production seat availability without mentioning the term available-to-promise. However, the approach taken in the production seat system is completely different from the approach and cannot be directly compared.

The approach on solving the stated problem is based on Christou (2006) and utilizes three models for production planning and allocating demand and production capacity. These models together with some straight-forward search algorithms decide whether to accept a customer order, and if so, how to select inventory and possibly modify the production schedule to satisfy all accepted customer orders. In doing so, the original aggregate long-term and medium-term plans of the company, remain unchanged. The models formulated operate on different time-granularities on inventory and production controls.

More specifically, at the push-control level, the multi-commodity aggregate production planning (MCAP) model Christou, Lagodimos, and Lycopoulou (2007) provides production plans to meet aggregate product demand for each aggregate period. This optimization model solves an aggregate production planning problem that takes into account the available production lines capacities, personnel availability, forecasting of demand for each product for each aggregate period, product life-time constraints, and soft constraints representing "reservations" on line capacities during periods where forecast (which may be viewed also as a sales target) is expected to be overly conservative. The model is a mixed-integer programming problem (MIP), with the only integer variables being the number of shifts needed for each line during each period. Its solution produces an aggregate production plan that optimally allocates production among the available lines so as to respect all hard constraints and maximize customer service levels and products' freshness while minimizing inventory costs and overtime expenses.

Then, the demand allocation ATP (DAATP) model provides a way to ration the aggregate production of a period among fine-grain level periods and among customer demand classes in a way to maximize company profits. This model takes into account raw materials availability as well as production costs and constraints, including life-time constraints for perishable products, and using data regarding customer profitability, it allocates inventory and production capacity for each customer demand class. The model is a linear program (LP) whose solution provides an optimal allocation of existing and planned production among the available demand classes—which may form a hierarchy.

Finally, the multi-commodity fine-grain production planning (MCFP) problem, together with traditional allocated ATP search procedures, operates at the pull-control level of actual sales. This model operates at the fine-grain time scale and uses as input the available inventory as well as the planned production for each line during the current aggregate period. For the fine-level time periods contained in the current aggregate period, solution of the MCFP problem produces production plans for each line for each fine-level period, for each product and each customer class. Whenever a new order request arrives, the MCFP problem is solved again (warm-starting if the user wishes from the last solution accepted) to check if the same or a new production plan that obeys the production constraints plus the allocations produced by DAATP for the periods within the current aggregate period is feasible. If so, the customer order can be accepted, otherwise it has to be denied. The MCFP is also modeled as an LP, whose size however grows with the product of the number of customers, products, and periods considered. In particular, let M', Π, K, L, O be respectively the number of fine-grain periods in the short-term planning horizon, the number of different products being planned, the total number of customer classes, the total number of production lines in the organization, and the total number of orders to be received within the current planning horizon. The MCFP model is a linear program with

$$\left(\frac{M'(M'+1)}{2}+M'\right)\Pi LK$$

variables and $O(M'+1)+LM'\Pi K$ non-trivial constraints and

$$M'\Pi LK\left(\frac{M'+1}{2}+1\right)$$

variable non-negativity constraints. All the orders entered in the system can be represented with at most $M'\Pi K$ constraints. Indeed, every order to be considered is a set of quadruples of the form $(i, \pi, k, d_i^{\pi,k})$ representing period, product, customer-class, and quantity demanded respectively. Different orders for the same period, same product coming from the same customer class can be concatenated into one quadruple containing the sum of their individual demands.

The combination of these three models can give optimal solutions to the ATP scheduling problem. In the remainder of this section, the approach is further explained in the form of a step-by-step application roadmap. In particular, the whole system workflow consists of the following discrete steps:

1. Solve the MCAP problem to determine next periods' aggregate production requirements based on the latest updates of market forecasts for the company's products.
2. Solve the DAATP problem to determine how to allocate current and planned product inventory among the current aggregate period's finer level time intervals and customer classes.
3. Using the solution of the DAATP problem in Step 2, compute a customer/product/period cube that contains the allocated quantities of each product to each customer class in each fine-grain level period, as seen in Figure 1.
4. Using the same portion of the allocated products per customer class per period, allocate the total extra hours o_i^{π} of unused capacity

Figure 1. Customer/product/period allocated ATP inventory cube

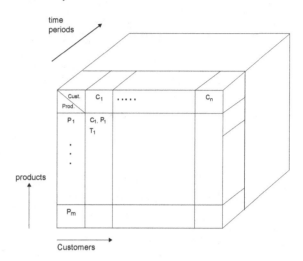

available during this aggregate period, to customer classes per period per product.
5. When a customer order request arrives, first check via simple search among the customer classes to which the customer belongs in a bottom-up fashion for available inventory in the periods up to the period requested. For any remaining product quantities that cannot be found in the inventory cube, proceed to Step 6.
6. Solve the MCFP problem to determine whether a production plan exists that can satisfy all current constraints and is able to provide the required remaining product quantities until the customer requested due-date. If such a plan exists, the order request is accepted and the appropriate book-keeping procedures are triggered to modify the production schedule to accommodate for the new order. If this is not the case then the order is rejected or countered by the quantities that can be found in Step 5.

Schematically, the activities involved in this advanced ATP approach are shown in Figure 2.

Figure 2. Coordination of activities for ATP among various functions

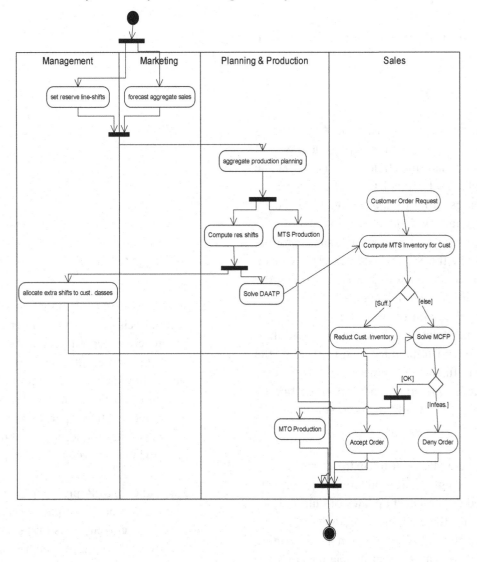

The solution of the MCAP and DAATP models is an off-line process that poses no serious constraints on the performance of the algorithms employed for their solution. Thus, the MCAP problem, in both cases, is easily solved on the NEOS servers in a few seconds. The real challenge lies, as mentioned earlier, in solving the MCFP problem in an almost real-time manner. To address this issue, real life data from the model's application in a Greek manufacturer operating in the food industry are presented in the next section.

The Prototype ATP Tool

It is no secret that the database model of all modern ERP systems are very complex as they are required to model all products, designs, functionalities, (business) processes, and activities that exist in the company. For this reason, thematic areas in the data model are developed, so as to decompose the overall model into smaller and more manageable sub-models.

The Compiere2 data model is generally divided in a first-level decomposition among the following

Figure 3. ERD expansion of the CMPCS module

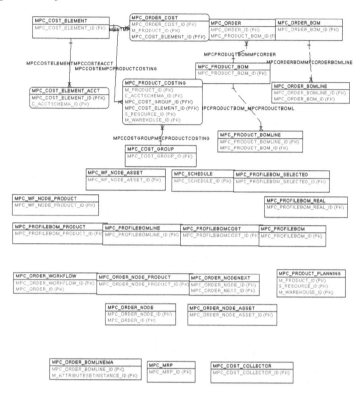

sub-models: a) assets related data, b) sales related data, c) requests related data, d) k-model, e) project related data, f) marketing campaigns related data, and g) manufacturing and production related data. The CMPCS manufacturing extension module to Compiere2 adds the entity relationship diagram shown in Figure 3. Note that only the relationship keys are shown for each table:

Overall, the Compiere2 tables used to compute the parameters and optimize the models presented in the previous section are shown in Figure 4. Note that for each table only primary and foreign keys are depicted in order to make the diagram more readable.

The operational system prototype formulates the MCFP problem as a GAMS model in the GAMS modeling language, converts it using the GAMS mps writer facility into standard MPS format for mathematical programming, and solves it using any of the following solvers, a) QSopt, b) lp_solve, and c) remote solution by submitting a job to the NEOS servers via the NEOSClient interface.

The results of the model, assuming that an optimal solution has been found—and that therefore the order can be accepted—are then saved in appropriately newly added tables in the Compiere user table-space. If the order request cannot be honored no changes to the ERP state are made, and the request is recorded as "not accepted." The proposed system design is depicted in Figure 5.

In Figure 6, the static structure of the MCFP module of the prototype is presented.

The described system has been implemented into a working prototype for checking whether an incoming order can be accepted or not in real time by the case company sales personnel. Food industry constitutes an ideal case for this study because it is characterized by strong seasonality in demand and short product life-time constraints. The case company is a 'meat and sausages' manufacturer.

Figure 4. Compiere2 tables for solving the ATP problem

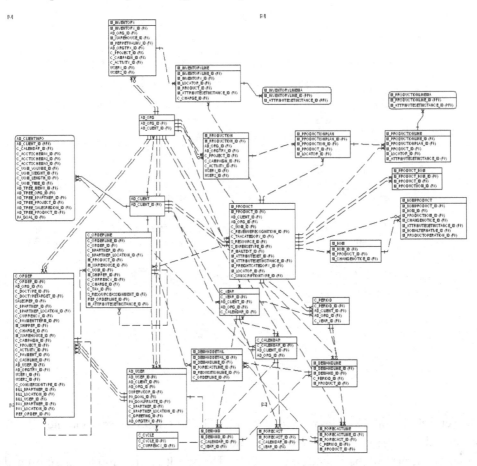

The prototype uses a client/server architecture, and the elaborated graphical user interface (GUI) follows a minimalist approach that allows users to learn how to use it very quickly and prevents confusion with side-effects that are irrelevant to the work-flow of order taking. The GUI allows the user to query about the planned production and inventory per customer class, period, and product or any such combination. It also allows querying on-the-fly the current production plans per line per period per product per customer class, and so forth. The prototype's user interface is shown in Figures 7 and 8.

In this case, the problems that need to be solved are quite complex, involving up to 360 products, 17 production lines, and 30 customer accounts. The CF60 [a-e] datasets are decomposed versions of the

Figure 5. System solution design architecture

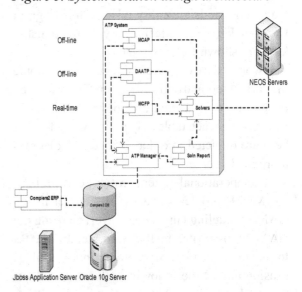

Figure 6. Static structure for MCFP module

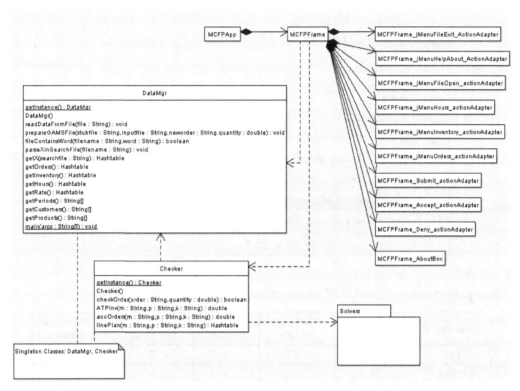

Figure 7. Checking for ATP availability using the MCFP (GUI actual customer codes are replaced)

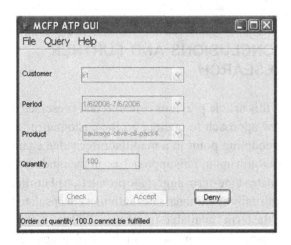

case-study manufacturer, involving 60 products, 14 production lines, and 30 customer accounts. Each meat product has a nominal life-time less than 2 months from production date. In that setting the size of the problem can reach up to 300.000 variables and more than 100.000 constraints. Interestingly, many of these constraints are redundant or not active in the solution. Solving a problem of that magnitude on the NEOS servers using GAMS/ BDLP was not possible.

However, solving the problem on a Pentium 4 (3.2 GHz) desktop, running Windows with 2GB of RAM using the QSOpt LP package, using the dual simplex method takes less than 15 seconds. The solution times do not vary significantly even as the data represent scenarios where the lines' utilization range from lightly loaded to heavily loaded requiring the use of all available "reserved" production capacity eventually leading to order rejections.

Figure 8. MCFP GUI—querying available inventory for a particular customer class/ product/ fine grain period

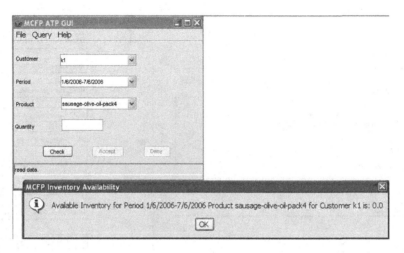

Table 1. Time performance of the MCFP problem solution for different data sets

Dataset Name	Number of Lines	Number of Products	Number of Periods	Number of Customers	MCFP Runtime (in seconds)
Ex7	2	2	4	2	0.8
CF60a	14	60	4	30	5.0
CF60b	14	60	4	30	7.0
CF60c	14	60	4	30	5.0
CF60d	14	60	4	30	10.0
CF60e	14	60	4	30	15.0
3E1	14	8	4	20	2.0

This response time allows a sales representative to service in real-time a customer placing an order request over the phone. The results of a number of tests with some of the hardest data set configurations are summarized in Table 1.

The Ex7 is a synthetic small data-set. 3E1 is a data-set whose size represents data from a juices-and-soft-drinks manufacturer in Greece. The run-time still allows for sales staff to respond in real-time to customer order requests.

CONCLUSIONS AND FURTHER RESEARCH

In this article previous research that presented a new approach to operate on the customer order decoupling point in a manufacturer value chain was built upon. This approach combines and coordinates long-term aggregate production planning with daily operational sales activities encapsulated in the term "available-to-promise." Three different optimization models, tightly coupled together, guide a system that helps manufacturers in markets exhibiting significant variations in demand decide in the best possible way on how to deal with any patterns in demand.

To support this system, a prototype software tool has been designed, implemented, and integrated within the open source Compiere2 ERP environment and provided immediate feedback to field personnel on the compatibility of an order request with current inventory levels and production plans.

A pilot demonstration of the prototype proof-of-concept system was very warmly received by the case-study food manufacturer's planning department. They made two major constructive suggestions for improvements: a) the system at the MCFP level should never deny an order but instead propose a later due-date when an order request arrives and b) the system should exhibit an internal feedback loop from the MCFP fine-grain problem level back to the aggregate MCAP level in that demand captured by incoming order requests—whether they are accepted as is or not—should be used as input to the computation of expected demand and the reservation of production capacity; such reservations are currently decided outside the system by management and planners, but the system could guide the planners' decisions by providing reasonable suggestions. Implementing both these recommendations is being worked towards.

This first implementation shows that the prototype provides significant support to the order receiving process. Still, a number of other open issues also remain, such as the business workflow and practices that have to be adopted by a company in order to successfully support the approach and furthermore the level of human intervention on the system prompts and the final decision making, based on the previously decided workflow. The experience from applying ATP scheduling processes in real life business applications proves that often, system prompts are opposed to specific business practices or more flexible managerial decisions, a fact that most of the times leads to system depreciation. Studying these issues in more detail will enhance the understanding of the ATP problem and would likely yield much

insight into the business models and practices that would make a company more capable of meeting its strategic goals such as profitability and high levels of customer service and satisfaction.

REFERENCES

APICS—*American Production and Inventory Control Society Dictionary* (1987) (6th ed.). Falls Church, VA.

Ball, M. O., Chen, C-Y., & Zhao, Z-Y. (2004). Available to promise. In D. Simchi-Levi, S. D. Wu, & Z-J. Shen (Eds), *Handbook of quantitative supply chain analysis—Modeling in the e-business era* (pp. 447-483). New York: Springer.

Brunelli, M. (2005). *Open source gaining traction in ERP market*. Retrieved January, 24, 2007, from http://searchopensource.techtarget.com/

Bryan, Garnier & Co. Technology Group. (2004). *The Restructuring of the ERP Market*. London.

Cecere L., Hofman, D., Martin, R., & Preslan, L. (2005). *The handbook for becoming demand driven*. Boston: AMR Research Inc.

Christopher, M. (2004). *Logistics and supply chain management: Creating value-adding networks* (3rd ed.). Harlow: Prentice Hall.

Christou, I. T. (2006). *Available-to-promise business scenario: Problem formulation, algorithmic expression and integration with open-source ERP systems*. MBA Thesis, National Technical University of Athens and Athens University of Economics and Business, Athens-MBA Program.

Christou, I.T., Lagodimos, A.G., & Lycopoulou, D. (2007). Hierarchical production planning for multi-product lines in the beverage industry. *Production Planning & Control, 18*(5), 367-376.

De Burca, S., Fynes, B., & Marshall, D. (2005). Strategic technology adoption: extending ERP across the supply chain. *The Journal of Enterprise Information Management, 18*(4), 427-440.

Ferguson, R. B. (2006). *Open source ERP grows up.* Retrieved December, 12, 2006, from http://www.eweek.com/article2/0,1759,1985895,00.asp

Gable, G., & Stewart, G. (1999). SAP R/3 implementation issues for small to medium enterprises. In *Proceedings of the 5th Americas Conference on Information Systems* (pp. 779-781). Milwaukee:

Gartner. (2005). *Market share: ERP software by company size.* Worldwide.

Hamerman, P., & Miller, B. (2004). *ERP applications—market maturity, consolidation and the next generation.* Forrester Research Report, ID No OR-TEECE 091574.

Harreld, H. (2001). *Extended ERP reborn in B2B.* Retrieved April, 14, 2006, from http://www.infoworld.com/articles/hn/xml/01/08/27/010827hnerp.html

Laudon, K. C., & Laudon, J. P. (2005). *Management information systems: Managing the digital firm* (9th ed.). London: Prentice-Hall.

Mason-Jones, R., Naylor, B., & Towill, D. R. (2000). Engineering the leagile supply chain. *International Journal of Agile Management Systems, 2*(1), 54-61.

McKie, S. (2001). *The great leap forward.* Retrieved www.business.technology.com/BT/Content/index.cfm/fuseaction/viewarticle/Content.id/109

Pibernik, R. (2005). Advanced available-to-promise: Classification, selected methods and requirements for operations and inventory management. *International Journal of Production Economics, 93-94*(1), 239-252.

Shehab, E. M., Sharp, M. W., Supramaniam, L., & Spedding, T. A. (2004). Enterprise resource planning: An integrative review, business process. *Management Journal, 10*(4), 359-386.

Tamura, T., Fujita, S., & Kuga, T. (1997). The concept and practice of the seat production system. *Managerial & Decision Economics, 18*(2), 101-112.

Zhao, Z., Ball, M. O., & Kotake, M. (2005). Optimization-based available-to-promise with multi-stage resource availability. *Annals of Operations Research, 135*(1), 65-85.

This work was previously published in International Journal of Enterprise Information Systems, Vol. 4, Issue 1, edited by A. Gunasekaran, pp. 18-33, copyright 2004 by IGI Publishing (an imprint of IGI Global).

Chapter 13
Developing an Enterprise Wide Knowledge Warehouse:
Challenge of Optimal Designs in the Media Industry

Amit Mitra
Cranfield University, UK

Laura Campoy
University of the West of England, UK

ABSTRACT

It has been common practice among organisations to develop standard operating procedures to gain advantages like standardisation, ensure continuity, and deal with contingency needs. Over time, processual perspectives of activity within organisations have enabled appreciation of such practices through what is commonly referred to as organisational knowledge. Whilst the process of knowledge development can be unique to the context, practical dimensions of development may be considerably different from those suggested by established theory. The present paper firstly reviews different frameworks that have come to be recognised as being effective in categorising organisational knowledge. Secondly, in the light of experiences of both authors in developing an interactive knowledge warehouse, the present paper discusses usefulness of these frameworks. Prevalence of non-disclosure conditions would mean that the mentioned organisation would need to remain anonymous. For the purposes of the present paper, the chosen organisation would be referred to as Kadrosi.

INTRODUCTION

Momentous developments in technology, products and services over the last few years have persuaded commercial organizations with a Web presence to reconsider their strategies to be able to survive and compete amidst unpredictable market conditions. With the advent of an ever-increasing variety of business models, facilitated by the Internet, emphasis of product development is gradually moving away towards an environment where service industries are likely to play a more dominating role (Westland & Clark, 1999). Somehow, such a proliferation of ventures has also influenced companies within the small and medium enterprise sector to look more carefully at their service offerings. Competence in bidding for new projects is directly related to sharing of previously acquired experiences among employees. In 2003, the Chief Executive Officer of Intel went on record by saying that businesses will cease to exist if they do not have a World Wide Web presence. At the same time a closer look will reveal (Elliot, 2002; Saloner & Spence, 2002; Timmers, 1999) that mere presence is not such a big challenge after all. Through the Web, sustenance of business and expansion of client base are areas that companies need to work on a continual basis. Some of such expansion is quite clearly dependent on assessing emergent opportunities. Others are based on ensuring that existing clients are sufficiently content with levels of available services. On the one hand, knowledge about emergent opportunities may be derived through new information, gleaned through market data. On the other, use of anecdotal client information could ensure fulfilment of expectations in relation to past experiences.

While recent dot-com failures have signalled the downfall of several large companies, many relatively smaller organisations have managed to attract business that would have hitherto gone to their larger rivals. Given such a shift in the direction of business, smaller organisations have tried to maximise their potential through a variety of measures. Storing information in formats that are reusable has been a more traditional means to ensure that organisations reduce redundancy and are able to learn from past experiences (Ruggles, 1998). But this has not necessarily meant that the organization will eventually succeed in maximizing ensuing advantages by reusing data. A

transition into knowledge use probably requires both a different kind of experience as well as expectation mindset of involved actors. With the advent of substantial improvements in technology, storage per se has not been a problematic issue, anymore. The rate at which relevance disappears from stored information seems to be an abiding complexity for organizations, keen on maximizing advantages through stored information. In other words, speed with which data becomes obsolete makes the whole process of sustained knowledge use quite complicated (Drucker, 1993; Lam, 2000; Nonaka & Takeuchi, 1995; Quinn, 1992; Reich, 1992; Teece, 1998; Zack, 1999). Hence, judgement would need to be exercised when information or data is being considered for storage as to its net worth to the organization, in future.

This article is intended to firstly review types of knowledge as identified in the emergent literature on knowledge management. Secondly the article considers the adopted processes of converting tacit into explicit knowledge within a media company based in Manchester, UK. Both of these two objectives of the article will be carried out with reference to experiences of both authors in developing an interactive knowledge warehouse for a media company called Kadrosi. The British Government's department of trade and industry (dti) has funded the development of the mentioned interactive knowledge warehouse project. As a just completed project, conditions of confidentiality require the use of a pseudonym instead of the actual name for the mentioned media company.

Like a data warehouse a knowledge warehouse is also usually the result of an IT infrastructure project. In line with Duncan (1995), a knowledge warehouse may be defined as a set of shared IT resources that can be interrogated by members of an organization to enable present and future business applications. Unlike a data warehouse that tends to support business processes (Ross, Beath, & Goodhue, 1996), a knowledge warehouse is primarily targeted to strategic enhancement of capacity and to a lesser degree some basic needs like development of bids and pitches. Wixom and Watson (2001) in the context of success factors for data warehousing talk about the need for a correspondence between data quality and system quality. At Kadrosi, the IT infrastructure was of a fairly advanced standard in that all users of the knowledge warehouse were IT literate, consequently they did not expect output of "clean data" as can be envisaged after undergoing reconciliation in a traditional data warehouse implementation. Mitra, Brown, and Hackney (2005) in their study in developing knowledge tools for an electronics component manufacturing plant found that formal and informal practices in training tended to be internalized by employees as they became habituated in using these tools. The context of Kadrosi is probably even more serious, given the amount of creativity that is necessary for employees of the organization at the operational level.

KNOWLEDGE FRAMEWORKS

With the growing recognition among organizations of harnessing advantages by leveraging existent knowledge assets within its workforce, a few research frameworks have become accepted as being standards in understanding and developing capacity. Research into understanding knowledge development may be categorized as being part of a couple of distinct approaches. Whereas the structuralist perspective concerns an understanding where knowledge is treated as being resident within people and organizations, the processual approach has developed through recognizing that knowledge is socially constructed and is embedded in practice (Newell, Robertson, & Scarborough, 2002).

For instance, Nonaka (1994) and Spender (1998) have developed frameworks to understand processes by which knowledge is created and used within organisations. Nonaka's (1994) framework

is based on the premise that individual cognition is essential to the knowledge creation process. According to Nonaka (1994) knowledge creation can only occur at the level of the individual. Socialization, externalization, internalization and combination are the four mechanisms according to Nonaka (1994) through which knowledge get created at the individual level, which is the realm where knowledge creation can occur. Exchange between individuals through socialization is likely to create new tacit knowledge. Interaction of members within an organization and those outside may lead to externalization that in turn may be able to create new explicit knowledge. Direction of knowledge creation through externalization is aimed at the outer world to the interacting organization. Explicit knowledge that exists in the outside world to the organizational context on the other hand may be able to be internalized by another simultaneous range of interactions by individual employees. Unattached knowledge creation, where explicit formats are used to create further explicit knowledge, is part of a process of combination where other processes may be subsumed. The distinctive aspect of Nonaka's (1994) framework is that knowledge is unlikely to exist among employees within an organization meaning the same thing to everybody. Every individual employee would have slightly different understanding of institutional knowledge.

Spender (1996, 1998) differs from Nonaka (1994) in highlighting a difference between individual and social knowledge. According to Spender's (1998) framework there exist contrasts and likely interactions between an individuals understanding of knowledge, which is possessed and the collective knowledge on which explicit knowledge is actually built upon. Unlike Nonaka (1994), Spender (1998) has distinguished between what constitutes individual explicit knowledge and what defines social or organizational knowledge. Again Spender (1998) has gone on to say that there may be some kind of an agreement among individuals within an organization as to what constitutes explicit organizational knowledge. Conscious, automatic, objectified and collective are the different formats according to Spender (1996) through which knowledge may be created within an organization. Whereas conscious and automatic are individual explicit and implicit mechanisms, objectified and collective refer to social means of acquiring knowledge according to Spender's (1996) framework. Social knowledge as a collective within an organization is highly beneficial to ensure strategic advantages in comparison to other competitors within the same sector. Spender's argument (1998) lends support to the notion that core competencies of an organization are crucial in bolstering strategic advantages in an aggressively competitive business environment. A different line of literature on "communities of practice" (Brown & Duguid, 1991) seems to have been emerging that is quite similar to Spender's (1998) framework where social understanding of knowledge plays a vital role.

Blackler (1995) has argued that there are in fact, five types of knowledge in embrained, embodied, encultured, embedded and encoded knowledge that may exist within an organization. In Blackler's (1995) framework, types of knowledge creation are either dependent on individual or collective effort. Embrained knowledge that is dependent on individual cognitive abilities and conceptual skills is similar to Nonaka's (1994) notion of tacit knowledge on the other hand, encultured knowledge is dependent on the processes of achieving a shared understanding through the development of organizational cultures is similar to Spender's notion of collective knowledge. Embedded knowledge is quite similar to what is commonly understood as standard operating procedures in that they are synonymous and resident within systemic rules of an organization. For instance, routines may be clearly publicised and made explicit through formal policies and procedures within organizations or informally tacit, in the minds of all workers. Essentially, therefore, Blackler (1995) has tried to suggest a framework where particular kinds of knowledge dominate in particular kinds of organizations. Such a framework is both quite different from both Nonaka's (1994) and Spender's (1996) frameworks as well as being nearer approximations of the real world. Traditional bureaucratised organizations, according to Blackler (1995) will rely on embedded knowledge found in rules and routines, on the other hand, more innovative and dynamic organizations would rely more on encultured knowledge if they are communication intensive or embrained knowledge if they are dependent on knowledge, skills and expertise of individual employees. Blackler's (1995) framework is therefore more meaningful in the context of the present article as it clearly suggests that the type of knowledge that dominates the firm's activities ought to determine the way in which it is managed.

Beyond the frameworks aforementioned is the realm of the processual perspective of knowledge that has simultaneously become more meaningful as management of knowledge moves away from first principles within organizations. A primary distinguishing feature of the processual perspective stems from its emphasis on processes and practices of knowing in order to understand what knowledge is. Process perspectives are derived through the appreciation of knowledge being socially constructed rather than being a static asset that is resident in people and organizations. Among the frameworks mentioned above, Spender (1996) has recognized the dynamic issues of knowledge creation. It tries to avoid the issue of absolute knowledge or notion of truth and in its place reinforces the importance of context where practice determines knowledge rather than orient understanding through a static or objective mindset. Intrinsic to the process perspective is the fact that the process of knowing is as important as knowledge itself. The link between the two is very strong.

In more recent times the processual perspective has been qualified by contributions from a variety of scholars including Cook and Brown (1999) and

Newell et al. (2002) where dimensions that were hitherto taken for granted have been questioned. For instance, Cook and Brown (1999) argue that not everything that people do are based on what they know rather it is both part of group action as well as part of the knowing process. Newell et al. (2002) argue that a substantial part of an individual's knowledge will always remain tacit. Such tacit knowledge exists as conscious experience and behaviour rooted in processes of knowing and action. Table 1 has been used to delineate the principal dimensions of the two perspectives.

It is clear from Table 1 that knowledge creation may be understood through a range of dimensions like nature, format, level, activity relationship and origin. These characteristics enable us to appreciate the basic distinction between the static and the dynamic formats of knowledge and how these might be captured within organizations. At a time when organizations are gradually becoming more knowledge intensive, that is every worker is becoming a knowledge worker as well as the fact that many organizations need to diminish costs, it is likely that there would be a transition of traditional bureaucratic firms to become more innovative and modern in the way that they use knowledge. While application of rules, regulations and procedures might continue to be the principal characteristic of certain traditional organizations, media companies like Kadrosi will certainly be driven by more innovative and modern ways of working where knowledge is resident in skills and expertise of employees. Kadrosi, being a strategic marketing company, is involved with promotion of products and services of a variety of client organizations that have included purely commercial organizations like Intel, Dell and Lever Faberge as well as nongovernmental organizations like Amnesty International and FairTrade. While it is routine for Kadrosi to develop Web based campaigns for its clients yet it is unique in trying to develop a strategic tool like an interactive knowledge warehouse to bolster competitive advantage within the sector that it operates in.

Given that Blackler's (1995) framework is the most amenable to variable formats of knowledge use, it was felt that it would be the most appropriate in classifying work within Kadrosi. Although a substantial amount of research has been (Blackler, 1995; Lam, 1997; Nonaka & Teece, 2001; Tsoukas, 1996) directed to the development of ways and means by which tacit knowledge can be made explicit yet it is clear from studies that context would need to play an important role in determining distinction and then establishing a connection between the tacit and the explicit. Essentially there are two complementary issues for a business's quest to lead within a particular industrial sector. The first concerns creation of knowledge and the second is to do with sharing and transfer

Table 1. Comparison of structural and processual approaches to classify knowledge (Source: Adapted from Newell et al., 2002)

Characteristic	Structural	Processual
Nature	Discrete cognitive entity that people and organizations possess	Rooted in practice, action and social relationships
Format	Objective and static	Dynamic where process of knowing is as important as knowledge
Level	Individual and collective level	Originates through the interplay between individual and the collective levels
Activity relationship	Different types of knowledge dominates in different types of organizations	Organizations are characterised by different types of knowledge and practices of knowing
Origin	Created via specific social processes	Knowing occurs via social processes

of it. For instance, Blackler (1995) argues that knowledge may be found to exist in various different formats. Table 2 has been used to enunciate different formats that Blackler (1995) identified, corresponding forms as discerned within Kadrosi have also been shown alongside.

It is clear from Table 2 that there may be several gradations through which types of knowledge may be categorised. Some of these may theoretically be unambiguous yet in practical terms may be found to have overlaps. For instance, it might involve a significant amount of complexity to distinguish between embrained, encultured and embedded knowledge. In general, it is commonplace to come across situations where cognitive abilities developed by individuals have actually contributed to the type of shared understanding that might be prevalent within groups and organizations. For instance, in the case of Kadrosi, a new coder working on a project on a repeat account may only attain knowledge of how to code for that client through shared understanding with the project team.

A knowledge store unlike other physical stores is different in that it is directed to delineate context rather than maintain unconnected pieces of data. While a physical library may contain books, journals, CDs and manuals, a knowledge store would require the embodiment of experiences and methods used. It is clear therefore that developing a physical library can be a simple objective where after infrastructure for the holding of material is created, inventory of archived material like books, journals and the like can easily be used to populate it. To some extent such a physical repository might provide a starting point to firstly take stock and arrange existent inventory and secondly to promote the idea that circulation of relevant material might be feasible when employees see a visible artefact where information sources are available. In the context of the present article it must be pointed out that both a physical as well as an intranet-based repository was planned and developed. Through such a phased approach it was possible to monitor uptake and popularity of the initiative within Kadrosi. Whereas usual data warehouses might be updated by a single person over fixed intervals, an interactive knowledge warehouse would be open to multiple update mechanisms as well as the fact that it would also cater to a diversity of knowledge needs of workers at Kadrosi.

Table 2. Categories of knowledge (Source: Adapted from Walsham, 2001)

Types of knowledge	Generic format	As obtained within Kadrosi
Embrained	Individual conceptual skills or cognitive abilities	The skill of graphic design, content management, creation of pitches, and so forth.
Embodied	Demonstrated through certain bodily and/or technical skills	The role of skilled coders and technical specialists
Encultured	Refers to the development of shared understanding at different levels like groups, organizations and societies	Understanding developed within specialist task forces focussing on individual domains like email campaigns, organizational procedure
Embedded	Taken-for-granted routines and interactions that could enable shared action for a team	Activities like developing Web pages that may have acquired a certain uniqueness within Kadrosi as being dependent on templates and style-sheets
Encoded	Explicit knowledge as representations available in books, computer databases, or Web sites	The company Web site of Kadrosi, databases within Kadrosi that contain project information

METHODS

The present article is based on experiences of both authors involved in a 24-month long teaching company project to develop an "interactive knowledge warehouse", funded by the Department of Trade and Industry (dti) of the British government. While the first author was involved with ensuring the overall academic input to the project, the second author provided extensive expert guidance on carrying out this research with particular aspects of organisational memory. The entire development spanned over two years, that is, between November 2001 and December 2003. A series of phases with consequent assessments at the end of each phase was the normative structure through which the teaching company scheme was driven. Teaching company schemes have now been renamed as Knowledge Transfer Partnerships (KTPs).

The knowledge warehouse project had a specific outcome designated at inception, i.e. the creation of an interactive knowledge warehouse. Within such a context, the research method conformed to an action research orientation. Following Baskerville (1999), it may be said that the setting in which the project was undertaken went on to conform to expectations of an ideal domain in which action research may be applied. Firstly, authors were actively involved in the work with clear expectations of developing the knowledge warehouse that would benefit Kadrosi as well as themselves. Secondly, the knowledge obtained was immediately applicable initially within Kadrosi and subsequently in client organizations where Kadrosi was involved in developing bespoke knowledge warehouses. Also, the authors worked throughout the 24-month project period using conceptual frameworks of established knowledge theories developed by, among others, Nonaka (1994), Spender (1998) and Blackler (1995). Thirdly, the project was cyclical and iterative, linking theory and applying it to practical work within Kadrosi.

Like the Straub and Welke (1998) action research study, a series of monthly interventions like educational sessions on estimating the range of expertise within Kadrosi were held during the second six-month period of the 24-month project. Normally groups identified in Figure 2 of this article would have somebody presenting the expertise within Kadrosi. A range of people would be present in the audience like the authors, the managing and commercial directors, the company supervisor and all other expertise personnel within Kadrosi. A second set of seminars were conducted to elaborate on questions within questionnaires for feedback, and to raise awareness of the knowledge warehouse in general before the physical model was created. In other words these seminar type events were also another mechanism to generate feedback and thus delineate expectations of users of the knowledge warehouse. Feedback generation on probable capabilities on knowledge warehouse was also carried out by the authors during second and third half year segment of the project. Normally a questionnaire would be sent to the concerned staff and then the authors would meet to discuss answers to questions before compiling them together in segmented reports.

An unintended development at the start of the project that turned out to be an advantage was the fact that Kadrosi was involved in restructuring its business and base it more on individual performance enhancement and expertise. Whereas the initial idea was to have different expert groups coming together on building parts of the knowledge warehouse, with every member of the organization being treated as an expert in a particular area, there was a different approach that needed to be used to understand firstly implications of sharing knowledge and secondly promoting usage of the knowledge warehouse. Initially the idea was to have reliance on expert groups involved in the development of knowledge in specific areas, like e-mail marketing, online advertising, mobile promotions, laws and regulations, customer relationship management, and research. Task forces—in an attempt to bolster development, dissemination and targeting of particular business interests within Kadrosi—specifically targeted individual domains of expertise. The second envisaged advantage that influenced the design of clusters was the interaction between different task forces to ensure that employees shared knowledge gained through experiences over time.

Although initially there was a drive to develop the artefact using the latest available software, yet it must be said that little was clear in the minds of both managers of Kadrosi as well as the academic supervisor and the first author for this article. It was clear that Kadrosi felt that they needed some kind of a tool through which productivity of the company could be enhanced. Also there was an implicit belief that through the project of the interactive knowledge warehouse, it might be possible to use unused documents to the advantage of Kadrosi. The academic supervisor, at that stage, had felt that what would be required is some kind of a rather flexible database that would both allow people to enter data as well as embed behaviour of objects that was going to be necessary to cater to a range of requirements of Kadrosi.

At one end of the spectrum of expectations, the idea of developing an interactive knowledge warehouse was simply to increase visibility of past experiences so that employees involved with creating new bids were able to review past successes and failures in similar project activities. By such reviews it was felt that employees would be able to discern potential and appropriately increase chances of success. Further, to this particular goal of creating a pool of resources from where competitor information could be effectively used, there were several goals that got added to the pool of expectations with the passage of time. These included:

- Knowledge sharing at an enterprise level
- Acquiring expertise in building repositories for clients
- Transforming culture of employees

- Making every employee an expert in a particular domain of activity

At the outset the aim of creating an intranet-based knowledge warehouse seemed a distant objective. This was so because it was unclear as to what would be the limits of knowledge that such a warehouse would hold. At that stage it was being envisaged that all activities of employees needed to be represented within the data warehouse. In such a scheme of things, apart from the challenge of inputting a vast and varied range of material that in itself would need some kind of vetting, it was necessary to ensure relevance and meaning in the wider context. Secondly, relevance of stored material would need careful monitoring, as knowledge that is meaningful at the organizational level might not be very useful at the level of the individual professional. The latter would expectedly volunteer knowledge firstly that is relevant to maintain professional expertise levels. Secondly, knowledge that will not in any way take away "trade secrets" so that individual employees may lose value in the job market of the media domain by surrendering any unique competencies.

Bearing these issues in mind, it was clear that embedding incentives within the knowledge capture process would be central for individuals to pass on professional knowledge. Such incentives would primarily contribute to trust development. The strategy therefore, for knowledge capture for the warehouse was to convey to individuals that, by sharing information in building of the knowledge warehouse, the resulting artefact would firstly be meaningful in what it contained and secondly such an artefact could add value to their activities by providing pointers and tips for at least quality assurance purposes, if not for other advantages. However, as we will see the individual dimension was quite a second order issue as the structure and remit of what was to be part of the knowledge warehouse were more important to figure out. In line with the work of Hansen, Nohria, and Tierney

(1999) it was clear that the individual dimension would be connected to the personalisation strategy that organizations might require to implement knowledge management.

Essentially therefore, the task at hand, taking into account goals and expectations of the project were phased out as shown in Table 3.

At the conclusion of the project in December 2003, we had achieved all of the goals set out for phase IV as shown in Table 3. The next phase was part of both implementation over time as well as how group culture would shape values like sharing along with how regularly material within the knowledge warehouse was updated and kept relevant.

Being a commercial company in a competitive business sector, it must be pointed out that following progression of different phases was not easy, as regularly new business demands would divert resources within Kadrosi. For instance, interviewing employees to incorporate feedback was a constant challenge as individuals working to deadlines of other company goals found it hard to talk to us and sit down with demonstration of the prototypes. A steering group within Kadrosi involving the industrial supervisor, managing director and commercial director regularly had difficulty in meeting up as they were all tied up with more pressing short term commercial concerns. In terms of technical resources, pro-

gramming and coding was also from time to time diverted to fulfil other needs of Kadrosi. In the process validation and ratification of progress at the mature end and basic technical development at the initial levels were held up during different phases of the project.

SIGNIFICANCE OF THE PHYSICAL (NONELECTRONIC) VERSION OF KNOWLEDGE STORE

After putting up shelving and other furniture to house documentation, and other material in place, most documentation—along with reports, manuals, disks and tapes—was housed by the research associate involved with the implementation of the plan on the ground. A categorization strategy was in place whereby all journals were alphabetically serialized and displayed through available display capable storage space. Other documentation, like manuals for software and any technical material, were made suitably visible. For instance, any journals of the advertising industry that Kadrosi subscribed to where placed using a serially ordered sequence across all display furniture like shelves. However, the important issue of use by employees of Kadrosi of such a physical store was a bigger challenge. To facilitate this process, a form was designed with initials of employees of

Table 3. Sequence of implementation of knowledge warehouse

Phase I	Develop a physical store containing all documentation currently available within Kadrosi. Such documentation would include magazines and journals subscribed to by the company. All videos and software accumulated over time. Technical journals, manuals and catalogs.
Phase II	Develop a categorization strategy to classify knowledge through extensive consultation with all 30 employees of Kadrosi. Review any relevant strategies of competitors involved in developing similar artefacts. Consider strategies used by large data repositories like university based libraries and Internet based databases. Review any software that may be used to develop the knowledge warehouse.
Phase III	Extend and build meaningful knowledge sharing capabilities by enriching material held in relation to individual expertise base within Kadrosi.
Phase IV	Develop expertise within Kadrosi to build and develop similar artifacts for clients as well as maximize profitability of current activities of Kadrosi.
Phase V	Facilitate culture change by making trust dependent on advantages of sharing and connecting profitability of activities of Kadrosi as a whole.

Figure 1. Activity map of developing physical knowledge repository

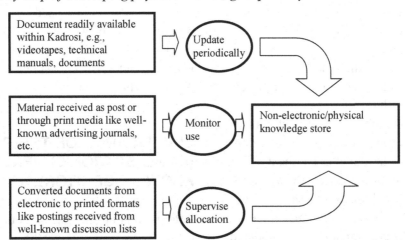

Kadrosi in boxes to be ticked off when material was read by particular individuals. It was through such a mechanism that a log could be created of the use of material available through the physical store. The idea of developing a physical store underpinned the dimension of seeing how the computer based knowledge warehouse may look like—implications may range from challenges of classifying data to the dimension of what may be relevant to employees and in the process contribute to knowledge oriented capacity building within Kadrosi.

In the end, the activity of populating shelves with journals and other material was down to a specific person. Such a dependency on periodic categorisation meant that there were resources that needed to be regularly directed to maintenance and sustenance of the physical knowledge store. The second dimension that required close monitoring was to do with the transfer of electronic media to the printed media. For instance, if a particular employee was subscribing to a discussion list like "mad.co.uk", the employee would be receiving periodic mailings. The latter would then need to be printed and made available through shelves for individual employees to circulate among themselves. Such a transfer required the willingness and cooperation of different employees to make individually received information corporately available.

A couple of needs of the physical knowledge repository in the end proved to be too resource intensive to expect rapid uptake and broad facility to envisage what may be expected in relation to a computer based resource. Firstly, the research associate involved with the development of the knowledge warehouse had to be constantly reviewing all journals and subscribed publications that routinely entered Kadrosi. Otherwise, by implication, material available would not be useful to the employees. Taking hard copies to be included into the repository also meant a substantial amount of interaction with all other staff on a regular basis. In a seriously competitive environment, the latter was quite a demanding proposition. Secondly, most staff were tied up with various projects at all times during the financial year. In this context, it was quite a high demand for them to read journals and magazines out of sheer interest in particular areas. In essence therefore, it could be concluded that without a dedicated individual who would periodically update material held in the repository both the objective of having up-to-date material that was shareable as well as the process of ensuring that publications got fed into the system were difficult to be successfully supported within Kadrosi.

DATA INTEGRATION INTO KNOWLEDGE WAREHOUSE

Businesses like those based in the insurance industry, medical, legal and engineering professions are increasingly dependent on retrospective data, warehoused in different formats. Checking of records, providing quotations for prospective work, reviewing histories of individual patients and clients are type of operational roles that data warehousing has been playing within dynamic business situations. Such a role of provision of information is certainly a crucial one, considering the short time spans within which decisions need to be arrived at. In the case of Kadrosi, we were concerned about the fact that strategic advantage involved consideration of both—past and contemporary data. Strategic direction is usually hard to discern in domains where mainly operational data and general information are being considered. Stenmark (2001) concludes that our interests as experts and professionals are an example of part of our tacit knowledge. Stenmark (2001) also goes onto prove that IT may be used to address knowledge that has not been made explicit. Firstly data needs to be contextualized and secondly, expectations from future prospects would need to be weighed against current business standing within the concerned sector/industry. Both of these functions are difficult to be carried out using traditional data warehousing approaches. Therefore, a dimension of the long term would need to be incorporated to arrive at strategic targets considering past experiences. In the context of Kadrosi, it was felt that this dimension could be fulfilled by the effective use of knowledge.

In simple terms, there appeared to be three formats of knowledge that were common within Kadrosi. Firstly there was knowledge that all employees within it as well as some who were outside it were aware of. Such knowledge could be referred to as explicit knowledge. Secondly, it was common within an innovative and modern organization like Kadrosi to have employees who were involved with creative work to be able to develop intuitive as well as professional knowledge insights into work processes that they were responsible for. This category of knowledge was shared at the discretion of the individual member within the organization. This was the most common type of tacit knowledge that came to occupy an important position in the final choice of the way the work on the interactive knowledge warehouse project developed over time. Thirdly, workflows within the organization over time generated an understanding of appropriateness within the media industry in general and Kadrosi in particular. Such knowledge was most commonly the type of embodied and embedded knowledge that were evident within Kadrosi.

In an endeavour to optimise outputs of its employees, Kadrosi had begun around late 2001, to reorganise its work force of about 30 employees into specialist clusters concentrating on individual areas to increase chances of success at bidding for new projects. These clusters as briefly touched upon earlier, were also known as task forces. Primarily Kadrosi had a couple of dimensions in mind when designing these task forces. The first was the delineation of individual domains of expertise as in task forces created to specifically look into the development, dissemination and targeting of particular business interests. The task force idea acquired clarity with the creation of nine task forces to look into, Web production, mobile marketing, email and viral marketing, tickets and voucher promotions, online advertising, interactive TV campaigns, Research and consultancy practices, and electronic payment practices. The second dimension that influenced design of clusters was the interaction between these different task forces to ensure that employees shared knowledge gained through experiences over time. A diagrammatic representation (Figure 2) of the envisaged infrastructure at this stage might be useful to appreciate expectations from the knowledge warehouse. It must be borne in mind here that individuals could be members of more than one task force and that interactivity between task forces was quite vital in the overall scheme of things within Kadrosi.

The diagram in Figure 2 illustrates the initial schema on which the knowledge model within Kadrosi was founded. It is clear from the diagram in Figure 2 that both the initial objectives of interactivity between task forces on different topics, viz. Research, E-mail marketing, Online advertising, Mobile, Laws and Regulations, and CRM as well as developing focused repositories on individual specialist areas would have been feasible within the model. The circle in the center, showing interactive knowledge warehouse actually includes the different categories under which knowledge was being stored. The six categories under which knowledge was being captured came about through filtering and putting together more than a hundred topics under which data was held within Kadrosi. The six categories shown in Figure 2 were not exhaustive but were capable of demonstrating a basic skeletal structure through which the important issue of categorisation was first approached.

The six topic areas mentioned in Figure 2 would contain different artefacts like films, documents, pitches, video clips, discussion list messages, e-mail messages from strategic players and the like. In the initial stages the plan was to develop a knowledge warehouse that would indicate location of the artefact to be found within Kadrosi. The knowledge warehouse is now fully operational and is hosted on the intranet facility of Kadrosi. With growth in usage of the warehouse it is planned that all artifacts now currently displayed would eventually be directly accessible.

Ever since the beginning of the research project it was gradually becoming clear that a link would have to be established between the work of the Kadrosi employees and the use of knowledge available within the intended warehouse. Otherwise,

Figure 2. Initial model of knowledge warehouse

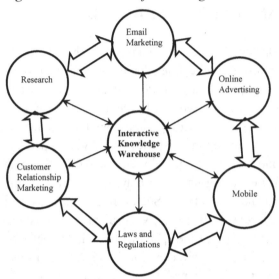

employees would find it mainly bureaucratic to input knowledge that they have had access to as a professional. To deal with this issue a series of feedback sessions were organised that reflected what were expected when employees wanted to use the system where they could find something that was going to be useful to carry out their current activities. In other words, to successfully build the knowledge warehouse, with voluntary surrender of knowledge from employees, the latter would need to trust the system. Research in interorganizational information systems carried out by Kumar, van Dissel, and Bielli (1998) indicates that some demonstrable benefit needs to accrue for the employee to be able to trust the system. It thus became important to establish how individual employees of Kadrosi could benefit from use of the knowledge warehouse to be willing to voluntarily surrender knowledge that may form a corporate resource. Kadrosi being an organization involved in the creation of strategic media solutions could not be said to have had the need to have specific roles in deployment of the intranet on which the knowledge warehouse would be based.

FLEXIBILITY OF KNOWLEDGE WAREHOUSE

Pomerol, Brzillon, and Pasquier (2002), in their research on operational knowledge representation, have found that operational practices are difficult to model because they are numerous besides being implicit within a community of practice with links between one and another. More importantly, Pomerol et al. (2002) contended that there is variation in the context in which these operational practices apply. In the Kadrosi case, this was quite valid as profitability and productivity of the bid development process was the primary objective of the knowledge warehouse. The created artefact sufficiently represented the bid development process that was the main plank on which profitability of Kadrosi's business depended.

At a stage when the development of the knowledge warehouse had reached a point where a design was expected, various formats were being considered. Sufficient representation of different states in which knowledge could exist was one issue that needed to be seriously considered. In other words, for the knowledge warehouse to be useful, both the detail as well as interactivity of knowledge indicators needed to be made available to the employees of Kadrosi. Admittedly, the detail would also need to be modelled. Here again, emergence of knowledge from that held within the organization was something that needed to encompass behavior and states of existence to sufficiently enable interactivity. In this context, the dynamic of change over time, flexibility and extensibility were all aspects that such modelling would need to sufficiently capture and represent.

Among the options that were available, entity relationship modeling was given significant consideration. However, several factors deterred adoption of the entity relationship model. The static nature of classifying data in layers meant that alterations at a later stage would be inconvenient. Representation of many-to-many relationships with numerous derived entities was also another

worry for the entity model. Use of primary and secondary keys to ensure uniqueness was also found to be unwieldy within a complex real time scenario. A simultaneous issue of knowledge existence in different states was also important to be captured within the model. Representation of subtle elements like formats of existence and more importantly behaviour was problematic within the entity model. Given these concerns of dynamism and flexibility as well as the need for adapting to Web-based infrastructure within Kadrosi, the object oriented model was found to be most appropriate for further development of the knowledge warehouse. To illustrate the application of the object model, a cross section of sample data is being presented in the following Table 4.

Table 4 indicates advantages of using the object model through which both issues of generalisation as well as specialisation are adequately captured. Class and super class design at one end of the model was capable of accommodating flexibility of representing task force/expertise focus within Kadrosi. The use of the class structure also provided advantages of extending the model to expand or collapse at different levels, depending on type of knowledge that got integrated into the warehouse. Specificity of individual items within the model shown in Table 3 may have been captured through use of objects and identifiers. Finally both representations of behaviour as well as states of existence made the object model eminently appropriate within the context of Kadrosi's knowledge warehouse needs.

After the object model was chosen and demonstrated to be robust enough to project management staff at Kadrosi it was clear that such a model could be the foundation of the warehouse. Another simultaneous argument that informed choice was the suitability of the object model to adapt to Web -based developments. Despite the suitability of the object model as shown in Table 3 above, extensive testing of modelling was not possible as time needed to be allocated for storyboarding the other front end of the application.

Table 4. Cross section of the object model (Source: Adapted from research data collected within Kadrosi)

Superclass	Class	Object	Identifier	Behaviour	States
E-mail Marketing	E-mail message	Sample	Period stamp	Read, send, receive, forward	Hard copy, e-mail, rich text format
	Electronic Newsletter	www.mad.co.uk	Date of publication	Read, send, receive, discuss, copy	E-mail, hard copy, Web sitesite
	Resource	Partner	Xpedite	Contact, receive, send, manage, deliver content, negotiate	E-mail, hard copy, word document, viral, Web site, presentation
			Digital impact	Contact, receive, send, manage, deliver content, negotiate	E-mail, hard copy, word document

Despite the technical nature of the object model that is shown in Table 3, it must be pointed out that the variations that were developed to arrive at Table 3 structure enabled better understanding of the knowledge warehouse and its different states in the future.

KNOWLEDGE DIMENSIONS AND STATES

Bearing in mind the earlier discussion in the article on frameworks of knowledge representation, it would be useful to compare experiences of authors in actually deriving the model that was eventually implemented within Kadrosi. Blackler's (1995) framework was the one that came nearest to estimating what happened during implementation of the knowledge warehouse. In a commercial environment somehow a combination of factors tends to decide whether a framework is going to be the most appropriate one. Mere flexibility or superior design is not reason enough for its use within development of facilities.

When the software engineers at Kadrosi were trying out interface development, a few options were closely examined. Initially the plan was to buy off-the-shelf knowledge management software that could fit into Kadrosi without any alterations. Prohibitive cost and limited flexibility meant that such options could not be taken for-

ward. Almost in tandem, there was Microsoft's Sharepoint that was being tested within Kadrosi as software that could be used for maintaining and administering its intranet infrastructure. After prolonged testing it was found to be unsuitable. However, the engineering team retained the basic design of Sharepoint within the solution that was being envisaged at that time. A little later, the engineering team within Kadrosi was working on development of an intranet solution for a major multinational computer hardware manufacturer in the USA. The type of requirements that this particular multinational had and the retained frame of Sharepoint enabled the team to develop a unique design that got to be implemented as the final prototype for the knowledge warehouse. So, in a way, the object-oriented design was what got implemented but in a more unconscious way.

From the perspective design of the knowledge warehouse, after considering a few alternatives like prevalent designs of the library storage systems, authors recommended the use of a system that would tie up more closely with the central gaps that existed in Kadrosi's areas of development and growth that was planned. The authors referred to these areas of improvement as knowledge gaps. There were six such gap areas that could have numerous subcategories. These subcategories under the "knowledge gaps" formed what came to be known as knowledge spaces. While knowledge gaps were restricted, the six

Figure 3. Structure of current knowledge tree

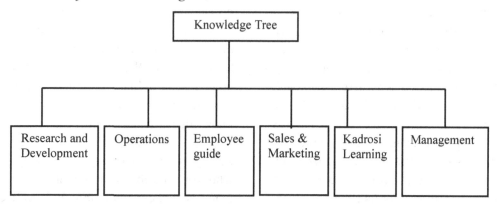

areas spaces could be infinitely extended. The intersection of gaps and spaces would produce a factual piece of retrievable information that users at Kadrosi could use.

The diagram in Figure 3 captures six areas that formed the principal knowledge gaps on which the entire knowledge warehouse now works within Kadrosi.

The diagram in Figure 3 clearly demonstrates how the new structure has become competent to handle different kinds of knowledge that may be saved within Kadrosi. The application has very recently been inaugurated within Kadrosi and continued support of the management team as well as the greater build up of documents and other material within it is going to provide an avenue to see how the knowledge warehouse can actually make a difference to the competitive advantage of Kadrosi.

If there is one challenge that stood out among all others in the development of the knowledge warehouse, it was the creation of the categorization structure that went through the largest amount of iterations and modifications. While initially, the objective was to develop a warehouse that would include all kinds of information, later, with the orientation of the mission statement and identification of principle areas where it was deemed necessary for Kadrosi to make progress, the structure became more manageable. Despite such simplification, a great deal of deliberation

and interactive sessions, generating feedback was necessary to arrive at the obtaining structure of the knowledge warehouse.

The categorization challenge was complicated partly due to need for embedding dynamic growth capabilities. Designing something static including every knowledge function was probably feasible within a three month period, however, developing something with a flexible capability to expand in the future with addition of different kinds of meta data was quite complicated. In essence, to arrive at the rationale of knowledge spaces and knowledge gaps required a wide variety of research permutations before the design was acceptable to all stakeholders of the project.

DISCUSSION

Within the Information Systems community an indifference to the existence of knowledge management as a subject of research along with a countervailing following of its practice seems to co-exist. It is clear that much of the generalizability of knowledge management stems from looking at existent knowledge within organizations through a new lens (Lee & Baskerville, 2003). Coerced by dynamic alterations to business environments, organizations are today trying to rediscover strengths that may have been overlooked as being unimportant. The Kadrosi content was no different. In many ways Kadrosi's task was to find out what it knew as Sieloff (1999) in the context of HP put it, "If only HP knew what HP knows", (p. 47). So, within such a context of discovering what it knew amidst a continual pressure of the need from commercial success. Kadrosi experimented with development of the knowledge warehouse. What began as an experiment to enable Kadrosi develop a tool to leverage competitive advantage eventually translated into an organizational product expertise that Kadrosi could put to use to develop similar artefacts for its clients.

In using "action research" as the method to develop the investigative dimensions of the study, authors were not free to pick and choose the problem that they wished to investigate. So from such a perspective, the study may be said to be an opportunistic ploy to develop research in the first place (Avison, Baskerville, & Myers, 2001; Baskerville, 1999). Despite such a limitation, action research enabled direct response to Kadrosi's needs and provided a rich research environment for the authors through which importance of knowledge sharing within a competitive business environment was tested.

The knowledge warehouse project demonstrated that frameworks are only as good as they make organizations more conscious of what is available within them. The context of a modern organization like Kadrosi already has some intrinsic advantages that make such awareness a reality. For instance, Kadrosi had an open office environment where all employees were colocated in different desks across the same office workspace. Managers of projects would usually walk around and be accessible all the time. Sharing and a high trust culture where employees socialised after office hours also meant that knowledge sharing was not going to be such a difficult transition after all.

Development of the knowledge warehouse provided a common platform whereby enterprise level knowledge sharing was feasible. Gradual modification of Kadrosi's organization meant

that professionals like graphic designers would provide support through outsourced supply. Given such a context, knowledge sharing would be a necessity rather than a hobby of the curious or the meticulous. Walsham (2001a) points out that homogeneity of knowledge does not enable constructive organizational learning. In this sense, the knowledge warehouse would enable learning from variety in practice and could theoretically lead to knowledge translators (Brown & Duguid, 1998) who would be able to frame interests of Kadrosi in terms of client community perspectives. With the creation of a new mission statement of Kadrosi every employee was reckoned to be an expert in a particular field of professional activity within Kadrosi. Partly this was true even before the project began as most employees come into Kadrosi as professionals anyway. However, whether culture of employees would further change to further facilitate the creation of a conscious knowledge based organization remains to be seen.

The present article set out to review types of theories that have commonly been used to understand knowledge management and then look at the type of experiences that the authors had in developing a knowledge warehouse within a media company. The article discovered various somewhat inevitable aspects that have ensured that a large part of knowledge management remained philosophical and theoretical. The present article found that Blackler's (1995) categorization of knowledge probably comes nearest to anything that is widely available in the modern organization. In so far as the experiences of the authors in implementing a knowledge management system was concerned a range of different skills eventually enabled production of the artefact that was being aimed for. In terms of Lee & Baskerville's (2003) paper, outcomes of the present research would fall in the third quadrant of type TE generalizability. Established theoretical frameworks were reviewed and empirical findings demonstrated that a limited fit could be attained in the new setting of a dynamic knowledge-creating environment. Processual knowledge therefore in a media enterprise has a significant innovative dimension. Concurring with Snowden (2003), the present study found that innovation would be both an objective as well as the basis of exploring challenges of knowledge sharing in processual contexts.

When the project had begun, cultural change of workers in terms of knowledge sharing practices was a stated objective. Alavi and Leidner (2001) developed a detailed research agenda for knowledge management systems. However, as noted by Shaw and Edwards (2005), they did not consider willingness to use such a system. For Kadrosi to be successful the knowledge warehouse has to be used, willingness to use the warehouse by non-supportive employees is the type of culture change that was an aim of the project. Culture change remains a second order objective and there remains a distance to go before anything concrete may be said to have been achieved by the project. As Stenmark (2003) found there needs to be a kind of attitude of the top management to ensure that a suitable uptake of intranets took place within the company. In so far as the artefact that was produced it is clear that no straight line or linear path could have led the development that in the end the project team did. So theories of knowledge management enable a different level of abstraction that has little to do with the world of practice. In the end a combination of traditional skills and understanding is actually what produces something that may be used by a dynamic organization like Kadrosi.

CONCLUSION

There were several important findings of the project at Kadrosi and consequently they made a contribution to knowledge. First, it was found that in an organization like Kadrosi that is involved in different sectors and areas of knowledge work, it

is best to connect knowledge codification from a need perspective. After identifying principal areas of growth of Kadrosi through its mission statement, categories of knowledge could be created that could then be uniquely identified through knowledge spaces and knowledge gaps within the knowledge tree. So had the project gone on to classify every component of knowledge that Kadrosi dealt with, the project could not have seen closure within its stipulated two year time frame.

Secondly, in a project where such a substantial amount of feedback needs to be incorporated, all the people of the organization need to be involved in one way or another. Being a 30-employee organization, in Kadrosi this was suitably achieved. Also the trust dimension tends to get highlighted within the development of any knowledge-based application. Employees are not going to volunteer in passing on their trade related information if they are unable to see some benefit to their work. This establishment of a trust factor is quite important in being able to appropriately represent useful knowledge. Miranda and Saunders (2003) have explored information sharing as an objective to enable social construction of meaning, instead of the traditional goal of decision-making. The knowledge warehouse project was typically aimed at enabling Kadrosi to achieve greater productivity and profitability. Coakes, Bradburn, and Sugden (2004) argue that process knowledge is different from tacit or explicit knowledge due to its domain specificity. The knowledge warehouse at Kadrosi showed that meaningful knowledge sharing is directly related to process knowledge.

Third, despite different approaches used in developing the initial structure of the knowledge warehouse, it is clear that classification or categorisation of knowledge is one of the most complicated issues in knowledge management (Galup, Dattero, & Hicks, 2003). For the Kadrosi case, the audience of ensuing outputs and the six priority areas within the mission statement enabled development of a structure. The use of knowledge spaces and knowledge gaps was motivated by the need for creating uniqueness in the retrieval of knowledge objects from the knowledge warehouse. The idea of ensuring sufficient interactivity was also something that required leaving documents in their original formats. The knowledge warehouse project clearly demonstrated that classification or categorisation of knowledge would need to be uniquely created for any similar knowledge application in other organizations. In this context Pomerol et al. (2002) work would be able to point out the need for sufficiently incorporating the contextual dimension and the dynamics of context.

In sum, it might be said that the study having been conducted in only one organization reduces generalizability, however, it increased correspondence to reality (Lee & Baskerville, 2003). Such a single organization study cannot be expected to provide generalizability of empirical results to other organizations (Lee & Baskerville, 2003), rather the purpose was to test and expand on established theory. Overall it must be said that Kadrosi was successful in achieving closure in the work because of a strong technical backup team. Despite the conceptual design and storyboarding of different facets of the project yet actually translating ideas into a usable intranet based facility needed substantial coding support. At Kadrosi this was readily available and hence the eventual black boxing. Any project like the knowledge warehouse development requires the support of sponsors. Kadrosi was no different. The managing director and the commercial director were themselves directly involved with the day-to-day progress of the project. This turned out to be crucial in ensuring that the quality of feedback and participation of other employees of Kadrosi could be sustained. Such a dimension of support and affiliation of important players within an organization is going to be significant in similar projects.

REFERENCES

Alavi, M., & Leidner, D. E. (2001). Review: Knowledge management and knowledge management systems: Conceptual foundations and research issues. *MIS Quarterly, 25*(1), 107-36.

Avison, D. E., Baskerville, R.L., & Myers, M. D. (2001). Controlling action research projects. *Information Technology & People, 14*(1), 28-45.

Baskerville, R. L. (1999). Investigating information systems with action research. *Communications of the Association for Information Systems, 2*(19), 1-32.

Blackler, F. (1995) Knowledge, knowledge work and organizations: An overview and interpretation. *Organization Studies, 16*(6), 1021-1046.

Brown, J., & Duguid, P. (1991). Organizational learning and communities of practice: Towards a unified view of working, learning and innovation. *Organization Science, 2,* 40-57.

Brown, J., & Duguid, P. (1998). Organizing knowledge. *California Management Review, 40*(3), 90-111.

Coakes, E., Bradburn, A., & Sugden, G. (2004). Managing and leveraging knowledge for organisational advantage. *Knowledge Management Research & Practice, 2*(2), 118-128.

Cook, S., & Brown, J. (1999). Bridging epistemologies: The generative dance between organizational knowledge and organizational knowing. *Organization Science, 10*(4), 381-400.

Drucker, P. (1993). *Post-capitalist society.* New York: Harper Collins.

Duncan, N. B. (1995). Capturing flexibility of information technology infrastructure: A study of resource characteristics and their measure. *Journal of Management Information Systems, 12*(2), 37-57.

Elliot, S. (Ed.) (2002). Electronic commerce: B2C strategies and models. *Wiley Series in Information Systems.* Chichester: John Wiley & Sons, Ltd.

Galup, S. D., Dattero, R., & Hicks, R. C. (2003). The enterprise knowledge dictionary. *Knowledge Management Research & Practice, 1*(1), 95-101.

Goodland, M., & Slater, C. (1995). *SSADM Version 4: A practical approach.* Berkshire, England: McGraw-Hill Publishing.

Hansen, M. T., Nohria, N., & Tierney, T. (1999). What's your strategy for managing knowledge? *Harvard business review* (pp. 106-116). Harvard University, Graduate School of Business Management.

Kumar, K., van Dissel, H. G., & Bielli, P. (1998). The merchant of Prato – Revisited: Toward a third rationality of information systems. *MIS Quarterly, 22*(2), 199-226.

Lam, A. (1997). Embedded firms, embedded knowledge: Problems of collaboration and knowledge transfer in global cooperative ventures. *Organization Studies, 18*(6), 973-996.

Lam, A. (2000). Tacit knowledge, organizational learning and societal institutions: An integrated framework. *Organization Studies, 21*(3), 487-514.

Lee, A. S., & Baskerville, R. L. (2003). Generalising generalizability in information systems research. *Information Systems Research, 14*(3), 221-243.

Miranda, S. M., & Saunders, C. S. (2003). The social construction of meaning: An alternative perspective on information sharing. *Information Systems Research, 14*(1), 87-106.

Mitra, A., & Brown, M. E. (2002). Challenges of modelling knowledge within dynamic environments: Case of application development within the media industry. In *Proceedings of the eSMART Conference*, University of Salford, November 16-18.

Mitra, A., & Lau, J. Z. Y. (2004). Challenges of developing an interactive knowledge warehouse within the media industry: Significance of emergent frameworks. In *Proceedings of the European Conference on Information Systems*, Turku, Finland, June 14 -16.

Mitra, A., Brown, M. E., & Hackney, R. (2005). Evolutionary knowledge management: A case of system development within the manufacturing industry. *International Journal of Technology Management, 31*(1/2), 98 -115.

Newell, S., Robertson, M., Scarbrough, H., & Swan, J. (2002). *Managing knowledge work.* Palgrave.

Nonaka, I. (1994). A dynamic theory of organisational knowledge creation. *Organisation Science, 5*(1), 14-37.

Nonaka, I., & Takeuchi, H. (1995). *The knowledge creating company: How Japanese companies create the dynamics of innovation.* New York: Oxford University Press.

Nonaka, I., & Teece, D. (Eds.) (2001). *Managing industrial knowledge: Creation, transfer and utilization.* Sage Publications.

Pisano, G. P. (1994). Knowledge, integration, and the locus of learning: An empirical analysis of process development. *Strategic Management Journal, 15*, 85-100.

Pomerol, J. C., Brézillon, P., & Pasquier, L. (2002). Operational knowledge representation for practical decision making. *Journal of Management Information Systems, 18*(4), 101-115.

Quinn, J. B. (1992). *Intelligent Enterprise: A knowledge and service based paradigm for industry.* New York: Free Press.

Reich, R. (1992). *The work of nations.* New York: Vintage Press.

Ross, J. W., Beath, C. M., & Goodhue, D. L. (1996). Developing long-term competitiveness through IT assets. *Sloan Management Review, 38*(1), 31-42.

Ruggles, R. (1998). The state of the notion: Knowledge management in practice. *California Management Review, 40*(3), 80-89.

Saloner, G., & Spence, A. M. (2002). *Creating and capturing value: Perspectives and cases on electronic commerce.* John Wiley & Sons, Inc.

Scharmer, C. O. (2001). Self-transcending knowledge: Organizing around emerging realities. In I. Nonaka & D. Teece (Ed.), *Managing industrial knowledge: Creation, transfer and utilization* (pp. 68-90). Sage Publications.

Shaw, D., & Edwards, J. S. (2005). Building user commitment to implementing a knowledge management strategy. *Information and Management, 42*(7), 977-988.

Sieloff, C. G. (1999). If only HP knew what HP knows: The roots of knowledge management at Hewlett-Packard. *Journal of Knowledge Management, 3*(1), 47-53.

Snowden, D. (2003). Innovation as an objective of knowledge management. Part I: The landscape of management. *Knowledge Management Research & Practice, 1*(1), 113-119.

Spender, J.-C. (1996). Organisational knowledge, learning and memory: Three concepts in search of a theory. *Journal of Organisational Change and Management, 9*(1), 63-78.

Spender, J.-C. (1998). Pluralist epistemology and the knowledge-based theory of the firm. *Organisation, 5*(2), 233-56.

Stenmark, D. (2001). Leveraging tacit organizational knowledge. *Journal of Management Information Systems, 17*(3), 3-24.

Stenmark, D. (2003). Knowledge creation and the web: Factors indicating why some intranets succeed while others fail. *Knowledge and Process Management, 10*(3), 207-216.

Straub, D., & Welke, R. J. (1998). Coping with systems risk: Security planning models for management decision-making. *MIS Quarterly, 22*(4), 441-469.

Sussman, S. W., & Siegel, W. S. (2003). Informational influence in organizations: An integrated approach to knowledge adoption. *Information Systems Research, 14*(1), 47-65.

Takeuchi, H. (2001). Towards a universal management concept of knowledge. In I. Nonaka & D. Teece (Ed.), *Managing industrial knowledge: Creation, transfer and utilization.* London: Sage Publications.

Teece, D. (1998). Research directions for knowledge management. *California Management Review, 40*(3), 289-292.

Timmers, P. (1999). *Electronic commerce: Strategies and models for business-to-business trading.* Chichester: John Wiley & Sons, Ltd.

Tsoukas, H. (1996). The firm as a distributed knowledge system: A constructionist approach [Special Issue]. *Strategic Management Journal, 17*, 11-25.

Tsoukas, H., & Mylonopoulos, N. (2003). Part special issue introduction: Modelling organisational knowledge. *Journal of the Operational Society, 54*, 911-913.

Walsham, G. (2001). *Making a world of difference: IT in a global context.* Chichester: John Wiley & Sons Ltd.

Walsham, G. (2001a). Knowledge management: The benefits and limitations of computer systems. *European Management Journal, 19*(6), 599-608.

Westland, J. C., & Clark, T. H. K. (1999). *Global electronic commerce*. The MIT Press.

Wixom, B. H., & Watson, H. J. (2001). An empirical investigation of the factors affecting data warehousing success. *MIS Quarterly, 25*(1) 17-41.

Zack, M. H. (1999). Developing a knowledge strategy. *California Management Review, 41*(3), 125-45.

This work was previously published in International Journal of Enterprise Information Systems, Vol. 4, Issue 2, edited by A. Gunasekaran, pp. 34-53, copyright 2008 by IGI Publishing (an imprint of IGI Global).

Chapter 14
Exploring the Influence Sources of ERP Adoption and the Y2K Effect in Taiwan

Hsiu-Hua Chang
National Central University and Tajen University, Taiwan

Chun-Po Yin
Haiching Vocational High School of Technology and Commerce and Cheng Shiu University, Taiwan

Huey-Wen Chou
National Central University, Taiwan

ABSTRACT

Based on diffusion-of-innovation models, in this study, we investigate the influence sources of ERP adoption in Taiwan and explore if the Y2K can be viewed as a critical point. The results demonstrate that the main influence source of ERP adoption is the mixed influence source for all adopters. Before the Y2K, the internal model shows the higher power of explanation. And after the Y2K, the main influence becomes external influence source. With different diffusion patterns before and after the Y2K, the results confirm that the Y2K is a critical point. Besides contributing to the application of diffusion-of-innovation in Taiwan's ERP adoption, the results of this study can provide suggestions for ERP suppliers' marketing strategy.

INTRODUCTION

In the age of the information and knowledge, organizations depend heavily on information systems to support regular operations, solve problems, and make flexible responses to the competition around the world. In the early stages, organizations tended to develop stand-alone systems for a single functional area or business unit; maintaining many different systems led to enormous costs. Organizations faced many problems because of the lack of integration, especially at the global level (Ives & Jarvenpaa, 1993). Enterprise Resource Planning (ERP) systems which incorporate commercial software packages, also known as integrated enterprise computing systems, and attempt to integrate all departments and functions across a company, constitute one of the fastest growing segments in the software market

DOI: 10.4018/978-1-60566-968-7.ch014

and one of the most important developments in recent years (Sprott, 2000; Seethamraju, 2005). Most of this are clearly attributable to the Y2K effect (Sprott, 2000). The Y2K rectification is a key driver in the decision to move to ERP software (Jacobs & Weston, 2007; Scott & Kaindl, 2000).

The ERP is the most important development in information technology use in the 1990s (Davenport, 1998). In the past decade about $300 billion was invested in ERP worldwide (Gefen & Ragowsky, 2005). And in Taiwan, according to the investigation of MIC (Market Intelligence & Consulting Institute), the market for ERP grew from 2.13 billion NT dollars in 1997, to 4.68 billion NT dollars in 1998. During the year 2000, the ERP market grew 26% and the market scale was up to 7.72 billion NT dollars. Nevertheless, the ERP market has generated 9.535 billion NT dollars in year 2003 and only up to 9.841 billion NT dollars in year 2004. MIC indicated that ERP market became mature after 2002. The CAGR (Compound Annual Growth Rate) of ERP market scale would reach 28% for three years after 2001, but also that the growth of the ERP market would decrease below 5% after 2004 (MIC, 2004).

The diffusion of innovation model (DOI model) is usually applied to explore the spread of an innovation such as a new technology, a new idea and a practice (Rogers, 2003). Schmitt, Thiesse, and Fleisch (2007) indicated that the diffusion of innovation theory provides well-developed concepts and quantities of empirical results which are useful for the study of technology evaluation, adoption and implementation. For example, Anat et al. (2004) applied the DOI model to investigate adoption of Internet standard IPV6. Ko, Yin and Kuo (2008) employed the innovation-diffusion model to analyze message diffusion within the blog community. Schmitt et al. (2007) used the concepts of DOI to explore the factors of Radio Frequency Identification (RFID)'s diffusion in the automotive industry. ERP packages can be characterized as an innovation, which has the potential to trigger

change at organizational and inter-organizational levels (Light & Papazafeiropoulou, 2004); the DOI model has the potential to investigate ERP adoption. The imitation hypothesis has generally guided researches on the organizational adoption of administrative innovations. The hypothesis states that, within a relevant population of firms, such adoption results in a predictable diffusion pattern. Members of a social system have different propensities for relying on mass media or interpersonal channels when seeking information about an innovation (Mahajan, Sharma, & Bettis, 1988; Rogers, 1995; Rogers, 2003).

In this study, we applied the DOI perspective to examine the impact of various forms of influence in the adoption of ERP in Taiwan. First, we examined the sources of influence (internal, external, and mixed) that could explain the diffusion pattern of ERP by adopting ordinary least square (OLS) estimation methods and specification tests. Second, because previous research showed that the Y2K effect is a key driver for the adoption of ERP; we treated the Y2K as a 'critical point' in delineating two regimes: "pre-Y2K" and "post- Y2K", to assess the different impacts of the influence sources within each of the regimes.

THEORETICAL PERSPECTIVES

The theoretical perspectives begin with the introduction of ERP and diffusion of innovation in first two sections, and then explain why this study regards ERP as an administrative innovation in next section. Following by a description of three diffusion models, namely influence sources. In the end, the theoretical perspectives highlight the crucial role that the Y2K drives the diffusion pattern of ERP.

Enterprise Resource Planning

The term "ERP" was addressed first by the Gartner Group in the early 1990s. It evolved from MRP,

Closed-Loop MRP in the 1970s and MRP II in the 1980s. ERP is designed to manage a production facility's orders, production plans and inventories. ERP integrates inventory data with financial, sales and human resources data, and has become the pervasive infrastructure (Jacobs & Weston, 2007; Markus, Tanis, & Fenema, 2000; Moller, 2005; Seethamraju, 2005).

Unlike the requirements of other information technology tools, companies should move out of their traditional "functional silo" mode of thinking to an organizational mode of planning and thinking in the implementation of ERP, because ERP will impact the entire organization and its cultures (Jacobs & Weston, 2007; Light & Papazafeiropoulou, 2004; Palaniswamy & Frank, 2002), radically reshaping how business is done and exploiting the new automated, seamless enterprise system capabilities in the processes, the real value-adding opportunity offered by ERP. To improve "how business is done" is not just about integrating and creating more efficient transactional processes, the ERP route to business

value is also dependent on major human, culture, and organizational changes (Willcocks & Sykes, 2000), see Figure 1.

Diffusion-of-Innovation

Since Rogers addressed the diffusion concept in 1962, researches on the diffusion of innovations have resulted in a large body of literature (Schmitt et al., 2007). According to Rogers' (1995, p. 11) definition, "an innovation is an idea, practice, or object that is perceived as new by an individual or other unit of adoption". The perceived newness of the idea determines the individual's reaction to it. Rogers (1995, p. 5) stated that "diffusion is the process by which an innovation is communicated through certain channels over time and among the members of a social system". This definition indicates that diffusion is a special type of communication, in that the messages concern a new idea. According to the definition, there are four main elements in the diffusion of innovations: (1) the innovation; (2) communication channels;

Figure 1. ERP: comparing change equations (Source: Willcocks & Sykes, 2000)

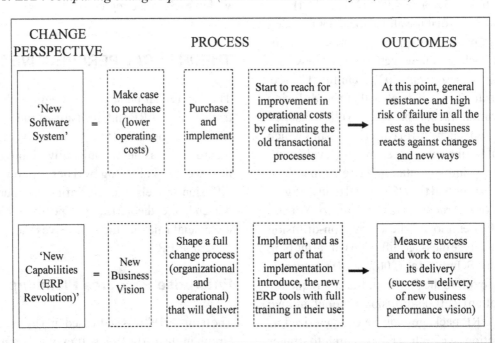

(3) time and (4) the social system (Rogers, 1995, 2003). These elements are described below:

- **Innovation:** A new product or service, a new production process technology, a new structure or administrative system, or a new plan can all be viewed as innovation. Damanpour (1991) argued that an innovation is a means of changing an organization, either as a response to changes in its internal or external environment or as a preemptive action taken to influence an environment.

- **Communication channels:** The essence of the diffusion process is the information exchange through which individuals communicate a new idea each other. A communication channel is the means by which messages get from one individual to another. It takes two forms: mass media channels and interpersonal channels. Mass media channels, involving all those means of transmitting messages such as radio and television are often the most rapid and efficient means to inform an audience of potential adopters about the existence of an innovation. Interpersonal channels, involving face-to-face exchanges among individuals, are more effective in persuading individuals to accept a new idea (Rogers, 1995, 2003).

- **Time:** Rogers (1995, p. 20) stated that "the time dimension is involved in diffusion (1) in the innovation-decision process by which an individual passes from first knowledge of an innovation through its adoption or rejection, (2) in the innovativeness of an individual or other unit of adoption, that is, the relative earliness/lateness with which an innovation is adopted, compared with other members of a system, and (3) in an innovation's rate of adoption in a system, usually measured by the number

of members of the system who adopt the innovation in a given time period" .

- **The social system:** A social system is a set of interrelated units that are devoted to joint problem-solving, to accomplish a common goal (Rogers, 1995). In the diffusion of innovation, it means the community of individuals and/or organizations that are potential adopters of the innovation (Loh & Venkatraman, 1992).

In this study, the innovation is the ERP and the relevant social system is the set of organizations that potentially adopt ERP. The communication channels in ERP take two forms: mass media channels (for example, through promotional efforts by ERP vendors, consulting firms or trade periodicals), and interpersonal channels (for example, through the members of a social system interacting with one another).

The innovation can be distinguished into two types: administrative innovation and technical innovation. According to Damanpour's (1991, p. 560) conceptualization, "technical innovations pertain to products, services and production process technology; they are related to basic work activities and can concern either product or process", whereas "administrative innovations involve organizational structure and administrative processes; they are indirectly related to the basic work activities of an organization and are more directly related to its management." Similarly, Venkatraman et al. (1994, p. 497) defined an administrative innovation as "involving significant changes in the routines (or behavioral repertoires) used by the organization to deal with its tasks of internal arrangements and external alignments". Furthermore, the implementation of administrative innovations often involves an enormous change in functions, tasks, responsibilities, systems and culture (Mahajan et al., 1988).

The diffusion of innovation perspective has been utilized for the study of technical innovations and administrative innovations. Detecting types of innovation is necessary for understanding organizations' adoption behavior and identifying the determinants of innovation in organizations (Downs & Mohr, 1976; Knight, 1967; Rowe & Boise, 1974).

ERP as an Administrative Innovation

According to the definitions of administrative innovation as described above, it captures: (1) the critical opinion of first-time adoption by an organization (Rogers, 1995); (2) the changes in the routines and procedures of organization and management that involve significant "set up" costs and organizational disruption (Teece, 1980); (3) a broader view of administrative tasks as an organization-environment co-alignment, that reflect both internal arrangements as well as external alignments (Thompson, 1967; Snow & Miles, 1983).

The arguments supporting the consideration of ERP as an administrative innovation are described below. First, it represents a significant shift in the mode of governance: ERP permits the injection of more discipline into their organizations. Some companies exert more management control and impose more-uniform processes on freewheeling, highly entrepreneurial cultures. Nevertheless, some companies use ERP to break down hierarchical structures, freeing their people to be more innovative and more flexible (Davenport, 1998). For example, a semiconductor company says, "we plan to use SAP as a battering ram to make our culture less autonomous." Union Carbide uses ERP to give low-level managers, workers, and even customers and suppliers much broader access to operating information (Davenport, 1998). In fact, such a shift in the mode of governance is an ally in achieving profound transformations in the strategic and operational mechanisms that are necessary for an organization to position itself within its current mission or scope (Markus et al., 2000; Loh & Venkatraman, 1992).

Second, ERP represents significant changes in the internal processes of the organizations. Karim, Somers, and Bhattacherjee (2007) found that the extent of ERP implementation influences business process outcomes, and both ERP radicaless and delivery system play moderating roles. Generally, organizations often modify themselves to fit the ERP. Therefore, ERP could drive the business process reengineering. Lee (1998) argued that organizations should make reengineering and ERP implementation simultaneously, to maximize value derived from the implementation. Besides, ERP is a software package that manages and integrates business processes across organizational functions and locations. It costs millions of dollars to buy and necessitates disruptive organizational change (Soh, Kien, & Tay-Yap, 2000). It is consistent with Teece's (1980) view of administrative innovation as often involving significant "set up" costs and organizational disruption.

Third, ERP constitutes a significant change in the organizational routines used to deal with the external environment. For instance, ERP adopters are found to reduce their turnover days of account receivables or inventories, and prolong turnover days of unpaid accounts permitted by their suppliers, thus causing a substantial efficiency elevation after ERP implementation (Tsai, 2008). ERP is evolving to support other functionalities that are offered separately, like supply chain management (SCM), customer relationship management (CRM), professional service automation (PSA) and others (Shakir, 2000; Shuai, Su, & Yang, 2007). ERP could integrate planning and resources of financial procedures and inter-enterprise collaborative operations. It emphasizes integration enterprise, customers, and supplier chains. Organizations build long-term relationships with partners through the sharing of information.

Influence Sources

Traditionally, diffusion model has three basic models: internal influence (word-of-mouth or interpersonal communication), external influence (mass-media communication), and mixed influence (Loh & Venkatraman, 1992; Mahajan, Muller, & Bass, 1990; Rogers, 1995; Venkatraman, Loh, & Koh, 1994). A diffusion model permits prediction of the continued development of the diffusion process over time as well as facilitates a theoretical explanation of the dynamics of the diffusion process in terms of certain general characteristics (Mahajan & Perterson, 1985). The essence of the diffusion is the information exchange through one individual (or other unit) communicates a new idea (or an innovation) to one or several others (Rogers, 2003). Internal and external sources are two influences for adopters. Internal influence source means the unit adopted an innovation is influenced by the members of the social system (inside). External influence source means the unit adopted an innovation is influenced from outside of the social system. Mass media, vendors, consulting firms or trade periodicals are usually external influence sources outside of the social system. These factors are explored by estimation of model fit.

Internal influence. Mansfield (1961) suggested the internal-influence model. It purports that diffusion occurs through channels of communication within a social system and is appropriate for testing the imitation hypothesis. The diffusion is driven from imitative behavior within the social system. The model can be stated as:

$$\frac{dN(t)}{dt} = qN(t)[m - N(t)] \qquad (1)$$

where *N(t)* is the cumulative number of adopters at time *t*, *m* is the total number of adopters who will eventually adopt the innovation, and *q* is the coefficient of internal influence. In this model, the diffusion rate is a function of the number who have already adopted the innovation, and the remaining number of potential adopters. Mahajan and Peterson (1985) argued that the model is

Figure 2. Internal influence diffusion curve (Source: Mahajan & Peterson, 1985)

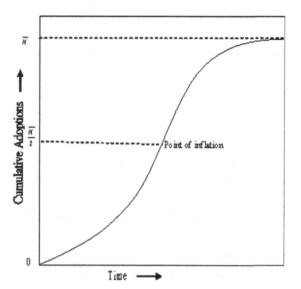

structurally equivalent to the imitation model, as seen in Figure 2. Applied to our study, the adoption of ERP in an organization may imitate other organizations which have adopted it.

External influence. Much of the popularity of the external-influence model is due to the work of Coleman et al. (1966). Diffusion processes are hypothesized as only being "driven" by information from a communication source external to the social system. The model assumes that the rate of diffusion at time *t* is dependent only on the potential number of adopters present in the social system at time *t*. That is to say, the model does not consider interaction between prior adopters and potential adopters (Mahajan & Peterson, 1985). The model can be represented as:

$$\frac{dN(t)}{dt} = p[m - N(t)] \qquad (2)$$

where *p* is the coefficient of external influence and a nonnegative constant. *N(t)* with t results in a curve that increases at a decreasing rate, as shown in Figure 3. In our study, external influence on the potential adopters of ERP includes:

mass media, vendors, consulting firms or trade periodicals.

Mixed influence. This formulation combines both the internal- and external-influence models (Bass, 1969). The mixed-influence model can be stated as:

$$\frac{dN(t)}{dt} = [p + qN(t)][m - N(t)] \qquad (3)$$

The cumulative distribution of the model brings about a generalized logistic curve whose S-shape depends on the coefficients p and q. The model is the most general form and is widely used to combine both internal and external influences concurrently. The diffusion of the model was due to a combination of coverage by the media and early adoption.

RESEARCH QUESTION 1: What source of influence best characterizes the diffusion of ERP?

The Y2K as a Critical Point

In the late 1990s, most enterprise information systems included some legacy systems; the Y2K was a serious problem for these old systems. ERP could provide a solution to fix the Y2K problem for firms (Jacobs& Weston, 2007). During the last three years of the 1990s, the ERP market was one of the fastest growing and most profitable areas of the software industry (Davenport, 1998). Sprott (2000) indicated that most of this was clearly attributable to the Y2K effect. The package software got a huge boost when companies began to realize the full impact of the Y2K problem.

By 1998, nearly 40% of companies with annual revenues of more than $1 billion had implemented ERP (Caldwell & Stein, 1998). The largest ERP vendor, SAP Inc., had revenues of $3.3 billion in 1997, which had soared from less than $500 million in 1992 (Davenport, 1998). AMR research predicted that the ERP market would reach $66.6

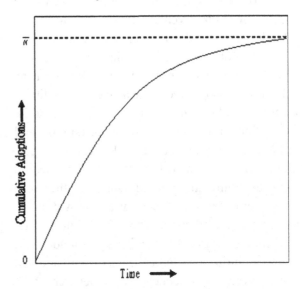

Figure 3. External influence diffusion curve (Source: Mahajan & Peterson, 1985)

billion by 2003. But, because many companies have already implemented ERP in response to the Y2K concerns, the ERP and its services of market have cooled somewhat at present (Markus & Tanis, 2000). The Y2K issue provided an added incentive to address the inflexibility of legacy systems, enabling the introduction of ERP. That is, the Y2K problem drove the demand for ERP software packages (Jacobs & Weston, 2007; MIC, 2004; Scott & Kaindl, 2000). Based on above discussion, we treat the Y2K as a critical point in the adoption of ERP. In particular, we test whether the types of underlying influence are different before and after this critical point.

The term "Y2K effect" is used to signify the importance of the Y2K critical point in driving the diffusion pattern of ERP. For this purpose, we consider the period: January 1997 to December 2000, as the first diffusion regime, and the period: January 2001 to December 2004, as the second diffusion regime.

RESEARCH QUESTION 2: What source of influence best characterizes the diffusion of ERP before and after the Y2K?

Method

The Adoption Data

The sample comprises companies which have adopted ERP in Taiwan. The data are collected from the TTS (Transmission Text Retrieval System) Web Server. TTS is the products of Transmission Books and Microinfo Co., Ltd. (TBMC). It has been providing various publications and services to academic libraries since 1981. TTS contains indexes of several major daily newspapers in Taiwan (such as United Daily News, Economic Daily News, China Times, and The Commercial Times). Related reports and statistical data on ERP in Taiwan mostly begin from 1997 (MIC, 2004). Besides, since we view the Y2K as a critical point, we perform a search of related information sources from 1997 to 2004 for the symmetric periods. Time-series adoption data are developed by the year function.

Table 1 shows these data (on 82 firms), and by year, provides the number of firms that adopted the ERP. Figure 4 illustrates the non-cumulative number of adopters. Figure 5 shows the cumulative number of adopters. It shows a similar "S" curve" and the pattern of diffusion process. It also

finds that the Y2K is possible the inflection point of the curve on the figure.

Analytical Framework

The model of Bass (1969) assumes that potential adopters of an innovation are influenced by two means of communication: (1) mass media and (2) word of mouth. This further assumes that the adopters of an innovation comprise two groups: (1) those influenced by mass media communication (an external influence) and (2) those influenced by interpersonal communication (an internal influence) (Mahajan et al., 1990). Mahajan et al. (1988) studied the adoption for the M-form organization structure and used linear regression analogue equation (OLS estimation) to test different models. Based on the Bass model and the analysis methods suggested by Mahajan et al. (1988), this study adopted the OLS analysis method.

Research Procedures

The Null hypothesis. A stringent null hypothesis assumes that the diffusion pattern follows a white-noise or a random walk process (Majahan et al., 1988; Loh & Venkatraman, 1992). The white-noise process clarifies the difference between the

Figure 4. Non-cumulative adoption

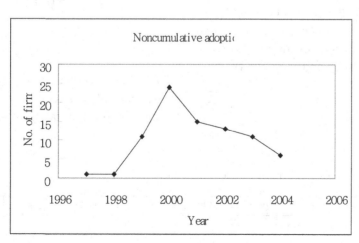

Figure 5. Cumulative adoption

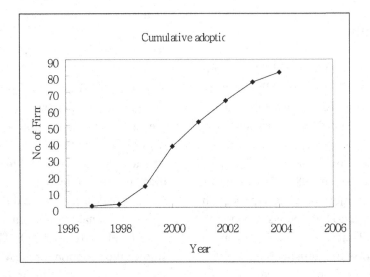

numbers of adopters at *t* and *(t-1)* is random. That is, in time-series data, the rate of diffusion will be driven by the error term only when:

$$x(t) = x(t-1) + \varepsilon(t) \qquad (4)$$

where $x(t)$ is the number of adopters at time *t*, and the residuals $\varepsilon(t)$ have a zero mean that is uncorrelated with $\varepsilon(t-k)$ for all nonzero *k*. The model indicated that in the adoption of time-series, progression occurs via a sequence of unconnected steps, starting each time from the previous value of the adoption time-series.

The External-influence Model. The regression analogue of the external-influence model, equation (2), for describing a time-series adoption pattern, can be stated as (Mahajan and et al, 1988):

$$x(t) = \beta_2 x(t-1) + \varepsilon(t) \qquad (5)$$

where $x(t) = N(t)-N(t-1)$ is the number of adopters at time *t*, $N(.)$ is the cumulative number of adopters, $\beta_2 = (1-p)$ and $\beta_2 < 1$, and the residuals, $\varepsilon(t)$, have zero mean, and $\varepsilon(t)$ is uncorrelated with $\varepsilon(t-k)$ for $k \neq 0$. Besides, if $\beta_2 = 1$, equation (5) is reduced to the white noise model.

The Mixed-influence Model. Two popular innovation diffusion models that generate the S-shape adoption pattern and, in particular, capture the imitation behavior, are those suggested by Mansfield (1961) and Bass (1969). The Bass model can be stated as:

$$\frac{dN(t)}{dt} = p(m - N(t)) + \frac{q}{m}(m - N(t))N(t) \qquad (6)$$

where the second term in equation (6) represents the "contact" between adopter and non-adopters and reflects the imitation behavior. Consequently,

Table 1. Adoption data (Non-cumulative)

Year	1997	1998	1999	2000	2001	2002	2003	2004
Number of adopters	1	1	11	24	15	13	11	6

the non-negative constant q is usually defined as the coefficient internal influence. Note when $q=0$ and $\beta_2 <1$, as in equation (6), it yields the Coleman model (external-influence), equation (3).

One possible regression analogue of both imitational (mix and internal) models can be derived as:

$$x(t) = \beta_2 x(t-1) + \beta_3 N * (t-1) + \varepsilon(t) \qquad (7)$$

where $\beta_2 = 1+q-p$ for the Bass (mixed-influence) model and $\beta_2 = 1+q$ for Mansfield (internal-influence) model and $\beta_2 >1$, $\beta_3 <0$, and $N*(t-1) = N^2(t-1) - N^2(t-2)$ (Mahajan et al., 1988).

The Internal-influence Model. In the mixed-influenced equation (7), $\beta_2 = 1+q-p$ for the Bass (mixed-influence) model and $\beta_2 = 1+q$ for the Mansfield (internal-influence) model and $\beta_2 >1$, $\beta_3 <0$. In the external-influenced equation (5), $\beta_2 = (1-p)$ and $\beta_2 <1$. So, we derive that internal-influenced β_2 is 1+ (mixed-influenced β_2) - (external-influenced β_2).

$$x(t) = \beta_2 x(t-1) + \beta_3 N * (t-1) + \varepsilon(t) \qquad (8)$$

where $\beta_2 = 1+ (1+q-p)-(1-q)$ and $\beta_2 >1$, $\beta_3 <0$. Table 2 summarized the model specification and parameter values.

Finally, we employed the F-test (Mahajan et al., 1988, Venkatraman et al., 1994) to test the significance of the explanatory power of alternative models.

Evaluating the Two Research Questions. The first research question, based on the analytical framework, is employed to test the entire diffusion regime, to assess the relative adequacy of an influence model against the white-noise model with the three influence models. The second research question is appraised in the two regimes. According to Loh and Venkatraman (1992), the approach we used is in accordance with the standard econometric technique of testing structural change by breaking up a full-time series into separate regimes, using some conceptually conceived cutoff points. The research question is to be evaluated by comparing the separate analysis results within each of the regimes, and to interpret the results in terms of the dominant type of influence in the two regimes.

RESULTS

Research question 1: Influence sources in the diffusion of ERP

Table 3 summarizes the parameter estimates and the fit statistics (R^2 and significance values) for the three alternative models and white noise

Table 2. Summary of hypothesized model specifications

Hypothesis	Model name	Model Specification	Parameter Values $-- \beta_2 \beta_3$
Null	White-noise	$x(t) = x(t-1) + \varepsilon(t)$	$-- =1 -$
Alternative	External Mixed Internal	$x(t) = \beta_2 x(t-1) + \varepsilon(t)$ $x(t) = \beta_2 x(t-1) + \beta_3 N * (t-1) + \varepsilon(t)$ $x(t) = \beta_2 x(t-1) + \beta_3 N * (t-1) + \varepsilon(t)$	$-- <1 -$ $-- >1 <0$ $-- >1 <0$

Table 3. Parameter estimation of ERP diffusion

Model	Coefficients				
	β_2	β_3	R^2	F	Sig.
White-noise	1.00	–	0.649	15.768	0.005***
External	0.857	–	0.672	17.369	**0.004***
Mixed	1.270	-0.006	**0.675**	9.326	**0.014***
Internal	1.413	−0.007	0.670	9.120	**0.015****

* p<0.1; ** p<0.05; *** p<0.01

model. The white noise's R^2 value is smaller than those of other models. Three alternative models are significant. Main influence sources are mixed influence sources. We may think external influence has more influence if we consider that mixed sources are combined with internal and external influence sources; however, there is no significant difference compared with these models.

Research question 2: What source of influence best characterizes the diffusion of ERP before and after the Y2K?

Table 4 summarizes the parameter estimates and fit statistics for the three alternatives model and the white-noise model before the Y2K (included). The results show that white-noise and external models are not significant, while mixed and internal models are significant (0.1 significant level). Mixed and internal models have the same influence (equal R^2 value), explaining the quite high variance (about 84%). From the above analysis, the main influence sources are internal channels before the Y2K.

Table 5 summarizes the parameter estimates and the fit statistics for the three alternatives model and the white noise model after the Y2K. Only the external model is significant with 0.05 significant level (mixed model is significant with 0.1 significant level). The results show that the main influence sources are the external channels. It explains the 96.1% variance. Table 4 and Table 5 show the main influence sources differing before and after the Y2K. These results confirm that the Y2K is a critical point.

DISCUSSION

An innovation is an idea, practice, or object perceived as new by an individual or other unit of adoption (Rogers, 2003). In this study, we view ERP as administrative innovation and the unit of adoption is an organization. We explore the influence sources of the adoption of ERP and also examine the Y2K effect by different diffusion models in Taiwan. The results show that the mixed model is a better fit for the total period.

Table 4. Parameter estimation of ERP diffusion before the Y2K

Model	Coefficients				
	β_2	β_3	R^2	F	Sig.
White-noise	1.00	–	0.485	1.589	0.297
External	1.00	–	0.485	1.589	0.297
Mixed	6.119	-0.262	**0.838**	11.364	0.081*
Internal	6.119	-0.262	**0.838**	11.464	0.081*

* p<0.1; ** p<0.05; *** p<0.01

Table 5. Parameter estimation of ERP diffusion after the Y2K

Model	Coefficients				
	β_2	β_3	R^2	F	Sig.
White-noise	1.000	–	0.724	3.833	0.145
External	0.700	–	**0.961**	33.438	**0.010****
Mixed	1.000	-0.003	0.855	12.830	**0.072***
Internal	1.300	-0.006	0.669	4.861	0.171

* $p<0.1$; ** $p<0.05$; *** $p<0.01$

More specifically, external communication channels show more influence. Perhaps mass media reports about the Y2K effect and the benefits of ERP create effective innovation knowledge and change attitudes toward ERP adoption. Considering the Y2K effect, before the Y2K, mixed model and internal model show the same power of explanation ($R^2 = 83.8\%$). While the internal communication channels are important influence sources behind ERP adoption before the Y2K, interpersonal channels are more effective in forming and changing opinions concerning the adoption of ERP. However, after the Y2K, the external influence sources become the main influences ($R^2 = 96.1\%$). That is, mass media and other external channels (such as consulting firms) are the major influence sources for ERP adoption in this period.

The Y2K is arguably the single "event" that signals both the maturing of ERP industry and the consolidation of large and small ERP vendors (Jacobs & Weston, 2007). After the Y2K, ERP concept and ERP market reach maturity. The Y2K effect is not the important factor anymore for ERP adoption. Enterprises focus on business strategy planning, critical process reengineering and organization change management for adopting ERP. External channels, such as reports of mass media about ERP, promotions of ERP providers and consulting firms play the major influence sources. The external diffusion model shows an exponential distribution, but also shows slow growth at a later stage. This finding is in accord with the MIC annual report about software in-

dustry development (Liu, 2006). The report also indicates that most large-sized (>89%) companies have already implemented ERP.

This study expands the application of the diffusion model to ERP adoption. The research results indicate the Y2K is the critical point that can significantly differentiate the pattern of ERP diffusion. The findings also reveal that the market's growth rate of ERP is decreasing in Taiwan. In particular, large firms turn their software system demands to other systems, such as customer relationship management, knowledge management, and business intelligence. Comparatively, medium and small-size firms have still been demanding ERP recently (MIC, 2008). For practitioners, because of the slow growth of the ERP market, ERP providers should provide multiple services and continue to maintain original customers. Moreover, because of the lower demand of large firms, they could exploit ERP applications for small and medium-size firms.

There are some limitations in this study. First, the sample is collected from the TTS Web Server, perhaps inducing some biases in terms that almost large companies reported in these sample sources. Some medium or small companies could have been missed. Nevertheless, due to their lower visibility, we could believe that smaller companies are not a critical impetus underlying imitative behavior in ERP diffusion. Next, this study is conducted in Taiwan, and the result might differ if conducted elsewhere since the social factors may differ in other countries. Finally, this study does not consider several dimensions, such as incorporating the effects of social structure and organizational characteristics. Future researcher could expand the scope of the constructs.

REFERENCES

Anat, H., Ravi, P., & David, S. (2004). A model of Internet standards adoption: The case of IPv6. *Information Systems Journal, 14*, 265–294. doi:10.1111/j.1365-2575.2004.00170.x

Bass, F. M. (1969). A new product growth for model consumer durables. *Management Science, 15*(5), 215–227. doi:10.1287/mnsc.15.5.215

Brown, C., & Vessey, I. (1999). *ERP implementation approaches: toward a contingency framework.* Paper presented at the Proceedings of the Twentieth International Conference on Information Systems, Charlotte, NC.

Caldwell, B., & Stein, T. (1998). New IT agenda. *Informationweek, 30*, 30–38.

Center, M. I. (2004). 2004 yearbook of information service industry. Institute *for Information Industry.*

Center, M. I. (2006). Information application demand analysis of large companies in Taiwan.

Coleman, J. S., Katz, E., & Menzel, H. (1966). *Medical innovation: A diffusion study.* Indianapolis: Bobbs-Merrill.

Daft, R. L. (1978). A dual-core model of organizational innovation. *Academy of Management Journal, 21*, 193–210. doi:10.2307/255754

Damanpour, F. (1991). Organizational innovation: a meta-analysis of effects of determinants and moderators. *Academy of Management Journal, 34*(3), 555–590. doi:10.2307/256406

Davenport, T. H. (1998). Putting the enterprise into the enterprise system. *Harvard Business Review*, 121–131.

Davidson, R., M., J.G. (1981). Several tests for model specification in the presence of alternative hypotheses. *Econometrica, 49*(3), 781–793. doi:10.2307/1911522

Downs, G. W., & Mohr, L. B. (1976). Conceptual issues in the study of innovation. *Administrative Science Quarterly, 21*(4), 700–714. doi:10.2307/2391725

Gefen, D., & Ragowsky, A. (2005). A multi-level approach to measuring the benefits of an ERP system in manufacturing firms. *Information Systems Management, 22*(1), 18–25. doi:10.1201/1078/44912.22.1.20051201/85735.3

Institute, M. I. C. (2004). Ch12 Information Service Industry. *2004 Information Service Industry Yearbook.*

Institute, M. I. C. (2004). Ch12 Information Service Industry. *2006 Information Service Industry Yearbook.*

Institute, M. I. C. (2008). CH4 The Trend and Situation of Market. *2008 Information Service Industry Yearbook.*

Ives, B., & Jarvenpaa, S. (1993). Organizing for global competition: The fit of information technology. *Decision Sciences, 24*(3), 547–580. doi:10.1111/j.1540-5915.1993.tb01293.x

Jacobs, R. F., & Weston, F. C. (2007). Enterprise resource planning (ERP)—A brief history. *Journal of Operations Management, 25*(2), 357–363. doi:10.1016/j.jom.2006.11.005

Karim, J., Somers, T. M., & Bhattacherjee, A. (2007). The impact of ERP implementation on business process outcomes: A factor-based study. *Journal of Management Information Systems, 24*(1), 101–134. doi:10.2753/MIS0742-1222240103

Knight, K. E. (1967). A descriptive model of the intra-firm innovation process. *The Journal of Business, 40*, 478–496. doi:10.1086/295013

Ko, H. C., Yin, C. P., & Kuo, F. Y. (2008). Exploring individual communication power in the blogosphere. *Internet Research, 18*(5), 541–561. doi:10.1108/10662240810912774

Lee, R. (1998). An enterprise decision framework for information system selection. *Information Systems Management, 15*(4), 7–18. doi:10.1201/1078/43186.15.4.19980901/31145.2

Liu, T. H. (2006). *The Analysis of Business Software Companies' Development.* Market Intelligence Consulting Institute.

Loh, L., & Venkatraman, N. (1992). Diffusion of information technology outsourcing: Influence sources and the Kodak effect. *Information Systems Research, 3*(4), 334–358. doi:10.1287/isre.3.4.334

Mahajan, V., Muller, E., & Bass, F. M. (1990). New product diffusion model in marketing: a review and directions for research. *Journal of Marketing, 54*, 1–26. doi:10.2307/1252170

Mahajan, V., & Peterson, R. A. (1985). *Models for innovation diffusion.* Beverly Hills: Sage Publications.

Mahajan, V., Sharma, S., & Bettis, R. A. (1988). The adoption of the M-form organizational structure: A test of imitation hypothesis. *Management Science, 34*(10), 1188–1201. doi:10.1287/mnsc.34.10.1188

Mansfield, E. (1961). Technical change and the rate of imitation. *Econometrica, 29*, 741–766. doi:10.2307/1911817

Markus, M. L., & Tanis, C. (2000). The enterprise systems experience-from adoption to success. In R. W. Zmud (Ed.), *Framing the Domains of IT Research: Glimpsing the Future Through the Past* (pp. 173-207). Cincinnati: Pinnaflex Educational Resources.

Markus, M. L., Tanis, C., & Fenema, P. C. (2000). Multisite ERP implementations. *Communications of the ACM, 43*(4), 42–46. doi:10.1145/332051.332068

Moller, C. (2005). Unleashing the potential of SCM: adoption of ERP in large Danish enterprises. *International Journal of Enterprise Information Systems, 1*(1), 39–52.

Palaniswamy, R., & Frank, T. G. (2002). Oracle ERP and network computing architecture: implementation and performance. *Information Systems Management, 19*(2), 53–69. doi:10.1201/1078/43200.19.2.20020228/35140.6

Rogers, E. M. (1995). *Diffusion of innovations.* New York: The Free Press.

Rogers, E. M. (2003). *Diffusion of innovations.* New York: The Free Press.

Rowe, L. A., & Boise, W. B. (1974). Organizational innovation: current research and evolving concepts. *Public Administration Review, 34*, 284–293. doi:10.2307/974923

Schmitt, P., Thiesse, F., & Fleisch, E. (2007). *Adoption and diffusion of RFID technology in the automotive industry.* Paper presented at the 15th ECIS, Switzerland.

Scott, J. E., & Kaindl, L. (2000). Enhancing functionality in an enterprise software package. *Information & Management, 37*(3), 111–122. doi:10.1016/S0378-7206(99)00040-3

Seethamraju, R. (2005). Enterprise resource planning systems-implications for managers and management. *Australian Accounting Review, 15*(3), 90–96. doi:10.1111/j.1835-2561.2005.tb00308.x

Shakir, M. (2000). *Decision making in the evaluation, selection and implementation of ERP.* Paper presented at the Proceedings of the Americas Conference on Information Systems.

Shuai, J. J., Su, Y. F., & Yang, C. (2007). *The impact of ERP implementation on corporate supply chain performance.* Paper presented at the 2007 IEEE International Conference on Industrial Engineering and Engineering Management, Singapore.

Snow, C. C., & Miles, R. E. (1983). The role of strategy in the development of a general theory of organizations. In R. Lamb (Ed.), *Advances in Strategic Management* (pp. 237-259). Greenwich: JAI Press.

Soh, C., Kien, S. S., & Tay-Yap, J. (2000). Cultural fits and misfits: Is ERP a universal solution? *Communications of the ACM, 43*(4), 47–51. doi:10.1145/332051.332070

Sprott, D. (2000). Componentizing the enterprise application packages. *Communications of the ACM, 43*(4), 63–69. doi:10.1145/332051.332074

Srinivasan, V., & Mason, C. H. (1986). Nonlinear least squares estimation of new product diffusion models. *Marketing Science, 5*, 169–178. doi:10.1287/mksc.5.2.169

Sumner, M. (1999). *Critical success factors in enterprise wide information management systems.* Paper presented at the Proceedings of the American Conference on Information Systems, Milwaukee.

Teece, D. J. (1980). The diffusion of an administrative innovation. *Management Science, 26*(5), 464–470. doi:10.1287/mnsc.26.5.464

Thompson, J. D. (1967). *Organizations in action.* New York: McGraw-Hill.

Tsai, B. H. (2008). *The impact of enterprise resource planning systems on the efficiency of Taiwanese firms.* Paper presented at the Proceedings of the 2008 IEEE Asia-Pacific Services Computing Conference.

Venkatraman, N., Loh, L., & Koh, J. (1994). The adoption of corporate governance mechanisms: a test of competing diffusion models. *Management Science, 40*(4), 496–507. doi:10.1287/mnsc.40.4.496

Willcocks, L. P., & Sykes, R. (2000). The role of the CIO and IT function in ERP. *Communications of the ACM, 43*(4), 32–38. doi:10.1145/332051.332065

Chapter 15
IS Success Factors and IS Organizational Impact:
Does Ownership Type Matter in Kuwait?

Abdulrida Alshawaf
Kuwait University, Kuwait

Omar E. M. Khalil
Kuwait University, Kuwait

ABSTRACT

This research investigated the possible ownership type effect on the information systems (IS) success factors and IS impact on organizational performance in Kuwaiti organizations. Four IS success factors—IS strategy and resources, end user support, IS sophistication and IS organizational level & user involvement—and three IS organizational impact factors—improving work efficiency, improving decision making, and improving work effectiveness—were identified. Ownership type was found to affect the profiles of the IS success factors and IS organizational impact. Public organizations tend to commit less IS resources; their managers get less involved in IS strategy formulation, and their users get less involved in systems development. Yet, they tend to rate their IS organizational impact higher. This "IS expectation-performance gap" is further explained in the article, along with research implications, limitations, and future research.

INTRODUCTION

Information systems (IS) success has long generated much interest and consequent research (Almutairi & Subramanian, 2005; Kim & Kim, 1999; Palvia, Palvia, & Zigli, 1992). However, consistent results on the determinants of IS success have yet to emerge (Seliem, Ashour, Khalil, & Miller, 2003).

A plausible reason for such inconsistent findings is that IS management issues are perhaps context-sensitive and are related to the particular country's unique political, legal, economic, cultural and technological characteristics. Consequently, findings from Western-based investigations are not necessarily generalizable to other settings or countries (Aharoni & Burton, 1994; Rosenzweig, 1994; Seliem & Turunen, 2003).

A significant part of the research on IS success and its determinant factors is based on findings drawn from investigations of private organizations in developed countries (Jain, 1997; Seneviratne, 1999; Seliem et al., 2003). Therefore, the value of such findings in guiding IS decisions and policies in public organizations in the developing countries is inadequate until their external and international generalizability is verified. In addition, IS management practices and IS effects on performance may vary in the public and private organizations because of possible environmental and organizational differences between them (Bretschneider, 1990; Bretschneider & Wittmer, 1993; Jayasuriya, 1999; Margetts & Willcocks, 1994).

Identifying issues that may be distinctive to certain cultures (Khalil & Elkordy, 1997) and certain organizational types are essential for effective IS management practices. The few studies that investigated IS practices, characteristics and effectiveness in a Kuwaiti context (e.g., Aladwani, 2001, 2002; Almutairi & Subramanian, 2005; Alshawaf, Ali, & Hasan, 2005) did not address in their research designs the possible differences in IS management practices and IS organizational impacts across private and public organizations. IS policy makers in the Kuwaiti public and private organizations need to be aware of the IS success factors that may be specific to their organizations in order to make decisions that deem necessary to the enhancement of IS contributions to organizational performance.

This research explores whether IS success factors and IS impact on organizational performance are common across the public and private organizations in Kuwait. The article is organized accordingly. It starts with a background on the research variables and context, research method, results, discussion of the research findings, implications, limitations and future research, and the article ends with conclusions.

BACKGROUND

IS Success Factors

Mangers in public and private organizations are well aware that investments in a successful deployment of information technology (IT) for information acquisition, processing, and communication can influence decisions and, in turn, affect the efficiency and effectiveness of organizational performance. The literature on IS success offers a number of research frameworks and models describing the potential impact of organizational and technical factors on IS success, measured by user satisfaction, system use, impact on user's performance, and/or impact on organizational performance.

Delone and McLean's (1992) model may be considered to be one of the most comprehensive and popular IS success models. The model identifies six interrelated dimensions of success, including information quality, system quality, system use, user satisfaction, individual impact and organizational impact. The model has generated a great deal of research that aimed at validating the applicability of the model in different contexts and for different information systems types. Ten years later, Delone and McLean (2003) revisited and revised their model to include a new service quality dimension, the modification of the use dimension into intent to use, and the combination of the individual and organizational impact into an overall net benefits dimension.

Nevertheless, IS research has explored a broad range of factors that are considered to be critical to the success of information systems. In spite of its lack of a robust theoretical basis and the absence of consistent procedures for identifying the factors that are considered relevant to IS success, the methodology has been long used as a methodology in IS research (Boynton & Zmud, 1994). Lam (2005) adds that CSF studies continue to be valuable for making sense out of problems where there are many potential factors that may affect the outcome, and where the researcher hopes to make a set of practical recommendations based on the most influential factors.

Based on a review and synthesis of the literature on IS effectiveness/success, an initial set of IS situational factors that are believed to affect IS success has been identified. These factors include the age of the IS organizational unit, the organizational level of the IS unit, clarity of the IS strategy, top management involvement in the formulation of IS strategy, locus of the IS financial decisions, IS resources, user involvement in systems development, end-user training, end-user support and IS sophistication. These factors are briefly discussed next.

1. The age of the IS organizational unit. As the importance of IS services increases, organizations tend to establish organizational units and provide them with the resources needed to undertake their responsibilities. Over time, IS units are expected to draw more managerial support and resources, gain more technical and managerial experience, and acquire and manage more and better IT applications. Consequently, the longer an IS unit has been in existence in an organization the more it is expected to positively impact organizational performance. Contrary to expectation, however, Atiyyah (1989) found older computer units have a negative influence on organizational effectiveness in the public organizations of Saudi Arabia.

2. The organizational level of the IS unit. The organizational infrastructure and the reporting level of the IS unit in an organization is considered critical to the allocation of sufficient resources and the deployment of IT applications (Davenport & Prusak, 1998; Ein-Dor & Segev, 1978; Franz & Robey, 1986). The higher the reporting level of the IS unit, the higher the organizational commitment to the mission and needs of the unit; the more the impact that IS is expected to

have on organizational performance. Atiyyah (1989) found that having the computer unit report to top management to positively impact information systems effectiveness in the public organizations of Saudi Arabia. Compared to their counterparts in private organizations, IS managers in public organizations are usually placed lower in the organizational structure (Bretschneider, 1990). Davenport and Prusak (1998) and Gold, Malhotra, and Segars (2001) found the organizational infrastructure to be critical to the deployment and success of knowledge management systems (KMS). Al-Busaidi and Olfman (2005) found organizational infrastructure to correlate with knowledge management systems (KMS) success in Omani organizations.

3. Clarity of IS strategy. A clear IS strategy is essential to effective IS planning, operation, and control. Clearly stated and understood strategies provide a sense of direction and help identify priorities and allocate resources. Therefore, organizational benefits from IS services are expected to be superior when IS operates under clearer and better understood strategies. Davenport and Prusak (1998) found vision clarity to be critical to the deployment of knowledge management systems (KMS). Also, Al-Busaidi and Olfman (2005) found vision clarity to correlate with KMS success in Omani organizations.

4. Top management involvement in the formulation of IS strategy. Top management support for IS takes different forms, including, but not limited to, commitment of resources, involvement in IS strategy formulation, and sponsorship of, and involvement in, systems development (e.g., Igbaria, 1992; Lee & Kim, 1992; Thong, Yap, & Raman, 1996; Yap, Soh, & Roman, 1992). The focus in this research is on top management involvement in the articulation and formulation of IS strategies. A collaborative approach to

IS strategic planning can produce effective planning processes and significant IS based competitive advantages (Kearns & Lederer, 2000; Rai & Lee, 2003). In addition, Aladwani (2001) found IT planning effectiveness to positively associate with management involvement in the planning process in the Kuwaiti private organizations.

The level of top management involvement in IS strategy formulation unveils the extent to which top management is committed to IS mission and role in the organization. High involvement assures that IS strategies are well aligned with the organization's strategies as well as the strategies of the other functional areas in the organization. Therefore, more involvement in the formulation of IS strategies is expected to lead to more successful systems, which are expected to have higher impact on organizational performance.

5. Locus of the IS financial decisions. IS management in an organization may have the technical competency to assess the needed IT investments. However, it is rather difficult to justify IS investments solely on tangible benefits. On the other hand, top management's understanding of the potential intangible benefits of IS investments makes it necessary to secure the needed IS financial resources. Therefore, balanced roles of top-level management and IS management is required in order to reach productive accords when making IS related financial and budgeting decisions. This locus of the IS financial decisions is expected to result in more IS investments, which may, in turn, improve organizational performance.

6. IS resources: In order to serve the organization and affect its performance, IS must have the necessary human and technical resources. In a meta-analysis of empirical research on IS success factors. Mahmood and Swanberg (1999) found a significant impact of organizational support to IS

success. Shin (1999) found IT spending to strongly associate with a decline in coordination costs, and thereby can improve the organization's performance and productivity. Teo and Wong (1998), however, found no correlation between the intensity of IT investment and organizational impacts in their Singapore-based study. Therefore, the possible relationship of availability of IS resources and IS impact on organization performance needs further investigation in public and private organizations in a developing country context.

7. End user support. With the increasing role of end user computing and the expanding use of personal productivity tools, end-user support is considered a critical factor in IS success (e.g., Igbaria & Chakrabarti, 1990; Mirani & King, 1994). In order to provide end users with the necessary technical and logistical support, organizations have established and staffed internal specialized units or centers. The existence of such support units is expected to enhance user satisfaction and systems use, and consequently, improve organizational performance.

8. IT training. User training is essential for effective adoption and use of IT applications. User training is particularly important in the developing countries because of the widespread of computer illiteracy and improper IT training in the formal educational programs. Al-Busaidi and Olfman (2005) found end user training to correlate with KMS success in Omani organizations. Therefore, IT training is expected to impact organizational performance.

9. End user involvement. User involvement in the design, development, and implementation of systems is believed to affect systems acceptance and use (Franz & Robey, 1986; Gyampah & White, 1993; Torkzadeh & Doll, 1994). Involvement of end users is particularly important in the developing countries

because it gives users the opportunity to provide first-hand information on their needs and to learn about the potential benefits of IT from IT specialists. Atiyyah (1989) found user involvement to have positive impact on information systems effectiveness in public organizations in Saudi Arabia. Aladwani (2001) found IT planning effectiveness to be positively correlated to user involvement in the planning process in the Kuwaiti private organizations. Therefore, user involvement is expected to affect IT usage and acceptance, which, in turn, enhance organizational performance.

10. IS sophistication. Typically, organizations operate, manage and maintain a diverse portfolio of IS applications (Cummins, 2002). IS sophistication refers to the depth and breadth of IT applications and services offered by the IS unit to users in an organization. IS success is expected to result from the institutionalization and use of such IT applications (Li, Rogers, & Chang, 1994; Mahmood & Becker, 1985; Raymond & Bergeron, 1992; Seliem et al., 2003). Davenport & Prusak (1998) found technical infrastructure to be critical to the deployment of knowledge management systems (KMS). In an exploratory study of participants from 12 countries, Alavi and Leidner (1999) found technical infrastructure to be essential to KMS implementation success. Gold et al. (2001) found technology to be important to KMS success. Al-Busaidi and Olfman (2005) found technical infrastructure to correlate with KMS success in Omani organizations. Therefore, higher IS sophistication is expected to enhance organizational performance.

IS Organizational Impact

In their 1992 model, DeLone and McLean (1992) proposed measuring IS success through individual and organizational impacts, which were later combined into an overall net IS benefits dimension in their revised model of 2003 (DeLone & McLean, 2003). Yet, the ultimate goal of IT investments is the improvement of organizational performance; and IS researchers have adopted various ways to operationalize organizational performance and used different surrogate measures to test the IS impact on that performance.

Kraemer et al. (1994), for example, measured the perceived business value of IS in organizations using a 40-item scale. These items were grouped along ten dimensions: organizational effectiveness, organizational efficiency, economies of production, new business innovation, customer relations, supplier relations, product and service enhancement, interorganizational coordination, marketing support, and competitive dynamics. In the United Arab Emirates, Yousef (1994) used a 10-item measurement scale to measure the perceived organizational improvements as a result of IS adoption, including organizational planning, organizational monitoring, problem solving, simplified work processes, speeding accomplished work, work accurateness, decreasing operating cost, departmental communications, training and decision making.

Noble (1995) identified three major contributions of IT to organizations. These contributions include improved efficiency through speed of processes and quality of service, organizational boundary spanning (handling relations with the environment), and coordination of relations among organizational units. Ramamurthy and Premkumar (1995) measured IS success in terms of IS contribution to the standardization of work processes. In addition, Thong et al. (1996) measured IS success using staff productivity, operating costs and quality of decision-making. Jurison (1996) used perceived improvement in organizational effectiveness as organizational impact measures. In addition, Yoon, Guimaraes, and Clevenson (1998) measured IS impact on organizational performance in terms of decreased task time, decreased number of steps, simplified process, increased derived benefits and decreased process costs.

Lastly, Mirani and Lederer (1998) identified three categories of organizational benefits from IT: strategic, informational and transactional. Subdimensions of transactional benefits include communications efficiency, systems development efficiency and business efficiency (including employee productivity). Teo and Wong (1998) adopted improved management and increased productivity as measures of IS contribution to organizational performance.

This investigation adopts a 13-item scale to measure IS impact on organizational performance. The items were selected in light of the reviewed literature and the context of this investigation.

Public vs. Private Organizations

Governments around the world are the largest consumers of IT products and services (Caudle, 1990). Compared to private organizations, public organizations have unique characteristics that may influence IS management and IS contribution to organizational performance. Robertson and Seneviratne (1995) speculate that these characteristics include absence of market incentives, the existence of multiple, conflicting goals, a political context with a broader range of constituent groups, a higher level of accountability, lower work satisfaction and organizational commitment, and more rules regulations, and constraints.

Robertson and Senevirante (1995) and Margetts and Willcocks (1994) also speculate that, in public organizations, changes in work settings are more difficult to implement, and the risk involved in IT development is more exacerbated. Compared to their counterparts in the private sector, IS managers in the public sector often have to deal with higher levels of interdependence across organizational boundaries, operate with higher levels of red tape, use less tangible criteria for evaluation of IS investments, get more concerned with extra

organizational linkages rather than with internal coordination, and are usually placed lower in the organizational structure (Bretschneider, 1990). Frequent political leadership changes, lack of long-range planning, rigidity of governmental personnel and procurement processes may impose constraints on IS resources and IS planning and control within public organizations (Newcomer & Caudle; 1991; Salmela & Turunen, 2003).

Overall, compared to their private counterparts, public organizations tend to focus on formalities and abiding to rules and work procedures rather than processes and outcomes. This constraining operating environment in public organizations has implications on the respective capacity to effectively manage IS in such organizations (Thong & Yap, 2000). Bretschneider (1990) found the differences between public and private sectors to be mainly related to organizational interdependence, red tape, criteria for evaluating hardware and software, the planning process and the organizational level of the IS manager. Also, Bretschneider and Wittmer (1993) and Aggarwal and Mirani (1999) argue that public and private organizations differ in their propensity towards IT assimilation. Furthermore, the different operating environments in the two sectors are expected to influence IS characteristics such as size, location, age, scope, task structuredness, human resources, systems development methods, and hardware and software resources (Salmela & Turunen, 2003; Seliem et al., 2003), which may, in turn, influence IS success factors and IS organizational impact in these organizations.

The role of IT in public organizations has been delineated in many studies in the context of the developed world, particularly in the U.S. (Caudle, 1990). Nevertheless, in one of the few studies in the Arab World, Seliem et al. (2003) found dissimilarities between the Egyptian private and public manufacturing companies in terms of location of processing facilities, years of systems use, and size of the IS unit. Compared to private organizations, public organizations were found to have more experiences with IT applications, tend to have larger IS units, and more matured IS functions. In addition, ownership type (public vs. private) was found to influence the relationship of the organizational determinants of top management support, user involvement, and IS maturity to IS effectiveness, measured by user information satisfaction.

As to the context of Kuwait, Aladwani (2002) reported management advocacy (e.g., encouragement, allocation of IS resources) and users attitudes to positively associate with user satisfaction in a sample of public organizations. Later, Alshawaf et al. (2005) found that ownership type (public vs. private) to have no effect on the managers' ratings of IS issues. Using a sample of private organizations and Delone and McLean's (1992) IS success model, Almutairi & Subramanian (2005) found information quality to affect system quality and user satisfaction, system quality to affect user satisfaction, and system usage to affect individual impact. Nevertheless, these investigations neither addressed all of the IS success factors that this investigation does nor did they adopt the IS organizational impact as the dependent variable that measures IS success.

RESEARCH METHOD

The aforementioned literature review suggests that public and private organizations differ in their managerial practices, managerial climate and management systems (Aladwani, 2002; Bozeman & Bretschneider, 1986; Bretschneider, 1990; Bretschneider & Wittmer, 1993; Margetts & Willcocks, 1994; Seliem et al., 2003), and Kuwaiti organizations may be of no exception. This difference, which is a consequence of the type of ownership, may intervene in the relationship between the IS success factors and IS potential organizational impact. Figure 1 describes these hypnotized relationships.

Specifically, this investigation addresses two questions:

1. Does ownership type affects mangers' perceptions of the IS success factors in Kuwaiti organizations?
2. Does ownership type affects mangers' perceptions of the IS organizational impact factors in Kuwaiti organizations?

Research Variables and Measurement

This investigation includes ten independent variables (IS success factors) and one dependent variable (IS organizational impact), and one intervening variable (ownership type). These research variables were chosen in light of the IS success research models, prior research results, and our familiarity with the Kuwaiti environment within which the investigated organizations operate. Table 1 depicts the research variables and the way they were measured in this investigation.

With the exception of IS impact on organizational performance (13-items) and the locus of IS financial decisions (2-items), all variables were measured using single-item scales. Although single-item measures may limit the reported research findings, the researchers had to adopt them in order to shorten the questionnaire response time and improve the response rate.

In the IS Organizational impact scale, each measuring item was formulated as a statement with a 5-point Likert scale. The scale was developed, logically evaluated and validated using a panel of experts consisting of three IS academicians and three IS executives.

Sampling

Our sample was drawn from the governmental organizations and private companies that were listed in the Kuwait Stock Exchange. Only organizations with formal IS departments were chosen

Figure 1. The research model

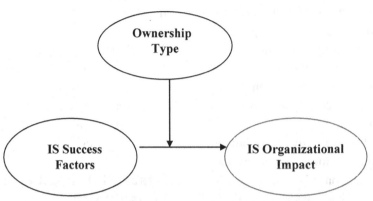

Table 1. Research variables and measurements

Research Variables	Measurement
The Independent variables:	
The age of the IS unit	Number of years the unit has been in existence (one item)
The organizational level of the IS Unit	The management level that the IS unit manager reports to (one item)
Clarity of IS strategy	The extent to which IS strategy is clear (one item using a 5-point Likert scale: 1= v. low, 5 = v. high)
Top management involvement in IS strategy formulation	The extent to which top management is involved in formulating IS strategies (one item using a 5-point Likert scale: 1= v. low, 5 = v. high)
Locus of IS financial decisions	The extent to which the roles of top management and IS management in making the IS financial decisions are balanced (two items using a 5-point Likert scale: 1= v. low, 5 = v. high)
IS resources	Availability of the resources needed for IS (one item using a 5-point Likert scale: 1= v. low, 5 = v. high)
End-user support	Whether the organization has a special organizational unit to support end-user computing (one item)
IT training	Whether the organization holds regular training programs on computer applications (one item).
End user involvement in systems development	The extent to which end users participate in systems development (one item using a 5-point Likert scale: 1= v. low, 5 = v. high)
IS sophistication	The breadth (number) of IT applications in the organization (one item)
The Dependent Variable:	
IS organizational impact	The extent to which IS contributes to different aspects of the organizational performance (13-item scale using a 5-point Likert scale: 1= v. low, 5 = v. high)
The Intervening variable:	
Ownership Type	An organization is private if it is not totally owned by the government

as a target population. A total of 105 organizations that met the selection criteria were identified for the target sampling-frame, and consequently were contacted and officially invited to participate in this research. Fifty-two organizations agreed to participate, providing approximately 50% response rate. Twenty-seven of the participant organizations were from the public sector and the rest (25) were from the private sector. In general, the participant organizations represented a broad cross section of Kuwaiti organizations.

Data Collection

A self-administered questionnaire was used for data collection. The informants were department heads, one informant per organization. Middle level managers were selected to participate in this investigation because we found from our preliminary evaluation of the computer-based systems that existed in the participant organizations at the time of our investigation were mostly transactions processing systems (TPSs) and management information systems (MISs). Middle level managers were the primary users of the systems, and, therefore, they were considered to be appropriate informants for our investigation.

The questionnaire was administered to a head of a department that was considered to be a heavy user of IS services. The questionnaire consists of three sections. The first section contains questions to collect data on the ten IS success factors. The second section has the 13-item scale that measures the IS organizational impact variables. The third section includes personal demographics questions. To eliminate selection bias, first, the IS manager in each organization was asked to identify three departments or organizational functions that were considered to be heavy users of IS services. Then, only one department head was selected to respond to the questionnaire. The questionnaires were handed directly to the respondents and later collected from them.

Reliability

The overall reliability, the internal consistency, of the 11-item scale used to measure the ten IS success factors, as measured by Cronbach's alpha based on standardized items is .678. Also, Cronbach's alpha for the 13-item scale of the IS organizational impact is .893. These two alpha coefficients are greater than .60, which is the acceptable lower level for exploratory research such as this one (Hair, Anderson, Tatham, & Black, 1998).

RESULTS

Public vs. Private Organizations Analysis with the Original Data Set

Chi Square and t-tests were conducted in order to explore the similarities/dissimilarities of the ten IS success variables in the public and private organizations (Tables 2 & 3). The results suggest that the organizations in the public sector in the sample had more end user support units ($p < .01$), and more balanced roles of top management and IS management in IS financial decisions ($p < .10$) than their counterparts in the private sector did.

On the other hand, the organizations in the private sector were found to have more resources committed to IS ($p < .01$), more top management involvement in IS strategy formulation ($p < .05$), more end users involvement in systems development ($p < .05$), and more IT training for their end users ($p < .10$) than their counterparts in the public sector. Nonetheless, the organizations in the public and private sectors were found to be similar (no significant differences) in the ages of their IS units, IS organizational levels, IS sophistication, and perceived clarity of IS strategies.

The t-test results for the IS organizational impact variables are presented in Table 4. The results illustrate that the perceived IS organizational impact items were generally higher in the public organizations than in their private counterparts. More specifically, 10 of the 13 IS organizational impacts—information for planning and scheduling ($p < .05$), monitoring of work activities ($p < .05$), adherence to work rules and procedures ($p < .10$), relationship with customers and clients ($p < .05$), communication and information sharing ($p < .10$), employees' skills ($p < .10$), collaboration among work groups ($p < .05$), work accomplished ($P < .05$), work quality ($p < .01$), and work cost ($p < .01$)—were significantly higher in the public organizations than in their private counterparts.

Table 2. Chi square test of two independent samples (IS auccess variables)

Success Factors		Organization group		Total
		Public	Private	
End-User Support Units	Yes	19	4	23
	No	8	21	29
Total		27	25	52
Statistics: Chi Square = 15.556 df = 1 P < .01				
IT training	Yes	18	22	40
	No	9	3	12
Total		27	25	52
Statistics: Chi Square = 3.328 df = 1 P < .10				

Table 3. t-test of two independent samples (IS success factors)

Variable	Type	Mean	Sd	t-value	Sig.
Age of the IS unit	1	1.96	.759	.952	.346
	2	1.76	.779		
Organizational level of the IS Unit	1	.59	.501	-1.281	.206
	2	.76	.436		
Clarity of IS strategy	1	2.26	.903	-1.641	.107
	2	2.64	.757		
Top MGT involvement in IS strategy formulation	1	3.15	1.167	-2.382	.021
	2	3.84	.898		
Locus of IS financial decisions	1	2.44	1.251	-1.845	.071
	2	3.04	1.060		
Availability of IS resources	1	3.22	.934	-3.149	.003
	2	3.96	.735		
End user involvement in systems development	1	2.67	1.109	-2.455	.018
	2	3.36	.907		
IS sophistication	1	19.26	2.443	1.114	.270
	2	18.60	1.732		

(Type: 1 = Public (N =27), 2 = Private (N = 25)), df = 50

Public vs. Private Organizations Analysis with the Reduced Data Set

A factor analysis was applied on the original data set in order to remove redundancy in the data and reveal the underlying pattern that existed between the items (variables), reduce the number of factors, and measure their reliability coefficients. The extraction method used is the principle component analysis, and the rotation method is the Oblique rotation method. The Oblique rotation method is appropriate when the factor scores are computed for each response and used for subsequent analysis (Hair et al., 1998). It maintains correlations

Table 4. t-test of two independent samples (IS organizational impact variables)

Variable	Type	Mean	sd	t-value	Sig.
Simplifying work procedures	1	3.70	1.103	1.199	.236
	2	3.40	.645		
Providing information for planning and scheduling	1	3.37	.884	2.177	.034
	2	2.88	.726		
Monitoring overall work activities	1	3.44	.892	2.274	.027
	2	2.92	.759		
Assuring adherence to official work rules and procedures	1	3.11	.974	1.989	.052
	2	2.64	.700		
Enhancing decision making processes	1	3.26	.944	1.668	.102
	2	2.80	1.041		
Improving relationships with customers and clients	1	3.78	1.251	2.612	.012
	2	2.96	.978		
Reengineering organizational work processes	1	3.11	1.155	0.822	.415
	2	2.88	.833		
Facilitating communication and information sharing within the organization	1	3.52	1.122	1.854	.070
	2	3.00	.866		
Developing/enhancing employees' skills	1	3.00	.877	1.769	.083
	2	2.56	.917		
Facilitating collaboration among work groups	1	3.26	.764	2.499	.016
	2	2.72	.792		
Increasing the overall work accomplished	1	3.70	1.171	2.613	.012
	2	2.96	.841		
Increasing work quality	1	3.81	1.111	3.364	.001
	2	2.92	.759		
Decreasing the overall cost of work	1	3.89	1.121	3.778	.000
	2	2.84	.850		

(Type: 1 = Public (N =27), 2 = Private (N = 25)) df = 50

among the factors, since they're conceptually linked. Varimax rotation is orthogonal, meaning that the factors remain uncorrelated through out the rotation process.

The results of the initial factor analysis for the IS success variables showed positive and negative loadings on the factors. Therefore, the variables with negative signs have been reverse scored in order to produce positive correlations and loadings. The ten original IS success variables were reduced into four constructs (factors), and the 13 IS organizational impact variables were reduced into three constructs (factors). Table 5 depicts the factors and their loadings. The loadings range from .667 to .889, which are higher than the recommended .55 for exploratory studies such as this one (Hair et al., 1998).

The Kaiser-Meyer-Olkin (KMO) Measures of Sampling Adequacy (MSA) indicate the appropriateness of the factor analysis. The Kaiser-Meyer-Olkin (KMO) Measures of Sampling Adequacy (MSA) for the factor analysis of the IS success

Table 5. The factors, loadings, and reliability coefficients

Factors	Loadings	Reliability Coefficients*	Explained Variance
IS Success Factors		.678	.635
1. IS Strategy & Resources (F1-IS-SUC):		.740	.302
Clarity of IS strategy	.817		
IT training	.770		
IS Resources	.769		
Top MGT involvement in IS strategy formulation	.685		
2. End user Support (F2-IS-SUC):		.314	.135
End user support unit	.765		
Locus of IS financial decisions	.700		
3. IS Sophistication (F3-IS-SUC):		.224	.122
Age of the IS unit	.770		
IS sophistication	.740		
4. IS Org. level and User Involvement (F4-IS-SUC):		.447	.106
IS organization level	.799		
End user involvement in systems development	.765		
IS Organizational Impact Factors		.893	.635
1. Improving work efficiency (F1-IS-CON):		.893	.452
Decreasing overall work cost	.853		
Increasing work quality	.822		
Increasing the amount of completed work	.802		
Facilitating communication & information sharing	.756		
Monitoring work activities	.717		
Facilitating collaboration among work groups	.704		
Simplifying work procedures	.688		
Improving relationships with customers	.667		
2. Improving decision making (F2-IS-CON):		.619	.104
Providing information for planning and task scheduling	.856		
Enhancing decision making processes	.826		
3. Improving work effectiveness (F3-IS-CON:		.737	.079
Reengineering work processes	.889		
Developing employees work skills	.773		
Assuring adherence to work rules & procedures	.693		

* Cronbach's Alpha based on standardized items

variables and IS organizational impact variables are .688 and .813, respectively. These indexes indicate a relatively high degree of interconnections among the variables, and, consequently, verify the appropriateness of the factor analysis.

Table 6. Pearson correlations of the IS success factors and ownership type and IS organizational impacts (N = 52)

Factors	Type	F1-IS-Con	F2-IS-Con	F3-IS-Con	F1-Suc	F2-Suc	F3-Suc	F4-Suc
Type	1	-.439**	-.294*	-.201	.421**	-.286*	.328*	.017
F1-IS-Con		1	.289*	.496**	.026	.278*	-.107	-.066
F2-IS-Con			1	.159	.110	.110	-.176	-.181
F3-IS.Con				1	.143	-.010	-.194	.043
F1-IS-Suc					1	-.169	.007	-.004
F2-IS-Suc						1	.019	-.049
F3-IS-Suc							1	-.024
F4-IS-Suc								1
** *P < .01; * P < .05 (2-tailed)*								

Table 7. t-Test for two independent samples (IS critical success factors)

Factors	Type	Mean	Std. Deviation	t-Value	Sig.
IS strategy & resources	1	-.3054209	1.14345399	-2.392	.021
	2	.3298545	.70019717		
End user support	1	-.4465401	.88261826	-3.747	.000
	2	.4822633	.90248302		
IS sophistication	1	.1472164	1.06133829	1.106	.274
	2	-.1589937	.92410881		
IS org. level & user involvement	1	-.2595140	1.05265983	-2.001	.051
	2	.2802751	.87576998		
(Type: 1 = Public (N = 27), 2 = Private (N = 25)), df = 50					

Pearson correlations were computed in order to explore the relationships among the IS success factors (independent variables), the contingent variable (ownership type), and the IS organizational impact factors (dependent variables) in the entire sample. Table 6 summarizes the results.

The results suggest that the only significant relationship between the independent and dependent variables (factors) is the positive relationship between end user support and improvement of work efficiency (p < .05). However, strong correlations do exist between ownership types, on one hand, and IS success factors and IS organizational impact factors, on the other hand. As to its relationship with the IS organizational impact

factors, ownership type correlates negatively with improving work efficiency (p < .01) and improving decision-making (p < .05). As to its relationship with the IS success factors, ownership type correlates positively with IS strategy & resources (p < .01) and IS sophistication (p < .05), and negatively with end user support (p < .05).

Furthermore, to test whether significant differences exist between the public and private organizations in terms of the IS success factors and IS organizational impact factors, a t-test was performed. The results, depicted in Table 7, of the IS success factors indicate that, generally, the private sector organizations have established clearer IS strategies and committed more resources to

Table 8. t-test for two independent samples (IS organizational impact factors)

Factors	Type	Mean	Std. Deviation	t-value	Sig.
Improving work efficiency	1	.418449	1.1310217	3.456	.001
	2	-.451925	.5739816		
Improving decision making	1	.2799619	1.01736012	2.173	.035
	2	-.3023580	.90571576		
Improving work effectiveness	1	.1913485	1.15723024	1.449	.153
	2	-.2066560	.76716634		
(Type: 1 = Public (N = 27), 2 = Private (N = 25)) df = 50					

there IS units (p < .05), provide more support for their end users (p < .01), and their IS units report to higher management levels and their end users get more involved in systems development (p < .10) than their counterparts in the public sector. The two groups (private and public organizations), however, seem to have similar level of IS sophistication.

As to the IS organizational impact factors, Table 8 presents the t-test results for the public and private organizations. The results show that IS was perceived to have more impact on improving work efficiency (p < .01) and improving decision-making (p < .05) in the public organizations than in their private counterparts. The two groups, however, seem to be similar in their perceptions of the IS impact on improving work effectiveness.

DISCUSSION

This investigation was designed in order to explore whether the perceptions of IS success factors and IS organizational impact vary depending on ownership type in Kuwaiti organizations.

The results of the preliminary analysis of the ten IS success factors imply that, compared to their counterparts in the private sector, the public sector organizations in Kuwait have established more end user support units, and their top managers and IS managers play more balanced roles in making IS financial decisions. Conversely, the organizations

in the private sector appear to have more top management involvement in the formulation of IS strategies, make more resources available to their IS departments, have more involvement of end users in systems development, and conduct more IT training for their end users than their counterparts in the public sector. These results support Seliem's et al. (2003) findings that private organizations in Egypt commit more resources to their IS units than what public organizations usually do.

The IS unit age, IS organizational levels, IS sophistication and clarity of IS strategies emerged in our analysis as IS characteristics that are similar in the two groups—private and public organizations. These findings provide no support to Bretschneider's (1990) view that IS units are usually placed lower in the organization structure within public organizations, but are in agreement with Seliem's et al. (2003) findings of no significant difference in the organizational location of the IS units in the private and public Egyptian organizations.

The aforementioned findings may be interpreted in light of the two different operating environments of the public and private organizations. Compared to private organizations, public organizations are likely to have higher levels of accountability, more rules and regulations, lower organizational commitment, and less clear objectives (Robertson & Seneviratne, 1995). These characteristics are likely to influence the relevant capacity to effectively manage IS in such organizations (Thong & Yap, 2000).

Managers in the investigated public organizations appear to underline compliance with regulations and formalities while their counterparts in private organizations tend to focus on the processes and resources required to achieve clearly stated strategies and objectives. Emphasis on compliance and accountability may have led the Kuwaiti public organizations to institutionalize IS units and closely follow formal procedures when making IS related financial decisions. On the other hand, emphasis on processes and resources may have caused managers in the Kuwaiti private organizations to get deeply involved in the formulation of IS strategies, commit the needed IS resources, and support end user involvement in systems development.

The data reduction procedure (factor analysis) has resulted in identifying four IS success factors and three IS organizational impact factors. The IS success factors include IS strategy & resources, end user support, IS sophistication, and IS organizational level & user involvement. The three IS organizational impact factors include improving work efficiency, improving decision making, and improving work effectiveness. The results of the correlation analysis for the whole sample indicate that end user support is the only IS success factor that correlates with improving work efficiency as an IS organizational impact factor.

This means that organizational commitment to end user support and provision of required financial resources, that is through balanced roles of top management and IS managers in making IS financial decisions, may enhance systems usage and consequently, improve work efficiency. In addition, the significance of improving work efficiency, as an IS organizational impact, is logical, since most of the IT applications in the investigated organizations are typically transactions processing systems (TPS) and management reporting systems (MIS), which are adopted in these organizations mainly for the purpose of improving efficiency and reducing cost.

It is noteworthy, however, that ownership type, the contingent variable in this study, was found to correlate with three of the four IS success factors, namely IS strategy and resources, end user support, and IS sophistication and to correlate with two of the three IS organizational impact factors, namely improving work efficiency and improving decision making. This finding suggests that ownership type does matter when it comes to IS success factors and IS organizational impacts. Public and private organizations differ in their managerial practices, managerial climate, and management systems (Aladwani, 2002; Bozeman & Bretschneider, 1986; Bretschneider, 1990; Bretschneider & Wittmer, 1993; Margetts & Willcocks, 1994; Seliem et al., 2003), and Kuwaiti organizations are of no exception. Ownership type (public vs. private) appears to intermediate the relationship of the investigated IS success factors and IS organizational impact, measured as improving work efficiency and improving decision-making.

Furthermore, our results suggest that ownership type affects IS success factors and IS organizational impact differently across the public and private organizations. The four IS success factors of IS strategy and resources, end user support, IS sophistication, and IS organizational level and user involvement are consistently lower in the public organizations than in their private counterparts (Figure 2). However, the three IS organizational impact factors of improving work efficiency, improving decision-making, and improving work effectiveness are consistently higher in the public organizations than in their private counterparts (Figure 3).

Compared to their counterparts in the public organizations, managers in the private organizations perceive their organizations to develop clearer IS strategies and devote more resources to IT, provide more support to their end users, have more sophisticated IT applications, better position IS units in the organizational structure and experience greater participation of their users in systems development activities. Yet, compared to their counterparts in the public organizations, managers in the private organizations perceive the organizational impact (e.g., improving work efficiency, improving decision making, and improving work effectiveness) of IS to be lower and, consequently, less successful.

This finding may appear to be counterintuitive. It suggests that having clearer IS strategies and devotion of more IS resources, more support to end users, more sophisticated IT applications, higher reporting level for the IS unit in the organizational structure and greater users' involvement in systems development would result in less IS impact on organizational performance. Conversely, having less clear IS strategies and devotion of less IS resources, less support to end users, less sophisticated IT applications, lower reporting level for the IS units in the organizational structure and less users' involvement in systems development would result in more IS impact on organizational performance.

This seemingly contradictory result may be attributed to problems related to this research, including possible measurement errors, relatively

Figure 2. Ownership type and IS success factors

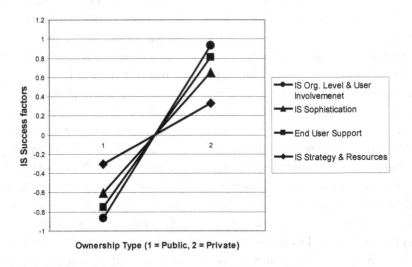

Figure 3. Ownership type and IS organizational impact

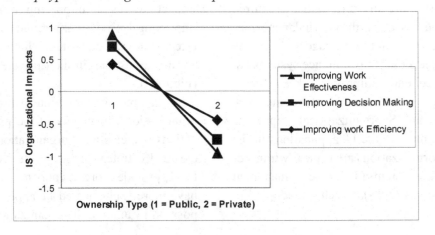

small sample size, and/or the exclusion of other important contextual factors. Or, it may imply that the public organizations in our sample are simply more efficient in their use of IT resources (i.e., producing higher IS impact with less resources and organizational commitment) than their counterparts in the private sector. This interpretation, however, is dubious, since the characteristics of the public organizations, discussed in an earlier section of the article, are likely to create an operating environment that is acquiescent to inefficiencies.

A third, and may be a more sound, explanation of this finding can be made in light of what might be called "*IS expectation-performance gap.*" Our findings suggest that the expectation-performance gap is bigger in the private organizations than in their public counterparts. Compared to their counterparts in public organizations, when managers in private organizations develop clearer IS strategies and commit more IS resources, make more support available to end users, assure accessibility to the needed IT applications, position their IS units properly high in the organizational structure and facilitate greater users' involvement in systems development, they expect higher IS contribution to their organizational performance; and, consequently, they may apply more rigorous performance targets when rating IS actual performance.

The differing operating environments of the public and private organizations, again, lend further support to this interpretation of our finding based on the "IS expectation-performance gap." Compared to private organizations, public organizations are likely to have lower organizational commitment, less clear objectives (Robertson & Seneviratne, 1995), more emphasis on compliance to regulations and work procedures rather than on achievement of measurable objectives, experience lower competition and motivation, and, consequently, operate less efficiently (Aladwani, 2002).

These differences are likely to influence IS roles, objectives, resources, and expected performance. Driven more by the bottom line, IS objectives and performance are more likely to be better articulated and measured in the private sector, and, therefore, managers' perception of IS contribution to organizational performance tend to be more objective and realistic. Consequently, the gap between the actual and expected IS performance may be greater within the private sector organizations, compared to the gap within the public sector organizations.

IMPLICATIONS

The findings of this research should be of interest to both practitioners and researchers. As to practitioners, our findings indicate that improvement in work efficiency in both public and private organizations associates with organizational commitment to end user support and provision of required financial resources. Decision and policy makers in the Kuwaiti public and private organizations should continue to commit resources that are necessary to maintain and upgrade their applications portfolios, through effective collaborative roles by top management and IS managers in making IS financial decisions, and enhance their support to end users, through the institutionalization of end user support units and staffing them with the requisite technical capabilities.

Private organizations in Kuwait should consider establishing more organizational units and staffing these units with skilled IT professionals in order to support their end users. They need also to develop policies that allow their top managers and IS managers to play more balanced roles in IS financial decision making. However, the Kuwait public organizations should consider raising IT awareness among their managers, especially at the top level, in order to enhance their understanding of the capabilities and limitations of IT applications. Their top managers should get more involved in the formulation of IS strategies, commit more resources to their IS departments, encourage and enable more involvement of end users in systems development, and hold more IT training to their end users.

Top management in public organizations should also have higher expectations for what IS may contribute to their goals. More IT spending and more top management involvement must be met with clearer understanding and agreement on IT goals and strategies. In addition, IS managers must be proactive in managing executives' expectations of IT contributions and help them set more realistic ones.

As to researchers, effective utilization of information systems in public organizations is under studied. The results of this research should contribute to the evolving literature on IS success in public organizations and in developing countries. Future research models designed to investigate IS success in a Kuwaiti context is expected to include ownership type as a research variable or a covariate.

Our results also suggest that although public organizations may have as many IT applications as private organizations do (i.e., level of IS sophistication), managers in public organizations may be willing to accept lower IS contribution levels as satisfactory. This does not bode well for the improvement of public services through the effective use of IT. Further research is needed to give guidance to the public organizations' executives as to how to measure and improve IS contributions to organizational performance.

RESEARCH LIMITATIONS AND FUTURE RESEARCH

Our findings should be interpreted and generalized in light of the limitations of this research. Possible measurement errors, the relatively small sample size, the exclusion of other contextual factors, and the use of cross-sectional data are among these

limitations. Single item measures were used to measure a number of IS success factors; and perceived measures were used to measure the impact of IS on organizational performance instead of objective ones. These measurement problems may have negatively affected the reliability and validity of the results.

Future research should adopt research designs that employ more multi-item scales in order to measure IS success factors and include new dimensions to the IS organizational impact construct. Given that IS impact includes tangible and intangible benefits, such an impact should be measured as a function of multiple financial and non-financial variables. Use of nonfinancial measures, however, is particularly imperative, since financial measures may be confounded by other business, economic, and environmental factors.

Future research should also adopt larger samples in order to minimize sampling error, and to further validate the results of this investigation. Also, other possible intermediary effects such as organizational culture and climate, organizational size, and organizational age should be considered in future IS success research. For instance, culture was found to affect knowledge management systems (KMS) (Alavi & Leidner, 1999; Gold et al., 2001), and therefore, should be explicitly considered in future cross-cultural IS success research designs.

Lastly, a cross-sectional data was used in this research with assumed causal flows from IS success factors to organizational performance. Future longitudinal investigations are recommended in order to conclusively replicate the findings presented in this research. Future longitudinal IS success research in Kuwait will be particularly valuable in order to properly assess the organizational impact of the emerging IT applications in the private sector (e.g., ERPs and Internet-based applications) and the implementation of the Kuwaiti e-government initiative that has recently started in a number of public organizations.

CONCLUSION

This research aimed at investigating ownership type as possible intermediary in the relationship between IS success factors and IS organizational impact in a Kuwaiti setting. Four IS success factors (IS strategy & resources, end user support, IS sophistication, and IS organizational level & user involvement) and three IS organizational impact measures (improving work efficiency, improving decision making, and improving work effectiveness) were investigated. The results suggest that ownership type intermediates in the relationship between the IS success factors and IS organizational impact.

Kuwaiti public and private organizations appear to differ in their managerial practices, managerial climate, and management systems. These differences have implications on the relevant capacity to manage IS in these organizations as well as the IS impact on organizational performance. Compared to public organizations, private organizations appear to have clearer IS strategies and devote more IS resources, provide more support to end users, have more sophisticated IT applications, position their IS units higher in the organizational structure, experience greater users' involvement in systems development, and adopt clearer and more measurable IS objectives.

Yet, public organizations tend to rate their IS contribution to organizational performance higher than their private counterparts, creating an "IS expectation-performance gap" between the two sectors. Private organizations' managers appear to be tougher raters of IS organizational impact than their counterparts in the public organizations, and are unwilling to accept lower IS contribution levels as satisfactory. While top management in public organizations must provide more support and resources to their information systems, they must also have higher expectations for the impact that IS should have on organizational performance. Nevertheless, further research is needed to corroborate these findings and extend them to other contexts.

REFERENCES

Aggarwal, A., & Mirani, R. (1999). DSS model usage in public and private sectors: Differences and implications. *Journal of End User Computing, 11*(3), 20-28.

Aharoni Y., & Burton, R. M. (1994). Is management science international: In research of universal rules. *Management Science, 40(*1), 1-3.

Aladwani, A. M. (2001). IT planning effectiveness in a developing country. *Journal of Global Information Technology Management, 4*(3), 51-65.

Aladwani, A. M. (2002). Organizational actions, computer attitudes, and end-user satisfaction in public organizations: An empirical study. *Journal of End User Computing, 14*(1), 42-49.

Alavi, M., & Leidner, D. (1999). Knowledge management systems: Issues, challenges and benefits. *Communications of AIS, 1*(7), 37.

Almutairi, H., & Subramanian, G. (2005). An empirical application of the DeLone and McLean model in the Kuwaiti private sector. *Journal of Computer Information Systems, 45*(3), 113-122.

Alshawaf, A. H., Ali, J. M. H., & Hasan, M. H. (2005). A benchmarking framework for information systems management issues in Kuwait. *Benchmarking: An International Journal, 12*(1), 30-44.

Al-Busaidi, K. A., & Olfman, L. (2005). An investigation of the determinants of knowledge management systems success in Omani organizations. *Journal of Global Information Technology Management, 8*(3), 6-27.

Atiyyah, H. S. (1989). Determinants of computer system effectiveness in Saudi Arabian public organizations. *International Studies of Management & Organizations, 19*, 85-103.

Boynton, A. C., & Zmud, R. W. (1994). An assessment of critical success factors. *Sloan Management Review, Summer*, pp. 17-27.

Bozeman, B., & Bretschneider, S. (1986). Public management information systems: Theory and prescription. *Public Administration Review, 55*(6), 559-566.

Bretschneider, S. (1990). Management information systems in public and private organizations: An empirical test. *Public Administration Review, 50*(5), 536-545.

Bretschneider, S., & Wittmer, D. (1993). Organizational adoption of microcomputer technology: The role of sector. *Information Systems Research, 4*(1), 88-108.

Caudle, S. L., (1990). Managing information resources in state government. *Public Administration Review, 50*, 515-524.

Cummins, F. (2002). *Enterprise integration.* New York: John Wiley.

Davenport, T. H., & Prusak, L. (1998). *Working knowledge.* Boston, MA: Harvard Business School Press.

DeLone, W. H., & McLean, E. R. (1992). Information systems success: The quest for the dependent variable. *Information Systems Research, 3*(1), 60-90.

DeLone, W. H., & McLean, E. R. (2003). The DeLone and McLean model of information system success: A ten year update. *Journal of Management Information Systems, 19*(4), 9-30.

Ein-Dor, P., & Segev, E. (1978). Organizational context and success of management information systems. *Management Science, 24*, 1064-1077.

Franz, C., & Robey, D. (1986). Organizational context, user involvement and usefulness of information systems. *Decision Sciences, 17*, 329-355.

Gold, A. H., Malhotra, A., & Segars, A. H. (2001). Knowledge management: An organizational capabilities perspective. *Journal of Management Information Systems, 18*(1), 185.

Gyampah, K., & White, K. (1993). User involvement and user satisfaction: An exploratory contingency model. *Information & Management, 25*, 1-10.

Hair, J. F., Anderson, R. E., Tatham, R. L., & Black, W. C. (1998). *Multivariate data analysis* (5th ed). Englewood Cliffs, NJ: Prentice-Hall.

Igbaria, M. (1992). An examination of microcomputer usage in Taiwan. *Information & Management, 22*, 19-28.

Igbaria, M., & Chakrabarti, A. (1990). Computer anxiety and attitudes towards microcomputer use. *Behavior & Information Technology, 9*, 229-241.

Jain, R. (1997). A diffusion model for public information systems in developing countries. *Journal of Global Information Management, 5*(1), 4-15.

Jayasuriya, R. (1999). Managing information systems for health services in a developing country: A case study using a contextualist framework. *International Journal of Information Management, 19*(5), 335-349.

Jurison, J. (1996). The temporal nature of IS benefits: A longitudinal study. *Information & Management, 30*, 75-79.

Kearns, G. S., & Lederer, A. L. (2000). The effect of strategic alignment on the use IS-based resources for competitive advantage. *Journal of Strategic Information Systems, 9*, 265-293.

Khalil, O., & Elkordy, M. (1997). The relationship of some personal and situational factors to IS effectiveness: Empirical evidence from Egypt. *Journal of Global Information Management, 5*(2), 22-34.

Kim, Y., & Kim, Y. (1999). Critical issues in the networking area. *Information Resources Management Journal, 4*(4), 14-23.

Kraemer, K. L., Moony, J., Dunkle, D., & Vitalari, N. (1994). The business value of Information technology in corporations. Special Report, CRITO and CSC Consulting.

Lam, W. (2005). Investigating success factors in enterprise application: A case-driven analysis. *European Journal of Information Systems, 14*(2), 175-187.

Lee, J., & Kim, S. (1992). The relationship between procedural formalization in MIS development and MIS success: A contingency analysis. *Information & Management, 22*, 89-111.

Li, E., Rogers, J., & Chang, H. (1994). An empirical reassessment of the measure of information systems sophistication. *Information Resources Management Journal, 7*, 3-19.

Mahmood, M., & Becker, J. (1985). Effect of organizational maturity on end users' satisfaction with information systems. *Journal of Management Information Systems, 11*, 37-64.

Mahmood, M., & Swanberg, D. (1999). Factors affecting information technology usage: A meta-analysis of the experimental literature. In *Proceedings of the 1999 IRMA International Conference,* pp. 359-364.

Margetts, H., & Willcocks, L. (1994). Informatization in public sector organizations: Distinctive or common risks? *Informatization and the Public Sector, 3*(1), 1-19.

Mirani, R., & King, W. (1994). The development of a measure for end-user computing support. *Decision Sciences, 25*, 481-498.

Mirani, R., & Lederer, A. L. (1998). An instrument for assessing the organizational benefits of IS projects. *Decision Sciences, 29*(4), 803-838.

Newcomer, K., & Caudle, S. L. (1991). Evaluating public sector information systems: More than meets the eye. *Public Administration Review, 51*(5), 377-388.

Noble, F. (1995). Implementation strategies for office systems. *Journal of Strategic Information Systems, 4*, 239-253.

Palvia, P. C., Palvia, S. C., & Zigli, R. M. (1992). In M. Khosrowpour (Ed.), *Global information technology management.* Harrisburg, PA: Idea Group.

Rai, R., & Lee, G. (2003). Organizational factors influencing the quality of the IS/IT strategic planning process. *Industrial Management & Data Systems, 103*(8/9), 622-632.

Ramamurthy, K., & Premkumar, G. (1995). Determinants and outcomes of electronic data interchange diffusion. *IEEE Transactions on Engineering Management, 42*, 332-351.

Raymond, I., & Bergeron, F. (1992). Personal DSS success in small enterprises. *Information & Management, 22*, 301-308.

Robertson, P. J., & Seneviratne, S. J. (1995). Outcomes of planned organizational change in the public sector: A meta-analytic comparison to the private sector. *Public Administration Review, 55*(6), 547-558.

Rosenzweig, P. M. (1994). When can management science research be generalized internationally? *Management Science, 40*(1), 28-39.

Salmela, H., & Turunen, P. (2003). Competitive implications of information technology in the public sector. *International Journal of Public Sector Management, 16*(1), 8-26.

Seliem, A., Ashour, A., Khalil, O., & Miller, S. (2003). IS characteristics and effectiveness in private and public Egyptian companies. *Arab Journal of Administrative Sciences, 10*(1), 71-91.

Seneviratne, S. J. (1999). Organizational change and information technology in the public sector. In G. D. Garson (Ed.), *Information technology and computer applications in public administration: Issues and trends* (pp. 41-61). Hershey, PA: IGP.

Shin, N. (1999). Does information technology improve coordination? An empirical analysis. *Logistics Information Management, 12*(1/2), 138.

Teo, S. T., & Wong, P. K. (1998). An empirical study of the performance impact of computerization in the retail industry. *Omega International Journal of Management Science, 26*, 611-621.

Thong, J. Y. L., Yap, C. S., & Raman, K. S. (1996). Management support, external expertise and information systems implementation in small businesses. *Information Systems Research, 7*, 248-266.

Thong, J. Y. L., & Yap, C. (2000). Business process reengineering in the public sector: The case of the Housing Development Board in Singapore. *Journal of Management Information Systems, Summer*, 245-270.

Torkzadeh, G., & Doll, W. (1994). The test retest reliability of user involvement instruments. *Information & Management, 26*, 21-31.

Yap, C., Soh, C., & Roman, K. (1992). Information systems success in small business. *OMEGA, 20*, 597-609.

Yoon, Y., Guimaraes, T., & Clevenson, A. (1998). Exploring expert systems success factors for business process reengineering. *Journal of Engineering and Technology Management, 15*, 179-199.

Yousef, D. A. (1994). Top management attitudes towards the use of computer in managerial practices: An empirical study in the United Arab Emirates government Sector. *Arab Journal of Administrative Sciences, 1*(May), 295-329.

This work was previously published in International Journal of Enterprise Information Systems, Vol. 4, Issue 2, edited by A. Gunasekaran, pp. 13-33, copyright 2008 by IGI Publishing (an imprint of IGI Global).

Chapter 16
An ASP-Based Product Customization Service System for SMEs:
A Case Study in Construction Machinery

Yan Su
Nanjing University of Aeronautics and Astronautics, China

Wenhe Liao
Nanjing University of Aeronautics and Astronautics, China

Yu Guo
Nanjing University of Aeronautics and Astronautics, China

Shiwen Gao
Nanjing University of Aeronautics and Astronautics, China

Huibin Shi
Nanjing University of Aeronautics and Astronautics, China

ABSTRACT

A product customization system with integrated application services is helpful for small to medium-sized enterprises (SMEs). The mode of application service provider (ASP) particularly targets SMEs by providing integrated applications. The current product customization system seldom considers integrating with ASPs and orienting product lifecycle. In this article, an ASP-based product customization service system operating in lifecycle-oriented customization mode is proposed. Resource share, product data transform, and product configuration are three important aspects for effectively supporting lifecycle-oriented product customization service. A resource collection method for distributed resource share is put forward. An XML-based data mapping model for isomeric/isomorphic product data transform is presented. A new algorithm for rapid product configuration is designed, and an interactive virtual environment for collaborative configuration is suggested. Using this system, SMEs can develop their Internet-based sales and customization systems smoothly, in a short time, and at low cost. A construction machinery oriented product customization service platform is introduced as a case study.

INTRODUCTION

Due to the ever-increasing economic globalization, product variation and customization is a trend in current market-oriented manufacturing environments. The success of mass customization systems depends on a series of external and internal factors, given as follows (Silvira, Borenstein & Fogliatto, 2001):

- Products should be customizable
- Customer demand for variety and customization must exist
- The willingness and readiness of suppliers, distributors, and retailers to attend to the system demands
- Technology must be available
- Knowledge must be shared.

To achieve those, a firm has to face the particular challenge of quick response to dynamic customer needs, wide variations, increasing complexity of product design, rapid design, and product technology changes. It is important to evolve e-business environment by improving an enterprise-competitive capability to meet the customers' individual demands efficiently (Yang, Zhang, Liu, & Xie, 2005). However, small to medium-sized enterprises (SMEs) may not make socially optimal investments in product customization. It is even difficult for SMEs to develop Internet-based customization systems because of technology difficulties (Wang Li, & Jiang, 2003; Zhao, Ju, Wang, & Yin, 2003). In fact, reports suggest that SMEs in China are not keeping up with new information technology and manufacturing cases and most of them do not have enough money to buy or have no technical capability to utilize advanced software such as CAD, CAM, PDM, SCM, and CRM. An integrated service platform, which evolves e-business environment by integrating knowledge, technologies, and resources among customers, suppliers, and other business partners to improve SMEs' competitive capability and meet customers' individual demands efficiently has been a trend in recent years.

Application service provider (ASP), which is viewed as a subset of e-commerce (Heart & Pliskin, 2001), is a third party service organization whose core value propositions are to lower total cost of ownership, make monthly fees predictable, reduce time to market, provide access to market-leading applications, and allow businesses to focus on their core competencies (Jaruzelski, Ribeiro, & Lake, 2000; Kern, Lacity, & Willcocks, 2002). ASP stresses the roles of collaboration and interaction between a provider and a consumer as a key feature. ASPs particularly target SMEs by providing applications that these firms normally cannot afford (Nigel & David, 2005). The ASP mode is helpful by setting up an ASP service platform that provides services such as system development, system integration, and technology support (Yang et al., 2005; Pan & Jia, 2005; Xu, Li, & Zhang, 2004). The integration of the product customization system and ASP is seldom considered in current researches of product customization systems.

In this article, an ASP-based product customization service system for SMEs operating in lifecycle oriented product customization mode is proposed. Key technologies to support the system are studied in detail. The purpose of this study is to effectively reduce the time and cost of product customization for SMEs by providing an integrated product customization service environment. The rest of this article is organized as follows. First, the system structure is presented. Next, a lifecycle-oriented product customization mode driving the system operation is described. Key technologies to support product customization are examined in depth. Then, as a case study, a construction machinery oriented product customization service platform is developed based on the system and used to verify the studies. Finally, this article is concluded avenues for future work are suggested.

SYSTEM STRUCTRUE

According to a marketing study of product customization and a background of the low engagement of SMEs in e-business (Rodney, Gerard, & Ashwin, 2002; Wang, Li, & Jiang, 2003; Zhao et al., 2003), ASP-based product customization service systems mainly serve as a software resource rental center, a design/manufacture knowledge share center, and a technology consultation center. It provides open, reconfigurable and Web-enabled applications to support product customization for SMEs. The framework of an ASP-based product customization service system includes four layers—a resource support layer, a management layer, an application service layer, and a user layer, as shown in Figure 1. The four layers cover the total lifecycle of product customization—from requirements analysis, product configuration, design, manufacturing, to managing and marketing.

Resource Support Layer

The foundation of an ASP-based product customization service system is the resource support layer. It includes a system database, a sharing resource base, and a product configuration knowledge base. The sharing resource base—which consists of a number of product development software, manufacture resources, and enterprise information—is

Figure 1. Framework of ASP-based product customization service system

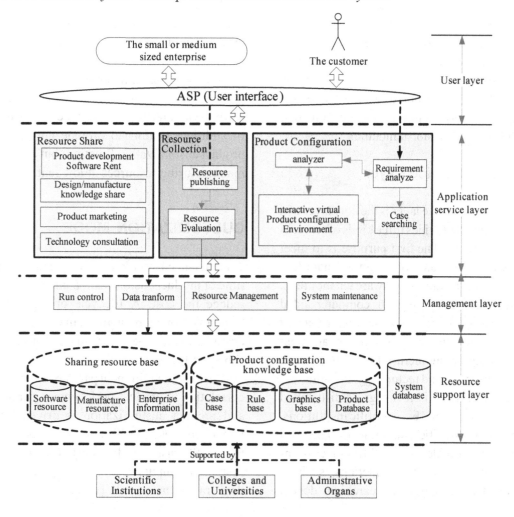

available to all enterprises in an industry. The system database is used to drive the whole service system running smoothly. The product configuration knowledge base supplies sufficient knowledge of product configuration. It includes the case base, the rule base, the graphics base, and the products database.

Management Layer

The management layer consists of four main function modules which are used to manage the integrated platform. The four modules are the run control module, data transform module, resource management module, and system maintenance module. The resource management module serves mainly for product customization and emphasizes particularly on the management of the product hierarchy tree, product data, and product version. The run control and system maintenance modules are designed to make system and all function modules act smoothly. The isomeric/isomorphic product data from distributed customers or enterprises are transformed into uniform data format through the data transform module.

Application Service Layer

The application service layer is the core layer of a service system. It provides three kinds of services for three purposes. The first purpose is to meet SMEs' resource demands of design and manufacturing including advanced software tenancy (e.g., computer aided design (CAD), computer aided manufacturing (CAM), supply chain management (SCM), and customer relationship management (CRM)), design/manufacture knowledge share, product marketing, and technology consultation. The second purpose is to integrate distributed resources owned by SMEs, scientific institutions, colleges and universities, and so forth. The third purpose is to provide users (SMEs or customers) product customization functions, such as requirement analyzing, case searching, design type analyzing, virtual product configuring, and configuration validity analyzing.

User Layer

The user layer presents users the following interactive function interfaces: information upload/download, software tools upload/download, resource evaluation, requirements analysis, product configuration, product assembly and disassembly, design validity analysis, configuration validity analysis, and so on. These interfaces are embedded within the portal of an ASP. Using these interfaces, SMEs and other customers can access all the tools and application services provided by the product customization service system.

High-tech process innovation (e.g., computer hardware and software) offers enterprises the potential of reducing production costs and enhancing product quality. The whole product customization service system is supported by scientific institutions, colleges and universities, and administrative organizations, which can act as a high-tech software and technology service center as well. In addition, it aims to provide not only rapid product customization functions but also design/manufacturing resources at low rent.

CUSTOMIZATION MODE

An efficient customization mode can shorten the time of product customization and consequently reduce the cost. A lifecycle oriented product customization mode which can help cut product customization time is proposed. The model is shown in Figure 2.

Customer requirement parameters have strong correlation to product performance parameters, and product customization is driven by customer requirements. When a customer logs on to an ASP-based product customization service system and inputs requirement parameters, the data transform module parses them into XML

Figure 2. Lifecycle oriented product customization mode

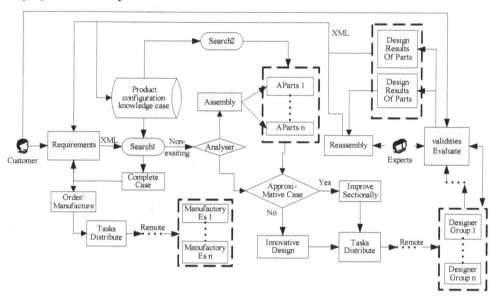

documents. Then, a case-based search module makes the first search (see "Search 1" in Figure 2) for a counterpart case from the resource support layer. If none of the counterparts is found, the analyzer starts up and analyzes exported XML model documents from CAX scene. For an assembly product, every child node in XML model documents is captured for further search. If there is not any counterpart or similar part and the child-node can be divided further, the second search (see "Search 2" in Figure 2) continues until gaining a counterpart or a similar part or until the child node not being divided any more. When a similar product is achieved, an approach of partially improved design is adopted. If neither a counterpart nor a similar product is found from database, an innovation design is appointed. Distributed design groups who receive design tasks can rent software tools of product development provided by the product customization service system weekly or monthly. Domain experts take part in evaluating the design results together with customers and designers in interactive virtual product configuration environment. Design results of assembly parts are reassembled and submitted to the analyzer for validity analysis. All finished

parts and assembly parts are submitted into the product configuration knowledge base for future reuses. After the customer is satisfied with results of the design, product orders are sent to remote distributed manufactories for production. If necessary, distributed designers and manufacturers can also obtain information or technology support from the ASP-based product customization service system at low cost.

KEY TECHNOLOGIES

It can be seen from Figure 1 and Figure 2 that distributed resource collection, data transform, requirement analysis, and product configuration are four important aspects for supporting product customization effectively. Requirement analysis has been studied in detail by Lou, Zhang, and Tan (2004) and Tan, Zhang, and Dai (2005). The remainder of this article focuses on a distributed resource collection method, an information mapping technology between isomeric/isomorphic data for data transform, a quick retrieving algorithm, and an interactive virtual product configuration environment for product configuration.

Figure 3. Resource collecting

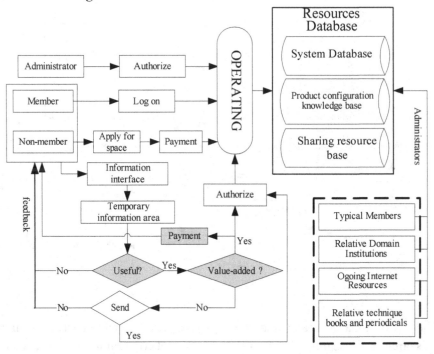

Distributed Resource Collection

Regardless of which category is focused on and which method or logical structure is adopted, the fundamental and central element determining failure or success of product customization is product resources (Choi & Lee, 2003), including design knowledge, manufacture resource, product cases, product data, and so forth. At the same time, distributive resource share is one of the important reasons why the business mode of application service providers cannot diffuse effectively in China, as expected. Since the proposed product customization service system is based on the ASP model, distributive resource share is a bottleneck of realizing product customization.

However, recent studies consider issues on how to make use of an existing resource base to accelerate product development and improve the quality of product design. Very little work has been done on studying resource collection for resource sharing. In order to encourage resource-holders to build and update resource support

layer cooperatively and attract more customers to provide useful feedback messages, a dynamic resource collection method with some incentive mechanism is proposed in this article (shown in Figure 3).

Original resources of resource support layer are collected by administrators from typical members, relative domain institutions, ongoing Internet resources, and relative technique books and periodicals. The newest resources are gathered dynamically from different clients. System administrators have the highest authorization to operate the whole resource, involving constructing the resources database and collecting distributed resources. Non-members must register and pay for special resources or for resource space to deposit their private resources into the resources database. Any uploaded resources will be absorbed in the resources database when it is evaluated to be useful. When a newly added resource is evaluated to be a value-added resource, certain reward is given to the resource provider. Resource evaluation model and certain incentive mechanism are crucial aspects to promote resource share.

Resource Evaluation

In order to evaluate the value of a resource provided by a client and judge whether it is a value-added resource or not, appropriate evaluation indexes and evaluation algorithm are established as follows:

Hypothetically set U is an evaluation index,

$$U = (u_1, u_2, u_3, u_4, u_5),$$

where $u_1, u_2, u_3, u_4,$ and u_5 are specialization degree, innovation degree, credit degree, quality level, and forecast-value respectively.

If set W is a relevant weight aggregate of U and ω_i is the weight of element u_i (i=1, 2, 3, 4, 5), then $W = (\omega_1, \omega_2, \omega_3, \omega_4, \omega_5)$ and $\sum_{i=1}^{5} \omega_i = 1$. Each index is divided into six grades, that is, very high, high, general, low, very low, and none. Each grade is marked by evaluation experts. Let R^* be the mark matrix of u_i (i=1, 2, 3, 4, 5) and P be the matrix of the number of evaluation experts, then

$$R^* = \begin{bmatrix} r_{11} & r_{12} & r_{13} & r_{14} & r_{15} & r_{16} \\ r_{21} & r_{22} & r_{23} & r_{24} & r_{25} & r_{26} \\ r_{31} & r_{32} & r_{33} & r_{34} & r_{35} & r_{36} \\ r_{41} & r_{42} & r_{43} & r_{44} & r_{45} & r_{46} \\ r_{51} & r_{52} & r_{53} & r_{54} & r_{55} & r_{56} \end{bmatrix},$$

$$P = \begin{bmatrix} N_{11} & N_{12} & N_{13} & N_{14} & N_{15} & N_{16} \\ N_{21} & N_{22} & N_{23} & N_{24} & N_{25} & N_{26} \\ N_{31} & N_{32} & N_{33} & N_{34} & N_{35} & N_{36} \\ N_{41} & N_{42} & N_{43} & N_{44} & N_{45} & N_{46} \\ N_{51} & N_{52} & N_{53} & N_{54} & N_{55} & N_{56} \end{bmatrix}$$

Let A be the evaluation matrix, then

$$A = W \oplus R^* \oplus P = W \bullet (R^* \bullet P^T) = (a_1, a_2, a_3, a_4, a_5).$$

Log files memorize the frequency τ of submitting the resource done by each client and the number of resources provided by each client at a time. The context of resources and other information are memorized in a temporary information area. Domain experts and task-assigners mark each item. In general, the amount of resources provided by a client changes along with time t. Let $g(t, \tau)$ be the quantity of resources per second at a time and G_k k=1, 2, 3, 4, 5 be the total quantity of the Kth kind of resource, then

$$G_k = \iint g(t, \tau) dt d\tau,$$

Suppose ξ_i (i=1, 2, 3, 4, 5) is the value of unit mark and N is the number of experts who attend evaluation. ξ_i is appointed by the task-assigner. Let Val be the final evaluation result, then

$$N = \Sigma\Sigma N_{ij}, i = 1, ..., 5, j = 1, ..., 6,$$
$$Val = (\xi_1 G_1, \xi_2 G_2, \xi_3 G_3, \xi_4 G_4, \xi_5 G_5) \bullet A/N$$

Set U=(u1, u2, u3) represents the grade of useful degree, where u1, u2, and u3 respectively represent very useful, useful, and useless. Therein, $0 \le u_i \le 1$ and $\sum_{i=1}^{3} u_i = 1$. Hypothetically, $Vper = Val/ (\sum_{i=1}^{6}(\xi_i G_i))$ and λ is a constant appointed by task-assigner, then

if $Vper \ge u_1$, the resource is very useful;
if $u_2 \le Vper \le u_1$, the resource is useful;
if $Vper \le u_3$, the resource is useless;
if the resource is useful and $Vper \ge \lambda$, the resource is value-added.

Uploaded resources from non-administrators are first deposited in a temporary information area and divided into experience knowledge, innovation knowledge, cases, product development tools, and market feedback information. Task-assigners and experts start up the resource evaluation module to evaluate uploaded resources, and give results of useful degree and value-added degree. Useful resources are deposited in the sharing

Table 1. Incentive mechanism

Approach	Explanation
Payment	Assign the rate of exchange of *Val* according to market requirements and knowledge application foreground. Pay cash or post goods to the knowledge supplier directly.
Awarded marks	When new knowledge is submitted, the evaluation module starts up. Calculated value per time is added to *Val* and deposited as a type of awarded marks. The supplier of resources can exchange services provided by the ASP-based product customization service provider at any time.
Widen authorization	When *Val* is larger than a certain value, the supplier of resources has the following choices: a) To be a member when his/her present status is non-member b) To be an advanced member if he/she has been a general member c) To prolong the period of validity to operate ASP-based product customization service system

resource base, product configuration knowledge base, and system database, respectively, according to characteristics of the resource.

Incentive Mechanism

To encourage resource-holders to publish knowledge and attract more customers to provide helpful feedback information, relevant incentive mechanisms are raised. According to the value of *Val*, three reward approaches are established as incentive mechanism (Table 1).

XML-Based Data Mapping

Collected product data from distributed customers are usually expressed in different file formats. It is necessary to transform these isomeric/isomorphic product data into uniform format for product data share and data exchange. Here, isomeric product data are upon different data models, and isomorphic product data are based on the same data model but expressed in different methods. For example, a product tree-structure set up for assembly and BOM (bill of material) established for production are isomeric product data, while a bill of material (BOM) designed in tree-structure style and BOM designed in table style are isomorphic product data. Those are because a product tree-structure is built on an assembly relationship and a BOM

is based on a manufacturing process. XML is primarily a data modeling language which offers a method for describing and formatting messages and for allowing data to be passed between applications. The proposed service system employs XML as isomeric/isomorphic product data exchange standards. The reason of choosing this notation is as follows (Nazmul, 1999; Holman, 2000; Quin, 2004). First, it is because of its feature of standard language and its interoperability. An advantage of XML is that it would allow, by means of eXtensible Stylesheet Language Transformations (XSLT), the generation of eXtensible HTML (XHTML) pages which are visual on a browser with a representation of the domain or the problem or any other document that includes their elements. Second, 3D model information is especially important to design and can be easily exported in XML language from CAX.

On an ASP-based product customization service system, a relational database is used as a back-end database and an XML document is only used to exchange and search among different modules. To realize data mapping between XML documents and relational database, two mapping models are designed—template-driven mapping (Figure 4) and object-oriented mapping (Figure 5).

According to the XML template, data are retrieved from a relational database and expressed

Figure 4. Template-driven mapping

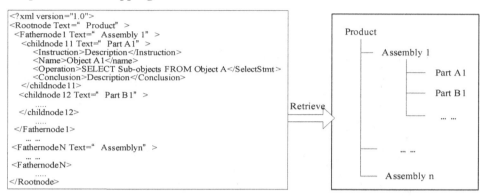

Figure 5. Object-oriented mapping

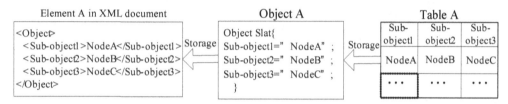

in XML. Then, the XML document is displayed in the user interface in a relative table or a hierarchy tree. According to object-oriented mapping, data in the table or nodes of hierarchy tree are transformed into XML document and deposited into a relational database. Figure 6 illustrates the mentioned mapping relationships in a product hierarchy tree of road-surface machinery. When the original product list is going through analyzing customers' requirement, an object list is produced by searching matching elements from the XML document. Then, on one hand, the object list is organized as a product hierarchy tree through tree-node information mapping and a new product list is deposited in the database through mapping into the XML document again. On the other hand, the object list is mapped into the product order in table type.

Product Configuration

Quick and efficient product configuration is important for cutting product development time and cost. The process of retrieving similar cases is an important task in product configuration. From the requirement-driven product customization process graph (Figure 2), it is obvious that searching counterparts or similar cases from the resource support layer is the key technology for smooth product customization. There are two main strategies that are used for retrieval, namely the generalization hierarchy strategy and the parallel strategy (Watson, 1996). Here, the generalization hierarchy strategy and parallel strategy are integrated according to the product hierarchy tree and two searching algorithms are applied—text similar degree algorithm and parameter gray correlative degree algorithm.

Text Similar Degree Algorithm

Let set $OT_0 = (b_1, b_2,...)$ be the retrieving object, $OT_l = (c_1, c_2,...)$ the product case deposited in product resource base, where b_j is the keyword of OT_0 and c_j the keyword of OT_l, and $sim(OT_0, OT_l)$ expresses the similarity degree, then

Figure 6. Product hierarchy tree of road-surface machinery

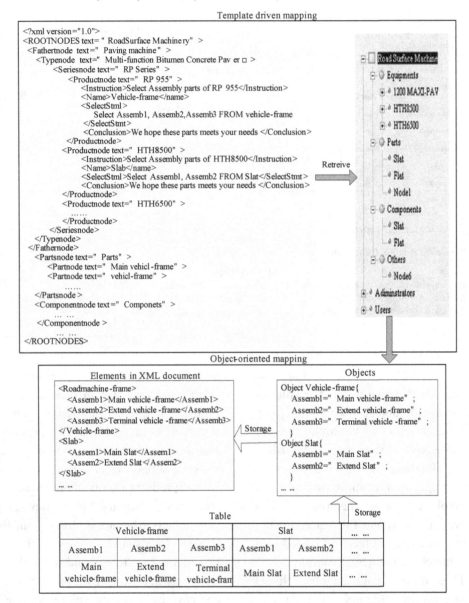

$$sim(OT_0, OT_l) = \frac{count(OT_0 \cap OT_l)}{count(OT_0) + count(OT_l) - count(OT_0 \cap OT_l)}$$

(4.1)

if $sim(OT_0, OT_l) = 1$, the retrieved case is taken as a counterpart of product object;

if $0 < sim(OT_0, OT_l) < 1$, the retrieved case is a similarity with similar degree of $sim(OT_0, OT_l)$;

if $sim(OT_0, OT_l) = 0$, there is not any similarity.

Parameter Gray Correlative Degree Algorithm

Let set $P_0 = [p_0(1), p_0(2), ..., p_0(n)]$ be performance parameters of a product required by the customer, set $P_i = [p_i(1), p_i(2), ..., p_i(n)]$ (i=1, 2,..., m) is performance parameters of the ith product case deposited in database, and $r(P_0, P_i)$ expresses correlative degree. Using the gray correlative grade model (Xiao, Song, & Li, 2005), P_0 is a reference sequence and P_i is a compare sequence. Formula 4.2 is used as product configuration according to performance parameters.

$$r(P_0, P_i) = \sum_{k=1}^{n} \omega_k r(p_0(k), p_i(k)) =$$

$$\sum_{k=1}^{n} \omega_k \frac{\Delta \min_i \min_k |p_0(k) - p_i(k)| + 0.5 \Delta \max_i \max_k |p_0(k) - p_i(k)|}{|p_0(k) - p_i(k)| + 0.5 \Delta \max_i \max_k |p_0(k) - p_i(k)|}$$

(4.2)

Where ω_k is the weight of performance parameter k, $0 \le \omega_k \le 1$ and $\sum_{k=1}^{n} \omega_k = 1$.

The text similar degree algorithm (Formula 4.1) is applied in nodes of a product hierarchy tree. The text-name of the tree node is regarded as a retrieving object. The retrieving process starts from the root-node and downwards when none of the counterparts or similarities is retrieved at the current level, and ends when the current node is a leaf-node. If multi-similarities of a retrieving object are found, customer requirements are decomposed into performance parameters. A further search based on the parameter gray correlative degree algorithm (Formula 4.2) is done according to the performance parameters. When a text-type parameter is met with in parameter table, the text similarity degree algorithm is utilized and the value of $sim(OT_0, OT_i)$ is added into Formula 4.2. When one parameter item is a scale number, the center value of a scale is regarded as a performance parameter for the compare sequence.

For example, a multi-function Bitumen-concrete paver is required by customers (Table 2). The text-name "multi-function Bitumen-concrete paver" is an object to be retrieved. First, the text similar degree algorithm is applied and multi-similar products are retrieved (Table 3). In order to get the most similar product from Table 3, the parameter gray correlative degree algorithm is used for further search according to performance parameters. When the item of engine type is met, the text similar degree algorithm is utilized and the text item is replaced by $sim(OT_0, OT_9)$. Results indicate that RP955 is the most similar. Then improvement design and innovation design are performed on retrieved similar parts of RP955. Tests show that case-based product configuration, by use of the proposed retrieval method, can significantly improve retrieval efficiency and reduce the development time and cost for design and assembly. It also suggests a good start point for further product development activity.

Table 2. Performance parameters of multi-function Bitumen-concrete paver put forward by customer

	Basic working width (ω_1)	Max working width (ω_2)	Max paving thickness (ω_3)	Paving speed (ω_4)	Traveling speed (ω_5)	Theoretic productivity (ω_6)	Hopper capacity (ω_7)
Multi-function Bitumen-concrete paver	3.0	9~9.5	350	0~18	0~2.4	600~700	14
	Gradient ability (ω_8)	Engine type (ω_9)	Rated output (ω_{10})	Generator power (ω_{11})	Weight (ω_{12})	Overall dimension (ω_{13})	
	20	BF6M1013	133	28	21~28.4	6759×3000×3850	

$(\omega_1 = \omega_2 = \omega_3 = \omega_4 = \omega_5 = \omega_6 = \omega_7 = \omega_8 = \omega_{10} = \omega_{11} = \omega_{12} = \omega_{13} = 0.08, \ \omega_9 = 0.04, \sum_{i=1}^{13} \omega_i = 1)$

Table 3. Cases of multi-function Bitumen-concrete paver retrieved from case base

Item\Parameter / Product-type	RP601J/701J	RP955	RP951A	RP602	RP802	...
Basic working width	3.0	3.0	3.0	2.5	3.0	...
Max working width	6.0/7.0	9.5	9.5	6.0	8.0	...
Max paving thickness	300	350	350	380	380	...
Paving speed	1.54~4.64	0~18	0~18	0~14	0~14	...
Traveling speed	0.44-3.01	0~2.4	0~2.4	0~3.0	0~3.0	...
Theoretic productivity	300	700	700	400	600	...
Hopper capacity	13	14	14	13	13	...
Gradient ability	20	20	20	20	20	...
Engine type	4135AZKa	BF6M1013E	BF6M1013	BF6M1013C	BF4M1013C	...
Rated output	90	137/2300	133	112	112	...
Generator power	1500	28	28	20	20	...
Weight	16~21	21.3~28.6	21.3~28.6	15.8~21.5	16.5~23.5	...
Overall dimension	6136×3000×3635	6731 ×3000 ×3850	6757 ×3000 ×3650	6230 ×2500 ×3855	6230 ×3000 ×3855	...

Interactive Virtual Product Configuration Environment

At present, end users often want to configure a product with individual preference and are allowed to change product characteristics with real-time update in the product appearance or overall shape. Only supplying bills of product configuration or 2D images for showing customer's configurations may not be effective when product styling (shape, color, and appearance in 3D space) is a crucial factor that influences the purchase decision. There is a need for a web-based interactive visualization environment.

Lots of virtual assembly systems have been studied and developed in recent years. It is a good way to improve existing virtual assembly systems to meet the need of visual product configuration. In order to allow end users to participate in product configuration vividly and make products to meet customers' individual requirements, an interactive virtual product configuration environment needs to contain five major components—a product configuration hierarchy organization, a virtual configuration scene, a match colors module, a PDM module, and an intercommunication module. A configuration product hierarchy tree is structured by the product configuration hierarchy organization. Product data are well integrated with a product hierarchy tree by the PDM module. Participants in product configuration—including customers, designers, and experts—exchange their opinions via an intercommunication module, and change colors of 3D model via the match colors module to meet individual favorites.

A CASE STUDY

As production automation technologies are improving constantly, information technologies are being applied widely and individuation and diversification of customers' requirements are increasing continually, construction machinery in China must reflect the era of individuation. In order to better cater to different customers' requirements, construction machinery is now being developed for product serialization, large-scale production, and general parts. Those make it possible to carry out product customization in construction machinery. Jiansu Province has the largest industry base of construction machinery in China with the majority of the companies' SMEs. Many SMEs in Jiangsu Province lack professional staffs, technology ability, and economy strength. It is difficult for them to self-develop a product customization system operating in lifecycle-oriented customization mode. In addition, SMEs united into one industry chain for lifecycle-oriented product customization service is an inevitable trend for winning competitive market predominance.

Thus, based on the aforementioned studies and supported by China National 863 Projects, a construction machinery oriented product customization service platform was developed by utilizing object oriented technologies, modularization design method, and Internet technologies. The resource support layer was built upon an SQL Server 2000 system. All modules were implemented in the .NET framework by making use of ASP.NET with Visual Basic and JavaScript. The interactive virtual product configuration environment was developed by improving a self-developed Web-based interactive virtual assembly system (Yi, Cheng, & Guo, 2006). The virtual configuration scene was developed by use of EAI technologies of Cortona (ParallelGraphics, 2005) on a Java development platform. The virtual configuration environment was developed based on virtual reality modeling language (VRML) and embedded in an IE6.0 browser that allows end users to access the system over the Internet.

Figure 7 shows several typical interfaces that were developed. Figure 7(a) is a typical interface of the resource evaluation system for collecting product customization resources for road-surface machine. It is based on the proposed dynamic resource collecting method with certain incentive mechanisms. Figure 7(b) and Figure 7(c) are typical interfaces for product configuration. Figure 7(b)

provides customers rapid configuration functions for primary case search by keywords, specifically configuration by performance parameters and a product tree-structure reconstruction. Figure 7(c) offers all users functions of product preview and collaborative analysis, including seven main modules shown at the left of Figure 7(c). The configuration tree management module takes charge of organizing and maintaining the configuration product hierarchy tree. The product data management module, the product version management module, and the parts management module are responsible for managing and maintaining detailed information of products or parts linked on tree-nodes. The 3D model control module bears two functions: one is to control 3D model assembly/disassembly and movement; the other is to mark the 3D model when any modification is demanded. The match colors management module provides customers auto-match colors function of 3D model according to customers' favorites. Customers, experts, designers, and system managers have different authorizations respectively in operation, management, and maintenance. Their authorizations are managed by the users authorization management module. The interface of the interactive virtual product configuration environment is divided into four display plats. The center of it consists of an above-part and under-part. The above-part is a virtual scene of 3D model display and the under-part lists the performance parameters for the configuration product. The right of it is divided into a display area of a product tree-structure and a communication area. The product hierarchy trees in Figure 7(b) and Figure 7(c) are created by XML-based template-driven mapping. Parameter tables in Figure 7(c) are retrieved by the combination of the text similar degree algorithm and the parameter gray correlative degree algorithm and created by XML-based object-oriented mapping. ASP is responsible for customization maintenance and management.

Figure 7. Typical interfaces of Construction machinery oriented product customization service platform

(a) resource evaluation

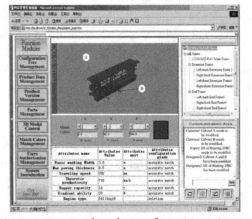

(b) product configuration

(c) interactive virtual product configuration environment

The construction machinery oriented product customization service platform has been applied in some SMEs in construction machinery in the Jiangsu province, P.R. China. Jiangsu Zhenjiang Huachen Huatong Road Machinery Co., Ltd. (simply referred to as Huachen Huatong) is a typical, successful application enterprise. Huachen Huatong is one of the important road machinery and concrete machinery companies producing in Jiangsu. Any product using these two kinds of machines is composed of hundreds or even thousands of parts and many of these parts have several selections to meet with different needs. Configuring such complex products artificially is not only hard work but also responds slowly to individual requirements. In order to meet customers' individual requirements and efficiently expand markets, it was necessary for Huachen Huatong to develop an Internet-based product customization system. However, if the enterprise itself funds the developing and maintaining of a product customization system, it will increase product cost and also make the enterprise unable to concentrate on its core-competitiveness completely.

Thus, Huachen Huatong turned to the construction machinery oriented product customization service platform for implementing product customization. Huachen Huatong submitted their product resources to the resource support layer of the customization service platform and left the customization service management and maintenance to the service provider. Huachen Huatong only pays low, yearly rent and updates its product resources in time. Customers who want to order individual products of road machinery or concrete machinery produced by Huachen Huatong just need to login onto the platform and customize products through product configuration module and interactive virtual product configuration environment. Designers, experts, and even customers, can carry out collaborative configuration analysis in the interactive virtual product configuration environment.

In the following, the customization of machinery and equipment for multi-function cement concrete pavement is used as an example. If a customer wants to customize a multi-function cement concrete paver produced by Huachen Huatong, the customer logins onto the construction machinery oriented product customization service platform and first inputs keywords of paver, machinery, cement concrete, and Huachen Huatong. Three counterparts of 1200MAXI-PAV, HTH6000, and HTH8500, and some selections of relevant parts are listed at the left of Figure 7(b). Then the customer is asked to continue inputting detailed parameters. After the customer inputs parameters of basic paving width 4.4m, max paving width 8m, paving thickness 380mm, paving speed 0~4m/min., and so on, the product listing is updated and only 1220MAXI-PAV and its parts are remained. According to different paving widths, each kind of frames of 1220MAXI-PAV has several selections. For instance, left-back extension frame has three selections, that is, left-back extension frame1, left-back extension frame2, and left-back extension frame3. The customer can select favorite or more suitable parts to form equipment through function modules of add nodes, delete selected nodes, and reconstruct tree-structure (see at the center of Figure 7(b)). After initializing the product configuration, the customer switches to the interactive virtual product configuration environment to preview and carry out individualized design. If the customer expects Cabinet A to be coffee color and Cabinet B with a chamfer angle of 45 degree, the relevant location of the 3D model in a virtual scene can be labeled and modification information is published in the communication area. The customer himself can modify the color of Cabinet A through the function module of match colors. Designers and experts can execute collaborative design and validity analysis, and feed back results to the customer. If the customer puts forward further individuation needs, the same process can continue until the configuration product meets with

the customer's requirements completely. When the configuration process is completed, the bill of parts of configuration product is delivered to the customer in table style which is transformed by XML language. Detailed BOM of the configuration product is distributed to relevant manufacture enterprises or parts suppliers.

Feedback information shows that after using this service platform, Huachen Huatong responded to customers' individual requirements more quickly and offered more perfect pre-sale services and after-sale services on time. The enterprise is able to develop its Internet-based sales and customization systems smoothly in shorter time and at lower cost than before. Road pavers have more than a 38% occupation ratio in the Chinese market with an increase of about 11% compared to the same period of the previous year when this customization service was not used. Machines of Huachen Huatong are approbated and welcomed in Chinese road machinery area and the building construction machinery area.

CONCLUSION AND FUTURE WORK

In this article, an ASP-based product customization service system operating in a lifecycle oriented product customization mode has been proposed. Key technologies to support the lifecycle-oriented product customization service effectively were discussed in detail. A resource evaluation model and relevant incentive mechanism to facilitate distributed resource share was established. Template-driven mapping and object-oriented mapping based on XML for isomeric/isomorphic product data transform were presented. A text similar degree algorithm and parameter gray correlative degree algorithm were combined to speed up product configuration. In order to meet end users' individualized requirements and allow end users to participate in product configuration vividly, an interactive virtual product configuration environment through improving existing virtual assembly system was presented. A construction machinery oriented product customization service platform was developed as a case study which has verified the results. Practices show that SMEs could develop their Internet-based sales and customization effectively in a shorter time and at lower costs by using the service system.

In the future, it is intended to constitute a set of uniform evaluation criterion through statistical analysis of historical data to make resource evaluation more effective. In addition, product configuration validity analysis and system service mechanism need further investigation.

REFERENCES

Choi, B., & Lee, H. (2003). An empirical investigation of KM styles and their effect on corporate performance. *Information & Management, 40*, 403-417.

Heart, T., & Pliskin, N. (2001). Is e-commerce of IT application services (ASP) alive and well? *Journal of Information Technology Theory and Application, 3*(4), 33-41.

Holman, G. K. (2000). *What is XSLT*. Retrieved November 16, 2004, from http://www.xml.com/pub/a/2000/08/holman/index.html

Jaruzelski, B., Lake, R. M, & Ribeiro, F. M. (2000). *ASP101: understanding the application service provider model*. Retrieved May 12, 2004, from http://www.bah.com

Kern, T., Lacity, M., & Willcocks, L. (2002). *Netsourcing: renting business applications and services over a network*. New York: Prentice-Hall.

Lou, J. R., Zhang, S. Y., & Tan, J. R. (2004). Research on expressing and processing client demands for mass customization. *Chinese Mechanical Engineering, 15*(8), 685-687.

Nazmul, I. (1999). *Benefits of using XML*. Retrieved January 12, 2005, from http://www.developerlife.com/xmlbenefits/default.htm

Nigel, J. L., & David, H. B. (2005). An SME perspective of vertical application service providers. *International Journal of Enterprise Information Systems, 1*(2), 37-55.

Pan, X. H., & Jia, Z. Y. (2005). Research and implementation of networked manufacturing platform based on ASP. *Manage Technique, 9*, 99-101.

ParallelGraphics. (2005). *Cortona 3D viewer*. Retrieved March 22, 2005, from http://www.cortona3d.com/cortona3d

Quin, L. (2004). *Extensible markup language (XML)*. Retrieved December 13, 2004, from http://www.w3.org/XML/

Rodney, L. S., Gerard, A. A., & Ashwin, W. J. (2002). Managing seller-buyer new product development relationships for customized products: a contingency model based on transaction cost analysis and empirical test. *Journal of Product Innovation Management, 19*(6), 439-454.

Silvira, G. D., Borenstein, D., & Fogliatto, F. S. (2001). Mass customization: Literature review and research directions. *International Journal of Production Economics, 72*, 1-13.

Tan, J. R, Qi, F., Zhang, S. Y., & Dai, R. Y. (2005). Research on technology of design retrieve based on fuzzy customer requirement. *Chinese Journal of Mechanical Engineering, 41*(4), 79-84.

Wang, Z. Q., Li, X. N., & Jiang, C. Y. (2003). Networked manufacturing for high technology industry region of Shannxi Province's center. *Computer Integrated Manufacturing Systems, 9*(8), 710-715.

Watson, I. D. (1996). Case-based reasoning tools: An overview. Progress in Case-Based Reasoning. In *Proceedings of the 2nd UK Workshop on Case Based Reasoning*. University of Salford, UK.

Xiao, X. P., Song, Z. M, & Li, F. (2005). *The basis and application of gray technology*. Beijing: Science Press, China.

Xu, L. Y., Li, A. P., & Zhang, W. M. (2004). Networked manufacturing base on ASP and relational technologies. *China Mechanical Engineering, 15*(19), 1755-1759.

Yang, Y., Zhang, X. D., Liu, F., & Xie, Q. (2005). An Internet-based product customization system for CIM. *Roboties and Computer-Integrated Manufacturing, 21*, 109-118.

Yi, L., Cheng, X. S, & Guo, Y. (2006). Development and implementation of Web-based interactive virtual assembly platform. *Machine Building & Automation, 35*(1), 75-79.

Zhao, H. J., Ju, W. J., Wang, S. Y., & Yin, C. F. (2003). Software resource sharing and its application in networked manufacturing system. *Computer Integrated Manufacturing Systems, 9*(7), 608-612.

This work was previously published in International Journal of Enterprise Information Systems, Vol. 4, Issue 1, edited by A. Gunasekaran, pp. 1-17, copyright 2008 by IGI Publishing (an imprint of IGI Global).

Chapter 17
Monitoring Enterprise Applications and the Future of Self-Healing Applications

Shuchih Ernest Chang
National Chung Hsing University, Taiwan

Boris Minkin
National Chung Hsing University, Taiwan

ABSTRACT

With the drastic growth of the Internet and the advance of hardware and software technologies, the enterprise information systems supporting business operations and functions have become more and more complex. The need of monitoring the behavior of such systems is becoming apparent, since it allows detecting problems early and resolving them before they become fatal and affect business seriously. In addition to covering the concept and related technologies of various monitoring approaches and their corresponding advantages and disadvantages, this article illustrates how self-healing application monitoring can facilitate the performance and availability management of Java based enterprise applications. The creating of enterprise strength monitoring solutions, together with the criteria of monitoring technology adoption and vendor selection, is also presented in this article.

INTRODUCTION

Application monitoring is essential for observing and improving the performance and availability of enterprise applications which are usually large-scale, distributed, multi-tiered and complicated. In general, the monitoring process should be carried out with appropriate techniques and mechanism to examine and control the applications for serv-ing the needs of businesses. In terms of business needs, people's life and living styles have been, in recent years, deeply influenced by the Internet and the World Wide Web, which enable electronic commerce (EC) for companies and their business partners to conduct business and perform electronic transactions. In addition to the purchase of products and services over the Internet, EC also encompasses all electronically conducted business activities, operations, and transaction process-ing within and cross companies. Through EC, companies can alleviate constraints (upon time, space and cost) to enhance the way they connect to and interact with their EC counterparties by serving customers and collaborating with business partners electronically and intelligently. However, to catch this revolutionary opportunity offered by EC, enterprises are facing complex challenges. "Cost-effectively protecting the availability of mission-critical applications has as much to do with business planning than with technical ca-pability," and "A solid decision-making process must be followed to remove the fear factor from the equation", stated by Meta Group (Garry, 2004), may serve as examples of such highly important challenges in ensuring a responsive management of EC applications.

Availability is defined as a function of *mean time between failures* (MTBF) and *mean time to repair* (MTTR) (Zimmerman, Yuhanna, Heffner, Schreck, Rankine, & Garbani, 2004). It is calcu-lated much like a probability of failure, using the following formula:

Availability = MTBF/(MTBF+MTTR)

In an IT system, the application availability is the result of the aggregation of all the availability factors of all architectural components supporting the application. This aggregation differs whether the components are serial or parallel, and it is a commonly agreed goal that single points of fail-ure (in terms of considering serial components) tend to be avoided, and critical components are doubled or clustered (in terms of building parallel components). The Information Technology Infra-structure Library (ITIL), which is the most widely accepted approach to IT service management in the world, provides a set of service management best practices which include availability manage-ment (Behr, Kim, & Spafford, 2005). According to ITIL, availability management ensures that users can use IT services when they need them, at the

level agreed to in the Service Level Agreement (SLA), by managing factors such as the reliability, complexity, serviceability, and maintainability of software, hardware, contracts and procedures.

The definition of what highly available means with respect to a particular application is crucial in determining what problem is really being solved. If the application is performing poorly, it might be considered unavailable by its users. If mobile users cannot connect because the phone organization's cable is accidentally cut, the ap-plication is unavailable. If a table in the database is currently off-line, the entire application could be unavailable. From the users' perspective, the answer may be different depending on when they connect, how they connect, and what they access. Therefore, every user has a different definition of "highly available". In general, the user requirements for availability are defined in the SLAs, the agreements between business and IT departments on the major characteristics that application shall provide. Good SLAs should ad-dress availability and stability issues, as well as security, performance and others. The industry measures availability in nines (e.g., 99%, 99.99%, 99.999%), representing the percentage of time the application is deemed available throughout an entire year. Vendors use terms such as basic availability (95%—e.g., tape backup), enhanced availability (e.g., 99.9%—RAID disks), highly available (99.999%—application data protection), and fault tolerant (>99.9999%—life and death applications).

According to a survey conducted by Contin-gency Planning Research (Kembel, 2000), mission critical brokerage applications have much higher costs for downtime and require higher availability and performance requirements than retail appli-cations. A later Contingency Planning Research survey conducted in 2001 found that 18% of the participating companies reported an hourly loss of downtime between $251,000 and $1,000,000, and another 8% of the companies reported an hourly downtime damage of over one million US dollars (Eagle Rock Alliance, 2001). According to Patterson (2002), a simple way to estimate cost of downtime can be summarized as follows:

Estimated Average Cost of one hour of downtime =
Employee costs per hour * Fraction employees affected by outage +
Average revenue per hour * Fraction revenue affected by outage

Where:

- Employee costs per hour is the total salaries and benefits of employees per week divided by the average number of working hours.
- Average revenue per hour is the total revenue per week divided by average number of business hours.
- "Fraction employees affected by outage" and "Fraction revenue affected by outage" are just educated guesses or reasonable ranges.

Managing performance for Java based enterprise applications is closely related to management of availability. For example, once the performance of a mission critical financial application degrades, it can be considered unavailable by the users with highly sensitive time requirements. Monitoring is necessary to ensure continuous performance and availability requirements in accordance with the defined SLAs. Monitoring allows detecting problems early and resolving them before they become fatal and affect end users. A variety of

monitoring methods exists in the industry. This article addresses the important issue of monitoring enterprise applications by identifying appropriate and feasible monitoring approaches for performance tuning and availability management, describing their corresponding quality of services (QoS) benefits, and spelling out the advantages and disadvantages of various approaches.

APPLICATION MONITORING REQUIREMENTS

Monitoring applications to detect the problems before they happen is a common application and system requirement, especially in revenue-generating production environments. Application monitoring should be more than just collecting data showing how an application is performing technically. It should be proactive. It should identify the problem before the catastrophic production failure happens. It should contain history—how the application performed overtime so the persons responsible for monitoring and management of applications can determine the periods of maximum load and trends of the application usage in order to set up an optimal configuration. It should provide reports with insights on how application performed and what particular problems of different severities have occurred. It should give the possibility to correlate the events in different layers of the application to identify the root cause of the problem. Figure 1 shows a typical multitiered (layered) infrastructure of an enterprise EC application may look like.

Figure 1. The typical infrastructure of an enterprise EC application

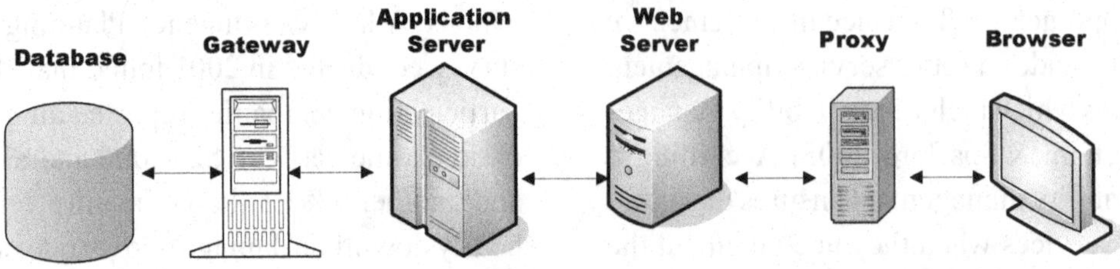

Performance problems may occur in any one of those layers. It is very hard to identify the root cause of the problem without being able to correlate the events occurring in different layers and understanding how they are interrelated together and what have caused what. Another important characteristic of application monitoring is the *alert*. Alerting the operations department before the problem becomes critical so they can mitigate it in a timely manner is important for any respectable infrastructure. A wide variety of alert means are available such as beepers, e-mail, screen alerts and so forth. Alerts can be also of varying severity. For instance, a fatal alert would be issued if the critical production application is down, and warning or informational alert might be issued when a possibility of the problem is on the horizon.

It all comes to how one wants to approach the production problems, and there are generally and philosophically two ways to do it: one is through the continuous data collection of up-to-date statistics for the health, status and performance of the system—the proactive way. Another one is through a trial-and-error theorizing method or a random log parsing using whichever data is available—often unreliable scripts and heroic efforts of a few operation and infrastructure personnel.

MONITORING APPROACHES

Monitoring Through Logging

Logging may work well for small-scale applications that do not require stringent up time defined by their service level agreements. Managing logs in the clustered environment where multiple application server instances and clones are dedicated to the single application through both vertical and horizontal scaling topologies may pose a credible threat to the feasibility of log administration and coordinating events that occur in those logs. One of the attempted solutions was to log to a central network file system with synchronized file write access. However, this presents a major performance problem as soon as logs start growing fast, and with high volume applications, it would not take weeks or months for this to happen—it might be just a few hours. Another problem with logging is the severity level at which logging is attempted. Logging in the production environment needs to be performed at least at the warning level. Debug and informational messages should be disabled, which requires high level of discipline from the administration team. Timestamp differences between multiple logs may contribute to the problems of coordinating events and correlating them to identify root cause of the problem. Maintaining the logging code is another important consideration—multiple applications

Figure 2. Multiple applications on different servers may log into the same JMS queue

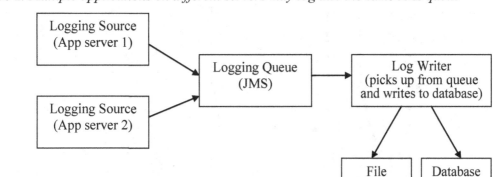

have to reuse the common logging library for the monitoring operations to be able to interpret logs in a common format. Inconsistent logging format will break any possibility of correct interpretation for the log files.

One of the possible ways of mitigating problems of log monitoring is using a consistent logging framework with a standard logging format throughout the corporation. One example of such framework is Apache Log4J (Gülcü, 2004). It can resolve a number of aforementioned problems—including ones with severity levels, inconsistent logging format and logging in the clustered environment. It is possible to configure Log4J to enable appending logs through Java Message Service (JMS) in an asynchronous way, and thus, allowing multiple logging sources to log into the same logging queue, where a queue listener could pick up the messages and write them to the common log or a database. As shown in Figure 2, applications hosted on different application servers may be able to log into the same JMS queue, and a central component called Log Writer will pick up messages from that queue and write them to a file and/or a database. This way, it is possible to overcome the performance hit of logging since it will be done in an asynchronous way. In addition, the problem with coordinating

logging from multiple sources (such as application servers) goes away, since they will all go into the same queue. The problem with this approach is however, a requirement for an extra middleware and infrastructure to host the JMS service.

One useful note on logging is related to monitoring Java Virtual Machine (JVM) garbage collection statistics. In order to debug it, it could be beneficial sometimes to turn the **verbose:gc** option on for the particular JVM—this helps analyze the performance issues with the application memory management—however, interpreting the results would be best with some graphical tool, such as the GCViewer, a free open source tool available at www.tagtraum.com. As shown in Figure 3, the tool parses the log and shows the chainsaw of garbage collection with information on pauses, throughput and overall application performance.

Monitoring Through Viewing

Modern Java application servers provide tools that help monitoring some of the major characteristics inside the applications that run on them. For example, BEA WebLogic provides WebLogic Resource Monitor that analyzes performances of things like connections pools, servlets, Enterprise Java Beans (EJBs), user sessions, and so forth. It

Figure 3. An example of the visualized logging information on JVM performance

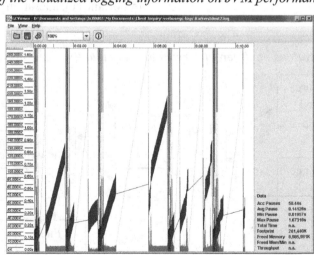

also provides graphs based on the current snapshot of the system. IBM WebSphere Application Server comes with a similar concept—called Tivoli Performance Viewer, formerly called Resource Analyzer, which also gives a snapshot of application at a given point of time—allowing monitoring various resources within Java (such as Java EE) containers—Web container, EJB container, connection pools, JVM heap sizes, HTTP sessions, and others.

The problem with this monitoring solution is that it only provides very limited history and limited reports, and it does not provide ability to do alerts or correlation of events to investigate and/or identify the root cause of the problem. These simple tools may be good if administrator knows exactly what to monitor for—for instance, JVM heap size. However, if the cause of the problem were not known, it would be very hard to see which particular problem is causing the issue by using this kind of tools. In addition, since it is an online monitoring tool, the administrator will have to literally sit in front of it while the application is under load and try to understand what the root cause of a particular problem is. There are no historical reports available, neither historical data are preserved. Analyzing the results of the monitoring tool can be a challenge in its own, since variety of data of most granular level can be provided, and it is hard to arrive at any particular conclusion given an immense volume of those data. Some help has been given by IBM by providing Tivoli Performance Advisor module, which helps interpret results of the Tivoli Performance Viewer data collection, but the advice it provides is mostly related to configuration parameters, and would not necessarily help with the application-related problems.

Java Performance Monitoring Interface

The Java Platform, Standard Edition (Java SE) provides comprehensive support for monitoring and management of Java applications. It not only defines the management interfaces for the JVM, but also provides out-of-the-box remote monitoring and management on the Java platform of applications that run on it. Starting with release 5, Java SE provides the Java Monitoring and Management Console (JConsole) tool for not only managing Java applications, but monitoring and managing Java virtual machines. It uses the extensive instrumentation of the Java virtual machine to provide information on performance and resource consumption of applications running on the Java platform using Java Management Extension (JMX) technology. The JConsole tool helps analyze garbage collections scenarios and JVM heap usage, by extensively using JMX.

JMX consists of three tiers: Instrumentation tier, Agent tier, and Distributed Services tier. The instrumentation tier is a collection of manageable resources instrumented through Mbeans (i.e., Managed Beans), Java classes that expose a management interface for a managed resource. Agent tier contains the Mbean Server—Java class that manages a group of MBeans registered with the server and services such as dynamic class loading, monitors, timers, relation service between Mbeans. Distributed Services tier includes adapters to provide access to Mbeans, and connectors to expose Mbeans to other protocols (RMI, CORBA, etc.).

There is no single optimal method to get all monitoring information. JMX is necessary for optimal management solutions of Java SE and Java EE artifacts. At the method invocations level, byte-code instrumentation might be a more appropriate solution—for which one needs to use Java Virtual Machine Profiling Interface (JVMPI) (Sun Microsystems, 2004) or Java Virtual Machine Tool Interface (JVMTI) (Sun Microsystems, 2006). Lots of it is part of Java 5. JVMPI allows more detailed monitoring of internal JVM characteristics such as garbage collection statistics in both new and old spaces of JVM heap, number of allocation failures and so forth. JVMTI, a new native interface in Java 5 and Java 6, supersedes JVMPI, which has been deprecated in Java SE since release 5, and includes all the functionality that JVMPI had with the additional debug capabilities and byte code instrumentation. Migration guides from JVMPI to JVMTI are available from Sun Microsystems (O'Hair, 2004).

IBM WebSphere Application Server provides an interfaces called Performance Monitoring Infrastructure (PMI) that helps collect variety of metrics within the server such as CPU, I/O and memory utilization, servlet/EJB response times, the number of HTTP sessions, Web server threads, Web container thread pools, connection pool statistics, and JVM performance heaps. As a matter of fact, there are more than a hundred different metrics within WebSphere.

CREATING ENTERPRISE STRENGTH MONITORING SOLUTION

The Challenge

To perform effective enterpriser level application monitoring, it is necessary to manage and monitor Java EE applications in conjunction with the underlying infrastructure. One way to do it is through synthetic transactions (simulations) to help measure end-to-end time—from the browser all the way to the backend server. Another approach, which may be more appropriate for some environments since Java EE does not exist in isolation, is to do the real monitoring of the production infrastructure under load. Java continually evolves and Java 6 is seen on the horizon, although many of us still run Java 1.4 or Java 5. Starting with its release 5, Java EE as mentioned above has substantial management enhancements. JMX is also being updated with support for new schemas. Tools are often selected over the process. It is necessary to look for tools, processes, and organizational structures on the

path to success. More information about the challenges on the path to a success of Java EE monitoring and management is available in Haight and Brodie (2005).

Application dependencies and different implementations of Java EE specifications often are issues for monitoring the applications optimally. Different application server vendors introduce variety of proprietary technologies although the core is compliant with Sun's spec. Continuous evolution of technology and variety of evolving standards, such as JSRs (Java Specification Requests), are making confusion even more. The challenges on the path to success of Java EE monitoring and management include:

1. Infrastructure Challenges
    a. Application Stack dependencies
    b. Multiple vendors for Java EE application Servers (WebLogic, WebSphere, Tomcat, etc.).
2. Technology issues
    a. Complexity of Java EE specification (includes variety of specs—EJB, Servelts, JSP, etc.)
    b. Continues Java EE evolution—we are seeing lots of changes and enhancements in latest Java EE versions, particularly on the backend EJB front—where the spec has been practically entirely rewritten.
3. Standards establishment
    a. Many different standards are evolving outside of Java EE scope. Plain Old Java Objects (POJOs) are taking front pages. Frameworks such as Spring and Hibernate often outrun standard Java EE way of doing things, and many customers consider standards such as EJB a hurdle rather than an advantage.
    b. JMX management standard is widely accepted but needs more enhancements to enable management of SNMP traps and vendor integration.
4. Management / ISVs

a. Many technical approaches exist on how to optimally approach management of ISVs, especially in the areas of monitoring and management of systems. Managing vendor chum, establishing correct criteria and selecting right vendor is a complex process that had to be developed.

5. Testing process
   a. Insufficient testing and buggy problems cannot be addressed alone through monitoring.
   b. Tracking problems is important once they are identified.

6. Organizational issues
   a. Stakeholder commitment is an important factor in resolving issues within the organization, as well as defining the right strategy for optimal monitoring and management.

7. Finally, Business Impact is the driving force to achieve availability demands and establish proper monitoring.

This path to success is not without obstacles and requires vehement dedication particularly in the areas of vendor selection and standards definition.

VENDOR SELECTION AND TECHNOLOGY ADOPTION

For the optimal enterprise application monitoring and management solution, it is necessary to select a commercial vendor product with multifaceted capabilities. The following criteria for vendor selection might be very useful in order to determine their suitability in a particular company's environment.

- Technical criteria:
  o Supported application server versions
  o Supported operating systems
  o Supported monitoring APIs (PMI, JMX, JVMTI, JVMPI, SNMP)
  o Support for both live and synthetic transactions monitoring
  o Metrics gathered (EJB, Servlets, Connection Pools, etc.)
  o Reporting and correlation abilities
    • Can the reports be introduced?
    • Can the metrics be correlated to one another to identify the root cause?
  o Overhead introduced
    • Need to analyze this with regards to the detail that is gathered—the more details, the bigger is overhead.
  o Intrusiveness
    • Altering application logic, needs for agents, byte-code instrumentation, changing JVM options
  o Alarms and notification
    • Must be able to notify operations in the event of failure, warning and so forth.
  o SLA monitoring capabilities
    • Can monitor satisfaction of application requirements?
  o Integration with other monitoring technology
    • Since companies may already have vendors or existing technology in place that monitors their databases and OS, it might be good to be able to integrate with this vendor or technology at the interface level in order to process and analyze the complete picture for ultimate root cause analysis.
- Criteria not as technical:
  o Vendor stability
  o Use in the industry
  o Market penetration
  o Schedule of major releases
  o Online documentation availability
  o Product training
  o Technical support

In the past several years, we have seen rise and fall of many Java EE providers. While technology is important, viability of the vendors is very important as well. One should look away from the coolness of the product to the viability of the vendor and their vision. It is necessary to understand the application's role within the business process and be able to monitor and manage it in conjunction with other applications and underlying infrastructure. You have to know your environment and your transactions. IBM produced some documents on typical bottlenecks in several industries, such as banking, shopping and trading (IBM, 2004). As shown in Figure 4, the most latency is in the database server for banking. For others, it is usually the application server. One needs to classify how different transactions perform and what to look for when problems arise. For example, based on the study from IBM, around 26% of the problems reported in trading industry were related to the database, 34% related to memory, 23% related to configuration, and 11% related to coding. Therefore, the technology adopted for the purpose of application monitoring and management should always reflect the environment and the transaction patterns of a specific business.

Monitoring of various aspects of a Java EE application is a great way to get to the root cause of a problem, but it is still a reactive approach—it addresses the problem post-factum. The following section proposes the solution that would address the problem even before it is seen.

DESIGN FOR SELF-HEALING

It would be better to have a Java EE application that would solve its own problems, right? Obviously, we cannot create a system that would be completely self-healing; there will be a need to implement various reporting characteristics that would allow the system to report to its owner what it is attempting to do. The following are the basic characteristics of the self-healing system, as we would propose:

1.   Self-configuring

A system should be able to reconfigure itself when asked by its self-healing engine. Whenever particular error/issue occurs; the system would adjust its configuration accordingly and will be

Figure 4. How latency varies based on workload patterns (of various industries) and tiers (Source: IBM (2004))

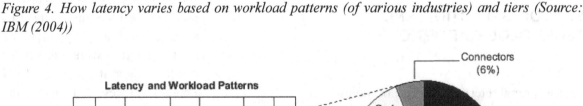

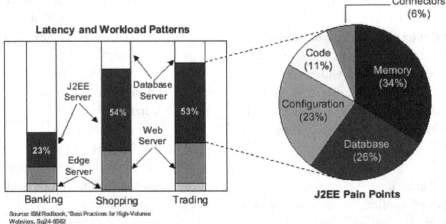

able to restart itself if necessary in a manner that would be transparent to the users.

2. Self-healing

A system should be able to cure its own issues in an automatic or semi-automatic manner. For example, if a particular application thread is failing (not responding), the application may be able to terminate this thread or if a particular part of the application is throwing exceptions, the application will handle it gracefully, making this application part unavailable to the user accompanied by an appropriate message while, at the same time, notifying the operations and/or development team of a fatal problem in production.

3. Self-optimizing

A system can optimize itself based on changing throughput and user load. For example, if a Java EE application is running out of JDBC connections, the system should be able to increase the maximum setting of JDBC connection pool. If a Java EE application is running low on memory, the system should be able to automatically adjust its maximum allowable memory size for its Java Virtual Machine (such as the Xmx parameter).

The proposed architecture of this self-configuring, self-healing, self-optimizing system should contain an autonomic manager and elements managed and monitored by this manager. The manager has to monitor, analyze, plan and execute actions on those various elements. Managed elements are parts of application that need to expose the interface to be managed. This can be easily done using JMX interface. The monitor elements collect, aggregate and filter events from the managed elements. Once this is done analyzers kick in that try to analyze the information collected by monitors and determine if any problematic patterns have been observed. Then, a plan is constructed based on the analysis and one

of the possible solutions is selected. The executors carry out the plan by performing the necessary actions for the purpose of self-configuring, self-healing or self-optimizing.

How does the targeted enterprise application architecture fit into our proposed paradigm of self-configuring, self-healing and self-optimizing system? The short answer is by categorizing the problematic patterns and plans into these three categories. The longer answer would involve the usage of complex rule-based engine that can help define which rules are associated with which particular scenario. Actions taken in order to fix or address the problems will also fit in one of these three scenarios. The importance or priority factor can be assigned to various actions or problematic patterns. For instance, self-configuring and self-healing may be given higher priority than self-optimizing, as the latter is more of the issue of application working better rather than application working at all.

The simple UML diagram, seen in Figure 5, outlines the relationships between various elements within the scheme described above.

In Java EE terms, the various elements of this system may take more concrete meaning. For example, the managed application in Figure 5 will likely be a Java EE application packaged in the form of an Enterprise Archive. Managed elements of each application can be extensions of generic managed element class—providing the interface for capturing events associated with them. For instance, if one were to monitor the database connection pooling, the managed element would be the Connection Pool (or some wrapper object around it). Various events associated with connection pool object could be things like getting the exceptions when the pool runs out of connections (such as the ConnectionWaitTimeoutException in WebSphere), or getting an exception when the connection becomes unreliable—stale—such as when a network link is broken or a database went down, or for any other reason. The complexity of

Figure 5. Class diagram for the autonomic management of the problems in the system

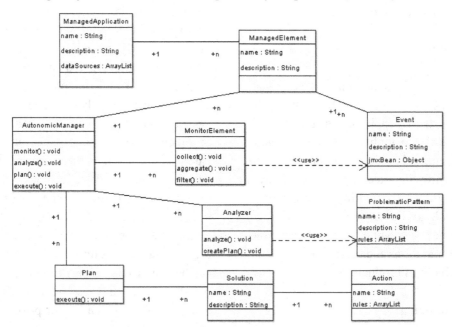

these events can be as deep as one can possibly imagine.

Once events are associated with the particular managed element (such as the connection pool), monitor elements will have to be established to deal with those events. The most important tasks of the monitor elements are to collect proper events based on the defined scenario, aggregate them and filter for future analysis. Filters can be defined to only separate particular types of events, say, back to our example, only events when stale connection is experienced.

An analyzer will then kick in to analyze events collected by monitors vs. various problematic patterns that have been defined. A problematic pattern is a class in its own that can contain rules based on which events are dependent on each other or manifest particular problem, such as an application is running out of available database connections. Based on the problem manifestation, the analyzer will come up with a plan that may consist of several possible solutions, each solution comprising of set of actions to be taken. For

example, one possible solution to the maximum connection pool size being too small could be a self-optimizing action of increasing the connection pool size. Another one could be the self-healing action of killing unresponsive database threads that occupy significant portion of application pool. Self-configuring actions of changing particular parameters within an application or underlying application server can certainly take place and be part of self-optimizing or self-healing actions in both scenarios.

At this point, we come to the dilemma about whether let the system do it all in automatic or semi-automatic manner. Should the system select the best solution and go ahead—execute it, or should the operator/administrator be involved? This is a configuration question for the self-configuring, self-healing and self-optimizing system. Perhaps, both options should be presented to the user in reality and allow the system administrator to either have it on the manual mode or on the cruise control. All possible three scenarios are discussed and detailed here:

1. Let the system execute everything automatically. This will require the definition of some extra rules to be associated with a Plan object so it is intelligent enough to select the best solution. This may also require this Plan object to be aware of the history and culture of how this is done at the particular company or place—once again rules engine mechanisms could be quite valuable in this situation. The obvious advantage of this approach is that everything is proactive and automatic. The obvious disadvantage is that this may bypass the human at all. An extensive logging facility (perhaps, based on monitoring through logging as described in the previous section) can be implemented to address those concerns.

2. Present the user with possible solutions to select from. This will require the implementation of the user interface, such as console that the user will see and have to act upon. Utilizing a workflow engine might be helpful. Generally, not as proactive as the first, fully automatic solution, but this solution gives more control to the human, particularly the system administrators, and this approach could be more comfortable and desirable in more conservative environments.

3. Not only present the user with the list of possible solutions but also with the list of actions that each of these solutions encompasses. This way the conscientious administrator can take actions one at a time and see possible effect on the system.

By using the proposed autonomic computing system with the capability of self-configuring, self-healing and self-optimization, enterprises can achieve better and more efficient ways of managing complicated system resources as suggested by Ganek and Corbi (2003).

CONCLUSION

It is very important to understand latency and workload patterns about the enterprise applications within your company. Operations need to involve from the development time, otherwise it will be too late for achieving the overall goal of performance and availability management. When applications are experiencing major problems in production, it is too late—the users will reject such applications. Application support costs are necessary to be determined early and not just for Java, but for all applications. This needs to include managed application design—costs for monitoring and managing the application. One key point is that enterprise application management needs to be a team effort, instead of individual heroics. Developers need to know where to patch and improve the code. QA needs to determine the code quality. A release team needs to check interdependencies. Lines of business need ROI indicators. New technologies are initially niche focused. Overtime, though, value increases and cost decreases. It is going to cost money to introduce the Java EE application management, spend time to introduce changes to the environment and require even more (money, time, efforts and management process) to overcome uncomfortable learning curves. Results may not be good immediately, and frankly speaking, there could be more costs than results initially, but they will get better eventually. Benefits can be enormous as a well-performed infrastructure is a magnet for both customers and users.

By using self-configuring, self-healing and self-optimizing methodologies, development teams and infrastructure managers can gain even bigger advantages of not having to worry about reactively changing and tuning the system parameters once a monitoring tool reports it. Instead, the system will proactively tune and change itself, perhaps, fixing the issue even before it becomes a critical production problem and is noticed by users or has any business impact.

REFERENCES

Behr, K., Kim, G., & Spafford, G. (2005). *The visible ops handbook: Implementing ITIL in 4 practical and auditable steps*. Oregon: Information Technology Process Institute.

Eagle Rock Alliance (2001). *Online survey results—2001 cost of downtime*. West Orange, New Jersey: Eagle Rock Alliance. Retrieved January 14, 2008, http://www.contingencyplanningresearch.com/2001%20Survey.pdf

Ganek, A. G., & Corbi, T. A. (2003). The dawning of the autonomic computing era. *IBM Systems Journal, 42*(1), 5-18. Retrieved January 14, 2008, from http://researchweb.watson.ibm.com/journal/sj/421/ganek.pdf

Garry, C. (2004). *Downtime as a business expense*. Infrastructure Strategies, Meta Group.

Gülcü, C. (2004). *The complete Log4j manual, Version 1.2*. Switzerland: QoS.Ch Publisher.

Haight, C., & Brodie, S. (2005). *Managing the J2EE application lifecycle for performance and availability—Part III*. Mercury Webinar. Retrieved January 14, 2008, from http://www.mercury.com/

IBM (2004). *More about high-volume web sites*. IBM Redbook.

Kembel, R. W. (2000). *Fibre channel: A comprehensive introduction* (Revised ed). Tucson, Arizona: Norwest Learning Associates.

O'Hair, K. (2004). *The JVMPI transition to JVMTI*. California: Sun Microsystems. Retrieved January 14, 2008, from http://java.sun.com/developer/technicalArticles/Programming/jvmpitransition/

Patterson, D. A. (2002). A simple way to estimate the cost of downtime. In *Proceedings of LISA '02: the Sixteenth USENIX Conference on Systems Administration*, Pennsylvania, USA (pp. 185-188), November 3-8, 2002.

Sun Microsystems (2004). *Java virtual machine profiler interface (JVMPI)*. California: Sun Microsystems. Retrieved January 14, 2008, from http://java.sun.com/j2se/1.5.0/docs/guide/jvmpi/jvmpi.html

Sun Microsystems (2006). *JVM tool interface, Version 1.1*. California: Sun Microsystems. Retrieved January 14, 2008, from http://java.sun.com/javase/6/docs/platform/jvmti/jvmti.html

Zimmerman, B., Yuhanna, N., Heffner, R., Schreck, G., Rankine, C., & Garbani, J. (2004). *An executive guide to high availability*. Cambridge, Massachusetts: Forrester Research.

This work was previously published in International Journal of Enterprise Information Systems, Vol. 4, Issue 1, edited by A. Gunasekaran, pp. 1-17, copyright 2008 by IGI Publishing (an imprint of IGI Global).

Chapter 18
Managing the Implementation of Business Intelligence Systems:
A Critical Success Factors Framework

William Yeoh
University of South Australia, Australia

Andy Koronios
University of South Australia, Australia

Jing Gao
University of South Australia, Australia

ABSTRACT

The implementation of a BI system is a complex undertaking requiring considerable resources. Yet there is a limited authoritative set of CSFs for management reference. This article represents a first step of filling in the research gap. The authors utilized the Delphi method to conduct three rounds of studies with 15 BI system experts in the domain of engineering asset management organizations. The study develops a CSFs framework that consists of seven factors and associated contextual elements crucial for BI systems implementation. The CSFs are committed management support and sponsorship, business user-oriented change management, clear business vision and well-established case, business-driven methodology and project management, business-centric championship and balanced project team composition, strategic and extensible technical framework, and sustainable data quality and governance framework. This CSFs framework allows BI stakeholders to holistically understand the critical factors that influence implementation success of BI systems.

BACKGROUND

Engineering asset management organizations (EAMOs), such as utilities and transportation enterprises, store vast amounts of asset-oriented data (Lin et al., 2007). However, the data and information environments in these organizations are typically fragmented and characterized by disparate operational, transactional and legacy systems spread across multiple platforms and diverse structures (Haider & Koronios, 2003). An ever-increasing amount of such data is often collected for immediate use in assessing the operational health of an asset, and then it is either archived or deleted. This lack of vertical integration of information systems, together with the pools of data spread across the enterprise, make it extremely difficult for management to facilitate better learning and make well-informed decisions thus resulting in suboptimal management performance. Yet large volumes of disperse transactional data lead to increased difficulties in analyzing, summarizing and extracting reliable information (Ponniah, 2001). Meanwhile, increased regulatory compliance and governance requirements have demanded greater accountability for decision making within such organizations (Logan & Buytendijk, 2003; Mathew, 2003). In response to these problems, many EAMOs are compelled to improve their business execution and management decision support through the implementation of a BI system.

According to Negash (2004), "BI systems combine data gathering, data storage, and knowledge management with analytical tools to present complex and competitive information to planners and decision makers." Implicit in this definition, the primary objective of BI systems is to improve the timeliness and quality of the input to the decision making process (Negash, 2004). Data is treated as a corporate resource, and transformed from *quantity* to *quality* (Gangadharan & Swami, 2004). Hence, actionable information could be delivered at the right time, at the right location, and in the right form (Negash, 2004) to assist individual decision makers, groups, departments, divisions or even larger units (Jagielska et al., 2003). Fisher et al. (2006) further posited that a BI system is primarily composed of a set of three complementary data management technologies, namely data warehousing, online analytical processing (OLAP), and data mining tools.

A successful implementation[1] of BI system provides these organizations with a new and unified insight across its entire engineering asset management functions. The resulting unified layer, in reporting, business analysis, and forecasting assures consistency and flexibility (Gangadharan & Swami, 2004). Critical information from many different sources of an asset management enterprise can be integrated into a coherent body for strategic planning and effective allocation of assets and resources. Hence, the various business functions and activities are analyzed collectively to generate more comprehensive information in support of management's decision-making process.

BI systems come as standardized software packages from such vendors as Business Objects, Cognos, SAS Institute, Microstrategy, Oracle, Microsoft and Actuate, and they allow customers to adapt them to their specific requirements. In recent years, the BI market has experienced extremely high growth as vendors continue to report substantial profits (Gartner, 2006a; IDC, 2007). Forrester's recent survey indicated that for most CIOs, BI was the most important application to be purchased (Brunelli, 2006). The results of the latest Merrill Lynch survey into CIO spending similarly found that the area with the top spending priority was BI (White, 2006). These findings are echoed by Gartner's CIOs priorities surveys in 2006 which revealed that BI ranked highest in technology priority (Gartner, 2006b). In the most recent survey of 1400 CIOs, Gartner likewise found that BI leads the list of the top ten technology priorities (Gartner, 2007).

INTRODUCTION AND RESEARCH MOTIVATION

While BI market appears vibrant, nevertheless the implementation of a BI system is a financially large and complex undertaking (Watson et al., 2004). The implementation of an enterprise-wide information system (such as a BI system) is a major event and is likely to cause organizational perturbations (Ang & Teo, 2000). This is even more so in the case of a BI system because the implementation of a BI system is significantly different from a traditional operational system. It is an infrastructure project, which is defined as a set of shared, tangible IT resources that provide a foundation to enable present and future business applications (Duncan, 1995). It entails a complex array of software and hardware components with highly specialized capabilities (Watson & Haley, 1998).

BI project team need to address issues foreign to the operational systems implementation, including cross-functional needs, poor data quality derived from source systems that can often go unnoticed until cross-systems analysis is conducted; technical complexities such as multidimensional data modeling; organizational politics, and broader enterprise integration and consistency challenges (Shin, 2003). Consequently, it requires considerable resources and involves various stakeholders over several months to initially develop and possibly years to become fully enterprise-wide (Watson & Haley, 1997). Typical expenditure on these systems, includes all BI infrastructure, packaged software, licenses, training and entire implementation costs, may demand a seven-digit expenditure (Watson & Haley, 1997). The complexity of BI systems is exemplified by Gartner's recent study that predicted more than half of systems that had been implemented will be facing only limited acceptance (Friedman, 2005).

Much IS literature suggests that various factors play pivotal roles in the implementation of an information system. However, despite the increasing interest in, and importance of, BI systems, there has been little empirical research about the critical success factors (CSFs) impacting the implementation of such systems. The gap in the literature is reflected in the low level of contributions to international conferences and journals. Although there has been a plethora of BI system studies from the IT industry, nonetheless, most rely on anecdotal reports or quotations based on hearsay (Jagielska et al., 2003). This is because the study of BI systems is a relatively new area that has primarily been driven by the IT industry and vendors, and thus there is limited rigorous and systematic research into identifying the CSFs of BI system implementation. Therefore, the increased rate of adoption of BI systems, the complexities of implementing a BI system, and their far-reaching business implications justify a more focused look at the distinctive CSFs required for implementing BI systems.

Research Objective

Given the background and motivation of this research, the authors used Delphi method to:

- explore and identify the CSFs, and their associated contextual elements that influence implementation of BI systems
- consolidate a CSFs framework for BI system implementation

Essentially, the authors argue that there is a set of factors influencing the implementation of BI systems and such antecedents (i.e., CSFs) are necessary. In alignment with Sum et al.'s (1997) argument, this research also recognizes that the associated contextual elements that make up each factor provide more specific, useful and meaningful guidelines for BI systems implementation. As asserted by Sum et al. (1997), Top management support has often been cited as a CSF, but what exactly constitutes top management support is not really known. Good performance of the CSFs requires that their elements (or constituents) be known so that management can formulate appropriate policies and strategies to ensure that the elements are constantly and carefully being managed and monitored. Lack of clear definitions of the CSFs may result in misdirected efforts and resources.

Furthermore, the CSFs identified can be consolidated into a framework to provide a comprehensive picture for BI stakeholders, and hence allowing them to optimize their resources and efforts on those critical factors that are most likely to have an impact on the system implementation. Thereby ensuring that the initiatives result in optimal business benefits as well as maintaining effective uptake.

The remainder of this article has been structured as follows. The following section describes the research methodology, before elaborating on the CSFs finding. The next section then presents the CSFs framework and detail of each CSF. In the last section the authors state the conclusion, research contribution and future study.

RESEARCH METHODOLOGY

In the absence of much useful literature on BI system, this study seeks to explore and identify a set of CSFs that are jointly agreed by a group of BI system experts who possess substantial experience in EAMOs. The Delphi method was deemed to be the most appropriate method for this study because it allows the gathering of subjective judgments which are moderated through group consensus (Linstone & Turoff, 1975; 2002; Helmer, 1977). Moreover, this research assumes that expert opinion can be of significant value in situations where knowledge or theory is incomplete, as in the case of BI systems implementation in EAMOs (Linstone & Turoff, 2002). Unlike focus group method, this Delphi method is particularly suitable for this research situation where personal contact among participants and thus possible dominance of opinion-leaders is

not desirable because of concerns about the difficulty of ensuring democratic participation.

For this study, a Delphi panel composed of fifteen BI systems experts in EAMOs was established. Ziglio (1996) asserts that useful results can be obtained from small group of 10-15 experts. Beyond this number, further increases in understandings are small and not worth the cost or the time spent in additional interviewing (Carson et al., 2001). Thus, the size of such a Delphi panel is deemed suitably representative. As shown in Table 1, the Delphi participants have all been substantially involved in the implementation of BI systems within EAMOs in Australia and the United States.

In addition, the range of engineering asset management organizations represented by these experts was diverse and included public utilities (such as electricity, gas, water, and waste management) and infrastructure-intensive enterprises such as telecommunications and rail companies. It should be noted that some of the large organizations in which the participants have been involved have implemented BI projects in a series of phases. Most of the EAMOs are very large companies with engineering assets worth hundreds millions of dollars and have committed immense expenditure to BI projects. So the expertise of the Delphi participants represents 'state of the art' knowledge of BI systems implementation in a broad range of engineering asset-intensive industries.

The Delphi study comprised three rounds. During the first round the authors conducted face-to-face interviews with each participant (and phone interviews in some cases due to geographical constraints), and these varied in duration from one to one and half hours. Rather than having an open-ended question, the authors adopted a different approach from traditional Delphi methods by beginning with a list of factors derived from data warehousing literature, which is the core component of a BI system. Having a prior theory has advantages such as allowing the opening and probe questions to be more direct and effective, and helping the researcher recognize when

Table 1. Delphi participants and their BI systems experience in EAMOs

Current Position	Organization Type	BI System	EAMOs' Industry Sector
Principal consultant, Committee, Author, Speaker	BI Consultancy, TDWI Committee	Business Objects, Information Builder, Cognos, Oracle	Electricity, gas, water & waste utilities, oil & gas production, defense, public transportation
Principal consultant, Committee	BI Consultancy, DWAA Committee	Cognos, Business Objects, Actuate	Telecommunications, airlines, municipal utility
Principal consultant, Author, Speaker	BI Consultancy, TDWI Summit	Cognos, Business Objects, Hyperion, Oracle, SAS	Energy utilities, transportation, mining industries
Principal consultant, Committee	BI Consultancy, DWAA Committee	Actuate, Microstrategy, Business Objects	Transportation & municipal utility, logistics
Principal consultant, Author, Speaker	BI Consultancy, TDWI Summit	Hyperion, Informatica, Oracle, Actuate, Business Objects	Electricity, gas, water utilities, telecommunications
Principal consultant	BI Consultancy	Business Objects, Cognos, Oracle	Electricity, gas, water & waste utilities
Principal consultant	BI Consultancy	SAS, Business Objects, Cognos, Microsoft, Oracle, Informatica	Rail infrastructure and fleets, public transportation, mining industries
Principal consultant	BI Consultancy	Oracle, IBM, Hyperion, Informatica, Cognos, Microsoft	Telecommunications, electricity, gas, water utilities,
Executive VP (global consulting), Speaker	BI Consultancy, Conferences	Hyperion, Informatica, Oracle	Utilities, telecommunications, public transportation
Principal consultant	BI Consultancy	Oracle, Business objects	Energy utilities, logistic transportation company
Principal consultant	BI Consultancy	Informatica, Oracle, Hyperion	Rail infrastructure and fleets
Principal consultant	BI Consultancy	Cognos, SPF Plus	Energy utilities
Principal consultant	BI Consultancy	Business Objects, SAS, Oracle	Utilities & logistics
Academic, Consultant, Author, Speaker	Academia, BI Consultancy	Oracle, Business Objects, Hyperion Microstrategy	Utilities, telecommunications & manufacturing
Principal consultant	BI Consultancy	Oracle, IBM	Municipal utilities

something important has been said (Carson et al., 2001). However, the existing literature is not comprehensive in regard to CSFs for an entire BI system, but mainly focuses on data warehousing. Therefore, those factors were mainly used to start each discussion. When the mention of particular factors elicited relevant responses then further probing questions would follow in order to gather more details on those factors. The panelists were

indeed encouraged to suggest other factors that they deemed critical.

At the commencement of the interviews, it was explained that the study focused on CSFs that facilitated the implementation success of BI systems in terms of infrastructure performance and process performance. The infrastructure performance consists of three major IS success dimensions proposed by Delone and McLean

Table 2. Ratings of critical success factors by Delphi participants

Critical Success Factors	Mean	Std. Dev
• Committed management support and sponsorship	4.16	0.99
• Business user-oriented change management	4.10	1.00
• Clear business vision and well-established case	4.09	0.90
• Business-driven methodology and project management	4.08	0.88
• Business-centric championship and balanced project team composition	3.94	0.89
• Strategic and extensible technical framework	3.90	0.89
• Sustainable data quality and governance framework	3.82	0.91

(1992; 2003), namely system quality, information quality, and system use, whereas process performance is composed of meeting time-schedule and budgetary constraints (Ariyachandra & Watson, 2006). After the interview, further clarifications (if any) were made by follow-up phone calls and e-mail communications. Subsequently, the data gathered from the first round of interviews were analyzed thoroughly by content analysis technique, a constant comparison ('grounded') technique, to identify major themes (Glaser & Strauss, 1967). This technique encourages the emergence of a finding from the data set by constantly comparing incidents of codes with each other and then abstracting related codes to a higher conceptual level (Glaser, 1992; 1998). In other words, the qualitative data were examined thematically and emergent themes were ranked by their frequency and later categorized. The objective of the present research was to identify the CSFs that influence the implementation of BI systems. Hence, it is considered to be very important to determine what emerges from the data regarding interpretations of the CSFs for implementing BI systems.

In the subsequent round, the suggested factors of all the participants were consolidated into a single list. The list was then distributed among the participants to facilitate comparison of the expert's perceptual differences. However, none of them nominated any additional factors of their own. Also, based on feedback from participants, some further minor changes were incorporated. In addition, the participants confirmed that the classification of factors and their associated contextual elements is appropriate. For instance, several elements are grouped together because of the closed interrelationship. During the third round, the list of candidate CSFs was surveyed by the Delphi participants using a structured questionnaire survey approach. Specifically, a 5-point Likert scale was applied to rate the importance of the candidate CSFs in the process of seeking statistical consensus from the BI experts. The purpose of using a 5-point scale from 1 to 5 (where 1 meant 'not important,' 2 of 'little importance,' 3 'important,' 4 'very important,' to 5 'critically important') was to distinguish important factors from critical success factors. From the survey feedback, only those factors with average rating of 3.5 and above were shortlisted as CSFs (as shown in Table 2). These CSFs ratings are considered legitimate because the participants were directly drawing on their hands-on experience in EAMOs' BI system implementations. The details of the results are discussed below.

CSFS FINDING AND DISCUSSION

Table 2 depicts the average rating results for the respective CSFs in descending order of importance. It contains the consensus outcomes and shows that the Delphi study captured the importance of the seven critical factors, namely committed management support and sponsorship, business user-oriented change management, clear business vision and well-established case, business-driven methodology and project management, business-centric championship and balanced project team composition, strategic and extensible technical framework, sustainable data quality and governance framework.

Notably, data and technical-related factors did not appear to be the most critical in relation to other organizational factors. According to most interviewees, technological difficulties can be solved by technical solutions. However, it was found that achieving management and organizational commitment for a BI initiative poses the greatest challenge, because the BI teams considered them to be outside their direct control. The organizational support is reflected in the attitudes of the various business stakeholders; that is, their attitudes to change, time, cost, technology, and project scope. Based on a large-scale survey result, Watson and Haley (1997) pointed out that the most critical factors for successful implementations were organizational in nature. Committed management support and adequate resources were found to determine the implementation success, because these factors worked to overcome socio-political resistance, address change-management issues, and increase organizational buy-in. This finding was also converging with Gartner's recent observation that "overcoming complex organizational dynamics will become the most significant challenge to the success of business intelligence initiatives and implementations" (Burton et al., 2006).

In fact, the effort of implementing BI systems is highly regarded by the Delphi participants as a business-driven program as opposed to a technological one. The fulcrum of BI program success is thus dependent on the business personnel, whereas technical people are expected to support the analytical requirements via technologies and tools. The definition of strategic BI framework, project scoping and data quality initiatives were considered within the realm of business personnel.

That is, this new understanding emphasizes the priority of business aspects, not the technological ones, in implementing BI systems.

While the specific CSFs may seem to vary slightly between BI systems and general IS studies, the actual contextual elements of these CSFs are substantially different from the implementation effort required for conventional operational systems. Unlike those transactional systems, business stakeholders need to be involved interactively in order to meet their dynamic reporting and ever-changing analytical needs. Owing to the evolutionary information requirements, the BI team has to provide continual support not only on tools application, but also at broader data modeling and system scalability issues. This is in line with the adoption of an incremental delivery approach for implementing an adaptive decision support system, such as a BI system (Arnott & Pervan, 2005). Moreover, organizational and business commitment to a BI system implementation is critical to solve the complex organizational issues, especially in the democratization process of data ownership, selection of funding model, change of business process, definition of the scoping study, data stewardship and quality control, and the provision of domain expertise and championship. The following section presents the CSFs framework consolidated from these CSFs findings.

DEVELOPMENT OF A CRITICAL SUCCESS FACTORS FRAMEWORK

Based on the research finding, these seven critical factors were integrated with the implementation success measures to provide a comprehensive CSFs framework for implementing BI systems. As illustrated in Figure 1 below, this CSF framework outlines how a set of factors contribute to the success of a BI system implementation. It postulates that there is a set of CSFs influencing the implementation success that takes into account two key measures: infrastructure performance and process

Figure 1. A critical success factors framework for the implementation of business intelligence systems

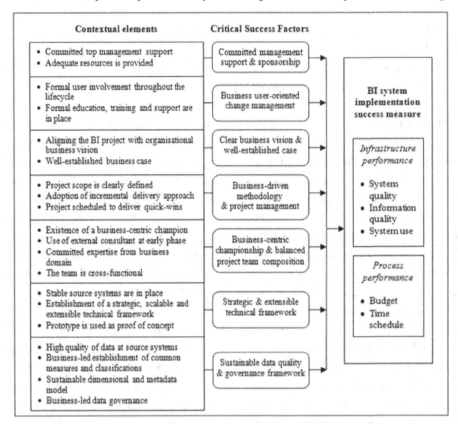

performance. The infrastructure performance has parallels with the three major IS success variables described by (Delone & McLean, 1992; 2003), namely system quality, information quality, and system use, whereas process performance can be assessed in terms of time-schedule and budgetary considerations. Specifically, system quality is concerned with the performance characteristics of the information processing system itself, which includes ease-of-use, functionality, reliability, flexibility, integration, and response time (Delone & McLean, 1992; Rai et al., 2002). Information quality refers to accuracy, timeliness, completeness, relevance, consistency, and usefulness of information generated by the system (Delone & McLean, 1992; Fisher et al., 2006). System use is defined as "recipient consumption of the output of an information system" (Delone & McLean, 1992). These success criteria serve as the opera-

tionalizations of this study's dependent variables (i.e., the critical success factors).

In brief, this framework treats the CSFs identified as necessary factors for implementation success, whereas the absence of the CSFs would lead to failure of the system (Rockart, 1979). Within the framework, each of the CSFs identified by the Delphi study is described as follows.

Committed Management Support and Sponsorship

Committed management support and sponsorship has been widely acknowledged as the most important factor for BI system implementation. All Delphi participants agreed that consistent support and sponsorship from business executives make it easier to secure the necessary operating resources such as funding, human skills, and other requirements throughout the implementation process (Watson et al., 2001). This observation is reasonable and expected because the whole BI system implementation effort is a costly, time-consuming, resource-intensive process (Watson et al., 2004).

Moreover, the Delphi experts further argued that BI system implementation is a continual information improvement program to leverage decision support. They believed that the typical application-based funding for implementation of transactional systems does not apply to BI systems that are adaptive in nature. That is, a BI system evolves through an iterative process of systems development in accordance to dynamic business requirements (Arnott & Pervan, 2005). Therefore the BI initiative, especially for the enterprise-wide scale, requires consistent resource allocation and top-management support to overcome organizational issues. These organizational challenges arise during the course of the cross-functional implementation, as it often uncovers many issues in such areas as business process, data ownership, data quality and stewardship, and organizational structure. Many functional units tend to focus on tactical gains, ignoring the rippling effects imposed on other business units, and one expert observed that,

The whole BI effort cut across many areas in the organization that's making it very difficult, it hits a lot of political barriers. For instance, for a systems owner, they are only interested in delivering day to day transaction, as long as all that done... that's what they care about.

Also, without dedicated support from top management, the BI project may not receive the proper recognition and hence the support it needs to be successful. This is simply because users tend to conform to the expectations of top management and so are more likely to accept a system backed by their superiors (Lambert, 1995).

Business User-Oriented Change Management

Having an adequate user-oriented change management effort was deemed critical by the Delphi participants. The experts perceive that better user participation in the change effort can lead to better communication of their needs, which in turn can help ensure the system's successful implementation. This is particularly important when the requirements for a system are initially unclear, as is the case with many of the decision-support applications that a BI system is designed to sustain (Wixom & Watson, 2001). Significant numbers of Delphi participants shared the same view that formal user participation can help meet the demands and expectations from various end users. No doubt, the user groups know what they need better than a secluded architect or developer that does not have day to day user experience. Hence, key users must be involved throughout the implementation cycle because they can provide valuable input that the BI team may overlook. The data dimensions, business rules, metadata, and data context that are needed by business users should be considered and incorporated into the system (Wixom & Watson, 2001). Furthermore, users can provide input to the process through review and testing to ensure that it meets the goals that they think it should.

Furthermore, when users are actively involved in the effort, they have a better understanding of the potential benefits and this makes them more likely to accept the system on completion (Hwang et al., 2004). Thus through this 'implicit' education approach, it create a sense of ownership by the users. Most interviewees also agreed that consistent support for, and systematic training of, end users must not be ignored when aiming for successful BI system implementation (Ang & Teo, 2000). Many participants emphasized that training should focus on the technology itself as well as on the associated management and maintenance issues. This training is important to equip users to understand and experience the features and functions, and to learn about the configured environment and business rules of the BI applications.

Clear Business Vision and Well-Established Case

As a BI initiative is driven by business, so a strategic business vision is needed to direct the implementation effort. The Delphi participants indicated that a long-term vision, primarily in strategic and organizational terms, is needed to enable the establishment of BI business case. The business case must be aligned to the corporate vision because it would eventually impact the adoption and outcome of the BI system. Otherwise they will not receive the executive and organizational supports that are required to make them successful. Consequently, the investment return of a BI system implementation should be included in those of the business process as a whole (Liautaud & Hammond, 2000). Majority interviewees indicated that the mindset of 'setting an excellent system there, then people will come to use it' is totally inappropriate. In fact, one interviewee claimed that:

A BI system that is not business-driven is a failed system! BI is a business centric concept. Sending IT off to solve a problem rarely results in a positive outcome. There must be a business problem to solve.

Most participants stressed that a solid business case that was derived from a detailed analysis of business needs would increase the chances of winning support from top management. Thus, a substantial business case should incorporate the proposed strategic benefits, resources, risks, costs and the timeline. Hence, a solid business case would provide justifiable motivations for adopting a BI system to change the existing reporting and analytical practices.

Business-Driven Methodology and Project Management

The next factor to be considered is business-driven methodology and project management. According to the Delphi experts, adequate project scoping and planning allows the BI team to concentrate on the best opportunity for improvement. To be specific, scoping helps to set clear parameters and develops a common understanding as to what is in scope and what is excluded (Ang & Teo, 2000). For instance, a Delphi expert gave insight into his experience:

The success of 90% of our project is determined prior to the first day. This success is based on having a very clear and well-communicated scope, having realistic expectations and timelines, and having the appropriate budget set aside.

Hence, adequate scoping enables the project team to focus on crucial milestones and pertinent issues while shielding them from becoming trapped in unnecessary events. Many experts further indicate that it is advisable to start small and adopt an incremental delivery approach. Large-scale change efforts are always fraught with greater risks given the substantial variables to be managed simultaneously (Ang & Teo, 2000). Moreover, business changes very fast and is always looking to see immediate impact, and such an incremental delivery approach provides the tools for delivery of needed requirements in a short time (Greer & Ruhe, 2004). Also, an incremental delivery approach allows for building a long-term solution as opposed to a short term one, as is the case for an evolutionary BI system development (Arnott & Pervan, 2005).

Besides that, some interviewees commented that a BI program that starts off on a high-impact area is always valuable to provide tangible evidence for both executive sponsors and key users (Morris et al., 2002). According to them, adopting this so-called 'low hanging fruits' approach—

projects with the greatest visibility and monetary impact— demonstrates to leadership that there is a payback (ROI) for their investment and it shows it in a short timeframe. This will increase leadership support and help the other associated initiatives to be supported readily. One interviewee elaborated that:

You cannot role out the whole BI system at once but people want to see some key areas. You need to do data marts for a couple of key areas and then maybe a small number of other key reports in an attempt to keep all stakeholders happy. Then when the first release is done and you get some feedback, you can work on other data mart areas and enhance existing subject areas over time.

Therefore, a 'low hanging fruits' approach allows an organization to concentrate on crucial issues, so enabling teams to prove that the system implementation is feasible and productive for the enterprise.

Business-Centric Championship and Balanced Project Team Composition

The majority of Delphi experts believed that having the right champion from the business side of the organization is critical for implementation success. According to them, a champion who has excellent business acumen is always important since he/she will be able to foresee the organizational challenges and change course accordingly. More importantly, this business-centric champion would view the BI system primarily in strategic and organizational perspectives, as opposed to one who might over-focus on technical aspects. For example, as noted by an interviewee:

The team needs a champion. By a champion, I do not mean someone who knows the tools. I mean someone who understands the business and the technology and is able to translate the business requirements into a (high-level) BI architecture for the system.

All interviewees also agreed that the composition and skill sets of a BI team have a major influence on the implementation success. The project team should be cross-functional and composed of those personnel who possess technical expertise and those with a strong business background (Burton et al., 2006). As most interviewees stressed, a BI system is a business-driven project to provide enhanced managerial decision support, and so a suitable mix of IT expertise is needed to implement the technical aspects, whereas the reporting and analysis aspects must be under the realm of business personnel.

Furthermore, most experts posited that the BI team must identify and include business domain experts, especially for such activities as data standardization, requirement engineering, data quality analysis, and testing. Many respondents also agreed with the critical role played by external consultants, especially at early phase. They believed that the lack of in-house experience and competencies can be complemented by external consultants who have spent the majority of their time working on similar projects. As well as being a subject matter expert, the interviewees indicated that an external consultant could provide an unbiased view of solution to a problem. This is because the organizational structure of an engineering asset management enterprise is traditionally functional-oriented and culturally fragmented with siloed information systems design (Haider & Koronios, 2003). There may even be situations where the client possesses the expertise to solve a particular problem, but are conflicted on the organizational ground. An external consultant hence can evaluate and propose an unbiased course of action without having fear of political repercussions (Kaarst-Brown, 1999).

Strategic and Extensible Technical Framework

In terms of strategic and extensible technical framework, most experts asserted that stable source/back-end systems are crucial in implementing a BI system. A reliable back-end system is critical to ensure that the updating of data works well for the extraction, transformation and loading (ETL) processes in the staging area (Ponniah, 2001). Hence the data can be transformed to provide a consistent view into quality information for improved decision support. It is therefore crucial for BI team to assess the stability and consistency of source systems before embarking on a BI effort. Otherwise after the system implementation, the cost of changes in terms of time and money can be significant. A BI expert explained the importance of this factor in detail:

It's more important you got a reliable, consistent, stable back-end system, in my experience, I'm working with a mining company now, in their case, they don't have consistent back-end systems, in some departments, they have just large number of spreadsheets, which call production data into their spreadsheets, it is scary. It's a major impediment to BI system, and you got multiple bits over all the places.

Another prime element concerned by the respondents was that the technical framework of a BI system must be able to accommodate scalability and extendibility requirements. Having a strategic view embedded in the system design, this scalable system framework could include additional data sources, attributes, and dimensional areas for fact-based analysis, and it could incorporate external data from suppliers, contractors, regulatory bodies, and industry benchmarks (Watson et al., 2004). It would then allow for building a long-term solution to meet incremental needs of business.

The majority of interviewees also agreed that a prototype is always valuable as proof of a concept. That is, constructing a fairly small BI application for a key area in order to provide tangible evidence for both executive sponsors and general users (Watson et al., 2001). They perceive that a prototype that offers clear forms of communication, and better understanding in an important business area, would convince organizational stakeholders on the usefulness of a BI system implementation. As a result of a successful prototype, senior management and key users would be more likely and more motivated to support larger-scale BI efforts.

Sustainable Data Quality and Governance Framework

The Delphi findings indicate that the quality of data, particularly at the source systems, is crucial if a BI system is to be implemented successfully. According to the interviewees, a primary purpose of the BI system is to integrate 'silos' of data sources within enterprise for advanced analysis so as to improve the decision-making process. Often, much data related issues within the back-end systems are not discovered until that data is populated and queried against in the BI system (Watson et al., 2004). Thus corporate data can only be fully integrated and exploited for greater business value once its quality and integrity are assured.

The management are also urged to initiate data governance and stewardship efforts to improve the quality of the data in back-end systems because unreliable data sources will have a ripple effect on the BI applications and subsequently the decision outcomes (Chengalur-Smith et al., 1999). For instance, an expert expressed his concern:

This is the most underrated and underestimated part of nearly every BI development effort. Much effort is put into getting the data right the first time, but not near enough time is spent putting in place the data governance processes to ensure the data quality is maintained.

Some interviewees further argued that a sound data governance initiative is more than ad-hoc data quality projects. Indeed, it should include a governing committee, a set of procedures, and an execution plan. More specifically, the roles of data owners or custodians and data stewards must be clearly defined (Watson et al., 2004). Frontline and field workers should be made responsible for their data source and hence data quality assurance. Meanwhile, a set of policies and audit procedures must be put into place that ensures ongoing compliance with regulatory requirements as most EAMOs like utilities are public-owned company.

Apart from that, the Delphi participants believed that common measures and definitions address the data quality dimension of representational consistency. This allows all stakeholders to know that this term has such definition no matter where it is used across the source systems. Furthermore, it is typical for an EAMO to have hundreds of varying terms with slightly different meanings, because different business units tend to define terms in ways that best serve their purposes. Often accurate data may have been captured at the source level; however, the record cannot be used to link with other data sources due to inconsistent data identifier. This is simply because data values that should uniquely describe entities are varied in different business units. Once an organization collects a large number of reports it becomes harder to re-architect these areas. As a result, a cross-system analysis is important to help profiling a uniform 'master data set' which is in compliance with business rules. The development of a master data set on which to base the logical data warehouse construction for BI system will ease terminology problems (Watson et al., 2004).

In order to have consistent measures and classification across subject areas, most interviewees asserted that business-led commitment is pivotal to establish consensus on data measurement and definition. Indeed, a BI system implementation is a business driven initiative to support the reporting and analytical requirements of business. As a result, the BI team would use those common definitions to develop an enterprise-wide dimensional model that is business-orientated. Many participants asserted that a correct dimensional data model is the absolute cornerstone of every BI project. A faulty model will surely lead to failure of the project as it will fail to deliver the right information. As noted by an interviewee:

Not understanding dimensional modeling will cause lots of grief later on and make it difficult to answer some questions. Once you have a large number of reports, it becomes harder to re-architect these areas. Better to get it right the first time with a star schema and well-designed dimensions and fact tables. Good use of aggregates can speed report results and make people happy.

Also, a sustainable metadata model on which to base the logical and physical data warehouse construction for a BI system was deemed critical by many experts. Therefore, the metadata model should be flexible enough to enable the scalability of the BI system while consistently providing integrity on which OLAP and data mining depend (Watson & Haley, 1997).

CONCLUDING REMARKS AND FUTURE RESEARCH

This theory building research presents a CSFs framework derived from a Delphi study with 15 BI systems experts within engineering asset management domain. An analysis of the findings demonstrated that there are a number of CSFs peculiar to successful BI system implementation. More importantly, this study revealed a clear trend towards multi-dimensional factors in implementing BI systems. Organizational factors were perceived to be more important than the technological ones because the BI team considered them to be outside their direct control. Furthermore, the contextual elements of these CSFs appear to be substantially different from the implementation effort of conventional operational systems.

The research is likely to make both theoretical and practical contributions to the field of BI systems implementation. First, this study fills in the research gap by building theory of CSFs, addresses issues of concern to practitioners and supplements the current limited understanding on implementation issues of BI systems. Moreover, this research provides thought-provoking insights into multi-dimensional CSFs that influence the BI systems implementation. The contextual elements identified alongside for each of the critical factors and the consolidated CSFs framework provides a comprehensive and meaningful understanding of CSFs.

Not only does this research contribute to the academic literature but it benefits organizations in several ways as well. Essentially, BI practitioners (both current and potential) will be better able to identify critical factors for successfully implementing BI systems. The findings will enable them to better manage their implementation of BI systems if they understand that such effort involves multiple dimensions of success factors occurring simultaneously and not merely the technical aspects of the system. With the CSFs framework, it could enable BI stakeholders to better identify the necessary factors, and to possess a comprehensive understanding of those CSFs. Such outcomes will help them to improve the effectiveness and efficiency of their implementation activities, by obtaining a better understanding of possible antecedents that lead to successful BI system implementation. For senior management, this research finding can certainly assist them by optimising their scarce resources on those critical factors that are most likely to have an impact on the BI systems implementation. Moreover, the management can concentrate their commitment to monitor, control and support only those key areas of implementation.

In the next stage, it is planned to conduct case study with multiple engineering asset management organizations to further validate the CSFs findings. The multiple case studies will examine whether these critical factors and/or any other alternative factors influence the implementation success of BI systems.

ACKNOWLEDGMENT

This research is conducted through the Cooperative Research Centre for Integrated Engineering Asset Management (CIEAM). The support of CIEAM partners is gratefully acknowledged. This article is based on a previous version presented at the IFIP TC8 CONFENIS 2007 Conference.

REFERENCES

Ang, J., & Teo, T. (2000). Management issues in data warehousing: Insights from the housing and development board. *Decision Support Systems, 29*(1), 11-20.

Ariyachandra, T., & Watson, H. (2006). Which data warehouse architecture is most successful?. *Business Intelligence, 11*(1).

Arnott, D., & Pervan, G. (2005). A critical analysis of decision support systems research. *Journal of Information Technology, 20*(2), 67-87.

Brunelli, M. (2006). *BI, ERP top 2007's IT spending list.* Retrieved July 8, 2007, from http://searchoracle.techtarget.com/originalContent/0,289142,sid41_gci1233170,00.html.

Burton, B., Geishecker, L., & Hostmann, B. (2006). *Organizational structure: Business intelligence and information management.*

Carson, D., Gilmore, A., Gronhaug, K., & Perry, C. (2001). *Qualitative research in marketing.* London: Sage.

Chengalur-Smith, I., Ballou, D., & Pazer, H. (1999). The impact of data quality information on decision making: An exploratory analysis. *Knowledge and Data Engineering, IEEE Transactions on, 11*(6), 853-864.

Delone, W., & McLean, E. (1992). Information systems success: The quest for the dependent variable. *Information System Research, 3*(1), 60-95.

Delone, W., & McLean, E. (2003). The DeLone and McLean model of information systems success: A ten-year update. *Management Information Systems, 19*(4), 9-30.

Duncan, N. (1995). Capturing flexibility of information technology infrastructure: A study of resource characteristics and their measure. *Management Information Systems, 12*(2), 37-57.

Fisher, C., Lauria, E., Chengalur-Smith, I., & Wang, R. (2006). *Introduction to information quality.* Cambridge, MA: MITIQ Press.

Friedman, T. (2005). *Gartner says more than 50 percent of data warehouse projects will have limited acceptance or will be failures through 2007.* Retrieved February 21, 2007, from http://www.gartner.com/it/page.jsp?id=492112.

Gangadharan, G., & Swami, S. (2004). Business intelligence systems: Design and implementation strategies. *Paper presented at the 26th International Conference Information Technology Interfaces ITI.*

Gartner Press Release. (2006a). *Gartner says business intelligence software market to reach $3 billion in 2009.* http://www.gartner.com/press_releases/asset_144782_11.html.

Gartner Press Release. (2006b). *Gartner survey of 1,400 CIOs shows transformation of IT organization is accelerating.* http://www.gartner.com/press_releases/asset_143678_11.html.

Gartner Press Release. (2007). *Gartner EXP survey of more than 1,400 CIOs shows CIOs must create leverage to remain relevant to the business.* Retrieved February 21, 2007, from http://www.gartner.com/it/page.jsp?id=501189.

Glaser, B., & Strauss, A. (1967). *The discovery of grounded theory.* Chicago, IL: Aldine.

Glaser, B. (1992). *Basics of grounded theory analysis.*

Glaser, B. (1998). *Doing grounded theory: Issues and discussions.* Sociology Press.

Greer, D., & Ruhe, G. (2004). Software release planning: An evolutionary and iterative approach. *Information and Software Technology, 46*(4), 243-253.

Haider, A., & Koronios, A. (2003). Managing engineering assets: A knowledge-based approach through information quality. *Paper presented at the International Business Information Management Conference.* Cairo.

Helmer, O. (1977). Problems in futures research: Delphi and causal cross-impact analysis. *Futures, 9*(S 17), 31.

Hwang, H., Ku, C., Yen, D., & Cheng, C. (2004). Critical factors influencing the adoption of data warehouse technology: A study of the banking industry in Taiwan. *Decision Support Systems, 37*(1), 1-21.

IDC Press Release. (2007). *Top-ranked business intelligence tools vendors maintain positions.* Retrieved July 3, 2007, from http://www.idc.com/getdoc.jsp?containerId=prUS20767807.

Jagielska, I., Darke, P., & Zagari, G. (2003). Business intelligence systems for decision support: Concepts, processes and practice. *Paper presented at the 7ᵗʰ International Conference of the International Society for Decision Support Systems.*

Kaarst-Brown, M. (1999). Five symbolic roles of the external consultant: Integrating change, power and symbolism. *Journal of Organizational Change Management, 12*(6), 540-561.

Lambert, S. (1995). An investigation of workers' use and appreciation of supportive workplace policies. Best papers 1995*: Proceedings of the Academy of Management.*

Liautaud, B., & Hammond, M. (2000). *E-business intelligence: Turning information into knowledge and profit.* New York, NY: McGraw-Hill.

Lin, S., Gao, J., Koronios, A., & Chanana, V. (2007). Developing a data quality framework for asset management in engineering organizations. *International Journal of Information Quality, 1*(1), 100-126.

Linstone, H., & Turoff, M. (1975). *The Delphi method: Techniques and applications.* Reading, MA: Addison-Wesley.

Linstone, H., & Turoff, M. (2002). *The Delphi method: Techniques and applications (Electronic version).*

Logan, D., & Buytendijk, F. (2003). *The Sarbanes-Oxley Act will impact your enterprise.*

Lucas, H. (1978). The evolution of an information system: From key-man to every person. *Sloan Management Review, 39*(52).

Mathew, J. (2003). *CIEAM business plan V1.0.* Brisbane, Australia: Centre for Integrated Engineering Asset Management (CIEAM)

Morris, H., Moser, K., Vesset, D., & Blumstein, R. (2002). *The financial impact of business analytics.* Framingham, MA: IDC.

Negash, S. (2004). Business intelligence. *Communications of the Association for Information Systems, 13,* 177-195.

Ponniah, P. (2001). *Data warehousing fundamentals.* New York, NY: Wiley-Interscience.

Rai, A., Lang, S., & Welker, R. (2002). Assessing the validity of IS success models: An empirical test and theoretical analysis. *Information Systems Research, 13*(1), 50-69.

Rockart, J. (1979). Chief executives define their own data needs. *Harvard Business Review, 57*(2), 81-93.

Shin, B. (2003). An exploratory investigation of system success factors in data warehousing. *Journal of the Association for Information Systems, 141*(170), 170.

Sum, C., Ang, J., & Yeo, L. (1997). Contextual elements of critical success factors in MRP implementation. *Production and Inventory Management Journal, 38*(3), 77-83.

Watson, H., Abraham, D., Chen, D., Preston, D., & Thomas, D. (2004). Data warehousing ROI: Justifying and assessing a data warehouse. *Business Intelligence Journal,* 6-17.

Watson, H., & Haley, B. (1998). Managerial considerations. *Communications of the ACM, 41*(9), 32-37.

Watson, H., Annino, D., Wixom, B., Avery, K., & Rutherford, M. (2001). Current practices in data warehousing. *Information Systems Management, 18*(1), 1-9.

Watson, H., Fuller, C., & Ariyachandra, T. (2004). Data warehouse governance: Best practices at Blue Cross and Blue Shield of North Carolina. *Decision Support Systems, 38*(3), 435-450.

Watson, H., & Haley, B. (1997). Data warehousing: A framework and survey of current practices. *Journal of Data Warehousing, 2*(1), 10-17.

White, C. (2006). *New CIO spending survey.* Retrieved July 11, 2007, from http://www.b-eye-network.co.uk/blogs/white/archives/2006/09/new_cio_spending_survey.php.

Wixom, B., & Watson, H. (2001). An empirical investigation of the factors affecting data-warehousing success. *MIS Quarterly, 25*(1), 17-41.

Ziglio, E. (1996). *The Delphi method and its contribution to decision-making. Gazing into the oracle. The Delphi method and its application to social policy and public health* (pp. 3-33). London: Jessica Kingsley Publishers.

ENDNOTE

[1]   Implementation refers to an on-going process which includes the entire development of an information system from the original suggestions through the feasibility study, system analysis and design, programming, training, conversion, and installation of the system (Lucas, 1978).

This work was previously published in International Journal of Enterprise Information Systems, Vol. 4, Issue 3, edited by A. Gunasekaran, pp. 79-94, copyright 2008 by IGI Publishing (an imprint of IGI Global).

Chapter 19
Rule–Based Approach for a Better B2B Discovery

Youcef Aklouf
University of Science and Technology –USTHB, Algeria

El Kindi Rezig
University of Science and Technology –USTHB, Algeria

ABSTRACT

This chapter improves the exchange model proposed in Aklouf and Drias (2008). This model has three levels; the authors focus on the discovery level and how organizations find each other more efficiently through the use of a Web service directory like UDDI. The discovery approach that this chapter depicts strengthens the partner discovery process. With the evolution of organizations' Web services and their widespread use, searching for them based on what they provide has become a real challenge. A functionality-based Web service discovery mechanism is then necessary since the functionalities are the most important thing partners look for. This chapter presents an approach that targets the discovery of organizations' Web services according to what they provide to other organizations that might become potential partners using a functionality-based model. The proposed model attempts to express without ambiguity the functionalities of the organization's Web services operations by using an ontology. Moreover, the proposed approach exploits expert systems that aim at adding new business functionalities to Web services according to their rule-base defined by the organization knowledge engineer or the system administrator. The authors have also added a semantic layer between the ontology and the expert systems to make them more ontology-aware. A JAVA implementation has been done to validate the authors' proposal.

INTRODUCTION

As B2B architectures become increasingly more complex though the discovery of what organiza-

tions provide is still limited, the actors in a B2B exchange should know what other organizations provide in terms of their Web services functionalities to choose the appropriate partners to deal with. The classical discovery process is made through Web services directories like ebXML and UDDI which

DOI: 10.4018/978-1-60566-968-7.ch019

are a bit limited in describing the Web services functionalities and what they provide to other businesses.

Web services discovery and ontology usage have become a must in business to business (B2B) interchanges, we noticed this need through some B2B-related works (Aklouf, Y., Pierra, G., Ait Ameur, Y., & Drias, H., 2005). The necessity to discover and publish Web services in a centralized environment has given birth to the UDDI standard (UDDI specification, n.d.) that allows the Web services publication and discovery. This standard has become very popular since it permits the publication and diverse discovery methods of Web services, but the evolution of the business world has provoked a set of critics on that standard, these critics are numerous, we're going to state some of them that we have addressed on this chapter.

The Web services discovery with UDDI is purely syntax-based, this made the UDDI registry little efficient with the evolution of the users' requirements, in a business environment, it would be well to introduce some discovery mechanisms that are more accurate and less ambiguous.

The diverse searching modes provided by the UDDI inquiry API (tModel name, business name, service name, etc…) don't always reflect the Web service functionalities. It would be useful to have a formal way to look for the functionalities provided by the Web services.

The Web services publication methods provided by the UDDI publish API don't imply a formal model to express what the Web services provide to users (business capabilities), thus, the discovery of the Web services functionalities can't be performed efficiently.

Numerous related works have been done to improve the UDDI registry by integrating some semantic Web techniques, for example the approach (Sivashanmugam, K., Verma, K., Sheth, A., & Miller, J., 2003) aims at introducing semantic annotations within the description of the] (Patil, A.A., Oundhakar, S.A., Sheth, A.P., & Verma, K.,

2004). This led to a semantic discovery of Web services (WSs) based on multiple parameters (IOPE: Input, Output, Precondition, Effect), this model has the advantage of allowing a semantic Web services discovery but the WS publisher must be aware of the semantic specification in order to make his Web services reachable with a semantic discovery, in addition, this approach doesn't express efficiently what the Web service really provides to users.

Another approach has been proposed (Patil, A.A., Oundhakar, S.A., Sheth, A.P., & Verma, K., 2004), it consists of publishing for each Web service its corresponding DAML-S profile that contains pertinent information concerning the Web services like the IOPE, this approach is efficient, but it doesn't adhere to the WSDL standard which represents the WS description. Moreover, the Web service publisher must know how to describe his Web services with DAML-S.

Multiple other related works have been done like Akkiraju, R., Farrell, J., Miller, J., Nagarajan, M.Schmidt, M., Sheth, A., & Verma, K. (2005); Benna, A., Boudjlida, N., & Talantikite, H. (2008); and Aklouf Y., & Drias, H. (2007) which tend to integrate the semantic Web with the Web services technology, in order to have a semantic-based Web services discovery, but these approaches still remain incapable to truly express the functionalities provided by the Web services.

In our approach, we focus on what the Web services provide (their functionalities or business capabilities), to achieve this, we have proposed a formal model to express the Web services functionalities supported by an ontology. We have also made the discovery more dynamic by introducing expert systems that aim at adding new capabilities (functionalities) to the Web services.

This chapter begins with an overview of the exchange model we want to improve, then, we present a brief description of the approach objectives. These objectives are detailed from section 4 to section 8, we present the conceptual architecture of the proposed approach in section 9. Section 10 describes the validation of our proposal, section 11 presents a short evaluation between our system and the standard UDDI. Finally we conclude and present some future work in section 12.

THE EXCHANGE MODEL ARCHITECTURE OVERVIEW

This section proposes an exchange model represented by a layered architecture (Aklouf, Pierra, Ait Ameur, & Drias, 2005) gathering the various classes of information necessary to ensure completely an automatic exchange between partners. This exchange model is inspired from several infrastructure proposed in the literature such as ebXML (ebXML, 2001), RosettaNet (RosettaNet, 2001a) OAGI (Randy, 2001), etc. The model with its three layers is also called an integration model within the company processes. This model makes it possible to integrate remotely processes between several companies.

These processes can be industrial or logistic. Integration can require the installation of a workflow system between organizations (Trastour, Preist, & Colemann, 2003). This business model has as main objectives, the reduction of the coordination costs as well as the reduction of durations of exchange of goods and services.

The most categories of information (classes) identified by the model are summarized in the following:

1. Information that allow a system to locate and discover automatically a partner, which provides the service required by the consumer

Figure 1. The layered infrastructure representing the exchange model

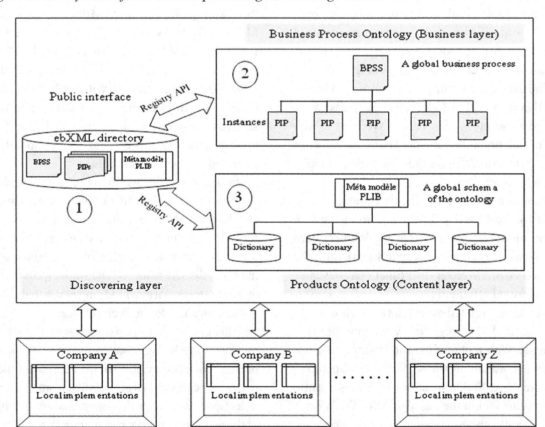

(like a specific search engine for companies and services);

2. Information about the supported business process, gathering different steps to be followed during collaboration. This is defined by several languages and protocols;

3. Information describing products and services used in the exchange (products ontologies describe this category of information).

Figure 1 illustrates the architecture of the model with these three components.

This architecture allows exchange between two or several partners represented by the systems as A, B ...Z, via some interfaces between layers. These interfaces provide services making it possible to deliver the necessary information to the adjacent layer. The three levels represent three parts of the system and can work conjointly to increase the automaticity of the B2B exchange model.

The partner must give some technical solutions describing various measurements taken and standards chosen to adapt the company local system to support a communication with others partners. This requires on one hand, the extension of the internal information system by tools belonging to these various levels and, in addition, the integration of these tools at the local level, allowing each company to have a uniform global system in accordance with the suggested B2B model (Aklouf, & Drias, 2007).

As stated previously, to carry out exchanges between companies using this model, it is necessary to develop the following points.

- Firstly, to use the discovering layer (1) and to have the possibility to locate in an automatic way, the company having the capabilities to answer the requests with the customer requirements whatever their nature might be;

- Then, once the localization of partner is accomplished, a collaboration agreement is established by the layer business process

(2). This layer provides all steps to be followed and executed during the exchange;

- Finally, the exchange can start with the use of a format of contents accepted by both actors (3). This supposes that a preliminary consensus on the nature and the representation of the product catalogs of data exchanged was established previously.

Objectives of the Proposed Architecture

The objective of the suggested model is to set up an adaptive architecture which can be used as a horizontal or a vertical system. A vertical standard is a system which is specific to some kind of activities or some particular products. For instance, RosettaNet is a standard specific to semiconductors and electronic information commerce. A horizontal standard is a general system which defines exchange protocols and information formats without referencing any product or service. The standard ebXML is an example of a model which proposes generic and standardized services for the most industry branches and which can be adapted to particular fields and contexts. This model provides also a collaborative environment allowing industrial managers, the consortia and the developers of standards, to work conjointly or in collaboration in order to have an effective and a reliable exchange system in which the integration of the companies is done with lower cost.

The main objectives of this architecture are:

- the description of an infrastructure that proposes an intelligent module for discovering and localizing partners who propose services and eBusiness catalogues: the most known standards are UDDI (Dogac, Cingil, Laleci, & Kabak, 2002) and the ebXML registry.

- the proposition of a business process ontology model based on the existing standards such as PIP of RosettaNet (RosettaNet,

2001c), ebXML BPSS (ebXML, 2005), BPMN (Business Process Management Notation), BPEL (Business Process Execution Language), etc.

- and finally, the integration of the existing industrials catalogues of components describing objects or services from several industrial sectors. Among them we find, RNTD, RNBD of RosettaNet (RosettaNet, 2001b), PLIB (ISO 10303-11, 1994), etc.

Our principal focus is on the definition of an open architecture allowing the integration of different technologies and knowledge coming from heterogeneous communities. This architecture requires the modeling of business processes adaptable to the needs and the requirements dictated by the specificity of these exchanges.

Architecture Functionalities

This model presents a set of useful functionalities:

1. the possibility of adding new functionalities to the system as a product catalogues models or as a separately developed dictionaries;
2. the possibility of managing applications and data locally or remotely;
3. the factorization of a set of knowledge as standards and business rules useful for the various parts of the system;
4. the possibility of modifying the topology of the model, following the adoption of new standards or the implementation of a new tool (ensure evolution of the system – scalability-);
5. the flexibility of the model accepting the adhesion of new partners without modifying the architecture;
6. the possibility offered by the loosely coupled aspect of the model, which offers the possibility to take into account competences and tools proposed by partners in order to

be used by the defined architecture (Aklouf, Pierra, Ait Ameur, & Drias, 2003).

In the next section we shed light on the discovery layer which is the scope of this chapter.

Discovering Layer

The first task which must be realized by the exchange system consists in finding the partners with whom to collaborate. This part of the system must provide exactly the required service and the contact information about the supplier of services. To satisfy this requirement, a repository (directory) containing business documents, data, meta-data and necessary mechanisms to research and discover partners, must be developed. This module must be carried out with the collaboration of all partners involved on the development of a technical specification making it possible to publish and retrieve information, the companies' profiles and the provided services.

We take advantage of a new approach in discovering partners' Web services, this approach emphasizes the Web services operations by describing them through a new model driven by an ontology. The presented approach also takes advantage of expert systems in order to add new capabilities to the organization Web services using the business rule base.

Objectives of the Discovery Layer

The overall objectives are shortly described below:

- **Objective 1. A formal description of the partner's Web service operations (functional couples):** The proposed discovery approach focuses on what the Web service provides to users, thus, we have added some semantic annotations in the Web service description document by using the

OWL language, this model is described later.

- **Objective 2. A functionality-based Web services discovery:** The clients (users) search for Web services based on the functionalities they provide, this is achieved by making queries that take advantage of the model we have proposed to express the Web service functionalities, the model is detailed later.
- **Objective 3. Automatically adding new functionalities to companies' Web services using expert systems:** We addressed this objective by using an expert system that interacts with the UDDI registry and makes inferences stated in its rule-base to add new functionalities to the Web services.
- **Objective 4. Automatically adding possible compositions between WSs operations based on a rule-base:** We addressed this objective like we did in the previous one, the difference is that the inferences are made based on the functionalities provided by different Web services to make a functionality-based composition.
- **Objective 5. A functionality-based Web services publication with unburdening the WS publisher from providing advanced specifications on his WS:** In order for Web services to be discovered in terms of their functionalities, they must be published according to our proposed model, the publisher **doesn't have to give advanced details about his WS.** This would greatly help organizations that don't have an advanced expertise to describe semantically their Web services.

The objectives are addressed in detail in the next parts.

Objective 1: A Formal Description of the Web Service Operations (Functional Couples)

To describe the Web service functionalities, we associate a couple (action, task) that we called: functional couple which is associated to the Web service operations by adding extra annotations to the WSDL.

Every operation in the Web service has an **action** that is performed against a given **task** for example: (book, flight) where "book" is the action and "flight" is the task.

The tasks and actions are all represented in an ontology to formalize the vocabulary to avoid ambiguities and to add a semantic layer to the functional couples.

Example: The "flight" Web service has three operations that are represented as follows in its WSDL (some parts are omitted for simplicity purposes):

```
<wsdl:operation name="Order"
parameterOrder="t f">
...
</wsdl:operation>
<wsdl:operation name="Book"
parameterOrder="s">
...
</wsdl:operation>
<wsdl:operation
name="Destination"
parameterOrder="x y">
...
</wsdl:operation>
```

To express the Web service functionalities we add a functional couple to every operation in the "flight" Web service:

```
Order => (process, order)
Book => (book, flight)
Destination => (pick, destina-
tion)
```

After adding the functional couples to the WSDL, we get the following WSDL which we called WSDL' (some parts are omitted for simplicity purposes):

```
<wsdl:operation concept="
http://www.owlontologies.com/
Ontology120 7402766.owl#process
*http://www.owl-ontologies.com/
Ontology12074 02766.owl#order"
name="Order" parameterOrder="t
f">
...
</wsdl:operation>
<wsdl:operation concept="
http://www.owlontologies.com/
Ontology120 7402766.owl#book
```

```
*http://www.owl-ontologies.com/
Ontology1207402 766.owl#flight"
name="Book" parameterOrder="s">
...
</wsdl:operation>
<wsdl:operation concept="
http://www.owlontologies.
com/Ontology120 7402766.
owl#pick *http://www.owl-
ontologies.com/Ontolo-
gy12074027 66.owl#destination"
name="Destination"
parameterOrder="x y">
...
</wsdl:operation>
```

Figure 2.

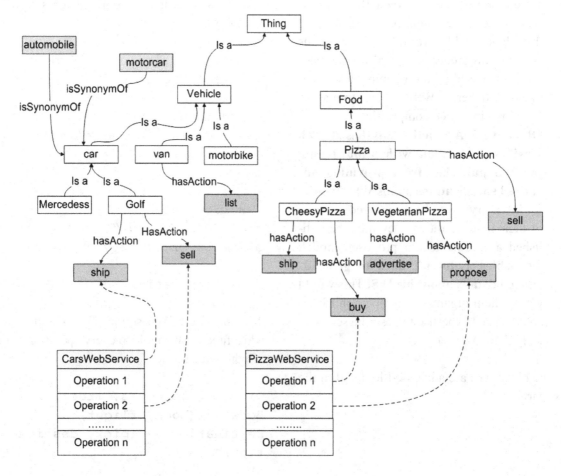

As described by the above WSDL' excerpt, we add a "concept" attribute to every operation in the WSDL, that attribute contains the operation functional couple in this format: action*task, action and tasks are classes of the ontology where they are defined with the appropriate properties as illustrated in Figure 2 of an example ontology

Figure 3 shows how the WS operations are mapped to the functional couples that are represented in the ontology. Action classes are colored in blue, and are linked to their corresponding task classes using the property (hasAction). Task classes are colored in white. Synonym classes are colored in grey.

Objective 2: A Functionality-Based Web Services Discovery

Figure 3 illustrates the process of functionality-based discovery.

1. **Discovery module:** This module retrieve the informal query from the client, an informal query is written in a natural language, the client isn't supposed to know how our system works (functional couples), that's why we send this query to the ESQI.
2. **Expert system of query interpretation (ESQI):** This ES (expert system) objective is to facilitate a functional-based search, by keeping track of specific patterns of all existing functional couples in the UDDI registry, this way, the user who searches for a specific functionality doesn't have to write the query in a formal way (action followed by its task), the query can be written in a natural language, and this ES is responsible of converting it (the query) to a valid functional couple.

Example: Here is a rule named: R of the ESQI. (The asterisk represents whatever character sequence)

Figure 3.

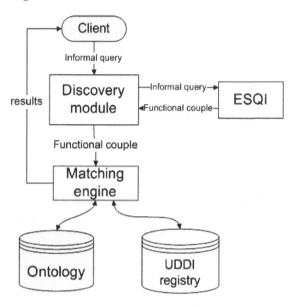

```
R = * boo* flig* => (book,
flight)
```

If the client's query is: "I want a Web service that books a flight" the ESQI returns the functional couple (book, flight) based on what exists in its rule base that is updated automatically when publishing a new Web service.

3. **Matching engine:** Retrieves the functional couple from the ESQI to query the UDDI registry. two matching modes are possible:
    3.1. **Matching with a normal search:** Nine matching levels are applied to the returned result of a normal search (see Table 1).
    3.2. **Matching with a composite search:** Five matching levels are applied to the returned results of a composite search (see Table 2)

Table 1.

Level	Description
Exact	Exact match with the searched functional couple
Synonym	Functional couples whose tasks are synonyms (using the ontology) to the searched one, for example: car, automobile, the synonyms are provided by the ontology.
Plug-in	Functional couples whose tasks are encompassed by the searched one for example (buy, car) is encompassed by (buy, vehicle)
Subsumes	Functional couples whose tasks subsume (using the ontology) the searched one, for example (buy, vehicle) subsumes (buy, car).
Inferred_exact	The functional couples that have been added by the expert systems.
Inferred synonym	The inferred functional couples whose tasks are synonyms (using the ontology) to the searched one.
Inferred plug-in	The inferred functional couples whose tasks are encompassed by the searched one.
Inferred subsumes	The inferred functional couples whose tasks subsume (using the ontology) the searched one.
Failure	No match found.

Table 2.

Level	Description
Exact	Compositions that have the exact match with the searched functional couple.
Synonym	Compositions that have functional couples whose tasks are synonyms (using the ontology) to the searched one.
Plug-in	Compositions that have functional couples whose tasks are encompassed by the searched one.
Subsumes	Compositions that have a functional couple whose tasks subsume (using the ontology) the searched one.
Failure	No match found.

Objective 3: Automatically Adding New Functionalities to Web Services Using Expert Systems

Local Inference Expert System (LIES)

This expert system task is to add new business functionalities that are represented as functional couples to the Web services based on the ES rule base. This ES makes inferences based on the functional couples that exist in the same Web service (no Web service composition) that's why it is called local. This ES contains knowledge rules that are domain-specific (finance, health, ...). The rules are defined using functional couples as the following example shows:

```
R = (authenticate, customer)
(list, product) (receive, order)
```

```
=> (buy, product)
```

The rule R adds the inferred functional couple (buy, product) to every Web service that has the functional couples (authenticate, customer), (list, product), (receive, order).

Objective 4. Automatically Adding Possible Compositions Between WSs Operations Based on a Rule-Base

Composition Inference Expert System (CIES)

This ES is similar to the local inference ES in the way that it adds new capabilities to Web services, but this ES makes inferences based on the functional couples that exist in different Web services.

Example:

```
R = (estimate, car) (publish,
carAuction) (check, creditCard)
(transfer, money) => (buy, car)
```

The rule R adds the inferred functional couple (buy, car) to the composition of the Web services that have the functional couples (estimate, car), (publish, carAuction), (check, creditCard), (transfer, money).

Objective 5. A Functionality-Based Web Services Publication with Unburdening the WS Publisher from Providing Advanced Specifications on His WS

Figure 4 illustrates the process of functionality-based WS publication.

1. **Publication module:** Retrieves the Web service information (WSDL, service name, business name) and the functional couple of every WS operation.
2. **Mapping module:** Annotates the WSDL with the functional couples that must be present in the ontology. This produces the WSDL'.
3. **ESQI:** Retrieves the functional couples and add them to its rule base in order to resolve the informal search queries sent by the discovery module.
4. **WSDL'/UDDI mapper:** converts the functional couples added in the WSDL' to tModels. Afterwards, the Web service is published and the service key is retrieved.
5. **LIES & CIES:** The Web service servicekey along with its functional couples are injected into the working memory of those two ESs as facts in order to trigger their rules and add new capabilities to the published Web service through the Web service updater.
6. **Web service updater:** Whenever there's a match in the rules of the LIES or CIES, new functional couples must be added to the Web services that have triggered the rule, the inferred functional couples are represented in tModels and published on the UDDI registry.

The Discovery Layer Architecture

Figure 5 illustrates the global conceptual architecture of the proposed discovery approach, the crucial parts of our proposal were detailed separately in the previous sections.

Figure 5 illustrates our architecture components along with the interaction between them. The front-end interface is what the client sees, the publication interface allows publishers to advertise their WSs, the discovery interface allows the

Figure 4.

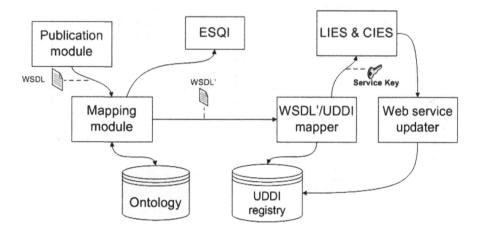

clients to search for WSs, and finally, the administration interface allows the system administrator or the knowledge engineer to manage the expert systems through the rules manager.

The Validation Infrastructure

In order to validate the proposed approach, the architecture has been implemented using JAVA SE (JAVA language, n.d.) and the inference engine JESS (JESS the Rule Engine for the Java Platform, n.d.) to implement the expert systems, we have also used a set of other tools: Apache Tomcat (Apache Tomcat, n.d.), jUDDI (JAVA UDDI implementation) (Apache jUDDI, n.d.), Axis (JAVA SOAP implementation) (Apache Axis, n.d.), SPARQL (Simple Protocol and RDF Query Language) (SPARQL Query Language for RDF, n.d.), OWL (Web Ontology Language) (OWL Web ontology Language Reference, n.d.), Protégé (Ontology editor and knowledge acquisition system) (Protégé, OWL Web ontology Language Reference, n.d.), UDDI4J (JAVA UDDI API) (UDDI4JAVA, n.d.).

Figure 5.

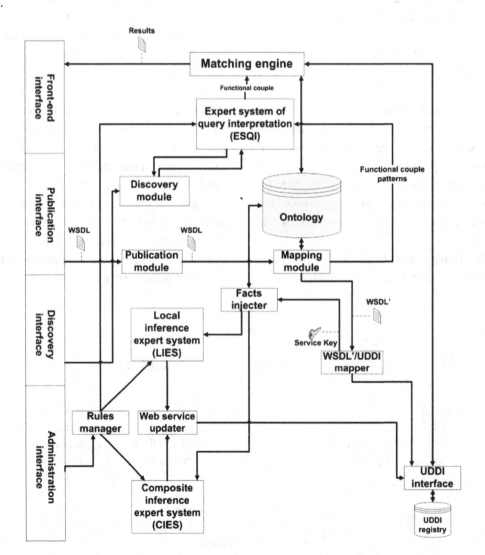

The application has been developed as a Web service, in order to consume it we have also developed a client application. The Figure 6 illustrates the technical architecture.

Figure 6 illustrates a layer-based division of our system, the storage layer which is server-side contains the persistent entities of our system like the UDDI registry, ontology…, the processing layer is the core of our systems and contains all the processing components, this layer is implemented as a Web service, therefore, it is server-side, finally, the presentation layer represents the consumer application.

Our Proposal's Evaluation

We chose to express the functional relevance with a scale of 5 (0 means no functional relevance and 5 means the best functional relevance), the histogram depicted in Figure 7 illustrates an evaluation between and our system in terms of functional accuracy.

- **Semantic-aware search:** Our system honors an ontology-driven search, which increases its semantic abilities comparing to the standard UDDI.
- **Inferred search:** Due to the use of business rule-bases, our system allows users to find inferred WS capabilities. This feature isn't yet possible with the standard UDDI.
- **Composite search:** The composite capabilities of the standard UDDI are decent, though, there's no functionality-based composition which can bring a better mean of WSs discovery.

Figure 6.

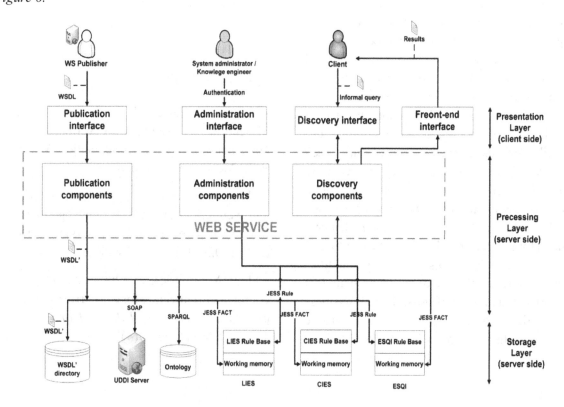

Figure 7.

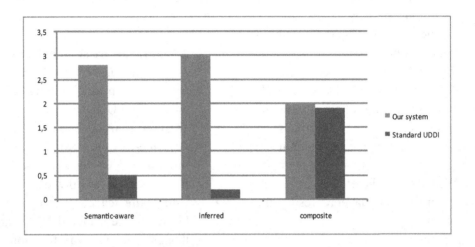

CONCLUSION

We conclude that the way organizations find each other is a crucial part in a B2B process, and, the proposed exchange model that we have previously published had the lack of describing and exposing the functionalities of the businesses Web services to other organizations in order to have potential partners, now that we presented the discovery approach we used, the discovery process is more efficient due to the use of and ontology-enabled discovery on one hand, and rule-based systems to enrich what an organization can offer.

The UDDI extensibility made the design and the validation of our approach possible, our contribution has targeted a functionality-based discovery in order to make Web services more reachable by clients who have specific needs that must be satisfied without ambiguity, we avoided this latter through the use of an ontology that provides a formalized knowledge representation, we have also made the Web services functionalities dynamic through the use of expert systems that can infer a great deal of possible new business capabilities according to the business knowledge provided by human experts. Some perspectives to enhance our proposal are listed below:

- Adding new ontology patterns in order to achieve a more accurate level of semantics.
- Developing a process that adds the rules to the expert systems automatically.
- Developing the principle of functional couples to describe the WSs functionalities in a more accurate way.

REFERENCES

Akkiraju, R., Farrell, J., Miller, J., Nagarajan, M.Schmidt, M., Sheth, A., & Verma, K. (2005, November 7). Web service semantics - WSDL-S. W3C Member Submission.

Aklouf, Y., & Drias, H. (2007). Business process and Web services for a B2B Exchange Platform. International Review on Computers and Software (I.RE.CO.S). Prize Worthy Prize.

Aklouf, Y., & Drias, H. (2008). An adaptive e-commerce architecture for enterprise information exchange. *International Journal of Enterprise Information Systems, 4*(4), 15–33.

Aklouf, Y., Pierra, G., Ait Ameur, Y., & Drias, H. (2005). PLIB ontology: A mature solution for products characterization in B2B electronic commerce. International Journal of IT Standards and Standardization Research, 3(2). UDDI specification (n.d.). Retrieved from http://www.uddi.org/

Apache Axis (n.d.). Retrieved from http://ws.apache.org/axis/

Apache jUDDI (n.d.). Retrieved from http://ws.apache.org/juddi/

Apache Tomcat (n.d.). Retrieved from http://tomcat.apache.org/

Benna, A., Boudjlida, N., & Talantikite, H. (2008). SAWSDL, mediation and XQUERY for Web services discovery. In *Proceedings of the 8th International Conference on New Technologies in Distributed Systems*.

JAVA language (n.d.). Retrieved from http://java.sun.com

JESS the Rule Engine for the Java Platform (n.d.). Retrieved from http://herzberg.ca.sandia.gov/

OWL Web ontology Language Reference. (n.d.). Retrieved from http://www.w3.org/TR/owl-ref/

Paolucci, M., Kawamura, T., Payne, T. R., & Sycara, K. (2002). Importing the Semantic Web. In Proceedings of E-Services and the Semantic Web Workshop.

Patil, A.A., Oundhakar, S.A., Sheth, A.P., & Verma, K. (2004). METEOR-S Web service annotation framework.

Protégé. OWL Web ontology Language Reference. (n.d.). Retrieved from http://www.w3.org/TR/owl-ref/

Sivashanmugam, K., Verma, K., Sheth, A., & Miller, J. (2003). Adding semantics to Web services standards. In Proceedings of the 1st International Conference on Web Services (ICWS'03), Las Vegas, Nevada (June 2003) (pp. 395-401).

SPARQL Query Language for RDF. (n.d.). Retrieved from http://www.w3.org/TR/rdf-sparql-query/

UDDI4JAVA (UDDI4J). (n.d.). Retrieved from http://uddi4j.sourceforge.net/

Chapter 20
Generic Object Oriented Enterprise Modeling Approach Utilizing a Strategic Abstraction Mechanism

Islam Choudhury
Kingston University, Kingston-upon-Thames, UK

Sergio de Cesare
Brunel University, UK

Emily Di Florido
Brunel University, UK

ABSTRACT

A Generic Object-Oriented Enterprise Modeling Process (GOOEMP) is a set of partially ordered steps intended to reach the objective of building a fully integrated, dynamic, object-oriented model of the enterprise. An abstraction mechanism is proposed to enable this process. The process is generic because it applies to most types of enterprises. Enterprise models are the products developed from the process and these can be used by various stakeholders in an organization to: a) give them an understanding of the enterprise; b) design integrated information systems; c) respond to business changes by evolving their enterprise models and information systems in a coordinated and coherent manner; and d) enable the enterprise models built within a particular industry to be reused and applied to many other industries.

INTRODUCTION

High level competition in a global market requires organizations to deliver high quality customized and short life span products and services at a low cost, low lead time, and provide full customer sat-

isfaction at all times. This involves products and services being developed at a higher rate and in reduced time. Enterprises need to be agile, respond rapidly to changes and new ideas. This requires the enterprise to adopt an effective information systems strategy that maps the business needs accurately. The business processes, functions, data and systems must be fully understood, stored, made accessible,

DOI: 10.4018/978-1-60566-968-7.ch020

integrated and supported by a well designed information infrastructure. At present most of the information within an enterprise has been developed in a piecemeal manner. Information is stored in disorganized, disintegrated, incomplete company wide databases. Also the information models that were developed separated out the processes, functions, data, and systems. It is very difficult to access accurate and useful information as and when required quickly and efficiently. Computer-aided modeling of the enterprise is a powerful tool for analyzing business structures and the associated information infrastructures. Enterprise wide computer models represent the business structure, process, functions, classes, resources, strategy, token, flow and information of an enterprise and can be used to develop a suitable information systems infrastructure (Graefe & Chan, 1993; Hu, Harding, & Popplewell, 2000).

Enterprise models can be developed using object-orientation; a powerful concept that can be applied to almost all aspects of the lifecycle of a product from analysis, design, implementation and maintenance. The main benefit gained from using one paradigm throughout the lifecycle is that the difficulties of conceptual transformation from one level to other levels of the lifecycle are reduced. Object-orientation modeling constructs help in understanding, abstracting and representing different levels of knowledge within the enterprise and encapsulating that knowledge within object components. Componentizing the enterprise helps to: a) reduce and mange the complexity within an enterprise; b), provides better understanding of the enterprise; c) helps to develop and represent an enterprise in a model; and d) help in integration, reuse and evolution of the enterprise model. The authors have developed an object-oriented enterprise modeling process by synthesizing, adapting and enhancing previous work in enterprise modeling.

There have been a variety of research approaches, methodologies, and frameworks and modeling approaches in enterprise and business modeling including the following:

- The Information Engineering (IE) approach developed by Martin (1989);
- The Enterprise Integration methodologies and Enterprise Architectures and Reference Models, developed by various researchers such as 'PERA' (Barber, Dewhurst, Burns, & Rogers, 2003; Hu et al., 2000; Vallespir, Chen, Zanettin.M., & Doumeingts, 1991), 'GRAI integrated methodologies' (Williams, 1993 and Chen et al 1997), 'CIM-OSA' (Barber et al., 2003; Dewhurst, Barber, & Pritchard, 2002; Kim, Weston, & Woo, 2001; Vernadat, 1992), 'TOVE' (Fox, 1992), and 'Component-oriented methodologies' (Dogru, 2005; Stojanovic, Dahanayake, & Sol, 2005); A summary of various enterprise integration reference architectures can be found in Chalmeta et al. (2001) and Bernus et al (2003);
- Generic enterprise architectures, frameworks, methodologies and modeling approaches, such as the 'Generic Reusable Business Object Modelling' (Choudhury, Sun, & Patel, 1997; Choudhury 1999; Papazoglou & Van den Heuvel, 2000; Versteeg & Bouwman, 2006), the 'Generic Enterprise Reference Architecture and Methodology' (Bernus & Nemes, 1996) and 'Information Systems Architecture' (Zachman, 1987); Enterprise architecture at work: modelling, communication, and analysis (Lankhorst 2005)
- Object-oriented business engineering and enterprise modeling such as 'Reengineering with Object Technology' (Jacobson, Ericson, & Jacobson, 1995), 'Business Engineering with Object Technology' (Taylor, 1995), 'Object Oriented Business Engineering' (Shelton, 1994), Object Oriented Enterprise Modeling' (Gale & Eldred, 1996), Object Oriented Principles

in Information Systems Alignment with Enterprise Modelling (Strimbei 2006), and the suitability of UML Activity diagrams for Business Process Modeling (Russel et.al. 2006)

- Ontology-driven business modeling'(Partridge, 1996; Daga, de Cesare, Lycett, & Partridge, 2004, 2005).

All the above research has one goal in common, that is to help build enterprise models that can serve as a basis to understand the business and integrate all the appropriate aspects of the enterprise including the strategy, operations, people, processes, information, applications, systems and technology. Some of the main problems with enterprise modeling are: a) managing the complexity inherent in enterprises; b) abstracting the appropriate level of knowledge; c) representing that knowledge in an appropriate manner that is understandable by various stakeholders of the enterprise; d) time and cost overheads; e) reusing and evolving the models over time and as the business changes; f) capturing reusable elements within an industry that is applicable to various other industries; g) evaluating and usefully applying the enterprise models; and h) describing a process to develop enterprise models that would be generic and reusable.

To address the above issues, a comprehensive enterprise modeling process using the object-oriented paradigm was developed by the authors. Such a modeling process is very useful as it provides steps for the business to follow which will allow it to develop an integrated set of enterprise models. The object-oriented paradigm, and especially the concept of business objects, contains modeling constructs which allow for the knowledge within the enterprise to be fully captured and represented in a form that is meaningful both to the business and information systems people. The object-oriented paradigm also allows for the modeling of the data, functions, processes

and systems within the company. These can be encapsulated into different types of components, which can be effectively developed, stored, used and reused. The enterprise models that are built are integrated and coordinated within the company in such a way that the models can easily respond to changes. This will allow companies, safe in the understanding that their information systems can cope and evolve with business changes, to concentrate on improving their business by responding positively to change.

This paper describes an enterprise modeling process which concentrates and develops on, as well as integrating, the work of the following researchers: Bernus and Nemes (1996), Choudhury et al.(1997) and Gale & Eldred (1996). Bernus and Nemes (1996) have developed a framework to define a generic enterprise reference architecture and methodology unifying and developing on the basis of 'PERA' (Barber et al., 2003; Hu et al., 2000; Vallespir et al., 1991), 'GRAI integrated methodologies' (Williams, 1993), 'CIM-OSA' (Barber et al., 2003; Dewhurst et al., 2002; Kim et al., 2001; Vernadat, 1992), and 'TOVE' (Fox, 1992). Choudhury et al.(1997) have developed a Generic Reusable Business Object Modeling Framework based on the work of Jacobson et al. (1995), Taylor (1995), and the idea of business objects by Arrow, L., Barnwell, R., Burt, C., & Anderson, M. (1995). Gale and Eldred (1996) have developed the 'future strategy business planning' methodology to build object-oriented enterprise models which are comprehensive and formal descriptions of the enterprise. They develop their model from general systems theory, conceptual modeling, information theory, and business theory.

Section 2 provides an overall description of the GOOEMP. Sections 3, 4 and 5 explain each of the three levels, conceptual, representational and instance level in detail and with examples. Finally, section 6 presents some conclusions.

AN OVERALL DESCRIPTION OF THE GOOEMP

To understand the modeling process a description of a model is first provided. Essentially, there are three types of models: The conceptual model, the representational model, and the instance model (Burkhart et al., 1992). These models have two main functions:

- Filter out irrelevant detail and thereby display only information that is essential to the task (this involves abstraction)
- To represent that information in a useful and appropriate way to address the goal of modelling.

Burkhart et al. (1992) defines a model as:

'...the explicit interpretation of one's understanding of a situation, or merely one's ideas about that situation. It can be expressed in mathematics, symbols or words, but essentially a description of entities, processes or attributes and relationships between them. It may be prescriptive or illustrative, but above all, it must be useful.'

The goal of the GOOEMP in the context of this paper is to represent the enterprise in a model, taking into account ideas from the business as well as the information systems. It enables the stakeholders to gain knowledge about the business and to integrate the business components including processes, functions, data areas and their relations to one another. The business object models built from the GOOEMP can also be used as a reference point or starting point for design and implementation of information systems and for the analysis of change. The stakeholders of the models could be a number of people such as business process designers, business developers, business managers, systems analysts and software engineers. A generic enterprise model is one that is sufficiently general to be used in several contexts (e.g., by different industries). The generality of the model must be optimized because if it were too general it would be of little use as the conceptual difficulty to convert the general to the specific would be too high. GOOEMP makes use of an abstraction technique, using the genericity dimension (see Choudhury et al., 1997) to abstract appropriate industrial sectors and business domains that are to be modeled. Once a domain has been identified, the model of that domain is built according to the abstraction mechanism explained in Figure 1. This shows the abstraction levels for modeling, mapping and optimizing the enterprise model. It explains the relationships between the business domain and the information systems domain to define an optimum generic level to enable effective reuse of the model. This takes into consideration i) the conceptual difficulty of the transition from business domain modeling to analysis, design and implementation, ii) flexibility and (iii) ease with which the model can cope with change.

The object-oriented paradigm provides appropriate modeling constructs and symbols to enable the effective capture and representation of information and knowledge within an enterprise at the conceptual, representational and instance levels. The object-oriented modeling constructs that are useful for enterprise modeling include objects, abstraction, encapsulation, instantiation, inheritance, specialization, polymorphism, composition, containment and association. The abstraction, encapsulation and representation of things meaningful to a business are referred to as business objects (Arrow et al., 1995). A business object model is an object-oriented representation of a business domain, and is both methodology and language independent. Business object models can be developed at the three levels as described in Figure 2. The three levels correspond with the concept of abstract class, derived class and object in an object-oriented approach. The business object models are refined by either specializing or generalizing the models as required by the designer of the business object model to an appropriate optimum

Figure 1. Abstraction levels for modeling, mapping and optimizing the enterprise model

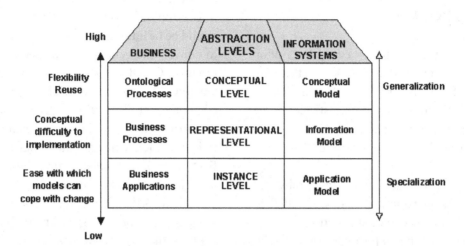

level to enable reuse in different contexts. The different contexts of reuse are: reuse within the same organization that has developed the model; reuse across vertical industries (i.e., companies within the same industrial sector, for example, financial, telecommunications, health, etc.); or reuse across all industries. The final enterprise model would be a collection of all the business object models built and would be referred to as a generic object oriented enterprise model (GOOEM).

The following sections explain the conceptual level, representation level and instance levels in detail. These sections also explain through examples the steps required to build models at each level and the mappings between each level.

CONCEPTUAL LEVEL OF THE GOOEMP

This refers to the generic concept objects within an enterprise such as Actor, Event, Process, Resource, etc. and their inter-relations. These terms are based on and developed from the enterprise ontology (Fox, 1992). These are the most basic terms that exist in all enterprises and can be the starting point to identifying the generic business domains and generic processes in an enterprise.

Figure 3 shows part of a conceptual business object model containing the conceptual business objects and their interrelations.

REPRESENTATIONAL LEVEL OF THE GOOEMP

The business domain can be divided up into various functional domains and the representational level refers to particular industrial domains being modeled, e.g. the customer services domain, business management domain or people and work management domain. The representational domain is built with the Generic Reusable Business Object Modeling (GRBOM) Framework (Choudhury et al., 1997). The interactions of the conceptual business objects allow model developers to identify patterns with which to represent particular business processes and these business processes can be generalized to generic business processes. An example of one pattern that could be extracted from the conceptual model is the Actor - Event - Process - Resource (AEPR) pattern. The AEPR pattern can be found in several domains within an enterprise such as the customer services domain and can be generalized to the core, generic business processes of a domain. Figure 2, section 2 shows

Figure 2. Mapping and reuse potential of the business object models at different abstraction levels

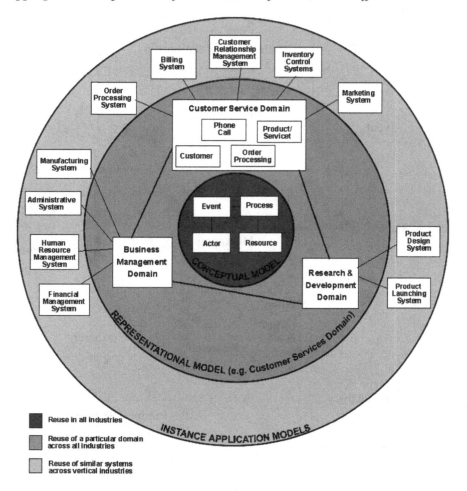

an example of mapping from the conceptual level to the representational level: Actor (Customer) is responsible for an Event (Phone Call) to a Process (Order Processing) to place an order for a Resource (Product/ Service). This pattern can be generalized to the Gain Business Generic Business Process of the Customer Service Domain. The authors have identified many business patterns and generic business processes of the Customer Services Domain of the Telecommunications Industry (Choudhury et al., 1997).

Another important pattern that can be identified is the Process, Role, Actor, Capability (PRAC) pattern. This pattern is extremely important to the next stage of building an object-oriented repre-

sentational model. Figure 4 shows the transformation from generic business processes to business objects with attributes and methods. The tool used to develop the objects and subsequently the overall object oriented business object models was Rational Rose using the Unified Modeling Language (UML). The core generic business processes are identified for the industry. The core generic business processes in the telecommunication customer services domain have been represented in a core business model and is made up of five core generic business processes: Gain Business, Develop Product/ Service, Bill & Collect, Maintain Product/ Service, Launch & Withdraw Product/ Service (Choudhury et al., 1997).

Figure 3. An example part of a conceptual model of an enterprise (For simplicity the details of each link are omitted from this diagram)

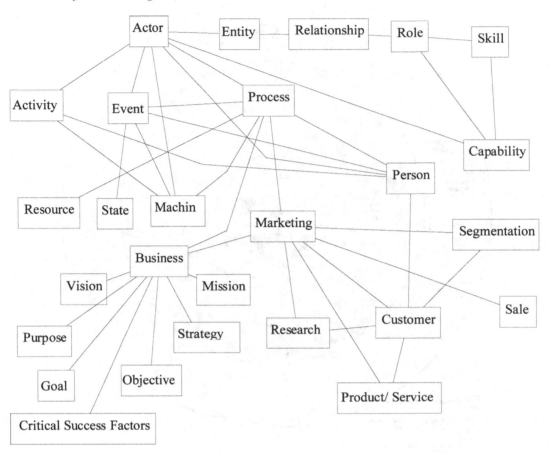

Further studies into the customer services of the retail banking and fashion retail industries have shown similar core generic business processes. PRAC matrixes can be developed for each core Generic Business Process.

Table 1 is a Process-Role-Activity-Capability Matrix for the core generic business process, Gain Business. It is not in the scope of this paper to present all the results but a representative sample of the results is reproduced. The Generic Business Processes can be translated into roles played by actors with particular capabilities that allow them to carry out the process. The roles played by actors can be easily converted to objects with attributes and behavior.

As an example it can be seen that the Gain Business Generic Business Process can be converted to Gain Business Role which has to be carried out by a Business Gainer Actor object. The capability of that actor can be mapped to the responsibility of that object. The capability of an actor object is the total of all the business activities required to fulfill the responsibility of gaining business and is mapped to the operations of the business gainer actor object. The information required to fulfill the business gaining role is mapped to the attributes of the business gainer actor object. The attributes and operations are abstract at this stage. The activities of gain business can be further viewed as processes and the PRAC pattern can be repeated for each activity. This process is repeated until

Figure 4. Transformation of process to objects (PRAC pattern)

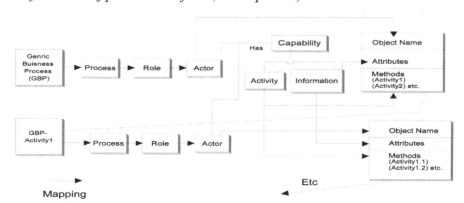

Table 1. Part of a process role activity capability matrix for generic business process gain business found in telecommunications, retail banking and fashion retail industries

PATTERN TYPE	PROCESS	ROLE	ACTOR	CAPABILITY	
				ACTIVITY	INFORMATION
Generic Business Process (GBP)	Gain Business	Gain Business	Business Gainer	1.Handle Customer Contact (in)	Customers, Customer Events
				2.Handle Marketing	Product and Services Portfolio, Orders, Marketing Plan
				3.Manage Sales/ Lead and Prospects	Customers, Customer Events, P&S Portfolio, Sales Leads and Prospects
				4.Manage Sales Account	Customers, Customer Events, P&S Portfolio, Sales Leads and Prospects
GBP - Activity1 to Process	Handle Customer Contact (in)	Handling Customer Contact (in)	Customer Contact Handler	1.1 Manage Customer Dialogue	Customers, Customer Events
				1.2 Identify Reason for Contact	Customers, Customer Events
				1.3 Capture Customer Information	Customers, Customer Events
				1.4 Co-ordinate Customer Contacts	Customers, Customer Events
				1.5 Close Customer Contact (in)	Customers, Customer Events
GBP- Activity2 to Process	Handle Marketing	Handle Marketing	Marketing Handler	2.1 Develop Marketing Programme	P&S Portfolio, Orders, Marketing Plan
				2.2 Establish Monitoring Mechanism	Orders, Marketing Plan
				2.3 Run Marketing Program	Orders, Marketing Plan

Figure 5. Business object component composition for solution designs using the Rational Rose Repository of models and objects - Instance Level Model

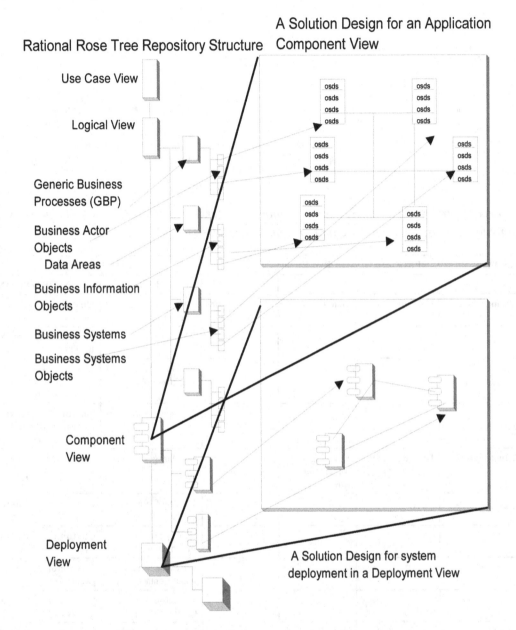

the discrete tasks carried out by each actor and the data areas required to fulfill these tasks are identified and represented in an object-oriented model. The generic business processes can then be represented in an object collaboration diagram and an object interaction diagram. Once all the objects are identified the object collaboration diagram is developed to represent these processes.

The final result of this representational level modeling is a set of PRAC matrixes for all the generic business processes. A large static reference diagram of all the objects with their attributes and operations and links between all the objects

Figure 6. Modeling to implementation

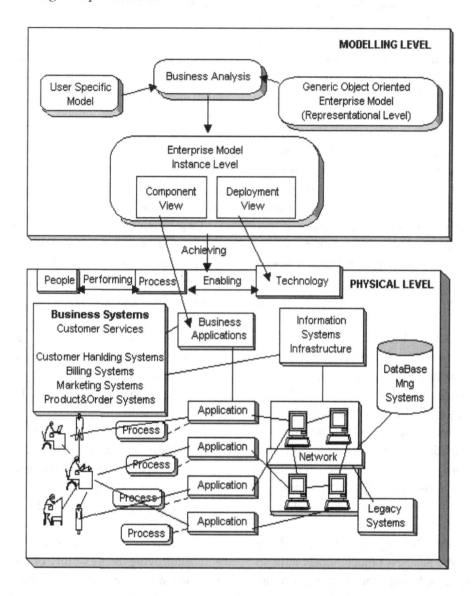

is also developed. Finally, Object collaboration diagrams for all the generic business processes are developed. All these models are stored within the Rational Rose repository, for easy access of all the models, generic business concept objects, business process objects, business actor objects and business information objects.

INSTANCE LEVEL

The representational model can be used as a starting reference model to identify the systems that need to be built within a particular domain such as the Customer Services Domain. The instance model refers to actual instances of systems being built within the domain of interest. Jacobson's Use Case Engineering (Jacobson et al., 1995) approach was used to develop such systems. Each process is a use case containing an appropriate interaction of business interface objects, business control objects and business entity objects. Firstly it is important to identify the main areas of systems development. It was found that in the customer services domain of the telecommunications, retail banking and fashion retail industry four major areas were identified. These were Customer Handling Systems, Order and Product Management Systems, Billing Systems and Marketing Systems. Within each system various integrated applications need to be built. It is left to each industry to develop these systems and applications that suit the requirements of their particular organization. The representational model would aid them in this task.

The instance model is developed from the repository of objects that have been built so far. Figure 6 shows how the various business objects could be used as building blocks and the subsequent interactions would be a solution to a particular business problem. A number of solutions could be proposed. These solution models are referred to as instance level models. These models would be provided to the systems, applications and technology experts to design actual systems for the organization. Figure 5 shows the transformation from the Modeling level to the Physical Level via the Instance Level Model. Application developers and technology experts would have access to all the business object models built so far and they could adopt the most appropriate solution by discussing with the business experts and manipulating the business object models in such a way that the integrity of all the systems within the organization would be maintained. As the business is represented as business objects, business people can communicate their needs with the systems and technology people in a language that everyone can understand.

CONCLUSION

In this paper we have proposed a generic object-oriented enterprise modeling process referred to as 'GOOEMP' for describing the steps required to build an integrated set of business object models within an organization. Object-oriented modeling constructs and the concept of business objects were invaluable for representing the various enterprise components at three different abstraction levels, which are conceptual, representational and instance levels.

Case studies carried out in British Telecommunications showed that the GOOEMP can be usefully applied in a real environment and some of the results were presented. It was important to evaluate the various issues addressed in Figure 1 and Figure 2, section 2. To enable this, two further case studies were carried out, one in the retail banking industry and the other in the fashion retail industry.

The issues that were addressed for evaluation purposes include:

- Identifying the reuse potential of various models at the conceptual, representational and instance levels;
- Identifying the reuse potential of various other components, models and objects identified within the enterprise;
- Improving the flexibility of modeling;
- Handling the conceptual difficulty of implementing a solution to a problem starting from models at each of the three abstraction levels; and
- Checking the correctness, consistency, and usefulness of the information in the model.

From Figure 1 and Figure 2, it can be seen that reuse and flexibility is very high at the conceptual level. This is because the very general ontological concept objects can be found in all industries and this model can be adapted and reused easily in all industries. At the instance level, the models are too specific, and usually apply to one organization. It is possible, if the model is built using the GOOEMP that some of the systems built would be similar to systems required in other organizations in the same industrial domain, e.g. if a billing system is built in a company within the telecommunications industry, a similar billing system could apply to another telecommunications company. However, the systems would be proprietary and very inflexible to change.

It was found that the most important issue being addressed is the conceptual difficulty to implementation. At the conceptual level, it is very difficult to map all the various concept objects on to an application, system or solution design, even though the reuse potential was high. At the instance level, it is quite easy to map on to an implementation but the reuse potential was low. It was found that the most appropriate and useful level for model reuse across industries is at the representational level. At this level generic domains are identified that are common across all industries, e.g. 'customer services domain', 'business management domain', 'people and work management domain', etc. The models built in these domains can be usefully mapped on to an implementation model and the models can also be usefully reused by different companies across several industrial sectors.

The main problem with obtaining information from an organization, and reusing it, is that this information is usually confidential; it represents a company's knowledge and expertise so the company will be reluctant to share their model. However, we can foresee more of this knowledge becoming public over time especially if we can identify the right level of abstraction, generality and granularity. The most useful information that is required is that at the representational level for reasons identified earlier. Related work has been conducted at the Massachusetts Institute of Technology (MIT) which has developed a

handbook of organizational processes (Malone et al., 2003).

Further work is underway to analyze, handle and evaluate the effects of change on these models and the impact it has on reuse using the change dimension of the GRBOM framework (Choudhury et al., 1997). Further work is also underway to carry out a quantitative evaluation of reuse of the 'telecommunications industry customer services representation model', to measure the reuse potential of that model in the retail banking and fashion retail industry. This would be done by carrying out a statistical analysis of totaling up all the generic business processes objects, business activities, business information objects, business systems objects, business application objects, etc. discovered and developed from the case study. One-to-one mappings of each of the objects onto retail banking and fashion retail companies would be attempted. Correlation results will be a measure of the reuse potential.

REFERENCES

Arrow, L., Barnwell, R., Burt, C., & Anderson, M. (1995). *OMG Business Object Survey*.

Barber, K. D., Dewhurst, F. W., Burns, R. L. D. H., & Rogers, J. B. B. (2003). Business-process modelling and simulation for manufacturing management. A practical way forward. *Business Process Management Journal, 9*(4), 527–542. doi:10.1108/14637150310484544

Bernus, P., & Nemes, L. (1996). A framework to define a generic enterprise reference architecture and methodology. *Computer Integrated Manufacturing Systems, 9*(3), 179–191. doi:10.1016/S0951-5240(96)00001-8

Bernus, P., Nemes, L., & Schmidt, D. (2003) *Handbook on enterprise architecture*. Springer.

Burkhart, R., Fulton, J., Gielingh, W., Marshall, C., Menzel, C., Petrie, C., et al. (1992). *The notion of a model.* Paper presented at the Proceedings of the First International Conference on Enterprise Integration.

Chalmeta, R., Campos, C., & Grangel, R. (2001). References architectures for enterprise integration. *Journal of Systems and Software, 57*(3), 175–191. doi:10.1016/S0164-1212(01)00008-5

Chen, D., Vallespir, B., & Doumeingts, G. (1997). GRAI integrated methodology and its mapping onto generic enterprise reference architecture and methodology. *Computers in Industry, 33*(2-3), 387–394. doi:10.1016/S0166-3615(97)00043-2

Choudhury, I. (1999). *Generic reusable business object modeling.* PhD Thesis, South Bank University, London.

Choudhury, I., Sun, Y., & Patel, D. (1997). *Generic reusable business object model - A framework and its application in British telecommunication plc.* Paper presented at the OOIS97 Proceedings of 4th International Conference on Object-Oriented Information Systems, London.

Daga, A., de Cesare, S., Lycett, M., & Partridge, C. (2004). *Software stability: Recovering general patterns of business.* Paper presented at the Tenth Americas Conference on Information Systems, New York.

Daga, A., de Cesare, S., Lycett, M., & Partridge, C. (2005). *An ontological approach for recovering legacy business content.* Paper presented at the 8th Annual Hawaii International Conference on System Sciences, Los Alamitos, California.

Dewhurst, F. W., Barber, K. D., & Pritchard, M. C. (2002). In search of a general enterprise model. *Management Decision, 40*(5), 418–427. doi:10.1108/00251740210430416

Dogru, A. (2005). Toward a component-oriented methodology to build-by-integration. In S. de Cesare, M. Lycett & R. D. Macredie (Eds.), *Development of component-based information systems* (pp. 49-69). New York: M.E. Sharpe.

Fox, M. S. (1992). The TOVE Project, Towards a common sense model of the enterprise. In C. Petrie (Ed.), *Enterprise integration modeling* (pp. 189-204). Cambridge, MA: The MIT Press.

Gale, T., & Eldred, J. (1996). *Getting results with the object-oriented enterprise model.* New York: SIGS Publications.

Graefe, U., & Chan, W. (1993). An enterprise model as a design tool for information infrastructure. In H. Yoshikawa & J. Goossenaerts (Eds.), *Information infrastructure systems for manufacturing* (Vol. B-14, pp. 183-192): North-Holland.

Hu, B., Harding, J. A., & Popplewell, K. (2000). A reusable enterprise model. *International Journal of Operations & Production Management, 20*(1), 50–69. doi:10.1108/01443570010301083

Jacobson, I., Ericson, M., & Jacobson, A. (1995). *The object advantage: Business process reengineering with object technology.* ACM Press.

Kim, C., Weston, R., & Woo, H. (2001). Development of an integrated methodology for enterprise engineering. *International Journal of Computer Integrated Manufacturing, 14*(5), 473–488. doi:10.1080/09511920010029254

Lankhorst, M. (2005) *Enterprise architecture at work: Modelling, communication, and analysis.* Springer.

Malone, T. W., Crowston, K. G., & Herman, G. A. (2003). *Organizing business knowledge: The MIT Process Handbook.* MIT Press

Martin, J. (1989). *Information engineering: Introduction.* Englewood Cliffs, NJ: Prentice Hall.

Papazoglou, M. P., & Van den Heuvel, W. (2000). Configurable business objects for building evolving enterprise models and applications (LNCS 1806, pp. 328-344).

Partridge, C. (1996). *Business objects. Re-Engineering for re-use.* UK: Butterworth-Heinemann.

Russell, N., van der Aalst, W., Hofstede, A., & Wohed, P. (2006). On the Suitability of UML 2.0 Activity Diagrams for Business Process Modelling. In *Proceedings of the 3rd Asia-Pacific conference on Conceptual modelling - Volume 53.*

Shelton, R. E. A. (1994). *Object-oriented business engineering: delivering the distributed enterprise.* Paper presented at the OOP'94, London.

Stojanovic, Z., Dahanayake, A., & Sol, H. (2005). An Approach to component-based and service-oriented system architecture design. In S. de Cesare, M. Lycett & R. D. Macredie (Eds.), *Development of component-based information systems* (pp. 23-48). New York: M.E. Sharpe.

Strimbei, C. (2006). *Object oriented principles in information systems alignment with enterprise modelling.* Social Science Research Network Economy Informatics Working Paper No. 1/2005

Taylor, D. A. (1995). *Business engineering with object technology.* John Wiley & Sons.

Vallespir, B., & Chen, D. Zanettin.M., & Doumeingts, G. (1991). Definition of a CIM Architecture within the ESPRIT Project `IMPACS'. In G. Doumeingts, J. Browne & M. Tomljanovich (Eds.), *Computer applications in production engineering: Integration aspects* (pp. 731-738). Amsterdam: Elsevier.

Vernadat, F. B. (1992). CIMOSA - A European development for enterprise integration. Part 2: Enterprise modelling. In C. Petrie (Ed.), *Enterprise integration modeling* (pp. 189-204). Cambridge, MA: The MIT Press.

Versteeg, G., & Bouwman, H. (2006). Business architecture: A new paradigm to relate business strategy to ICT. *Information Systems Frontiers, 8,* 91–102. doi:10.1007/s10796-006-7973-z

Williams, T. J. (1993). The Purdue enterprise reference architecture. In H. Yoshikawa & J. Goossenaerts (Eds.), *Information infrastructure systems for manufacturing* (Vol. B-14, pp. 183-192). North-Holland.

Zachman, J. A. (1987). A framework for information systems architecture. *IBM Systems Journal, 26*(3), 276–292.

Chapter 21

Semantic Web Services for Simulation Component Reuse and Interoperability:
An Ontology Approach

Simon J. E. Taylor
Brunel University, UK

David Bell
Brunel University, UK

Navonil Mustafee
Brunel University, UK

Sergio de Cesare
Brunel University, UK

Mark Lycett
Brunel University, UK

Paul A. Fishwick
University of Florida, USA

ABSTRACT

Commercial-off-the-shelf (COTS) Simulation Packages (CSPs) are widely used in industry primarily due to economic factors associated with developing proprietary software platforms. Regardless of their widespread use, CSPs have yet to operate across organizational boundaries. The limited reuse and interoperability of CSPs are affected by the same semantic issues that restrict the inter-organizational use of software components and web services. The current representations of Web components are predominantly syntactic in nature lacking the fundamental semantic underpinning required to support discovery on the emerging Semantic Web. The authors present new research that partially alleviates the problem of limited semantic reuse and interoperability of simulation components in CSPs. Semantic models, in the form

DOI: 10.4018/978-1-60566-968-7.ch021

of ontologies, utilized by the authors' Web service discovery and deployment architecture, provide one approach to support simulation model reuse. Semantic interoperation is achieved through a simulation component ontology that is used to identify required components at varying levels of granularity (i.e. including both abstract and specialized components). Selected simulation components are loaded into a CSP, modified according to the requirements of the new model and executed. The research presented here is based on the development of an ontology, connector software, and a Web service discovery architecture. The ontology is extracted from example simulation scenarios involving airport, restaurant and kitchen service suppliers. The ontology engineering framework and discovery architecture provide a novel approach to inter-organizational simulation, by adopting a less intrusive interface between participants Although specific to CSPs this work has wider implications for the simulation community. The reason being that the community as a whole stands to benefit through from an increased awareness of the state-of-the-art in Software Engineering (for example, ontology-supported component discovery and reuse, and service-oriented computing), and it is expected that this will eventually lead to the development of a unique Software Engineering-inspired methodology to build simulations in future.

INTRODUCTION

Commercial-Off-The-Shelf (COTS) Simulation Packages (CSPs) offer an interactive and visual modeling development environment for creating computer models of existing and proposed systems as well as for experimenting with the models themselves. Simulation practitioners in industry extensively use CSPs such as Simul8 (Concannon, et al., 2003), Witness, AnyLogic, AutoMod and Arena to model their simulations. These packages allow reuse of standard simulation components like workstations, queues, conveyors, resources, etc. and thereby provide the building blocks which facilitate the creation of larger models. As these models grow larger and more complex the prospect of simulation model reuse and interoperability is appealing as it has the potential to reduce the time and cost incurred in developing future models. An extension of model reusability is the concept of separate development and user groups, whereby models are developed and validated by one group and then used to specify simulations by another group (Bortscheller & Saulnier, 1992). This is collaborative model building. Collaborative model building is increasingly gaining prominence as

models become large and complex and there is an increasing need among modelers, who may be specialising in different domains, to join together to conduct a simulation study. A few software vendors have started integrating solutions that facilitate such parallel and co-operative model development, for example, the Teamwork and Concurrent Version System (CVS) Integration provided by AnyLogic (XJ Technologies). In particular, the opportunity to interoperate models (running together in separate CSPs on separate computers linked via a network) is attractive as this approach avoids the costs of "cut and paste" integration. In this paper we look at the *discovery and import* of CSP-created models across organizational boundaries within the context of industrial supply chains, thus enabling development and user groups to exist in different organizations. This approach does not allow model information hiding between enterprises and contrasts with the *distributed simulation* approach to model reuse that enables an organization to hide model specific information and data from the other participants.

To motivate our approach, consider the area of Supply Chain Management (SCM). This consists of a series of tasks such as manufacturing, transport and distribution that are undertaken by organizations with the aim of delivering products to their customers. Simulation of the supply chain can identify manufacturing bottlenecks, resources required for on time delivery, adequate stock levels for distribution etc. and help to improve the performance of the underlying supply chain. Each organization that forms a part of the supply chain normally develops models that simulate their own part of the supply chain using CSPs (Fujimoto, 2000). Assuming that all necessary individual simulation components are available then the question is how to link or interoperate them together. Distributed simulation offers one such solution. Distributed simulation can be defined as the distribution of the execution of a single run of a simulation program across multiple processors (Taylor et al., 2001). It allows each organization to run its model within its own site (thereby encapsulating model details within the organization itself) and participating with other sites through information exchange using distributed simulation middleware. Gan et al. (2000), Boer et al. (2002), Mertins et al. (2000), Gan et al. (2005), Taylor et al. (2005), Mustafee & Taylor (2006), Mustafee et al. (2009) are examples of successful distributed simulation using CSPs. There is a growing body of research dedicated to creating distributed simulation with CSPs and the High Level Architecture (HLA), the IEEE 1516 standard for distributed simulation. In an attempt to unify this research, the COTS Simulation Package Interoperability Product Development Group (CSPI-PDG), a Simulation Interoperability Standards Organization (SISO) standardization group, began operation in October 2004 (http://www.sisostds.org/).

The distributed simulation approach to achieving reusability in the context of CSPs faces the following challenges: (1) A lack of widespread demand for distributed simulation in industry has meant that the CSP vendors have not currently incorporated distributed simulation support into their products. Consequently, the organizations

that want to use this approach do not have ready-made solutions; (2) Research projects that create CSP-based distributed simulations do not have access to the source code and are thus limited by the functionality offered by the vendor; and (3) Execution of a distributed simulation tends to be much slower than traditional standalone simulation. For example, the straightforward use of the conservative HLA time advance mechanisms results in a simulation that runs extremely slowly, at times a few factors slower that its corresponding sequential runs (Gan et al., 2005). However, for larger and more complex models, distributed simulation could be a feasible alternative (Mustafee et al., 2009). In order to progress, these issues have to be resolved before the industry can fully benefit from the application of CSP-based distributed simulation. Our approach is a step towards this as it facilitates the discovery of models.

Our discovery and import approach to model reuse in the context of CSPs offer an alternative to the distributed simulation approach. By *discovery* we mean that individual simulation models, which are created by organizations to model their activity in the supply chain, are discovered from among an inter-organizational repository of models spread across the web. The selected models are then loaded into a CSP, modified according to the requirements of the new model and executed. We believe that our approach to enabling CSP-based supply chain simulation has fewer technical limitations, especially when compared to using distributed simulation technique to connect different CSP-based components of the supply chain simulation. Mustafee et al. (2006, 2009) have previously implemented such an approach to model the UK National Blood Service (NBS) blood supply chain through use of the HLA. The authors have concluded that the level of technical expertise required to implement a CSP-based distributed simulation is significant, and for wider adoption of this approach it may be required that distributed simulation middleware be integrated with the CSP packages. This, in turn, would generally require intervention of the COTS package vendors, as source code changes may be necessary. However, the alternative approach to reusing CSP-based components that we present in this paper will alleviate the steep-learning curve that is associated with learning distributed simulation technique. Furthermore, the requirement for the CSP vendor to intervene in the short run may also be by-passed. We therefore refer to this CSP-model reuse approach as the "lighter" approach (the distributed simulation approach being considered "heavier").

Our vision is a web of Simulation Component (SC) models that are accessible to the practitioner. The current representations of web components are predominantly syntactic in nature lacking the fundamental semantic underpinning required to support discovery on the emerging Semantic Web (Bell et al., 2005). Semantic models, in the form of web ontologies, utilized by web service discovery and deployment architectures provide one approach to support simulation model reuse. Improved component reuse supported by ontological models has already been proposed in simulation (Fishwick & Miller, 2004). When considering COTS simulation packages, intrusive activities are not possible when dealing with packaged software as only import or export capabilities are achievable. The tools of the Semantic Web provide a means to construct external descriptions of the CSP models. This external description, or ontology, can then be used to support the reuse of simulation components. Consider a scenario where a large multinational organization uses CSPs to model many of its business activities. Two human processes are undertaken when a simulation is required – the creation of the model and its execution. In order to fully utilize the capabilities within the organization we propose that *model parts* be reused more effectively, better utilizing the expertise within distinct models. In order to support component reuse, methods for describing the models that enable semantic discovery are

proposed. The system supports the discovery of specific model components and their loading into the COTS simulation package. Semantic interoperation is achieved through the use of simulation component ontology to identify required components at varying levels of granularity (including both abstract and specialized components). Once selected, simulation components are loaded into a CSP, modified according to the requirements of the new model and executed. The ontology is derived from existing CSP simulation components and is contrasted to the current simulation ontology. We propose that the evolutionary construction of domain-grounded simulation component ontology better supports the semantic discovery of simulation components. In addition, when combined with hard simulation semantics (i.e., state), concepts from both vocabularies provide improved matching terms.

The chapter is organized as follows. Section 2 presents a summary of pertinent literature. Section 3 describes the Discrete Event Simulation Component (DESC) ontology and the process undertaken to engineer it. Section 4 covers the software tools that use the DESC ontology – the semantic search and component integration software. A conclusion summarizes the work presented.

RELATED LITERATURE

Three areas of research are relevant to the work presented here: *COTS simulation package interoperability*, *semantic web services* and *grid resource discovery*. Together they provide an insight into the decoupling of component simulation models from their execution environment and are used for discovery and synthesis. To outline reuse and interoperability problems in this area we first discuss *COTS simulation package interoperability*. We then introduce the precepts to our approach: *semantic search and ontology*.

COTS Simulation Package (CSP) Interoperability

The simple act of linking together, or interoperating, two or more CSPs and their models, can be extremely complex. This is due to time synchronization requirements and the complexity of distributed simulation algorithms and/or software used to create the link (such as the runtime infrastructures based on the IEEE 1516 High Level Architecture standard (IEEE 2000)) (Fujimoto, 2000). This complexity can often hide the precise nature of what is being shared between these interoperating CSPs. To attempt to simplify this, the Simulation Interoperability Standards Organization's (SISO) COTS Simulation Package Interoperability Product Development Group (CSPI PDG) are developing approaches to the standardization and simplification of CSP interoperability. The first major development by the CSPI PDG is a set of Interoperability Reference Models (IRMs) to help make this simplification possible. First introduced in detail in Taylor, et al. (2006), these IRMs are effectively design patterns for CSP interoperability. The IRMs are a set of guidelines for CSP interoperability and were first introduced in Taylor et al. (2008). The IRMs are discussed next.

IRMs or "interoperability design patterns" are effectively a set of simulation patterns or templates, which enable modelers, vendors and solution developers to specify the interoperability problems that must be solved. The Interoperability Reference Models (IRMs) are intended to be used as follows:

- To clearly *identify* the model/CSP interoperability *capabilities* of an *existing* distributed simulation, e.g. the distributed supply chain simulation is compliant with IRMs Type A and B.
- To clearly *specify* the model/CSP interoperability *requirements* of a *proposed* distributed simulation, e.g. the distributed

hospital simulation must be compliant with IRMs Type A and C.

An IRM is defined as the simplest representation of a problem within an identified interoperability problem type. Each IRM can be subdivided into different subcategories of problem. As IRMs are usually relevant to the boundary between two or more interoperating models, models specified in IRMs will be as simple as possible to "capture" the interoperability problem and to avoid possible confusion. These simulation models are intended to be representative of real model/CSPs but use a set of "common" model elements that can be mapped onto specific CSP elements. Where appropriate, IRMs will specify time synchronization requirements and will present alternatives. IRMs are intended to be cumulative (i.e. some problems may well consist of several IRMs). Most importantly, IRMs are intended to be understandable by *simulation developers, CSP vendors and technology solution providers.*

There are presently four different types of IRMs. These are described in Table 1. The reader is referred to Taylor et al. (2008) for an extensive discussion on the IRMs.

An example of **Type A Entity Transfer IRM** is presented next in relation to a distributed blood supply chain simulation created using CSP Simul8.

UK National Blood Service (UK NBS) is a public funded body in the UK that is responsible for distributing blood and associated products. The analysis of this health care supply chain is of particular interest as blood donors are in short supply, the shelf-life of blood products is relatively short and blood product ordering policies are potentially complex. The UK NBS is a part of the National Health Service (NHS) Blood and Transplant (NHSBT) organization. The NBS is responsible for collecting blood through voluntary donations, testing the blood for ABO and Rhesus grouping and infectious diseases such as HIV, processing the blood into around 120 different

Table 1. Interoperability reference models

IRM Type	IRM Name	IRM Description
Type A	Entity Transfer	Deals with the requirement of transferring entities between simulation models, such as an entity *Part* leaves one model and arrives at the next.
Type B	Shared Resource	Deals with sharing of resources across simulation models. For example, a resource R might be common between two models and represents a pool of workers. In this scenario, when a machine in a model attempts to process an entity waiting in its queue it must also have a worker. If a worker is available in R then processing can take place. If not then work must be suspended until one is available.
Type C	Shared Event	Deals with the sharing of events across simulation models. For example, when a variable within a model reaches a given threshold value (a quantity of production, an average machine utilization, etc.) it should be able to signal this fact to all models that have an interest in this fact (to throttle down throughput, route materials via a different path, etc.).
Type D	Shared Data Structure	Deals with the sharing of variables and data structures across simulation models. Such data structures are semantically different to resources, for example a bill of materials or a common inventory.

products (of which the main three are Red Blood Cells, plasma and platelets), storing the stockpile and transferring excess stock between different NBS centers, and finally issuing the different blood products to the hospitals as per their needs. The NBS infrastructure consists of 15 Process, Testing and Issuing (PTI) centers which together serve 316 hospitals across England and North Wales.

Blood products are stored in the PTI Centers until they are requested by the hospitals served by that Center. A hospital places an order for blood products when its inventory falls below a predetermined order point, or when rare products not held in stock are requested for particular patients. Hospitals normally receive their orders daily and the blood remains in the hospital bank until it is cross-matched (tested for compatibility) for a named patient. It is then placed in "assigned inventory" for that patient for a fixed time after the operation. If it is not used, it is returned to "unassigned inventory" and can be cross-matched again for another patient. On average a unit will be cross-matched four times before it is used or outdated. In practice, however, only half of the cross-matched blood is actually transfused. The original simulation ran on one PC and is described in (Katsaliaki and Brailsford 2006).

The problem faced by this simulation is speed. Mustafee et al. (2009) developed a distributed simulation that demonstrated that considerably length runtimes on a single computer could be reduced by distributing the simulation over several PCs. Without the use of the IRMs it would be difficult to write down the interoperability requirements in a common "language." With the IRMs this task becomes quite straightforward. There are no shared resources, events or data structures; the distributed simulation only requires the exchange of entities. There are two types of entity: orders and blood units. There are no bounded buffers in this model and there is no need to preserve queuing discipline when multiple entities arrive simultaneously. There is a travel time between the PTI Centre and hospitals. We can therefore quite clearly and simply state that the NBS distributed simulation implementation is compliant with **IRM Type A Entity Transfer.**

The distributed simulation (interoperability) implementation of the NBS blood supply chain shows how other supply chain simulations might be implemented (and some of the associated issues). However, the models still need to be found/discovered. This is particularly difficult if models exist across organizational boundaries. To began to explain our approach we now discuss the background to semantic search and ontologies.

Semantic Web Services, Semantic search and Ontology

Semantic search has been applied to both semantic web services and grid resource discovery with a common reliance on knowledge modeled through ontologies. Ontology itself is a specification of a representational vocabulary for a shared domain of discourse – with definitions of classes, relations, functions, and other objects (Gruber, 1993). It is an explicit specification of a conceptualization. The term is borrowed from philosophy, where an ontology is a systematic account of existence (Gruber, 1993). In borrowing the term ontology and placing it into an engineering discipline, two distinct usage types emerge in the creation of these specifications: The theoretic (deductive) approach and the pragmatic (inductive approach) (Geerts & McCarthy, 1999). It is the pragmatic approach that is adopted in this paper – focusing on the engineering of knowledge from CSP models.

The Semantic Web provides the knowledge structure and reasoning about a web of models. Such knowledge is applied within the context of a grid of CSPs that are able to execute discovered models. The Semantic Web (Berners-Lee et al, 2001) aims to uncover knowledge about domains so as to better support discovery, integration and understanding of resident objects. Semantic web services (SWS) refine this vision (McIlraith et al., 2001) making web services "computer-interpretable, use apparent, and agent-ready". With this web of services comes a need to describe explicitly and in a form able to be read by computers.

Current intersections between web services and the Semantic Web have delivered a diverse body of research. The agent community (McIlraith et al., 2001; Gibbins et al., 2003; Martin et al., 1999) has recognized the benefit of ontology if computer-to-computer web architectures are to be achieved. Combining service and domain ontology is seen as a key to achieving service synthesis (Chen et al., 2003). Work on service ontology is currently centered on the OWL-S and WSMO

groups. Recognizing the progress, by the DAML Consortium and others, attention has moved from ontology languages to specific application areas like services. A discussion of semantic web services would not be complete without coverage of the OWL-S upper ontology model (WSMO being similar in nature). The OWL-S high level model describes the relationship between the differing service decompositions (see Figure 1) (Chen at al., 2003; Ankolekar et al., 2001). A resource provides a service that is represented by the ServiceProfile, described by the ServiceModel and supported by the ServiceGrounding. Generally, the profile describes the service in a high level way (enough to discover the service), the model describes the detail of how it works and can be used to: (1) perform more in-depth analysis of whether the service meets a need, (2) to compose service descriptions from multiple services to perform a specific task, (3) during enactment, to co-ordinate activities from participants and (4) to monitor execution (Ankolekar et al., 2001). The service grounding details practical access and has converged with WSDL.

OWL-S (and WSMO) (Lara et al., 2004) provide generalized models for describing services. Others have identified the need for specialized common concepts within a web service context (Lara et al., 2004; Cardoso & Sheth, 2003; Paolucci et al., 2002; Curbera et al., 2002; Tosic et al, 2002), with one example being quality of service. These concepts represent glue homogenizing a wealth of asymmetrically described web resources. New issues become pertinent in a Semantic Web of a "great number of small ontological components consisting largely of pointers to each other" (Hendler, 2001). This semantic web service environment, with recognition of the need to combine service and domain ontologies, warrants research that identifies practical approaches for businesses to combine the service ontology with existing or new domain ontologies. The foremost question in semantic service orientation is how best this should be undertaken in the context of simulation.

Figure 1. OWL-S upper ontology

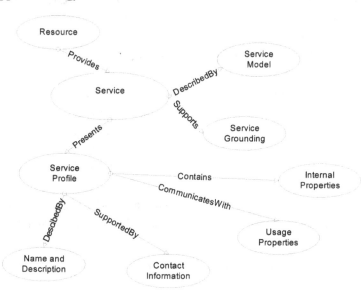

Transporting this vision to a simulation environment with a web of simulation components has several challenges. Combining distributed SC models into a new model requires that they are discovered. Consequently, explicit, computer readable knowledge is required for such search tasks. Knowledge in the form of ontologies has already been applied to simulation (Fishwick & Miller, 2004) with work by the University of Florida on simulation translation and University of Georgia on a taxonomy of simulation objects called DeMO. DeMO provides a precise description of simulation models with hard semantics. In order to realize a vision for SCs, similar to that of SWS, requires that the domain being simulated is represented explicitly (an OWL ontology (Smith et al., 2004)). The DeMO ontology (Fishwick & Miller, 2004) is an upper ontology that details events, activities and processes. Hard semantics work perfectly if all stakeholders adopt the single model. If this is not the case, and with only the CSP SCs, a transformation directly to such a model will likely miss tacit domain concepts that may help any subsequent SC search activity.

The eXtensible Modeling and Simulation Framework (XMSF) is defined as a set of composable standards, profiles and recommended practices for web-based modeling and simulation. XMSF prescribes the use of ontologies for the definition, approval and interoperability of complimentary taxonomies that may be applied across multiple simulation domains (Bhatt et al., 2004). In military modeling and simulation, the study of ontology is recognized as important in developing techniques that would allow semantic interoperability between simulation systems and to this effect the ontology of C2IEDM (Command and Control Information Exchange Data Model) has been created to further studies on enabling interchange of data between two or more systems (Tolk & Turnitsa, 2004). Work is also underway for creating an ontology for physics which would represent physics-based model semantics in modeling and simulation. Its intention is to capture the concepts of physical theories in a formal language so as to support various forms of automated processing that are currently not supported (Collins, 2004). An ontology for the representation of data pertaining to a Synthetic Environment called sedOnto (Synthetic Environment Data Representation Ontology) has been proposed Bhatt et al., 2004). Finally, ongoing work is looking into establishing an ontology for BML, an unambiguous language to command and control forces and equipment (Tolk & Blais, 2005). We now present our ontology-based approach.

SIMULATION COMPONENT ONTOLOGY

Requirement for Semantic Search

The globalization of many organizations and industries often results in a fragmentation and heterogeneity of knowledge produced by its domain experts. In order to synthesize the most appropriate knowledge in a model, the best available model parts must first be found. Syntactic and taxonomic approaches limit the precision in which SCs can be related to the domain. Typical

Figure 2. DESC-restaurant ontology structure

Figure 3. DeMO ontology structure

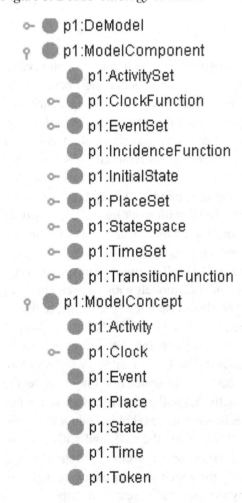

issues are that a component may not fit neatly into a prescribed category or simple use of synonyms to describe the component.

The Discrete Event Simulation Component Ontology

The Discrete Event Simulation Component (DESC) ontology resulted from two distinct research activities: (1) the transformation of CSP models into OWL ontology files and (2) semantic search scenarios being carried out against the OWL files. Snapshots of DeMO and DESC ontologies are presented in figures 2 and 3. The differences are apparent with DeMO focus-

ing on the component properties and DESC on the component in relation to the domain. Links between the two models are achieved through referencing the DeMO:ModelComponent from the DESC:SimulationConcept when it relates to an available component model. Additionally, the DeMO ontology is imported by the DESC ontology so that the latter can use classes and properties of the former (for example, when describing a business concept that is a specific *state* or *activity* in the simulation).

The ontology was created using the Protégé tool from Stamford University (with OWL plugins) (http://protege.stanford.edu/). A decision was made to ground the ontology in the domain

Table 2. Process for deriving semantic content from CSP models

Activities	Description	Impact
Component Extraction	Specific components are extracted to form distinct models. These are stored in the DESC library (a standard web server).	CSP models SC Models
Component Typing	A new class is added to the OWL ontology to represent the SC. Similar classes are grouped under a type.	OWL Classes
Component Dependency Models	Extended DeMO properties are used to define dependencies between services. E.g. StateDependency. Reference DeMO concepts when describing business properties (e.g. ThinkingTable has a DeMO state property). New classes and properties are created for previously implied activities etc. (e.g. Serving is a created from an analysis of table in ordering and eating).	OWL Properties New OWL Classes and properties implied from the model
Ontology Testing	The finalized ontology is loaded into the SEDI4G server and several search tasks are undertaken.	DESC OWL File

Figure 4. Simul8 model

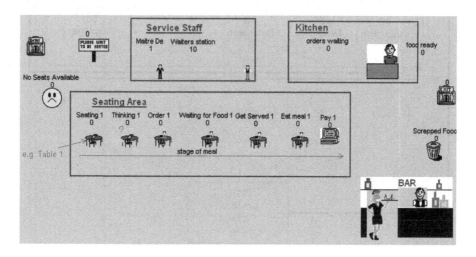

language of existing SCs as opposed to using a particular service ontology such as OWL-S or WSMO.

Ontology Engineering

A number of activities were carried out to transform three CSP models into an ontological form, i.e. as files written in the Web Ontology Language (OWL). The process included the decoupling of the SCs from the model by placing distinct component models into a web-based component library (URI accessible). The framework of the activities carried out in this work is detailed in Table 2. The framework evolved as each CSP

model was deconstructed and transformed into ontology classes (including relations to dependent or related classes). Realization of the need for a DESC ontology resulted from this process – which included the adoption of DeMO for hard component semantics.

The ontology engineering process resulted in DESC-RESTAURANT (Figure 2), DESC-KITCHEN and DESC-AIRPORT models (OWL Files). Each provided more component returns as concept inferencing was able to traverse the concept tree and return additional suitable candidates. The process undertaken to engineer the domain simulation ontology provides the basis for subsequent modelers to reference and extend

Figure 5. Discovery architecture

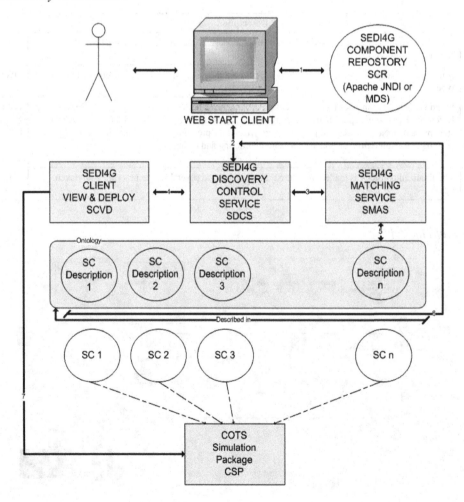

the domain ontology; thus achieving richer search results and evolving into a large component ontology. The ontology engineering process systematically analyses the CSP model, of which figure 4 is a simple example.

DISCOVERY AND IMPORT OF SIMULATION COMPONENTS

Our *discovery and import* approach aimed at CSP model reuse enables us to (1) semantically search for the desired simulation models and (2) parse and import the identified models into a simulation package. For our demo application we have used CSP Simul8. Simul8 enables users to rapidly construct accurate, flexible and robust simulations using an easy-to-use visual modeling interface (Curbera et al., 2002). However, our discovery and import architecture has the potential to support any CSP that allows an external program to perform basic operations such as opening the CSP and loading a model through its Component Object Model (COM) interface (Gray, et al., 1998). COM is a Microsoft technology that allows different software components to communicate with each other by means of interfaces (Tosic et al, 2002). The discovery component of our architecture (described in section 4.1) can be used with very little change to support other CSPs. The parse and import component, however, would require implementation of a CSP specific parser (described in section 4.2) and cannot be reused.

Design of Component Discovery System

The component discovery system is an extension of the SEDI4G architecture (Bell & Ludwig, 2005). Extending the application to support simulation component (model) (SC) descriptions as well as grid services required only minor configuration changes to support the new OWL DESC ontology. The semantic discovery system shown is figure

5 comprises a set of web services (SCVD, SDCS and SMAS).

The discovery process begins by identifying the web services and ontology required to carry out semantic search. The choices are directed by the ontology size and service placement on the network (represented by the grey flexible services and data in Fig. 1). Thus, Step 1 involves the selection of which discovery control service (SDCS), knowledge base and matching service best fit the user requirement – specified as text strings. This information is sent to SDCS together with the search parameters (2). SDCS then calls the KB based matching service SMAS (based on OWLJessKB (http://edge.cs.drexel.edu/assemblies/software/owljesskb/)) (3) that in turn loads the KB and rules (5). The matching is carried out and returned to SDCS for use in one of the client components (4). The SDCS service can optionally provide the resource properties, the dynamic state of each service, alongside the service choices (6). Finally the returned components are displayed in a web start client (SCSV holding the component options on the server side) allowing selected components to be deployed into the CSP. The deployment is simple in nature, loading server side XML into the CSP. A more robust solution would provide transformation capabilities as has been done by Fishwick and Miller (2004).

The matching algorithm is semantic and uses an ontology and a reasoning engine. The assumption in this paper is that an ontology is a catalogue of the types of "things" derived from existing simulation models. Types in the ontology represent the predicates, word meanings, or concepts and relation types of the language when used to discuss topics in the domain (Bell and Ludwig, 2005) – in this paper these are SCs.

To summarize, the matching algorithm comprises two steps; the initialization of the knowledge base and the search. During the initialization phase the ontology is loaded transforming ontological classes into facts that have rules applied using the Rete algorithm (Forgy, 1982). During the search inferences are made from the facts (using Java Expert System Shell (Jess) queries to identify similarities in properties and subclass relations – see (Bell and Ludwig, 2005)) identifying semantically matched SCs. For example, when searching for a component to simulate a restaurant table – several are returned that model different states.

Design of CSP Model Parser and Importer

The discovery architecture detailed in the previous section is used by the CSP Model Parser and Importer (CMPI) software to conduct a semantic search for existing models. This search is conducted by calling a web service defined in the component discovery architecture, which takes a search string as parameter and returns an enumeration of unique resource names (URN) and corresponding unique resource locators (URL) for each model returned by the matching algorithm. CMPI then provides the user an option to (1) download the models into the local system for introspection or (2) import them directly into the new model being built through reuse of the discovered components.

If the user chooses option (1) the model can be downloaded into the local system by clicking on the URL, as with any file download from the Internet. The file downloaded is an XML representation of the Simul8 model that was discovered. If the user chooses option (2) the URN is passed as a parameter to yet another web service, which returns the XML representation of the model as a SOAP attachment. The nature of this web service is synchronous and this allows the CMPI to block further execution of the code until the XML file has been received.

The merging of the existing model (being built through reuse of discovered models and model components) with the new model requires a CSP specific parsing operation. Since both the models in question have an XML representation, we employ a text parsing mechanism which traverses

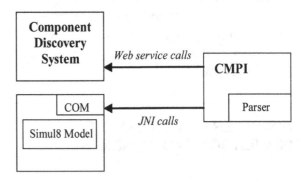

Figure 6. Architecture of dependencies of CMPI

through the XML hierarchy of these models and outputs a third XML file containing assimilated results from both. This new XML file is now loaded into the CSP and the user is presented with the overall model. It should be added that the text parsing mechanism is heavily dependent on the specific knowledge of Simul8. However, this is not a major problem because a model can be opened in Simul8, copied into the clipboard and pasted into another Simul8 model. This solution would alleviate the need for a model parser.

The CMPI software is written in Java and it uses the Simul8 COM interface to interact with Simul8 using Java Native Technology (Sun, 2003). CMPI invokes web service calls to communicate with the component discovery system. It also includes a CSP specific parser component which, as has been discussed in the previous paragraph, can be considered optional. The architecture and dependencies of CMPI is shown in Figure 6.

CONCLUSION

The paper presents a novel approach to CSP model reuse and interoperability. The approach adopts a simulation component ontology and semantic search architecture. The approach to modeling simulation components focuses on the specific application domains. In relating each component to a type collection and each other enables the search process to better identify likely semantic matches. Several Simul8 models are transformed into OWL ontologies and then used by a web service based semantic search and component deployment architecture. The research has demonstrated: (1) a new, lighter approach to CSP model reuse and (2) the benefits of semantic search to this field of research. We now critically discuss the shortcomings of this research with regards to each of the aforementioned points in order to provide an overview of how we intend to address these limitations in our future work.

Although it can be argued that our 'lighter' semantics-based approach has a shorter learning curve when compared to the 'heavier' distributed simulation approach, it is still true that the simulation modeler in industry will have to be well acquainted with Software Engineering concepts such as semantics-based interoperability, software component reuse and ontologies. Furthermore, our approach is currently based on a particular simulation package (Simul8). Although it may be intuitive to imagine a scenario in which model components, developed in heterogeneous CSPs by different modelers, are discovered and then imported to a specific CSP to facilitate intra-CSP model reuse, in reality this is a distant objective. One reason for this is that the CSPs are "black boxes" and have been designed and implemented to exist in isolation.

Thus, one model component developed in a specific CSP can only be imported in other instance of the same CSP. In order to circumvent this limitation of our otherwise CSP-neutral ontology-based SEDI4G architecture, we plan to conduct further research using CSP AnyLogic and a three-phase CSP emulator. We intend to conduct a "proof-of-concept" study which would attempt to show that simulation model reuse across CSPs is achievable. The choice of CSP AnyLogic and the CSP emulator, which had been implemented for an earlier study by Mustafee and Taylor (2006), is dictated by the fact that both AnyLogic and the CSP emulator support the Java language. Thus we plan to investigate the scope for simulation component discovery (using the DESC ontology and

the SEDI4G architecture) and reuse in the context of heterogeneous CSPs. We would consider CSP AnyLogic and CSP emulator as the exemplar CSP application for our study.

This research has also demonstrated the benefits of semantic search to the field of simulation. Semantic search and reusable software components are two concepts we have borrowed from Software Engineering. There is scope to learn more. The authors are particularly interested in building a framework, which would help create reusable simulation components and would ultimately enable modelers to build models using these reusable and interoperable components.

REFERENCES

Ankolekar, A., Burstein, M., Hobbs, J. R., Lassila, O., Martin, D., McDermott, D., et al. (2001). DAML-S: Semantic Markup for Web Services. *International Semantic Web Working Symposium (SWWS)*, 348-363.

Bell, D., de Cesare, S., & Lycett, M. (2005). Semantic transformation of Web services. *On The Move 2005 (SWWS 2005 Workshop)*, 2005, 856-865.

Bell, D., & Ludwig, S. A. (2005). Grid Service Discovery in the Financial Markets Sector. *Journal of Computing and Information Technology*, *13*(4), 265–170. doi:10.2498/cit.2005.04.02

Berners-Lee, T., Hendler, J., & Lassila, O. (2001). The Semantic Web. *Scientific American*, *284*, 34–43.

Bhatt, M., Rahayu, W., & Sterling, G. (2004). sedOnto: A Web enabled ontology for synthetic environment representation based on the SEDRIS specification. *Fall Simulation Interoperability Workshop*, Boer, C. A., Verbraeck, A., & Veeke, H. P. M. (2002). Distributed simulation of complex systems: Application in container handling. *European Simulation Interoperability Workshop*

Bortscheller, B. J., & Saulnier, E. T. (1992). Model reusability in a graphical simulation package. In *Proceedings of the 1992 Winter Simulation Conference* (pp. 764-772).

Cardoso, J., & Sheth, A. (2003). Semantic e-workflow composition. *Journal of Intelligent Information Systems, 21*, 191–225. doi:10.1023/A:1025542915514

Chen, L., Shadbolt, N. R., Goble, C., Tao, F., Cox, S. J., Puleston, C., & Smart, P. (2003). Towards a knowledge-based approach to semantic service composition. *Second International Semantic Web Conference (ISWC2003)*.

Collins, J. B. (2004). Standardizing an ontology of physics for modeling and simulation. *Fall Simulation Interoperability Workshop*.

Concannon, K. H., Hunter, K. I., & Tremble, J. M. (2003). Dynamic scheduling II: SIMUL8-planner simulation-based planning and scheduling." In *Proceedings of the 2003 Winter Simulation Conference* (pp. 1488-1493).

Curbera, F., Duftler, M., Khalaf, R., Nagy, W., Mukhi, N., & Weerawarana, S. (2002). Unraveling the Web services Web - An introduction to SOAP, WSDL, and UDDI. *IEEE Internet Computing, 6*, 86–93. doi:10.1109/4236.991449

Fishwick, P. A., & Miller, J. A. (2004). Ontologies for modeling and simulation: Issues and approaches. In *Proceedings of the 2004 Winter Simulation Conference* (pp. 259-264).

Forgy, C. L. (1982). Rete: A Fast Algorithm for the Many Pattern/Many Object Pattern Match Problems. *Artificial Intelligence, 19*, 17–37. doi:10.1016/0004-3702(82)90020-0

Fujimoto, R. M. (2000) *Parallel and Distributed Simulation Systems*. New York: John Wiley & Sons Inc.

Gan, B. P., Liu, L., Jain, S., Turner, S. J., Cai, W., & Hsu, W. (2000). Manufacturing supply chain management: Distributed supply chain simulation across enterprise boundaries. In *Proceedings of the 2000 Winter Simulation Conference* (pp. 1245-1251).

Gan, B. P., Yoke, M., Low, H., Wang, X., & Turner, S. J. (2005). Using manufacturing process flow for time synchronization in HLA-based simulation. *IEEE International Symposium on Distributed Simulation and Real-Time Applications* (pp. 148-157).

Geerts, G. & McCarthy, W.E. (1999). An accounting object infrastructure for knowledge-based enterprise models. *IEEE Intelligent Systems & their Applications*.

Gibbins, N., Harris, S., & Shadbolt, N. (2003). Agent-based semantic Web services. In *Proceedings of the 12th International Conference on World Wide Web* (pp. 710-717). Budapest, Hungary: ACM Press.

Gray, D. N., & Hotchkiss, J., LaForge, Shalit, S. A., & Weinberg, T. (1998). Modern languages and Microsoft's component object model. *Communications of the ACM, 41*, 55–65. doi:10.1145/274946.274957

Gruber, T. R. (1993). A translation approach to portable ontology specifications. *Knowledge Acquisition, 5*, 199–220. doi:10.1006/knac.1993.1008

Hendler, J. (2001). Agents and the Semantic Web. *IEEE Intelligent Systems, 16*, 30–37. doi:10.1109/5254.920597

IEEE. (2000). IEEE Standard 1516 (HLA Rules), 1516.1 (Interface Specification) and 1516.2 (Object Model Template).

Katsaliaki, K., & Brailsford, S. C. (2007). Using Simulation to Improve the Blood Supply Chain. *The Journal of the Operational Research Society, 58*(2), 219–227.

Lara, R., Roman, D., Polleres, A., & Fensel, D. (2004). A conceptual comparison of WSMO and OWL-S. *European Conference on Web Services* (pp. 254-269).

Martin, D., Cheyer, A. J., & Moran, D. B. (1999). The Open Agent Architecture: A Framework for Building distributed Software Systems. *Applied Artificial Intelligence*, *13*, 91–128. doi:10.1080/088395199117504

McIlraith, S. A., Son, T. C., & Zeng, H. L. (2001). Semantic Web Services. IEEE *Intelligent Systems & their Applications*, 16, 46-53,

Mertins, K., Rabe, M., & Jaekel, F. (2000). Neutral template libraries for efficient distributed simulation within a manufacturing system engineering platform. In *Proceedings of the 32nd Conference on Winter Simulation*, 1549-1557.

Mustafee, N., & Taylor, S. J. E. (2006). Investigating distributed simulation with COTS simulation packages: Experiences with Simul8 and the HLA. *Operational Research Society Simulation Workshop* (pp. 33-42).

Mustafee, N., Taylor, S. J. E., Katsaliaki, K., & Brailsford, S. (2006). Distributed Simulation with COTS Simulation Packages: A Case Study in Health Care Supply Chain Simulation. In *Proceedings of the 2006 Winter Simulation Conference* (pp. 1136-1142), Monterey, CA, USA.

Mustafee, N., Taylor, S. J. E., Katsaliaki, K., & Brailsford, S. (2009). Facilitating the Analysis of a UK NBS Chain Using the HLA. *SIMULATION: Transactions of the Society of Modeling and Simulation International*, *85*(2), 113–128. doi:10.1177/0037549708100530

Paolucci, M., Kawamura, T., Payne, T. R., & Sycara, K. (2002). Semantic matching of web services capabilities. *International Semantic Web Conference* (pp. 333-347). Berlin: Springer-Verlag.

Smith, M. K., Welty, C., & McGuinness, D. L. (2004) OWL Web Ontology Language, W3C Recommendation 10 February 2004. Retrieved from http://www.w3.org/TR/owl-guide/

Sun Microsystems. (2003). Java Native Interface. Retrieved from http://java.sun.com/j2se/1.4.2/docs/guide/jni/.

Taylor, S. J. E., Bohli, L., Wang, X., Turner, S. J., & Ladbrook, J. (2005). Investigating Distributed Simulation at the Ford Motor Company. In *Proceedings of the Ninth IEEE International Symposium on Distributed Simulation and Real-Time Applications. IEEE Computer Society* (pp. 139-147).

Taylor, S. J. E., Sudra, R., Janahan, T., Tan, G., & Ladbrook, J. (2001). Towards COTS distributed simulation using GRIDS. In *Proceedings of the Winter Simulation Conference* (pp. 1372-1379).

Taylor, S. J. E., Turner, S. J., & Strassburger, S. (2008). Guidelines for commercial off-the-shelf simulation package interoperability. In *Proceedings of the Winter Simulation Conference* (pp. 193-204).

Taylor, S. J. E., Wang, X., Turner, S. J., & Low, M. Y. H. (2006). Integrating Heterogeneous Distributed COTS Discrete-Event Simulation Packages: An Emerging Standards-Based Approach. *IEEE Transactions on Systems . Man & Cybernetics: Part A*, *36*(1), 109–122. doi:10.1109/TSMCA.2005.859167

Tolk, A., & Blais, C. (2005). Taxonomies, ontologies, and battle management languages – recommendations for the coalition BML study group. *Spring Simulation Interoperability Workshop*.

Tolk, A., & Turnitsa, C. (2004). Ontology of the C2IEDM - further studies to enable semantic interoperability. *Fall Simulation Interoperability Workshop*.

Tosic, V., Esfandiari, B., Pagurek, B., & Patel, K. (2002). On requirements for ontologies in management of web services. *Web Services, E-Business, and the Semantic Web* (pp. 237-247). Berlin: Springer-Verlag.

Compilation of References

Achjari, D., & Quaddus, M. A. (2003). Roles of formal/informal networks and perceived compatibility in the diffusion of world wide web: The case of Indonesian banks. In *Proceedings of the 36th Hawaii International Conference on System Science.*

Adelman, S., Moss, L., & Rehm, C. (2005). What are some of the concerns we should be aware of in integrated planning? *DMReview.com.* Retrieved December 20, 2006 from http://www.dmreview.com/article_sub.cfm?articleId=1027080

Agarwal, R., & Karahanna, E. (1998). The antecedents and consequents of user perceptions in information technology adoption. *Decision Support Systems, 22*(1), 15–29. doi:10.1016/S0167-9236(97)00006-7

Agarwal, R., & Tanniru, M. R. (1990). Knowledge acquisition using structured interviewing: an empirical investigation. *Journal of Management Information Systems, 7,* 123–140.

Aggarwal, A., & Mirani, R. (1999). DSS model usage in public and private sectors: Differences and implications. *Journal of End User Computing, 11*(3), 20-28.

Agrawal, M., & Chari, K. (2007, March). Software Effort, Quality and Cycle Time: A Study of CMM Level 5 Projects. *IEEE Transactions on Software Engineering, 33*(3), 145–156. doi:10.1109/TSE.2007.29

Aharoni Y., & Burton, R. M. (1994). Is management science international: In research of universal rules. *Management Science, 40*(1), 1-3.

Aier, S., & Schönherr, M. (2006). Evaluating integration architectures – A scenario-based evaluation of integration technologies. In D. Draheim, & G. Weber (Eds.), *Trends in enterprise application architecture, revised selected papers* (LNCS 3888, pp. 2-14).

Ajzen, I., & Fishbein, M. (1980). *Understanding attitudes and predicting social behavior.* Prentice Hall.

Akkiraju, R., Farrell, J., Miller, J., Nagarajan, M. Schmidt, M., Sheth, A., & Verma, K. (2005, November 7). Web service semantics - WSDL-S. W3C Member Submission.

Aklouf, Y., & Drias, H. (2007). Business process and Web services for a B2B Exchange Platform. International Review on Computers and Software (I.RE.CO.S). Prize Worthy Prize.

Aklouf, Y., & Drias, H. (2008). An adaptive e-commerce architecture for enterprise information exchange. *International Journal of Enterprise Information Systems, 4*(4), 15–33.

Aklouf, Y., Pierra, G., Ait Ameur, Y., & Drias, H. (2005). PLIB ontology: A mature solution for products characterization in B2B electronic commerce. International Journal of IT Standards and Standardization Research, 3(2). UDDI specification (n.d.). Retrieved from http://www.uddi.org/

Al- Mashari. M. (2000). Constructs of Process Change Management in ERP Context: A Focus on SAP R/3. In *Proceedings of AMICS.*

Aladwani, A. M. (2001). Change management strategies for successful ERP implementation. *Business Process Management Journal, 7*(3), 266–275. doi:10.1108/14637150110392764

Aladwani, A. M. (2001). IT planning effectiveness in a developing country. *Journal of Global Information Technology Management, 4*(3), 51-65.

Aladwani, A. M. (2002). Organizational actions, computer attitudes, and end-user satisfaction in public organizations: An empirical study. *Journal of End User Computing, 14*(1), 42-49.

Alagar, V. S., & Periyasamy, K. (1998). Specification of Software Systems. New York: Springer-Verlag.

Alavi, M., & Leidner, D. (1999). Knowledge management systems: Issues, challenges and benefits. *Communications of AIS, 1*(7), 37.

Alavi, M., & Leidner, D. E. (2001). Review: Knowledge management and knowledge management systems: Conceptual foundations and research issues. *MIS Quarterly, 25*(1), 107-36.

Al-Busaidi, K. A., & Olfman, L. (2005). An investigation of the determinants of knowledge management systems success in Omani organizations. *Journal of Global Information Technology Management, 8*(3), 6-27.

Al-Gahtani, S., & King, M. (1999). Attitudes, satisfaction and usage: Factors contributing to each in the acceptance of information technology. *Behaviour & Information Technology, 18*(4), 277–297. doi:10.1080/014492999119020

Al-Mashari, M., Al-Mudimigh, A., & Zairi, M. (2003). Enterprise resource planning: A taxonomy of critical factors. *European Journal of Operational Research, 146*(2), 352–364. doi:10.1016/S0377-2217(02)00554-4

Almutairi, H., & Subramanian, G. (2005). An empirical application of the DeLone and McLean model in the Kuwaiti private sector. *Journal of Computer Information Systems, 45*(3), 113-122.

Alshawaf, A. H., Ali, J. M. H., & Hasan, M. H. (2005). A benchmarking framework for information systems management issues in Kuwait. *Benchmarking: An International Journal, 12*(1), 30-44.

Altobello, S., Grandon, E., & Mykytyn, P. (2008). Predicting electronic commerce adoption in Chilean SMEs. *Journal of Business Research, 61*(6), 697–705. doi:10.1016/j.jbusres.2007.06.047

Amoako-Gyampah, K., & Salam, A. F. (2004). An extension of technology acceptance model in an ERP implementation environment. *Information & Management, 41*, 731–745. doi:10.1016/j.im.2003.08.010

Anat, H., Ravi, P., & David, S. (2004). A model of Internet standards adoption: The case of IPv6. *Information Systems Journal, 14*, 265–294. doi:10.1111/j.1365-2575.2004.00170.x

Anderson, G. (2000). From Supply Chain to Collaborative Commerce Networks: The Next Step in Supply Chain Management. [). Montgomery Research Inc.]. *Achieving Supply Chain Excellence Through Technology, 2*, 101–105.

Anderson, J. C., & Gerbing, D. W. (1998). Structural equation modeling in practice: A review and recommend two-step approach. *Psychological Bulletin, 103*(3), 411–423. doi:10.1037/0033-2909.103.3.411

Andresen, K., Levina, O., & Gronau, N. (2008). *Design of the evolutionary process model for adaptable software development processes.* Paper presented at the European and Mediterranean Conference on Information Systems 2008 (EMCIS2008)

Ang, J., & Teo, T. (2000). Management issues in data warehousing: Insights from the housing and development board. *Decision Support Systems, 29*(1), 11-20.

Angeles, R., & Nath, R. (2000). An empirical study of EDI trading partner selection criteria in customer-supplier relationship. *Information & Management, 37*, 241–255. doi:10.1016/S0378-7206(99)00054-3

Ankolekar, A., Burstein, M., Hobbs, J. R., Lassila, O., Martin, D., McDermott, D., et al. (2001). DAML-S: Semantic Markup for Web Services. *International Semantic Web Working Symposium (SWWS)*, 348-363.

APICS—*American Production and Inventory Control Society Dictionary* (1987) (6th ed.). Falls Church, VA.

Appleton, E. L. (1997). How to Survive ERP. *Datamation, 43*(3), 50–53.

Arb, R. v. (1997). *Vorgehensweisen und Erfahrungen bei der Einführung von Enterprise-Management-Systemen dargestellt am Beispiel von SAP R/3.* Institute für Wirtschaftsinformatik der Universität Bern.

Argote, L. & Ingram, P. (2000). Knowledge transfer: A basis for competitive advantage in firms. *Organizacional behavior and human decision processes, 82*(1), 150-169.

Ariyachandra, T., & Watson, H. (2006). Which data warehouse architecture is most successful?. *Business Intelligence, 11*(1).

Arnott, D., & Pervan, G. (2005). A critical analysis of decision support systems research. *Journal of Information Technology, 20*(2), 67-87.

Arrow, L., Barnwell, R., Burt, C., & Anderson, M. (1995). *OMG Business Object Survey.*

Arunchalam, V. (1997). Electronic data interchange: issues in adoption and management. *Information Resources Management Journal, 10*(2), 22–31.

Atiyyah, H. S. (1989). Determinants of computer system effectiveness in Saudi Arabian public organizations. *International Studies of Management & Organizations, 19*, 85-103.

Atkinson, H. (1999). ERP software requires good planning. *Journal of Commerce, 9*, 14.

Avison, D. E., Baskerville, R.L., & Myers, M. D. (2001). Controlling action research projects. *Information Technology & People, 14*(1), 28-45.

Avshalom, A. (2000); A new approach to ERP customisation. Retrieved April 15, 2009 from www.erpfans.com/erpfans/eshbel.htm

Bacharach, S. B., & Aiken, M. (1977). Communication in administrative bureaucracies. *Academy of Management Journal, 18*, 365–377. doi:10.2307/255411

Bagozzi, R. P., & Yi, Y. (1988). On the evaluation of structural equation models. *Academy of Marketing Science, 16*(1), 74–94. doi:10.1007/BF02723327

Baki, B., & Caker, K. (2005). Determining the ERP package selecting criteria: The case of Turkish manufacturing companies. *Business Process Management Journal, 11*(1), 75–86. doi:10.1108/14637150510578746

Ball, M. O., Chen, C-Y., & Zhao, Z-Y. (2004). Available to promise. In D. Simchi-Levi, S. D. Wu, & Z-J. Shen (Eds), *Handbook of quantitative supply chain analysis—Modeling in the e-business era* (pp. 447-483). New York: Springer.

Bancroft, N., Seip, H., & Sprengel, A. (1998). *Implementing SAP R/3: How to introduce a large system into a large organization.* Manning Publishing Company, USA.

Barber, K. D., Dewhurst, F. W., Burns, R. L. D. H., & Rogers, J. B. B. (2003). Business-process modelling and simulation for manufacturing management. A practical way forward. *Business Process Management Journal, 9*(4), 527–542. doi:10.1108/14637150310484544

Barkema, H., & Vermeulen, F. (1998). International expansion through start-up or acquisition: A learning perspective. *Academy of Management Journal, 41*(1), 7–26. doi:10.2307/256894

Barki, H., & Hartwick, J. (1989). Rethinking the concept of user involvement. *MIS Quarterly, 13*(1), 55-63.

Baroudi, J., Olson, M., & Ives, B. (1986). An empirical study of the impact of user involvement on system usage and information satisfaction. *Communications of the ACM, 29*(3), 232-238.

Barwise, P., Elberse, A. & Hammond K. (2002). Marketing and the Internet: A research review. No. 01-801.

Basili, V. R., & Weiss, D. M. (1981). Evaluation of a software requirements document by analysis of change data. In *Proceedings of 5th International Conference on Software Engineering* (pp. 314-323).

Baskerville, R. L. (1999). Investigating information systems with action research. *Communications of the Association for Information Systems, 2*(19), 1-32.

Basoglu, N., Daim, T., & Kerimoglu, O. (2007). Organizational adoption of enterprise resource planning systems: A conceptual framework. *The Journal of High Technology Management Research, 18*, 73–97. doi:10.1016/j.hitech.2007.03.005

Bass, F. M. (1969). A new product growth for model consumer durables. *Management Science, 15*(5), 215–227. doi:10.1287/mnsc.15.5.215

Behr, K., Kim, G., & Spafford, G. (2005). *The visible ops handbook: Implementing ITIL in 4 practical and auditable steps.* Oregon: Information Technology Process Institute.

Behrens, S., Jamieson, K., Jones, D., & Cranston, M. (2005). Predicting system success using the technology acceptance model: A case study. *16th Australian Conference on information Systems*, Nov 9- Dec 2, Sydney

Bell, D., & Ludwig, S. A. (2005). Grid Service Discovery in the Financial Markets Sector. *Journal of Computing and Information Technology, 13*(4), 265–170. doi:10.2498/cit.2005.04.02

Bell, D., de Cesare, S., & Lycett, M. (2005). Semantic transformation of Web services. *OnTheMove 2005 (SWWS 2005 Workshop), 2005*, 856-865.

Benna, A., Boudjlida, N., & Talantikite, H. (2008). SAWSDL, mediation and XQUERY for Web services discovery. In *Proceedings of the 8th International Conference on New Technologies in Distributed Systems.*

Bennett, R., Härtel, C., & McColl-Kennedy, J. R. (2005). Experience as a moderator of involvement and satisfaction on brand loyalty in a business-to-business setting 02-314R. *Industrial Marketing Management, 34*, 97–107. doi:10.1016/j.indmarman.2004.08.003

Bentler, P. M. (1995). *EQS structural equations program manual.* Inc. CA: Multivariate Software.

Benyon, D. (1993). Adaptive systems: A solution to usability problems. *User Modeling and User-Adapted Interaction, 3*(1), 65–87. doi:10.1007/BF01099425

Berchet, C., & Habchi, G. (2005). The implementation and deployment of an ERP system: An industrial case study. *56*(6), 588-605.

Berman, F., Fox, G., & Hey, T. (2003). *Grid computing. Making the Global infrastrucure a Reality.* Wiley.

Berners-Lee, T., Hendler, J., & Lassila, O. (2001). The Semantic Web. *Scientific American, 284*, 34–43.

Bernroider, E., & Koch, S. (2001). ERP selection process in midsize and large organizations. *Business Process Management, 7*(3), 251–257. doi:10.1108/14637150110392746

Bernroider, E., & Koch, S. (2001). ERP selection process in midsize and large organizations. *Business Process Management Journal, 7*(3), 251–257. doi:10.1108/14637150110392746

Bernus, P., & Nemes, L. (1996). A framework to define a generic enterprise reference architecture and methodology. *Computer Integrated Manufacturing Systems, 9*(3), 179–191. doi:10.1016/S0951-5240(96)00001-8

Bernus, P., Nemes, L., & Schmidt, G. (Eds.). (1998). *Handbook on Architectures of Information Systems* Heidelberg: Springer.

Bettman, R. J., Luce, M. F., & Payne, J. W. (1998). Constructive consumer choice process. *The Journal of Consumer Research, 25*, 187–217. doi:10.1086/209535

Bhatt, M., Rahayu, W., & Sterling, G. (2004). sedOnto: A Web enabled ontology for synthetic environment representation based on the SEDRIS specification. *Fall Simulation Interoperability Workshop,* Boer, C. A., Verbraeck, A., & Veeke, H. P. M. (2002). Distributed simulation of complex systems: Application in container handling. *European Simulation Interoperability Workshop*

Bingi, P., Sharma, M. K., & Godla, J. (1999). Critical issues affecting an ERP implementation. *Information Systems Management, 16*(3), 7–15. doi:10.1201/1078/43197.16.3.19990601/31310.2

Bingi, P., Sharma, M. K., & Godla, J. K. (1999). Critical success factors affecting an ERP implementation. *Information Systems Management.*

Bingi, P., Sharma, M., & Godla, J. (1999). Critical Issues Affecting an ERP Implementation. *Information & Management,* 7–14.

Bjerkness, G., & Bratteteig, T. (1995). User participation and democracy: A discussion of Scandinavian research on system development. *Scandinavian Journal of Information Systems, 7*(1), 73-98.

Bjørn-Andersen, N., & Hedberg, B. (1977). Designing information systems in an organizational perspective. *Studies in the Management Sciences Perscriptive Models of Organizations, 5.*

Blackler, F. (1995) Knowledge, knowledge work and organizations: An overview and interpretation. *Organization Studies, 16*(6), 1021-1046.

Blau, P. M., & Scott, W. R. (1962). *Formal Organizations.* Chandler Publishing.

Boehm, B. W., & Papaccio, P. N. (1988). Understanding and controlling software costs. *IEEE Transactions on Computers,* 1462–1467.

Booker, E. (1999). Web to ERP - - ERP Stage II: Outsiders Invited In. *Internet Week,* October 25, pp. 86.

Bortscheller, B. J., & Saulnier, E. T. (1992). Model reusability in a graphical simulation package. In *Proceedings of the 1992 Winter Simulation Conference* (pp. 764-772).

Botta–Genoulaz, V., & Millet, P. (2006). An investigation into the use of ERP systems in the service sector. *International Journal of Production Economics, 99,* 202–221. doi:10.1016/j.ijpe.2004.12.015

Botta-Genoulaz, V., Millet, P. A., & Grabot, B. (2005). A survey on the recent research literature on ERP systems. *Computers in Industry, 56*(6), 510–522. doi:10.1016/j.compind.2005.02.004

Boudreau, M., & Robey, D. (2005). Enacting integrated information technology: Human agency perspective. *Organization Science, 16*(1), 3-18.

Boynton, A. C., & Zmud, R. W. (1994). An assessment of critical success factors. *Sloan Management Review, Summer,* pp. 17-27.

Bozeman, B., & Bretschneider, S. (1986). Public management information systems: Theory and prescription. *Public Administration Review, 55*(6), 559-566.

Bradley, J. (2008). Management Based Critical Success Factors in the Implementation of Enterprise Resource Planning Systems. *International Journal of Accounting Information Systems, 9,* 175–200. doi:10.1016/j.accinf.2008.04.001

Bradley, J., & Lee, C. C. (2007). ERP training and user satisfaction: A case study. *International Journal of Enterprise Information Systems, 3*(4), 33–50.

Brakely, H. H. (1999). What makes ERP Effective? *Manufacturing Systems, 17*(3), 120.

Brehm, L., Heizl, A., & Markus, L. (2001). Tailoring ERP systems: a spectrum of choices and their implications. In *Proceedings of the 34th Hawaii International Conference on System Sciences*, Hawaii, USA (pp. 8017-8025).

Bretschneider, S. (1990). Management information systems in public and private organizations: An empirical test. *Public Administration Review, 50*(5), 536-545.

Bretschneider, S., & Wittmer, D. (1993). Organizational adoption of microcomputer technology: The role of sector. *Information Systems Research, 4*(1), 88-108.

Brewer, G. (2000). On the road to successful ERP. *Instrumentation & Control Systems, 73*(5), 49–58.

Brooks, F. P. (1975). *The Mythical Man-month: Essays on Software Engineering.* Reading, MA: Addison-Wesley Publishing Company

Brooks, F. P. (1987). No Silver Bullet: Essence and Accidents of Software Engineering. *IEEE Computer, 20*(4), 10–19.

Brown, C. V. (2003). Managing the Next Wave of Enterprise Systems. *MIS Quarterly, 2*(1), 65–77.

Brown, C., & Vessey, I. (1999). *ERP implementation approaches: toward a contingency framework.* Paper presented at the Proceedings of the Twentieth International Conference on Information Systems, Charlotte, NC.

Brown, J., & Duguid, P. (1991). Organizational learning and communities of practice: Towards a unified view of working, learning and innovation. *Organization Science, 2,* 40-57.

Brown, J., & Duguid, P. (1998). Organizing knowledge. *California Management Review, 40*(3), 90-111.

Bruges, P. (2002). ERP Implementation Methodologies. *MSIS, 488.*

Brunelli, M. (2005). *Open source gaining traction in ERP market.* Retrieved January, 24, 2007, from http://searchopensource.techtarget.com/

Brunelli, M. (2006). *BI, ERP top 2007's IT spending list.* Retrieved July 8, 2007, from http://searchoracle.techtarget.com/originalContent/0,289142,sid41_gci1233170,00.html.

Bruner, G. C. II, & Kumar, A. (2005). Explaining consumer acceptance of handheld Internet devices. *Journal of Business Research, 58,* 553–558. doi:10.1016/j.jbusres.2003.08.002

Brusilovsky, P. (2001). Adaptive hypermedia. *User Modeling and User-Adapted Interaction, 11*(1/2), 87–110. doi:10.1023/A:1011143116306

Bry, F., Nagel, W., & Schroeder, M. (2004). Grid computing. *Informatik Spektrum, 27*(6), 542–545.

Bryan, Garnier & Co. Technology Group. (2004). *The Restructuring of the ERP Market.* London.

Bryman, A., & Ducan, C. (2001). *Quantitative data analysis with SPSS Release 10 for Windows*. London: Routlege Publishing.

Buckhout, S., Frey, E., & Nemec, J. (1999). Making ERP Succeed: Turning Fear into Promise. *IEEE Engineering Management Review*, Second Quarter, 116-123.

Bull, C. (2003). Politics in Packaged Software Implementations. In *Proceedings of the 11th European Conference on Information Systems, June*.

Buonanno, G., Faverio, P., Pigni, F., Ravarini, A., Sciuto, D., & Tagliavini, M. (2005). Factors affecting ERP system adoption. A comparative analysis between SMES and large companies. *Journal of Enterprise Information Management*, *18*, 384–426. doi:10.1108/17410390510609572

Buonanno, G., Faverio, P., Pingi, F., Ravarini, A., Sciuto, D., & Tagliavini, M. (2005). Factors affecting ERP system adoption. *Journal of Enterprise Information Management*, *18*(4), 384–426. doi:10.1108/17410390510609572

Burbeck, S. (2000). The Tao of e-business services. *IBM Corporation*. Retrieved October 7, 2006, from http://www.ibm.com/software/developer/library/ws-tao/index.html

Burkhart, R., Fulton, J., Gielingh, W., Marshall, C., Menzel, C., Petrie, C., et al. (1992). *The notion of a model*. Paper presented at the Proceedings of the First International Conference on Enterprise Integration.

Burton, B., Geishecker, L., & Hostmann, B. (2006). *Organizational structure: Business intelligence and information management*.

Caldwell, B., & Stein, T. (1998). New IT agenda. *Informationweek*, *30*, 30–38.

Cardoso, J., & Sheth, A. (2003). Semantic e-workflow composition. *Journal of Intelligent Information Systems*, *21*, 191–225. doi:10.1023/A:1025542915514

Carr, S. (1999). The Intelligence Game. *Upside*, *11*(10), 75–78.

Carson, D., Gilmore, A., Gronhaug, K., & Perry, C. *(2001)*. *Qualitative research in marketing*. London: Sage.

Carton, F., & Adam, F. (2003). Analysing the Impact of ERP Systems Roll-Outs in Multi-National Companies.

Electronic Journal of Information Systems Evaluation, *6*(2), 21–32.

Caudle, S. L., (1990). Managing information resources in state government. *Public Administration Review, 50*, 515-524.

Cavaye, A. (1995). User participation in system development revisited. *Information Management, 29*, 311-323.

Cebeci, U. (2009). Fuzzy AHP-based Decision Support System for Selecting ERP Systems in Textile Industry by using balanced Scorecard. *Expert Systems with Applications*, *36*, 8900–8909. doi:10.1016/j.eswa.2008.11.046

Cecere L., Hofman, D., Martin, R., & Preslan, L. (2005). *The handbook for becoming demand driven*. Boston: AMR Research Inc.

Center, M. I. (2004). 2004 yearbook of information service industry. Institute *for Information Industry*.

Center, M. I. (2006). Information application demand analysis of large companies in Taiwan.

Chalmeta, R., Campos, C., & Grangel, R. (2001). References architectures for enterprise integration. *Journal of Systems and Software*, *57*(3), 175–191. doi:10.1016/S0164-1212(01)00008-5

Chau, P. Y. K., & Hu, P. J. (2002). Examining a model of information technology acceptance by individual professionals: an exploratory study. *Journal of Management Information Systems*, *18*(4), 191–229.

Chen, D., Vallespir, B., & Doumeingts, G. (1997). GRAI integrated methodology and its mapping onto generic enterprise reference architecture and methodology. *Computers in Industry*, *33*(2-3), 387–394. doi:10.1016/S0166-3615(97)00043-2

Chen, I. J. (2001). Planning for ERP Systems: Analysis and Future Trend. *Business Process Management Journal*, *7*(5), 374–386. doi:10.1108/14637150110406768

Chen, L., Shadbolt, N. R., Goble, C., Tao, F., Cox, S. J., Puleston, C., & Smart, P. (2003). Towards a knowledge-based approach to semantic service composition. *Second International Semantic Web Conference (ISWC2003)*.

Chengalur-Smith, I., Ballou, D., & Pazer, H. (1999). The impact of data quality information on decision making:

An exploratory analysis. *Knowledge and Data Engineering, IEEE Transactions on, 11*(6), 853-864.

Chiasson, M., & Davidson, E. (2005). Taking industry seriously in IS research. *MIS Quarterly, 29*(4), 591–606.

Cho, V. (2006). Factors in the adoption of third-party B2B portals in the textile industry. *Journal of Computer Information Systems, 46*(3), 18–31.

Choffray, J. M., & Lilien, G. L. (1980). Industrial market segmentation by the structure of the purchasing process. *Industrial Marketing Management, 9*, 331–342. doi:10.1016/0019-8501(80)90049-8

Choi, B., & Lee, H. (2003). An empirical investigation of KM styles and their effect on corporate performance. *Information & Management, 40*, 403-417.

Choudhury, I. (1999). *Generic reusable business object modeling.* PhD Thesis, South Bank University, London.

Choudhury, I., Sun, Y., & Patel, D. (1997). *Generic reusable business object model - A framework and its application in British telecommunication plc.* Paper presented at the OOIS97 Proceedings of 4th International Conference on Object-Oriented Information Systems, London.

Christopher, M. (2004). *Logistics and supply chain management: Creating value-adding networks* (3rd ed.). Harlow: Prentice Hall.

Christou, I. T. (2006). *Available-to-promise business scenario: Problem formulation, algorithmic expression and integration with open-source ERP systems.* MBA Thesis, National Technical University of Athens and Athens University of Economics and Business, Athens-MBA Program.

Christou, I.T., Lagodimos, A.G., & Lycopoulou, D. (2007). Hierarchical production planning for multi-product lines in the beverage industry. *Production Planning & Control, 18*(5), 367-376.

Chung, S. H., & Snyder, C. A. (1999). ERP Initiation: A Historical Perspective. In. *Proceedings of Americas Conference on Information Systems, 11*(3), 33–45.

Clegg, S. R. (1989). *Frameworks of Power.* London: Sage.

Clement, A., & Van den Besselar, P. (1993). A retrospective look at PD projects. *Participatory Design: Special Issue of the Communications of the ACM, 36*, 29-39.

Cliffe, S. (1999). ERP Implementation. *Harvard Business Review*, (January-February): 16–17.

CMS Watch. (2009). The ECM Suites Report 2009, Version 3.1. *CMS Works, CMS Watch Olney.*

Coakes, E., Bradburn, A., & Sugden, G. (2004). Managing and leveraging knowledge for organisational advantage. *Knowledge Management Research & Practice, 2*(2), 118-128.

Cohen, B. (1989). Justification of formal methods for systems specifications. *Software Engineering Journal, 4*(1), 26–35. doi:10.1109/32.21723

Coleman, J. S., Katz, E., & Menzel, H. (1966). *Medical innovation: A diffusion study.* Indianapolis: Bobbs-Merrill.

Collins, J. B. (2004). Standardizing an ontology of physics for modeling and simulation. *Fall Simulation Interoperability Workshop.*

Concannon, K. H., Hunter, K. I., & Tremble, J. M. (2003). Dynamic scheduling II: SIMUL8-planner simulation-based planning and scheduling." In *Proceedings of the 2003 Winter Simulation Conference* (pp. 1488-1493).

Cook, S., & Brown, J. (1999). Bridging epistemologies: The generative dance between organizational knowledge and organizational knowing. *Organization Science, 10*(4), 381-400.

Cooper, R. B., & Zmund, R. W. (1990). Information Technology Implementation Research: A Technological Diffusion Approach. *Management Science, 36*(2), 123–139. doi:10.1287/mnsc.36.2.123

Cover, R. (2004). *Web standards for business process modeling, collaboration, and choreography.* Retrieved October 7, 2001, from http://xml.coverpages.org/bpm.html.

Cummins, F. (2002). *Enterprise integration.* New York: John Wiley.

Curbera, F., Duftler, M., Khalaf, R., Nagy, W., Mukhi, N., & Weerawarana, S. (2002). Unraveling the Web services Web - An introduction to SOAP, WSDL, and UDDI. *IEEE Internet Computing*, *6*, 86–93. doi:10.1109/4236.991449

Curran, T., & Lad, A. (2000). *SAP R/3 Business Blueprint* (2nd ed.). Prentice Hall.

D'aspremont, C. & Jacquemin, A. (1988). Cooperative and Non-Cooperative R&D Industry with Spillovers. *The American Economic Review*, *78*(December), 1133–1137.

Daft, R. L. (1978). A dual-core model of organizational innovation. *Academy of Management Journal*, *21*, 193–210. doi:10.2307/255754

Daga, A., de Cesare, S., Lycett, M., & Partridge, C. (2004). *Software stability: Recovering general patterns of business.* Paper presented at the Tenth Americas Conference on Information Systems, New York.

Daga, A., de Cesare, S., Lycett, M., & Partridge, C. (2005). *An ontological approach for recovering legacy business content.* Paper presented at the 8th Annual Hawaii International Conference on System Sciences, Los Alamitos, California.

Damanpour, F. (1991). Organizational innovation: a meta-analysis of effects of determinants and moderators. *Academy of Management Journal*, *34*(3), 555–590. doi:10.2307/256406

Damian, D., & Chisan, J. (2006). An Empirical Study of the Complex Relationships between Requirements Engineering Processes and Other Processes that Lead to Payoffs in Productivity, Quality, and Risk Management. *IEEE Transactions on Software Engineering*, *32*(7), 433–453. doi:10.1109/TSE.2006.61

Daneva, M. (2003). Lessons Learnt from Five Years of Experience in ERP Requirements Engineering. In *Proceedings of the 11th IEEE International Requirements Engineering Conference.*

Daneva, M. (2004). ERP Requirements Engineering Practice: Lessons Learned. *IEEE Software*, 26–33. doi:10.1109/MS.2004.1270758

Daneva, M., & Wieringa, R. J. (2006). A Requirements engineering framework for cross-organizational ERP systems. *Requirements Engineering*, *11*, 194–204. doi:10.1007/s00766-006-0034-9

Davenport, T. (1998). Putting the enterprise into the enterprise system. *Harvard Business Review*.

Davenport, T. H. (2000). *Mission Critical: Realizing the Promise of Enterprise Systems*. Harvard Business School Publishing.

Davenport, T. H., & Brooks, J. (2004). Enterprise Systems and the Supply Chain. *Journal of Enterprise Information Management*, *17*(1), 8–19. doi:10.1108/09576050410510917

Davenport, T. H., & Prusak, L. (1998). *Working knowledge*. Boston, MA: Harvard Business School Press.

Davidson, R., M., J.G. (1981). Several tests for model specification in the presence of alternative hypotheses. *Econometrica*, *49*(3), 781–793. doi:10.2307/1911522

Davis, A. M. (1990). *Software Requirements–Analysis and Specification*. Prentice Hall.

Davis, F. D. (1989). Perceived usefulness, perceived ease of use and user acceptance of information technology. *MIS Quarterly*, *13*(3), 319–339. doi:10.2307/249008

Davis, F. D., Bagozzi, R., & Warhaw, P. (1989). User acceptance of computer technology: A comparison of two theoretical models. *Management Science*, *35*(8), 982–1002. doi:10.1287/mnsc.35.8.982

Davis, R. (2008) *ARIS Design Platform. Advanced Process Modelling and Administration*. Springer-Verlag.

Dawes, P. L., Lee, Y. D., & Dowling, G. R. (1998). Information control and influence in emergent buying centers. *Journal of Marketing*, *62*, 55–68. doi:10.2307/1251743

Dawson, J., & Owens, J. D. (2007). *The Fundamental Challenge: Human and Organisational Factors in an ERP Implementation*. First European Conference on Information Management and Evaluation, University of Montpellier, France, 20-21 September.

Dawson, J., & Owens, J. D. (2008). ERP Non-implementation: A Case Study of a UK Furniture Manufacturer. *International Journal of Enterprise Information Systems*, *4*(3).

De Burca, S., Fynes, B., & Marshall, D. (2005). Strategic technology adoption: extending ERP across the supply chain. *The Journal of Enterprise Information Management*, *18*(4), 427-440.

De Jong, M., & Van der Geest, T. (2000). Characterizing web heuristics. *Technical Communication, 47*(3), 311–326.

Deep, A., Guttridge, P., Dani, S., & Burns, N. (2007). Investigating factors affecting ERP selection in made-to-order SME sector. *Journal of Manufacturing Technology Management, 19*(4), 430–446. doi:10.1108/17410380810869905

Deloitte Consulting (2000). ERP's Second Wave.

Deloitte Touche (2002). *Achieving, Measuring and Communicating IT value, and IDG Research Services Group report.*

DeLone, W. H., & McLean, E. R. (1992). Information systems success: The quest for the dependent variable. *Information Systems Research, 3*(1), 60-90.

DeLone, W. H., & McLean, E. R. (2003). The DeLone and McLean model of information system success: A ten year update. *Journal of Management Information Systems, 19*(4), 9-30.

Delone, W., & McLean, E. (1992). Information systems success: The quest for the dependent variable. *Information System Research, 3*(1), 60-95.

Delone, W., & McLean, E. (2003). The DeLone and McLean model of information systems success: A ten-year update. *Management Information Systems, 19*(4), 9-30.

DeMarco, T. (1978). *Structured analysis and system specification.* New York: Yourdon press.

Dewar, R. D., & Dutton, J. E. (1986). The adoption of radical and incremental innovation: An empirical analysis. *Management Science, 32*, 1422–1433. doi:10.1287/mnsc.32.11.1422

Dewhurst, F. W., Barber, K. D., & Pritchard, M. C. (2002). In search of a general enterprise model. *Management Decision, 40*(5), 418–427. doi:10.1108/00251740210430416

Dobson, P., Myles, J., & Jackson, P. (2007). Making case for critical realism: Examining the implementation of automated performance management systems. *Information Resources Management Journal, 20*(2), 138–152.

Dogru, A. (2005). Toward a component-oriented methodology to build-by-integration. In S. de Cesare,

M. Lycett & R. D. Macredie (Eds.), *Development of component-based information systems* (pp. 49-69). New York: M.E. Sharpe.

Doherty, N. F., & King, M. (1998). The importance of organizational issues in systems development. *Information Technology & People, 11*, 104–123. doi:10.1108/09593849810218300

Downs, G. W., & Mohr, L. B. (1976). Conceptual issues in the study of innovation. *Administrative Science Quarterly, 21*(4), 700–714. doi:10.2307/2391725

Drucker, P. (1993). *Post-capitalist society.* New York: Harper Collins.

Duncan, N. (1995). Capturing flexibility of information technology infrastructure: A study of resource characteristics and their measure. *Management Information Systems, 12*(2), 37-57.

Dyer, J. D., Cho, D. S., & Chu, W. (1998). Strategic supplier segmentation: The next 'best practice' in supply chain management. *California Management Review, 40*(2).

Eagle Rock Alliance (2001). *Online survey results—2001 cost of downtime.* West Orange, New Jersey: Eagle Rock Alliance. Retrieved January 14, 2008, http://www.contingencyplanningresearch.com/2001%20Survey.pdf

Eastin, M. S. (2002). Diffusion of e-commerce: an analysis of the adoption of four e-commerce activities. *Telematics and Informatics, 19*, 251–267. doi:10.1016/S0736-5853(01)00005-3

Eckhouse, J. (1999, January 25). ERP vendors plot a comeback. *Information Week, 718*, 126–128.

Ehie, I. C., & Madsen, M. (2005). Identifying critical issues in enterprise resource planning (ERP) implementation. *56*(6), 545-557.

Ein-Dor, P., & Segev, E. (1978). Organizational context and success of management information systems. *Management Science, 24*, 1064-1077.

El Sayed, H. (2006). ERPs and accountant's expertise: the construction of relevance. *Journal of Enterprise Information Management, 19*(1), 83–96. doi:10.1108/17410390610636896

Elbanna, A. R. (2003). Achieving Social Integration to Implement ERP Systems. In *Proceedings of the 11th European Conference on Information Systems, June.*

Elbertsen, L., Benders, J., & Nijssen, E. (2006). ERP use: exclusive or complemented? *Industrial Management & Data Systems, 106*(6), 811–824. doi:10.1108/02635570610671498

Elliot, S. (Ed.) (2002). Electronic commerce: B2C strategies and models. *Wiley Series in Information Systems.* Chichester: John Wiley & Sons, Ltd.

Emmanouilides, C., & Hammond, K. (2000). Internet usage: predictors of active users and frequency of use. *Journal of Interactive Marketing, 14*(2), 17–32. doi:10.1002/(SICI)1520-6653(200021)14:2<17::AID-DIR2>3.0.CO;2-E

Equey, C. (2006). *Etude du comportement des PME/PMI suisses en matière d'adoption de système de gestion integré* (HES-SO/HEG-GE/C Working paper series N° 06/12/1-CH). HEG: Dept. of Economie d'Entreprise.

Equey, C., & Rey, A. (2004*). La mise en place d'une solution de gestion moderne (ERP/PGI), quels enjeux pour une PME/PMI? 1ère partie: étude de cas détaillés,* (HES-SO/HEG-GE/C Working paper series N° 06/1/4-CH). HEG: Dept. of Economie d'Entreprise.

Erl, T. (2008). *Web service contract design and versioning for SOA.* Prentice Hall International.

Esteves, J. (2009). A benefits realisation road-map framework for ERP usage in small and medium-sized enterprises. *Journal of Enterprise Information Management, 22*(1), 25–35. doi:10.1108/17410390910922804

Esteves, J., & Pastor, J. (1999). An ERP Lifecycle-based Research Agenda. In *Proceedings of the 1st International Workshop on Enterprise Management and Resource Planning Systems, November.*

Esteves, J., & Pastor, J. (2000). Towards a Unification of Critical Success Factors for ERP Implementations. In *Proceedings of the 10th Business Information Technology Conference, Manchester, UK.*

Esteves, J., & Pastor, J. (2001). Enterprise resource planning systems research: an annotated bibliography. *Communication of AIS, 7*(8), 51–52.

Esteves, J., & Pastor, J. (2004). Organisational and Technological Critical Success Factors Behaviour Along the ERP Implementation Phases. In *Proceedings of the 6th International Conference on Enterprise Information Systems, April.*

Esteves, J., & Pastor, J. A. (2001). Analysis of critical success factors relevance along SAP implementation phases. *Seventh Americas Conference on Information Systems.*

Esteves-Sousa, J., & Pastor-Collado, J. (2000). Towards the unification off critical success factors for ERP implementations. *Proceedings of the 10th Annual Business Information Technology conference.* Manchester, UK.

Evangelista, P. (1998). ERP Systems Strategies. *American Production and Inventory Control Society- Cleveland Chapter,* Speech Proceedings, June.

Fang, L., & Patrecia, S. (2005). *Critical Success Factors in ERP Implementation.* Jonkoping International Business School, Jonkoping University.

Ferguson, R. B. (2006). *Open source ERP grows up.* Retrieved December, 12, 2006, from http://www.eweek.com/article2/0,1759,1985895,00.asp

Ferman, J. E. (1999). Strategies for Successful ERP Connections. *Manufacturing Engineering, 123*(4), 48–60.

Fisher, C., Lauria, E., Chengalur-Smith, I., & Wang, R. (2006). *Introduction to information quality.* Cambridge, MA: MITIQ Press.

Fishwick, P. A., & Miller, J. A. (2004). Ontologies for modeling and simulation: Issues and approaches. In *Proceedings of the 2004 Winter Simulation Conference* (pp. 259-264).

Fitzpatrick, D. (1998). *Regional Development and the Information Society.* TIMMERS.

Flynn, B. B., Schroeder, R. G., & Sakakibara, S. (1994). A framework for quality management research and an associated measurement instrument. *Journal of Operations Management, 11*(4), 339–575. doi:10.1016/S0272-6963(97)90004-8

Forgy, C. L. (1982). Rete: A Fast Algorithm for the Many Pattern/Many Object Pattern Match Problems. *Artificial Intelligence, 19,* 17–37. doi:10.1016/0004-3702(82)90020-0

Fox, M. S. (1992). The TOVE Project, Towards a common sense model of the enterprise. In C. Petrie (Ed.), *Enterprise integration modeling* (pp. 189-204). Cambridge, MA: The MIT Press.

Francalanci, C. (2001). Predicting the implementation effort of ERP projects: empirical evidence on SAP/R3. *Journal of Information Technology, 16*(1), 33–48. doi:10.1080/02683960010035943

Franz, C., & Robey, D. (1986). Organizational context, user involvement and usefulness of information systems. *Decision Sciences, 17*, 329-355.

Freeman, C., & Soete, L. (1997). *The Economics of Industrial Innovation* (3rd ed.). Cambridge, MA: The MIT Press.

Friedman, T. (2005). *Gartner says more than 50 percent of data warehouse projects will have limited acceptance or will be failures through 2007.* Retrieved February 21, 2007, from http://www.gartner.com/it/page.jsp?id=492112.

Friedrich, C. J. (Ed.). (1958). *Authority.* Cambridge: Harvard University Press.

Fujimoto, R. M. (2000) *Parallel and Distributed Simulation Systems.* New York: John Wiley & Sons Inc.

Fuller, M. A., Hardin, A. M., & Scott, C. L. (2007). Diffusion of virtual innovation. *The Data Base for Advances in Information Systems, 38*(4), 40–45.

Gable, G., & Stewart, G. (1999). SAP R/3 implementation issues for small to medium enterprises. In *Proceedings of the 5th Americas Conference on Information Systems* (pp. 779-781). Milwaukee:

Gable, G., & Stewart, G. (1999). *SAP R\3 Implementation Isses for Small to Medium Enterprises.* American Conference on Information Systems, Milwaukee, USA.

Gale, T., & Eldred, J. (1996). *Getting results with the object-oriented enterprise model.* New York: SIGS Publications.

Galup, S. D., Dattero, R., & Hicks, R. C. (2003). The enterprise knowledge dictionary. *Knowledge Management Research & Practice, 1*(1), 95-101.

Gan, B. P., Liu, L., Jain, S., Turner, S. J., Cai, W., & Hsu, W. (2000). Manufacturing supply chain management: Distributed supply chain simulation across enterprise boundaries. In *Proceedings of the 2000 Winter Simulation Conference* (pp. 1245-1251).

Gan, B. P., Yoke, M., Low, H., Wang, X., & Turner, S. J. (2005). Using manufacturing process flow for time synchronization in HLA-based simulation. *IEEE International Symposium on Distributed Simulation and Real-Time Applications* (pp. 148-157).

Ganek, A. (2007). Overview of autonomic computing: Origins, evolution, direction. In M. Parashar, & S. Harir (Eds.), *Autonomic computing* (pp. 3-18). New York: Taylor & Francis Group.

Ganek, A. G., & Corbi, T. A. (2003). The dawning of the autonomic computing era. *IBM Systems Journal, 42*(1), 5-18. Retrieved January 14, 2008, from http://researchweb.watson.ibm.com/journal/sj/421/ganek.pdf

Gangadharan, G., & Swami, S. (2004). Business intelligence systems: Design and implementation strategies. *Paper presented at the 26th International Conference Information Technology Interfaces ITI.*

Gargeya, V. B., & Brady, C. (2005). Success and Failure factors of adopting SAP in ERP System Implementation. *Business Process Management Journal, 11*(5), 501–516. doi:10.1108/14637150510619858

Garry, C. (2004). *Downtime as a business expense.* Infrastructure Strategies, Meta Group.

Gartner Press Release. (2006a). *Gartner says business intelligence software market to reach $3 billion in 2009.* http://www.gartner.com/press_releases/asset_144782_11.html.

Gartner Press Release. (2006b). *Gartner survey of 1,400 CIOs shows transformation of IT organization is accelerating.* http://www.gartner.com/press_releases/asset_143678_11.html.

Gartner Press Release. (2007). *Gartner EXP survey of more than 1,400 CIOs shows CIOs must create leverage to remain relevant to the business.* Retrieved February 21, 2007, from http://www.gartner.com/it/page.jsp?id=501189.

Gärtner, J., & Wagner, I. (1996). Mapping actors and agendas: Political frameworks of systems design and participation. *Human-Computer Interaction, 11*(3).

Gartner. (2005). *Market share: ERP software by company size*. Worldwide.

Gatignon, H., & Robertson, T. S. (1985). A propositional inventory for new diffusion research. *The Journal of Consumer Research, 11*(4), 859–867. doi:10.1086/209021

Geerts, G. & McCarthy, W.E. (1999). An accounting object infrastructure for knowledge-based enterprise models. *IEEE Intelligent Systems & their Applications.*

Gefen, D., & Ragowsky, A. (2005). A multi-level approach to measuring the benefits of an ERP system in manufacturing firms. *Information Systems Management, 22*(1), 18–25. doi:10.1201/1078/44912.22.1.20051201/85735.3

Gena, C., & Weibelzahl, S. (2007). Usability engineering for the adaptive web. In P. Brusilovsky, A. Kobsa & W. Nejdl (Eds.), *The adaptive web* (pp. 720-762). Berlin: Springer.

Ghingold, M., & Wilson, D. T. (1998). Buying center research and business marketing practice: meeting the challenge of dynamic marketing. *Journal of Business and Industrial Marketing, 13*(2), 96–108. doi:10.1108/08858629810213315

Gibbins, N., Harris, S., & Shadbolt, N. (2003). Agent-based semantic Web services. In *Proceedings of the 12th International Conference on World Wide Web* (pp. 710-717). Budapest, Hungary: ACM Press.

Glaser, B. (1992). *Basics of grounded theory analysis.*

Glaser, B. (1998). *Doing grounded theory: Issues and discussions.* Sociology Press.

Glaser, B., & Strauss, A. (1967). *The discovery of grounded theory.* Chicago, IL: Aldine.

Gold, A. H., Malhotra, A., & Segars, A. H. (2001). Knowledge management: An organizational capabilities perspective. *Journal of Management Information Systems, 18*(1), 185.

Goodacre, A., & Tonks, I. (1995). Finance and technological change. In Stoneman (Ed.), *Handbook of the Economics of Innovation and Technological Change* (pp. 298-341). Oxford: Blackwell

Goodland, M., & Slater, C. (1995). *SSADM Version 4: A practical approach*. Berkshire, England: McGraw-Hill Publishing.

Goodpasture, V. (1995). Easton Steps up to the Plate. *Manufacturing Systems, 13*(9), 58–64.

Grady, R., & Caswell, D. (1999). *Software Metrics: Establishing a Company-wide program.* Prentice Hall.

Graefe, U., & Chan, W. (1993). An enterprise model as a design tool for information infrastructure. In H. Yoshikawa & J. Goossenaerts (Eds.), *Information infrastructure systems for manufacturing* (Vol. B-14, pp. 183-192): North-Holland.

Granlund, M., & Malmi, T. (2002). Moderate impact of ERPs on management accounting: a lag or permanent outcome? *Management Accounting Research, 13*, 299–321. doi:10.1006/mare.2002.0189

Gray, D. N., & Hotchkiss, J., LaForge, Shalit, S. A., & Weinberg, T. (1998). Modern languages and Microsoft's component object model. *Communications of the ACM, 41*, 55–65. doi:10.1145/274946.274957

Greer, D., & Ruhe, G. (2004). Software release planning: An evolutionary and iterative approach. *Information and Software Technology, 46*(4), 243-253.

Gronau, N. (2003). Web services as a part of an adaptive information system framework for concurrent engineering. In R. Jardim-Goncalves, J. Cha, & A. Steiger-Garcao (Eds.), *Concurrent engineering: Enhanced interoperable systems.*

Gruber, T. R. (1993). A translation approach to portable ontology specifications. *Knowledge Acquisition, 5*, 199–220. doi:10.1006/knac.1993.1008

Gülcü, C. (2004). *The complete Log4j manual, Version 1.2*. Switzerland: QoS.Ch Publisher.

Guha, S., Grover, V., Kettinger, W. J., & Teng, J. T. C. (1997). Business process change and organizational performance: exploring an antecedent model. *Journal of Management Information Systems, 14*(1), 119–154.

Gulick, L. H., & Urwick, L. F. (Eds.). (1937). *Papers on the Science of Administration.* Institute of Public Administration, New York.

Gupta, A. (2000). Enterprise Resource Planning: The Emerging Organizational Value System. *Industrial Management & Data Systems, 100*(3), 114–118. doi:10.1108/02635570010286131

Gyampah, K., & White, K. (1993). User involvement and user satisfaction: An exploratory contingency model. *Information & Management, 25*, 1-10.

Haider, A., & Koronios, A. (2003). Managing engineering assets: A knowledge-based approach through information quality. *Paper presented at the International Business Information Management Conference.* Cairo.

Haight, C., & Brodie, S. (2005). *Managing the J2EE application lifecycle for performance and availability—Part III.* Mercury Webinar. Retrieved January 14, 2008, from http://www.mercury.com/

Hair, J. E., Anderson, R. E., Tatham, R. L., & Black, W. C. (1998). *Multivariate Data Analysis* (5ᵗʰ ed.). Englewood Cliff, NJ: Prentice Hall.

Hallikainen, P., Kimpimäki, H., & Kivijärvi, H. (2006). Supporting the Module Sequencing Decision in the ERP Implementation Process. In *Proceedings of the 39th Hawaii International Conference on System Sciences - 2006*, 1-10.

Hamerman, P., & Miller, B. (2004). *ERP applications—market maturity, consolidation and the next generation.* Forrester Research Report, ID No OR-TEECE 091574.

Hammer, M., & Champy, J. (1993). *Reengineering the Corporation.* New York: Harper Business.

Hammersley, M. (1991). *What's Wrong With Ethnography?: Methodological Explorations.* London: Routledge.

Hammersley, M., & Atkinson, P. (1995). *Ethnography: Principles in Practice* (2ⁿᵈ ed.). London: Routledge.

Hansen, M. T., Nohria, N., & Tierney, T. (1999). What's your strategy for managing knowledge? *Harvard business review* (pp. 106-116). Harvard University, Graduate School of Business Management.

Hardt, A., & Schrepp, M. (2008). Making business software usable for handicapped employees. In K. Miesenberger, J. Klaus, W. Zagler & A. Karshmer (Eds.), *Computers helping people with special needs* (pp. 502-509). Berlin: Springer.

Harreld, H. (2001). *Extended ERP reborn in B2B.* Retrieved April, 14, 2006, from http://www.infoworld.com/articles/hn/xml/01/08/27/010827hnerp.html

Hartwick, J., & Barki, H. (1994). Explaining the role of user participation in information systems use. *Management Science, 40*(4), 440–465. doi:10.1287/mnsc.40.4.440

Heart, T., & Pliskin, N. (2001). Is e-commerce of IT application services (ASP) alive and well? *Journal of Information Technology Theory and Application, 3*(4), 33-41.

Hecht, B. (1997). Choose the right ERP software. *Datamation, 43*(3), 56–58.

Helmer, O. (1977). Problems in futures research: Delphi and causal cross-impact analysis. *Futures, 9*(S 17), 31.

Henderson, R., & Divett, M. J. (2003). Perceived usefulness, ease of use and electronic supermarket use. *International Journal of Human-Computer Studies, 59*(3), 383–395. doi:10.1016/S1071-5819(03)00079-X

Hendler, J. (2001). Agents and the Semantic Web. *IEEE Intelligent Systems, 16*, 30–37. doi:10.1109/5254.920597

Hendricks, K. B., Singhal, V. R., & Stratman, J. K. (2006). (in press). The impact of enterprise systems on corporate performance: A study of ERP, SCM, and CRM system implementations. [*Corrected Proof.*]. *Journal of Operations Management.*

Hicks, D. A., & Stecke, K. E. (1995). The ERP Maze: Enterprise Resource Planning and Other Production and Inventory Control Software. *IIE Solutions, 27*(8), 12–16.

Hickson, D. J., Hinings, C. R., Lee, C. A., Schneck, R., & Pennings, J. M. (1971). A strategic contingency theory of intraorganizational power. *Administrative Science Quarterly, 16*, 216–229. doi:10.2307/2391831

Hildebrandt, L. (1987). Consumer retail satisfaction in rural areas: A re-analysis of survey data. *Journal of Economic Psychology, 8*, 19–42. doi:10.1016/0167-4870(87)90004-3

Hill, S. (1997). The Wait is Over. *Manufacturing Systems, 15*(6), 11–X.

Hill, T. (2000). *Manufacturing Strategy*. Boston: McGraw-Hill.

Hinchey, M. G., & Sterritt, R. (2006). Self-managing software. *Computer, 40*(2), 107–111. doi:10.1109/MC.2006.69

Hiquet, B., & Kelly, A. F. (1998). SAP R/3 implementation guide: A manager's guide to understanding SAP. India: Macmillan Technical.

Ho, C. F., Wu, W. H., & Tai, Y. M. (2004). Strategies for the Adaptation of ERP systems. *Industrial Management & Data Systems, 104*(3), 234–251. doi:10.1108/02635570410525780

Holland, C. P., & Light, B. (1999). A Critical Success Factors Model for ERP Implementation. *IEEE Software*, (May-June): 30–36. doi:10.1109/52.765784

Holland, C. P., & Light, B. (1999, May/June). A Critical success factor model for ERP implementation. *IEEE Software*, 30–36. doi:10.1109/52.765784

Holland, C., & Light, B. (1999). A critical success factors model for ERP implementation. *IEEE Software, 16*(3), 30–36. doi:10.1109/52.765784

Holland, C., Light, B., & Gibson, N. (1999). A critical success model for enterprise resource planning implementation. *Proceedings of the 7th European Conference on Information Systems*. Copenhagen, Denmark: Copenhagen Business School.

Holman, G. K. (2000). *What is XSLT*. Retrieved November 16, 2004, from http://www.xml.com/pub/a/2000/08/holman/index.html

Hong, K. K., & Kim, Y. G. (2002). The Critical Success Factors for ERP Implementation: An Organisational Fit Perspective. *Information & Management, 40*, 25–40. doi:10.1016/S0378-7206(01)00134-3

Horling, B., Benyo, B., & Lesser, V. (2001). *Using self-diagnosis to adapt organizational structures* (Tech. Rep. TR-99-64). University of Massachusetts.

Howard, M. S. (1994). *Quality of Group Decision Support Systems: a comparison between GDSS and traditional group approaches for decision tasks*. Eindhoven University of Technology, Eindhoven.

Hu, B., Harding, J. A., & Popplewell, K. (2000). A reusable enterprise model. *International Journal of Operations & Production Management, 20*(1), 50–69. doi:10.1108/01443570010301083

Humphrey, W. (2005). *Managing the software process*. Addison-Wesley.

Hunter, M. G., & Lippert, S. K. (2007). Critical Success Factors of ERP implementation. *Information Resources Management Proceedings*. Hershey, PA: IGI Publishing.

Hurbean, L. (2006). Factors Influencing ERP Projects Success in the Vendor Selection Process. Retrieved June 22, 2009 from http://papers.ssrn.com/sol3/papers.cfm?abstract_id=946746

Hussein, R., Karim, N. S. A., Mohamed, N., & Ahlan, A. R. (2007). The influence of organizational factors on information systems success in e-government agencies in Malaysia. *The Electronic Journal on Information Systems in Developing Countries, 29*(1), 1–17.

Hwang, H., Ku, C., Yen, D., & Cheng, C. (2004). Critical factors influencing the adoption of data warehouse technology: A study of the banking industry in Taiwan. *Decision Support Systems, 37*(1), 1-21.

IBM (2004). *More about high-volume web sites*. IBM Redbook.

IDC Press Release. (2007). *Top-ranked business intelligence tools vendors maintain positions*. Retrieved July 3, 2007, from http://www.idc.com/getdoc.jsp?containerId=prUS20767807.

IEEE. (2000). IEEE Standard 1516 (HLA Rules), 1516.1 (Interface Specification) and 1516.2 (Object Model Template).

Igbaria, M. (1992). An examination of microcomputer usage in Taiwan. *Information & Management, 22*, 19-28.

Igbaria, M., & Chakrabarti, A. (1990). Computer anxiety and attitudes towards microcomputer use. *Behavior & Information Technology, 9*, 229-241.

Igbaria, M., Zinatelli, N., Cragg, P., & Cavaye, A. L. M. (1997). Personal computing acceptance factors in small firms: a structural equation model. *MIS Quarterly, 21*(3), 279–302. doi:10.2307/249498

Illa, X. B., Franch, X., & Pastor, J. A. (2000). Formalising ERP selection criteria. In *Proceedings of the 10th International Workshop on Software Specification and Design* (pp.115). IEEE Computer Society, Washington, DC, 5-7 November.

Im, K. S., Dow, K. E., & Grover, V. (2001). A reexamination of IT investment and the market value of the firm: an event study methodology. *Information Systems Research, 12*(1), 103–117. doi:10.1287/isre.12.1.103.9718

Institute, M. I. C. (2004). Ch12 Information Service Industry. *2004 Information Service Industry Yearbook.*

Institute, M. I. C. (2004). Ch12 Information Service Industry. *2006 Information Service Industry Yearbook.*

Institute, M. I. C. (2008). CH4 The Trend and Situation of Market. *2008 Information Service Industry Yearbook.*

Ives, B., & Jarvenpaa, S. (1993). Organizing for global competition: The fit of information technology. *Decision Sciences, 24*(3), 547–580. doi:10.1111/j.1540-5915.1993.tb01293.x

Ives, B., & Olson, M. (1984). User involvement and MIS success: A review of research. *Management Science, 30*(5), 586-603.

Jackson, D. W., Keith, J. F., & Burdick, R. R. (1984). Purchasing agents' perceptions of industrial buying center influence: a situational approach. *Journal of Marketing, 48*, 75–83. doi:10.2307/1251512

Jacobs, R. F., & Weston, F. C. (2007). Enterprise resource planning (ERP)—A brief history. *Journal of Operations Management, 25*(2), 357–363. doi:10.1016/j.jom.2006.11.005

Jacobson, I., Ericson, M., & Jacobson, A. (1995). *The object advantage: Business process reengineering with object technology.* ACM Press.

Jagielska, I., Darke, P., & Zagari, G. (2003). Business intelligence systems for decision support: Concepts, processes and practice. *Paper presented at the 7ᵗʰ International Conference of the International Society for Decision Support Systems.*

Jain, R. (1997). A diffusion model for public information systems in developing countries. *Journal of Global Information Management, 5*(1), 4-15.

Jalote, P. (1999). *CMM in Practice, Processes for executing project at Infosys.* Addison-Wesley

Jalote, P. (2002). *Software Project Management in Practice.* Addison-Wesley.

Jameson, A. (2007). Adaptive interfaces and agents. In J.A. Jacko & A. Sears (Eds.), *Human-computer interaction handbook* (pp. 433-458). Mahwah, NJ: Erlbaum.

Janssens, G., Kusters, R., & Heemstra, F. (2008). A small survey into the importance of and into a concept for estimating effort-related costs of ERP implementation projects. *Working papers Management Sciences, 14.*

Jaruzelski, B., Lake, R. M, & Ribeiro, F. M. (2000). *ASP101: understanding the application service provider model.* Retrieved May 12, 2004, from http://www.bah.com

JAVA language (n.d.). Retrieved from http://java.sun.com

Jayasuriya, R. (1999). Managing information systems for health services in a developing country: A case study using a contextualist framework. *International Journal of Information Management, 19*(5), 335-349.

JESS the Rule Engine for the Java Platform (n.d.). Retrieved from http://herzberg.ca.sandia.gov/

Jiménez, J., & Polo, Y. (1998). International diffusion of a new tool: The case of electronic data interchange in the retailing sector. *Research Policy, 26*(7-8), 811–827. doi:10.1016/S0048-7333(97)00045-0

Jonker, C. M., & Treur, J. (2003). A temporal-interactivist perspective on the dynamics of mental states. *Cognitive Systems Research Journal., 4*, 137–155. doi:10.1016/S1389-0417(02)00103-1

Jöreskog, K. (1971). Statistical analysis of sets of congeneric tests. *Psychometrika, 36*, 109–133. doi:10.1007/BF02291393

Jöreskog, K., & Sörbom, D. (1993). *LISREL 8 Structural Equation Modeling with the Simples Command Language.* Scientific software International, Chicago-Illinois.

Judd, C. M., Smith, E. R., & Kidder, L. H. (1991). *Research Methods in Social Relations* (6th ed.). Fort Worth, TX: Harcourt Brace Jovanovich.

Jurison, J. (1996). The temporal nature of IS benefits: A longitudinal study. *Information & Management, 30,* 75-79.

Kaarst-Brown, M. (1999). Five symbolic roles of the external consultant: Integrating change, power and symbolism. *Journal of Organizational Change Management, 12*(6), 540-561.

Kaefer, F., & Bendoly, E. (2004). Measuring the impact of organizational constraint on the success of business e-commerce efforts: A transactional focus. *Information & Management, 41,* 529–541. doi:10.1016/S0378-7206(03)00088-0

Kamhawi, E. M. (2007). Critical factors for implementation success of ERP systems. *International Journal of Enterprise Information Systems, 3*(2), 34–49.

Kansel, V. (2006). Enterprise Resource Planning Implementation: A Case Study. *The Journal of American Academy of Business, Cambridge, 9*(1), 165–170.

Karat, M., Brodie, C., Karat, J., Vergo, J., & Alpert, S. R. (2003). Personalizing the user experience on ibm.com. *IBM Systems Journal, 42*(4), 686–701.

Karim, J., Somers, T. M., & Bhattacherjee, A. (2007). The impact of ERP implementation on business process outcomes: A factor-based study. *Journal of Management Information Systems, 24*(1), 101–134. doi:10.2753/MIS0742-1222240103

Karsak, E. E., & Ozogul, C. O. (2009). An integrated decision making approach for ERP system selection. *Expert Systems with Applications, 36,* 660–667. doi:10.1016/j.eswa.2007.09.016

Katsaliaki, K., & Brailsford, S. C. (2007). Using Simulation to Improve the Blood Supply Chain. *The Journal of the Operational Research Society, 58*(2), 219–227.

Kauffman, R. G. (1996). Influences on organizational buying choice process: future research directions. *Journal of Business and Industrial Marketing, 11*(3/4), 94–107. doi:10.1108/08858629610125496

Kawalek, P., & Wood-Harper, T. (2002). Finding of thorns: User participation in enterprise system implementation. *Advances in Information Systems, 33*(1), 13-22.

Kearns, G. S., & Lederer, A. L. (2000). The effect of strategic alignment on the use IS-based resources for competitive advantage. *Journal of Strategic Information Systems, 9,* 265-293.

Kearns, G. S., & Sabhewarl, R. (2007). Antecedents and consequences of information systems planning integration. *IEEE Transactions on Engineering Management, 54*(4), 628–643. doi:10.1109/TEM.2007.906848

Kembel, R. W. (2000). *Fibre channel: A comprehensive introduction* (Revised ed). Tucson, Arizona: Norwest Learning Associates.

Kensing, F., & Blomberg, J. (1998). Participatory design: Issues and concerns. *Computer Supported Cooperative Work, 7,* 167-185.

Kerimoglu, O., Basoglu, N., & Daim, T. (2008). Organizational adoption of information technologies: Case of enterprise resource planning systems. *The Journal of High Technology Management Research, 19,* 21–35. doi:10.1016/j.hitech.2008.06.002

Kern, T., Lacity, M., & Willcocks, L. (2002). *Netsourcing: renting business applications and services over a network.* New York: Prentice-Hall.

Khalil, O., & Elkordy, M. (1997). The relationship of some personal and situational factors to IS effectiveness: Empirical evidence from Egypt. *Journal of Global Information Management, 5*(2), 22-34.

Kien, S., & Soh, C. (Eds.). (2003). An exploratory analysis of the sources and nature of misfits in ERP implementations (1st ed.). In: G. Shanks, P. Seddon, & L. Willcocks (Eds.), *Second-wave enterprise resource planning systems, implementing for effectiveness* (pp. 373-387). Cambridge, UK: Cambridge University Press.

Kim, C., Weston, R., & Woo, H. (2001). Development of an integrated methodology for enterprise engineering. *International Journal of Computer Integrated Manufacturing, 14*(5), 473–488. doi:10.1080/09511920010029254

Kim, Y., & Kim, Y. (1999). Critical issues in the networking area. *Information Resources Management Journal, 4*(4), 14-23.

Kim, Y., Lee, Z., & Gosain, S. (2005). Impediments to Successful ERP Implementation Process. *Business Process Management Journal, 11*(2), 158–170. doi:10.1108/14637150510591156

Klein, H., & Myers, M. (1999). A set of principles for conducting and evaluating interpretive field studies in information systems. *MIS Quarterly, Special Issue on Intensive Research, 23*(1), 67-93.

Klopping, I., & McKinney, E. (2004). Extending the technology acceptance model the task-technology fit model to consumer e-commerce. *Information Technology. Learning Performance Journal, 22*(1), 35–48.

Knight, K. E. (1967). A descriptive model of the intra-firm innovation process. *The Journal of Business, 40*, 478–496. doi:10.1086/295013

Ko, H. C., Yin, C. P., & Kuo, F. Y. (2008). Exploring individual communication power in the blogosphere. *Internet Research, 18*(5), 541–561. doi:10.1108/10662240810912774

Koch, C. (1996, June 15). Flipping the switch. *CIO, 9*(17), 43–66.

Koch, C. (1999). The Most Important Team in History. *CIO, 13*(2), 40–52.

Kositanurit, B., Ngwenyama, O., & Osei-Bryson, K.-M. (2006). An exploration of factors that impact individual performance in an ERP environment: an analysis using multiple analytical techniques. *European Journal of Information Systems, 15*, 556–568. doi:10.1057/palgrave.ejis.3000654

Kostopoulos, K. C., Brachos, D. A., & Prastacos, G. P. (2004). Determining factors of ERP adoption: an indicative study in the Greek market. In *Proceedings of the IEEE Engineering Management Conference,* Oct 18-21 (pp. 287-291).

Kraemer, K. L., Moony, J., Dunkle, D., & Vitalari, N. (1994). The business value of Information technology in corporations. Special Report, CRITO and CSC Consulting.

Krause, D. R., Pagell, M., & Curkovic, S. (2001). Toward a Measure of Competitive Priorities for Purchasing. *Journal of Operations Management, 19*, 497–512. doi:10.1016/S0272-6963(01)00047-X

Kujala, S. (2003). User involvement: a review of the benefits and challenges. *Behaviour & Information Technology, 22*(1), 1–16. doi:10.1080/01449290301782

Kumar, K., & Hillegersberg, J. (2000). ERP experiences and evolution. *Communications of the ACM, 43*(4), 23–26. doi:10.1145/332051.332063

Kumar, K., van Dissel, H. G., & Bielli, P. (1998). The merchant of Prato – Revisited: Toward a third rationality of information systems. *MIS Quarterly, 22*(2), 199-226.

Kumar, V., Maheshwari, B., & Kumar, U. (2002). ERP systems implementation: Best practices in Canadian government organizations. *Government Information Quarterly, 19*, 147–172. doi:10.1016/S0740-624X(02)00092-8

Kumar, V., Maheshwari, B., & Kumar, U. (2003). An investigation of critical management issues in ERP implementation: empirical evidence from Canadian organizations. *Technovation, 23*(10), 793–807. doi:10.1016/S0166-4972(02)00015-9

Kuropka, D., Bog, A., & Weske, M. (2006) Semantic enterprise services platform: Motivation, potential, functionality and application scenarios. In *Proceedings of the tenth IEEE international EDOC Enterprise Computing Conference, Hong Kong* (pp. 253-261).

Kusters, R. J., Heemstra, F. J., & Jonker, A. (2009). ERP Implementation Costs: A Preliminary Investigation. In *Enterprise []*. Berlin: Springer.]. *Information Systems, 12*, 95–107.

Kwon, T. H., & Zmud, R. W. (1987). Unifying the fragmented models of information systems implementation. In *Critical issues in information systems research* (pp. 227-251). John Wiley & Sons, Inc.

Lam, A. (1997). Embedded firms, embedded knowledge: Problems of collaboration and knowledge transfer in global cooperative ventures. *Organization Studies, 18*(6), 973-996.

Lam, A. (2000). Tacit knowledge, organizational learning and societal institutions: An integrated framework. *Organization Studies, 21*(3), 487-514.

Lam, W. (2005). Investigating success factors in enterprise application: A case-driven analysis. *European Journal of Information Systems, 14*(2), 175-187.

Lambert, S. (1995). An investigation of workers' use and appreciation of supportive workplace policies. Best papers 1995: *Proceedings of the Academy of Management.*

Lämmer, A., Eggert, S., & Gronau, N. (2008). A procedure model for a SOA-Based integration of enterprise systems. *International Journal of Enterprise Information Systems, 4*(2), 1–12.

Lankhorst, M. (2005) *Enterprise architecture at work: Modelling, communication, and analysis.* Springer.

Lansley, P., Sadler, P. J., & Webb, T. D. (1975). *Organization Structure, Management Style and Company Performance,* Omega, London.

Lara, R., Roman, D., Polleres, A., & Fensel, D. (2004). A conceptual comparison of WSMO and OWL-S. *European Conference on Web Services* (pp. 254-269).

Latif-Shabgahi, G., Bass, J. M., & Bennett, S. (1999). Integrating selected fault masking and self-diagnosis mechanisms. In *Proceedings of the Seventh Euromicro Workshop on Parallel and Distributed Processing* (pp. 97-104). IEEE Computer Society.

Latvanen, H., & Ruusunen, R. (2001). Management of Risks in an ERP Implementation Project. In T. S. o. Economics (Ed.), (pp. 20).

Laudon, K. C., & Laudon, J. P. (2006). *Management Information Systems.* NJ: Pearson Education.

Laudon, K. C., & Laudon, J. P. (2007). *Essentials of Management Information Systems: Managing The Digital Firm* (6th Ed). NJ: Prentice Hall.

Lauesen, S. (2002). *Software requirements. Styles and techniques.* London: Addison-Wesley.

Laukkanen, S., Sarpola, S., & Hallikainen, P. (2005). ERP system adoption – Does the size matter? In *Proceedings of the 38th IEEE Annual Hawaii Conference on System Sciences,* Jan 03-06, 2005. Track 8 (pp. 1-9).

Law, C.C.H., & Ngai. (2007). ERP systems adoption: An exploratory study of the organizational factors and impacts of ERP success. *Information & Management, 44*(4). doi:10.1016/j.im.2007.03.004

Lee, A. S., & Baskerville, R. L. (2003). Generalising generalizability in information systems research. *Information Systems Research, 14*(3), 221-243.

Lee, J., & Kim, S. (1992). The relationship between procedural formalization in MIS development and MIS success: A contingency analysis. *Information & Management, 22,* 89-111.

Lee, R. (1998). An enterprise decision framework for information system selection. *Information Systems Management, 15*(4), 7–18. doi:10.1201/1078/43186.15.4.19980901/31145.2

Lee, Y., Kozar, K. A., & Larsen, K. R. T. (2003). The technology acceptance model: past, present, and future. *Communications of the Association for Information Systems, 12,* 752–780.

Legare, T. L. (2002). The Role of Organisational Factors in Realising ERP Benefits. *Information Systems Management, 19*(4), 21–42. doi:10.1201/1078/43202.19.4.20020901/38832.4

Legris, P. J., Ingham, J., & Collerette, P. (2003). Why do people use information technology? A critical review of the technology acceptance model. *Information & Management, 40*(3), 191–204. doi:10.1016/S0378-7206(01)00143-4

Lehmann, D. R., & O'Shaughnessy, J. (1982). Decision criteria used in buying different categories of products of products. *Journal of Purchasing and Materials Management, 18,* 9–14.

Leung, L. (2001). College student motives for chatting on ICQ. *New Media & Society, 3*(4), 483–500. doi:10.1177/14614440122226209

Leymann, F., & Roller, D. (2000). *Production workflow - Concepts and techniques.* Prentice Hall International.

Leymann, F., & Roller, D. (2006). Modeling business processes with BPEL4WS. *Information Systems and E-Business Management, 4*(3), 265–284. doi:10.1007/s10257-005-0025-2

Li, E., Rogers, J., & Chang, H. (1994). An empirical reassessment of the measure of information systems sophistication. *Information Resources Management Journal, 7,* 3-19.

Liautaud, B., & Hammond, M. (2000). *E-business intelligence: Turning information into knowledge and profit.* New York, NY: McGraw-Hill.

Liaw, S. S., & Huang, H. M. (2003). An investigation of user attitudes toward search engines as an information retrieval tool. *Computers in Human Behavior, 19*(6), 751–765. doi:10.1016/S0747-5632(03)00009-8

Liaw, S. S., Chang, W. C., Hung, W. H., & Huang, H. M. (2006). Attitudes toward search engines as a learning assisted tool: approach of Liaw and Huang's research model. *Computers in Human Behavior, 22*(3), 501–517. doi:10.1016/j.chb.2004.10.007

Light, B. (2005). Going beyond 'misfit' as a reason for ERP package customization. *Computers in Industry, 56*, 606–619. doi:10.1016/j.compind.2005.02.008

Lin, S., Gao, J., Koronios, A., & Chanana, V. (2007). Developing a data quality framework for asset management in engineering organizations. *International Journal of Information Quality, 1*(1), 100-126.

Linstone, H., & Turoff, M. (2002). *The Delphi method: Techniques and applications (Electronic version).*

Liu, T. H. (2006). *The Analysis of Business Software Companies' Development.* Market Intelligence Consulting Institute.

Logan, D., & Buytendijk, F. (2003). *The Sarbanes-Oxley Act will impact your enterprise.*

Loh, L., & Venkatraman, N. (1992). Diffusion of information technology outsourcing: Influence sources and the Kodak effect. *Information Systems Research, 3*(4), 334–358. doi:10.1287/isre.3.4.334

Loh, T. C., & Koh, S. C. L. (2004). Critical elements for a successful ERP implementation in SMEs. *International Journal of Production Research, 42*(17), 3433–3455. doi:10.1080/00207540410001671679

Lotto, P. (2006). Befriending your ERP system. *Electrical Wholesaling.* Retrieved March 20, 2007 from http://www.infor.com/7343/14397/12565/23954/23965

Lou, J. R., Zhang, S. Y., & Tan, J. R. (2004). Research on expressing and processing client demands for mass customization. *Chinese Mechanical Engineering, 15*(8), 685-687.

Lu, H. P., & Yeh, D. C. (1998). Enterprise's perceptions on business process re-engineering: A path analytic model. *OMEGA. International Journal of Management Science, 26*(1), 17–27.

Lucas, H. (1978). The evolution of an information system: From key-man to every person. *Sloan Management Review, 39*(52).

Lucas, H., Walton, E., & Ginzberg, M. (1988). Implementing package software. *MIS Quarterly, 12*(4), 537-549.

Lübke, D., Lüecke, T., Schneider, K., & Gómez, J. M. (2006). Using event-driven process chains fo model-driven development of business applications. In F. Lehner, H. Nösekabel, & P. Kleinschmidt (2006), *Multikonferenz Wirtschaftsinformatik 2006* (pp. 265-279). GITO-Verlag.

Luftman, J., Kempaiah, R., & Nash, E. (2005). Key Issues for IT Executives. *MIS Quarterly, 5*(2), 81–99.

Mabert, V. A., Soni, A., & Venkataramanan, M. A. (2001). Enterprise resource planning: common myths versus evolving reality. *Business Horizons, 44*(3), 69–76. doi:10.1016/S0007-6813(01)80037-9

Mabert, V. A., Soni, A., & Venkataramanan, M. A. (2003). Enterprise resource planning: Managing the implementation process. *European Journal of Operational Research, 146*(2), 302–314. doi:10.1016/S0377-2217(02)00551-9

Mabert, V. A., Soni, A., & Venkataramanan, M. A. (2005). Model based interpretation of survey data: A case study of enterprise resource planning implementations. *In Press, Corrected Proof.*

Maguire, M. (2001). Methods to support human-centred design. *International Journal of Human-Computer Studies, 55*(4), 587–634. doi:10.1006/ijhc.2001.0503

Mahajan, V., & Peterson, R. A. (1985). *Models for innovation diffusion.* Beverly Hills: Sage Publications.

Mahajan, V., Muller, E., & Bass, F. M. (1990). New product diffusion model in marketing: a review and directions for research. *Journal of Marketing, 54*, 1–26. doi:10.2307/1252170

Mahajan, V., Sharma, S., & Bettis, R. A. (1988). The adoption of the M-form organizational structure: A test of imitation hypothesis. *Management Science, 34*(10), 1188–1201. doi:10.1287/mnsc.34.10.1188

Mahmood, M., & Becker, J. (1985). Effect of organizational maturity on end users' satisfaction with information systems. *Journal of Management Information Systems, 11*, 37-64.

Mahmood, M., & Swanberg, D. (1999). Factors affecting information technology usage: A meta-analysis of the experimental literature. In *Proceedings of the 1999 IRMA International Conference,* pp. 359-364.

Maiden, N. (2006). Improve you Requirements: Quantify them. *IEEE Software*, 68–69. doi:10.1109/MS.2006.165

Malone, T. W., Crowston, K. G., & Herman, G. A. (2003). *Organizing business knowledge: The MIT Process Handbook*. MIT Press

Mansfield, E. (1961). Technical change and the rate of imitation. *Econometrica, 29*, 741–766. doi:10.2307/1911817

Manzano, M. (1996). *Extensions of First Order Logic*. Cambridge University Press.

Marakas, G., & Elam, J. (1998). Semantic structuring in analyst acquisition and representation of facts in requirements analysis. *Information Systems Research, 9*, 37–63. doi:10.1287/isre.9.1.37

March, J. (1991). Exploration and exploitation in organizational learning. *Organization Science, 2*(special issue), 71–87. doi:10.1287/orsc.2.1.71

Margetts, H., & Willcocks, L. (1994). Informatization in public sector organizations: Distinctive or common risks? *Informatization and the Public Sector, 3*(1), 1-19.

Markus, L. (1983). Power, politics and MIS implementation. *Communication of the ACM, 26*(6), 430-444.

Markus, L., Axline, S., Petrie, D., & Tanis, C. (2000). Learning from Adopters' Experience with ERP Problems Encountered and Success Achieved. *Journal of Information Technology*, 245–265. doi:10.1080/02683960010008944

Markus, M. L., & Tanis, C. (2000). The enterprise systems experience-from adoption to success. In R. W. Zmud (Ed.), *Framing the Domains of IT Research: Glimpsing the Future Through the Past* (pp. 173-207). Cincinnati: Pinnaflex Educational Resources.

Markus, M. L., Axline, S., Petrie, D., & Tanis, C. (2001). Learning From Adopters' Experiences With ERP: Problems Encountered and Success Achieved. *Journal of Information Technology, 15*, 245–265. doi:10.1080/02683960010008944

Markus, M. L., Tanis, C., & Fenema, P. C. (2000). Multisite ERP implementations. *Communications of the ACM, 43*(4), 42–46. doi:10.1145/332051.332068

Markus, M., & Tanis, C. (2000). The enterprise system experience—from adoption to success. In: R. Zmud & M. Price (Eds.), *Framing the domains of IT management: Projecting the future through the past.* Cincinnati, OH: Pinnaflex Educational Resources.

Marnewick, C., & Labuschagne, L. (2005). A conceptual model for enterprise resource planning (ERP). *Information Management & Computer Security, 13*(2), 144–155. doi:10.1108/09685220510589325

Martin, D., Cheyer, A. J., & Moran, D. B. (1999). The Open Agent Architecture: A Framework for Building distributed Software Systems. *Applied Artificial Intelligence, 13*, 91–128. doi:10.1080/088395199117504

Martin, J. (1989). *Information engineering: Introduction.* Englewood Cliffs, NJ: Prentice Hall.

Mason-Jones, R., Naylor, B., & Towill, D. R. (2000). Engineering the leagile supply chain. *International Journal of Agile Management Systems, 2*(1), 54-61.

Mathew, J. (2003). *CIEAM business plan V1.0.* Brisbane, Australia: Centre for Integrated Engineering Asset Management (CIEAM)

McDonald, R. (1981). The dimensionality of test and items. *The British Journal of Mathematical and Statistical Psychology, 34*, 110–117.

McIlraith, S. A., Son, T. C., & Zeng, H. L. (2001). Semantic Web Services. IEEE *Intelligent Systems & their Applications, 16*, 46-53,

McKie, S. (2001). *The great leap forward.* Retrieved www.business.technology.com/BT/Content/index.cfm/fuseaction/viewarticle/Content.id/109

McLaren, T. (2006). Why has the adoption of ERPs by SMEs lagged that of larger firms? Retrieved August 5, 2007 from http://www.ryerson.ca/~tmclaren/erpsme.html

McQuiston, D. H. (1989). Novelty, complexity, and importance as critical determinants of industrial buyer behavior. *Journal of Marketing, 53*, 66–79. doi:10.2307/1251414

Melnyk, S. A., & Stewart, D. M. (2002). Managing Metrics. *APICS- The Performance Advantage, 12*(2), 23-26.

Meredith, J. R., & Mantel, S. J. J. (2003). *Projectmanagement: a managerial approach* (5th ed.). John Wiley & Sons Inc.

Mertins, K., Rabe, M., & Jaekel, F. (2000). Neutral template libraries for efficient distributed simulation within a manufacturing system engineering platform. In *Proceedings of the 32nd Conference on Winter Simulation,* 1549-1557.

Millman, G. J. (2004). What did you get from ERP and what can you get? *Financial Executive*, May, 38-42.

Min, H., & Galle, W. (2003). E-purchasing: profiles of adopters and non-adopters. *Industrial Marketing Management, 32*(3), 227–233. doi:10.1016/S0019-8501(02)00266-3

Mintzberg, H. (1979). *The Structuring of Organizations.* Englewood Cliffs, NJ: Prentice Hall.

Miranda, S. M., & Saunders, C. S. (2003). The social construction of meaning: An alternative perspective on information sharing. *Information Systems Research, 14*(1), 87-106.

Mirani, R., & King, W. (1994). The development of a measure for end-user computing support. *Decision Sciences, 25*, 481-498.

Mirani, R., & Lederer, A. L. (1998). An instrument for assessing the organizational benefits of IS projects. *Decision Sciences, 29*(4), 803-838.

Mirchandani, D., & Motwani, J. (2001). End-user perceptions of ERP systems: A case study of an international automotive supplier. *International Journal of Automotive Technology and Management, 1*(4), 416–420. doi:10.1504/IJATM.2001.000049

Mitra, A., & Brown, M. E. (2002). Challenges of modelling knowledge within dynamic environments: Case of application development within the media industry. In *Proceedings of the eSMART Conference*, University of Salford, November 16-18.

Mitra, A., & Lau, J. Z. Y. (2004). Challenges of developing an interactive knowledge warehouse within the media industry: Significance of emergent frameworks. In *Proceedings of the European Conference on Information Systems*, Turku, Finland, June 14 -16.

Mitra, A., Brown, M. E., & Hackney, R. (2005). Evolutionary knowledge management: A case of system development within the manufacturing industry. *International Journal of Technology Management, 31*(1/2), 98 -115.

Miyazaki, A. D., & Fernández, A. (2001). Consumer perceptions of privacy and security risks for online shopping. *The Journal of Consumer Affairs, 35*(1), 27–44.

Molla, A., & Bhalla, A. (2006). ERP and competitive advantage in developing countries: The case of an Asian company. *The Electronic Journal on Information Systems in Developing Countries, 24*(1), 1–19.

Moller, C. (2005). Unleashing the potential of SCM: adoption of ERP in large Danish enterprises. *International Journal of Enterprise Information Systems, 1*(1), 39–52.

Møller, C., Kræmmergaard, P., & Rikhardsson, P. (2004). A Comprehensive ERP bibliography - 2000-2004. *Department of Marketing, Informatics and Statistics, Aarhus School of Business, IFI Working paper series*(12), 54.

Monk, E., & Wagner, B. (2005), Concepts in enterprise resource planning (2nd ed.). Boston: Thomson Course Technology.

Morgan, D. L. (1996). Focus groups. *Annual Review of Sociology, 22*, 129–153. doi:10.1146/annurev.soc.22.1.129

Morris, H., Moser, K., Vesset, D., & Blumstein, R. (2002). *The financial impact of business analytics.* Framingham, MA: IDC.

Mos, A., & Murphy, J. (2001). *Performance monitoring Of Java component-oriented distributed applications.* Paper presented at the IEEE 9th International Conference on Software, Telecommunications and Computer Networks - SoftCOM 2001.

Motiwalla, L., Khan, M. R., & Xu, S. (2005). An intra- and inter-industry analysis of e-business effectiveness. *Information & Management, 42*(5), 651–667. doi:10.1016/j.im.2003.12.001

Motwani, J., Mirchandani, D., Madan, M., & Gunasekaran, A. (2002). Successful Implementation of ERP Projects: Evidence From Two Case Studies. *International Journal of Production Economics, 75*(1-2), 83–96. doi:10.1016/S0925-5273(01)00183-9

Mumford, E. (2003). *Redesigning human systems* (p. 303). Hershey, PA: Information Science Publishing.

Muscatello, J. R. (1999). ERP and its Effects on the Supply Chain. APICS Manufacturing Symposium, Erie, PA.

Muscatello, J. R. (2002). The Potential Use of Knowledge Management for Training: A Review and Direction of Future Research. *Business Process Management Journal, 9*(3), 382–394. doi:10.1108/14637150310477948

Muscatello, J. R. (2006). The Usefulness of Reengineering for Enterprise Resource Planning (ERP) Systems Implementations: A Comparison of Practitioners and Consultants Beliefs. *Applied Computing and Informatics, 2*, 54–66.

Muscatello, J. R., & Parente, D. H. (2006). Enterprise Resource Planning (ERP): A Post Implementation Cross Case Analysis. *Information Resources Management Journal, 7*(3), 61–80.

Muscatello, J. R., Small, M. H., & Chen, I. J. (2003). Implementing enterprise resource planning (ERP) systems in small and midsize manufacturing firms. *International Journal of Operations & Production Management, 23*, 850–871. doi:10.1108/01443570310486329

Mustafee, N., & Taylor, S. J. E. (2006). Investigating distributed simulation with COTS simulation packages: Experiences with Simul8 and the HLA. *Operational Research Society Simulation Workshop* (pp. 33-42).

Mustafee, N., Taylor, S. J. E., Katsaliaki, K., & Brailsford, S. (2006). Distributed Simulation with COTS Simulation Packages: A Case Study in Health Care Supply Chain Simulation. In *Proceedings of the 2006 Winter Simulation Conference* (pp. 1136-1142), Monterey, CA, USA.

Mustafee, N., Taylor, S. J. E., Katsaliaki, K., & Brailsford, S. (2009). Facilitating the Analysis of a UK NBS Chain Using the HLA. *SIMULATION: Transactions of the Society of Modeling and Simulation International, 85*(2), 113–128. doi:10.1177/0037549708100530

Myers, M. D. (1999). Investigating Information Systems with Ethnographic Research. *Communications of the Association for Information Systems, 2*, 23.

Nah, F. F., & Delgado, S. (2006). Critical Success Factors for Enterprise Resource Planning Implementation and Upgrade. *Journal of Computer Information Systems*, 99–113.

Nah, F. F., & Lau, J. L. S. (2001). Critical Factors for Successful Implementation of Enterprise Systems. *Business Process Management Journal, 7*(3), 285–296. doi:10.1108/14637150110392782

Nah, F. F., & Lau, J. L. S. (2003). ERP Implementation: Chief Information Officers' Perceptions of Critical Success Factors. *International Journal of Human-Computer Interaction, 16*(1), 5–22. doi:10.1207/S15327590IJHC1601_2

Nazmul, I. (1999). *Benefits of using XML*. Retrieved January 12, 2005, from http://www.developerlife.com/xmlbenefits/default.htm

Negash, S. (2004). Business intelligence. *Communications of the Association for Information Systems, 13*, 177-195.

Neves, D., Fenn, D., & Sulcas, P. (2004). Selction of Enterprise Resource Planning (ERP) Systems. *South African Journal of Business Management, 35*(1), 45–52.

Newcomer, K., & Caudle, S. L. (1991). Evaluating public sector information systems: More than meets the eye. *Public Administration Review, 51*(5), 377-388.

Newell, S., Robertson, M., Scarbrough, H., & Swan, J. (2002). *Managing knowledge work*. Palgrave.

Newman, M., & Noble, F. (1990). User involvement as an interaction process: A case study. *Information Systems Research, 1*(1), 89-113.

Newman, M., & Robey, D. (1992). A social process model of user-analyst relationships. *MIS Quarterly, 16*(2), 249-266.

Newman, M., & Zhao, Y. (2008). The process of enterprise resource planning implementation and business process re-engineering: Tales from two Chinese small and medium-sized enterprises. *Information Systems Journal, 18*, 405–425. doi:10.1111/j.1365-2575.2008.00305.x

Ngai, E. W. T., Law, C. C. H., & Wat, F. K. T. (2008). Examining the critical success factors in the adoption of enterprise resource planning. *Computers in Industry, 59*(6), 548–564. doi:10.1016/j.compind.2007.12.001

Nicolaou, A. I., & Bhattacharya, S. (2006). Organizational Performance Effects of ERP Systems Usage: The Impact of Post-Implementation Changes. *International Journal of Accounting Information Systems, 7*, 18–35. doi:10.1016/j.accinf.2005.12.002

Nielsen, J. (1994). Heuristic evaluation. In J. Nielsen & R.L. Mack (Eds.), *Usability inspection methods* (pp. 25-62). New York: John Wiley & Sons.

Nigel, J.L., & David, H.B. (2005). An SME perspective of vertical application service providers. *International Journal of Enterprise Information Systems, 1*(2), 37-55.

Noble, F. (1995). Implementation strategies for office systems. *Journal of Strategic Information Systems, 4*, 239-253.

Nonaka, I. (1994). A dynamic theory of organisational knowledge creation. *Organisation Science, 5*(1), 14-37.

Nonaka, I., & Takeuchi, H. (1995). *The knowledge creating company: How Japanese companies create the dynamics of innovation.* New York: Oxford University Press.

Nonaka, I., & Teece, D. (Eds.) (2001). *Managing industrial knowledge: Creation, transfer and utilization.* Sage Publications.

Noori, B., & Salimi, M. H. (2005). A decision-support system for business-to-business marketing. *Journal of Business and Industrial Marketing, 20*(4-5), 226–236. doi:10.1108/08858620510603909

Noyes, J., Starr, A., & Frankish, C. (1996). User involvement in the early stages of the development of an aircraft warning system. *Behaviour & Information Technology, 15*(2), 67-75.

O'Brien, J. A., & Marakas, G. M. (2007). *Enterprise Information Systems* (13th ed). Boston: McGraw-Hill International.

O'Hair, K. (2004). *The JVMPI transition to JVMTI.* California: Sun Microsystems. Retrieved January 14, 2008, from http://java.sun.com/developer/technicalArticles/Programming/jvmpitransition/

Ojedokim, A. A. (2006). *The Impact of Computerization on Productivity in Botswana: A case study of two state corporations.* PhD thesis, Department of Library and Information Studies, University of Botswana.

Oliver, R. (1999). ERP is Dead! Long Live ERP. *Management Review, 88*(10), 12–13.

Olson, D. L., Chae, B., & Sheu, C. (2005). Issues in Multinational ERP Implementations. *International Journal of Services and Operations Management, 1*(1), 7–21. doi:10.1504/IJSOM.2005.006314

Oman, P. W. (1990). CASE Analysis and Design Tools. *IEEE Software, 7*, 37–44. doi:10.1109/52.55226

Oslen, K. A., & Saetre, P. (2007). IT for niche companies: Is an ERP system the solution? *Information Systems Journal, 17*, 37–58. doi:10.1111/j.1365-2575.2006.00229.x

Ostadzadeh, S. S., Shams Aliee, F., & Ostadzadeh, S. A. (2007) A Method for Consistent Modeling of Zachman Framework Cells. In K. Elleithy (ed.), *Advances and Innovations in Systems, Computing Sciences and Software Engineering* (pp. 375-380). Springer-Verlag.

OWL Web ontology Language Reference. (n.d.). Retrieved from http://www.w3.org/TR/owl-ref/

Palaniswamy, R., & Frank, T. G. (2002). Oracle ERP and network computing architecture: implementation and performance. *Information Systems Management, 19*(2), 53–69. doi:10.1201/1078/43200.19.2.20020228/35140.6

Palvia, P. C., Palvia, S. C., & Zigli, R. M. (1992). In M. Khosrowpour (Ed.), *Global information technology management.* Harrisburg, PA: Idea Group.

Pan, X. H., & Jia, Z. Y. (2005). Research and implementation of networked manufacturing platform based on ASP. *Manage Technique, 9*, 99-101.

Paolucci, M., Kawamura, T., Payne, T. R., & Sycara, K. (2002). Importing the Semantic Web. In Proceedings of E-Services and the Semantic Web Workshop.

Paolucci, M., Kawamura, T., Payne, T. R., & Sycara, K. (2002). Semantic matching of web services capabilities. *International Semantic Web Conference* (pp. 333-347). Berlin: Springer-Verlag.

Papazoglou, M. P. (2007). *Web services: Principles and technology.* Prentice Hall.

Papazoglou, M. P., & Van den Heuvel, W. (2000). Configurable business objects for building evolving enterprise models and applications (LNCS 1806, pp. 328-344).

ParallelGraphics. (2005). *Cortona 3D viewer.* Retrieved March 22, 2005, from http://www.cortona3d.com/cortona3d

Park, J.-H., Suh, H.-J., & Yang, H.-D. (2007). Perceived absorptive capacity of individual users in performance of Enterprise Resource Planning (ERP) usage: The case for Korean firms. *Information & Management, 44*, 300–312. doi:10.1016/j.im.2007.02.001

Parr, A., & Shanks, G. (2000). A model of ERP project implementation. *Journal of Information Technology, 15*(4), 289–303. doi:10.1080/02683960010009051

Parr, A., & Shanks, G. (2003). Critical success factors revisited: A model for ERP project implementation. In: G. Shanks, P. Seddon, & L. Willcocks (Eds.), *Second-wave enterprise resource planning systems.* Cambridge, UK: Cambridge University Press.

Parsons, T. (1947). The institutionalization of Authority. In M. Weber (Ed.), *The Theory of Social and Economic organization.* New York: Oxford University Press.

Partridge, C. (1996). *Business objects. Re-Engineering for re-use.* UK: Butterworth-Heinemann.

Patil, A.A., Oundhakar, S.A., Sheth, A.P., & Verma, K. (2004). METEOR-S Web service annotation framework.

Patterson, D. A. (2002). A simple way to estimate the cost of downtime. In *Proceedings of LISA '02: the Sixteenth USENIX Conference on Systems Administration*, Pennsylvania, USA (pp. 185-188), November 3-8, 2002.

Paul, C. L. (2008). A modified delphi approach to a new card sorting methodology. *Journal of Usability Studies, 4*(1), 24.

Paulraj, A., & Chen, I. J. (2005). Strategic Supply Management: Theory and Practice. *International Journal of Integrated Supply Management, 1*(4), 457–477. doi:10.1504/IJISM.2005.006306

Peabody, R. L. (1964). *Organizational authority: superior-subordinate relationships in three public service organizations.* New York: Atherton Press.

Pibernik, R. (2005). Advanced available-to-promise: Classification, selected methods and requirements for operations and inventory management. *International Journal of Production Economics, 93-94*(1), 239-252.

Pisano, G. P. (1994). Knowledge, integration, and the locus of learning: An empirical analysis of process development. *Strategic Management Journal, 15*, 85-100.

Pitts., M. G., & Browne, G.J. (2007). *Improving requirements elicitation: An empirical investigation of procedural prompts*, 17, 89-110.

Pomerol, J. C., Brézillon, P., & Pasquier, L. (2002). Operational knowledge representation for practical decision making. *Journal of Management Information Systems, 18*(4), 101-115.

Ponniah, P. (2001). *Data warehousing fundamentals.* New York, NY: Wiley-Interscience.

Poon, P., & Wagner, C. (2001). Critical Success Factors Revisited: Success and Failure Cases of Information Systems for Senior Executives. *Decision Support Systems, 30*(3), 393–418. doi:10.1016/S0167-9236(00)00069-5

Popova, V., & Sharpanskykh, A. (2007a). Process-Oriented Organization Modeling and Analysis. In:J.C.Augusto, J. Barjis, U. Ultes-Nitsche (Eds.), *Proceedings of the 5th International Workshop on Modelling, Simulation, Verification and Validation of Enterprise Information Systems (MSVVEIS 2007)* (pp. 114-126). INSTICC Press.

Popova, V., & Sharpanskykh, A. (2007b). Modelling Organizational Performance Indicators. In F. Barros, et al. (Eds.), *Proceedings of the International Modeling and Simulation Multiconference IMSM'07* (pp. 165-170). SCS Press.

Popova, V., & Sharpanskykh, A. (2007c). A Formal Framework for Modeling and Analysis of Organizations. In J. Ralyte, S. Brinkkemper, & B. Henderson-Sellers (Eds.), *Proceedings of the Situational Method Engineering Conference, ME'07* (pp. 343-359). Springer Verlag.

Pozzebon, M. (2000). *Combining a Structuration Approach with a Behavioral Based Model to Investigate*

ERP Usage. Presentation at the Association of Information Systems.

Premkumar, G. & Roberts. (1999). Adoption of new information technologies in rural small businesses. *Omega, 27*(4), 467–484. doi:10.1016/S0305-0483(98)00071-1

Pressman, R. S. (2006). Software Engineering, A Practitioner's Approach, India: Tata McGraw-Hill.

Pries-Heje, L. (2006). ERP misfits: What is it and how do they come about?. *Proceedings of the 17ᵗʰ Australasian Conference on Information Systems*. Adelaid, Australia.

Procaccino, J., Verner, J., Overmyer, S., & Darter, M. (2002). Case Study: Factors for early prediction of software development success. *Information and Software Technology, 44*, 53–62. doi:10.1016/S0950-5849(01)00217-8

Protégé. OWL Web ontology Language Reference. (n.d.). Retrieved from http://www.w3.org/TR/owl-ref/

Quiescenti, M., Bruccoleri, M., La Commare, U., Noto La Diega, S., & Perrone, G. (2006). Business process-oriented design of Enterprise Resource Planning (ERP) systems for small and medium enterprises. *International Journal of Production Research, 44*(18-19), 3797–3811. doi:10.1080/00207540600688499

Quin, L. (2004). *Extensible markup language (XML)*. Retrieved December 13, 2004, from http://www.w3.org/XML/

Quinn, J. B. (1992). *Intelligent Enterprise: A knowledge and service based paradigm for industry*. New York: Free Press.

Rai, A., Lang, S., & Welker, R. (2002). Assessing the validity of IS success models: An empirical test and theoretical analysis. *Information Systems Research, 13*(1), 50-69.

Rai, R., & Lee, G. (2003). Organizational factors influencing the quality of the IS/IT strategic planning process. *Industrial Management & Data Systems, 103*(8/9), 622-632.

Rajagopal, P. (2002). An innovation-diffusion view of implementation of enterprise resource planning (ERP) systems and development of a research model. *Information & Management, 40*(2), 87–114. doi:10.1016/S0378-7206(01)00135-5

Ramamurthy, K., & Premkumar, G. (1995). Determinants and outcomes of electronic data interchange diffusion. *IEEE Transactions on Engineering Management, 42*, 332-351.

Ramayah, T., & Lo, M.-C. (2007). Impact of shared beliefs on "perceived usefulness" and "ease of use" in the implementation of an enterprise resource planning system. *Management Research News, 30*(6), 420–431. doi:10.1108/01409170710751917

Rao, S. (2000). Enterprise Resource Planning: Business Needs and Technology. *Industrial Management & Data Systems, 100*, 81–88. doi:10.1108/02635570010286078

Raymond, I., & Bergeron, F. (1992). Personal DSS success in small enterprises. *Information & Management, 22*, 301-308.

Raymond, L., Uwizeymungu, S., & Bergeron, F. (2005). *ERP adoption for e-government: An analysis of motivations*. e-Government Workshop '05 (eGOV05), Brunel University.

Reich, R. (1992). *The work of nations*. New York: Vintage Press.

Relevant Business Systems (n.d); The ERP selection process survival guide (2ⁿᵈ ed.). Retrieved February 20, 2007 from http://www.relevant.com/pdf/articles/ERPguide.pdf

Riemenschneider, C., Harrison, D. A., & Mykytyn, P. P. J. (2003). Understanding ICT adoption decisions in small business: integrating current theories. *Information & Management, 40*(4), 269–285. doi:10.1016/S0378-7206(02)00010-1

Rikhardsson, P., & Kraemmergaard, P. (2006). Identifying the impacts of enterprise system implementation and use: Examples from Denmark. *International Journal of Accounting Information Systems, 7*, 36–49. doi:10.1016/j.accinf.2005.12.001

Robertson, P. J., & Seneviratne, S. J. (1995). Outcomes of planned organizational change in the public sector: A meta-analytic comparison to the private sector. *Public Administration Review, 55*(6), 547-558.

Robey, D. & Farrow, D. (1982). User involvement in information system development: A conflict model and empirical test. *Management Science, 28*(1), 73-85.

Robey, D., Ross, J., & Boudreau, M. (2002). Learning to implement enterprise systems: An exploratory study of the dialectics of change. *Journal of Management Information Systems, 19*(1), 17-46.

Robinson, J. R. L., Marshall, G. W., & Stamps, M. B. (2005). Sales force use of technology: antecedents to technology acceptance. *Journal of Business Research, 58*, 1623–1631. doi:10.1016/j.jbusres.2004.07.010

Rockart, J. (1979). Chief executives define their own data needs. *Harvard Business Review, 57*(2), 81-93.

Rockley, A. (2003). *Managing enterprise content.* Pearson Education.

Rodney, L. S., Gerard, A. A., & Ashwin, W. J. (2002). Managing seller-buyer new product development relationships for customized products: a contingency model based on transaction cost analysis and empirical test. *Journal of Product Innovation Management, 19*(6), 439-454.

Rogers, E. M. (1983). *Diffusion of Innovations.* New York: The Free Press.

Rosenzweig, P. M. (1994). When can management science research be generalized internationally? *Management Science, 40*(1), 28-39.

Ross, J. W. (1999). Clueless executives still keep ERP from delivering value. *Computer World*, September 20, p.30.

Ross, J. W. (1999). Surprising Facts about implementing ERP. *IT Professional, 1*(4), 65–68. doi:10.1109/6294.781626

Ross, J. W., Beath, C. M., & Goodhue, D. L. (1996). Developing long-term competitiveness through IT assets. *Sloan Management Review, 38*(1), 31-42.

Rowe, L. A., & Boise, W. B. (1974). Organizational innovation: current research and evolving concepts. *Public Administration Review, 34*, 284–293. doi:10.2307/974923

Ruggles, R. (1998). The state of the notion: Knowledge management in practice. *California Management Review, 40*(3), 80-89.

Russell, N., van der Aalst, W., Hofstede, A., & Wohed, P. (2006). On the Suitability of UML 2.0 Activity Diagrams for Business Process Modelling. In *Proceedings of the 3rd Asia-Pacific conference on Conceptual modelling - Volume 53*.

Salmela, H., & Turunen, P. (2003). Competitive implications of information technology in the public sector. *International Journal of Public Sector Management, 16*(1), 8-26.

Saloner, G., & Spence, A. M. (2002). *Creating and capturing value: Perspectives and cases on electronic commerce.* John Wiley & Sons, Inc.

SAP AG. (1999). ASAP Methodology for Rapid R/3 Implementation: User Manual, Walldorf.

Sarker, S., & Lee, A. (2002). Using a Case Study to Test the Role of Three Key Social Enablers in ERP Implementation. *Information & Management, 40*(8), 813–829. doi:10.1016/S0378-7206(02)00103-9

Sarkis, J., & Sundarraj, R. P. (2003). Managing Large-Scale global Enterprise Resource Planning Systems: A Case Study at Texas Instruments. *International Journal of Information Management, 23*(5), 431–442. doi:10.1016/S0268-4012(03)00070-7

Satzger, B., Pietzowski, A., Trumler, W., & Ungerer, T. (2007). Variations and evaluations of an adaptive accrual failure detector to enale self-healing properties in distributed systems. In P. Lukowicz, L. Thiele, & G. Tröster (Eds.), *Architecture of computing systems - ARCS 2007* (LNCS 4415, pp. 171-184).

Scapens, R., & Jazayeri, M. (2003). ERP systems and management accounting change: opportunities or impacts? *European Accounting Review, 12*(1), 201–233. doi:10.1080/0963818031000087907

Schaik, P. V., Flynn, D., Wersch, A. V., Douglas, A., & Cann, P. (2004). The acceptance of a computerized decision support system in primary care: a preliminary investigation. *Behaviour & Information Technology, 23*(5), 321–326. doi:10.1080/0144929041000669941

Scharmer, C. O. (2001). Self-transcending knowledge: Organizing around emerging realities. In I. Nonaka & D. Teece (Ed.), *Managing industrial knowledge: Creation, transfer and utilization* (pp. 68-90). Sage Publications.

Scheer, A., & Habermann, F. (2000). Making ERP a success. *Communications of the ACM, 43*(4), 57–61. doi:10.1145/332051.332073

Scheer, A.-W., & Nuettgens, M. (2000). *ARIS Architecture and Reference Models for Business Process Management.* In W.M.P. van der Aalst, et al. (Eds.), LNCS 1806, pp. 366-389.

Schmitt, P., Thiesse, F., & Fleisch, E. (2007). *Adoption and diffusion of RFID technology in the automotive industry.* Paper presented at the 15th ECIS, Switzerland.

Scott, J. E. (1999). The FoxMeyer Drugs' Bankruptcy: Was it a Failure of ERP? *Americas Conference on Information Systems, August 13-15, Milwaukee,* 223-225.

Scott, J. E., & Kaindl, L. (2000). Enhancing functionality in an enterprise software package. *Information & Management, 37*(3), 111–122. doi:10.1016/S0378-7206(99)00040-3

Scott, W. R. (2001). *Institutions and organizations.* Thousand Oaks, CA: SAGE Publications.

Seethamraju, R. (2005). Enterprise resource planning systems-implications for managers and management. *Australian Accounting Review, 15*(3), 90–96. doi:10.1111/j.1835-2561.2005.tb00308.x

Seliem, A., Ashour, A., Khalil, O., & Miller, S. (2003). IS characteristics and effectiveness in private and public Egyptian companies. *Arab Journal of Administrative Sciences, 10*(1), 71-91.

Seneviratne, S. J. (1999). Organizational change and information technology in the public sector. In G. D. Garson (Ed.), *Information technology and computer applications in public administration: Issues and trends* (pp. 41-61). Hershey, PA: IGP.

Seyal, A. H., & Rahman, M. N. A. (2003). A preliminary investigation of e-commerce adoption in small and medium enterprises in Brunei. *Journal of Global Information Technology Management, 6*(2), 6–26.

Shainesh, G. (2004). Understanding buyer behavior in software services – strategies for Indian firms. *International Journal of Technology Management, 28*(1), 118–127. doi:10.1504/IJTM.2004.005056

Shakir, M. (2000). *Decision making in the evaluation, selection and implementation of ERP.* Paper presented at the Proceedings of the Americas Conference on Information Systems.

Shang, R. A., Chen, Y. C., & Shen, L. (2005). Extrinsic versus intrinsic motivations for consumers to shop online. *Information & Management, 42*(3), 401–413. doi:10.1016/j.im.2004.01.009

Shang, S., & Seddon, P. (2000, August 10-13). *A comprehensive framework for classifying the benefits of ERP systems.* Paper presented at the 6th America's Conference on Information Systems, Long Beach, California.

Shang, S., & Seddon, P. (2002). Assessing and managing the benefits of enterprise systems: The business manager's perspective. *Information Systems Journal, 12,* 271-299.

Shanks, G., et al. (2000). Differences in critical success factors in ERP systems implementations in Australia and China: A cultural analysis. *Proceedings from the 8th European Conference on Information Systems.* Venna, Austria.

Sharpanskykh, A., & Treur, J. (2006) Verifying Interlevel Relations within Multi-Agent Systems. In *Proceedings of the 17th European Conf. on AI, ECAI'06* (pp. 290-294). IOS Press.

Shaw, D., & Edwards, J. S. (2005). Building user commitment to implementing a knowledge management strategy. *Information and Management, 42*(7), 977-988.

Shaw, J., Giglierano, J., & Kallis, J. (1989). Marketing complex technical products: The importance of intangible attributes. *Industrial Marketing Management, 37,* 50–56.

Shehab, E. M., Sharp, M. W., Supramaniam, L., & Spedding, T. A. (2004). Enterprise resource planning: An integrative review, business process. *Management Journal, 10*(4), 359-386.

Shelton, R. E. A. (1994). *Object-oriented business engineering: delivering the distributed enterprise.* Paper presented at the OOP'94, London.

Sheth, J. N. (1996). Organizational buying behavior: past performance and future expectations. *Journal of Business and Industrial Marketing, 11*(3/4), 7–24. doi:10.1108/08858629610125441

Shikarpur, D. (1997). The dilemma of buying ERP. *Dataquest India*. Retrieved January 15, 2007 from www.dqindia.com/oct159/3ij1141101.html

Shim, S. J., & Viswanathan, V. (2007). User assessment of personal digital assistants used in pharmaceutical detailing: System features, usefulness and ease of use. *Journal of Computer Information Systems, 48*(1), 14–21.

Shin, B. (2003). An exploratory investigation of system success factors in data warehousing. *Journal of the Association for Information Systems, 141*(170), 170.

Shin, N. (1999). Does information technology improve coordination? An empirical analysis. *Logistics Information Management, 12*(1/2), 138.

Shore, B. (2001). Information sharing in global supply chain systems. *Journal of Global Information Technology Management, 4*(3).

Shuai, J. J., Su, Y. F., & Yang, C. (2007). *The impact of ERP implementation on corporate supply chain performance*. Paper presented at the 2007 IEEE International Conference on Industrial Engineering and Engineering Management, Singapore.

Sieloff, C. G. (1999). If only HP knew what HP knows: The roots of knowledge management at Hewlett-Packard. *Journal of Knowledge Management, 3*(1), 47-53.

Silvira, G. D., Borenstein, D., & Fogliatto, F. S. (2001). Mass customization: Literature review and research directions. *International Journal of Production Economics, 72*, 1-13.

Simon, H. A. (1957). *Administrative Behavior* (2nd ed.). New York: Macmillan Co.

Sivashanmugam, K., Verma, K., Sheth, A., & Miller, J. (2003). Adding semantics to Web services standards. In Proceedings of the 1st International Conference on Web Services (ICWS'03), Las Vegas, Nevada (June 2003) (pp. 395-401).

Skov, M. B., & Høegh, R. Th. (2006). Supporting information access in a hospital ward by a context-aware mobile electronic patient record. *Personal and Ubiquitous Computing, 10*(4), 205–214. doi:10.1007/s00779-005-0049-0

Smith, M. K., Welty, C., & McGuinness, D. L. (2004) OWL Web Ontology Language, W3C Recommendation 10 February 2004. Retrieved from http://www.w3.org/TR/owl-guide/

Sneed, H. M. (2000). Encapsulation of legacy software: A technique for reusing legacy software components. *Annals of Software Engineering, 9*, 293–313. doi:10.1023/A:1018989111417

Snider, B., Silveira, G., & Balakrishnan, J. (2009). ERP implementation at SMEs: Analysis of five Canadian cases. *International Journal of Operations & Production Management, 29*, 4–29. doi:10.1108/01443570910925343

Snow, C. C., & Miles, R. E. (1983). The role of strategy in the development of a general theory of organizations. In R. Lamb (Ed.), *Advances in Strategic Management* (pp. 237-259). Greenwich: JAI Press.

Snowden, D. (2003). Innovation as an objective of knowledge management. Part I: The landscape of management. *Knowledge Management Research & Practice, 1*(1), 113-119.

Soh, C., & Kien, S. S., & Tay-Yap. (2000). Cultural Fits and Misfits: Is ERP a Universal Solution. *Communications of the ACM, 41*(4), 47–51. doi:10.1145/332051.332070

Soliman, K., & Janz, B. (2004). A exploratory study to identify the critical factors affecting the decision to establish Internet based interorganizational information systems. *Information & Management, 41*(6), 697–707. doi:10.1016/j.im.2003.06.001

Somers, T. M., & Nelson, K. (2001). The impact of critical success factors across the stages of enterprise resource planning implementation. In *Proceedings of the 34th Hawaii international Conference of System Sciences*, Mavis Hawaii, January 3-6, 2001(CD-ROM)

Somers, T. M., & Nelson, K. G. (2004). A taxonomy of players and activities across the ERP project life cycle. *Information & Management, 41*(3), 257–278. doi:10.1016/S0378-7206(03)00023-5

Spender, J.-C. (1996). Organisational knowledge, learning and memory: Three concepts in search of a theory. *Journal of Organisational Change and Management, 9*(1), 63-78.

Spender, J.-C. (1998). Pluralist epistemology and the knowledge-based theory of the firm. *Organisation, 5*(2), 233-56.

Sprott, D. (2000). Componentizing the enterprise application packages. *Communications of the ACM, 43*(4), 63–69. doi:10.1145/332051.332074

Sproule, S., & Archer, N. (2000). A buyer behavior framework for the development and design of software agents in e-commerce. *Electronic Marketing Applications and Policy, 10*(5), 396–405.

Srinivasan, V., & Mason, C. H. (1986). Nonlinear least squares estimation of new product diffusion models. *Marketing Science, 5*, 169–178. doi:10.1287/mksc.5.2.169

Steenkamp, J. P., & Van Trijp, H. C. M. (1991). The use of Lisrel in validating marketing constructs. *International Journal of Research in Marketing, 8*(November), 283–299. doi:10.1016/0167-8116(91)90027-5

Stefanou, C. (1999). Supply chain management (SCM) and organizational key factors for successful implementation of enterprise resource planning (ERP) systems. *Proceedings of Americas Conference on Information Systems*. Milwaukee, WI.

Stenmark, D. (2001). Leveraging tacit organizational knowledge. *Journal of Management Information Systems, 17*(3), 3-24.

Stenmark, D. (2003). Knowledge creation and the web: Factors indicating why some intranets succeed while others fail. *Knowledge and Process Management, 10*(3), 207-216.

Stensrud, E. (2001). Alternative approaches to effort prediction of ERP projects. *Information and Software Technology, 43*(7), 413–423. doi:10.1016/S0950-5849(01)00147-1

Stensrud, E., & Myrtveit, I. (2003, May). Identifying High Performance ERP Projects. *IEEE Transactions on Software Engineering, 29*(5). doi:10.1109/TSE.2003.1199070

Stephenson, S. V., & Sage, A. P. (2007). Information and knowledge specifications in systems engineering and management for innovation and productivity through enterprise resource planning. *Information Resources Management Journal, 20*(2), 44–73.

Stoel, M. D., & Muhanna, W. A. (2009). IT capabilities and firm performance: a contingency analysis of the role of industry and IT capability type. *Information & Management, 46*, 181–189. doi:10.1016/j.im.2008.10.002

Stojanovic, Z., Dahanayake, A., & Sol, H. (2005). An Approach to component-based and service-oriented system architecture design. In S. de Cesare, M. Lycett & R. D. Macredie (Eds.), *Development of component-based information systems* (pp. 23-48). New York: M.E. Sharpe.

Stratman, J.K., & Roth, A.V. (2002). Enterprise Resource Planning (ERP) Competence Constructs: Two-Stage Multi-item Scale Development and Validation. *Decision Sciences, Fall.*

Straub, D. W. (1989). Validating instruments in MIS research. *MIS Quarterly, 13*(2), 147–169. doi:10.2307/248922

Straub, D., & Welke, R. J. (1998). Coping with systems risk: Security planning models for management decision-making. *MIS Quarterly, 22*(4), 441-469.

Strimbei, C. (2006). *Object oriented principles in information systems alignment with enterprise modelling.* Social Science Research Network Economy Informatics Working Paper No. 1/2005

Sum, C., Ang, J., & Yeo, L. (1997). Contextual elements of critical success factors in MRP implementation. *Production and Inventory Management Journal, 38*(3), 77-83.

Summer, M. (1999). Critical success factors in enterprise-wide information management systems projects. *Proceedings of the Americas Conference on Information Systems*. Milwaukee, WI.

Sumner, M. (2000). Risk factors in enterprise-wide/ERP projects. *Journal of Information Technology, 15*(4). doi:10.1080/02683960010009079

Sumner, M. (2005). Enterprise resource planning. NJ: Pearson Education.

Sun (2004). Predictive self-healing in the Solaris 10 operation system. A technical introduction. Retrieved from http://www.sun.com/bigadmin/content/selfheal/selfheal_overview.pdf

Sun Microsystems (2004). *Java virtual machine profiler interface (JVMPI)*. California: Sun Microsystems. Retrieved January 14, 2008, from http://java.sun.com/j2se/1.5.0/docs/guide/jvmpi/jvmpi.html

Sun Microsystems (2006). *JVM tool interface, Version 1.1*. California: Sun Microsystems. Retrieved January 14, 2008, from http://java.sun.com/javase/6/docs/platform/jvmti/jvmti.html

Sun Microsystems. (2003). Java Native Interface. Retrieved from http://java.sun.com/j2se/1.4.2/docs/guide/jni/.

Sun, A., Yazdani, A., & Overend, J. (2005). Achievement assessment for enterprise resource plan-ning (ERP) system implementations based on critical success factors. *International Journal of Production Economics, 98*(2), 189–203. doi:10.1016/j.ijpe.2004.05.013

Sussman, S. W., & Siegel, W. S. (2003). Informational influence in organizations: An integrated approach to knowledge adoption. *Information Systems Research, 14*(1), 47-65.

Takeuchi, H. (2001). Towards a universal management concept of knowledge. In I. Nonaka & D. Teece (Ed.), *Managing industrial knowledge: Creation, transfer and utilization*. London: Sage Publications.

Tamura, T., Fujita, S., & Kuga, T. (1997). The concept and practice of the seat production system. *Managerial & Decision Economics, 18*(2), 101-112.

Tan, J. R, Qi, F., Zhang, S. Y., & Dai, R. Y. (2005). Research on technology of design retrieve based on fuzzy customer requirement. *Chinese Journal of Mechanical Engineering, 41*(4), 79-84.

Taube, L. R., & Gargeya, V. B. (2005). An Analysis of ERP System Implementation. *The Business Review Cambridge, 4*(1), 1–6.

Tavolato, P., & Vincena, K. (1984). A prototyping methodology and its tool (pp. 334-346). Springer-Verlag.

Taylor, D. A. (1995). *Business engineering with object technology*. John Wiley & Sons.

Taylor, S. J. E., Bohli, L., Wang, X., Turner, S. J., & Ladbrook, J. (2005). Investigating Distributed Simulation at the Ford Motor Company. In *Proceedings of the Ninth IEEE International Symposium on Distributed Simulation and Real-Time Applications. IEEE Computer Society* (pp. 139-147).

Taylor, S. J. E., Sudra, R., Janahan, T., Tan, G., & Ladbrook, J. (2001). Towards COTS distributed simulation using GRIDS. In *Proceedings of the Winter Simulation Conference* (pp. 1372-1379).

Taylor, S. J. E., Turner, S. J., & Strassburger, S. (2008). Guidelines for commercial off-the-shelf simulation package interoperability. In *Proceedings of the Winter Simulation Conference* (pp. 193-204).

Taylor, S. J. E., Wang, X., Turner, S. J., & Low, M. Y. H. (2006). Integrating Heterogeneous Distributed COTS Discrete-Event Simulation Packages: An Emerging Standards-Based Approach. *IEEE Transactions on Systems. Man & Cybernetics: Part A, 36*(1), 109–122. doi:10.1109/TSMCA.2005.859167

Tchokogué, A., Bareil, C., & Duguay, C. R. (2005). (in press). Key lessons from the implementation of an ERP at Pratt & Whitney Canada. [*Corrected Proof.*]. *International Journal of Production Economics*.

Teece, D. (1998). Research directions for knowledge management. *California Management Review, 40*(3), 289-292.

Teece, D. J. (1980). The diffusion of an administrative innovation. *Management Science, 26*(5), 464–470. doi:10.1287/mnsc.26.5.464

Teo, S. T., & Wong, P. K. (1998). An empirical study of the performance impact of computerization in the retail industry. *Omega International Journal of Management Science, 26*, 611-621.

Themistocleous, M., Irani, Z., & O'Keefe, R. (2001). ERP and application integration: exploratory survey. *Business Process Management Journal, 7*(3), 195–204. doi:10.1108/14637150110392656

Thompson, J. D. (1967). *Organizations in action*. New York: McGraw-Hill.

Thong, J. Y. L., & Yap, C. (2000). Business process reengineering in the public sector: The case of the Housing Development Board in Singapore. *Journal of Management Information Systems, Summer*, 245-270.

Thong, J. Y. L., Yap, C. S., & Raman, K. S. (1996). Management support, external expertise and information systems implementation in small businesses. *Information Systems Research, 7*, 248-266.

Timmers, P. (1999). *Electronic commerce: Strategies and models for business-to-business trading.* Chichester: John Wiley & Sons, Ltd.

Tiwana, A., & Keil, M. (2006). Functionality risk in Information Systems Development: An Empirical Investigation. *IEEE Transactions on Engineering Management, 53*(3), 412–425. doi:10.1109/TEM.2006.878099

To, M., & Ngai, E. W. T. (2007). The role of managerial attitudes in the adoption of technological innovations: an application to B2C e-commerce. *International Journal of Enterprise Information Systems, 3*(2), 23–33.

Togur, D. M., & Bloomberg, E. (2003). *CIO Survey Series: Release 4.5*, Morgan Stanley Research Report, 2003.

Tolk, A., & Blais, C. (2005). Taxonomies, ontologies, and battle management languages – recommendations for the coalition BML study group. *Spring Simulation Interoperability Workshop.*

Tolk, A., & Turnitsa, C. (2004). Ontology of the C2IEDM - further studies to enable semantic interoperability. *Fall Simulation Interoperability Workshop.*

Torkzadeh, G., & Doll, W. (1994). The test retest reliability of user involvement instruments. *Information & Management, 26*, 21-31.

Tornatzky, L. G., & Klein, K. J. (1982). Innovation characteristics and innovation adoption-implementation: a meta-analysis of findings. *IEEE Transactions on Engineering Management, 29*(1), 28–45.

Tosic, V., Esfandiari, B., Pagurek, B., & Patel, K. (2002). On requirements for ontologies in management of web services. *Web Services, E-Business, and the Semantic Web* (pp. 237-247). Berlin: Springer-Verlag.

Toure, H. I. (2007). Competitiveness and Information and Communication Technologies (ICTs) in Africa. *World Economic Forum.* Retrieved July 21, 2007 from http://www.weforum.org/pdf/gcr/africa/1.5.pdf

Trepper, C. (1999). ERP Project Management is Key to a Successful Implementation. Retrieved from http://www.erphub.com.

Trochim, W. (1989). Concept Mapping: Soft Science or Hard Art? In W. Trochim (Ed.), *A Special Issue of Evaluation and Program Planning, 12*, 1-16.

Tsai, B. H. (2008). *The impact of enterprise resource planning systems on the efficiency of Taiwanese firms.* Paper presented at the Proceedings of the 2008 IEEE Asia-Pacific Services Computing Conference.

Tsoukas, H. (1996). The firm as a distributed knowledge system: A constructionist approach [Special Issue]. *Strategic Management Journal, 17*, 11-25.

Tsoukas, H., & Mylonopoulos, N. (2003). Part special issue introduction: Modelling organisational knowledge. *Journal of the Operational Society, 54*, 911-913.

Tung, F. C. (2007). Using e-CRM Information System in the High-Tech Industry: Predicting Salesperson Intentions. *Journal of American Academy of Business, 11*(2), 131–137.

UDDI4JAVA (UDDI4J). (n.d.). Retrieved from http://uddi4j.sourceforge.net/

Umble, E. J., & Umble, M. M. (2002). Avoiding ERP Implementation Failure. *Industrial Management, January / February*, 25-33.

Umble, E. J., Haft, R. R., & Umble, M. M. (2003). Enterprise Resource Planning: Implementation Procedures and Critical Success Factors. *European Journal of Operational Research, 146*, 241–257. doi:10.1016/S0377-2217(02)00547-7

Vallespir, B., & Chen, D. Zanettin.M., & Doumeingts, G. (1991). Definition of a CIM Architecture within the ESPRIT Project 'IMPACS'. In G. Doumeingts, J. Browne & M. Tomljanovich (Eds.), *Computer applications in production engineering: Integration aspects* (pp. 731-738). Amsterdam: Elsevier.

Van Velsen, L., Van der Geest, T., Klaassen, R., & Steehouder, M. (2008). User-centered evaluation of adaptive and adaptable systems: a literature review. *The Knowledge Engineering Review, 23*(3), 261–281. doi:10.1017/S0269888908001379

Vanderperren, W., Suvée, D., Verheecke, B., Cibrán, M. A., & Jonckers, V. (2005). Adaptive programming in JAsCo. In *Proceedings of the 4th international confer-*

ence on Aspect-oriented software development. ACM Press.

Velcu, O. (2007). Exploring the effects of ERP systems on organizational performance. *Industrial Management & Data Systems, 107*, 1316–1334. doi:10.1108/02635570710833983

Venkatesh, V., & Davis, F. D. (2000). A theoretical extension of the technology acceptance model: four longitudinal field studies. *Management Science, 46*(2), 186–204. doi:10.1287/mnsc.46.2.186.11926

Venkatraman, N., Loh, L., & Koh, J. (1994). The adoption of corporate governance mechanisms: a test of competing diffusion models. *Management Science, 40*(4), 496–507. doi:10.1287/mnsc.40.4.496

Vernadat, F. B. (1992). CIMOSA - A European development for enterprise integration. Part 2: Enterprise modelling. In C. Petrie (Ed.), *Enterprise integration modeling* (pp. 189-204). Cambridge, MA: The MIT Press.

Versteeg, G., & Bouwman, H. (2006). Business architecture: A new paradigm to relate business strategy to ICT. *Information Systems Frontiers, 8*, 91–102. doi:10.1007/s10796-006-7973-z

Verville, J., & Halingten, A. (2003). A six-stage model of the buying process of ERP software. *Industrial Marketing Management, 32*, 585–594. doi:10.1016/S0019-8501(03)00007-5

Verville, J., Bernades, C., & Halingten, A. (2005). So you're buying an ERP? Ten critical factors for successful acquisitions. *Journal of Enterprise Information Management, 18*(60), 665–677. doi:10.1108/17410390510628373

Vidgen, R., Wood-Haper, T., & Wood, R. (1993). A soft systems approach to information systems quality. *Scandinavian Journal of Information Systems, 5*, 97-112.

Wagner, W., & Antonucci, Y. L. (2004). An analysis of the imagine PA public sector ERP project. *System Sciences, 2004. Proceedings of the 37th Annual Hawaii International Conference on*, 8.

Walsham, G. (2001). *Making a world of difference: IT in a global context*. Chichester: John Wiley & Sons Ltd.

Walsham, G. (2001a). Knowledge management: The benefits and limitations of computer systems. *European Management Journal, 19*(6), 599-608.

Wang, Z. Q., Li, X. N., & Jiang, C. Y. (2003). Networked manufacturing for high technology industry region of Shannxi Province's center. *Computer Integrated Manufacturing Systems, 9*(8), 710-715.

Ward, S., & Webster, F. E. (1991). Organizational buying behavior. In T.S. Robertson, & H.H. Kassarjian (Eds), *Handbook of Consumer Behavior* (pp. 419-458). Englewood Cliffs, NJ: Prentice Hall.

Watson, H., & Haley, B. (1997). Data warehousing: A framework and survey of current practices. *Journal of Data Warehousing, 2*(1), 10-17.

Watson, H., & Haley, B. (1998). Managerial considerations. *Communications of the ACM, 41*(9), 32-37.

Watson, H., Abraham, D., Chen, D., Preston, D., & Thomas, D. (2004). Data warehousing ROI: Justifying and assessing a data warehouse. *Business Intelligence Journal*, 6-17.

Watson, H., Annino, D., Wixom, B., Avery, K., & Rutherford, M. (2001). Current practices in data warehousing. *Information Systems Management, 18*(1), 1-9.

Watson, H., Fuller, C., & Ariyachandra, T. (2004). Data warehouse governance: Best practices at Blue Cross and Blue Shield of North Carolina. *Decision Support Systems, 38*(3), 435-450.

Watson, I. D. (1996). Case-based reasoning tools: An overview. Progress in Case-Based Reasoning. In *Proceedings of the 2nd UK Workshop on Case Based Reasoning*. University of Salford, UK.

Weber, M. (1958). *From Max Weber: Essays in Sociology*. In H.H. Gerth & C. Wright Mills (Eds.). New York: Oxford University Press.

Webster, F. E., & Wind, Y. (1972). A general model for understanding organizational buying behavior. *Journal of Marketing, 36*(2), 12–19. doi:10.2307/1250972

Wei, C.-C., & Wang, M.-J. J. (2004). A comprehensive framework for selecting an ERP system. *International Journal of Project Management, 22*(2), 161–169. doi:10.1016/S0263-7863(02)00064-9

Wei, C.-C., Chien, C.-F., & Wang, M.-J. J. M.-J. J. (2005). (in press). An AHP-based approach to ERP system selection. [*Corrected Proof*]. *International Journal of Production Economics*.

Weibelzahl, S., Jedlitschka, A., & Ayari, B. (2006). Eliciting requirements for an adaptive decision support system through structured interviews. In *Proceedings of the 5th Workshop on User-Centred Design and Evaluation of Adaptive Systems,* Dublin, Ireland (pp. 470-478).

Weinberg, G. (1971). *The Psychology of Computer Programming.* New York: van Nostrand Reinhold Co.

Welti, N. (1999). *Successful SAP R/3 Implementation: Practical Management of ERP Projects.* Addison Wesley Publications.

Westland, J. C., & Clark, T. H. K. (1999). *Global electronic commerce.* The MIT Press.

Weston, F. C. W. J. (2001). ERP implementation and project management. *Production and Inventory Management Journal, 42*(3/4), 75.

Whalen, P. J. (2007). Strategic and Technology Planning on a Roadmapping Foundation. *RES Technology Management*, May-June, pp. 40-51.

White, C. (2006). *New CIO spending survey.* Retrieved July 11, 2007, from http://www.b-eye-network.co.uk/blogs/white/archives/2006/09/ new_cio_spending_survey.php.

Willcocks, L. P. (2000). The role of the CIO and IT function in ERP. *Communication of ACM.*

Willcocks, L. P., & Sykes, R. (2000). The role of the CIO and IT function in ERP. *Communications of the ACM, 43*(4), 32–38. doi:10.1145/332051.332065

Willcocks, L., & Skykes, R. (2000). Enterprise resource planning: The role of the CIO and its function in ERP. *Communications of the ACM, 43*(4), 32–38. doi:10.1145/332051.332065

Williams, T. J. (1993). The Purdue enterprise reference architecture. In H. Yoshikawa & J. Goossenaerts (Eds.), *Information infrastructure systems for manufacturing* (Vol. B-14, pp. 183-192). North-Holland.

Willis, T. H., Willis-Brown, A. H., & McMillan, A. (2001). Cost containment strategies for ERP system implementations. *Production and Inventory Management Journal, 42*(2), 36.

Wixom, B. H., & Watson, H. J. (2001). An empirical investigation of the factors affecting data warehousing success. *MIS Quarterly, 25*(1) 17-41.

Wixom, B., & Watson, H. (2001). An empirical investigation of the factors affecting data-warehousing success. *MIS Quarterly, 25*(1), 17-41.

Wright, S., & Wright, A. (2002). Information system assurance for enterprise resource planning systems: unique risk considerations. *Journal of Information Systems, 16*, 99–113. doi:10.2308/jis.2002.16.s-1.99

Wu, J. H., & Wang, Y. M. (2006). Measuring ERP Success: the Ultimate Users View. *International Journal of Operations & Production Management, 26*(8), 882–903. doi:10.1108/01443570610678657

Wu, J. W., Chen, Y. C., & Lin, L. M. (2007). Empirical evaluation of the revised end user computing acceptance model. *Computers in Human Behavior, 23*(1), 162–174. doi:10.1016/j.chb.2004.04.003

Wu, J.-H., & Wang, Y.-M. (2006). Measuring ERP success: the ultimate users' view. *International Journal of Operations & Production Management, 26*(8), 882–903. doi:10.1108/01443570610678657

CIMOSA – Open System Architecture for CIM. *ESPRIT Consortium AMICE* (1993). Berlin: Springer-Verlag.

Xiao, X. P., Song, Z. M, & Li, F. (2005). *The basis and application of gray technology.* Beijing: Science Press, China.

Xu, L. Y., Li, A. P., & Zhang, W. M. (2004). Networked manufacturing base on ASP and relational technologies. *China Mechanical Engineering, 15*(19), 1755-1759.

Xu, Q., & Ma, Q. (2008). Determinants of ERP implementation knowledge transfer. *Information & Management, 45*, 528–539. doi:10.1016/j.im.2008.08.004

Yang, Y., Zhang, X. D., Liu, F., & Xie, Q. (2005). An Internet-based product customization system for CIM. *Roboties and Computer-Integrated Manufacturing, 21*, 109-118.

Yap, C., Soh, C., & Roman, K. (1992). Information systems success in small business. *OMEGA, 20*, 597-609.

Yi, L., Cheng, X. S, & Guo, Y. (2006). Development and implementation of Web-based interactive virtual assembly platform. *Machine Building & Automation, 35*(1), 75-79.

Yi, M. Y., Jackson, J. D., Park, J. S., & Probst, J. (2006). Understanding information technology acceptance by individual professionals: toward an integrative view. *Information & Management, 43*(3), 350–363. doi:10.1016/j.im.2005.08.006

Yin, R. K. (2003). *Case study research. Design and methods* (3rd ed.). Thousand Oaks, CA: Sage publications.

Yoon, Y., Guimaraes, T., & Clevenson, A. (1998). Exploring expert systems success factors for business process reengineering. *Journal of Engineering and Technology Management, 15*, 179-199.

Yousef, D. A. (1994). Top management attitudes towards the use of computer in managerial practices: An empirical study in the United Arab Emirates government Sector. *Arab Journal of Administrative Sciences, 1*(May), 295-329.

Yusuf, Y., Gunasekaran, A., & Abthorpe, M. S. (2004). Enterprise information systems project implementation: A case study of ERP in Rolls-Royce. *International Journal of Production Economics, 87*(3), 251–266. doi:10.1016/j.ijpe.2003.10.004

Zablah, A. R., Johnston, W. J., & Bellenger, D. N. (2005). Transforming partner relationships through technological innovation. *Journal of Business and Industrial Marketing, 20*(7), 355–364. doi:10.1108/08858620510628597

Zachman, J. A. (1987). A framework for information systems architecture. *IBM Systems Journal, 26*(3), 276–292.

Zachman, J.A. (2003). *The Zachman Framework: A Primer for Enterprise Engineering and Manufacturing.*

Zack, M. H. (1999). Developing a knowledge strategy. *California Management Review, 41*(3), 125-45.

Zhao, H. J., Ju, W. J., Wang, S. Y., & Yin, C. F. (2003). Software resource sharing and its application in networked manufacturing system. *Computer Integrated Manufacturing Systems, 9*(7), 608-612.

Zhao, Z., Ball, M. O., & Kotake, M. (2005). Optimization-based available-to-promise with multi-stage resource availability. *Annals of Operations Research, 135*(1), 65-85.

Ziglio, E. (1996). *The Delphi method and its contribution to decision-making. Gazing into the oracle. The Delphi method and its application to social policy and public health* (pp. 3-33). London: Jessica Kingsley Publishers.

Zimmerman, B., Yuhanna, N., Heffner, R., Schreck, G., Rankine, C., & Garbani, J. (2004). *An executive guide to high availability.* Cambridge, Massachusetts: Forrester Research.

Zmud, R., & Cox, J. (1979). The implementation process: A change approach. *MIS Quarterly, 3*(2), 35-43.

About the Contributors

Angappa Gunasekaran is Professor of Operations Management and Chairperson of the Department of Decision and Information Sciences in the Charlton College of Business at the University of Massachusetts (North Dartmouth, USA). Previously, he has held academic positions in Canada, India, Finland, Australia, and Great Britain. He has a BE and ME from the University of Madras and a PhD from the Indian Institute of Technology. He teaches and conducts research in operations management and information systems. He serves on the Editorial Board of twenty journals and edits a journal. He has published about 200 articles in journals, sixty articles in conference proceedings, and three edited books. In addition, he has organized several conferences in the emerging areas of operations management and information systems. He has extensive editorial experience that includes the guest editor of many high profile journals. He has received outstanding paper and excellence in teaching awards. His current areas of research include supply chain management, enterprise resource planning, e-commerce, and benchmarking.

Timothy Shea, D.B.A., is an Associate Professor of Management Information Systems. Dr. Shea first worked in industry and management consulting developing large systems applications and early CASE tools. He received his D.B.A. in Management Information Systems from Boston University. Dr. Shea's research has focused on the delivery and management of web-based learning and teaching technologies, corporate universities, end-user training, implementation issues around ERP's, ecommerce, and communities of practice. He has 18 journal articles published, 7 book chapters, 4 training manuals, and over 50 conference presentations. He teaches undergraduate and graduate MIS classes including Advanced Projects, Database, Networking, and E-Business.

* * *

Richard Oladele Abiola is a Professor of Business Administration at the Federal University of Technology, Akure, Nigeria. He obtained BSc in Business Education (1976), MBA (1982), and PhD in Business(1995). He is currently the Head, Department of Management Technology of the Federal University of Technology, Akure. His research interests are: Marketing Innovations, Business Policy and Strategic Management, Organizational Behavior and Organizational Aspects of Information Systems

Youcef Aklouf (PhD) is an associate professor at the computer science department of the University of Science and Technology Houari Boumediene (USTHB), and is a member of Artificial Intelligence Laboratory. He got his PhD from the USTHB University in April 2007 and from the University of Poitiers-FRANCE- in June 2007 where he was a member of the data engineering team of LISI/ENSMA.

Aklouf received his engineering and MS degrees in computer science from the University of Science and Technology of Algiers (USTHB) in 1998 and 2002, respectively. He also teaches at USTHB several courses: compiling, databases, algorithmic, web-programming tools, operating systems, etc. His research areas include: e-commerce, business–to-business, web-services, ontology and multi-agents system, Grid services.

Abdulridha Alshawaf is an associate professor of management information systems at Kuwait University. He has a PhD in Information Systems from Virginia Commonwealth University. His publications have appeared in journals such as Journal of Global Information Technology Management, Research in Accounting in Emerging Economies, Journal of Global Information Management, and Benchmarking an International Journal. His research interest includes information technology impact on organizations, information ethics, and e-commerce.

David Bell (david.bell@brunel.ac.uk) is a Lecturer at Brunel University, West London (UK), carrying out research into pervasive and service oriented software engineering. He holds a BSc (Hons) in Computing and Electronics (Swansea), a MBA (Warwick) and a PhD in Information Systems (Brunel). As part of his research into the adoption and application of novel technologies in a business setting, Dr. Bell is investigating the use of semantic technologies to facilitate software re-use in business grid and pervasive environments. Prior to returning to academia, Dr. Bell spent 15 years working in the IT industry in roles from developer to technology director. Dr. Bell has continued with technology and business consultancy and has authored and presented a number of papers on Semantic Service Discovery, Web Services and Grid Computing.

Laura Campoy is a senior lecturer in information systems in the Department of Operations and Information Management at Bristol Business School. After gaining significant research and teaching experience in the area of knowledge management technologies in the UK and overseas, she joined the University of the West of England in 2005. Campoy's research has been published in several peer reviewed journals. Over the years, she has worked in a number of projects and is currently researching knowledge architectures and tools for collaborative environments.

Hsiu-Hua Chang is a doctoral student in Department of Information Management, National Central University; she is also a lecturer in Department of Management Information Systems, Tajen University in Taiwan. Her research interests include knowledge management, electronic commerce, and ERP.

Shuchih Ernest Chang is an associate professor at the Institute of Electronic Commerce, National Chung Hsing University (NCHU) in Taiwan. He received his MSCS and PhD degrees from the University of Texas at Austin. He has 15 years of working experience in major computer and financial service firms in USA, including: Unisys, IBM, Sun Microsystems, JP Morgan, Bear Stearns, and UBS. His research interests are in e-learning technologies, electronic commerce, enterprise application architecture, information security management, and voice-enabled web systems. His publications have appeared in IEEE Pervasive Computing, Information and Software Technology, Expert Systems with Applications, International Journal on Artificial Intelligence Tools, Industrial Management & Data Systems, International Journal of Enterprise Information Systems, International Journal of Technology Management, and International Journal of Production Research.

Injazz J. Chen is the Nance Professor of Operations and Supply Chain Management in the Nance College of Business at Cleveland State University, where he received several awards for research and teaching excellence. He received his MS in Operations Research and D.B.A. in Operations Management from the University of Kentucky. His current research focuses on supply chain management (SCM), green/sustainable supply chains, and management of information and manufacturing technologies. His research findings appear in a wide variety of journals such as Journal of Operations Management, Journal of Supply Chain Management, International Journal of Production Research, European Journal of Operational Research, International Journal of Operations and Production Management, and Omega. His 2004 paper, "Strategic Purchasing, Supply Management, and Firm Performance" (with A. Paulraj and A. Lado), published in the Journal of Operations Management (JOM), was invited for presentation in the JOM Best Paper Award session at the Academy of Management annual meeting in August 2005. He recently received the 2007 JPSM Best Paper Award for a paper he published (with A. Paulraj and J. Flynn) in the Journal of Purchasing and Supply Management. Dr. Chen has served on the Editorial Review Boards of six academic journals, including Journal of Operations Management and Journal of Supply Chain Management.

Huey-Wen Chou is a Professor at National Central University. Her research interests include team dynamics, ERP, organizational change. She received her PhD from University of Illinois Urbana-Champaign

Islam Choudhury has been a lecturer in information systems for several years. He has worked at South Bank University, London Guildhall University, London Metropolitan University and Kingston University. He holds a BSc from the University of Wales College of Cardiff and a PhD, funded by BT, from South Bank University. His research interests include the general systems theory, generic business modeling, enterprise integration, workflow modeling, software process improvement and eBusiness.

Ioannis T. Christou holds a professional diploma in electrical engineering from NTUA (Greece) (1991), an MSc (1993) and PhD (1996) in Computer Sciences from the University of Wisconsin at Madison (USA), and an MBA from the AthensMBA program at NTUA and AUEB (2006). Dr. Christou has participated in several research and industrial projects in the areas of EIS, SCM, web & GRID services infrastructure and applications. He has been with Delta Technology Inc. (Atlanta USA) as project leader for Advanced Decision Support Systems, with Intracom S.A. as "Knowledge and Data Engineering" area leader, and with Lucent Technologies Bell Laboratories. Dr. Christou was adjunct assistant professor at the University of Patras Comp.Eng.&Informatics Dept. (Greece). He is currently assistant professor at Athens Information Technology.

Julie Dawson is Operations Manager at a UK furniture manufacturer undertaking a part time postgraduate research degree at the Lincoln Business School, University of Lincoln, United Kingdom. Her research interests include the implementation of information systems in organisations, particularly ERP systems. The human and organisational issues experienced throughout the planning and implementation of ERP systems are of particular interest. She is a Member of the Chartered Institute of Management.

Sergio de Cesare holds a PhD in information systems from LUISS Guido Carli in Rome (Italy). He is currently a lecturer at Brunel University where he teaches object-oriented modeling and Semantic

Web technologies. Sergio's broad research interests lay in the areas of business and software modeling, model driven information systems development and the Semantic Web. His current research focuses on the development of ontological models for systems development/re-engineering and the subsequent transformation of such models into platform-independent and platform specific application models. Sergio has (co-)authored several papers published in international journals and conference/workshop proceedings related to object oriented, component-based and ontological modeling.

Ma José Martín De Hoyos holds a Ph.D. in Business Administration and is senior lecturer in the Department of Marketing and Business Management at the University of Zaragoza (Spain). Her main research line is online consumer behaviour and e-commerce. Her work has been published in several journals, such as Industrial Marketing Management, Journal of Business and Industrial Marketing, Internet Research, Technovation, Online Information Review and European Journal of Innovation Management.

Emily Di Florido is a PhD student at the School of Information Systems, Computing and Mathematics at Brunel University. She has a degree in electronic engineering (Università La Sapienza, Rome) and an MSc in information system development (London Metropolitan University). Her broad research interests lay in the areas of model driven information systems, E-Government and digital engagement. Her current research focuses on strategic alignment between information technology and business processes within the public sector. She also has experience as an IT consultant for the voluntary and public sector and as a transport planner in the urban context.

Sandy Eggert is a research assistant at Potsdam University and scientific editor of the journal "ERP Management". Her research activities concentrate on the areas of adaptability of Enterprise Content Management Systems and the integration of enterprise systems. Before her job at Potsdam University she worked as a consultant at BearingPoint GmbH, focussing on enterprise information portals and knowledge management.

Catherine Equey is a UAS Professor of Accounting and Finance at the Haute Ecole de Gestion of Geneva, Switzerland. Professor Equey teaches all facets of accounting, with a particular focus on Management Accounting. She also focuses on the topical domain of Internal Control and the COSO framework. She spent many years in Swiss audit firms as an accounting auditor, and has now taken on a teaching and management role within a local management school. More recently, she has been CFO of a group of schools, for which she was equally in charge of the implementation of Oracle financials. A specialist in the areas of integrated management systems and Enterprise Resource Planning implementation, Professor Equey devotes a large part of her current activities to coaching companies wishing to implement financial and management accounting systems. Her consulting work is particularly dedicated to SMEs and public sector organisations. Her research areas are ERP and Finance.

Emmanuel Fragnière, CIA (Certified Internal Auditor), is a Professor of service management at the Haute Ecole de Gestion of Geneva, Switzerland. He is also a lecturer at the Management School of the University of Bath, UK. He was previously a commodity risk analyst at Cargill (Ocean Transportation), and a senior internal auditor at Banque Cantonale Vaudoise, the fourth-largest bank in Switzerland. Mr. Fragnière specializes in energy, environmental, and financial risk. He has published several papers in academic journals, such as the Annals of Operations Research, Environmental Modeling and Assessment, Interfaces, and Management Science. His research is partly focused on the development of risk management models for decision-makers in the fields of energy and production. One of his major achievements in the area was to make several successful bids for research projects from various public utilities in the Canton de Genève. The results of these projects have been implemented in the new long-range planning model used by the Energy Technology Systems Analysis Program (ETSAP) of the International Energy Agency. Mr. Fragnière's other research interests include modeling systems, for which he has also obtained considerable funding from the Swiss National Science Foundation.

Paul A. Fishwick (fishwick@cise.ufl.edu) is Professor of Computer and Information Science and Engineering at the University of Florida. Fishwick's research interests are in modelling methodology, aesthetic computing, and the use of virtual world technology for modelling and simulation. He is a Fellow of the Society of Modelling and Simulation International, and recently edited the CRC Handbook on Dynamic System Modelling (2007). He served as General Chair of the 2000 Winter Simulation Conference in Orlando, Florida.

Shiwen Gao is an advanced engineer of China National Space Administration. He holds an Enterprise information management master's degree in 2003 from Tsinghua University. He is currently pursuing his PhD degree in aerospace manufacture engineering from Nanjing University of Aeronautics and Astronautics, China. His research focuses on virtual manufacturing and enterprise information.

Yu Guo is an assistant professor of mechanical and electrical engineering at NUAA, China. He is currently the Supervisor of CAD/CAM research team. He holds a master's degree in mechanical and electrical engineering from Xin Jiang University in China, and a PhD degree in mechanical design from HuazhongUniversity of Science and Technology in China. His research interests include design theory and methodology, simulation optimization, and mass customization.

Norbert Gronau studied engineering and business administration at Berlin University of Technology, Germany. Currently he holds a chair of Business Information Systems and Electronic Government at the University of Potsdam. His main research activities concentrate on the areas of Corporate Architectures and Business Management.

Fred Heemstra is a full professor in Management Science and Computer Science at the Open University, the Netherlands. From 1994 until 2000 he was the Dean of the department of Economics, Business and Public Administration. He is also a partner at KWD Resultaatmanagement. Previously he worked at Twente University, Eindhoven University of Technology, Polytech Brabant and as a management consultant at Infoligic and Vreelandgroup. Heemstra holds a Master Degree and a PhD degree in Industrial Engineering from Eindhoven University of Technology. His work, interests and research focuses on Management of IT, particularly IT Risk Management, Software Management, IT Cost Benefit Management, Software Cost Estimation and Control, Software Quality Management, Software Requirement Management, IT Project Management and Information Economics.

Blanca Hernandez has a Ph.D. in Business Administration and is lecturer in the Department of Marketing and Business Management at the University of Zaragoza (Spain). Her research interests include the acceptance of new technologies, knowledge management systems, and e-commerce. Her work has been published in journals such as Industrial Marketing Management, Internet Research, Technovation, Journal of Business Research, Journal of Business and Industrial Marketing and Online Information Review.

Corrie Huijs, MSc is a consultant at M&I/Partnersbv with a focus on e-government services and information management in the area of education. Former research activities as a researcher in the Department of Computer Science of the University of Twente included business-IT alignment, architecture of information systems, requirements engineering, design methodology, e-government and collaborative learning. Her educational work at the University of Twente included supervision in projects for the design of industrial information systems.

Guy Janssens is, after several business functions in the field of information management, employed as assistant professor at the School of Management at Open Universiteit Nederland. He develops courses and teaches the subjects: Enterprise Resource Planning, Project Management and Management and Information Technology. He is currently doing Ph.D. research on the subject 'estimating costs of ERP implementation projects'.

Julio Jimenez has a Ph.D. in Business Administration and is professor in the Department of Marketing and Business Management at the University of Zaragoza (Spain). His research in adoption and diffusion of innovations has been published in several journals, such as Research Policy, Industrial Marketing Management, Internet Research, Online Information Review, European Journal of Marketing and Technovation.

Omar E. M. Khalil is currently a professor of information systems at Kuwait University. He has a PhD in information systems from the University of North Texas. His publications have appeared in journals such as the Journal of Global Information Management, Journal of Organizational and End-User Computing, Information Resources management Journal, International Journal of Production and Economics, International Journal of Man-Machine Studies, Journal of Business Ethics, and Journal of Informing Science. His research interest includes information systems effectiveness, global information systems, information quality, and knowledge management.

Rob Kusters obtained his master degree in econometrics at the Catholic University of Brabant in 1982 and his PhD. in operations management at Eindhoven University of Technology in 1988. He is professor of 'ICT and Business Processes' at the Dutch Open University in Heerlen where he is responsible for the master program 'Business process Management and IT'. He is also an associate professor of 'IT Enabled Business Process Redesign' at Eindhoven University of Technology where he is responsible of a section of the program in management engineering. He published over 90 papers in international journals and conference proceedings and co-authored six books. Research interests include process performance, enterprise modelling, software quality and software management.

Anne Lämmer is a software engineer at Capgemini sd&m AG in Germany. Her research activities concentrate on the development of robust and adaptable software architectures. The theme of her doctoral thesis is in the field of self-organisation and self-diagnosis in enterprise systems.

Wenhe Liao is a professor of mechanical and electrical engineering at NUAA, China. He received his master's and PhD degrees from the Department of Aerospace Manufacture and Engineering at NUAA, in 1990 and 1996, respectively. He is currently the director of Jiangsu Engineering Technology Research Center for Digital Design and Manufacture, the dean of Academy of Frontier Science. Prof. Liao takes charge of many different R&D projects, and concentrates his academic work on anufacturing information technology and CAD/CAM.

Mark Lycett (mark.lycett@brunel.ac.uk) is a Reader in Adaptive Information Systems at Brunel University, examining the complex dynamics that couple people, process, information and technology. His research interests relate to the principles and mechanisms of adaptation/evolution in the natural and social realm and how they can be brought to fruition using modern technologies, in particular to guide and improve people's experience with technology. Mark has published his work in a number of leading journals and conferences and is engaged in ongoing research with a number of organizations. Prior to returning to education, he spent a number of years in industry, primarily in project management.

Boris Minkin is a guest researcher at the Center for Electronic Commerce and Knowledge Economics Research, National Chung Hsing University (NCHU) in Taiwan. He has more than 16 years of experience working in the areas of information technology and financial services. In his professional career, Boris has successfully completed numerous IT projects, and become an IBM Certified WSAD Enterprise Developer, IBM Certified WebSphere Solution Developer, IBM Certified WebSphere Systems Expert, and Sun Certified Java Programmer. He received a BS in electrical engineering and computer science degree from St. Petersburg Marine Technical University, and a MS in information management degree from Stevens Institute of Technology, New Jersey. His professional interests are in Internet technology, enterprise application architecture, Java technology, multi-platform application, object oriented methodology & application, network management, and relational database design.

Amit Mitra lectures on information systems theory and practice at the Department of Information Systems of Cranfield University. Over the last decade Mitra has been active in a range of research areas including knowledge management, database management systems, electronic commerce, research methods in information systems and public sector information systems implementation. His work has been published in various peer reviewed journals. As a practice-based researcher, Amit is regularly invited to deliver talks in different research led fora within higher education.

Joseph R. Muscatello is an Assistant Professor of Business Management and Related Technology at Kent State University- Geauga. He received his Doctorate from the Cleveland State University and researches in the areas of enterprise systems, supply chain management, forecasting, project management and the impact of technology on organizations. He has published in Omega, International Journal of Operations and Production Management, Information Resource Management Journal, Applied Computing and Informatics, Journal of Business Forecasting, Journal of Safety Research, Business Technology Educator and the Business Process Management Journal. He has also published several book chapters and presented at academic and professional venues over 50 times! Dr. Muscatello is a former Director with Cap Gemini Ernst & Young and has Fortune 500 executive level manufacturing experience in the chemical and metal industries. He is APICS certified at the Fellow level and teaches APICS certification courses domestically and internationally. He is the owner of several businesses and sits on 2 for-profit and 2 non-profit Boards of Directors.

Navonil Mustafee (navonil.mustafee@brunel.ac.uk) received his Ph.D. in Information Systems and Computing from Brunel University. Presently he is working as a research fellow in Grid Computing and Simulation in the School of Information Systems, Computing and Mathematics, Brunel University. His research interests are in Grid Computing, Parallel and Distributed Simulation, Healthcare Simulation and Information Systems.

Jonathan D Owens is a Senior Lecturer in Operations and Logistics management at the Lincoln Business School, University of Lincoln, United Kingdom. He has track record for publishing in the fields of Operations, Logistics and Supply Chain Management. He is a Chartered Engineer registered with the UK engineering council and currently a Visiting Professor in Logistics Management at the Tecnológico de Monterrey University, México. He is on the editorial panel for numerous journals in his field.

S. Parthasarathy is a Senior Grade Lecturer in the Department of Computer Applications, Thiagarajar College of Engineering, Madurai, India. He is a B.Sc., (Mathematics), M.C.A. (Master of Computer Applications), M.Phil., (Computer Science), P.G.D.B.A. (Business Administration), P.G.D.P.M. (Planning and Project Management) professional. A habitual rank holder, he has been teaching at the post-graduate level since 2002. He has published research papers in peer reviewed international journals and international conferences. He has written two text books in his area of specialization and they were published by The New Age International Publishers (P), Ltd., New Delhi, India, in the year 2007. He has authored several chapters on Enterprise Resource Planning (ERP) in the Edited Books published by the IGI Global, USA in 2008. He is currently the Editor-in-Chief for the Edited Book "Enterprise Information Systems and Implementing IT infrastructures: Challenges and Issues" to be published by IGI Global, USA in 2010. He is the Principal Investigator for the research project "Requirements Management in COTS Software Projects" funded by the University Grants Commission, New Delhi, India. His current research interests include enterprise information systems, enterprise resource planning and software engineering.

S. T. Ponis is a lecturer in SIMOR/NTUA. Dr. Ponis holds a PhD from NTUA in the area of information systems analysis and design to support SMEs forming networked organizations. Dr. Ponis has worked as an IT Manager on behalf of a leading apparel enterprise, and was involved in several research projects on behalf of NTUA/SIMOR. He has contributed in the areas of production planning and control, supply chain management, business process modeling, networked and virtual enterprises and Web information systems. His current research interests are in supply chain management, knowledge management and logistics, UML and agent modeling, e-commerce.

Lene Pries-Heje is a PhD student in the Software Development Group at the IT University of Copenhagen, Denmark. She received her MSc in computer science and business administration from Copenhagen Business School in 1991 and has worked for more than 10 years as an ERP consultant, ERP project manager and consultant manager. Since 2002 she has worked as a part time lecturer in Information Systems at Copenhagen Business School and The IT University of Copenhagen. Her research interests include ERP systems, implementation methods, socio-technical design, and cooperative design.

Muthu Ramachandran is currently a principal lecturer in the Faculty of Innovation North: Information and Technology, Leeds Metropolitan University, Leeds, UK. Previously he spent nearlyeight years in industrial research (Philips Research Labs and Volantis Systems Ltd, Surrey, UK) where he worked on software architecture, reuse, and testing. Prior to that he was teaching at Liverpool John Moores University and received his PhD was from Lancaster University. His first career started as a research scientist from India Space Research Labs where he worked on real time systems development projects. Ramachandran has widely published articles on journals, chapters, and conferences on various advanced topics on software engineering and education. He did his master's degrees from Indian Institute of Technology, Madras and from Madurai Kamaraj University, Madurai, India. Muthu is also a member of various professional organizations and computer societies: IEEE, ACM, BCS, HEA.

Alexei Sharpanskykh is a postdoctoral researcher at the Vrije Universiteit Amsterdam. He received his PhD degree at the Vrije Universiteit Amsterdam in the area of artificial intelligence. Currently he is doing research in modeling and analysis of multi-agent organizations in the context of a number of projects in the areas of logistics, incident management and air traffic control.

Huibin Shi, associate professor, school of software engineering, Tongji University, China. Dr. Huibin Shi was awarded PhD in computer science and MSc in software engineering respectively by the University of York, UK. His research interests include: Software engineering, management information system, microprocessor design and performance measurement, instruction level parallelism, compiler techniques, benchmarking, (Stack) microprocessor architecture, system on chip (SOC) design.

Yan Su is a PhD candidate in the college of mechanical and electrical engineering at Nanjing University of Aeronautics and Astronautics (NUAA), China. She received a bachelors degree from the college of aerospace engineering and a master's degree from the college of mechanical and electrical engineering, at NUAA in 1998 and in 2002 respectively. Her research interests are in the areas of mass customization, enterprise information, and CAD/CAM, with emphasis on virtual manufacture and supply chain management.

Simon J.E. Taylor (simon.taylor@brunel.ac.uk) is the Founder and Chair of the COTS Simulation Package Interoperability Product Development Group (CSPI-PDG). He has served as the Chair of ACM's Special Interest Group on Simulation (SIGSIM) 2005 to 2008. He is a Reader in the School of Information Systems, Computing and Mathematics at Brunel University.

Faith-Michael Emeka Uzoka is Faculty in the Department of Computer Science and Information Systems, Mount Royal, Canada. He obtained MBA (1995), MS (1998), and PhD (2003) in Computer Science with focus on Information Systems. He also conducted a two year post doctoral research in the University of Calgary (2004-2005). He is on the editorial/review board of the following journals: International Journal of Biomedical Engineering and Consumer Informatics, International Journal of Scientific Research in Education, Evaluation and Program Planning Journal. His research interests are Organizational Computing and Decision Support Systems, Technology Adoption and Innovation, and Medical Informatics.

Lex van Velsen, MSc is working toward the PhD degree in the technical and professional communication department at the University of Twente, Enschede, The Netherlands. His research interests include personalized communication systems, electronic government services and user-centered design. His latest research projects focused on user requirements engineering for e-government services and a comparison of different methods for the evaluation of personalized systems.

Thea van der Geest, PhD is an associate professor at the communication studies/technical and professional communication department of the University of Twente, The Netherlands. She teaches courses in interface & interaction design and research methodology. Her research focuses on information and document design for interactive media, with a special interest on the design and evaluation process and user-centered research methods. She has conducted and supervised numerous user studies on requirement analysis, acceptance, personalization, usability and accessibility of systems. Her recent research projects are focusing on requirements engineering for and evaluation of e-government services and systems for Dutch and international government agencies.

Chun-Po Yin holds a PhD degree in Information Management from National Sun-Yat-Sen University, Taiwan. He is a teacher of Haiching Vocational High School of Technology and Commerce, and concurrently an Assistant Professor of Information Management at the Cheng Shiu University, Taiwan. His current research interests include group supporting systems, organizational communication, and issues of information society.

Index

Symbols

3D model 268, 272, 273, 275
3D model control module 273

A

ABC analysis 193
abstraction mechanism 322, 325
AcceleratedSAP (ASAP) 64
Accounting and Finance (AF) 108, 109
account manager 49
administrative innovation 224, 225, 227, 228,
        234, 238, 382
administrative innovations 225, 227
administrative organizations 264
administrative system 227
Advanced Manufacturing Research (AMR) 30
agent-oriented view 183
alert 281
Alfa's situation 88
American Production and Inventory Control
        Society (APICS) 6
American Productivity and Quality Center
        (APQC) 6
Analysts 33
analytic hierarchy process (AHP) 63
analytic hierarchy process (AHP) method 63
antecedent conditions 85, 88
application design 289
application layer 122, 124
application monitoring
        278, 281, 284, 285, 286
application roadmap 195
application service provider (ASP) 261, 262
application software 29

areas of function 125
ASP-based product customization service 261,
        262, 263, 264, 265, 268, 275
ATP approach 190, 193, 195
ATP function 190, 191, 192, 193
ATP functionality 189, 192, 193
ATP model 189
ATP problem 189, 193, 198, 201
authoritative communication 179
authority 174, 175, 176, 177, 178, 179, 180,
        182, 183, 184, 185, 186, 187, 376
authority structure 180, 182, 184
automatic solution 289
autonomy 181
available-to-promise 189, 192, 193, 200, 20
        2, 376, 386
available-to-promise (ATP) 188, 190, 192
Available-to-promise (ATP) procedures 188
average variance extracted (AVE) 163

B

back-end database 268
back-end systems 302
basic systems 162, 164
bidimensional structure 164
BI framework 297
big bang 128
BI infrastructure 293
bill of material (BOM) 268
BI market 292, 293
BI project 293, 299, 303
BI stakeholders 291, 294, 304
BI system 291, 292, 293, 294, 295, 296,
        297, 298, 299, 300, 301, 302, 303,
        304

BI team 297, 299, 300, 301, 302, 303
black boxing 220
BOM creation 192
BPR 18, 19, 20, 21, 23, 25, 26
brainstorming 66
broader data modeling 297
bureaucratic firms 207
business analyst 33
business-centric championship 291, 297
business-driven methodology 291, 297, 300
business-driven project 301
business efficiency 244
business environment 157, 159, 160, 161, 217
business execution and management 292
business functions 292
business gainer actor object 328
business intelligence 235
business intelligence software 40
business IS 156
business-led commitment 303
business model 327
business operations 278
business plan 145, 150
business processes 99, 100, 114
business process reengineering (BPR) 18, 19, 20, 32, 37, 38
business process standardization 35
business process, training 2
business user-oriented change management 291, 296
button-event 123
buying centre influence 106

C

Capability Maturity Model (CMM) 37
capable-to-promise (CTP) 192
capital investment 102
case-based product configuration 271
case-based search module 265
categorization 211, 217, 218
categorization strategy 211
categorization structure 217
CAX scene 265
check in/check out 130
CIMOSA 175, 186, 385

client/server architecture 198
CMM model 39
CMPCS solution 192
code fragments 124, 125, 128, 131
collaborative configuration 261, 274
collective knowledge 205, 206
Commercial-off-the-Shelf (COTS) 47
Commercial-off-the-Shelf (COTS) systems 47
commercial software package 135
commodity-off-the-shelf computers 188
communication channels 226, 227, 235
company arena 82
company local system 311
company-specific business process 35
complex management tools 18
complex projects 59
complex software 34, 36
complex systems 131, 132
complex tools 162, 164
complex undertaking 291, 293
composite reliability coefficient (CRC) 163
computer aided design (CAD) 264
computer aided manufacturing (CAM) 264
computer-aided modeling 323
computer-based systems 247
computer system applications 189
concept of service 121
conceptual design 220
conceptual frameworks 209
conceptual model 325, 326, 328
construction machinery orient-
    ed product customization
    261, 262, 273, 274, 275, 276
content management 120, 125, 127, 130
context 203, 205, 206, 207, 208, 209, 210, 212, 213, 215, 218, 220, 222, 384
contextual organizational factors 100
conventional operational systems 297, 304
co-ordination mechanism 138, 141
cost-failure paradox 99
COTS systems 47
counter-resistance according 142
critical success factors (CSFs) 62, 63, 135, 240, 293
CRM users 37
cross functional 141, 142, 146, 150

cross-functional 81, 90, 91, 293, 299, 301
cross functional executive level 8
cross-functional implementation 299
cross-functional implications 33
cross-functional team 103
cross-sectional mail survey 1
cross-system analysis 303
cross-system improvement 121
crucial milestones 300
CSFs framework
    291, 293, 294, 297, 303, 304
cultural foundations 100
current market-oriented manufacturing environ-
    ments 262
customer enquiry 140
customer order decoupling point (CODP) 191
customer relationship management
    209, 228, 235
customer relationship management (CRM) 30,
    31, 34, 37, 228, 264
customer service (CS) 108, 109, 188, 190,
    191, 193, 194, 201
customization 47, 56, 261, 262, 263, 264,
    265, 268, 269, 273, 274, 275, 276,
    277, 371, 380, 385
customization service 261, 262, 263, 264,
    265, 266, 268, 273, 274, 275, 276

D

DAML-S profile 309
data architectures 35
data collection 106
data dictionary (DD) 30
data envelopment analysis (DEA) 64
data flow diagrams (DFD) 30
data issues 35
data mining tools 292
data quality 291, 293, 296, 297, 299, 301,
    303, 305, 306, 358, 371
data repository 135, 136
data sources 302, 303
data transform 261, 264, 265, 275
data transform module 264
DD based 31
decision-making 243, 251, 252, 253
decision-making process 292, 302

degree algorithm 269, 271, 273, 275
Department of Trade and Industry (dti) 209
design/manufacture knowledge 263, 264
design-supporting 47
developing country context 106
development process 47
development software 263
DFD 30, 31
diagrammatic representation 213
diffusion concept 226
diffusion model 224, 225, 228, 229, 235,
    237, 371
diffusion-of-innovation 224
diffusion-of-innovation models 224
digital archiving 120
digitization 99
document management 120, 129, 130
DOI model 225
dynamic knowledge-creating environment 218
Dynamic properties 179
dynamic resource collecting method 273

E

e-business 159, 170, 262, 263, 373
e-business context 159
e-business environment 262
ECM solutions 120
ECM systems 120, 121, 125, 129, 130
economic globalization 262
EIS relevant 185
electronic commerce (EC) 278
electronic media 212
eliminate disparate systems 1
e-mail functionalities 127
e-mail marketing 209
embrained knowledge 206
emergent literature 204
end-users 81, 84
end-user support 241, 242
end-user training 241
engineering asset management
    291, 292, 294, 301, 303, 304
Engineering asset management organizations
    (EAMOs) 292
engineering method 31, 32, 34, 37, 38, 39,
    40, 42, 43

enterprise 322, 323, 324, 356, 325, 326, 358, 328, 361, 363, 364, 335, 366, 368, 376, 379, 381, 384, 385

enterprise architecture 323, 334, 370

enterprise architecture CIMOSA 175

enterprise content management system 120

enterprise information 263

enterprise information systems (EISs) 32, 174, 175

Enterprise Java Beans (EJBs) 282

enterprise resource planning (ERP) 1, 15, 16, 134, 135, 152, 374, 381

enterprise resource planning (ERP) systems 1, 13, 18, 27, 46, 99, 120, 134, 224, 374

enterprise strength monitoring solutions 278

enterprise systems 120, 121, 123, 125, 128, 129, 130, 131, 133, 370

enterprise-wide dimensional model 303

enterprise-wide information system 293

enterprise-wide scale 299

entity model 215

entrepreneurial cultures 228

ERP acquisition 100, 101

ERP activities 57, 60, 62, 66, 67

ERP activity 65

ERP adoption 21, 25, 27, 113, 114, 115, 117, 224, 225, 235, 369, 377

ERP applications 235

ERP applications vendors 191

ERP approach 147, 148, 150

ERP bibliography 62, 70, 373

ERP competence centre 84

ERP consultants 63

ERP customization 32, 37

ERP end users 37

ERP functionality 29, 30, 35, 40, 191, 192

ERP implementation 1, 3, 4, 5, 6, 8, 9, 10, 11, 13, 15, 19, 20, 21, 23, 24, 25, 27, 28, 354, 30, 31, 356, 32, 37, 38, 39, 40, 366, 44, 371, 380, 100, 102, 104, 115, 116, 117, 134, 135, 137, 138, 141, 142, 144, 145, 150, 151, 150

ERP implementation process 80

ERP implementation project 57, 58, 59, 60, 61, 62, 64, 66, 68, 69

ERP implementation projects 57, 58, 59, 60, 61, 64, 65, 69, 367

ERP implementations 1, 2, 4, 7, 8, 9, 11, 12, 13, 81, 82, 84, 362, 95, 368, 96, 97

ERP installation 23

ERP knowledge 11

ERP lifecycle 137, 138, 145

ERP market 1, 225, 230, 235

ERP maturity 29, 30, 35, 38, 40, 43

ERP maturity model 29, 30, 39, 40, 42

ERP maturity model (EMM) 29, 30, 35, 39, 40, 41, 43

ERP-oriented environment 12

ERP package 81, 84, 87, 88, 89, 91, 93, 94, 95, 96

ERP package software 81, 84, 88, 93, 95, 96

ERP performance gap 193

ERP phase 65

ERP problems 135, 136, 138

ERP product 99, 102, 103, 104, 189

ERP project 32, 35, 37, 42, 57, 58, 59, 60, 61, 62, 63, 64, 66, 70, 72, 73, 376, 380, 384, 81, 84, 86, 87, 88, 90, 92, 95, 97, 104

ERP Project Life Cycle Stages 63

ERP project manager 81, 84, 87, 88, 90, 95

ERP projects 29, 30, 31, 32, 34, 35, 37, 38, 39, 40, 42, 43

ERP project success 1

ERP purchase decision 106

ERP radicaless 228

ERP research 100

ERP resources 11

ERP selection 99, 100, 101, 102, 106, 108, 114, 115, 117, 118, 356, 367, 377

ERP software 2, 5, 10, 12, 13, 23, 29, 32, 37, 38, 40, 42, 43, 84, 355, 101, 102, 103, 106, 110, 365, 113, 114, 117, 119, 384, 115, 116

ERP software suppliers 62

ERP solution business 103

ERP solutions 189

ERP spending 1

ERP suppliers 224

ERP suppliers' marketing strategy 224

ERP system 3, 4, 5, 7, 8, 10, 11, 12, 18, 19, 20, 21, 22, 23, 24, 25, 26, 29, 30, 32, 34, 35, 37, 38, 39, 40, 42, 43, 45, 46, 47, 48, 51, 54, 55, 58, 356, 358, 368, 370, 371, 375, 385

ERP team 38, 40, 42, 43

ERP users 22, 26, 48, 54

ERP vendors 29, 30, 35, 43, 103, 104, 113, 116, 140, 141, 142, 145, 361

ERP worldwide 225

established theory 203, 220

evolutionary BI system 300

evolutionary BI system development 300

evolutionary information 297

explicit knowledge 204, 205, 213, 219

exploratory factor analysis (EFA) 7

exploratory research 247

eXtensible HTML (XHTML) 268

eXtensible Stylesheet Language Transformations (XSLT) 268

external alignments 227, 228

external consultants 81, 94

external influence 224, 229, 231, 234, 235

External-influence Model 232

external influence source 224

externalization 205

extraction, transformation and loading (ETL) 302

F

face-to-face exchanges 227

fact-based analysis 302

financial management 189

focus group 46, 48, 49, 50, 51, 54

four-stage procedure model 128

Functional evaluation 103

functionality-based model 308

functionality-based Web service discovery 308

functional silo 226

fundamental tool 156

G

Gain Business Generic Business Process 327, 328

Gain Business Role 328

GAMS model 197

GAMS modeling language 197

GCViewer 282

generalization hierarchy strategy 269

Generalized Enterprise Reference Architecture and Methodology (GERAM) 183

general model 105, 119, 384

general systems theory 324

generic 322, 324, 325, 326, 327, 328, 329, 330, 331, 332, 333, 334, 356, 358

generic enterprise reference architecture 323

generic object-oriented enterprise modeling process (GOOEMP) 322

generic reusable business object modeling (GR-BOM) 326

generic solution 103

geographic dispersion 137, 143

global CIOs 30

global effect 165

global expenditure 100

globalization 99

globalized view 189

global level 224

global practices 104

global sourcing 105

go-live 21, 81, 86, 92

governance framework 291, 296, 297

graphical user interface (GUI) 198

grid architecture 121

group culture 211

group structure 105

H

hardware 4, 6, 10, 13, 278, 279

hardware layer 123

hardware platform 191

heuristic evaluation 49, 50, 54

hierarchical approach 125

hierarchical levels 125, 127

hierarchical structure 181

hierarchy organization 272

hierarchy tree 264, 269, 270, 271, 272, 273

homogeneity 25

human-oriented 175, 186

human resources 2, 103, 114, 135, 136, 138, 141, 189, 244

human resources data 226

I

IBM WebSphere Application Server 283, 284
imitation hypothesis 225, 229, 237, 371
imposing sanctions 180
individual cognition 205
industry type 106, 113, 114
informal aspects 182
information and communications technology (ICT) 100
information engineering (IE) 323
information mapping technology 265
information quality 240, 245
information systems 239, 240, 241, 243, 247, 256, 257, 258, 259, 260, 322, 354, 323, 324, 357, 361, 363, 367, 367, 370, 372, 374, 381, 383, 386
information systems community 217
information systems design 301
information systems (IS) 99, 100, 156, 239
information systems (IS) success model 99
information technology 2, 8, 10
Information Technology Infrastructure Library (ITIL) 279
information technology (IT) 3, 100, 108, 109, 240
information technology (IT) projects 37
information technology (IT) utilization 100
information theory 324
infrastructure performance 295, 297, 298
innovation diffusion theory (IDT) 157
Institute for Supply Management (ISM) 6
integration of enterprise systems 120, 133, 370
interactive knowledge warehouse 203, 204, 207, 208, 209, 210, 213, 214, 221, 373
interactive virtual assembly system 273
intercommunication module 272
inter-enterprise collaborative operations 228
internal arrangements 227, 228
internalization 205
international competition 121
International Journal of Enterprise Information Systems (IJEIS) 18, 19
Internet-based sales 261, 275, 276
interorganizational information systems 214

inter-organizational levels 225
interpersonal channels 225, 227, 235
interpersonal communication 229, 231
inter-related systems 158
intranet-based repository 208
intranet infrastructure 216
intranet solution 216
inventory data 226
inventory levels 191, 193, 201
IS adoption 158
IS contributions 240, 256
IS impact 239, 240, 242, 243, 244, 245, 252, 254, 255, 256, 257
IS investments 242, 244
IS literature 293
IS management practices 240
IS manager 244, 247
isomeric/isomorphic data 265
isomeric/isomorphic product data 261, 264, 268, 275
IS organizational impact 239, 244, 245, 246, 247, 249, 250, 251, 252, 253, 254, 256, 257
IS organizational impact factors 239, 245, 251, 252, 253
IS organizational level 239, 253, 257
IS organizational unit 241
IS planning 241, 244
IS sophistication 239, 241, 243, 246, 247, 248, 250, 251, 252, 253, 256, 257
IS strategic planning 242
IS strategy 239, 241, 242, 246, 247, 248, 250, 251, 252, 253, 257
IS success 239, 240, 241, 242, 243, 244, 245, 247, 248, 249, 251, 252, 253, 254, 256, 257
IS success factors 239, 240, 242, 244, 245, 247, 248, 251, 252, 253, 254, 256, 257
IS unit 241, 243, 244, 246, 248, 250, 252, 254
IT industry 293
IT infrastructure 139, 204, 205
IT infrastructure project 204
IT investments 242, 243
IT issues 19

IT landscape 129
IT products 244
IT services 279
IT-system development 81
IT training 3, 4, 242, 246, 247, 248, 250, 252, 256

J

Jack-of-all-trades 48, 49, 52
Java applications 283
Java based enterprise applications 278, 280
Java EE application 284, 286, 287, 289
Java Message Service (JMS) 282
Java Virtual Machine (JVM) 282
Java Virtual Machine Profiling Interface (JVMPI) 283
Java Virtual Machine Tool Interface (JVMTI) 283
just-in-time (JIT) 191

K

Kadrosi 203, 204, 205, 207, 208, 209, 210, 211, 212, 213, 214, 215, 216, 217, 218, 219, 220
Kaiser Normalization (KMO) 108
key component 106
key factors 2
KM users 37
knock-out criteria 87
knowledge analysis 50
knowledge assets 205
knowledge base 263, 264, 265, 268
knowledge codification 219
knowledge creation 205, 206, 207, 221, 375
knowledge gaps 216, 217, 219, 220
knowledge intensive 207
knowledge management 204, 211, 216, 217, 218, 219, 220, 221, 222, 235, 354, 373, 379, 380, 382
knowledge management (KM) 30, 34, 37
knowledge management systems (KMS) 241, 243, 256
knowledge representation 215, 216, 221, 376
knowledge transfer partnerships (KTPs) 209

knowledge warehouse 203, 204, 205, 207, 208, 209, 210, 211, 212, 213, 214, 215, 216, 217, 218, 219, 220, 221, 373
knowledge warehouses 209
knowledge worker 207
Kuwaiti context 240, 256
Kuwaiti organizations 239, 245, 246, 252, 253

L

Large-scale 300
large-scale survey result 297
lifecycle-oriented customization 261, 273
lifecycle-oriented product 261, 262, 273, 275
lifecycle-oriented product customization service 261, 273, 275
life-time constraints 193, 194, 197
linear program (LP) 194
linear regression 231
linking theory 209
literature review 245
literature study 62
logical structure 266
logic-based specification language 174
logistic curve 230
long-term relationships 228
long-term solution 300, 302

M

make-to-order (MTO) 190
management decision-making 19
management information systems (MISs) 247
management software 156, 157, 160, 161, 162, 164, 165, 167, 173
managerial decisions 177, 178, 181, 182, 184
managerial literature 178
managing director 142
manufacture resources 263
manufacturing process 268
market-leading applications 262
market-oriented departments 181
mass media 225, 227, 230, 231, 235
mass-media communication 229
material management 103

material requirement planning (MRP) 23
mathematical models 114, 115
MCFP problem 194, 195, 196, 197, 200
mean time between failures (MTBF) 279
mean time to repair (MTTR) 279
media enterprise 219
M-ERP interface 51, 52
M-ERP screen 48
M-ERP users 48
meta-analysis 242, 259, 372
meta-data 312
metadata model 303
meta-information 51, 55
methodology 59, 63, 64, 70, 376
M-form organization structure 231
MIC annual report 235
migration path 101
mixed influence 224, 229, 234
Mixed-influence Model 232
mixed-integer programming problem (MIP) 194
mixed model 234, 235
mobile marketing 213
modeling framework 179, 186
Modeling methods 176
modelling imagery 131
Modern information systems 32
MPS data 193
multi-commodity aggregate production planning (MCAP) 194
multi-commodity fine-grain production planning (MCFP) 194
multi-dimensional CSFs 304
multi-dimensional factors 303
multidimensional structure 164
multi-function Bitumen-concrete paver 271, 272
multi-perspective user validation 37
multiple platforms 292
multi-tiered 278, 280

N

national arena 82
National Association of Accountants (NAA) 6
noise model 232, 233, 234
Nominal Group Technique (NGT) 65

non-adopters 158, 170, 373
non-disclosure conditions 203
Non-functional requirements 34
non-measurable benefits 166
non-necessity 22
non-response bias 161
non-response rate 22

O

object interaction diagram 330
object model 215, 216
object-orientation modeling 323
object-oriented model 322, 325, 330, 332
object-oriented paradigm 324, 325
object-oriented representational model 327
office environment 218
office manager 49
Office of Statistics (OFS) 22
online analytical processing (OLAP) 292
ontology 175, 179, 353, 308, 309, 311, 312, 313, 315, 316, 317, 318, 319, 320, 321, 375, 377
ontology-aware 308
open-ended questions 63
open source (OS) 189, 191, 192, 193, 201
operational problems 2
operational system prototype 197
order transaction 131
ordinary least square (OLS) 225
organic organization 182
organic organizational form 182
organisational knowledge 203, 221, 222, 375, 383
organisational memory 209
organizational adoption 225
organizational benefits 241, 244, 259, 373
organizational buying theory 115
organizational changes 2, 226
organizational characteristics 236
organizational commitment 241, 244, 252, 253, 255
organizational constraints 185
organizational documents 179
organizational effectiveness 241, 243
organizational efficiency 99, 100
organizational functions 228

organizational goals 176, 179, 180
organizational impact 239, 240, 243, 244,
        245, 246, 247, 249, 250, 251, 252,
        253, 254, 256, 257
organizational interdependence 244
organizational knowledge
        205, 206, 220, 222, 359, 381
organizational linkages 244
organizational performance 239, 240, 241,
        242, 243, 244, 245, 246, 254, 255,
        256, 257
organizational resources 181
organizational structure 35, 241, 244, 253,
        254, 255, 257, 299, 301
organizational tasks 182
organizational types 240
organization knowledge engineer 308
organization-oriented view 183
organizations managers 181
organization theories 174, 175
organization units 35
organization-wide coordination 189
out-of-the-box remote monitoring 283

P

paradox 99, 100
participatory design (PD) 82
PDM module 272
perceived ease 156, 160

perceived usefulness (PU) 156, 157, 160, 163,
        168, 169, 360, 365
performance indicators (PIs) 185
performance monitoring infrastructure (PMI)
        284
performance-oriented view 183
personalized software 54
personnel performance 188
pervasive infrastructure 226
phantom BOMs 192
physical knowledge repository 212
physical knowledge store 212
physical repository 208
pilot 89
planned production 188, 189, 190, 191,
        192, 194, 198

point-to-point 121
political context 244
polymorphism 325
post-implementation stages 62
power-related actions 175
power-related concepts 174, 175, 186
PRAC pattern 328, 329
predicate-based languages 183
procedure model 120, 125, 127, 128, 129,
        130, 131, 132, 133, 370
process model 80, 85, 86, 87, 97, 374
process model analysis 80
process-oriented 183, 186
process-oriented view 183, 186
processual knowledge 219
product configuration 261, 263, 264, 265,
        268, 269, 271, 272, 273, 274, 275,
        276
product constructs 102, 106
product data transform 261, 275
product experience 99, 106
product hierarchy tree
        264, 269, 271, 272, 273
production planning 103
production plans 226
production schedule 188, 190, 194, 195
production scheduling functions 193
production seat system 194
product lifecycle 261
product planner 49, 53
product-process centered 106
product variation 262
professional environment 54, 55
professional knowledge 210, 213
professional service automation (PSA) 228
profitable-to-promise (PTP) 192
program design language (PDL) 31
project champion 145, 150
project management 2, 9, 10, 13, 103
project management team 145
project manager 59, 73, 77
project support 2, 12
project team composition 291, 296, 297
proliferation 204
Promax 108, 110
prototype tool 188, 189, 191, 193

pseudonym 84
public organizations 354, 240, 355, 241,
    243, 244, 245, 247, 252, 253, 255,
    256, 257
pull-based controls 190

Q

quality control 189
quality of services (QoS) 280
quantity to quality 292
questionnaire-based survey 19

R

Radio Frequency Identification (RFID) 225
raw source code 121
real time extensions 31
real-time information 2
real-time sharing 87
real-world activities 49
re-architect 303
relational-oriented philosophy 105
representational model 325, 327, 331, 332
requirements engineering method (REM)
    29, 35, 37, 38, 39, 43
requirements engineering (RE) 30, 35
requirements engineering (RE) method 30
requirements engineering validation system
    (REVS) 31
requirements language processor (RLP) 31
research frameworks 240
resolution of process 35
resource collection 261, 265, 266
resource collection method 261, 265, 266
resource-intensive process 299
resource management 87, 89, 90, 264
resources database 266
Resource share 261
re-usage 121, 130
rotation method 108

S

SAP Requirement Engineering (SAPRE) 35
SAP's global ATP (GATP) 192
self-configuring 287, 288, 289
self-diagnosis 120, 121, 122, 123, 124,
    131, 133, 366, 370

self-healing 278, 286, 287, 288, 289
self-healing application monitoring 278
self-optimization 287, 288, 289
semantic discovery 309
semi-finished goods inventories 193
service index 121
Service Level Agreement (SLA) 279
service organization 262
service orientation 121
service-oriented architecture (SOA) 101, 120,
    128, 130, 131
service oriented concept 128
service oriented integration 128, 132
service platform
    261, 262, 273, 274, 275, 276
silver bullet 36
six-stage model 63
skeletal structure 214
small and medium sized enterprises' (SMEs)
    18, 31, 39, 47, 114, 261, 262
small-scale applications 281
SMEs 18, 19, 20, 21, 22, 23, 24, 25, 26,
    27, 371, 380
SOA approach 121
Socialization 205
social science 175
social structure 236
social system 225, 226, 227, 229
social theories 175, 176
society for information management 1
sociology 174, 175
socio-technical approach 82
socio-technical challenge 135
socio-technical design 82, 90, 91, 94
socio-technical implications 94
socio-technical model 64
socio-technical options 80, 93, 94, 95
socio-technical research 82
socio-technical solution 93
software 2, 3, 4, 5, 6, 10, 11, 12, 13
software change 33
software development
    32, 34, 35, 36, 45, 377
software development process 35
software engineering 30, 32, 33, 34
software intrinsic 102

software modifications 138, 143, 148, 149
software process management 37, 43
software project 3
software projects 30, 31, 32, 34, 37, 38, 39
software requirements specification (SRS)
    31, 33
software solution 29
software system 124, 128, 235
software technologies 278
software tools 36, 264, 265
software training 4
software vendor 113
source code 120, 121, 123, 124, 125, 127,
    128, 131
source code layer 124
source-code usage 124
specification and description language (SDL)
    31
stakeholders 33, 35, 43
standard ERP system 80, 84
standardisation 203
state charts 31
state-of-the-art IS 159
static structure 197
step-by-step transformation 128
storyboarding 215, 220
strategic apex 177
strategic enhancement 204
strategic ERP constructs 7
strategic media solutions 214
strategic planning 292
strategic tool 207
strategy business planning 324
structuralist perspective 205
sub-phase 31
Sun Microsystem 4
Superior-subordinate relations 178
Supply chain management functionality 192
supply chain management (SCM) 6, 30, 31,
    34, 103, 228, 264
supply chain management (SCM) software 30
supply chain systems 37
support quality 99, 106, 108, 113, 115
syntax-based 309
system administrator 308, 318
system framework 302

system integration architecture 32, 37
system maintenance modules 264
system quality 99, 106, 108, 110, 111, 113,
    240, 245
system resources 289
systems development efficiency 244
systems integration 6
system use 240

T

tacit knowledge 205, 206, 207, 213
TAM framework 160
TAURUS system 34
Technical architecture 103
technical material 211
technical resources 242
technological compatibility (TC) 158, 160
technological culture 158
technological decisions
    177, 178, 179, 180, 181, 182
technological development
    158, 159, 161, 164
technology acceptance model (TAM)
    99, 100, 106, 156, 157
technology-oriented 186
technology training 4, 5
TE generalizability 218
Temporal Trace Language (TTL) 179, 184
theoretical frameworks 218
Theory of Planned Behaviour (TPB) 157
Theory of Reasoned Action (TRA) 157
Theory of Reasoned Action, (TRA) 157
time-based view 65
traditional data warehouse 205
transactional data 29
transaction-oriented 105
transactions processing systems (TPSs) 247
tree management module 273
tree node 271
tree-structure 268, 273, 275
typology 49

U

UDDI 308, 309, 310, 311, 313, 315, 317,
    318, 319, 320, 321, 353
UML diagram 287

Unified Modeling Language (UML) 327
user-centered approach 48
user-centered methods 47
user-focused methods 46, 48
user-oriented change management
        291, 296, 297, 299
user participation 83, 96, 97, 356, 358, 368
user satisfaction 240, 242, 245, 257, 258,
        354, 365

V

variance inflation factor (VIF) 110
vendor constructs 102
vendor criteria 102
vendor evaluation 104
vendor selection 99, 107, 108, 111, 112,
        114, 115, 278, 285
viral marketing 213
virtual assembly systems 272
virtual product configuration
        265, 272, 273, 274, 275
virtual product configuring 264
virtual reality modeling language (VRML) 273

W

warehouse 203, 204, 205, 207, 208, 209,
        210, 211, 212, 213, 214, 215, 216,
        217, 218, 219, 220, 221, 373
Web -based developments 215
Web-based infrastructure 215

web-based interactive visualization environ-
        ment 272
Web procurement 156, 157, 158, 160, 162,
        165, 166
Web production 213
Web service 353, 308, 309, 312, 313, 315,
        316, 317, 319, 320, 321, 376
web service architecture 127
web service description language 128, 131
Web service directory 308
Web services 120, 131, 132, 133, 353, 308,
        309, 356, 313, 316, 317, 364, 320,
        321, 376, 380
Web service (WSDL) 309
Western-based investigations 239
white-noise model 233, 234
WS description 309

X

XML-based data mapping model 261
XML-based object-oriented mapping 273
XML language 268, 275
XML template 268

Y

Y2K 224, 225, 230, 231, 234, 235

Z

Zachman framework 175
zero-one goal programming 115